THE ART OF NOISE

THE ART OF NOISE

CONVERSATIONS WITH GREAT SONGWRITERS

DANIEL RACHEL

 ST. MARTIN'S GRIFFIN  NEW YORK

www.stmartins.com

The Library of Congress Cataloging-in-Publication Data is available upon request.

ISBN 978-1-250-05129-5 (trade paperback)
ISBN 978-1-4668-6521-1 (e-book)

St. Martin's Griffin books may be purchased for educational, business, or promotional use. For information on bulk purchases, please contact Macmillan Corporate and Premium Sales Department at 1-800-221-7945, extension 5442, or write specialmarkets@ macmillan.com.

A different version of this title was originally published in the United Kingdom under the title *Isle of Noises* by Picador/Pan Macmillan, a division of Macmillan Publishers Limited.

First U.S. Edition: October 2014

10 9 8 7 6 5 4 3 2 1

For Susie, Lily, Eleanor, and Lottie . . . XXXX

CONTENTS

What do you call that noise that you put on? This is pop.

'THIS IS POP,' ANDY PARTRIDGE

INTRODUCTION

> If the will of every man were free, that is, if every man could act as he pleased, all history would be a series of disconnected accidents.
>
> LEO TOLSTOY, *WAR AND PEACE*

5–4–3–2–1, counted down the introduction to Manfred Mann's 1964 top-five hit, signalling the start of *Ready Steady Go!* I was a teenager when I first watched a Channel 4 rerun of the show, and as the declaration THE WEEK-END STARTS HERE filled the screen in bold letters, I was transported back to the heyday of classic British songwriting—the time of The Beatles, The Who and The Kinks. The songs put to shame many of the superficial records of the Eighties and invited me to explore a popular music beyond the immediate present.

Having spent a lifetime listening to records and making my own music, I have always been intrigued by the creative process behind popular songs. I was instinctively drawn by the small mysterious piece of information that sat beneath each song's title: the name of the songwriter. I was fascinated to imagine Lennon and McCartney, Pete Townshend or Raymond Douglas Davies plucking words and melody out of the ether, and hunted for information about composition in biographies and magazines. Disappointingly the focus was invariably on the musicians' lifestyle. Meanwhile, across the Atlantic, Paul Zollo wrote a book called *Songwriters On Songwriting*. It was a collection of interviews with many of North America's most celebrated writers talking about their craft. It is a compelling and absorbing read. Sometime in the late 1990s I found myself in Borders bookshop on Charing Cross Road asking for the British equivalent. To my amazement, it did not exist. A seed was planted and ten years later I made up my mind to fill the gap.

To a songwriter, the question of what comes first, the words or the music, is a tired cliché. Writing a song is a highly personal process. If successful, the result is shared with an audience of thousands if not millions, something that requires composers to 'let go' of their precious creations. When I talked with the twenty-seven songwriters in this book I had all my questions laid out in front of me divided into neat themes: Words; Melody; Routine; Audience/ Performance; Musicality; Building a Song. I was fascinated by how differently each songwriter responded, and keen to follow up the unexpected insights they offered. Common themes began to emerge, as well as the idiosyncrasies of individual methods. They should be easy to find, whether you choose to read this book sequentially or just dip and skip. The most frequent phrase to appear is 'There is no one way to write'. It is no surprise. The book is a celebration of imagination, and its insights are gained not only from the artists' precise analysis of their own methods but also from their self-protective deflections.

In all but two of the conversations (Pet Shop Boys and Annie Lennox) my questions were not submitted ahead of talking with the artist. As a result, what you will read here is the transcription of songwriters' words as they collect their thoughts and search for the exact phrases to capture their meaning. It is likely that only a few of the musicians will remember what they said to me until they read this book (although Bryan Ferry, Mick Jones, Madness, Annie Lennox, Pet Shop Boys, Damon Albarn and Noel Gallagher all approved their chapters ahead of publication), but the threads of their thoughts reflect their deepest beliefs and working practices. A few stories may seem to be more rehearsed anecdotes from rock 'n' roll mythology, but whilst they may be known by one set of fans, they may be entirely new to the next. The artists are presented chronologically, loosely based upon the timing of their initial impact in musical history. This arrangement reflects developments in politics, social change and recording technology, all of which affect writing, from the language of the lyrics to the equipment of the recording studios and the devices songwriters employ to remember ideas.

I began writing the book by making a list of classic British rock and pop songwriters. Forty or fifty names immediately came to mind, but if the project was to cover fifty years, it felt right to condense the list to twenty-five artists. Since I was taking John Lennon and Paul McCartney's composition and recording of 'Love Me Do' in 1962 as the starting point of modern British music, I decided that the songwriters also needed to be performers. I also tried to give each of the decades from the Sixties to the present day roughly equal representation. By now the list of artists was slimming down to a more manageable thirty names. I discussed my ambition with Richard Thomas, a man renowned for his encyclopaedic knowledge of music and connected to both the rock and pop and the literary worlds. His response was encouraging but also realistic. Musing on why no one had ever attempted this before, he perhaps answered his own question by predicting that only a third of the list would agree to participate and that the project would take at least five years to complete. I then picked up the phone, searched the Internet for contact numbers and names, and began to send out invitations.

People say 'No' because they have not been persuaded to say 'Yes'—this was my maxim throughout the process. I have pestered, annoyed and cajoled in the pursuit of my ambition. I was convinced that the book belonged on the shelves of every music lover, musician, writer and social historian. I clung doggedly to this belief despite repeated rejections from within both the publishing and the music industries. Whilst this is not a definitive work by any stretch of the imagination, I would argue that the artists involved have all contributed uniquely to the progression of classic British songwriting. But what is meant by that term, 'classic'?

A song can get us from A to B as simply and effectively and with the same familiarity as a daily journey to work or a walk to the local pub. But some songwriters choose to take the scenic route. It's still the same starting and finishing point, but our minds have been opened along the way and our senses excited. Along with depth, originality and imagination, great music that makes a lasting impression has an honest craftsmanship running through it. Over time, and often with renewed appreciation, we bestow the word 'classic' upon it.

Equally tricky to pinpoint is the unique character of 'British' music. When we identify music in this way, we are making an association with the spoken voice of our language: dialect, slang, places and names. We recognize our accents and phrases, common codes of speech and our stresses of expression, but at the same time much of our island's musical heritage is imported. It would be a bold musician indeed who would lay claim to British modern instrumental originality. In the wake of The Beatles, Sixties songwriters drew from American R&B, Fifties rock 'n' roll and pre-war genres. Even punk, despite all its posturing and claims to raw self-expression, found its roots in the same music as its predecessors. The beat was simplified and the rhythm straightened, but the style and structures were still essentially American. Reflecting the classical compositions of Walter Carlos (*Switched-On Bach* and *A Clockwork Orange/ Music From The Soundtrack*), electronica, which found favour with so many artists in the Eighties, was born out of a European phenomenon, particularly the Seventies German movement that produced Faust, Can, Neu! and Kraftwerk. Musicians learn through imitation. Their originality is in the revoicing of an influence with creative imagination.

Only four female songwriters are questioned in the book. This is a reflection of historical male dominance, though a few artists turned down invitations to participate and some are no longer with us, namely Sandy Denny, Kirsty Mac-Coll and Amy Winehouse. I was keen to address the gender disparity by asking the songwriters I met for their thoughts on the subject. Their answers make for fascinating reading and it is no accident that the final chapters of the book, representing the most contemporary work, come from two female songwriters, Lily Allen and Laura Marling.

This book chronicles a golden age of British songwriting through the artists who have made their mark on the music of the twentieth and twenty-first centuries. The joy of their work will always be in the listening: the words best sung; the music best felt. But the conversations that follow offer a privileged insight into each writer's imagination. The techniques revealed range from editing and sharpening wordplay to finding rhythms and rhymes, and from pursuing melody in search of hooks to exploring studio possibilities. *The Art of Noise* challenges the notion that youth alone provides originality, whilst the wider conversation champions songwriters who have followed their artistic instincts, free from convention or commercial constraint. At a time when technological advances constantly distract listeners from the craft of songwriting—downloads without compositional credits; songwriting acknowledgements reduced to unreadable sizes on the iPod—there has never been a better moment to celebrate fifty years of classic British songwriting. God Save the Noise.

RAY DAVIES

And just when I wanted no one to be there / All of my friends were there / Not just my friends / But their best friends too.

Behind Ray Davies is the celebrated British music hall tradition: an era of song, laughter and alcohol. Music hall was riotous and unconstrained by the Royal Patent which regulated legitimate theatres, and its songs told stories in the folk tradition. Rogues, wastrels and criminals were remembered and even celebrated on the Victorian stage, like 'Sam Hall' or George Leybourne's comic character 'Champagne Charlie'. The created persona is also a characteristic of Ray Davies's songwriting. Just as the revered Vesta Tilley was the first music hall star to dress as a man, so 'Lola' was the first male pop character to dress as a woman. The molly houses of eighteenth-century London streamed with cross-dressers and effeminate masculine personalities. Following in the tradition, music hall stars were able to offer a contrast to contemporary prudishness just as modern pop can challenge archaic attitudes. Hoxton-born Marie Lloyd sang the saucy 'She'd Never Had Her Ticket Punched Before'. This story of a naive country girl arriving wide-eyed in London has echoes in the Davies ballads 'Big Black Smoke' and 'Polly'. His songbook runs riot with sexual ambiguity as well as an eye for male vulnerability: 'Out Of The Wardrobe' and the more directly *gay and fancy-free* figure of 'David Watts'. The Kinks, as their name suggested, played theatrical camp.

The London of 1860 had conspicuous parallels with the world Ray Davies would mirror in song a century later. More than 50,000 prostitutes were earning a living on the streets of the capital. The city was rife with disease and filled with an awful stench from the Thames, and tens of thousands of families lived packed into one-room tenements. Charles Booth's study of the working class revealed that almost a third of Londoners were living on or around the poverty line. In 1966, at the height of the media-proclaimed Swinging Sixties, the disparity between excess and bare existence was equally shocking. When England lifted the World Cup at Wembley the nation's number one singalong was 'Sunny Afternoon'. Davies had conceived the song in stark contrast to the mood of the age. Behind the knees-up rousing chorus the song attacked in subtle, cutting verse the *big fat momma*, symbol of an all-consuming, taxing government, and the *drunkenness and cruelty* of a broken-down aristocrat. 'Dead End Street' reflected the country's failings with equally devastating observation, referring to *a crack up in the ceiling* and family nourishment limited to bread and honey. The song was reminiscent of Fred W. Leigh and Charles Collins's standard 'My Old Man', which told of a couple fleeing from the burden of unpaid rent. Davies's compositions offered musical gaiety to sweeten bitter tales. The naked E major descending scale of 'The Money Go Round' robed itself in vaudeville delivery whilst attacking the theft of intellectual property. 'All Of My Friends Were There' described a *disguise of shame* with a worn moustache and parted hair. Out of the circus rhythm, falling notes in F major release the song's joviality into a beautifully segued half-time melancholy. Wit was a Davies tool of anger handled with precision blows.

The great British songwriting legacy is traditionally in defiance of the establishment. Like Jagger and Richards, the outspoken Davies paid little heed to convention. A century earlier Harry Clifton had accepted payment from factory owners to write songs encouraging employees to graft, but 'Work, Boys, Work and Be Contented' reflected a very different mood from the industrial world of the Sixties. Davies voiced the grievances and plight of the neglected working man. His songs recognized the hardship and struggle at the propping-up end of society. '(Wish I Could Fly Like) Superman' was a song of escapism from strikes and bills, whilst the celluloid dreamer of 'Oklahoma USA' asks *all life we work but work is a bore, if life's for livin' then what's livin' for?* Davies's songbook is a chronicle capturing the pulse and heart of the British working man. His stories show the realities with telling insights from everyday life, and his observations blend quaint and humorous storytelling with damning indictments of authority. He tells of prosaic characters and their everyday rituals, such as taking *afternoon tea* or *roast beef on a Sunday*, watching football or negotiating the weights and pulls of emotional attachment. His words are accessible and easy to understand, and there is a magnetism in the song construction that is deceptive in its simplicity. One of The Kinks' greatest achievements was *The Village Green Preservation Society*, celebrating a nostalgic image of a disappearing world. The village green acts as the focal point for the characters of 'Walter' and 'Johnny Thunder', representing a decaying of innocence. But it was not just a fondness for the past and the last *good old-fashioned steam-powered trains* that informed the album. There was an underlying sense of hope, determination and an ache for change. As the Seventies dawned, Davies would take these desires and re-examine his relationship to pop music.

The fountainhead of Ray Davies's imagination is London. 'Waterloo Sunset' conjures the unique atmosphere of the city's famous river. It is the nearest pop music has to Impressionism in art. The paintings of Whistler and Monet depict the fog of London shrouding the Thames, and Davies too draws the *dirty old river* with strokes of enduring symbolism. His eye for detail came from an art-school background. As a student at Croydon Art College he regularly crossed Waterloo Bridge, and this, coupled with a brief period as an in-patient at St Thomas' Hospital where he was able to watch the river flow, provided the idea for the song. His simple storytelling and eye for life's everyday detail bring to mind Hogarth's paintings and the fiction of Charles Dickens. Davies, though, connects with his audience via the highly accessible channel of popular melody. 'Waterloo Sunset' rests on three sets of five-note melodies working their way lazily down one octave. Another inspirational Londoner, William Blake, published in 1794 his collection *Songs Of Innocence And Of Experience*. The poems juxtapose the contrary states of humanity that interest Davies: good with corruption; childishness with adulthood; sexual purity with lust and jealousy. Two centuries may divide the writings, but the common ground is clear. Like Blake before him, Davies is keenly attuned to the city and the human beings who inhabit it.

In 1964, the newly elected Labour government, the first in thirteen years, boasted a straight-talking prime minister with a Yorkshire accent. The Kinks, too, traded on accent. Davies sang in his natural north London voice, establishing a semi-spoken delivery. Equally characteristic of The Kinks' early releases was the group's instrumentation. The sound of Dave Davies's guitar on 'You Really Got Me' and 'All Day And All Of The Night' was revolutionary. Both songs rested upon raw driven chord movement, abrupt key changes and fierce staccato. Fifty years later Metallica re-recorded 'You Really Got Me' for Ray's collaborations album. It represented a homecoming for heavy rock's founding influence. Before the invention of foot pedals to change frequency dynamics at the press of switch, Ray's younger brother experimented by skewering a knitting needle into his eight-amp guitar speaker. Dave's home-modelled Green Amp, once fed through a Vox AC30, emitted a cacophonous distorted effect. It was ahead of its time and defined the early Kinks sound.

The Davies brothers were born at 6 Denmark Terrace, Muswell Hill. Raymond Douglas arrived on 21 June 1944 as British troops advanced through Italy. Three years later David Russell Gordon completed the family of two boys and six girls. 'Come Dancing', written by Ray four decades on, and adapted in 2008 as an award-winning off-West End musical, nostalgically revisited his childhood memories: his sister dancing *at the local Palais* and he the unseen observer at the window watching *two silhouettes saying goodnight by the garden gate*. Tragically, on the eve of Ray's thirteenth birthday, his older sister Rene collapsed on a West End ballroom dance floor and never recovered consciousness. Her present to him was a Spanish guitar. It was the birth of Ray's complex relationship with music. The front room of Denmark Terrace offered a new space for night-time revelry. It was the home of the family piano and later the gramophone, and the room of entertainment, particularly when the boys' father came home drunk from the pub over the road. The finger-picking country-and-western-styled two chords of 'You Really Got Me' were radicalized with dramatic key shifts and repetition on the front-room upright. Davies would increasingly construct ideas at the piano. He told *Melody Maker* in 1966, 'The chords come first. The lyrics grow from fitting words to sounds . . . I'm not a good piano player. If you are reasonably good on an instrument and use it to compose on then you tend to get too complex—and that doesn't work in pop music.' Ray and Dave had served their apprenticeship in north London free-and-easies. In 1960 The Ray Davies Quartet, augmented by school friend Pete Quaife, performed their first shows, playing local dances. The band name changed from The Ramrods to The Boll Weevils to The Ravens until a settled line-up with the addition of Mick Avory on drums signed to Pye Records as The Kinks on 23 January 1964. Within a year the quartet was celebrating a trio of number-one singles.

For the next four years Davies's rapidly developing conversational tone demanded centre stage. Band arrangements become subservient to narrative storytelling. 'Where Have All The Good Times Gone' recalled *Daddy didn't have no toys and mummy didn't need no boys*; 'Well Respected Man' reflects Fifties conformity and class, but the main character secretly *adores the girl next door 'cause he's dying to get at her*; 'Dedicated Follower Of Fashion' points to the writer's interest in subterfuge: *they seek him here, they seek him there*; 'Situations Vacant' addresses upward social mobility and 'Mr Pleasant' superficial domestic happiness. Ray was the cruel observer with a fragile vocal delivery: *if I can't have you to myself / set me free*. The writing revelled in the elasticity of language: *my poor rheumatic back / yes, yes, yes it's my autumn almanac* and was sparing in the use of the word *love*. Davies brought an emotional and intellectual core to popular music delivered with subtle satire and social commentary. His trick was to favour imagination over reportage. Unfortunately in 1966, the American Federation of Musicians of the United States withheld permits, preventing The Kinks from touring the country. The Davies brothers' historical infighting on stage had fallen foul of an Anglo-American union agreement. In 1969 Ted Dreber, assistant president of the Federation, told *Rolling Stone* magazine that although there was no reference to the band on file the 'reciprocity agreement allows either union to withhold permits for a group if they behave badly on stage or fail to show for scheduled performances without good reason'. In 'Americana' Davies described the problem slightly differently: *. . . the English beat group known as The Kinks are banned from America / Their licence to perform has been revoked indefinitely*, before centring the disagreement on an altercation with a television union representative: *You with your red hunting jackets and your yellow frilly shirts . . . you're never gonna work in America again*. For Ray it was a disastrous and at the same time pivotal moment in his career. He responded by going underground. What emerged was exploratory and adventurous writing rewarded with commercial wilderness. Spirituality undercut 'God's Children'. Loss, depth and maturity blessed the *endless and sacred* 'Days'. The successful writer 'Sitting In My Hotel' *dressed in satin strides and two-tone daisy roots . . . writing songs for old-time vaudeville revues* was a sumptuous piano ballad with unexpected movement of chords and melody. As the Seventies began the American ban was lifted but Davies has always felt that The Kinks were denied their greatest opportunity. The country would embrace the band again, culminating with a performance (including the appropriately titled 'Give The People Want They Want') to a sold-out Madison Square Garden in 1981, but the momentum of the Sixties had been irrevocably crushed.

The British Music Hall Society motto, 'cherishing the jewels of Britain's musical past but actively supporting the interests of the future' might have been created for The Kinks. Much of the extensive commentary on the band's work would have you believe that Davies's writing career halted abruptly sometime around the end of the Sixties, then briefly reappeared in the early Eighties, before conducting a valedictory tour in the 2000s. Music chart statistics do a great disservice by suggesting that success is directly linked to artistic achievement. The songwriting of Ray Davies dispels this notion single-handedly. After a breathtaking run of magnificent singles in the Sixties, he began to look outside mainstream expectation. A series of records investigated the possibilities of the long-player and its relationship to popular music. They were bold and daring explorations. *Soap Opera* addressed the privileges of fame, using spoken-word links. *Schoolboys In Disgrace* was a collected song cycle examining education whilst *Preservation I* and *II* took Davies's theatrical leanings into scripted character parts. The release of *Arthur (Or The Decline And Fall Of The British Empire)* in 1969 coincided with The Who's rock opera, *Tommy*. The two albums, though vastly different in conception, embraced a thematic song cycle reminiscent of Italian cantata. But whereas Pete Townshend began to sidestep the structures of the popular song, verse, chorus, middle eight, Davies remained episodic, allowing each song to work independently within the greater theme. In his twenties Davies had taken orchestral lessons and their influence has affected various of his projects since. A commissioned piece, *Flatlands*, in the early Eighties, recorded with the Britten Sinfonia, used a choral offering to evoke the atmosphere of the Norfolk landscape. *The Kinks Choral Collection* in 2009 allowed long-forgotten gems such as the yearning 'Celluloid Heroes' and the suburban conformity of 'Shangri-La' to be arranged for the Crouch End Festival Chorus. Noel Gallagher employed the same voices in his debuting *Noel Gallagher's High Flying Birds* in 2011. It was a clear tribute and a reminder of a 66-year-old's influence in the new millennium.

In conversation Davies has consistently and perhaps deliberately given his songs ambiguous interpretations. *X-Ray: The Unauthorized Autobiography* was a master class in veiled truths and opacity. He is like a crossword: the pleasure is found in the challenge, not the personality of the game-setter. Meeting for our conversation was a flirtation of phone calls, theatre visits and backstage bonhomie. Ray has a kind, inviting manner and is a tease when explaining the songwriting process.

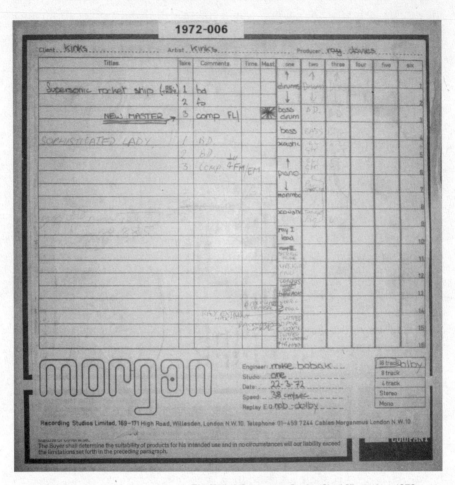

The Kinks' 'Supersonic Rocket Ship' 2" tape box, 1972

Carol Ann Duffy suggested in an interview that words take on a greater value when they are typed because in print they seem more glamorous and important.

Strangely enough, thinking back to 'Dedicated Follower Of Fashion', that was typed out, first draft, never changed a word, as was 'Come Dancing'. I use a pen quite a lot. I do like to write things out. I keep lots of notes. She's absolutely correct. It's maybe an age thing, but if I see something typed out on a screen I can only really evaluate it when it's in hard copy. So I'd go one step further: they have more power when you see the hard copy and even more value when they've been chiselled out in the lithograph.

When you have ideas how do you remember or capture them?

I've gone through periods of not writing anything down, believing if the idea is good it will stick. It's a really good question: whatever it takes. I literally do use serviettes in restaurants. I carry a bag round with me sometimes with various quite thick notepads. I've been a bit slack this year; I've only used two notepads up. There's always a few sheets of paper in my pocket.

When you're pulling ideas together do you need certain circumstances in which to write?

I remember writing when I had my first marriage. I had the television on. I was playing music. The two kids were crawling around the floor. All right, I was twenty-two years old, but I could work better in that situation than in silence. I liked being bombarded with external sources. My theory at that time was, if the idea's good it can survive all these onslaughts from the outside world.

Has the capacity stayed with you?

To a degree. I try to take the preciousness out of writing. Alone in a quiet room I tend to be too reverential of the space needed. It's the old Jimmy Webb theory: apparently when he wrote 'Up, Up And Away' and the hits for The 5th Dimension he lived in a car and had a very transient lifestyle. According to folklore he had all the success, bought a fantastic house, put a studio in it and then couldn't write.

Did that ever happen to you when you made the move from Muswell Hill to larger houses at the peak of your success?

It worked to a degree. Sometimes you need space. The tidier the space the tidier the ideas; and they're not always interesting.

I recently saw the Victoria & Albert exhibition dedicated to the artistic life of Annie Lennox. She explained how moving landscapes from taxi windows, tour buses or trains sparked her imagination.

I know what she means, people writing in transit, that's a good way to write. Like I say, the ideas have to be more durable and have to sustain themselves. If you're in perfect silence . . . that's why people drink, I suppose.

How developed are your ideas before they are committed to a written form?

I think the thought process is interesting. We didn't have tape recorders when I started writing songs. You couldn't tape ideas. I had to notate a lot of stuff. I've still got 'You Really Got Me' notated somewhere. Generally speaking, the good ideas stay in the head. I've got a couple of tunes going round my head and they won't leave me alone until they're finished. It's something I've built into my artillery. I use military words for songwriting: my artillery, my weaponry. I train my brain to remember incidents and people; sometimes they morph into one, certainly in a work like *Return To Waterloo*. That was an interesting project because for a couple of years I was going up on that same route making notes about imaginary people: people that I'd observed. Then I wrote the screenplay for it and it all just came out. It was all in my head. The discipline of that was interesting because each railway station along the line had a specific memory. I didn't realize it. I was writing that treatment for the two years I was taking that journey up on the train with it going through my head. When I got the commission to write it I took the journey on the train and said, 'Yes, I remember that man, this will happen at the second part of the story and this station reflects that emotion.' It's an interesting way, sort of Pavlov's theory of writing songs, writing a bigger piece.

Reading the *Waterloo Sunset* short stories gives the impression that your songs have developed backstories much as an actor's depth of character is implied by suggestion, not explicit explanation.

You can't do too much with a three-minute song. It's possible to layer it in such a way and throw in lyrics, ideas that trigger the imagination of the listener. All great songs can do that. I like to put in backstory. My theory is this: doesn't matter if you're writing a novel or doing an Edward Bond play or doing a short sketch on TV; if you've got the backstory right, you know the characters right.

Do you write in long form and then condense it down to a pop-song structure?

I believe in the three-act structure whether it be a film, play or song. It's a little test. Sometimes it doesn't work, but it's a good rule I have.

Aristotle would say the final act is resolution.

I guess you've got character, conflict and resolution. Sometimes it's bad to write to that sort of formula. It's a good thing to have in the artillery.

Much of your writing thrives on other people's lives; what is the attraction?

One of my favourite actors is Alec Guinness. I was shocked when he was interviewed saying the reason he's so good in all these great characters he played is because he's like an empty shell. Most good actors let the character consume them. One of the first books I bought after I started writing songs was Stanislavski's *An Actor Prepares*. I learnt that a lot of the rules that actors use can be applied to songwriting. It's not as profound being a songwriter, but

I am more interested in seeing other people. Other people's lives have to resonate in me or else I couldn't write the song. Sometimes it takes strangers that fascinate me to trigger off the creative urge. I like non-attractive people with big emotions.

What would make you reject an idea?

Feeling I'd done it before. I've got a high rejection rate and I reject too easily. There's only so many ideas, so many things you can write about. The secret is to put things in it that are unique. I'm writing a couple of love songs; it's really hard to write them. They're the ones that go through my head all the time and I'll put something unique in and I'll find something. It's like whittling down. I used to describe songwriting—I think it's when I was writing 'Waterloo Sunset'—it's like whittling down a stone and smoothing out the rough edges: it becomes perfect. You have to pitch songs to yourself. Sell it to yourself.

Have you had to overcome dried-up periods?

It's not drying out, when you sit down and write . . . like this morning I got up and I wrote some things and was finishing off some unfinished work. I realized sometimes the reason there's a problem with a particular song is it should be a bigger piece. So I started writing a bigger piece of music because that's what I was trying to do, but I thought I was doing a three-minute song. So I got it out of my system and put some samples in and created a more orchestral pad. Sometimes the orchestra's enough and you don't need the lyric. It's one of my ambitions to do an instrumental record with just as much narrative in it as some of my songs. Revisiting *The Village Green Preservation Society* was an overwhelming and humbling experience. I was amazed by the depth of the songs. I re-demoed every song to bring out the words. I did skeleton arrangements before they were orchestrated. I was very proactive in that area. There's a narrative to it which really worked for me. It made me realize I must have known something then when I did it. Being in a band is difficult . . . I think if I'd approached it as a piece in its own right without the band, I'm not saying it'd be more successful; I can't say that it stands as a great band album . . . there are many aspects on the record that no other band could have played, certainly some of the weirder Eastern European-sounding tracks. Only The Kinks could have done that.

Do you like re-visiting the past?

It's hell. The past is something you can't take back; it's wonderful. The joy of doing *Village Green*; it allowed me to interpret the songs. We didn't change any notes but the arrangements stretched and allowed the songs to breathe more, which was very rewarding for me.

Alcahol.

Demon alcahol.
Sad memories I cant recall
Never thought that I would fall,
a slave to demon alcahol.

Heres a sad and woefull story,
of a middle class executive
who enjoyed a life of prominent position
but the pressures at the office
and those socialite engagements
~~put his nerves in quite a serious condition~~.
and his selfish wifes fanatical ambition

~~Then~~ he got mixed up with a flusey
and she turned him on to booz
Then he beat his wife and ended up
in prison,
And it lled him to a life of indunion

Served his sentence lost his job
a bowl of soup   drink sudden lag at some
      at a Salvation army mission

'Alcohol' lyrics, handwritten by Ray Davies.

Do you go back and listen to your own records?

With songs I haven't done live for a long time, I just get the lyric sheet out and that tells me everything. It's interesting to note songs like 'Misfits' and 'Full Moon', how the songs thematically express themselves in a story-like narrative. I haven't sung 'Misfits' in years and it ends like it should end. The key phrases come out. Songs evolve over the years. 'Lola' writes its own arrangement; you just sing the song. It's always there. What I'm discovering is the value of doing things acoustically. If it works acoustically it will work with a big band. I never used to do that. When I was with The Kinks I always used to write songs that would suit them as an entity.

Can you recall the sentiment behind writing 'Lola'?

It was about love, but not directly. The song was designed. I didn't show the words to the band. We just rehearsed it with the *la-la la-la Lo-la* chorus which came first. I had a one-year-old daughter at the time and she was singing along to it. But I was bothered by the arpeggio guitar at the beginning. I said, 'It's got to be a hit in the first three seconds.' Later I went back in the studio and took the phrase at the end of the verse, C C C C D E, and replayed it at the beginning to grab people's attention. I had a new Martin acoustic guitar which I tracked three times all slightly out of time to give it character. And then I put a National guitar on top of it.

What was the ambition at the turn of the Seventies behind creating more theatrical works like *Arthur*, *Preservations I* and *II*, *Soap Opera* or *Schoolboys In Disgrace*?

The Who and The Kinks were both on a quest for the same destination but went about it in different ways. I did it with things like 'Shangri-La' and 'Australia', what people call the section songs: the thematic songs. I was trying to set up the idea that songs could be playlets, small theatre pieces. To put them in a format so they could be treated as more than a three-minute pop song. I will always aspire to write the great three-minute song. I've not written it yet. 'You Really Got Me', 'All Day And All Of The Night' and 'Tired Of Waiting For You' came close. I just know there's more juice in the tank. Better performances. There's always a better song to sing.

You once said 'Two Sisters' was like playing a chess game; a couple of more mediocre lines thrown in before the killer move *no longer jealous of her sister*. Similarly 'Wonderboy' is about the joy of life before the pay-off refrain *life is lonely*.

That's true. I can pick up on something Jackson Browne said to me. We were doing 'Waterloo Sunset' on the collaborations album. He said, 'I don't need *no* friends?' He said it twice. I said, 'Yeah.' He said, 'That's the most beautiful thing

I've ever had to sing. It doesn't make sense on the page but when you put it with the music . . .' I hadn't thought about it that way. The melody takes the curse off the grammar fault. The choice of words, the way they're pronounced, sometimes gives an emotion that's unexpected. *Don't* is the killer word because it's not correct. Great lines are only great because of what precedes them, maybe sometimes when they happen after. That's why I've got complete reverence for Shakespeare as I've got older. When we did *Schoolboys In Disgrace* I had the great joy of doing a mock Shakespeare in the live show when the headmaster had to give a speech. It's so great to liberate yourself to writing out the colours and the words used. It wasn't very good but it was effective. I did it in a Richard Burton impersonation (*laughing*). Speaking of Burton, I got a copy of *Under Milk Wood* recently and I played it in the car to drive to Wales. Why not have some Dylan Thomas? The language of Polly Garter is beautiful: she says *what a nose, there's a conk!* She's a loose woman and she's talking to one of the lovers, just great words and humour. Going back to the original question, I like to suppress certain words. 'Two Sisters' is a good example. It's mundane. It's ordinary and then you get a key change and that's the secret: a note change with a crucial word. Sometimes it gets that serious. There's a song called 'Motorway': *Motorway food is the worst in the world, you've never eaten food like you've eaten on the motorway, motorway food is the worst in the world* that goes on and on and on, goes to a chorus and at the end of the song is what the song is about: *Mama oh mama, my dear Suzie Q, this message is sent just for you . . . my back really hurts, I never thought I'd travel so far to work*. It's saying different things. It's setting it up like a list song at the beginning then it goes to the real emotion near the end. I do that. I set things up like that and sometimes I come in with a punchline at the end. The classic example is from an album called *Everybody's In Showbiz* from the early Seventies. I played the album to the head of the record company and he said, 'Why's this album called *Everybody's In Showbiz*?' There's a song at the end called 'Celluloid Heroes' which is about six and a half minutes long but he sat there and he sat there and on the last few bars I sing *everybody's a dreamer and everybody's a star and everybody's in showbiz, it doesn't matter who you are*. He said, 'I get it, you set it up, I understand.' The man took the time to listen to it. Without that delay . . . punchlines are great if they come in straightaway: *She loves you yeah, yeah, yeah*, but sometimes they need a set-up. I like the song called 'Maximum Consumption' from that album. It's just making wordplay with menus.

How important is truth as a starting point to a lyrical idea?

Oh, truth . . . well I'd say if I was looking at it as an assessment you can only write something if it's truthful to you, then you can believe it. Nothing can be honest if its premise is a lie. In fact there's a song I have about a compulsive liar. I've had it since I first started writing songs. It's a country song and I can't finish it. I wrote a lot of songs when I was living with my sister. Then when I joined the band I wrote a second bunch of songs. It's from then. I did a demo of it at home about four or five years ago. It's an exercise for me. I set myself impossible exercises to write songs about . . . to stretch. You've got to do a workout sometimes. It's like gymnasium exercises for your body: sometimes you need to work your brain out.

Do you believe you must hate something or have an element of cruelty to write from true emotion?

There's a song called 'Mr Reporter', it's one of my minor songs. Dave and I both did versions of it. He actually says *I hate you, Mr Reporter* but I don't believe it, the word *hate*. Songs have to land. Musical songs land, they have a finish, a button. 'Hello Dolly' will have a button. The audience knows it's over. You've got to convey ideas. A good song we did on *Phobia* was called 'Hatred': *the only thing that lasts forever.* Dave and I as a duet, and that worked. But in 'Mr Reporter' the word was not set up. It's such a big word, 'hate'. I didn't really do my writing properly and the song didn't land as a result.

A curious thought: did having your brother in The Kinks offer you security or freedom to be more artistically expressive?

When in doubt you . . . It was liberating to have him in the band. I did a song called 'Australia' years ago. I had to finish it really quickly; the back-track was down. I had *Opportunities are available in all walks of life in Australia*, and I thought, I don't know what to write next. I wanted to make Dave laugh so I said *no one beats around the bush in Australia* and he laughed! That's what's great about bands rather than being singer-songwriters. You can try out things on the rest of the band and if it works for them then it's good enough for me. I went through a phase of not letting the band hear the lyrics until we'd done the back-track 'cause I thought they'd laugh or be disparaging towards me, so I kept them secret. 'Waterloo Sunset' was like that. I didn't want them to know what it was really about.

Because of giving away something that's so personal to you?

I don't know. I just didn't want them to play duff notes over it or do something to screw it up, and certainly with 'Wonderboy': please be realistic, what's that lyric all about?

John Lennon said it was one of his favourite Kinks songs.

People strain their eyes to see, but I see you and you see me, and ain't that wonder? Sometimes the metre of songs . . . good lines are thrown away. Like I just said that line, that's the way I'd like to sing it, but you can't in the confines of four 4/4 bars, usually. Sometimes I let the words dictate. I'm notorious for sticking in 3/4 and 2/4 bars on top of a rock song and going to a 9/8 bar. I've done that before, to the constant frustration and sometimes amusement of the musicians working with me. The words dictate the metre. The difference about writing then, it sounds cruel and harsh because I was young; now I'm more considered with writing.

There's a beautiful song you wrote called 'Sweet Lady Genevieve' that has the lyrics *Once under a scarlet sky I told you never ending lies . . . I acted so slyly because you were acting so shy.*

Between that: *but they were the words of a drunken vagabond who knew very well he would break your heart before long. Oh forgive me, Genevieve.*

Do you use characters to confront or disguise your own realities? 'Mirror Of Love' might be a similar example.

I do use characters and that character is . . . as soon as the man starts speaking in 'Sweet Lady Genevieve' you don't trust him for one moment. Good character writing, I guess. 'Mirror Of Love' is completely benign, it's innocent. It's a man looking in the mirror saying, 'You're not such a bad guy after all'; two different emotions entirely. It sets up a thought pattern with people.

It's tempting to think the use of characters is a therapeutic device.

Yeah, it is a disguise.

No one can penetrate me, they only see what's in their own fancy. **How much of you is revealed in song?**

Less than you would imagine, more than you think. Around the later Sixties I was writing songs for a series on TV. They'd give me a brief on a Thursday, I'd write the song on a Friday and it'd be in the show on Saturday, but even in the songs that are just paid as a job something of you is inevitably going to transfer into that. I can't write a song without putting . . . an album like *Arthur*, for example, which was written for a script about a character. Something of me did end up in that. It's inevitable. There's a lot and a little.

You gotta be shrewd you gotta be strong, you've gotta convince yourself that you are not wrong. Whistle a tune and think of a catchy happy little song and look a little on the sunny side. **It's perplexing that some of your greatest writing has met with commercial silence. What gives you confidence to keep writing?**

Without going through that experience and those times I wouldn't have come out with those songs. Getting mediocre reviews puts you in the underground for a while—what's all that about?! It comes from a lack of awareness of your work. They've always done that with The Kinks. It's something to do with the name, me. We set a fairly high standard with our first bunch of singles.

They're now regarded as something to aspire to. I often think of Usain Bolt: how much faster has it got to go? He's a great runner but when he came second he was off the radar. It's staying on the radar within myself is the important thing. I had a chat with Damon Albarn when Blur were going through the Brit-pop war with Oasis. I said, 'You've just got to sit down and write your own songs and don't think about the publicity.' He did that, did his own thing and diversified. If I'm partly responsible for that I'm very happy.

Did school recognize talent in you as an artist?

I left school at fifteen to get some work experience. I then went back to art college and got all the qualifications I needed. The artistic side ran right beside the sporting side. I was captain of the sports team, fastest runner. The two worlds, art and sport, worked for me. I was acknowledged; I had something to say. I visualize songs before I write them, which comes from studying composition as a painter. Like the imagery in 'Waterloo Sunset'.

Where does melody come from? Do you believe in divine inspiration?

You can construct a melody. I studied orchestration in my late twenties and learnt a bit about melody structure, which didn't do me any favours as a song-writer because my whole philosophy of songwriting is untrained. The more I knew the less I could discover. I had a bunch of writers last week I was working with and I was trying to get to them to write more anthemic melodies. Great melodies are the most difficult to set lyrics to. You should interview Hal David. I had a long talk with him once at an awards ceremony. We were going to work together till we realized we both wrote lyrics. He said more often than not he got the melody from Burt Bacharach. They're quite complex melodies. The art of great lyric writing with great melody writers is to really know your scan and your vowels. 'Jerusalem' was a piece of text first, then Hubert Parry wrote the music and set it. It was a musical setting, not a melody. What an incredible set-ting. If he could have written that setting without that lyric *And did those feet in ancient times.* In those first few bars he created something immense. The way William Blake's lyrics scan, they don't rhyme, the great words he puts in, the images he conjures up. I'd love to have been around with Parry when he was writing that, doing his setting.

Do you develop vocal melody from your mind onto an instrument so you can see the notes you're working with?

See it in images, you mean? Interesting thing when I did the *Choral* album is how insignificant the melodies can look or sound if they're not written out properly and how the great melodies, Beethoven's Fifth, are very simple. Is it a triplet over 2/4 or is it a pick-up beat? 'You Really Got Me' if it was played on the downbeat, the first beat which is most people's (*hums riff*), it would be different totally, but it's a skip beat. It changes the whole emphasis. It's very important where those things are. So the writing of notes is crucial. My theory is—and I don't notate half as much as I should do—if it looks good it will sound great.

Are you trained to notate musical ideas?

I can to a degree; I can't do too much complex notation. In my late twenties I'd write out the classics. I did all the Bach Riemenschneider theories and Bartok's *Mikrokosmos*. I always got in trouble and irritated my piano teacher, the Colonel, because I was rewriting them all. I started singing in the school choir. When I did *Flatlands* for the Norwich Festival I had to write an entirely new piece of music especially for a choir, unlike *Village Green* which was adapted from an original rock record. I was more in control of the phonics. The thing I learnt by writing a new piece and using a mainly amateur choir—about forty per cent professionals—is to write simply. I learnt that very fast. If the notation looks good on paper it will sound good. Get the basis simple and articulated, then work on it to your heart's desire and be as tricky as you like.

The Kinks enjoyed greater stateside success in the Seventies and Eighties. Did your writing adapt for American consumption?

They say that Bartok when he moved to America used to notate conversations he heard in stores. There is a different language and tempo to the way people speak and pronounce words and that definitely had an effect on me with songs like 'Catch Me Now I'm Falling'. Being in the space does have an influence on the way you write.

Later you lived in New Orleans as a solo artist?

I went there primarily to write songs like 'The Real World'. 'The Getaway' I wrote in St Louis, Missouri, where I went for a weekend. I rehearsed 'Acute Schizophrenia Paranoia Blues' with the Preservation Hall Jazz Band for Meltdown. They acknowledged how much New Orleans music has influenced me. I was a fan of trad jazz and blues and Cajun music and country. It felt like a good place to go and write.

Is it important as both a writer and producer to see a song through from its origin to its end?

I've already got an idea of the way I want a song to sound before I write it. Sometimes songs are designed. I have an idea, something fires me up to write about it and I have a sound in mind. There's an album called *Give The People What They Want* from the Eighties. We were playing big auditoriums and I wanted the drums to sound like I was sitting in row sixty. It didn't work with some songs, I have to say. You never get it completely right. I certainly had that vision with '20th Century Man'. I'm singing as if I'm singing down to my chest.

I don't really want the listener in on everything I'm saying. The song almost needs subtitles.

Face To Face in 1966 marked the beginning of your producing career.

Shel Talmy was great at producing very quickly. It was at a time when we were trying to evolve and didn't want to be bracketed in one sound. Each song should have its own interpretation. 'Dead End Street' we felt was rushed; it had a whirligig-type organ on it played by our road manager and a French horn doing the phrase which made it sound like the Roman soldiers coming home to meet the Emperor. The French horn player was a man called Albert Hall. That name stuck with me. That's why there's a line in 'Session Man': *He never will forget at all the day he played at the Albert Hall.* I wanted 'Dead End Street' to be a bit dour and a bit earthy and a bit working-class, and the trombone fitted beautifully. Also it was more of a stomp. The version Shel wanted to make was more like a pop beat version. He finished the track and said, 'That's great,' and went home. Then we pretended to leave but came back to the studio and re-recorded the song. We played it to him the next day and he said, 'See what I mean, there's nothing wrong with it.' He thought we were playing him his version. I had some great times with Shel and we made some great records but it was clear it was time to move on.

Who or what did the character 'Dandy' represent?

I've thought a lot about this. Sometimes I write songs . . . I think it was about someone, probably me, who needed to make his mind up about relationships. Also about my brother, who was flitting from one girl to another. It's a more serious song than it seems. It's about a man who's trapped by his own indecision with relationships and lack of commitment. That's the way I'd write it now, but when I was twenty-two or twenty-three I wrote it about a jovial person who's a womanizer.

Do you remember writing the intro to 'Sunny Afternoon'?

I do. I'd bought a little white upright piano second hand. I hadn't written for a time. I'd been quite ill. It's a chromatic . . . writing scales practically on the piano. I was living in a very Sixties-decorated house. It had orange walls and green furniture. My one-year-old daughter was crawling around on the floor and I wrote the opening riff. I remember it vividly. I was even wearing a polo-neck sweater. All the times when I've had big success it's been at a time when I'm either ill or miserable or we're stuck. When 'You Really Got Me' got to number one we were stuck on a train that broke down on the way back from Torquay. The press were waiting to meet us. We all got flu, freezing cold in this carriage. It was a joy to have a hit with 'Sunny Afternoon'. England won the World Cup and we knocked 'Paperback Writer' off the number-one spot. It's

Ray Davies in Bergen, Norway, 17 June 1966
by Yan Calmeyer Friis

not one of their greatest singles but I'm a big admirer of The Beatles, an amazing band. It was quite significant.

Was it difficult as a writer, with the emerging dominance of The Beatles and The Stones?

You know what, sometimes they envied our freedom; we had one thing they didn't have and that was the right to fail. We failed but we tried something really radical. We didn't have the publicity machine The Beatles had. They were more accessible. They had more clearly defined roles within the show business society and hierarchy. With The Kinks, sometimes the audience are a little bit hesitant. It's like, 'What mood are they in today?', 'Are they going to please us or challenge us?' I think in a strange way it's paid off.

Do you remember a song called 'Yes Man' evolving into 'Plastic Man'?

I wanted to write a song about a person who has no self-identity. It's quite trendy now to be like everybody else.

And the song 'I'm Not Like Everybody Else'?

I used my brother as a model, as I did with 'Dandy'. Dave was always angrier; he's three and a bit years younger than me. He's a more outward person. He tells you what he thinks. It was great, liberating . . . casting a song for Dave's character. It's great now when I sing it. It's like if you cast something for actors each actor will bring to a play their own interpretation of it. My interpretation is more psychological whereas Dave's is more physical.

Is there a connection between your sister Rene playing the record 'Oklahoma' as described in your unauthorized autobiography, _X-Ray_, and the song 'Oklahoma USA'?

Yes, that was intentional: _She's walkin' on the surrey with the fringe on top._ She actually died whilst she was dancing to 'Surrey With The Fringe On Top' when she was at the Lyceum Ballroom. It was written on a battered Spanish guitar, nylon strings. I barre the A chord then do the quick movement with the fingers. I pedal the A note even though I change the chords. John Gosling played a beautiful piano part.

What was your thinking with the 1971 album _Muswell Hillbillies_? It was a radical change in sound and approach for The Kinks.

We'd gone through a phase of expanding through the Sixties. _Muswell Hillbillies_ was a return to what we thought we were as people. You reinvent to become yourself in the sense that we'd become these public personas with our haircuts and the way we dressed. We had longer hair and I was wearing country and western jackets. I figured the Muswell Hillbilly was like the Beverly

(N.W.B.)

Oaklahoma U.S.A.

All life we work but work is a bore,
If lifes not for living whats living for.
She lives in a house that is near decay,
Built for the industrial revolution
But in her dreams she is far away in
Oaklahoma U.S.A. with Shirly Jones and Gordon McRay.

As she goes to her job in the factory.
She dreams Errol Flynn gonna sweep her away
while she sits in line on the conveyor belt.
Shes Rita Hayworth or Doris Day.
In her dreams she is far away.
In Oaklahoma U.S.A. (That where Ive got my future made)
Shirly Jones and Gordon McRea.

Shes walking on the surrey with the fringe
on top.

As she still goes to her job in the factory,
She's Rita Hayworth or she is Day
When shes buying her paper
As she puts up her shopping at the corner shop
Shes thinking on the surrey with the fringe on
She goes to but sees in a daze (someone different)
She's Rita Hayworth or Doris Day every day
and Errol Flynn gonna take her away
to Oaklahoma U S A

'Oaklahoma USA' lyrics, handwritten by Ray Davies

Hillbillies. My parents come from inner Holloway, Islington. My mother was born in Barnsbury when it was a slum. People said, 'How upper-class,' but now it's become elevated to that level because Tony Blair lived there. My parents moved out to what was in those days . . . my mother took a bus out, she said, 'I've got to get out of the inner city.' For her it was like moving to the Hebrides, and it was Muswell Hill. It was more affluent and harder to fit in. It's a play on the Beverley Hillbillies. It was a change of identity. We felt like we were reverting back to our origins before we grew up in Muswell Hill.

It was inspired by the Archway Tavern. The family had drifted apart; last time we were with the family properly was before 'You Really Got Me' and then we went on tour. This pub my parents and sisters went to, there was the worst Irish country and western band you'd ever seen. A guy was playing the pedal steel but it sounded like a wild music. We had a great connection then. Dave used to turn up. He's very nostalgic for the family. *Muswell Hillbillies* came about after I went there with a writer friend of mine. It was an Irish pub then in the midst of all the Troubles. They burned the English flag. I made my apologies and left. It was a sign that there was undercurrent.

There was also lot of demolition and regeneration. If you look at the pictures on the record we're outside on a street that's boarded up and ready to be demolished. For '20th Century Man' I wrote a little script: it was a bigger story. He was a person that was holed up. He attached dynamite to all the doors and windows and threatened to blow himself up if they demolished the house. His was the last house standing in the street. That's a fiction. But I'd worked that out, and then wrote '20th Century Man'. That's why that emotion stays with me. And I still think of that when I perform it today.

Muswell Hillbillies seemed to be swimming against the tide after the enormous success of 'Lola'.

Yeah, I know, we were a success despite ourselves. I wanted to write songs that are not as light as they sound, like 'Acute Schizophrenia Paranoia Blues'. Songs about subjects that were close to me, and I wanted to write things that had an element of danger to them and an element of love. Sometimes love songs are so tender that you don't want people to hear them, they're so personal, and that's certainly the case with 'Oklahoma USA' and 'Holloway Jail'. When you're writing about real people you want to serve their memory well; doing a single about them doesn't always work.

Why are you a songwriter?

Good question. I still wake up in the mornings and wonder what I'm going to do when I grow up. Why am I a songwriter? That's the way it ended up. I'm going to write some long-form stuff, maybe a couple of small plays. Writing is writing; I just love writing tunes for them. I'm a very ambitious, creative person.

ROBIN GIBB

1964. The Beatles arrive in Australia. Barry, Robin and Maurice Gibb immediately recognize kindred musical spirits. 'The Three Kisses Of Love' with accompanying *yeah, yeah, yeah*'s was a sign. It had a three-part harmony. English pop was celebrating vocal unison and it was time for the brothers to come home.

The Bee Gees' affinity with The Beatles would impact throughout their career. At the height of their success they would recreate the classic album *Sgt. Pepper's Lonely Hearts Club Band* with George Martin producing. The sessions revealed the precise attention to vocal tuning of Barry Gibb and the unnerving ease with which the brothers could replicate John, Paul and George's complex arrangements. It was impressive, but by no means unexpected. The Gibb family had emigrated in 1958 in search of better work possibilities. Their fledgling talents were soon spotted by Brisbane disc jockey Bill Gates at a speedway meeting where they were singing between races. Gates steered the boys onto radio and television and soon landed them their own TV show, *The BG's Half-Hour*. Barry was the sole composer in these developing years, signing a publishing deal as a 15-year-old. Adelaide Radio recognized him as Composer of the Year for 'I Was A Lover' as his prolific writing provided hits for both his own group and for other artists.

The Bee Gees were a vocal group. It is an important distinction to make. The concentration on voice and melody is paramount in their approach and song construction. 'Let the melody dictate' is the simple maxim that dominates Robin's conversation. He contends that the lyrics and beat of a record are secondary to its vocal attraction. From early in the siblings' career, the method of finding melody, defining it note by note and then, later, adding words, has never faltered. Robin confesses to only a rudimentary ability with his instrument, the keyboard, but far from being a limitation, this has diverted his focus away from rhythm towards melodic development.

Five months before the original release of The Beatles' *Sgt. Pepper's Lonely*

Hearts Club Band in June 1967, the Gibb family returned to England and within two weeks signed a recording deal with Brian Epstein's working partner, Robert Stigwood. His first advice to the trio was: 'Write for the future, now. Don't write for now.' Augmented by a drummer and a lead guitar player, the newly formed Bee Gees soon found homeland success, relying heavily upon the British dominance of popular music. The influence of Lennon and McCartney's picturesque lyrics is most evident on their British debut single, 'New York Mining Disaster 1941'. Originally titled 'Have You Seen My Wife, Mr Jones?' the song was composed in the darkness of a back stairwell at Polydor Records, helping to invoke the images of people trapped in a mine. The song's inspiration came from the mining disaster in the small Welsh village of Aberfan in October 1966 which killed 116 children and 28 adults. Written by Barry and Robin, the opening guitar introduction sets the uneasy mood. Its sound is produced by a standard A minor open chord played by Maurice, mixed with an open D tuning of the same chord played by Barry. Karl Richardson, engineer of many Bee Gees sessions, asserts that Barry's characteristic rhythm playing, invariably tuned to an open chord, helped to distinguish their recordings from traditional R&B presentation. Often his guitar would be submerged in a song's mix to subtly lend weight to arrangements as a percussive driving force. By contrast, and despite record company reservations, it was Maurice's multi-layered rhythm track drum stomps on 'You Win Again' that were largely responsible for the Bee Gees' first number-one record of the Eighties. Had Barry not summoned himself from a creative slumber the track might never have existed. In the early hours he woke with a melody line and lyric running through his head. It was his habit to keep a Dictaphone by the side of the bed for such moments, but on this occasion the machine did not have a cassette in it. Fearing he might forget the melody, he located a blank tape and was able to record the song's key line, *There's no fight you can't fight / This battle of love with me / You win again.*

The three brothers always regarded themselves first as songwriters, second, recording artists and third, performers. Bee Gees song ideas were chiefly generated from Barry's acoustic guitar. Later Maurice would be more active in developing and arranging. He had an exemplary knowledge of Beatles bass lines and allowed his admiration of Paul McCartney's inventiveness to influence many early releases. 'I've Gotta Get A Message To You', recorded in B flat, is a clear homage to the booming bottom end of 'Paperback Writer' and 'Rain'. The bass harmonizes the alternating lead vocals of Robin and Barry with flourishing movement and octave leaps. At Stigwood's insistence the chorus melody was re-recorded with a three-part harmony to focus and strengthen the arrangement. The song imagined a prisoner on Death Row and their final thoughts before going to the chair. It was a typical narrative base with orchestral embellishment from the prodigious talents of Bill Shepherd that would define many of their first recordings.

The brothers placed great store by the use of titles to inspire compositions. Robin explained, 'We always believed there's no such thing as a title you can't write a song to.' 'Grease' was suggested by their manager, and Barry set about defining it for the song's chorus *grease is the word* before counselling its *groove* and *feeling*. 'Massachusetts' and 'Heartbreaker' invited immediate suggestion, but reserved revelation; they said something without revealing everything. 'Tragedy' uses its single-word heading with infectious repetition over a round of minor chords and an inventive explosion mid-song generated by Barry cupping his hands around the microphone and faking the noise. The verses are heralded by the distinctive first and fifth notes of D and A accenting, with on-the-beat quavers and crotchets, the oncoming drama. Where vocal lines stop, guitars and an overdriven synthesizer, played by Blue Weaver, bridge the changes with continuous and connecting phrases.

Such is the strength and imitable style of the Bee Gees in their fastidious attention to detail that even when they write for others, a song will always emerge bearing their unique hallmark. As young boys they began by pretending they were composing for famous artists. Incredibly, the imitation game of their childhood fantasies would become adult reality. Barry and Robin, in particular, spent a large part of the Eighties producing and writing for other artists. For Barbra Streisand 'Guilty' won best pop performance at the Grammys as she celebrated her first number-one studio album, whilst 'Woman In Love', her only career number-one single, won an Ivor Novello Award for Best Song. 'Heartbreaker' provided Dionne Warwick with her biggest hit since Bacharach and David's 'Do You Know The Way To San Jose', and in 1985, Diana Ross's interpretation of the Motown-styled 'Chain Reaction' earned the former Supremes lead singer accolades to parallel her mid-Sixties heyday. 'Islands In The Stream', written as an R&B song with Marvin Gaye in mind, took its name from an Ernest Hemingway book title. Recorded by Dolly Parton and Kenny Rogers, its country interpretation became the biggest-selling record in RCA history. In total, a staggering 2,500 artists have covered the songs of the Bee Gees, including Elvis Presley, Frank Sinatra, Nina Simone, Lulu and Roy Orbison.

The phenomenal success of the writing partnership of Barry, Robin and Maurice over five decades is without precedent. As the Bee Gees they have sold over one hundred million records and collected a multitude of awards, notably induction to the Songwriters' and Rock 'n' Roll Halls of Fame and Brit Lifetime Achievement and Legend awards. They are Grammy legends, have a star on the Hollywood Boulevard Walk of Fame and have been honoured with CBEs for services to music. Six consecutive number ones in the USA is a feat matched only by The Beatles. In fact, Lennon and McCartney are the only songwriters to have more US number ones, whilst the Gibb brothers have been responsible for twenty-two American top-spot positions. *Saturday Night Fever* was a recipient of four Grammy nominations and is the biggest-selling soundtrack album ever, with sales in excess of forty million.

Robin Hugh Gibb was born in Douglas on the Isle of Man on 22 December 1949, an hour before his non-identical twin, Maurice Ernest, and three years after his eldest brother, Barry Alan Compton. The boys' father was the leader of a dance band, the Hughie Gibb Orchestra, and when he returned with his family to Manchester in the Fifties, his drum kit took up residence in the front room alongside a stereogram and big band, opera and Bing Crosby records. One afternoon he heard voices coming from what he thought was the radio, singing in perfect harmony. He tracked down the sound to his three boys, practising singing with hairbrushes. The twins were a mere six years old, but confident enough to show off their precocious talent on stage at the local Gaumont Theatre in film intermissions. Hughie began to instil into the boys stage professionalism inspired by his love of the four-piece vocal group The Mills Brothers. Then Elvis Presley arrived.

Robin Gibb on a flight from Miami to London, circa 2003 by Dwina Gibb

Prepubescent male voices have a natural treble before the voice breaks. The quality is then lost but can be recaptured via countertenor by some adult males. It was the falsetto reverberation of Barry, Robin and Maurice that would impact in mid-Seventies America and revolutionize world pop. At the turn of the decade the Bee Gees' success had abruptly faltered. From the highs of selling out the Albert Hall their career had bottomed out to Variety Club dates as the pressures of initial stardom, touring, wealth and petty squabbling split the band, ending a glorious run of hit singles including 'To Love Somebody', 'World', 'Words', 'I Started A Joke' and 'First Of May'. New direction was to be found in groove and a reawakening passion for R&B. Encouraged by producer Arif Mardin, the brothers began to explore their formative doo-wop influences, and duly served up *Main Course*. It is an exceptional release that included the lead single 'Jive Talkin'' and the romantic 'Fanny Be Tender' in which Barry and Robin sing the verse melody in unison 'as one voice'. The effect is a trademark sound of the Bee Gees before the chorus opens out to a three-part harmony with Maurice's added texture. Significantly, the cleverly formed 'Nights On Broadway' featured Barry's first use of falsetto, pitched from middle A up to the octave above. His natural tenor crosses over between minor and major changes, *singing them sweet sounds* from vocal wholeness to vulnerability, supported by Maurice and Robin's backing. Mid-song the shuffle groove breaks from the tempo, and, over extended bars, the voices explore harmony as the patient lover waits *even if it takes a lifetime*.

The falsetto effect suited the brothers' voices, and, under the umbrella of disco, the world danced to the records of the Bee Gees. Pivotal to this success was a *New York Magazine* article, 'Tribal Rites of the New Saturday Night', by the British journalist Nik Cohn. The Bee Gees contributed seven tracks about survival without having seen the Stigwood-commissioned film. With John Travolta's downtown Brooklyn character seducing a nation to visit their nearest ballroom, a multitude of hits followed. 'Stayin' Alive' was the first record to utilize a drum loop, now standard recording practice. Two bars of real drums from a previous Bee Gees track were edited together and used as a groove foundation. The same loop was later employed on both 'More Than A Woman' and 'Woman In Love'. After the gender non-specific words of 'How Deep Is Your Love', 'Stayin' Alive' spent four weeks at number one before the cleverly alternating voices of 'Night Fever' completed a top-spot trilogy. American radio responded by having Bee-Gee-free weekends, such was their impact on the airways. On 12 July 1979, during a baseball game in Chicago, protestors filled a crate with disco records before blowing up its contents. The destruction was a crusade against eighteen months of number-one dance dominance, and either by design or coincidence the reign ended with the Bee Gees' sixth consecutive number-one single, 'Love You Inside Out', ahead of Gamble and Huff's ironically titled 'Ain't No Stopping Us Now'.

Robin Gibb died on 20 May 2012 after a long battle with cancer. Nine years earlier his twin, Maurice, had succumbed to a heart attack. They had both seen new generations of songwriters and artists inspired by their vast portfolio. Take That, Boyzone, Destiny's Child and Steps all found success in the pop world, whilst Richard Ashcroft, Oasis and Ocean Colour Scene offered admiration from the rock fraternity. Robin's belief was in the mass rather than the individual composition, and we shared a poignant afternoon in June 2010 discussing his thoughts and techniques in the grounds of his converted eleventh-century Oxfordshire medieval home. He was charming company, relaxed in the sunshine of his peaceful garden, and after revealing many of his songwriting methods, Robin picked a few of his favourite compositions from the heaped vinyl stretching across the table at his side. He cited 'How Deep Is Your Love' and 'Words' and then 'Emotion', which he recalled had been written with Barry and finished in half an hour, the brothers having said, 'Great title, let's write it.' He singled out 'Chain Reaction', stating 'It's the only song with fifteen key changes,' and then 'Nights On Broadway' because he was so proud of the song's construction. As a tribute to Maurice, I would like to recommend P. P. Arnold's interpretation of 'Bury Me Down By The River', which Maurice co-wrote with Barry. When I spent time with the former Ikette in the early Nineties she marvelled at the song's poignant and prophetic sentiment, *I wasn't born to be lucky 'cause luck had no future with me.* With tea and home-made biscuits served, Robin picked up the conversation . . .

'We see ourselves first and foremost as composers, writing for ourselves and other people. We started writing when we were eight years old in Manchester. We used to listen to the radio and imagine what other people's records would be. So we'd listen to a record and say, 'Let's imagine we're real songwriters.' We're still doing that, pretending we were writing their new record and we'd be in this imaginary world. It was a hobby with no friends.'

How much did you study other artists' records? Would you deconstruct an Elvis or a Beatles song?

It wouldn't be there to deconstruct, we weren't that savvy about music. We were completely self-taught. Our parents didn't even know what we were doing. It was a hobby that even we weren't aware of. We were just playing it the same way kids throw a ball around; we were just throwing music around. We didn't even have instruments, really, until Barry got a guitar for Christmas. He plays the guitar now the same way as he did when he taught himself then. There's been no musical education at all. Even today I don't know the name of musical notes. I can't read music.

Is your instrument the keyboard?

I play keyboards to compose music. I don't play instruments to entertain people: two different things. My dad used to play the piano brilliantly and me and Barry were always very impressed. We used to say to him, 'Why don't you compose music?' He'd say, 'Oh, no, I can play piano . . . I'll leave composing to others.' So whenever Barry and myself approach an instrument, it's really just to . . . how can we use it to inspire us to write a song: use chords, a chord progression, a sound.

What sparks your lyrical imagination?

Somebody in a conversation . . . your antennae are always up for a title; that can spark off a whole song. You hold it in your mind and because it stands out you don't usually forget it. When you get a line it becomes a statement, rather than a story. Principally, we go by the melody first, then write the lyrics to that melody; never the other way around. Let the melody dictate the lyric and the statement. It's very important it's not just a story. What we always did was, 'Let's come up with a title and then write it.' We always believed there's no such thing as a title you can't write a song to, like 'Massachusetts'. We wrote that on a boat in New York harbour as a challenge. When you look back it's quite a good exercise if you are songwriters to challenge yourselves to do something; we'd never been to Massachusetts. It's an unusual title with all the S's. (*Assumes pompous voice.*) 'How could anybody possibly write a song called . . .', so we did. We've always loved one-word titles like 'Emotion' and 'Heartbreaker', 'Words', 'Tragedy' without having to give too much away. It sparks the imagination for people, draws people. And colourful titles like 'Chain Reaction', 'Islands In The Stream'. I think 'You Win Again' came up in a conversation. Even though it's a very common expression it was very good: *this battle of love . . . we do nothing but compete*—it complements the title. I think the art of composition is not just the title but the statement, and also working the lyrics around the idea that it is a battle and you are competing: at the end it complements the statement you are making. 'Guilty' which we did for Streisand, the way *it oughta to be illegal* and building the legalities and crime into the song . . . There's different ways that you compose. Your brain tells you rather than the other way. When you start composing it can last for hours.

You often keep gender non-specific, which lends your songs universal appeal.

Yes, we do that on purpose. Love is not about a particular sex. A lot of people that started out in the music industry used *he* and *she*. Love is universal and we'd go out of our way not to mention *he* or *she*, so like a *you* or *babe*. It's a subtle way of doing it, but it has a way of crossing . . . there's a lot of people out there who can't really relate if you do use those expressions and we want our songs to relate to as many people as possible.

Do you scat lyrics: dress the melody with syllables before concentrating on the words?

We put down a pilot vocal over a basic recording for our own reference on a song we don't have lyrics to: we've got the melody and just make up words as we go along. Say it's 'You Win Again' (*hums melody and meaningless syllables*) then sing *You win again* where we think it should be. Then we'll have the lyric session: play it over and over again, listen to it and somehow within that umming and aahing words form, you hear it. It's almost like, what could we be saying there? You hear with your brain words that you weren't actually saying. It's a strange thing and that's the formula we've stuck to. It's amazing how much you can come up with like that. It's always worked.

When the three of you sat down to write words, how collaborative was the process?

It was very collaborative. The majority of the work was done by Barry and myself: the melody and the lyric session; the idea, of course; the vocalizing; the essence of everything. The thing is there wasn't a role; we'd both have ideas and come to the table with them. We'd both expand on them. We'd always go with the melody first and write the lyrics on another day. On the Streisand album, for instance, 'Guilty' and 'Woman In Love' and all that, we decided to do six or seven days in a row in Barry's bedroom, where we just did the melodies. On one day it would be this song, the next day 'Guilty'. The weekend we'd have off and then on Monday we'd come in and start on the lyrics of those melodies.

Bee Gees melodies are very infectious and memorable. Are they worked out exactly, note for note?

We don't like to waste notes. We are very conscious that melody is extremely important. You've got seven notes to work with, everybody in the whole world has: it's the order in which you use them. But melody is the most important thing about writing a song, and then you approach the lyrics and you must work them into it. If you take a lyric or a poem and try and adapt a song to that, I'm not saying it can't be done; we just have never done it. We don't think it works as well. You must let the melody dictate the flow of the song. It's also the most important thing that people are attracted to. They're not attracted to the story or the beat like everybody seems to think they are. It's the melody first, then the rest. The arrangement is secondary to that. We don't like to gild the lily too much. Space is as important. It creates an emotion and longing of its own is which also very infectious to people. A lot of people think that if you have a space you've got to fill it up with either an ad-lib or an instrument. We like to use our vocals and always use our harmonies. We're natural harmonizers and it sounds fantastic if you know how to use them. These days people don't know how to use harmonies unless they are shown on a piano where the notes go: otherwise they just can't do it, it's too hard for them.

Can you explain how melody comes to you? You've previously said 'I Started A Joke' was inspired by the sound of a Viscount . . .

. . . an engine. If the bells of that church over there went now I could hear a melody in that that other people couldn't, the harmonics for instance, and my ears will pick it out, only because I've been doing it so long. The extraordinary thing is you can hear melody if you've got your antennae up. The ear gets an extra sense to it. It's like playing Scrabble: you're constantly looking for seven-letter words. It's the same with songwriting: it's what you do. I expect if you're making movies you're constantly looking for the right light. If I've got someone to do a harmony with me, the natural thing is people will gravitate towards the melody, whereas I will naturally stick to the harmony.

When you start on a melody do you feel in control of its development, or are you trying to rein in something that's somehow already out there?

When you're in the mood for composing you don't always have a melody, but within five minutes of playing keyboards you could have a great one. If you're in the mood you're confident that . . . you get a buzz about something that you feel isn't there at the moment. It's a clean canvas: you play the keyboard, you shut the door; it's a kind of meditation moment. You fiddle around with one hand on the keyboard, and it doesn't really matter and you will find the melody. I'm not saying it's spiritual or anything like that, but it will come to you because you feel good about what you're doing, and you have patience. If it's a job, you've got to get a melody that feels good and you're sweating and don't find a melody in an hour: that's not how it works. It's the mood and you enjoy even the idea that you might not get a melody.

Do you record yourself trying to find an idea?

All the time. Both Barry and myself have a memo recorder on all the time because the simplest little melody here and there can sparkle and it can be a magical moment. Even in the studio you've got a seven-and-a-half-inch tape player going to record everything so you don't miss a thing. When you can't remember you go back: 'That's what we did there; we hummed that there.'

Does the number of chords in a song direct the development of the melody?

Too many chords . . . the chords are not a problem . . . the melody will find itself. Chords aren't the essence of a song. The melody is the essence. There are many variations of melody over a succession of the same chords. You could play me three or four chords of a very popular song, take the vocal or the melody off, and I could sing an entirely different melody and you wouldn't guess that those chords were from that song. It's quite normal in classical music. Billions of people all around the world only have seven notes available to them. As I said earlier, it is really how you use them, where you use them and the order you use them in—and not only necessarily the order that they fall, but also the spaces and the rests that you have and the way you let the song breathe and the speed at which the song goes. There are certain melodies that if you have just a little too fast, the song doesn't breathe; even the melody tends to lose its appeal. You've got to make it human as well. One thing technology can't really replace is the emotion of the human voice, much as they try; harmonies as well, and of course, they can't write the melodies that the mind can construct that affect the human psyche.

Does the instrument you use affect the writing of the melody?

That's arrangement really, improvisation. Once you've got the essence of the song that will either work or it won't. That's gilding the lily: if you have too much of a complementary instrument playing it has to really work and complement the song, otherwise there's no point in having it. It can't just be a guitar piece for the sake of it. Simple to me is pure. You mustn't lose track of that. It isn't necessarily 'throw everything on it' just so that it can be called a record. The pureness and the simplicity must come across so people can hear the human part of the song. That is everything. Everything must have a reason.

Your lyrics often have unusual turns of phrase, for example, *you're a holiday* **or** *nobody gets too much heaven any more.*

'Holiday' was written on an autoharp, again just 'Holiday' on its own. There have been songs called 'Holiday' since, but we were probably the first group to write a song called 'Holiday' about a relationship: *you're a holiday, such a holiday* and that was the way we worked it and it went top ten in America, and it made sense. But until you approach it, most people wouldn't think of it in that way. Songwriting is not so much about the obvious; it's about going around the houses and looking at it from a different angle. It's not about talking about rehab and vomiting in someone's shoes which some people do; it may be romantic to some. People love songs about human relationships, even those people that are not born yet; it's not something that goes in and out of fashion. It's the way you talk about them. The art of composition is that you approach it from an angle that most people would not and yet they can relate to it at the same time.

Robin's hands with an autoharp

Tim Rice said that love songs were the hardest to write because you not only had to be original, but also the vocabulary is more limited because you generally have to use fewer syllables.

Yes. I don't look at it from a technical point of view. I'm a great fan of Tim's. He's looking at it from a lyrical point of view and he's right. The problem with love songs is they are perennial as the grass and if you can get it right they will be played decades and decades from now and appeal to generations that are not around yet. If you try to be too fashionable . . . a lot of rap music I don't get because it's not my forte. I can't even relate to that. I love music. I love melody, I always will, but we'll stick to us and stick to what I know best. If you are going to try and be original . . . singing about *the moon in June* and *Jack and Jill went up the hill* and *we'll be in love forever*, that's the obvious and most boring route to take because that's not the art of composition. Anybody can sing about being happy in love. A great love song is not actually singing about being happy, they're not the ones that sell. The biggest sellers are torch songs: even if you get the hardest rockers, their biggest records are songs about missing people. The Police: their biggest record, 'Every Breath You Take', he's not with her, he's watching her with somebody else; he's longing for her, but he's always there. 'You Don't Have To Say You Love Me': *I'll be close at hand, You don't have to stay forever*—it's about going away. It's the happy/sad state of the human condition that people are attracted to. Even for people that are in happy relationships, there is something about these kinds of songs that produces longing. It's melancholic. It produces something unique in the human psyche that touches us. We all long for something, we don't know what it is, and this kind of music produces that. It's not because it's sad music, either. People are happy in this particular feeling for some reason. It's the kind of feeling that good music that affects people produces. It's not always celebratory music.

How much self-examination goes into your writing?

If you mean biographical, you'd have a nervous breakdown.

Having to pull out of yourself . . .

. . . I see what you mean, yes, of course. It's like acting: that can be draining. If you're going to convince people and make a record, the attitude has to be right. You've got to be, put yourself in the position of, the person in the song to get that over. If it's another person, they've got to do it, that's why you make sure you have the song to begin with.

So you have to draw on emotions deep within you. Are you always happy to go there for a song, do you have restricted areas that you won't go to?

You have a sense of what you know produces this kind of longing in people. If it does it with you, then it will do it with other people. In a way, what affects you will affect other people, and it's knowing it. A lot of men, I find, or boys, who start out in this business are very self-conscious about writing about human emotions. They feel it's not manly, it's not a guy thing, but they may want to. I know a lot of hard rockers who really like our music and sometimes they'll even perform it, but the soft underbelly of them is hidden. It's not because of the music; it's because singing about human emotions is very hard for people. What appeals to a woman generally is a male talking about emotions he's feeling. There's one ingredient in our emotions which one can miss out: apart from an angle that's different that you approach singing about love, it's also about the reflections of this guy's own emotions in it, which very few men sing about. They see it as a sign of weakness. But that doesn't mean he's any less a man. It does travel over the years, because human relationships are not a fashion. Some of our biggest records in America, 'How Can You Mend a Broken Heart', which was number one for weeks, that's a torch song. 'Too Much Heaven' for instance, there were twenty-two US number ones all about people you're missing. Very few about, 'Hey, we're happy, and we're just having a great time, the moon's up and let's party.' That's not something that appeals to people.

How far will you develop an idea before rejecting it?

Both Barry and myself will always self-check ourselves when writing. There are many songs we'll write and not use.

Will you always complete an idea?

Oh no, we won't complete a song . . . we'll know almost before we even get to the lyric stage. Sometimes it'll happen in the recording stage. Also you get a great song that doesn't translate well in the recording studio, right away. Sometimes you get a song that we call a work record; it's just not going to happen, then you finish it and it turns out to be a single and goes to number one. It's a very strange thing being a composer. When you've been a composer like ourselves for so long, eight years out of the womb and you're into this world and you haven't known any other in your life. It's a strange thing to look back and think that's all we've ever done.

How important is environment and the time of day to your writing?

I would have to say the early hours of the morning when it's quiet, about 2 a.m. You can't write when there are people around. It's a vexation to the spirit.

Are you self-conscious if you think people are listening to your developing ideas?

Absolutely. The creative process is a very personal thing. One problem is: don't invite anybody to say anything critical when you are developing a song.

It is crucial that you don't. If you feel that you're onto something special, that will uniquely come out special in the end, the last thing you want is somebody coming in, 'Oh, I don't like that . . .'. They may be the cleaning lady, for instance, but it has a psychological effect. You just don't want that kind of . . . you may think, well, what does she know, what do I know; it's not that. It can have a dramatic effect on how the song progresses, even to the point where you don't finish it. It's important even if you're getting off on it, don't always rush the idea. At that stage, everybody's gonna hear what you're hearing, because it isn't finished and that's why demos can be deadly. If you do a demo, which we don't really do any more, you tend to have a rough master and you always assume that people hear what you can hear on the finished record, but of course they don't, except for the person who's going to record the song. Record companies are the worst offenders; they don't always hear it the way you do. They always say they do, 'But it's only a demo.' 'It doesn't matter, we'll hear it . . . We know what we're talking about.' What's long and slippery and has no ears? Record company executives.

Do you remember the first song you wrote after introducing falsetto in 'Nights On Broadway'?

I'm trying to think . . . probably 'You Should Be Dancing' on the *Children of the World* album.

Did the framework of R&B songs like 'You Should Be Dancing' and 'Boogie Child' with the four on the floor beat demand a different writing approach?

First of all, I know people have said it looks like a definitive plan. As composers—I don't think American composers share the same attitude—we weren't afraid to go anywhere in terms of genre or what we wanted to work on; there's no such thing as a no-go area. 'Islands In The Stream' is the most successful and played country song in history. Not many people can get into the Nashville mafia and compose songs for country artists. R&B, American black music has always been appealing to us, as kids listening to it on Australian radio stations, playing twenty-four-hour pop every day: Sam and Dave, Otis Redding, soul music. One of our first R&B soul records was 'To Love Somebody', when we first arrived in England, which was huge in the States as well. We've always been in that world and when we met Arif Mardin we explored it further and it was always natural to us.

Working with Arif from *Mr Natural* on, I'm curious whether you approached creating songs as records as opposed to before when they were very definitely songs that became records.

Mr Natural I would describe as a transitional album. Where do we want to go from here? We wanted to stay on the same road, but as songwriters we needed to change, but also as artists we needed to adapt. As a composer you can do it easily, but you've got to be an artist at the same time. We were never conscious of an image as artists, but we were always very much composers first.

When you say 'we changed', how did you do that? It's extraordinary that as composers you varied your style so phenomenally.

If there was a change I don't know where the definitive line . . . where we could say, 'Oh, that's where we sat down and designed a change.' Because we weren't afraid to try and do anything, we were actually quite confident that we could, in the same way we could try and write a song around a title like 'Holiday'. We thought we could write any groove that came our way. We didn't feel any part of music was a no-go area because it was all part and parcel of the same thing. We never saw it as dance music; there's always been dance, either slow dance or fast dance from Glenn Miller to the Charleston, so music has always been danceable to. What we were doing was R&B music, which we loved: 'You Should Be Dancing', 'Jive Talkin'', just what we wanted to do at that particular point. We've always been a harmonizing group and when you do melody and harmonizing over those grooves it takes on a much more exciting feel. We spent a lot of time in the studio. If we had a choice between going to a nightclub we'd always go into the studio: workaholics, twenty-four hours a day, experimenting in the studio.

I read Barry experimented on the song 'Horizontal', recording eight pianos to be inspired by the sound.

In those days, thankfully, you didn't have the luxury of technology to give you the same sound that everybody had. You had to go in search of a sound that was different to other people. You looked at what was number one, listened to it, that was great, now let's do something different. Compete to be different rather compete to be the same, which is what a lot of people unfortunately do today because they all have the same sounds at their disposal. They don't go looking for sounds that are original.

Are you suited to writing on tap, to demand?

We love writing to deadline. If somebody says they want something you apply yourself: your mind is on it and you do it. Deadlines have always been an important part of our world. We write better with deadlines, actually. It inspires us, it focuses. When you've got open time, you don't apply yourself as well.

Is a Bee Gees melody led by the lead vocalist or by what the song requires?

Can do, if one of us is dominant in the vocal area on that idea, it might well work; that melody will work to that person's voice. I think there's a truth there, especially between me and Barry: one of us will allow the other to take over if it feels that's where the melody is finding itself. There is a lot in that, that if you are doing something that's special to that person's voice you'll find it and it'll be dominant and that melody will suit. It's not a decision, it's what feels right. It will be organic, natural, and it will be unquestioned. We won't say, 'Now you do this.' It wouldn't be like that, it's not as technical as that. It's just a sense of what is right in the composing period.

'I've Gotta Get a Message To You' is characterized by Barry singing the second verse and you the first . . .

. . . and third, like we do in 'How Can You Mend a Broken Heart'. There's another trick we play. If you listen to 'How Deep Is Your Love' you think it's a single voice but it's me and Barry singing in unison, which produces a nice sound, as it does on 'New York Mining Disaster'. There's a sound that we do, it's almost like a single voice, but it isn't, and it's not double-tracked, it's two voices together. It's something that we've done a lot.

How did the different writing combinations work between the three of you? As a listener I find it very hard to distinguish between songs you and Barry, or Barry and Maurice, have written.

Me too (*laughs*). We must talk about it one day; we must get to grips with it. It's a dichotomy wrapped in . . . whatever . . . an envelope. I don't really like composing on my own. I'm a team player. I like the camaraderie. I've enjoyed writing with Barry, I still do. He's the greatest songwriter in the world to work with and I wouldn't want to work with anybody else, and why should I? We've been writing together all our lives, but together is perfect. We're not bogged down by musical theory, or what's musically right and wrong, as long as it sounds good, and that's the whole idea. Emotionally it has to sound right; if it does, it's done.

What was the first song you all wrote together?

1958, it was called 'The Echo Of Your Love' (*sings*) *The echo is here to stay, the echo da da da, the echo is here to stay, the echo of your love*. I love the word *echo* by the way; even then I was drawn in by certain words. Love themes, eight years old: we were very young. Bill Gates the disc jockey, in Brisbane, invited us into his studio; he did the drive-time. He recorded these acetates and played them on his show. I'd like to get hold of them, I haven't had them since then, they must be around somewhere. 'Time Is Passing By', 'Let Me Love You' and 'The Echo Of Your Love'.

When you write for other people, does it open a different creative freedom?

We've always liked writing songs for other people, and seeing them have success with our songs is no different from having success ourselves because we see ourselves as composers and artists as well. The good thing about being an artist is you have the ability to express, get those songs out there, whereas a composer relies just upon artists. We've always enjoyed having that two-tier career . . . especially established artists who are already having hits putting out a record of yours is always a buzz. It's kind of an extension of what you do; it's not, 'Oh, why didn't you keep it?' It's still your song and it's a great thing. It's created a very broad catalogue and some of these songs are very much with these other artists and are very much part of their trademarks now because they are associated with them.

When you were working with artists such as Dionne Warwick or Barbra Streisand, did it bring out any unexplored areas of your writing?

Not really, they were songs we would have recorded ourselves. We've always felt that if we can get a buzz off a song, other people will too. When we were approached to do that Streisand album we said, 'Let's not listen to what she's already done, let's give her an album that we would do, a record that radio will love.' A lot of songwriters tend to write what the artist has already done. We wanted to give her a studio album with accessible songs and that's what we centred on. We didn't construct songs around what she'd already done.

Diana Ross's 'Chain Reaction' was the opposite of that.

We'd finished writing the album and I said, 'We don't have the quintessential single that should be off this album.' She thought it was finished. Barry and I got together one night and decided: what about writing a song like the Supremes would do, and the irony is it wouldn't be somebody else doing it; it would actually be one of the Supremes. Well, of course, when we played it to her it was shock and horror: 'I'm not doing a Supremes song . . . that's the last thing I want to do . . . I left that.' Revisiting a lot of skeletons there, we said, 'It's not a personal thing, we think it's a hit record . . .' We actually felt it was a smash, basically because '. . . you'd be doing it, and also because you are one of the Supremes, and what better person to do it than another one of the other Supremes?' Of course that clinched it. 'Yes, I see what you mean.'

Why do you think Americans have predominantly covered your songs?

Well, it's the biggest English-speaking and record market. There are more artists. Because of the way we were brought up, in actually being affected by American popular music, there is sophistication in the writing that doesn't really or hasn't existed in the UK, aside from The Beatles who were also affected by American music. Of course, there's Andrew Lloyd Webber, which is stage music, but in terms of the popular song, those British songwriters that have had success in the States, it's because they have been exposed to American music a tremendous amount, like Tim Rice, Andrew Lloyd Webber, Lennon and McCartney and various others. A lot of these reality TV programmes have dampened the infrastructure that encourages and supports and influences young, new songwriters to compose. The art of composition has been lost in this country to a degree. It's been buried. You've either got to be good for *X Factor* or it's the exit.

Historically there are very few successful female UK singer-songwriters.
There aren't any. I ask the same question: why there aren't that many really good woman politicians? They say we want our token woman, but what about talent? You've always got driven women in the States, in politics as in all fields. You're quite right: I don't know what the answer is. They're just not attracted to it the same way as guys are. It's a different world for females here; they feel intimidated, more so than if they were in the States, probably. It just feels different in America; it just feels that there's more opportunities, more possibilities. It's not very easy for women here if you're a composer or an artist, and again, if you're not selling yourself on sex or who you go out with, for a woman here, that's it. You've got to be controversial; you've got to look weird. Every record for a girl has to work. Your video has got to be sexual, controversial or quirky. They can't just be good composers and if they are, they don't want to be seen. There are a lot of dynamics at work. It's a hard business wherever you are, for women particularly, because you've got to be out of the house. You've got to be seen everywhere. Women by nature, without sounding sexist, really at the end of the day, if they do decide to have a partner and kids, it kind of takes over and becomes a priority. It's nature. Having a child is a serious thing to a woman and a guy can still plough on and be the reckless schoolboy that he always was.

Having sold millions of records, is there a point at which you ever feel overshadowed by your former glories?
No, why would I do that?

The pressure to keep up the success, to find new melody . . .
. . . How many people can have that? Don't you think McCartney suffers from that? Steven Spielberg could do that with his last movie. You've got to look at the bigger picture: very few people have achieved what we've achieved in this industry. If you're competing with yourself, that's the best people to compete with. If you've got one of the biggest catalogues in the world, how bad is that? You can go anywhere in America and turn on the radio station and hear one of our songs. That's a living catalogue. That's what you've worked for. It's not about individual songs and doing well. If Elton John releases an album today, the album may not do well, in spite of his catalogue. You can still have a number-one record; it may not be as big as *Goodbye Yellow Brick Road*, but the fact is, if you're one of the most successful artists in the world you're always

going to have those gigantic periods that have created you, but if you don't have the biggest-selling catalogue in the world, and you don't have all these people that have recorded your songs, you can't always stay at a level where every record is number one all the time, McCartney, Elton John, or anyone.

Can we talk about some of the specific songs in the Bee Gees' catalogue and whether you can recall writing them? 'Run To Me' and 'When The Swallow Flies' both illustrate a style of writing that features an understated verse followed by an explosive chorus, reserving the emotional high.

'When The Swallow Flies' goes way back and I can't remember the actual writing of that song. We've always had that formula, where we let the chorus blossom and the verse is a set-up for what we always call the pay-off, the chorus, the thing that draws everybody in. I find a lot of songs these days you feel like you never quite get to the song, you feel let down, or it's a continuation and you're back straight into the verse or what you consider the verse again and it never quite gets to another level. 'When The Swallow Flies' was typical of how we write, or was the start of what we were about, where we realized you had to have that emotional plateau to go to. If you start too big, emotionally, you don't have that. 'Run To Me' was a few years later. We wrote that in Ibiza because my parents had a house there. Wrote it in the living room and recorded it at IBC in Portland Place. It was a big hit for us but it was a transitory period from the ballad stage we'd been in and the more American black music that we wanted to be in. When we did 'When The Swallow Flies' and 'I Started A Joke' we were still teenagers, and 'Run To Me' about twenty-two, still young enough to be developing. We saw that as setting up the next stage, in between development. You either take time off to develop or you continue working in a transitory period.

'Stayin' Alive'?

That was written in the Honky Chateau in France. It's now compulsory to use 'Stayin' Alive' for paramedics in America because it emulates 103 beats per minute. It is the law. It sounds bizarre, but it is true. They trialled 2,000 songs in the past two years and it's the only song, if you think about, that gives you 103 bpm or more. It's now officially sanctioned by Washington as the song you have to use, in your mind or literally, in the ambulance or wherever to keep a person alive. It said on CNN, last year, that we weren't conscious of the human heartbeat, but that was quite incorrect. We thought when we were writing it that we should emulate the human heart. We got Blue Weaver who was the keyboard player at the time to lie on the floor and put electrodes on his heart and put it through the control room. Then we got the drummer to play to the heartbeat. We were the first people in the world to do a drum loop based on that.

Were you consciously choosing words to push the beat?

No. We weren't writing to the film. When Paramount said, 'We're making this film, *Tribal Rites Of A Saturday Night*, have you got any songs?' we said, 'Well, we're doing a new studio album, we haven't got time to sit down and write some songs for a B-movie.' We were a little bit sceptical because it wasn't the thing to write songs for a film in those days, you had to be cautious. We said, 'We've got some songs written, "More Than A Woman", "If I Can't Have You", "Night Fever", "How Deep Is Your Love", "Stayin' Alive", if you want to come over and have a listen?' So they did. About six or eight of them came trundling into the recording booth. As usual with people in the industry, everyone's afraid to say, 'Yeah, smash, number one.' ' "How Deep Is Your Love", a woman should sing that,' that was the first. Nothing sounds like a hit until it is a hit, until then it's crickets. Everybody looks at each other, they're reactive, they're not proactive. Nobody wants to go out on a limb and say, 'That's it.' The next comment was, 'Can we change the title "Saturday Night"?' 'No, there's too many songs called "Saturday Night".' ' "Stayin' Alive", mmm, sounds too much like "Buried Alive",' one guy said. We said, 'Well it's actually the opposite. "Buried Alive" is more pessimistic.' I said, 'We'll compromise with you. We don't like the title of the film *Tribal Rites Of A Saturday Night* but we have a song called "Night Fever". Call it *Saturday Night Fever*.' One of the guys said, 'It's too porn, sounds like a porn movie.'

The construction of 'Nights On Broadway' is typical of many of your songs, switching between major and minor chords, offering a darker edge to the music.

'Stayin' Alive' is the only dance record in history that is pure minor all the way through, practically. Nobody ever thought, including Arif, that any dance record could be made with all minors. We weren't even aware of that until afterwards. If you're not really conscious of musical theory you just don't think about it. You just do what you think sounds good. For instance, if you get an idea for something and it works, you wouldn't change it to be musically correct later. If it sounds good, keep it as it is.

One of my great favourite lyrics is *Fifteen kids and a family on the skids gotta go for a Sunday drive.*

Oh, 'Marley Purt Drive', that was done in the Stax Studios with Tom O'Dowd. *Odessa* was done in pieces, some in London and some in Atlantic Studios in New York; 'Marley Purt' did the vocals there and the back-track down in Memphis.

It's unusual for a Bee Gees song to tap into a folk structure.

Yeah, it's like folk but it's got some kind of Southern feel to it as well. A lot of what was vogue in the States at the time like The Band, *Music From Big*

Pink; elements of what underground bands were doing with a country, South feel to it.

Where did the chorus line come from?

It just blurted out. It's just what happens when you're writing songs. If you do everything by thought and design, you wouldn't be a songwriter. Sometimes afterwards you just want to keep it because it sounds right; it feels part of the song.

Was 'Jive Talkin'' inspired by the rhythm of a car driving over a bridge?

Yeah, Spielberg wants to do that in a life story about us. He's always been intrigued by that and the way we write songs because of the various documentaries he's seen on television about us. We were on our way to the recording studio and we didn't have an idea. We were crossing over the bridge and the tar ridges were making the rhythm noise against the tyres and it produced the rhythm of the record. When we got to the studio we gave the idea to Arif Mardin and we did the back-track that day.

Was 'jive' a reference to the Fifties dance?

It was originally; Arif, who lived in New York, said, 'Before you start writing the lyrics, you do know what jive talkin' means?', because we had the title. We'd done the backing and we were going upstairs to the toilet to write the lyric, we always wrote in the toilet. Arif said, 'It has a better meaning. It's black for lying. It'd be great, it's something unique now, it's spot on . . . catch it now, while you're doing the lyrics, and work with that premise.'

And *brother, mother* from 'Stayin' Alive', was that slang too?

It could be, but it just means you're surviving: *whether you're a brother or whether you're a mother you're stayin' alive, stayin' alive.* I don't think it was a black reference. The first Grammys after 9/11 they played 'Stayin' Alive' as a tribute to the people who *feel the city shakin'*. It's remarkable how it works with what happened.

I read that 'Harry Braff' was written under the influence of either drink or drugs.

Both.

How would you assess the role of stimulants in songwriting?

We found getting drunk gets in the way of the recording process. You can't be drugged and drunk in the studio if you want to be creative. It's just self-defeating. We didn't find alcohol particularly inspired you to write; you just wanted to go to sleep. That's the opposite of what you want to be in the studio.

You were normally up all night in the studio; you never knew what time it was. The creative process is such that the brain is over-stimulated, rather than the other way, and alcohol doesn't lend itself to that. We weren't party people. I'm not saying we were saints either, but when we were working we never did that kind of stuff. The studio was certainly no place to have a good time and get stoned. I'm not saying there weren't other places, but certainly not the studio. Working was our priority, we never used any excuse to take time off; the work was the most important thing. If anything we'd use it to get ideas, get inspired, but not in the studio. 'Harry Braff', it's still a favourite of the Gallagher brothers, all those records they love. It was written at the house of the head of Polydor at the time, Roland Rennie, in Reading. We wrote it one afternoon while we were hanging out. It was a fairly straightforward song about the racing driver.

I love you deeply with the sun in my eyes.
    I thank you very much, but let's move on (*laughs*). Personal feelings aside.

Did you play the Leslie organ on that song?
    Yes, it was written in the toilet at IBC because we loved the echo in there. All of our songs were, funnily enough, written in the studio at the time we were actually recording them. A lot of our songs are demos really. Two hours later we were putting down the back-track. It was as simple as that. We never wrote independently in another place. We just wrote in the studios as we went. When we first met Arif Mardin he was a bit frightened of that, because he was used to having songs ready to go when he got to the studio, but he got used to it. We saw the empty studio as a clean canvas: what could it be at the end of the day. Sometimes we had ideas, but half the time we loved the idea of not having anything to start from. Some people would be intimidated by that. We saw it as an adventure.

JIMMY PAGE

In 1955, the *Encyclopædia Britannica Yearbook* quaintly described rock and roll as 'concentrated on a minimum of melodic line and a maximum of rhythmic noise'. Thirteen years later Led Zeppelin unleashed the wailing cry *Stop what you're doing*. The electrifying 'Communication Breakdown' was bursting with staccato energy and vitality. It came from four musicians: John Bonham, John Paul Jones and the band's two principal songwriters, Robert Plant and Jimmy Page.

Led Zeppelin would release eight studio albums, each a musical statement capturing a given time and place. The single format was cast aside. Without the constraint and limitation of the three-minute pop song, the exploration of musical ideas was boundless. Page's designs would run to unorthodox lengths and were constructed in movements more usual in classical composition than pop music: 'Achilles Last Stand' required ten minutes to frame its two-chord sequence and intercut running scales; 'Ten Years Gone' was painstakingly pieced together, orchestrating multi-layered guitars; the majestic 'Kashmir' ran to over eight minutes, employing strings, augmented chordal positions and Eastern melody to reach its grand climax. They were ambitious, bold and groundbreaking in their execution, with musical virtuosity and, ironically, a return to the simplicity of pre-psychedelic and concept-album wanderings.

James Patrick Page was born on 9 January 1944, a date he shares with the American folk singer Joan Baez. When the boy was eight, the Page family moved from Hounslow to Epsom, Surrey. Soon afterwards, Jimmy was given a discarded guitar. He discovered an immediate and natural bond with the instrument and his untrained flair promptly attracted attention. As a 13-year-old he made an appearance on the BBC talent programme *All Your Own* playing his own composition, 'Mama Don't Allow No Skiffle Any More'. Page's schoolboy ambitions of biological research were sidelined in the quest for musical knowledge, as he studied the guitar. His record player knew no boundaries, playing music from Django Reinhardt and the rock 'n' roll styles of Cliff Gallup, Scotty Moore and James Burton to flamenco, classical and the blues licks of Hubert Sumlin, Freddie King and Elmore James. Once he had dismissed *Bert Weedon's Play In A Day* guitar book, which offered scant stimulation, Page absorbed, imitated and responded instinctively to the simple joy of listening to music.

Robert Plant, born 20 August 1948 in Worcestershire, was a jobbing Black Country musician motivated by food on the table and money in his pocket. By day his large hands were laying tarmacadam on West Bromwich High Street. One night when he was gigging as the frontman of the group Obs-Tweedle, Page was in the audience. The guitarist had travelled to Walsall having been tipped off about the incredible vocal range of this largely unknown singer. Page was flabbergasted. The kid was amazing and yet inexplicably undiscovered. Appropriate introductions were made and the pair spent a weekend together in Pangbourne discovering a similar taste in records. Plant was impressed by his host's arrangement of 'Babe I'm Gonna Leave You' and realized that an appropriate vocal melody would require thoughtful attention. Where the invention of Paul McCartney or Ray Davies sweetened chord progression, Page's constructions, assembled with great intricacy, demanded a more considered vocal expression. In response, Plant's acuity for weaving and placing melody broke with the conventions of Sixties pop. As Mick Jagger has since observed, the phrasing of 'Rock And Roll' was not in the tradition of a standard blues delivery. Bonham's drum introduction in 3/8 time sets the twelve bars each rounded off with the solo vocal line *been a long lonely, lonely, lonely, lonely, lonely time.* Plant's carriage of melody would add a mesmerizing dimension to the duo's writing, with the vocalist's role in partnership and not customarily or necessarily as a lead instrument. To 'pepper the music' was his way of describing his contribution in later years on a BBC documentary.

Led Zeppelin made musical declarations reflecting chapters of their surroundings. An uncle's farm in Northamptonshire had offered the young Page a playground of agricultural investigation. As an adult in a world-famous rock band, the serenity of rural life would have an impact on his writing partnership with Plant. The inner sleeve of their third release contained the telling note, 'Credit must be given to Bron-Y-Aur, a small derelict cottage in South Snowdonia, for painting a somewhat forgotten picture of true completeness which acted as an incentive to some of these musical statements.' The setting encouraged natural living amongst the elements and was conducive to acoustic instrumentation. New songs breathed Welsh air. Plant wrote *Hear the wind in the trees that Mother Nature's proud of you and me.* On one occasion the two writers found inspiration after a hike in the ragged borders. When they stopped to rest 'That's The Way' was written and hastily captured on Page's mobile cassette recorder, packed with his guitar in a haversack. Its dominant two-bar chordal palindrome in open tuning allowed Plant's gliding vocal to sashay with assurance. Acoustic leanings had been unmistakable since the group's first release. The notion of a one-dimensional rock band is a misguided judgement. The evolving range of music within Led Zeppelin's grooves was of devastating variety. As Page recognizes, his 'greatest achievement has been to create unexpected melodies and harmonies within a rock and roll framework'. The heavy riffs for which Page is lauded distract from the equally sensitive and gifted picking touch of his guitar approach.

Travel and location would fuel Page and Plant's writing through and beyond Led Zeppelin. Both artists represent a major strand of British songwriting that has travelled with global impact. Within the lyricism are Celtic images and names evocative of ancient Britain. In 'Thank You', Plant's first major contribution to the band's lyricism, he romanticized *If the mountains crumble to the sea there would still be you and me*. 'Immigrant Song' told of the *land of the ice and snow* and 'Ramble On' recalls *years ago in days of old* before conjuring up Gollum from the fiction of J. R. R. Tolkien and the *darkest depths of Mordor*. Plant rejoiced in the imagination of the past, with an increasing interest in the Dark Ages, Albion mythology and mysticism. The versatility of his range was the perfect foil for the bombastic musical approaches of Page and Bonham. Later, he recognized that his vocal style could at times stray into the hysterical, but naturally and with time his voice developed a richness of tone that has since been rewarded with solo and new collaborative success.

Page's apprenticeship as a session musician brought tremendous diversity to his songwriting and technical ability. When he was invited to contribute rhythm guitar on Jet Harris and Tony Meehan's 'Diamonds' in 1962, he couldn't read the musical notation placed before him. It was a steep learning curve, which he approached with youthful energy and a natural instinct for the way pop music was evolving. Page's guitar playing would help shape the sound of the decade. The range of Led Zeppelin was as eclectic as the records and groups he lent backbone to: Joe Cocker's 'With A Little Help From My Friends'; Shirley Bassey's 'Goldfinger'; 'Baby Please Don't Go' featuring a young Van Morrison; 'The Crying Game'; The Rolling Stones; Donovan, with John Paul Jones in attendance; Petula Clarke. Page's guitar was the Davies brothers' unwelcome guest on early Kinks recordings; the added staccato chords on The Who's 'I Can't Explain'; and even joined America's master of melody Burt Bacharach for an instrumental release of his greatest hits. In 1965, Page released a debut single, 'She Just Satisfies', playing all the instruments except the drums. He wrote songs with Jackie DeShannon and for other acts too, like Fifth Avenue, Gregory Phillips and Fleur De Lys. Most contentious was 'Beck's Bolero', claimed as a composition by both Page and his teenage friend Jeff Beck, with whom he was to play in The Yardbirds. As teenagers the pair had

regularly jammed and swapped records in Page's front room with another occasional visitor, Eric Clapton. The recording of the song has further historical
significance. During the sessions, it is said that Who drummer Keith Moon
quipped to Page with regard to his plan to form his own supergroup, 'That'll go
down like a lead Zeppelin.' It was left to manager Peter Grant to drop the 'a',
and a band was christened.

By the age of twenty-four, Page was bored. He was a highly accomplished
musician, greatly in demand, earning well, but finding little satisfaction in
playing on records he was unlikely to listen to. He had an urge for a wider creativity. In Led Zeppelin it was unleashed in concert. The band's live music
defied strict categorization. The four musicians jammed with dramatic spontaneity, embracing diverse musical references and genre shifts from Thirties
blues to Fifties rock 'n' roll. The effect was a celebration of music past and present. No boundaries. No rules. It was not unusual for shows to exceed three
hours. Considering that The Beatles never played beyond thirty minutes, this
was phenomenal. Songs were stretched way beyond their album times and it
was not uncommon for a four-minute piece to reach a crashing end over twenty
minutes later. Led Zeppelin thrived on their musical prowess and confidence.
By 1973, US dates were breaking attendance records previously held by the Fab
Four. In the UK, the band that had headlined the Albert Hall in 1970 closed
the decade with two nights at Knebworth. Their albums outsold all their rivals.
Led Zeppelin I leapfrogged The Beatles' *Abbey Road* to the number-one spot in
the US, spending a year and a half on the *Billboard* 100. By 1975, *Physical
Graffiti* had two million pre-orders in the States alone. *Led Zeppelin II* notched
up over five million copies worldwide, aided by a non-band-approved single
edit of 'Whole Lotta Love' which duly achieved over one million sales. Led
Zeppelin's fourth album ⚡🜚🜚Ⓘ carried no acknowledgement of their
name or songs on the outer sleeve. It has sold over thirty-two million copies
and is one of the ten biggest-selling albums of all time. Only three British bands
have matched or bettered the phenomenon: Pink Floyd, the Bee Gees and The
Beatles.

'I could play "Stairway To Heaven" when I was twelve. Jimmy Page didn't
actually write it until he was twenty-two. I think that says quite a lot.' Vim
Fuego may have been the lead guitarist of spoof rock band Bad News, but his
brag carries a potent charge. Page was actually twenty-seven and the song is a
rite of passage for any would-be instrumentalist across the world. It is a classic
anthem. Mystical lyrics, mostly written in a single outpouring, are backed by
wooden recorders and a mellotron flute played by John Paul Jones, and after
four minutes accompanying guitars give way to a complementary tom-drum
introduction. The song crystallized the essence of Page and Plant's writing
partnership. The technical demands of its intricate acoustic overture and compelling electric solo reveals a seasoned writer's creative imagination.

Customarily, and legally, a songwriter is regarded as the originator of both words and melody. Page compositions originate from a musical riff or chordal grouping and, alongside Keith Richards, Pete Townshend or Johnny Marr, he signifies how a guitarist's invention is a determining factor in a song's formation. Page contends that songs require arrangement and vision to achieve completeness. Yet more than any other songwriter in these pages, he has brought into question the fine line between sources of inspiration and original creation.

'Good artists borrow, great artists steal.' The difficulty in finding a definitive split between invention and interpretation is a historically blurred debate; even the aforementioned statement is variously credited to Oscar Wilde, Pablo Picasso and Salvador Dalí. The song 'Dazed And Confused' first appeared on the 1967 album *'The Above Ground Sound' Of Jake Holmes.* A radical rendering, complete with a violin-bowed guitar centrepiece, was performed by Page in his brief sojourn with The Yardbirds. Holmes's original arrangement with descending chords and mid-section breakdown was also evident in Led Zeppelin's self-credited version on their debut album a year later, with the important addition of a fresh top melody. Definitions of writing are further challenged in the band's use of traditional blues and folk song. Seeking lyrical inspiration for 'Whole Lotta Love', Robert Plant stumbled into Muddy Waters' version of a Willie Dixon melody, *Baby way down inside you need love.* The latter sued in 1985 when his daughter noticed a resemblance to her father's words. The usage had been significant but small, and musically there was no connection. Similarly, Memphis Minnie's 'When The Levee Breaks' is far removed from Zeppelin's account, yet she received a co-writing credit despite Page initiating most of the changes and riffs. Conversely, the derivation of the gospel song 'Nobody's Fault But Mine' remains undocumented. Led Zeppelin stamped the song with radical new invention on 1976's *Presence* with choreographed switches between major and minor keys and Plant hollering *Devil he told me to roll.* Correspondingly, by the time 'Gallows Pole' appeared on *Led Zeppelin III* the traditional European folk song had been through centuries of change since its first incarnation as 'The Maid Freed From The Gallows'. Its dramatic reading offered modern verse complete with banjos and mandolins. It is true to say that many Page and Plant compositions can be claimed in part: 'How Many More Times', 'Bring It On Home', 'In My Time Of Dying' and many other song titles have been noted or later adapted, but it is also important to remember that the Sixties were rife with interpretation and seen as legitimate ground for claiming writing credits. That they were difficult to challenge and therefore easier to get away with would be an ungentlemanly suggestion, and the tradition of folk further extends the complication. Page has sailed close to the ideas of Davey Graham and Bert Jansch, even segmenting their instrumentals into his own.

But it is important to maintain a level perspective. The Led Zeppelin catalogue is one of immense inventiveness and predominant originality. The records that inspired Page and Plant to become musicians naturally flowed into their work, but a writer's mettle is measured in surpassing influence and discovering unique artistry.

Astonishingly, all Led Zeppelin records were produced by Page. Like Ray Davies, he is responsible for having captured the growth of his band and navigated its multifaceted demands. Led Zeppelin had such talent at their disposal that to harness the musical ability was a prodigious achievement. From the outset, when Page's session work funded the group's first release, he was granted unprecedented creative freedom at the behest of Atlantic Records' president, Ahmet Ertegun. Within five years the band would account for a quarter of the label's annual sales. Led Zeppelin releases are models of recorded sound and experimentation; a two-second sample of John Bonham's playing was programmed into a Fairlight by producer Trevor Horn and used as the rhythm to Frankie Goes To Hollywood number one 'Relax'. Dynamics of light, shade, hard and soft are amongst the benchmarks of Page's masterful production abilities.

Four days before the murder of John Lennon on 8 December 1980, Led Zeppelin officially disbanded. A little over two months previously, at the age of thirty-two, John Bonham had died. It devastated the band. It would be fourteen years before Page and Plant's songwriting partnership was fully revived. Prompted by an *MTV Unplugged* series, Led Zeppelin songs were dusted down and rearranged with fresh musical vigour. Alongside a batch of new material and accompaniment from an Egyptian orchestral ensemble, the London Philharmonic and musicians from Marrakesh, *No Quarter* was a triumphant return. In 1998 the duo performed one hundred and fifteen gigs in nineteen countries to promote a further set of new recordings, *Walking Into Clarksdale*. In 2007, the three remaining Led Zeppelin members reunited on stage at the London O$_2$ for a valedictory concert in front of an audience of eighteen thousand. Twenty million applications had been received. The instant rapport between the players felt forty years earlier in a Chinatown rehearsal room was present once again, and the spirit of Bonham was summoned by his son, Jason. Jimmy Page was now OBE in recognition of his charity work in Brazil, and his band inductees of the UK Music Hall of Fame. It was a just reward for the barrage of critical abuse hurled at Led Zeppelin throughout their career.

As a result, Page has rarely granted interviews. We met in his management's offices close to west London's Shepherd's Bush Green. Elegant and dapper in a long black coat with silver hair combed back, he scanned the vinyl records of his music on the table between us and his eye was caught by a cassette (later referred to as his notebook) marked *Rehearsals 1970–71*. He took up the story of the tape's unofficial release: 'I was living with my first wife and some people came to the house who were sort of fans and involved in the bootleg market. They systematically started copying everything and then in the end, it just went. I lost a lot of soundboard tapes of Led Zeppelin that way. But let's see what I can remember.'

Do you have any introductory thoughts about songwriting?

I know what my contribution is and I know how that kicks off in the early stages. Coming from the guitarist's point of view, I'll start with the music first. That's the essence of the key ideas and then I'll work on those. Sometimes I've written the lyrics myself. For example, on the first Led Zeppelin album I had a number of things where I had the chorus, like 'Your Time Is Gonna Come' . . . well, that line gets repeated a number of times so there's not a lot of lyrics in that (*laughs*). 'Good Times Bad Times' I wrote the chorus. I had the music for it and I was writing for this thing that was going to be put together for the band. The whole thing on 'Good Times Bad Times' is recognized by John Bonham's bass drum, isn't it? Initially I had a sketch for it and then Robert supplied lyrics to the verses. I was very keen on concentrating on the music, and whoever I was going to be working with, for them to be coming up with lyrics. I didn't think that my lyrics were necessarily good enough. Maybe they were in certain cases, but I preferred that very close working relationship with whoever was singing, whether it be Robert Plant, Paul Rodgers or David Coverdale. The starting point would always be coming from the music, whether I had written that acoustically or electrically.

It's very noticeable in your music how song structures seem far more classical than pop in their construction.

Well, very much so, because I had very much the view that the music could set the scene. One of the things that you'll see in the Led Zeppelin music is that every song is different to the others. Each one has its own character; musically as much as lyrically. For example, 'Ten Years Gone' or 'The Rain Song', which has got a whole orchestral piece before the vocal even comes in. So yes, it was crafted in such a way that the music was really of paramount importance to setting the scene and most probably inspired the singer, in this case Robert, to get set into the overall emotion, the ambience of the track of what was being presented, and then hopefully inspire him to the lyrics.

Often we just had working titles. A good example of this and how it would change and mutate was 'The Song Remains The Same' leading into 'The Rain Song'. The original idea I had for that was an overture—as 'Song Remains The Same' is—leading into an orchestral part for 'The Rain Song'. I had a mellotron and I'd worked out an idea—John Paul Jones did it much better than me— coming into the very first verse. If it'd worked that way there wouldn't have been any vocal until the first verse, you would have had this whole overture of guitars and then into the orchestral thing that opened up into the first verse. But as it was, when we were rehearsing it then it actually became a song; the structure changed, there was another bit put in and then Robert started singing. That wasn't a bad idea to have an overture, a whole musical segment that took you into 'The Rain Song', but it worked out really well as it was (*laughs*). Whatever it was you were constantly thinking all the time about it.

Writing in movements was a very unusual step to take as a songwriter, considering Led Zeppelin was preceded by predominantly verse, chorus structures to suit the three-minute single format.

Although I've already said on the first album there were some choruses there, it got to the point where some of the things didn't have what you'd call the hook. The reason was we weren't actually writing music that was designed to go on the AM stations in the States at the time. You had FM, that were called the underground stations, and they would be playing whole sides of albums. Well, that's a dream, isn't it?—because people are going to get to hear—it's not necessarily a concept album—the whole body of work that you're doing on one side of an album and on the other. That was really a nice way to be able to craft the music into that. It was going to go like that anyway, but it was just really useful. The essence of the contents of these albums was going contraflow to everything else that was going on, and again this was intentional. Whereas on *Zeppelin II* you've got 'Whole Lotta Love', on *Zeppelin III* . . . with other bands it'd be something very close or reflective of if they'd got some sort of hit, and we just weren't doing that. We were summing up the overall mood and where we were on that musical journey at each point in time.

Did you write songs in sections and then join together collated ideas?

I worked very much in that way. I'd be working at home on various ideas and when we were working on something in a group situation I'd think, 'Oh, I know what I'm going to put in this,' if you hadn't already put it together. Some things, I had them really mapped out, and other things—this is as the group goes on—would be on the spot. 'Ramble On' and 'What Is And What Should Never Be': I had those structures complete.

Would 'Achilles Last Stand' have been written lineally?

On that one, yes it was. There was one section that sort of appeared from before and then I tied it all up from that. 'Achilles Last Stand' is quite an epic. It sort of grew. For me it was like, this is obviously the next part, and then this is obviously the next part. It's a long map. It gave a good excuse to be able to have all these sections and then orchestrate them with the guitar. I wanted to set something which was not impossible to do from my end of it, from what I was going to do guitar-wise and beyond the track, but was going to be very challenging. I welcome that sort of challenge. I didn't do that one at home. It was put together in Los Angeles in a studio rehearsing for the album and then it was recorded in Munich. We did that album (*Presence*) in three weeks. Literally, all recorded and all mixed. All the guitar overdubs were done in one evening. You can tell I must have been so focused at that point. I'd already heard what I wanted to do and then it was matter of pulling it off and getting it better than I'd heard in my head. It just goes to show the passion of what I was doing.

How did you use your eight-track at home to build a song?

By either putting down a riff that I'd know I was going to use in the situation of the rehearsals, of presenting it and saying, 'This is what I've got.' Or like 'Ten Years Gone', I had all the orchestrated parts mapped out at home beforehand. I did everything apart from the drums—the bass and the guitar parts. 'Friends', I'd already worked out the structure. Also at the same time I had the riff of 'Immigrant Song' and then that went into a rehearsal thing and it really kicked on. I knew how these things would work with the group.

Songbooks suggest your works have surprisingly few chords. Would you build riffs from simple progressions or even think in chordal segments?

I thought in whole chordal passages and 'The Rain Song' is a good example of that: there's quite a lot of chords, but that's relative to the melody—the movements of the chords. But as far as other things went it was minimalistic, if you like. Certainly a lot of it would be working from riffs. On the second album with 'Whole Lotta Love' I had that riff and the way of playing it.

Can you explain how a riff comes to you?

A riff will come out of . . . this whole thing of do you practise at home and all that. Well, I play at home and before I knew where I was things would be coming out and that's those little sections or riffs or whatever. At that stage it's selection and rejection. It's whether you continue with something or you go, 'No that's too much like something else,' and then you move into something else. If you've got an idea and you think that's quite interesting then I'd work and build on it at home. 'Rock And Roll' was something that came purely out of the ether. We were working on something else and John Bonham happened to play—just as you do sometimes, because we were recording—this intro from 'Keep A-Knockin'' from Little Richard and I went, 'Oh, that's it!'—I did this chord and half a riff that was in my head—'Let's do this.' It was really quick to do and we could write like that.

Did you use the acoustic guitar to write riff-based songs?

A lot of the material, believe it or not, was written on the acoustic on the first and second albums, quite clearly on the third one and the fourth one too. It depended on the circumstances. Mainly I'd get the ideas of the structure. 'Ramble On' was written on the acoustic, including the chorus, and was later on what people called a power chorus. It was working round the elements of the band too, because John Bonham was a really powerful drummer. I had this clear idea that it was useful to employ that power with the greatest benefit. So 'Ramble On', which is basically the acoustic and light verses coming into the heavy chorus, so you'd leave him out and then bring him in.

With the dynamic shifts already mapped out or imagined, before taking the song to the band?

Absolutely, oh yeah, certainly on a good number of those albums that's how it was.

Did you use a notebook to remember ideas?

I had a cassette player . . . not that I did 'Ramble On' like that. In those days the way to do things was to remember them, but sometimes I put things down on cassette just to make sure that I'd got something that had a really interesting little way of playing the sequence, if you like, the inflection and the extra notes, augmenting chords. Those sorts of notebooks (*points to cassette tape*) that got bootlegged just go to show all these different ideas that I was doing. That's not necessarily one of the best examples; I think a lot of that was just playing within the group.

If you were at home with a guitar would you just set the cassette to record and then go back to listen to any ideas you might have played?

I did that, yeah. I'd be expanding on an idea and then I'd go back and I'd review it. So a lot of it you can hear train wrecks as you're playing through the song—I'm just working and trying stuff. Then I'd come back, as you say, and extract what appeared to be the shining bits, if you like, as opposed to the dull bits, and then I'd lace them together. That's how the sequence of the song would arrive.

Would the tapes get recorded over?

No, I kept them. At the time I'd just be shaping stuff up because it would be for a particular purpose and that would be for the next album that was coming. As I say, a lot of it you'd remember, but sometimes I'd go back and check things out and implement them.

If you were away from instruments and studios and had ideas, did you have the ability to write dots?

That was the interesting thing of doing sessions, that I had to read music. I didn't read music when I went in there. I could read chord charts, but not all the notes put down on a stave. But if it was A and D and E suspended, or fourth, whatever, I could play all of that no problem. But it got to the point where I had to read music. Of course, if you can read it you can write it down. So what you're saying there, yes, I did that sometimes, but really I preferred to just lay it down on cassette as a point of reference.

Rehearsals 1970–71 by Led Zeppelin, cassette tape and liner

Did you ever sing ideas, or hear ideas before you physicalized them on an instrument?

Not really, I'd see it in my head and try and play it . . . theoretically if you can sing something you should be able to play it. So I didn't start singing things, because I wanted to be playing it.

After being a session player were you able to creatively blank your knowledge to explore new ideas, or would you think technically: I'm in an Aeolian or pentatonic scale here?

No, I didn't think about the scales at all, but you've got a good point because the whole thing about sessions was timing, and you shouldn't speed up, and the whole thing has to be very metred. That didn't fit necessarily for me with the aspect of classical music because you're conducting; you're slowing down the speed, and not only that, I thought that if you had music which would speed up the adrenalin would go with it, even for listening. That became very apparent hearing Berber music from Morocco, where that's exactly how they do it. Najat Aatabou was one of the early ones I heard. I heard that afterwards, but I thought, 'This is absolutely the plot.' 'Gallows Pole' is a good example of something that is purposely speeding up as it goes through. Another good one is 'Over The Hills And Far Away': the opening guitars are accelerating as they're moving up towards . . . it's all different ways of looking at it that I knew other people didn't do. They wouldn't think about it that way. But for me it felt like a natural way to be presenting music and again laying out this plot for the vocals and the lyrics to be inspired.

There are wild variations in time signatures in songs like 'The Ocean', 'Four Sticks' or 'Black Dog'. Was that natural or did you want to consciously play with rhythm?

I used to think like that. What you have to understand: when I was saying I'd plot out ideas before, I knew with the ability of the band that really you should be able to play any sort of music at all. The thing with the timing and the trick beats was, whatever it was that you presented the other two could play, and play it well.

And that would be starting point for a song; you'd say I want it in this time signature?

I wouldn't say it like that, I'd just play it. If they couldn't get a feel for what it was, then probably it wasn't very good. I would believe the riffs that I had; certainly something like 'The Ocean' would be pretty compelling because it would be a challenge to play it for everybody.

And presumably challenging and pushing yourself . . .

. . . I was constantly pushing myself just to keep moving it on.

Did that ever hinder your creativity?

No, because if one thing didn't work another thing would. From being a player, even on sessions playing acoustic and electric, the whole thing of my application to both was just constantly moving and building all the way through my process of writing. I have to say Led Zeppelin because that's a major body of work, but even in The Yardbirds it was like that.

How important is the level of noise you can make at the writing stage?

My early stuff I did was when I was still living at home with my parents, when I was doing studio work. I had a multi-track, sort of sound-on-sound recorder . . . it had echo—it was fantastic. I'd written things; some of them were all right, but some of them were eccentric, shall we say. That was the equivalent of a home studio on a domestic level, but nevertheless it worked to be able to try out various ideas. So from that to having an eight-track in the house. I didn't really need to turn up things loud because I'm only putting things down in a musical sketchbook. 'Ten Years Gone' is a good example but it doesn't have really loud electric guitar on it. At the time I would just plug in; I'd go into the machine direct, inject and process the sound so it wouldn't need to be loud.

There's a beautiful irony that where your music was loud and bombastic it didn't have to be created with that spirit, because mentally you knew it could go there.

Because of the dynamics of the music it could be more gentle if you like and then it could have an aggressive hit to it and then be gentle again. For example, 'Babe I'm Gonna Leave You', which for me is quite a major, important track on the first album. I heard that on a Joan Baez in-concert album. I thought, 'That's such a good song.' I assumed it was a public domain song because a lot of artists around that time were doing traditional folk songs and it was the only song that didn't have a credit on it. I worked out this arrangement using a more finger-style method and then having a flamenco burst in it. Again, it's light and shade and this drama of accents; using the intensity of what would be a louder section for effect.

Can sounds or the choice of guitar inspire a songwriting direction?

Yeah, definitely: you could try a guitar or new amp and suddenly the sound of what you're hearing . . . all guitars sound different anyway. Electric guitars all have their own characteristics . . . and then before you know where you are you've got a riff. 'The Battle of Evermore': I'd never played the mandolin before and there was John Paul Jones's mandolin and I just came up with that literally on the spot and we recorded it like that. I was just inspired by an instrument: the sound of something. I didn't know how to chord a mandolin or anything. It was a really inspiring time at Headley Grange.

When you were advancing musical ideas, would you ever have a narrative or images playing in your mind's eye?

The music is lyrical without lyrics. The lyrics are telling the story and they're conveying a situation or a person or a reflection or an observation, and the construction of the music I felt was doing the same sort of thing. It was lyrical in the way it was being played. So, for example, 'Ten Years Gone', which wasn't of course called that when it was first put together . . . by the time everybody got a feel for it and was playing it through in its entirety, Robert started writing these lyrics to it and he said, 'What do you think of this?' 'Well, that's absolutely perfect,' but I wouldn't have the idea to say, 'Can you write about a relationship that's ten years past?' That was the sort of connection that we had. Let's go for another one, 'Kashmir'. Now this comes back to my rehearsal tapes. I had this other song, 'Swan Song', I was working on which had this complicated finger-style piece and right at the end of it I just did this cascade and then I did what actually are the notes of 'Kashmir'. I thought, 'I'm going to try that as a riff and then I'm going to interlace the cascade over it.' So we worked and worked on getting this intensity and feel, and I did the overdub of the cascade, which is on brass on the final record. I just knew that this was fantastic. It was like nothing else that anybody had ever done before. Most of the stuff that we did I said, 'Nobody's ever done this before.' I saw that as being big and as something with orchestral overdubs to it right from the beginning of working with John Bonham. I wanted to have an intensity and majestic feeling.

Was 'Kashmir' in a guitar tuning from the beginning when you first captured the cascade on tape?
Yeah.

How did you use tunings creatively?
I'd use tunings that had been around, like the ones that the country blues players had used like open G, open D. And then there was G A G D A D which as far as I know Davey Graham came up with. It's very much like the feeling of a sitar tuning. I started playing around that, so just experimenting to come up with other things. For example, 'Dancing Days' is written in a country blues tuning open G and so is 'Bron-Y-Aur Stomp'. But then I started making up my own ones that no one had ever used before, for 'Friends' and 'The Rain Song' again.

Was that in open C tuning?
No, neither of those tunings are open. You have to put a finger on it to complete the chord. I was just exploring. It was different ways of looking at making a piece from just a standard tuning. It gave different options and voicings in your head, and that inspires you to play with it and stick with it, and before you know where you are you're coming up with a perspective that hasn't been done before, certainly by you, and probably hasn't been done by others.

Switching our attention to live situations, did your writing purposely have room built in for improvisation?
As a guitarist, although it was more contained, I was invited to do sessions because I could create stuff on the spot. The other musicians were a good number of years older than I was, and being the youngest session musician at the time, that was obviously my forte. The bands that I'd been in up to that point were usually the same line-up as Zeppelin, with the front singer, bass player, drummer and guitar. I learnt from those records of rock, and rockabilly, and blues. I had a feel for that sort of thing and how things worked under those circumstances. I knew what the guitarist's role was in it. Like the early Presley stuff, how Scotty Moore's whole part was the backbone to things, really. Presley would just fly vocally—marvellous stuff! So it got from there, and even in the bands I was in, like Neil Christian and the Crusaders, there was improvising and extended

solos. I'd always come through that tradition. The Yardbirds was a great band to play with because you'd have the structure of the song and then areas where you'd stretch out and try things, and I definitely wanted to do that. With Zeppelin we'd got these numbers, and as I said, the albums were summing up where we were at that point in time, collectively, I might say. Once those numbers went into the set then they would change because of the fact that we were improvising every night. So the character of the song would change as well.

It was an organic process.

Yes, it was, and a result of having the best musicians that there were going at that point of time, without any doubt. They were unparalleled.

And in reverse, was it a challenge if songs had been generated out of live improvisation to hone them for the vinyl version?

What do you mean, if things had come out of the jamming sections? Sometimes things went back into other songs. There's one called 'Walter's Walk' that I remember. I did that in a version of 'Dazed and Confused' and I hit this whole bloody thing. Then later we recorded it. There's loads of examples.

Led Zeppelin snapped unofficially on a Minolta SRT-IOI from the
back of the Marquee, 23 March 1971 by Lawrence Impey

Spontaneity and improvisation is a fascinating concept in freeing creative ideas and riffs.

I was employing the same thing I was doing at home in a much better situation, where you could really stretch ideas there and then. What it is, is that the creative process, whether it was at home, whether it was in a rehearsal situation, whether it was in the studio or whether it was live: it was always there. I was really fortunate and even still it hasn't dried up.

You once said you were fortunate that the audience agreed with your taste. When you write, do you think of the audience?

(*Laughs*) No, I'm not thinking about the audience. I'm just thinking about moving on whatever it is that I can contribute to music and getting it better and better. *Death Wish II* is a good example of something where I was presented with a project. There was forty-five minutes of music in a ninety-minute film and at that point of time it could be anything from a stab through to—I think the longest piece of music on that is four minutes and thirty-four, called 'The Chase', which is made up of all different pieces. I was writing to the visuals. So that was a totally different way of approaching writing, for me. Knowing where Michael Winner wanted the music, 'cause you'd see the visuals and a little stripe go down where the music starts and a little stripe at the end, so I wrote accordingly to that: to the mood or the movements or whatever. I had a set period to do this music and present it. It all really fitted well. I had to really work this musically: I had to do bars, get the tempos from what was going on . . . this is the way I approached it, anyway, very eccentric. Then it was said I had to do an album, so I had to lace all the little pieces together; some bits of music I doubled the lengths of them. There were a couple of areas I wrote lyrics. 'Who's To Blame', I wrote that one about a divorce. All the lyrics were relative to a divorce. As far as the lyric writing goes they weren't as strong as the music, so I was quite happy to let somebody else do the lyrics, especially if they were going to sing them.

I'd like to broach a subject that I must confess I know less about. I understand Aleister Crowley wrote technical works around releasing free will and writing true to the inner self? Do you believe there is a connection between the occult, mysticism and songwriting?

Well, you could say there's a certain ritual to it. You could say there's definitely an element of trance state. Crowley was a poet, but I didn't put any of it to music. I think the creative process can certainly be related to a trance state. But, just insomuch as there's a variety of music, it came in a variety of ways. There wasn't any one particular formula that I would apply. It could come from all manner of situations. In a rehearsal room playing with musicians I could just come up with stuff like that, and before I knew where I was I would have something that was the equivalent of a riff and a chorus area and a bridge and a solo area and a verse. I could do all of that. 'Friends': I wrote that after a massive argument, and yet you wouldn't know. I was inspired, I guess, by this feeling: I've just got to release this somehow. Fortunately I had one of my eccentric tunings and I channelled it into that. Everyone must have that sort of thing, but for me there's no one thing. There's a number of portents that have manifested this music and that's good, it's not just a one-trick thing. I'm going away for a break and I'll be writing when I'm over there. I'll take an acoustic with me and I'll definitely throw the guitar into a tuning to see what comes out. So that is one definite method I would employ. I don't know what tuning I'm going to use; could be one of half a dozen or I might make one up. It's an ongoing process of creativity. It should always be, all the time you've still got a pulse.

Would you say that you can spark inspiration at the moment you want to write?

Well, I don't do that, well, I can do. What would I do? There's only a small percentage of these songs that are written in a tuning, but this is just an example: I'd arrive at a tuning probably that I'd never worked on before and I'd start experimenting with it and seeing what works and what doesn't work. I'll keep doing that, and before I know where I am, this movement from these chords here to this inversion over here is actually pretty good and worth furthering. Then I'll keep going and going, and then hopefully, unless I've shot myself in the foot by telling you this, then you know something will appear.

I'm very interested in the idea of creativity being trapped and having the right vehicle to want to write. So taking the period after the split of Led Zeppelin, can a desire to want to create be held back because . . .

No, because *Death Wish* is the perfect example. That was the first project that I did after. There are a lot of ideas in there that I didn't even do with Led Zeppelin. I might have thought of those sorts of things but I didn't do them, certainly some of the bowing that's on there. I wasn't constricted by anything.

A curious quote I read of yours from the early Eighties was that you were afraid of writing.

Did I . . . afraid? It depends on the context of that. I wouldn't really subscribe to that. I'm reluctant to write lyrics. I just didn't think my lyrics were very good. Whatever situations I've been in, I've been able to write and present material or move material on.

Do you think that drugs—cocaine and heroin—can reach a creative force in writing that wouldn't otherwise be released?

That's a tricky one, because you don't want to advocate drug-taking because it'll kill people. Shall I just say, it certainly it wasn't out of the equation. The important thing is, no matter what you're doing and however you're applying yourself to what you're trying to do, the most important thing is that you are able to do it and keep moving it on rather than get stuck.

Were you ever intimidated by surpassing your achievements?

No . . . no . . . no, because the whole thing is, if you've done something that's measured up as being a musical milestone, that's great. As I've said, the whole policy with Led Zeppelin as opposed to other groups at the time was not to replicate your hit single or two hit singles of the first album and make things that are very similar. No, that's done: move on.

It's an enormous challenge to lay down: I will not repeat myself.

Hopefully not repeat myself. When you've got so much there that has preceded you it shouldn't become a millstone: it should inspire you to be moving on. The last album, *In Through The Out Door*, is the one where John Paul Jones had more ideas. He had this keyboard, this dream machine that he'd been working on and written quite a lot of stuff. So that album, as opposed to *Presence*, has got a lot more writing from that department.

I really get a sense of your creativity being sparked by an unknown.

I like that quote. I like that.

Can we talk about your collaboration with Robert? How would you give your ideas to him?

I'd play the ideas to him a lot of the time.

On guitar?

Yeah, and sometimes he'd go away not just with my ideas but with a backing track that was already done. Then he would do his lyrics to that. It's all different ways again. Sometimes he would start writing lyrics and melodies, of course, during the course of band rehearsals when things were being put together. Sometimes he'd do guide vocals and then go away and finesse those lyrics and then come back. Sometimes we'd do things right from scratch. When we went to Bron-Yr-Aur, for example, 'That's The Way' was done there and then under those conditions—not necessarily of going on a writing sabbatical, but having the guitar there it was a natural thing for us to be doing. It wasn't, 'We've got to go in, we've got to write something.' It was never that. It was just something that was done because we were musicians and we had a group. And for me it was always, What's going to appear out of the ether next? Whether it was a live recording or me playing the guitar at home or whether it was in the situation of band rehearsals. He would get inspired in exactly the same way and come up with whole lyrical plots. I thought Robert's lyrics were great.

Could you write in the same room?

Oh yeah, we would definitely write together, but it was always different. On 'Kashmir', for example, the whole of this piece was put together and he said,

'You know, I've got some lyrics that I wrote in Morocco that would be really great for this.'

Would you suggest to Robert where vocals would fit into the music; did you imagine their place when you were writing?

I would say this is going to lead to that. As I said, with 'The Rain Song' there was this whole introduction to the first verse, so I would say this isn't a vocal part but it's leading to this. 'Whole Lotta Love' it's pretty obvious where his vocal is going to come in.

Some instrumentalists have been shocked where vocalists have put their melodic ideas.

That definitely could happen with Robert, no doubt about it. It wasn't competitive, but we definitely got the best out of each other.

There are many unexpected vocal melodies in your music that in a lot of respects are more suggestive of how you would approach a guitar line. Would you initiate the vocal melody by . . .

. . . sometimes, yeah, and other things Robert would sing at a counter-point which was of his doing.

'Misty Mountain Hop', for example, has a very unusual verse melody.

He's singing with what's going on under the verse, but then he does start doing some cross-timing stuff as he goes on, which is really brilliant. He was really a creative vocalist as well. Don't forget the whole of the thing with Led Zeppelin was improvising. The way that piece had developed was the way I'd played it on stage; hopefully I never played it twice the same, but I was finding things and slotting them in on another night. The point of reference was certainly Indian, Arabic and Celtic music. I was listening to music that went right across the board. I delved into areas of music that not everybody else was listening to. They might have been in that particular field. Listening to Penderecki of course wasn't necessarily what anybody else was doing, but they might have been in the world of modern classical and avant-garde.

How did you balance what was the right key musically for a song and what was right for Robert to sing in?

You sort of usually knew his keys, plus there's certain keys that fit in rock music: key of E is pretty good and the key of A and variants of that, whether it's D or G and tunings. However, on the other more experimental things . . . let's put it this way, I would hear Robert's voice on things that I was doing. I was writing for the band. I wasn't writing to have a whole cache of songs to put on my solo album. It wasn't that.

Do you think writing for other musicians steers you in directions you might not otherwise naturally go?

But whatever you did, if you were creating in isolation something that was most unusual and not necessarily within the band's format, you'd try it out with the band because it should work.

Can you remember how 'Trampled Under Foot' originated?

Yeah, I do, that originated with John Paul Jones on the keyboard. He started playing this vamping riff. That was one that was put together from that being a really good idea. Bonzo did this sort of stomp. On the rehearsals you can hear I'm doing quite a number of different approaches to what's going to be in the verse. But the movement of it, the little links between verses, came up quite early. I can't remember who did what. I might have said, 'Let's move to this bit and this bit and then back to the verse,' and then John Paul Jones might well have said, 'Well OK, then, at the end of it let's do this bit and extend it.' Some things I can remember in detail, but not that one because it was really quite an organic thing. But I know the guitar riff I certainly didn't play at the beginning, but John's piano thing was constant all the way through.

How would you define songwriting? Traditionally it's words and melody.

It's not just words and melody. Again, there's no one hat that fits this, certainly not for me, and I don't think for most of the people whose writing I respect, either.

Arrangement to you is by definition part of songwriting?

I think it's a major part, maybe not for anybody else, but yes, I see the whole thing as a sort of piece. Yes, I do see it like that: definitely arrangement, absolutely. But also in recording you need to capture the edge of it, the thing that drove it in the first place, the energy. You don't want to it to be like I heard of other bands that would do ninety takes on something then come back the next day—I would never do that. Everybody knew if we'd got it, and if it just wasn't happening then you'd move onto something else and come back to this other thing the next day. So that was constantly creating and moving as opposed to labouring a point and getting bored of it. Well, I never get bored of the music I'm making.

Can you recall how 'Please Read The Letter' was written with Robert? Was the writing process different, coming eighteen years after your Led Zeppelin writing relationship?

Yeah, it's quite interesting. I can't remember what the original title for it was. He had a title that was from the lyrics. So we did this song and Robert said, 'I'm not really happy with this. I'm going to rewrite the lyrics.' We were in the studio and he went home overnight and came back with 'Please Read The Letter'. The melody had changed somewhat but he sang it over the original track. We didn't recut it. He'd changed his vocal perspective, if you like. That could have happened way back with Zeppelin; we'd have a guide vocal and he'd come back with an alternative plot. It wasn't the rule nor definitely the exception. That's just how that worked that time. Of course he recut it later with Alison Krauss.

Had your collaborative process changed in the Nineties, writing songs like 'Wah Wah' and 'City Don't Cry'?

No, we were definitely working together on those things like 'Yallah' and 'Wonderful One'. So what was the catalyst of all of that? Robert said, 'I've got these tape loops that Martin Meissonnier sent me'—I think he might have tried it out with some other guitarists and maybe that hadn't worked—and he said, 'Can you come up with anything?' I said, 'Sure.' We wrote what became the core of the new writing for that Unledded project across a couple of days. 'Wonderful One' and 'Yallah' were done on the first day. Then we had other stuff that we never used and it was really quite good. I came up with the riffs and that inspired him because he had the loops and we were firing off each other.

Can you recall the initial vision behind 'Stairway To Heaven'?

The initial idea was to have this quite fragile guitar that would open up this piece of music and for something that would accelerate as it went through from beginning to end. This thing that I was saying earlier on that I'd arrived at way back, even from leaving sessions, but to actually pull this idea off properly. So it just went like a whole . . . it's not quite an unravelling puzzle . . . OK, from the guitar point of view and the pad of it; something that was going to keep accelerating and changing its whole perspectives, from that first guitar into the bit where the electric twelve-strings are coming in in the verses; that the whole structure is going to change from one presentation, or mood, if you like, into another one that opens up with the twelve-strings on the verses and then that will move through. Then there will be chord fanfares that take it into a solo because it's all moving, it's all accelerating.

How much of this was in your imagination before recording the song?

I already had that, and then at the end have this whole bit.

When you say you already had this, before you played a note?

No, I had an idea. I had that opening bit and I thought, 'This is the way to take it from here.'

Do you remember writing the opening passage?

What, coming up with it? Yeah, I was just experimenting on the guitar and I came up with this thing and I thought, 'I'm not losing that!' It's not necessarily orchestrating on that but it's overdubbing, increasing the texture as it goes through.

The outro, A minor, G to F, is a traditional sequence?

Those chords go back, back, back, back, back, don't they? 'Hit The Road Jack' is those chords . . . slightly different.

Was Dylan's 'All Along The Watchtower' in your mind?

Not necessarily, no, but it might have been. That's the other thing: after a while I didn't want to listen to other guitarists in case it went in and regurgitated. The same chords, but they'd been around all over the place for years.

Originality is in presentation.

The application, yeah. That's like saying the chord of E was used in so many of those songs and a million other songs . . . it's the chord of E (*laughs*)!

BRYAN FERRY

On 24 August 1972, Roxy Music appeared on *Top of the Pops*. A wash of colour and glamour flooded the screen. 'Virginia Plain' spoke of wanton escapism *far beyond the pale horizon*. Its lyrical stream of consciousness was characterized by the vocalist's slurred delivery, as whirling electronics and echoes filtered bass synth, guitars and competing oboe. There was no chorus. The singer's unorthodox poetic eye was turned away from the harsh realities of Britain's economic difficulties. The following year saw the introduction of a three-day working week, unemployment rising to one million and Ted Heath's Conservative government battling with strikes and oil crises, pay freezes and five states of emergency. Art reacted: with bombast! Roxy Music turned the lights back on. At the helm was the son of a miner, now in his twenty-ninth year, who created a landscape of fantasy and escapism: a world of extravagance and lavishness. The group's detailed attention to costume and style made an immense impact, in combination with elements of Fifties rock 'n' roll banality, Sixties idealism and Seventies futurism. The vision was Bryan Ferry's.

Born on 26 September 1945 in the working-class community of Washington, County Durham, Bryan Ferry was raised within the North East triangle of Newcastle, Durham and Sunderland. He shared a birthdate with both George Gershwin and T. S. Eliot. The 2012 release *The Jazz Age*, by The Bryan Ferry Orchestra, featured selections from his back catalogue rearranged in the style of the Roaring Twenties, bringing a teenage musical journey full circle. Eliot is perhaps a less obvious influence, but, as an art student, Ferry would pin on his wall the poet's verse, cut out from a newspaper serialization. Bryan's first memory of music is hearing The Inkspots when he was five. His musical education primarily came from America. He learnt every note of the Charlie Parker Quartet EP and would memorize the solos of Miles Davis. Jazz was fundamental to his vocabulary. 'I loved the way the great soloists would pick up a tune and shake it up—go somewhere completely different—and then return gracefully back to the melody, as if nothing had happened.' His teenage influences were eclectic: Leadbelly, Fats Domino, Humphrey Lyttelton, folk and blues. When the Stax-Volt tour came to London's Roundhouse in 1967 Bryan was beguiled by the sharp suits of soul men Sam and Dave. He proclaimed it a 'road to Damascus' experience, showing music's power as a receptacle for art.

Art school has played an important role as a breeding ground for British musicians, and for Bryan Ferry it supplied a fundamental connection to his musical vision. John Lennon, Keith Richards, Ray Davies and Ian Dury all found value in artistic tuition. For Pete Townshend and Mick Jones, its more bohemian lifestyle after the rigidity of school meant escape from post-war nine-to-five conformity and an opportunity to develop artistic talent. With the aid of local and government grants, art school was an environment of great social opportunity. Art would come to dominate Ferry's compositional approach, channelling his love of collage and encouraging him to deliver a complete package of sound, fashion and theatrics with an *auteur*'s vision. Enrolling in the Fine Art department of Newcastle University in 1964, he was tutored by a pioneer of modernism, Richard Hamilton, the Pop Art designer of the Beatles' *White Album* cover. Hamilton validated Ferry's 'romantic leanings towards American culture' and fostered ways of thinking about and exploring the immediate present. His 1965 collage *Just What Is It That Makes Today's Homes So Different, So Appealing?* acted as 'a kind of talisman' for the intellectually stimulated student. The constant cross-fertilization of music and art lends a scholarly, thoughtful perspective to Ferry's work. The 2010 release *Olympia* shares its title with the controversial painting by Édouard Manet. Kate Moss was chosen for the album cover as a modern-day femme fatale, echoing the young courtesan who had shocked mid-nineteenth-century French society. Ferry's fifth solo album in 1978 took its name from a Marcel Duchamp canvas, *The Bride Stripped Bare By Her Bachelors, Even.*

A further tribute to the surrealist painter was Ferry's appropriation of Duchamp's phrase 'readymades' to describe existing songs which could be given a new stamp. By the time *These Foolish Things* was released in 1973 Ferry had already achieved great success with two Roxy Music albums, but this new recording revealed his natural ability as an interpreter of song. It was a daring move for a relatively fresh pop star. The record included a radical reworking of Bob Dylan's 'A Hard Rain's A-Gonna Fall'. Ringo Starr exclaimed in a telegram, 'Congratulations on your new record . . . Fanfuckingtastic.' Ferry's musical heritage dated back to the Thirties, blending such opposites as soul and electronica, French chanson and rock. A familiarity with the songs of Cole Porter, Tin Pan Alley and pre-war Hollywood musicals supplied a resource that he could explore and reinvent for his own songbook. In the Nineties, *Taxi* and *As Time Goes By* once again revisited unfashionable decades to enrich modern pop music. Ferry has always plotted his own course. Through the Seventies and Eighties Roxy Music released a series of vogue records, each furnished with a fresh image and a new musical statement. Ferry's infinite artistic palette was simply defined in his song 'If It Takes All Night': *every singer to his song.*

At twenty-four, never having played an instrument or written a song, Ferry invested in a piano and began to create. He had simply worked out that pop music had greater mass commercial appeal than art. If he could exploit the perceived gaps, then his creative visions could achieve mainstream recognition. Working by day as a ceramics teacher in a Hammersmith girls' school, he taught himself the rudiments of music theory. His writing output demonstrated staggering originality and soon attracted like-minded instrumentalists. The band's name, *Roxy* Music, was a statement in itself, echoing the name of a British cinema chain and at the same time suggesting an interest in glamour, art and style. Ferry assembled an extraordinarily disparate group of people resolved on combining art school and intellectual backgrounds to create a phenomenon unheard of in British musical history. Strong and allusive words, dramatic arrangements, idiosyncratic chords and abrupt tempo changes all combined to create some breathtaking recordings. Ferry instructed *stay hip, keep cool to the thrill of it all,* as they brought together radically different musical forms and ideas. The debut album, simply titled *Roxy Music,* was raw and packed with tremendous excitement and exhilaration. 'Re-Make/Re-Model', a title inspired by Derek Boshier's 1962 painting *Rethink/Re-entry,* opens with the chink and chat of a cocktail party before each individual member of the band lays down their musical manifesto in solo four-bar spots; snatches of 'C'mon Everybody', 'Day Tripper' and 'Ride Of The Valkyries' are heard after Ferry choruses the number plate of a girl's motor vehicle, *CPL593H.* The six-minute 'If There Is Something' delivers a country-tinged verse segueing into a second movement of band instrumentals, with the vocalist's desperate cry yearning for a simple romantic gesture: *roses around the door . . . growing potatoes by the score.* Ferry has always been adept at employing distinctive playfulness in his voice: quivering vibrato, sexy and cool bass, and as Alison Goldfrapp reflected, even a touch of Marlene Dietrich. The juxtaposition of unlikely lyrical ideas, laments fused with gilded rock, and the avant-garde musicality of the band was a bold statement. Roxy Music had the hallmarks of an English Velvet Underground and shared the propensity for sweet melody cut by abrupt musical incision. Like Lou Reed with John Cale, Ferry formed a dazzling alliance with an artistic renegade: Brian Eno. They traded ideas over two records before their relationship imploded.

Twenty years later the pair began to collaborate again. 'Mamouna', meaning 'good luck' in Arabic, rubbed off and Eno enhanced and treated the sounds for the joint composition 'Wildcat Days'. 'I Thought', from *Frantic* in 2002, was a wonderful example of Casio drum rhythm used against the velvet cushion of

Ferry's deep baritone. Much has been made of Eno and Ferry's separation, yet the band's invention never faltered after the Eno releases. Into the mid-Seventies, Ferry showed a considerable consolidation of songwriting invention. 'Mother Of Pearl' calls for the *lights* to be turned *down* and the music turned up, as spirited voices are layered in questioning and answering montage. Phil Manzanera's guitar, reflecting his Latin American upbringing, soars until abruptly broken by a wistful piano and a recession in the rhythm and melody. 'Amazona' connected a succession of simple chord-led parts predominantly in common time with subtle 7/8 variation. The open arrangement allowed the co-writer Manzanera room for expression before Ferry contributed words evoking the fantasy of Spanish imagination.

Melancholy and a sense of loss reflect the loner image of Ferry's songwriting personality. His ambition had been to invest pop music with greater depth, so that like jazz it could provide instrumental feeling without words. Within the various stages of his career, Ferry's writing has always developed and sought these aims. He favours impressionistic lyrics capturing the essence of a subject, rather than its details. The writer's bold brushstrokes concentrate on the emotional and visceral effect of his surroundings. His economical use of words, reduced often to three or four short syllables, explores the recurring themes of unrequited and unobtainable love. An outsider seems to be looking in and observing the mystery and attractions of adult sexuality: *if you're looking for love in a looking-glass world it's pretty hard to find*. Ferry is concise and pointed. Witty, too: *Well I've been up all night / Party time-wasting is too much fun*. Touches of impishness and humour counter the elegant, considered lyrics, as 'Prairie Rose' promised: *I will compose in fancy rhyme or just plain prose*. 'Do The Strand' throws in *Lolita* and *Guernica* amongst a litany of sophisticated art history and dance references, whilst 'Street Life' compared the benefits of study and pleasure: *Education is an important key—yes, but the good life's never won by degrees—no*. The construction of that song represented a new departure in Ferry's writing techniques. Andrew Mackay, Paul Thompson, Eddie Jobson, Johnny Gustafson and Phil Manzanera completed the backing track without sight of Ferry's intended words or melody. On this occasion, the singer's finalizing contribution brought a cheer from the control room as a track destined to be a B-side was transformed—and a third straight top-ten hit ensued.

Roxy Music would only release only half a dozen singles in their first incarnation, since Ferry's writing was more often suited to the freedom afforded by the long-player. 'In Every Dream Home A Heartache', from the second album, *For Your Pleasure*, tells of an inflatable doll bought mail order. The song culminates in the line *I blew up your body but you blew my mind*. In 2003, extended passages from the song's first draft of lyrics were revisited on Ferry's solo recording 'San Simeon', co-written with former Eurythmic Dave Stewart. He wrote in the notes to the album *Frantic*, 'The song is inspired by Orson Welles' movie *Citizen Kane*, with a castle haunted by the ghosts of a thousand Hollywood parties.'

'Body', 'Soul', 'Love' and 'Hate' are the section headings of Germaine Greer's 1970 publishing phenomenon *The Female Eunuch*. The book examined historical definitions of women's perception of self, but the four sections might as easily have described the themes of Bryan Ferry's oeuvre. Greer, however, was calling for the liberation of women from being viewed as objects of male desire, whilst Bryan Ferry was reflecting on his album covers advertising's liberal use of female sexuality to sell everyday products. He brought Hollywood fashion to the centre of his creative imagery. Designers, photographers and artists were credited on sleeves, and models were eroticized, from *Country Life*'s two unknown models in provocative states of undress to Jerry Hall as the Siren on Roxy Music's fifth offering. Yet the images challenged protestors by drawing parallels with the history of art and female representation through the ages.

After five albums released between 1972 and 1976, in a style frequently operating outside the traditional pop model, Ferry put Roxy Music's fluctuating line-up on hold. A set of compelling solo releases followed. 'When She Walks In The Room' typified an arresting period of melodic evocation. Ferry's re-emergence in 1979 was one of dramatic songwriting reinvention. By the time Roxy Music's sixth studio album appeared, the colour and temper of their lead singer's work had radically altered. 'Manifesto' was driven by a new intent and mystique: *I am that I am from out of nowhere*, an inspiration taken from Claes Oldenburg's 1961 work *I Am For An Art*. The single and accompanying LP sent the band off in a new direction, acknowledging both the influence of Seventies punk and the emergence of disco. Both 'Dance Away' with its cutting wordplay (*You're dressed to kill and guess who's dying*) and 'Angel Eyes' made the top five, and Ferry, like his compatriot David Bowie, was at the cutting edge of London's New Romanticism. Now mood and atmosphere informed the landscape of the writing, and with it came a second wave of success. 'Over You', 'Oh Yeah (On the Radio)' and 'More Than This' exemplified the new approach. Ferry had found a sophisticated and mature bent to his creativity. Sensual musical landscapes suited the sparse, minimalist, often ambiguous words. 'Jealous Guy', a tribute to its writer, the murdered John Lennon, reached number one in February 1981. It had all the trademarks of a Ferry original composition. Ironically, the writer had once again found his voice in the song of another. The *coup d'état* of Ferry's progressiveness came with the release of 'Avalon', a beautifully moving song with three simple verses divided by its one-word chorus. Ferry was increasingly drawn to plaintive melody, and would soon produce another chart-topper with *Boys And Girls*. 'Slave To Love', the pivotal piece, was another defining song of the decade's production identity and represented an immense progression from Ferry's compositions of the early Seventies. Oozing sexuality for nightclub smoochers, the vocals suggested *We're too young to reason / Too grown up to dream*. International sales rocketed, but from this high point in the mid-Eighties Ferry's output has slowly reduced to just four original studio albums in twenty-five years. Perhaps in some ways it makes sense of the writer's claim that he struggles to write satisfactory words and his joke about the benefits of hiring a lyricist.

I met Bryan, newly married and recently awarded a CBE, in his studio in the Olympia area of west London. The building, set over three floors, is an odd mix of past and present. Framed album-cover photographs of Roxy Music hang beside images from solo records and multiple Andy Warhol prints. Home for more than twenty years, Studio One houses recording facilities, offices and opulent relaxation rooms. Surrounded by shelves lined with books and fashion magazines, Bryan was immaculately dressed in bespoke shirt, tie and matching pullover. He spoke in a low voice as if drawing his thoughts from the middle distance, or from the collection of his vinyl releases that lay between us. More than thirty records have earned Ferry an Ivor Novello Award for Outstanding Contribution to Music, yet his conversation revealed an unassuming songwriter very insecure about his lyrical abilities. He is regularly cited by musicians as a source of inspiration. Morrissey declared his all-time favourite album to be *For Your Pleasure*, making it his only listing from a possible ten. A line from Roxy's 'Casanova': *Now you're nothing / But second hand / In glove* is likely to have provided inspiration for the title of the Mancunian's own debut single. A former Smiths instrumental written by Johnny Marr was given vigour with Ferry's lyrics on 1987's 'The Main Thing'. Nile Rodgers cites *Country Life* and particularly 'Love Is The Drug' as having the greatest influence on Chic. 'Same Old Scene' was clearly the blueprint for Duran Duran's early albums, while Lee Thompson of Madness wrote '4BF' in dedication and response to Ferry's own Humphrey Bogart tribute '2HB'. Even Sex Pistol Steve Jones has declared Roxy Music his all-time best band.

Roxy Music brought together multiple identities, pre-rock and roll memories, Weimar Republic decadence, space-age wild, ad hoc instrumental landscapes, textured canvases and lyrical double meanings. More recently, Ferry's records have featured collaborations with the Scissor Sisters and members of Radiohead and The Stone Roses. For an artist who claimed in a BMI Icon Award acceptance speech that songwriting was a lonely experience, he has a catalogue, spanning more than forty years, with a remarkable number of accolades, friends and admirers.

Do you need solitude or have a preferred time of day to write?

Well, yes, generally at night I find it easier when phones aren't ringing so much. There's more time to be creative. It's the only time I'm on my own, really; during the day most of the time I'm working in music I'm with a lot of people: the engineer, the producer, musicians. That's what I enjoy the most.

The writing process is in two parts: one is composing the melodies, which I quite enjoy doing. Normally I then take the musical ideas to the studio and work them up and see where to take it. I don't normally work on lyrics until later on, and that I must do on my own. I wish I knew a good lyric writer, actually: I probably would have used one before now. I find it difficult to find the right words to match the mood of the music. It takes a long time. Sometimes things happen immediately; most of the time you reject ideas constantly until you find the right one and then you think, 'Ah right . . . yeah.' It's a great feeling when you suddenly feel you've got the right words for a piece of music and it all melds together.

When you're creating the mood of the music do you have pictures or images in your mind?

Not really . . . it depends. When I'm writing the words I do, of course, and sometimes the music does build up pictures and you then follow that direction with the lyric. I don't normally say, 'I'm going to go and write a song about a flower,' or something. I just play the piano and hopefully some melodic thing which I like comes up. The melody is what I'm probably good at. I also like arranging. To me, the whole songwriting process is more than just being alone at the piano or a typewriter because I kind of change the songs when I'm in the studio working. So I'm kind of sculpting away at it with the various instruments. The song isn't finished for me until it's mixed, until the whole record is completed, because otherwise things can change, lyrics can change—I've thought of something better. It's a very fluid process. Some people in the old days would just sit at the piano and scrawl down the words and eureka, they've got a song. I don't work like that.

Do you structure whole songs before taking ideas to the studio?

No, not at all. You might have a verse idea and think, 'This feels like a good verse,' and then later on—it might not come the same day—a chorus or bridge idea. It's a case of collaging things together. I don't think I've ever sat and written a song from beginning to end in one go.

I'm surprised to hear that. Do you collect segments?

Sometimes, yeah, and say, 'This would be great in that piece of music to have this coming after it.' There's no fixed way of working. It's always quite slow! Also songwriting is quite a special thing, so I don't try and write every day. I like to keep it as a special event. That's why after two albums of my own things with Roxy, I did this record (*picks up These Foolish Things*) basically to get away from the pressures of songwriting and to make something with a different flavour. There's millions of great songs out there in the world, written by a lot of talented people. Obviously I like my own songs and probably my main musical statement is via songs I've written. This record started a whole career of interpretation of other songs and that's been very interesting for me to discover how simple certain songs are actually. It's good to discover different moods you wouldn't have necessarily written yourself.

Having leant into other writers' catalogues so much, do you ever find yourself borrowing chord progressions to resolve or initiate ideas?

Not really, not consciously.

Can you write at will or do you sense inspiration coming?

It's all a matter of chance, really. If I'm on my own near a piano in the right mood . . . the odds against that are quite high. I spend loads of hours working on bits of music downstairs in the studio. If it's one of my songs then I'm constantly shaping it and to me it's part of the writing process. Songwriting now is a very small part of my life, of my own inventing, especially if I'm on tour. I've never been someone who could write on the road. That's two separate things to me, performing and creating.

When you write words do you work from an idea or just let meanings unfold?

One word leads to another. You want to get the right feeling in the words. To try and get the emotion of the music in words without destroying the mystique of the music is the hard part. Sometimes you try and bring or throw in one or two intelligent ideas that you think might be good. This record 'Do The Strand' is an example of that. It's not a love song, which most songs are, it's a different kind of thing. In that song I was influenced by people like Cole Porter who played around with words . . . using real names for places. That illustrates what your interests are, which is always quite interesting for the listener, I think, to have you referring to other things you like in song.

Would you say your life has been one as a songwriter always absorbing ideas, or do you fall into that mode when the time is right?

When the time is right, then I think, 'Oh God, I need to work on this.' I haven't had the pressure of doing an annual album for quite a long time . . . and sometimes taken years to do. There's one there called *Mamouna*; that took a long time. Sometimes you make things more complex than you should, especially with solo work where you work with lots of different musicians and you get lots of different flavours, which makes it more interesting for me.

Is there an art you've discovered to writing strong melody?

No, it's just luck. I don't know where it comes from. I'm always amazed . . . it's just a case I suppose of putting the right notes in the right order. Some of the melodies are better than others and they last longer and you find, 'Oh, I must sing that one tonight,' if you're in a show. Others, they don't get performed live at all. Quite a few have just been recorded and that was it.

I just noticed your hand gesture: do you try to find melody on the keyboard as opposed to vocalizing ideas?

It's a bit of both. Sometimes what you play on the piano, the chords, suggest a melody in your head which you sing until you get the two things together. Other times you're kind of tinkering around . . . this is a top-line idea . . . this is the lead melody. It varies. It's always different. I don't have a formula, that's the thing. I was always intrigued by Elton John's procedure. He writes melodies to a given lyric, doesn't he? Which is the opposite? I'm sure it must be fun to do but I've never had any particular interest in doing that.

You've never written a set of words first?

I don't think so. Not to say that lyrics aren't important. They're really important to me, too important maybe. You never know how much people listen to them. I love reading and literature so I kind of almost felt what I was writing maybe wasn't good enough, so I tried harder and came up with . . . some lyrics I still like.

Do you try to make the words stand alone from the music or do they belong together?

Sometimes they do and sometimes they really need to be in the music to make the most impact or the most sense. It's different from writing poetry, really, because you have to make it flow with the music so they're working together. Sometimes you think, 'That reads very well.' Other times you think it sings better than it reads.

Many of your lyrics incorporate Latin, French or German, which Tolstoy would do as a measure of social standing and character aspiration.

That was for a bit of fun, just to make things more interesting. I haven't done it very often. 'Song For Europe' was the first song I co-wrote with Andy Mackay. It's always interesting to write with somebody else. He provided the chord structure. The progressions were very different from what I would have written: more complex and more musical, I guess, and less rock 'n' roll. I thought, 'Oh, that sounds great, it sounds very European,' so I came up with the title. I thought it would be amusing to have one of the verses in French, then a bit in Latin as well because the music seemed to be taking me all round Europe: Paris and Venice. I thought it was quite an interesting song. It became one of the favourite Roxy live songs. Then in the following year we did the song 'Bitter-Sweet' from the *Country Life* album with Andy's basic structure and chord progressions: that kind of real German, Berlin feeling. I always did the top line melody, so I really tried to bring that out in the lyrics.

Gestrandet an leben und kunst.

Exactly.

Stranded between life and art: it's tempting to see that as an analogy of your life?

Yeah. I was writing the lyrics to *Country Life* in Portugal. It's where we met the girls who graced the cover. They were German and they helped me do the translation for that chorus because I didn't study German. It's a good line. Sometimes you come up with lines and say, 'Oh, God, I got it right there.' Sometimes you don't get it right, but when you do it's a great feeling in song-writing. What you don't really want to do as a writer is to keep repeating yourself. It's very good having self-written albums interspersed with these sorts of records which give you some respite from the treadmill of writing. You always want it to be a pleasure of some kind.

May I ask you about your first forays into writing? If I've understood correctly, at twenty-four you'd never played an instrument or written a song.

Yes, I think so. The first batch of songs were on this album (*picks up first Roxy Music LP*), apart from 'Psalm', but for some reason we didn't record it till the third album, *Stranded*. Interesting, maybe I hadn't finished the lyric; I can't remember. Very simple and almost like a gospel, New Orleans kind of religious song.

Was it instinctive to know how to construct a song?

Yeah . . . it's a great feeling of discovery writing the first song. Some of those first songs were written not on the piano but on the harmonium. It was quite a great sound. Sometimes as you're writing the music or inventing the melody you'll come up with one of the major lines which is maybe the key line of the song, which sets the whole mood. Then it's hard work after that. Sometimes you get inspired and the right phrase just comes into your mind immediately as you're writing the tune. That's great if that happens.

Do you work from titles?

Good question. Sometimes you write something down: 'Oh, that's a great title for a song.' I always try to have notepads lying around and scribble ideas down, but never in the daytime. I'm very busy in the day doing other things.

Has that always been the case, even in your twenties and thirties?

Yes, I'd say so, unless I've been working flat out on an album, completing an album of lyrics; then I'll try and work on it all day long. I haven't really done that for quite a while. Sometimes you work on an album and you've got about fifteen songs that you're working on, and maybe twelve make it to the album and you have three things left over that you didn't complete. Sometimes I leave them around for a long time thinking, 'I'll go back to this another day.' That can be great, going back with a fresh energy. Instead of dealing with a blank canvas you've got something already there. I'll now do this to it and that to it . . . and then finish it off, hopefully. That's quite unusual: maybe not many people do that, perhaps, I don't know? You have scraps of paper lying around, song ideas and titles. You think, 'This might be a good line for a song.' It's always good to hang on to what you think are good ideas. I used to have a book, but I haven't been using it. I think some people carry books around with them all the time; is that what you find?

Yes, but now more with recording devices like phones.

It's funny; I've got one of those phones but I don't really use it. I still actually like cassettes. I normally have a cassette player on top of my piano, just perched there in case I write something that I like and press record. Sometimes I don't listen back for about a year or so.

Really?

Oh yeah (*laughs*), and then I'll see if there's anything on this cassette and there might be something, there might not. It might be the same idea going around and round for minutes.

Presumably you have stacks of cassettes.

There's a few; we've been through most of them. There's one at the moment I'm working on which I haven't listened to for a long time. I don't know how old it is. It might have been there for a year or two.

Would you let the cassette player run in record mode to capture any missed ideas?

Not normally, no. There was one song which was quite interesting in the way it was made, called 'When She Walks In The Room'. I played it on the piano and for the first time I pressed the thing, 'Oh, I like this,' and recorded it. We transferred that from the cassette onto the master tape and the song was built around that. So the piano was actually done from my cassette.

It's a beautiful song, with Ann Odell's strings.

Yes, exactly, it was a beautiful arrangement. She was great. I don't know what happened to her. She did fantastic strings for me on that and 'I Can't Let Go' and a cover called 'Feel The Need'—really brilliant string arrangement.

Do you remember writing 'Avalon'?

I remember being in a panic to complete it, 'cause everything on the album was complete, and mixed even, and I was still struggling with this song. Until about the last two days it didn't have a name. The last weekend of recording I was in New York working on the lyric and finally came up with the title 'Avalon' and it all kind of worked. And then I went into the studio about five o'clock on the Sunday afternoon and sang it and there was a girl there in another studio with this wonderful voice which I heard down the corridor. She came in and did the scat vocal on it and made the record what it was. She was brilliant. A girl from Haiti. That's an important part of the song now, such a beautiful invention.

Your use of the voice on so many of your records is really playful. I would be intrigued to know if you made stylistic choices when you were on your own or once you were recording in the studio.

I suppose more when you're recording . . . I don't know, really. Different songs suggest different styles of singing them. I'm not quite sure if I have a style at all.

If you took 'Mother Of Pearl', for example, it is a daring montage of ideas.

Oh yeah, that's one of my favourite ones. I did a remake of that, I think it came out on a B-side. I wasn't quite happy we'd ever really completed it. I must work on that again. I had Ronnie Spector singing on the remake. I've always loved her voice. I love working with other singers. I find that very inspiring. I like girls' voices. I like Dylan's voice. I like John Lennon's voice. Sinatra. Elvis. Lots of black American singers I love. I love soprano—high voices.

Do you ever assume the identity of another songwriter just for the fun of sparking an idea? What would Dylan write if he was here? How would John Lennon . . .

Not really, it's complicated enough as it is (*laughs*). But I am a fan of other people's songs. Dylan, obviously. I've done a lot of his songs because I like singing those words. He's very gifted.

Can you recall writing 'I Thought'?

Ah, yeah. That was another co-write with Brian Eno. It's one of the nicest things. People don't really notice that record. It started in St Petersburg. I was over visiting Brian; I was staying there. We thought we'd try and write a couple of things together. He had this one sequence which I thought sounded great. I quite like the lyric of that. I don't really analyse what I write. I had the title; it came quite fast. I like to write things that move people. I like to write things that move myself. The best songs that I've written have been ones where you shed a tear in the writing. It sounds silly, but, where you've been actually very moved doing it, that's when you know it really works and means something. You don't have to do that with all of the songs, but occasionally you get that and think, 'Ah, this is going to last.'

The most recent time was on my last album, *Olympia*. I've a song called 'Reason Or Rhyme', but it's happened before, I think it's a good song. Sometimes you get inspired not only by the melody but by the performance of other people. Marcus Miller is a wonderful bass player and great musician, and he really got inside that song. I found that very inspiring when I was completing the lyrics. The piano playing I did I liked. Sometimes I've kept away from playing on records . . . there's a lot of great keyboard players. My style is a bit unusual: it's very primitive but it works for me.

Is it true you don't put the third in your chords?

I try not to. I like fifths . . .

Because it opens it out musically?

Yeah, it does. It gives you more options. I like suggestion rather than statement.

You haven't labelled it a major or minor key.

Exactly. Musicians sometimes say, 'Is that a major or a minor?' '. . . Mmm . . . what do you feel?' Sometimes you get some odd things happening, which is good.

Do you think the audience play a part in the songwriting process?

Mmm . . . if you're writing something you think . . . you can't write to your audience; a certain part of my audience would like this line or like this lyric or get this; others won't. If you think you've written something particularly clever you think, 'Ah, that's good.' You've got to do it for yourself. You've got to follow your own taste or you'd get completely lost.

Do you have any thoughts as to why in all the years of your writing so few British female songwriters have emerged?

That's an interesting question. Cathy Dennis is a great, prolific writer. I know what you mean: there's no Carole King. It's the same thing, why aren't there any female producers? I think that's crazy. There's so many women around who have great musical instincts. I've often been more interested in what women thought about a piece of music than men.

Do you seek approval?

I think everybody does. 'Course the only time you really get that is when you play to a live audience. I suppose if you get an amazing review. I've always been very wary about analysing songwriting. It's always been a mystery to me where ideas come from. The lucky thing for me is I listened to loads of music at a very early age: jazz and blues, everything really. It helps if you have a lot of influences. It makes thing more interesting. I better go and write a song!

JOAN ARMATRADING

DANIEL RACHEL

9 December 1950: *I was born on an Island, St Kitts, in a little biddy town.* Within three years the infant's life would be shattered. Joan Anita Barbara Armatrading watched her family cross the waters to *spread their wings and fly away*, leaving her on the island of Antigua to be fostered by her grandmother. The separation would mark the child. She became independent, a loner, and as an adult would define her character with the poignant song title 'Me Myself I'. At the age of seven Joan arrived at New Street Station in Birmingham to be reunited with her parents and two elder brothers and raised in the white neighbourhood of Brookfields. In 'Mama Papa' she sang *Seven people in one room / No heat / One wage.*

Armatrading's early musical interest was limited to playing the recorder and singing in the school choir at Canterbury Cross Secondary, Perry Bar. Whilst her musically minded father worked on the buses, his guitar was kept locked up on a high shelf, a forbidden temptation. Eventually, she persuaded her mother to trade two prams for a three-pound pawned guitar. Later, as a 14-year-old, Joan began picking out melodies she had composed on her mother's piano (bought as 'a piece of furniture'). Her intention was to write for and about others; the unseen, offstage songwriter. She left school early, writing songs and performing in a covers duo whilst jobs came and went. An audition for Robert Stigwood's musical *Hair* took the adventurous teenager to London where she met the gregarious Guyanese-born songwriter Pam Nestor. Over three years as musical partners, with more than a hundred songs written between them, Armatrading would take the essence of her collaborator's prose and then compose separately on a piano or guitar. A primitive demo tape was accepted at Essex Music publishers, and, fortuitously, the recording was then stumbled upon by Mike Noble, who in turn played it to the acclaimed producer Gus Dudgeon. Borrowing members from both Elton John's and Cat Stevens's bands, she recorded a debut album, *Whatever's For Us*, in 1972 which went on to sell a healthy 2,000 copies and led to a two-week residency, as the first non-jazz artist, at London's Ronnie Scott's.

Alexandra Elene Maclean Lucas at the age of thirty-one fell into a coma. Four days later she was declared dead as the result of a traumatic mid-brain haemorrhage. On her headstone were the chiselled words 'The Lady'. The song-writer, better known as Sandy Denny, had combined a shattering vocal beauty with a matchless interpretation of folk music. For a short period, the country was blessed with two unique female songwriters. Both were observers of de-tailed emotions, exploring the infinite complexities of love and relationships. But whereas Denny's personal demons intruded into her haunting confessional voice, Armatrading declares of her own writing that there is too much for it all to be about one person. Her insights into other people's lives have often coaxed listeners towards unfamiliar lyrical angles. 'No Love For Free' reads from the point of view of a hooker, whilst 'Rosie' depicts a teasing and all-too-willing transvestite: *Aw Rosie, don't you do that to the boys*. In 'Down To Zero' the com-poser creatively diverts the narrative from an upstaging *scene stealer* who *walks through the crowd and takes your man* to a private self-affirming after-scene: *Sends you rushing to the mirror / Brush your eyebrows and say there's more beauty in you than anyone*. Armatrading may avoid self-exposure, but she gladly cele-brates in verse a rich view of life and a *blessed heart that sings*.

As a black woman emerging in a decade of heightened racial tensions, Armatrading forged her own natural sound, then used and transcended her background with untutored talent. It is a gift she attributes to God. In the mu-sic papers, a few critics scented a potentially vulnerable target: 'How Cruel' reflected: *I had someone say once I was way too black / And someone answers she's not black enough for me*. In 'Ma-Me-O-Beach', her detractors are met with humour: *Me I'm brown enough / In fact I'm overdone / Turn me over*. Three decades has made a huge difference to multicultural acceptance and the popu-larity of non-white British female solo artists. Sade, Melanie B, Shaznay Lewis, Corinne Bailey Rae, Ms Dynamite, Jamelia, Leona Lewis, Alexandra Burke and Laura Mvula head a roll-call of songwriters with varying degrees of sustained chart success, whilst Emeli Sandé appeared at the 2012 Olympics opening ceremony singing Henry Francis Lyte's Christian hymn 'Abide With Me' and as a result helped push her debut album to the top of the year's best-selling records. The change in attitudes owes a great deal to Armatrading's front-line profile in the Seventies and Eighties as the first independent female performer-cum-writer.

In 2007, *Into The Blues* propelled the 57-year-old artist to the top of the American *Billboard* blues chart. It was a supreme feat for a female writer, earn-ing her a Grammy nomination and a twelve-week stand at number one. Arma-trading is rightly proud of her achievement. She is a writer, producer and multi-instrumentalist. She has a recording career spanning six decades. Her seventeenth studio album is rich in melodic invention and emotionally drawn guitar playing. The songs may have a blues foundation, but the variation and unexpected turns within the writing reveal a creative imagination at odds with easy genre categorization. On the lead track, 'A Woman In Love', she sings, *When the morning comes like shifting sands in a desert storm*. The ubiquitous *Woke up one morning* blues opening is subtly toyed with and grounded by solid electric guitar interplay. Then unexpectedly the bridge rises out of a G minor verse with a melodic lift to B flat major and then F. It is characteristic of Armatrading to exalt harmony intersections out of flatlined verse.

Musical originality may be understood via a small record collection. Although the radio was a feature in the Armatrading household alongside the LPs of Sarah Vaughan, Nat King Cole, Jim Reeves and classical records, Joan, despite being an avid listener, to this day still buys few releases. The tradition of classic songwriting which links Lennon and McCartney to the majority of artists in this book, and is indeed a badge of honour for many, is neglected by Armatrading in favour of pursuing individualism without influence. That attitude is rare amongst her peers. A third album, simply titled *Joan Armatrading*, in 1976, proved to be the songwriter's breakthrough. Produced by Glyn Johns (The Beatles, The Rolling Stones, The Who, Led Zeppelin), it showed a recording approach in great contrast to the difficulties of the preceding *Back To The Night*: a studio ethos centred on working quickly, keeping it simple, and allowing instruments to retain their natural sounds. This record has become her enduring classic, with its stand-out track 'Love And Affection', a beautifully expressed craving for unadorned romance: *Now if I can feel the sun in my eyes and the rain on my face / Why can't I feel love?* Performed with members of Fairport Convention in attendance, including B. J. Cole, the man who found Sandy Denny collapsed at the bottom of her friend's narrow dog-leg stairs, the sparse production highlighted the emotional intensity of Armatrading's vocal delivery. She effortlessly glides across the beat before smoothly opening her full range to the principal three-chord picked guitar accompaniment. When the vocal line demands that the lead note reach up to G sharp and then slide a further half-tone to top A, she escorts the change with considered chord inversions: at first the guitar rests on C sharp with the root and fifth notes doubled with octaves played by her little finger. The jazz-sounding second chord that follows and hangs is an A sharp major seventh with octaves again doubled, this time with major seventh and third notes complemented on the instrument's top two strings. The result is a suspended atmosphere, rare to pop communication, but perfectly suited to the sentiment of the word *feel*, which Armatrading projects with rhetorical appeal. A further two studio albums produced by Johns, *Show Some Emotion* and *To The Limit*, explored and captured the dynamic

Joan with house key, circa 1980–83

range of the artist's vocal capabilities. 'Save Me' repeated the soloist's bewitching facility to switch from vulnerable falsetto to mid-range, wistful melancholy. 'Show Some Emotion' involved a multipart, jazz-centred chord progression taking in flattened fifths, sevenths and elevenths; major, minor and diminished chords. The sophisticated guitar playing belied a relaxed melody and a song founded on a groove-driven riff composed of an omnipresent Western rock anhemitonic pentatonic scale. Armatrading had the technical ability to bring together composite styles and write with accessible melody pushing the weight of voice, not just high into light head sounds, but also into baritone depth.

By the late 1980s, having established a home studio, Bumpkin, for the recording of *The Shouting Stage*, Armatrading was issuing a succession of albums that saw her play, arrange and produce all her output. The artistic freedom she gained by taking control of her music has been a major factor in her career. As for Kate Bush, the assertion of creative independence of industry machinations and media expectation liberated the artistic spirit from imposed time constraint. Armatrading's naivety in forgoing co-production credits on her early releases, however, deflected recognition of her quickly honed arrangement skills. As she pointed out in conversation, 'I'm not a control freak, but when I go in a studio I know exactly what I want.' She writes string arrangements and drum patterns, plays bass and piano and devises all the hooks of her songs. With touching modesty she qualified, 'I say these things because I'm very proud to be able to do them.'

Joan Armatrading is an artist with a determined musical temper. From her first release, when acoustic balladeers were selling profusely on both sides of the Atlantic, to her pop forays in the early Eighties, she has intuitively carved a career out of a love for and belief in songwriting. Her durable classic 'Willow' continues to echo around concert halls, with dedicated fans drawn by the song's heartfelt integrity: *I'm strong / Straight / Willing to be a shelter in a storm / Your willow . . . when the sun is out.* I met with Joan at the University Women's Club in Mayfair on a break from her 2010 world tour. Nine years earlier she had graduated from the Open University with an honours degree in history. In 2013 she was awarded an honorary doctorate in music by the same body. The achievements crown a career of accolades including an Ivor Novello Award for Outstanding Contemporary Song Collection, a five-year presidency of the highly prestigious Women of the Year Lunch, and an MBE. She has received three Grammy and two Brit Award nominations, and in addition to being given the keys to the city of Sydney, was invited in 2001 to write and perform a special tribute song, 'The Messenger', for Nelson Mandela. She also has the rare distinction of having appeared in an edition of the *Dandy* comic. In concert, Joan rids the stage of amplifiers and microphone stands, preferring a clean and tidy *mise en scène*. For a woman who has never touched drink,

smoked, used drugs nor sworn, it seemed appropriate that we chatted in the
healthy environment of the club's dining room.

Johnny Marr said he started playing the guitar as if he was a one-man symphony. Do you recognize that way of trying to cover all the bases?

That's exactly how I got my guitar style. I was trying to play the guitar, play the rhythm, play the bass bits, do whatever piano bits: trying to do everything all at once. So when I did that first record (*Whatever's For Us*) I had to really tone down how I played because I was getting in other people's way. Because you can hear it and you want to hear it, you try and do it. So I'm definitely like Johnny Marr (*laughs*).

Did you learn to play guitar and piano from other artists' songs?

I never did that. I just wrote my own songs. I never played or learnt other people's songs or played along to them. I used to write limericks, funny little stories and things like that. Then my mother bought the piano, put it in the front room and thought it was a great piece of furniture. As soon as it arrived I started making up my own songs. That's how my songwriting started and then I got my guitar and carried on from there. I'm sure at some point I would have written songs, but as soon as the piano arrived that was the catalyst. I love other people's songs. There's so many really good songwriters and so many great, great songs, but I'm so busy trying to write a great, great song that I tend to not sing other people's songs. Not because I don't like them but because I'm trying all the time to find a way to write something that is so good that you think, 'Oh, that's the song. You don't need to write anything else. You've done it.'

Has that song been written by another person?

No, no. I've heard songs that are just phenomenal but there's no songs that make me think there's no good anybody else writing a song, because that's what would have to happen.

Are you a Beatles fan?

I don't know how to answer that question. I'm completely appreciative of The Beatles. I know the importance of Lennon and McCartney and The Beatles' music, but I've never bought a Beatles record. I don't buy a lot of records and I don't listen to a lot of music. I know the songs; I hear them all the time. I really liked Paul's album *Ram*; the rawness, the jazziness.

Are there benchmarks in your own catalogue?

There are songs that absolutely I love. I love all of them, that's why they get on the record. But it's the same thing: I want to write a song that's better than 'The Weakness In Me' or 'Love And Affection' or 'This Charming Life' or 'Crazy'. I want to write a song that's better than all of the songs that I've written. I absolutely love writing songs, that's when I'm at my absolute happiest. That's always been a constant. There's a great sense of achievement when you write something and you feel really, really good about it; where you think, 'Yeah, I like that.' When I write I don't think about will you like it: I haven't a clue what you like. So I write purely for myself.

Can you remember the first song you wrote?

No, I can't. I can remember one called 'When I Was Young', but I was young then. I had no idea what I was saying.

Journalists have speculated that song was inspired by seeing Marianne Faithfull on television.

No! Oh, it's so annoying: some of these things that come out you think, 'Where did you get that information?' 'Who made these up?' And then they become a truth.

Can you write in any state of mind?

I'm in that frame of wanting to write at the moment. It's like a pull: 'Come on, Joan, write.' When I'm on tour I can't settle to write. I've only written 'Call Me Names' on tour. I can think of things but I can't physically do what I'm supposed to do. Whether it's the wandering from hotel to hotel, too many people, I don't know. I know when I've finished, I'll be writing. It's all going in my head. I don't know how that works, but there's an urge that comes. Then it goes. It's not that you don't want to write, it just doesn't enter your head. Nothing pulls you, nothing says, 'Here's an idea.' You don't even get that unconscious observation where you'll see something and think, 'That'll make a great song.' It's like it blanks out. It doesn't scare me because I know that it always comes. I don't think I could write if I was completely miserable; I might have ideas. Writing for me is a very, very happy time. It's a really energized, joyful . . . sometimes if you would see me writing you'd probably think I was mad because I'm quite animated: I move around, I jump around, I dance.

With your guitar in hand?

Yeah, I do all kinds of really silly things because you really get into it. It's a really nice, happy feeling to write. But singing makes you happy as well, so the two go together. People say to me, 'Why do you still write and still put records out?' It's simple: because I love it. I think it shows.

I'm not surprised to hear you are physical because predominantly your music is very up, even if the subject matter is not.

That's right, I'm glad you noticed because it's true, the music is up. I think music is kind of life, it's a joyful thing. If we didn't have music we'd have to invent it. We can't do without it. Because I'm so happy playing I can't help the music being up.

When you are generating ideas, how do you remember them?

Bit of all kinds of things: sometimes I'll immediately write something down, or I might put it in my iPhone now; write it down in the notes section, might take a piece of paper. Depending on the songs it's sometimes possible to keep it in your head; more often than not you forget. You think you'll remember but you'll forget. One song I didn't forget was 'Everyday Boy'. I met this chap at a friend's house and he had AIDS. He was telling me about his boyfriend's mother who didn't like him because she thought her son was going to die as well. But he was so kind about her, it was incredible. In the song I talk about him going to the mirror and looking at his hair and fixing himself, just his positiveness. Just watching and listening to him I could write all those words in my head, so when I got home I immediately wrote them down. Because it was so strong how he was, it allowed me to remember those words. But if you have something else, no matter how strong you think it is . . . sometimes you can't even remember the subject matter, let alone the words you thought of.

Do you find yourself filtering everyday conversations and tuning into your writing mind?

No, it doesn't really work like that. When I write I'm kind of not consciously looking for a song to write. If I've seen two people having an argument, I'm not listening in and thinking, 'That's going to make a great song.' Subconsciously I probably am. Sometimes a song will come from something that I've seen, I hadn't realized it was something that was going to give me a song. Then when I get away from it and something triggers it coming back, then there's the song.

Also, I've never written a song—and I get this often: 'Joan, this will make a great song' (*laughs*). I've had that so often: 'Listen to this, you're going to love this and I'm sure you're going to write about it.'

Would you ever set writing times or discipline yourself to a writing day? Glenn Tilbrook talks about digging trenches to generate inspiration.

Gilbert O'Sullivan, I read, would go in from nine to five to write. I tend to go in whenever the mood takes me. If I hadn't written anything in three months I don't panic, I just wait. I don't force myself to go and write. If I'm going to write, the whole feeling of the thing has to be in me to do it. Once you're in something, if it's not easy, you do have to keep going. But you don't realize that's what's going on. You suddenly wake up to: 'My goodness, it's been six hours, I'm still here,' or, 'It's four o'clock in the morning.' It's not like a chore, it's something you get completely lost and immersed in . . . you forget to eat and drink, forget to go to the loo.

At what point do you hear clarity and objectivity after you've created a song?

If you're talking about at what point during the recording process you hear it, that's a different thing to what point when you're writing you hear it. In writing I have to hear it very quickly, because if you don't you won't end the writing of the song. I must be quite clear that when I've written that verse, or that chorus, or that little bit of instrumental thing, that I'm happy that everything is connected: that the words make some kind of sense. I quite like it that there are little stories going through: a beginning, middle and an end. As I'm developing it I tend to think . . . how can I answer this? Different songs go different ways. If you go back to 'Everyday Boy', to me that was a story so I had to write the words first. But sometimes the song itself, as a whole, comes together with a kind of nonsense-verse thing happening that you're getting the sense of the song; you're getting the melody, the rhythm, the rhyming of the words with the melody, but what you're saying is rubbish. But you still have a sense of what you want to say, ultimately, but at that point it's not important. Once I've written the song and I've got the shape of it and I know what the thing is, then I'll go back and sort out the words. That's why it's not easy to answer that in that very simple way. Some songs, the melody comes first and I spend all my time just concentrating so the melody is right. Some songs, the words will come first and I'll spend all my time making sure that's right. Then some songs will come together as if you're singing something you know: it's not even writing a song, it's just singing something. So it's very different, each song dictates itself. This is the song that I am: I'm a piano song, or I'm a guitar song. You almost have no control over that. You just have to go with it. I always say when you write, people say, 'Aren't you clever, writing?' I think, 'Well, it's not so clever really because it's quite often just a bunch of accidents.'

watch the rain gently fall
like the tears running down my face

You sometimes ~~it feels~~ ~~like~~ the sky's
~~Sky is fall~~ Violence
Some ~~times~~ it feels like no one ~~hears~~ looks
Some ~~times~~ it feels like I'm an empty highway
and I'm on a road to ~~to~~ nowhere

As I watch the street lights flicker
like ~~the~~ dying embers of your ~~affection~~

Some ~~times~~ it feels like we never kissed
~~Some times~~ I've got so enthused in the push &
pull of the tide
Who cares if the world stops spinning
Cos I'm the lonely number one

As I lay me down to sleep
~~All~~ the little birds & bees
~~that~~ would sing to lovers
Pass me by

Ever in my dreams
                                  a
vivid colours turn to ~~grey~~ greyscale
And I turn to you and I ask
how can I make things better
And you say it's gone It's gone it's over
~~Now watch the gentle rain fall.~~
And I stand outside in just my ~~underwear~~
And I watch the gentle rain fall.

'Empty Highway' lyrics, handwritten by Joan Armatrading

Andy Partridge explains how 'Senses Working Overtime' came about from his fingers slipping on a chord, making a sound that suggested medieval serfs.

That's what I mean about accidents. When I said writing sounds very clever: writing isn't that clever, but it *is* clever. Quite often when you go to play a D your fingers will slip and you play a D7 or you hit an E or an F sharp. It's an accident, but the trick is to know you must keep that accident. A lot of writing is like that. The progression will be going along and you think, I know exactly what I'm going to do: this, this and this, and then, oh no, and that inspires the rest of it and takes you onto a road. The cleverness is in recognizing you've made a slip, but that's the genius. A lot of writing is like that. Some people won't want to admit that because they want to just be clever. The song will dictate. You need to follow the song: don't be the one pulling it in this direction, let it pull you.

Do you ever feel like you're writing a song that's already out there?

Yes, definitely, but not if you mean am I trying to rewrite 'Love And Affection'.

How do you explain the receiving of melody?

This is why I say nobody will be able to tell you how to write a song, because I could not tell you where I get any of my ideas, or my sense of rhythm, or melody, or that whole composition thing. I have no idea and I can do it. I know it's a God-given talent. I'm very sure of that because it's not something I gave to myself. So where did I get it from? I heard Wynton Marsalis, who I think is just brilliant, talking on an interview saying when he writes he hears a lot of the melody and the whole song; the rhythm of everything, and he writes everything in his head before he even gets to a keyboard. That's exactly what I do. If you look at 'Into The Blues' or lots of them, a lot of what's there I wrote in my head before I touched anything. I know exactly what I want to write about, the kind of shape of the thing and the melody of it, and it will stay in my head and it will work. Those ones, when they work they will work, as I said before. He's the only one I've heard who's said that. Then I said this to somebody the other day and they said, 'Oh yes, and with Mozart.' I'm not trying to put myself with Mozart, don't get me wrong (*laughing*). That's how he wrote his symphonies; he just did it in his head.

How long can you hold those ideas in your head?

Completely depends on the song. As I say, some songs you can hold and others, no matter how strong they feel, you're not going to remember them from here to the door. Here you think, 'Oh, that's too good, that's the song, I'll never forget that.' You walk two steps and it's gone. If you've played it that's a whole different thing, then you can hold it. When I write and I'm playing it and I've written the verse without recording it, then I'll remember that. But just in my head, without doing anything . . . Once you've committed to that physical thing: playing the chord, singing out loud, saying the words, then you can keep it for quite a while.

Joan Armatrading *Into the Blues,* 2007 by Andrew Catlin

There's a wonderful little scene in the *Track Record* documentary which shows you in a Boston hotel room laying down 'Heaven'. There's a recording machine in front of you, a drum machine, a guitar, and we see you putting down the vocal after.

That was for the cameras, but that's how I write. I would first of all write the song on the piano or the guitar and then once I'd written it I would involve the drum machine, then put in the bass bits and whatever harmonies and stuff.

When you started using a drum machine, did its regulating rhythm affect your writing?

If I was relying upon the drum machine to write the song that would make a big difference, but because I'm writing the song first . . . when I'm writing the song I'm looking for the rhythm that will work with that song, as opposed to having a rhythm and trying to make a song work with that rhythm. The song is dictating, as opposed to the other way round.

Does your writing style differ depending on whether you're using a piano or a guitar?

Songs on the piano tend to be more melodic. So 'The Weakness In Me' I can tell is written on the piano, but something like 'Back On The Road' I can tell is

written on the guitar: it's less melodic and very rhythm driven. 'Love And Affection': although that's melodic I can still tell that it's a guitar song. Guitar songs tend to be more rocky, more rhythmic, a little bit heavier or jazzier.

Does the instrument dictate the key you write in? For example, it would be more natural to write in E flat or B flat on the piano than on the guitar.

Not really. I tend to play in whatever key the song suits. I've done it where the song suits that key but actually my voice doesn't, but that's where the song needs to be.

In which case would you use a capo?

I can't use a capo. I get very confused because I know that the nut is there and suddenly the nut is here and I think, 'I don't know what I'm supposed to do now,' so I just change key.

Can you recall music before moving to Birmingham?

Not really, no. Because I was born in the West Indies and came to England when I was seven, people think the music had a huge influence while I was there, but it didn't. So any kind of influences in terms of Caribbean music would be British-tinged or American; that's where I'm hearing it.

You've crossed a multitude of genres throughout your career without compromising your individual style.

I personally like it as you've mentioned, throughout all the different styles I've done, from jazz, reggae, blues, rock, pop, whatever, and then when I did *Lovers Speak* I wanted to do something that was kind of acoustic-sounding but not being acoustic. Then I wanted to do just blues so I did *Into The Blues*, and then *This Charming Life* which is rock, pop, but I always want it to be me. So I'm not listening to loads of blues things; I just want it to be Joan Blues, or Joan Rock or whatever. I remember reading a review that said, 'Yeah, it's blues, but it's Joan blues.' I thought, 'Yeah, thank you, you've got it, that's exactly it.' I'm a songwriter so I want it to have my stamp on it. I want you to recognize what you're listening to. If it's *Into The Blues* I don't want you to think, 'Is that blues?' But at the same time, you know, I'm not trying to copy a blues song.

With the trilogy of records that you mentioned, *Lovers Speak*, *Into The Blues* and *This Charming Life*, did the broad definitions that you applied to each recording affect the writing process differently?

I'm used to flitting about when I'm writing . . . let's look what we've got here . . . *Secret Secrets*: 'Love By You' with Joe Jackson; that's a ballad, but then you've got 'Talking To The Wall', a very jazzy song. So when I've written that jazzy song I'm all into jazzy things. For some reason my mind doesn't say, 'OK, that was really good, why don't you write another jazzy one?' For some reason it says, 'I think you should write a real rock one now.' So I'll go off on these tangents all the time. Because I've been doing it for so long I'm very comfortable doing that. When I decided I wanted to write just a blues record it was actually quite difficult for me. I had to keep reining myself in and reminding myself, 'Don't go off and do a little jazzy thing now or a pop-rocky thing, this is blues so stay there and only think in those terms.' That's why when I say I did quite a lot of the writing in my head, that helped me keep myself focused. There are lots of different styles within the blues: Delta, swampy, Status Quo blues (*laughs*) . . . but they all gel very easily together. So if you go off and do one style and you mix it with another it stays in this blues thing. It's quite good. Rock isn't the same, it's very broad and if you don't mix it quite carefully it sounds like a strange compilation album. With *This Charming Life* I couldn't go off into heavy metal rock because it would jar against what's there. You had to be careful.

'A Woman In Love' starts with a very hard blues riff but then opens out into a typical melodic lift for your writing. Likewise 'Liza' suddenly jumps into a hip hop influenced section. Was that a natural part of the writing process?

No, I wanted to write a song that did that. It wasn't an accident that it went off into this other thing and then comes back to the place where it started. In that funny bit it doesn't mention 'Liza' in the way that it does in the beginning, and the melody is different. Somebody said to me, 'What you need to do is go back into the studio and link . . . it sounds like two separate songs,' but it wasn't about connecting the two. It was about making this bit be very different and strong on its own, in a way still stay connected but not in that I must make a melody that joins them together. It's like in 'Heading Back To New York City'; there's a very dancey bit in there. Again, I just like doing little quirky bits.

There's a lovely pair of photographs on the inner sleeve of *To The Limit* showing you writing lyrics, in one with a look of exasperation and the other relieved.

I can tell you exactly what happened there. Annie Leibovitz took these pictures; here she's saying, 'We've got to take one more picture,' and here's she's saying, 'We've finished.' (*Laughs.*)

How easily do words flow for you?

Very easily; they're the last thing I think about in terms of the song. That's why I said earlier on I'll write a song and the shape, the structure, the melody, the composition of it: how things are going to work with each other. I tend to concentrate on those the most. I'll very often know what I want to write and the structure so I don't have to worry about the real words. When I've written the song, then I'll write the words, and they tend to come very quickly. If you

C ♩♩♩♩ ♩♩♩♩

C
I was born on an island St Kitts

In a little biddy town

Had a mama and a papa
C

4 brothers and a sister   C E G C

Mama papa told us
C
Play hard

Fight fair

Live life

And love the Lord   ♩♩♩♩
                      C E G C

Said love the Lord

Said love the Lord

Cos one day you'll be
F F F F F
Walking on heaven's floor
E E E E E
Talking in the ear of God
F F F F F F F
What you gonna say to the man
      G G G G G
When he asks you what you've done

mid 8   Em F
             "   " G

Can you say you
gonna say
‡ did my best
with what I had
          you had

I know two people
Who saved up love
And a while lot more

They made us hold our
Sides with laughter all night long   ♩♩♩
made us laugh until we cried 'til we begged them stop
or well split our sides

C C always like the ♩♩♩♩ /♩♩♩♩

Their choice was the
That close
Mama Papa came to the United Kingdom
but settled in B/ham
made a home
when they wanted
to spread their
wings and
the fat of the land
fly away

Their choice was
They chose the
United Kingdom living in
and lived in Birmingham
when they wanted to
spread their wings
and fly away

7 people in one room
No heat
One wage
And bills to pay
bills to pay
gotta pay those bills
                            C E G
                            ♩♩♩ G

'Mama Papa' lyrics, typed and annotated by Joan Armatrading

look at Bonnie Raitt she didn't use to write; now writes, but only writes a certain amount. Writing, if you're not naturally drawn to it, is a hard process, to come up with melody, rhythm and lyrics that are different each time. As Noel Gallagher says, 'It's a struggle.' Lyrics seem to be the hardest thing for most people. There are a lot of writers who have spent five, ten years writing those ten, eleven, twelve songs but they will not be able to repeat the thing again. It's like the one novel in you. I write a lot because I have to.

Does there have to be a foundation of truth in the lyrics?

Tends to be, they tend to not be made up. 'Liza', for instance, that was someone I know; he was not rich, but from good parents, and she was from a poor family. Very different backgrounds, and all his friends were saying, 'Forget her. How are you going to make this work? She's from a council estate, you're in your posh little house, it's not going to work.' That's why you hear all the: you're from a part *where folks live on welfare*. It generally is from something that is real.

The music is staged reflecting the different social classes: do you generally try to make the music a reflection of the lyrical themes?

That's right, but it really depends on the songs, but yes, you want them to marry. I find New York very vibrant, very lively, very edgy. When you write something like 'Heading Back To New York City' you want it to be rocking along; it's not a little fairy-tale place so the music there has to match up to how I see it. You have to make the melody and the music match that sentiment. It's like when you watch a film and you can see two people: a chap with his arm around the woman when she's crying and you think that's quite sad, but as soon as you add the music that says you've got to cry now yourself, that's when the real emotion comes out. So the music really has to state the lyrics.

Are you ever surprised by what you've written?

Yeah, not so much in terms of music and melody, but the arrangements. I get pretty excited about the arrangements.

Do you ever listen back to past albums before creating a new one?

Not before creating it; after I will. I don't want to recreate anything, especially subconsciously. I tend not to listen to anything when I'm writing. Afterwards I'll get a couple of them out and see if the standard is still there (*laughs*).

I had a sense before today that you were very closed to other influences and yet when I listen to your records they very much follow the musical style of the different decades. Why is that?

Because I'm alive (*laughs*), I'm here, I hear music. I know what the music of the day is. For instance, if you listen to *Secret Secrets* and *Walk Under Ladders*, synthesizers were very prominent then; those were the keyboards and the sounds that you got. So unless I wanted not to be of the moment—and I don't mean of the musical moment, I mean in terms of living and being—then I wouldn't touch a synthesizer, I would only play a piano. But I'm here, we're meant to take part. If a synthesizer's the thing of the day then I'm definitely going to play it and include it in my music.

Are you chasing commerciality? Everybody wants their music to be heard . . .

I definitely want my music to be more successful than anybody in the world; however, there's a way of going about it that says, I'm doing it at any price, and there's a way of just doing it and saying, I'm just doing what I'm doing. I write my songs. I just go about my way. I hope people will like it but I don't want to have to do it in a way that makes me come across as false; as if I'm trying to chase that kind of commercial success, and I don't mean this music.

The metre of your words has great variation line by line; they don't often adhere to traditional rules or structure.

Part of it is probably because I'm not trained, so I don't know I shouldn't do certain things. That applies not to just melodies and metre but the whole musical thing. So you will get lots of odd, strange little two-bar turnaround things happening. For the musicians sometimes it's, 'What's going to happen here?' I like that quirky way of doing things and I do that very naturally.

Have you come across blocks as a writer?

No, I don't get that. What I get is writing rubbish. I always finish a song. I have to: doesn't matter how bad it is. I think if I don't finish I might never be able to start. I don't have any unfinished songs. If I couldn't finish I would be worried. They're not for anybody else to hear. I record them, listen to them; don't like them, they get erased. The ones that end up on the record are the ones that I like. I'm not going to let you hear it if I think it's rubbish. All these songs, they all at some point have been sung live on stage. I'm the constant; different bands over the years. I don't want to sing something I don't like, no matter if it's been a big hit. So it's really easy for me to sing 'Love And Affection' on stage every night because it's a great song: 'Willow', 'The Weakness In Me'. I like to feel comfortable.

You have a really strong gay following; does that influence your writing?

No, I have a strong everybody following; nobody influences my writing, only me.

There is enormous ambiguity in your writing, for example the line from 'Ma-Me-O-Beach': *pretty girls are there if you're good with chat.* **Whichever sex you are, it could appeal?**

It's not even that: the songs are written for everybody. If I see a pretty girl, just because I'm a woman I'm not going to think she's not a pretty girl. If people relate to the songs because I write them in the first person, I didn't do that intentionally, it's just the way I write; but when people hear the songs in that form they're able to relate to it because it's personal to them. The songs aren't written for men, for women, gay, not gay: they're just written for people and ultimately for me, but once they are out they're for people.

Where do you stand in the narrative of your songs?

Depends on the song. Some songs are written about me: 'Me Myself I', 'This Charming Life', 'Blessed', 'I'm Lucky'. You can tell: they say thank you for my life. A lot of the songs I'm the observer because I'm quite often near to the thing I'm writing about; I know the person or the situation or I have seen it happen. I'm able to write it quite personally as if it is me. I do have to get involved in the thing I'm writing about. If we go back to 'Liza', people thought that was a gay song but it's about a guy and his fiancée. I have to write a song in a way that allows you to realize it's meaningful. I do have to get involved in the song. A song like 'At the Hop', that's just a made-up song. It's not something that I do very often, just something to get the rhythm going. 'Barefoot And Pregnant': this chap that I knew was telling me about somebody that he knew, this woman who was in this situation of being almost a prisoner to this guy. He would shower her with all kinds, but he wouldn't allow her to go out and have her own life and be her own person. He was very controlling of her. As I say, you have to write in a way that allows people to identify with it. You don't want people to say, 'That's not true,' or 'That's not real,' or 'I have no interest in that.'

Billy Bragg says writing is simply very difficult because you have to reach inside yourself quite deep, to bring that out.

Yes you do, you kind of have to live it yourself, even if it's not you, you have to get inside that person's head. Here's a song: 'All A Woman Needs', a little bit like 'Barefoot And Pregnant': this was me and a friend of mine talking about someone that we both knew who was with this lady. All the woman wanted was for him to say, 'I love you,' just show the feelings he had for her by words and by touch. But if she said, 'I really like tennis,' he'd go and buy the most expensive racket or expensive lessons. Or if she said, 'I really like chocolate,' he'd get a table of chocolates. He'd never say or show in the way she wanted, it was always in this physical, material way: *Brings her flowers every day / And he phones her every night / Because she's his fancy / She's bound to love him too / And he's proved his feelings / He gives her all she needs / This boy can't understand / Though he holds her in his arms / He won't whisper words of love / He thinks it's alright / Love can come later.* All she wants, as it says here, *He has to woo her properly or he'll never win her heart.* She just wants (*girlie voice*) 'Ooh, darling, I love you.' (*Laughs.*)

Is your empathy for people connected to being separated from your parents at an early age? Has that provided a backbone to your writing?

It probably has; everything we've gone through makes us the person we are. When I got to England people say, 'What did you love? Was it arriving in this wonderful country?' No, the big deal was meeting my parents. I didn't know what England was. It had no significance for me, but coming to my parents had all the significance. So when we met, the tears and the whole thing, that was a real, real joy. I know I missed my parents terribly when I wasn't with them. I don't think about it but I wouldn't be surprised if that played a big part in shaping who I am, for sure. As a youngster, not having your parents for a while is not nice. It's not something I dwell on. I was always a loner person anyway; I'm no different now than when I was a youngster. I'm used to spending time on my own. That's where 'Me Myself I' comes from.

You wrote in 'If Women Ruled the World': *Women are carers / They were born that way.* **Is that a reason why women songwriters in this country haven't achieved the success of their male counterparts?**

I don't know, having done this for so long you still don't see many woman engineers, in terms of the music business, or producers. You get woman guitarists, but not many strong woman guitarists; it's often a very strummy, basic way of playing. It's not the way I play or the way Bonnie Raitt plays. Amy Winehouse was a really good strong woman writer in the UK. Did she write with other people? Quite often it's people writing together. On this first album *Whatever's For Us* Pam wrote the lyrics but she knew I wrote songs and asked me to put some music to words she'd written. I took the words away and changed them to make a song. I've never sat in a room with somebody to write a song. I don't think I'd be capable of it because I know so much about what I want to hear. I don't know that I'm particularly open to somebody else saying, 'Let's make this verse go like this.'

Can we talk about some of the songs you've written? *When you sing the blues, I'd take off all my clothes for you.*

'Play The Blues' was the first song I wrote for *Into the Blues*. I started the process in Cardiff on the *Lovers Speak* tour and started to write those lyrics. It's about the blues being so strong and somebody being so good at it, so magnetic, just to get them to sing, somebody would basically do anything (*laughs*).

I am not in love but I'm open to persuasion. **Did you write 'Love And Affection' in different pieces?**

Yes, it was a couple of songs; I can't remember the different bits too well. I've never said this before, but that opening line is really about me. I don't usually talk about this song.

Was the doo-wop backing vocals your idea?

Yes, it was. A lot of these things that people hear they tend to give the producer the credit, but as I say, I tend to write all these things that people like to hear.

Did you write it on a on a twelve-string?

Yes, if you hear a twelve-string it was written on a twelve-string.

'(I Love It When You) Call Me Names'.

That's the only song I've written on tour. It's actually about two chaps on tour who were in my band. Again, I think this is the first time I'm saying this. One of them was little and one was big and they were always arguing, always doing what it says in that song, but you kind of had the feeling that they loved it. Just getting at each other: you'd think, 'Get a room already.' They weren't gay. Like a little terrier, that just gets any big dog.

What does *drop the mahout* mean?

He's an elephant rider controlling it; its keeper. 'Drop The Pilot' is the only song I've written to be commercial, to be a hit single. I should do it again, because that worked. I came up with the title of it first, then had the idea, because it's about don't go out with that person, go out with me. I wanted to say it in a very different way. I've seen different people say 'Drop The Pilot' means all kinds of things. One thing I saw said, 'When ships go out to sea, the little tug boat . . .' something to do with fuelling, a link to the big ship; when the link is dropped it's called drop the pilot, apparently. I literally sat down and thought, 'What can I say that's quirky? It needs to be up, jolly and it needs to have that (*hums riff*)' . . . my music tends to go along with how the music goes; you don't always get a verse, chorus, a verse, chorus. Pop music that is a hit tends to have quite a formula: a verse, a chorus, another verse, a chorus, a middle-eighty bit, an instrumental, chorus. So I tried to do that structure and have all these hooky bits. It was very deliberate and I wanted the words to be quirky.

'Something's Gonna Blow' followed a far less conventional structure.

I wanted to write a song that was eight minutes long. I was on the Tube, the Northern Line, probably Tottenham Court Road. They announced there'd been a suicide so all the lines were being stopped. The platform was seriously packed and hot. People weren't annoyed by the suicide but by the wait and the heat, and before we got to the station the escalator had broken down, so all this was going on. When the train finally came I whipped out my pen and paper and wrote the words, so all of the things that you hear are what happened that day.

'I'm A Woman In Love' is an empowering statement in a male-dominated world.

Well, women do fall in love, don't they? I don't remember how that song came about. It's not about me.

'Willow' is a great audience favourite: *I may not be your best / You know good ones don't come by the score . . . A fight with your best girl / Prettiest thing you ever saw.*

I was in West Palm Beach, Florida. I remember that very well. I got to the gig. It was a funny bar thing. The room itself was half the size of this table: a little stage, a pool table, a gaming machine, a coffee bar thing, a booze bar thing, just this horrible place. I walked in and thought, 'There's no way I'm playing here, I'm going home.' So I went back to the hotel and it started to storm and outside of my hotel room was a willow tree. In my room, which I loved, little frogs, lizards like newts crawling up my room, which was sweet. But I thought, I don't really want to be here, and wrote 'Willow'.

It's not that I love myself, I just don't want company. **'Me Myself I' has a great one-note opening melody over the electric guitar introduction.**

Yes, it was written on the electric guitar as you hear it. The F sharp's very strong, it suits it.

'Best Dress On'.

In the show the audience sings that and as the tour goes on they've been getting louder and louder, more involved, it's so good. I think we were in Turnhout, Belgium; they wouldn't stop singing it. We stopped and they wouldn't stop. Then we had to start it again and they carried on even after we stopped a second time. 'Best Dress On' is really what it says. The whole album is about positivity; it's easy for people to tell you that things are not possible and for you to talk yourself into being down. I think there's always a bright side, generally it will always work out. That's one of the ones I would have written the *best dress on* part, the music would have followed and the words after but I would have known what I wanted to say.

If you search for me baby, better bring some more love than you declared.

Is that 'All The Way From America'? That's a song about somebody who was in America who wanted to go out with me. He would phone . . . nice bloke, but obviously just going to be a friend.

'**Down To Zero**' **is a good example of how you play with the rhythm of words:** *Now you walk with your feet back on the ground.*

That was about somebody who . . . very striking person, who couldn't believe or imagine somebody would choose somebody over them because they were so good-looking. If I'm not mistaken the words and melody came together. I would have known what the subject was and it's on the guitar as well so it's got that rhythmic thing going.

'The Weakness In Me' has three major chords and a minor. Is it difficult to write with simplicity?

I'll tell you what I think is absolutely amazing and I can't get over it at all: there's not a lot of notes. Twenty-six? C, D, E, F, G, A, B, then all the different sharps and flats. You think of all the different melodies that come out of these notes: it's staggering. You will get some things that repeat, but there's not a lot. It's incredible. So when you're trying to write simply or complicated you haven't got much to choose from. If you have a progression of say E, D, C, do you know how many tunes you can get out of that?

Have you ever challenged yourself by just using set chords?

I've done that just to see what you get out of it. It's not easy to be simple and clear and get the point across. It's easier to be complicated and twisty. I read a review of *Into The Blues* that said 'The simpleness . . .' of whatever song as if it was an insult. That's not an insult. If it works it works.

Was 'Love Bug' a euphemism for AIDS?

No, it wasn't actually, that's a good . . . it's what it says. You know Cab Calloway, an old black jazz dancer, blues . . . he sang comic types, *Hi de hi de hi de hi, Hi de hi de hi de ho.* I wasn't trying to be him but it makes me think of him. It's trying to be comic.

Do you remember writing 'Woncha Come On Home'? Was it written in a tuning?

That was written on a marimba and then I put the guitar bits around it. It's very, very simple. I was just messing about with that and watching the darkness from my window and picturing this. All the songs are in normal tunings apart from the first album. 'City Girl' was in open D or E. I don't remember where I learnt to do that. I did a radio programme when I interviewed five guitar players and Mark Knopfler was saying he still used open tuning. I thought, 'I haven't done that since *Whatever's For Us*. I bet that would sound good on "My Baby's Gone",' so on this tour I've used open tuning, it's really good for slide.

Did your shyness in the Seventies make it difficult to articulate ideas?

Not in terms of music: music I was always super-confident. I always knew what I wanted, but in terms of having a conversation, walking into a room . . . One of the luckiest things that ever happened to me was having Gus Dudgeon as my first producer. At the time Elton John was the biggest thing on the planet. One per cent of everything that sold was Elton, and Gus was *the* producer. When Gus started with me he didn't say, 'I'm the producer, do what I say.' He realized straight away that I knew what I wanted. He made sure that what I wanted happened. If there was something I couldn't articulate with the musicians and I spoke to Gus, he would make sure that it happened. If I'd had the working environment of *Back To The Night* as my first record I'd probably have never made another record. Whichever way I wanted to work, he worked. I'm very strong and very definite. I come in with a complete song. There's always someone who knows, this is how this song should go. Well, I wrote it, I reckon I know how it should go.

CHAZ JANKEL

''Ere, mate, do I know you? Well, fuck off, then!' Backstage, Chaz Jankel was caught off guard by Ian Dury's legendary abruptness. Jankel, on the look-out for a 'lyricist', had recently left his telephone number in a Shepherd's Bush music shop whilst purchasing a Wurlitzer electric piano. In response Chaz was invited to see Ian and the Kilburns the following night at the Nashville Rooms by the group's guitar player, Ed Speight. Jankel was 'riveted by Dury's off-beat dynamism' and image, with Ian wearing a fez and dark cabaret from the circus-styled troupe around him. With insults resolved, conversation swiftly led to collaboration and within a year the recording of what was destined to become a British classic album.

Arseholes, bastards, fucking cunts and pricks: it may have been the year of the Queen's Silver Jubilee, but regal it was not. The Anglo-Saxon abuse of 'Plaistow Patricia' fired out from many a teenager's record player, yet this was not simply a case of anti-Establishment filth. Dury came from the tradition of Victorian vaudeville, while Jankel represented a sidestep of modernist groove. It was a marriage made on a deep level, with spirit and energy. 'In a way the music transcends our own physical being. It's tapping into something quite eternal. Ian was a great person to write with because he showed passion. He didn't hide his emotions. A lot of people are polite, almost afraid to say what they think. Ian wasn't.' Following on from a tradition rife with coarse humour, Dury demonstrated an engagingly rampant wit, from the *caress* of the *clitoris* in 'You're More Than Fair', the promiscuous 'all mouth and trousers' of 'Billericay Dickie' reflecting on his love affair with Nina: *I got right up between her rum and her Ribena,* to the blatant 'Fucking Ada'. But 'bringing out the blue bag' came at a price for the band's writers. Dury's verbal originality inevitably prompted daytime radio to ban his records from the airways, thereby destroying any hope of commercial success. Notably, Jankel insisted swearing was taken off the lyric sheet. It distinguished the pair's compositions.

Dury's observations were often made from the perspective of the fool. His stage costumes, grimaces and comic timing all contributed to the pathos of his tales. In 'Dance Of The Crackpots' he insisted: *being daft is a therapy craft which sharpens up your wits.* The theatrical tradition of the buffoon endears clowns to the audience, and Dury's treasure trove of comedy and song nestled comfortably in the breast of his frank prose. 'This Is What We Find' offered, *Morning, Reg, meat and two veg . . . Hello, Brian, wash and iron?* Direct speech sat effortlessly in his lyrics, frequently enlivened by associations, Polari and cockney slang. Van Gogh's *eyeball pleasers* proved him to have been *a pencil squeezer* in the knowing 'There Ain't Half Been Some Clever Bastards', whilst 'Sueperman's Big Sister' was a *superior skin and blister.* Everyday humdrum life with its drama and tensions was made to sound colourful in the storyteller's voice. Later, in 'This Is What We Find', *home improvement expert Harold Hill of Harold Hill,* on discovery of *other gentlemen's kippers in the grill,* retaliates by *sanding off his winkle with his Black & Decker drill.* Dury tussled with the positioning of his rhymed character sketch between attention-grabbing farce at the top of the song and a third-verse climactic ending. The dilemma was an insight into the writer's craft. He would often happily rewrite ideas. 'Wake Up And Make Love With Me' was purged of all its American words and phrasing. 'Plaistow Patricia' underwent drastic revision, as did 'Billericay Dickie', which originally read as a set of announcements uncovering the mystery identity of *the king of Billericay; the flower of the east.*

Dury was like a sculptor, moulding his lyrics whilst sitting at his desk with a life-size cut-out of his hero Gene Vincent looking on. He had an artist's knack of finding the right angle or perspective. When writing he favoured a Rotring pen with coloured ink and a Planters Peanuts retractable pencil. His work pattern was random, but he wrote endlessly. 'The more you write the more likely you are to get a few out,' he told Channel 4 viewers. Equipped with his writing tools—a dictionary, a thesaurus and a collection of slang phrase-books—he might spend weeks, months, even years on an idea before he deemed it complete. On many of his drafts the alphabet is handwritten from A to Z, a device for ticking off rhyming repetitions. His exuberance in shaping internal rhymes helped craft lines such as *whybrows wonder whether Clevor Trevor's clever.* Music hall star Max Wall recorded a version of 'England's Glory', revelling in the alliteration: *winkles, woodbines, Walnut Whips, Vera Lynn and Stafford Cripps.* The song also featured a litany of the fictitious and the famous, from *Winston Churchill* and *Jane Austen* to *Lady Chatterley* and *Muffin the Mule.* Notes and conversational phrases lay scattered around his work desk. His daughter Jemima Dury, editor of *Hallo Sausages,* a collection of her father's lyrics, observed, 'In the Seventies he used foolscap or A4, in the Eighties he sometimes used A3 and then in the Nineties he started using A2.' Amongst the ordered chaos were turns of phrase like 'Uneasy Sunny Day Hotsy Totsy',

'Take Your Elbow Out Of The Soup (You're Sitting On The Chicken)' and the delightful 'Sex & Drugs & Rock & Roll', now part of the nation's vernacular.

Once he began to collaborate, Dury would often sit behind a drum kit to find a song's rhythm. In Jankel, he had a natural arranger. Chaz's gift at the piano or on guitar was not only for finding chords and melody, but for initiating riffs and placing instruments as the band sound built around new songs. 'Wake Up And Make Love With Me', set in E flat minor, creates a building groove withholding chord changes. It was effective, but unfashionable in English pop at the time. The first song the pair wrote together, 'Sink My Boats', from a set of words initially outlined in January 1974, had revealed the limitation of Dury's melodic ability. Jankel was adept at giving songs movement and setting the vocals within a rich musical canvas. Such was Dury's lyrical aptitude that it demanded Jankel's unpretentious but subtly dynamic accompaniment to float the verbose wordplay. On occasions, however, writing duties were reversed. The majority of the melody to 'I'm Partial To Your Abracadabra' came from Jankel and pushed Dury's narrow vocal range to the limits. In 2001, Paul McCartney tackled the song and stretched the vocal highs with unforgettable notes. Conversely, 'Sex & Drugs & Rock & Roll' was a rare occasion when Dury hummed the desired rhythmic melody to his writing partner. After Jankel had added the bridge and underlying chords, Dury let slip: 'I chinned the riff from a Charlie Haden bass solo on the album *Change Of The Century* by the Ornette Coleman Quartet.' Traces of the melody can also be heard in the Kentucky folk song 'Old Joe Clark'. In time, Dury also confessed to Coleman's trumpet player Don Cherry who nonchalantly responded, 'It goes that way.' For the BBC, 'Sex & Drugs & Rock & Roll' was too risqué and they duly banned the record. Dury's ironic sentiment betrayed his love of the broader arts and ended up in *The Oxford Book of Quotations*. Next to it sat a verse from 'What A Waste', beginning, *I could be the catalyst that sparks the revolution . . .*

Ian Robins Dury was born on Tuesday 12 May 1942 at home in Harrow. His favoured concert introduction, *Good evening, I'm from Essex,* disguised his Middlesex roots. Ian's mum was educated, and his 'Old Man' *drove a bus for London Transport* during the war, *dropped his aitches on occasion* and *said gorblimey now and then.* A decade later, Charles Jeremy Jankel was born into a middle-class Jewish family on 16 April 1952. At the age of seven, Chaz's first instrument was a Selmer Spanish guitar, bought in response to his excitement at seeing a photograph of skiffle artist Lonnie Donegan: 'I thought, that looks really cool: something horizontal coming out at an angle from a vertical human being.' Piano and guitar lessons followed, but reacting against the formality of the lessons and their Dickensian discipline, Chaz soon learnt just to trust his ears. 'It was like black dots on a white paper. It somehow smacked of the past and there was nothing futuristic about it. With guitar, I tend to get more into funk and Latin blues. With piano, I'm more harmonically based.' With his first chord learned (G7), new inspiration struck when he heard 'Get Out Of My Life Woman', written by its performer Lee Dorsey and pianist Allen Toussaint. The progressive drum introduction opened Jankel's musical mind. 'One early composition was "It's Allright, It's Okay". I wrote it with Matthew Linhart when I was nineteen. He had a great voice in the Rod Stewart mould. I was just dilly-dallying.' Like Dury, who would be tutored by pop artist Peter Blake, Jankel went to art college: 'I had a gift as a draughtsman but I couldn't see what I could do with it other than illustrate books.'

Soon the two former art students had reached the stage of writing songs together, playing any instrument they could get their hands on. 'Ian and I were demoing our songs at Alvic Studios, in Wimbledon. Ian was playing drums and singing and I was doing everything else: bass, guitar and keyboards.' Following a tip-off, Charlie Charles and Norman Watt-Roy, 'a frustrated rhythm section hiring themselves out to do sessions', were introduced. The foursome immediately gelled and new arrangements were recorded. 'On playback, Charlie was looking at the lyrics from "Blockheads" and it gets to the line, *You must have seen parties of Blockheads . . . shoes like dead pigs' noses*; he looked down at his footwear and said, "'Ere, Ian, that's me," and Norman as quick as a flash said, "Yeah, yeah, we're The Blockheads." Ian said, "Cracked it!" and there were high fives all round.' The album was completed at Workhouse Studios under the auspices of Peter Jenner and Laurie Latham, and the group were augmented for their first tour by Johnny Turnbull, Mickey Gallagher and saxophonist Davey Payne. It was the birth of Ian Dury And The Blockheads.

Jankel's relationship with Dury would prove to be a rollercoaster. He describes his writing partner as a control freak: 'If Ian wasn't controlling a situation he'd need to. He'd make a scene.' His methodology for writing the first full Blockheads album *Do It Yourself* was to split up the writers in his newly bought Kent home, Toad Hall. Despite the unpopularity of the strategy, the prize was a co-writing credit to capitalize on the success of the debut release *New Boots And Panties!!* In an unusually generous gesture Dury granted percentage points to the road crew—normally a system of remuneration strictly reserved for the creative team. Unfortunately, the strains of writing and recording were exacerbated by drink—in the later 'Delusions Of Grandeur' Dury quipped, *I'm a dedicated follower of my own success*—and midway through the second album sessions Jankel quit The Blockheads. In time the rift would be healed, but not before Jankel had ventured into the solo arena. 'Glad To Know You', ironically with lyrics authored by Dury, became the biggest-selling American dance record of 1982. The triple A-side also included '3,000,000 Synths' and a third song co-written with Kenny Young, famed for The Drifters' hit 'Under The Boardwalk'. 'We'd been playing a gig at the Paradiso in Amsterdam and after went back to the Hotel American, a huge, beautiful art deco building on one of the sides of the main square. I happened to meet a very attractive young lady who came back with me to my room: it was too good to be true, a highly charged evening. In the midst of it all suddenly this melody just popped into my head.' The resulting song found its way to Michael Jackson's producer Quincy Jones, who recorded it for his *Dude* LP. 'Years later Ian said, "It's great that you wrote 'Ai No Corrida' because by dint of association I know Quincy Jones!"' Throughout his career, Jankel has been hugely prolific and successful in both the dance and film score worlds, but it was his partnership with Ian Dury that defined and challenged his writing capabilities. Ian was fuelled by love of rockabilly and particularly Gene Vincent. 'When I joined I brought my influence to it, which was much more soul-based, Afro-American, albeit as a middle-class lad from north London.'

Back in August 1949, whilst swimming with a friend in an open-air pool on a day trip to Southend, Dury inadvertently swallowed contaminated water. With vaccination still a decade away, he contracted polio. Despite six weeks wrapped in a body cast to stop his frame from becoming twisted, and hospitalization for eighteen months, it was to mean a lifetime wearing a caliper. The 7-year-old had paralysis of the left arm and leg. 'As a result he sat longer than most people of his age and through that he became very perceptive about life. That's what I think gave him his intellectual edge.' Writing about the disability in 'Dance Of The Screamers', Dury exorcized his childhood anguish over a frenetic Jankel funk-jazz backing. In 1981, 'Spasticus Autisticus' was written in response to the International Year of the Disabled, but Dury's direct speech was once again deemed too much for radio. In addition to his disability Ian suffered an unhappy childhood. At nine, with his family now living in Upminster, Essex, the boy was sent to board at Chailey Heritage Craft School, a facility and hospital for disabled children. It was an experience that was later revisited in the writer's songbook. He recounts his agonies in 'Hey, Hey, Take Me Away'. Living with a weak and crippled body, Dury's power and defence rested in words, and in later years he mused: *do you blame your life on life and say it all began before the nappy?* Dury celebrated his differences: 'If we wish to package our uniqueness we take a risk with our souls,' he told television viewers. Temporary respite came when he passed his eleven-plus, but merciless bullying continued when he boarded at the Royal Grammar School in High Wycombe. Though he left school with O Levels in Art, English Language and Literature, Dury's education had been an awakening to the horrors of childhood abuse. Jankel observes that Dury felt uncomfortable with his lyrics until he found empathy and oneness with his fictitious characters. 'Mash It Up Harry' is a suburban tale with all the paraphernalia of work, pensions and domestic chores, but the writer found a compassionate connection with the character through football and the song's ending chorus, *We're on our way to Wembley*. 'What A Waste' used the power of suggestion over two chords. At the top of the song's typed lyric sheet is the bracketed self-direction: (*spoken but felt with feeling*). The verses begin *I could be . . .* before suggestions of careers ranging from *a lawyer . . . a poet . . . the driver of an articulated lorry* and *the ticket man at Fulham Broadway station*. Dury had no interest in social status. His craft was to question and not accuse the working man. He simply planted the idea of bettering oneself. His contradictory and troubled background promoted a sense of camaraderie with the less privileged in his lyrical world: *where bald is beautiful, we don't give a damn / Love-a-duck, we're as common as muck*.

Dury's lyrics were one-man travelogues of London, depicting a capital pulsating with life and populated with lively characters. Occasionally he would diversify from his native English with amusing results in 'This Is What We Find', using a touch of Latin, *O vanitas vanitatum*, and in 'Hit Me With Your Rhythm Stick' with French and German: *Das ist gut, c'est fantastique*. Closer to home, names and references reflected his Essex road map, taking in *Burnham-on-Crouch, Shoeburyness* and the *Isle of Thanet*. Essex-born songwriter Billy Bragg may have been influenced by Dury when he recorded his own version of the American standard 'Route 66', retitled 'A13, Trunk Road To The Sea'.

The writers in Madness owe much to Dury's song-book of 'words that don't have to join up'. Suggs's 'Baggy Trousers' acknowledged the debt with a nod and wink to the shopping-list style. Dury's 'Reasons To Be Cheerful (Part Three)' showed its lyrical sharpness with an inventory of rhyming random associations: *Hammersmith Palais, the Bolshoi Ballet . . . Health service glasses, gigolos and brasses,* and despite Jankel having to discard a large number of lyrics from 'Sweet Gene Vincent' to keep the song at a commercial length, the introduction itemized the uniform of Dury's hero in witty rhythmical metre: *white face, black shirt, white socks, black shoes, black hair, white Strat, bled white, died black*. The words proved Jankel's maxim: 'Every lyric has a precise tempo.' In 1976, Dury catalogued all of his songs by date and month, with a system of symbols including a £ sign to denote potential, or a *T* for Tune. The first entry is dated Dec 70 and titled 'I made mary cry in a lonely bus shelter'. He signs off the lyric sheet Duncan Poundcake. Jemima Dury identifies the pseudonym as taken from a phrase in William Burroughs's *Naked Lunch*, 'dunking pound cake with his dirty fingers'.

I met Chaz Jankel on a Wednesday afternoon in Crouch End, north London. In the local corner shop, the dailies all showed the face of America's first black president, Barack Obama. It was a momentous day, and our awareness of how the world had changed charged our conversation as we walked up the road and climbed the stairs to the top of his house. The studio room was an emporium of instruments, books and music. Chaz was relaxed and beaming at the opportunity to talk over his collaboration with Ian. After the uneasy Eighties and abortive attempts in the early Nineties to renew their writing partnership, differences plunged into insignificance when Dury was diagnosed with stomach cancer. The condition focused their creativity and fostered a firm desire to make new Blockheads albums, with Jankel back at the helm. Ian wrote: *when circumstances tell of death we keep our counsel, save our breath.* The returning records, *Mr Love Pants* and *Ten More Turnips From The Tip*, were great successes. Humour became a key weapon of protest. 'Jack Shit George' attacked the inadequacies of the welfare state and the education system. Jankel, although not in all the composition writing teams, harnessed the ideas and realized the songs' potential once again with his arrangement abilities. But it was to be a lyric written three decades before that carried a prophetic resonance: *the hope that springs eternal, springs right up your behind.* On Monday 27 March 2000, Ian died at 9 a.m. It was the end of 'The Passing Show'. Jankel and Dury were both opposite and analogous; their songbook a consummate celebration of technicality and art.

You started writing daily with Ian at his self-named Catshit Mansions in Kennington overlooking the Oval cricket ground, taking a Wurlitzer and an acoustic guitar. Can you describe those writing sessions?

It was very casual. He had a little typewriter, the type Len Deighton would have written on. He had a very simple workbench. I'd turn up and he'd have a little pile of A4 sheets with lyrics typed up sitting on top of the desk. He would write lyrics—I wouldn't get involved in that side at all—and we'd fashion the music together.

The first song you wrote together, 'Something's Going To Happen In The Winter', has a very straight high-octave harmony melody with Ian's vocal coming and going, often missing entry points, on the lower harmony. Had you melodically written the top line for Ian to copy?

Yes, often that would be the case. I'd maybe put a guide vocal down. Ian didn't consider himself a singer, more a wordsmith. I have a much more melodic angle, and he liked that. He wanted the songs to be musical and for me to push him in that respect. Sometimes it just wasn't possible for him to sing the melodies that I threw his way—but he would give it his best shot.

Did he ever come to you with melodies?

With 'Sex & Drugs & Rock & Roll': I'd see these lyrics on the pile and say, 'Yeah, we all know about that.' I was quite dismissive about it. I'd come back the next time and there it would be, either second or first on the pile. Then one day he said to me, 'Chaz, how about this?' and hummed this riff. I said, 'Blimey, that's really good.' I then knocked out a bridge for it. A couple of months later we recorded it and it was a big, massive underground hit, number one in *NME* and the indie charts. A couple of months after that I'm round his flat and he puts an album on in the living room where I'm sitting writing with him and goes off into the kitchen to make some coffee. I'm working on a tune and suddenly I hear in the background (*hums 'Sex & Drugs & Rock & Roll' riff*). I went, 'Hang on, where have I heard that before? Oh my God, I don't believe it.' I looked up and saw Ian standing in the doorway with two cups of coffee with a smile from ear to ear and I said, 'You so-and-so.' It was very interesting what happened after that, because he felt a little bit ashamed, a little bit of guilt; he somehow got in touch with Charlie Haden. He got this postcard back from him which said, 'Do not worry, this is not our music.' Ian loved jazz, it was probably his favourite idiom of all. Charlie Mingus was a hero. He had a very jazz sensibility with his lyrics and the offbeat way he lived. I suggested, 'Why don't you get an upright bass player, drummer and piano player and make some records like that?' He said, 'I'm not good enough.' He always felt jazz was higher up and never saw himself as that. He was much happier writing songs like 'Common as Muck' or songs that reached everybody, which they did. Another example was 'Sweet Gene Vincent': he knew he wanted to start slow and then get faster.

Did 'Sweet Gene Vincent' originally have much lengthier verses that needed editing down?

Oh yeah, he was prolific. It was really tough. You know how a single should be three minutes something?—we'd just about have got up to the middle eight if I kept all his verses. With song structure you can't get away with more than three choruses and more than six or seven verses, unless you're Bob Dylan.

Would Ian include you in the editing-down process?

I would make suggestions. I would say, 'Look, Ian, what about if we wrap it up round about here or we just use this verse?' He was always so up for it. He never questioned it.

How would you define songwriting? For example, why did Norman Watt-Roy not get a credit for his definitive bass part on 'Hit Me With Your Rhythm Stick'?

It's a tough question. 'Hit Me With Your Rhythm Stick' is such a famous bass part, a phenomenal line. Norman is recognized as one of the greatest bass players living today. Now and again Norman has played something that has influenced the development of a song and I have credited him, for example 'Number One' from one of my solo dance records. He made a mistake when learning the chords and it sounded really good and I said, 'Hey, that's really great.' In those instances I do honour it. With 'Rhythm Stick' I'd been jamming with Ian drumming. He'd rented a house in Kent and I went down there. I had this riff that I was sort of playing around with. It was a nice jam and we were happy just grooving on it and that was it, I went home. The next day I was listening to the first song, 'Wake Up And Make Love', on *New Boots And Panties!!* and I

SINK MY BOATS   (uptempo with crashdive on "Crash my plane")

XÏVSZgOXXÏXSZÏSSÏXZZZZZZZZZZZZZZZZZEXXzzzzEXz ZZ SxxzXzzzzXzzzZx²x SxzZ zzzx zzZZ

I've got the feeling, but I ain't got the skill

And I don't like your suggestion;

Will you still love me when I'm over the hill

Is another stupid question

Don't deny...that I show...disrespect

Ask me why...and I'll change...the subject

Justify...but it has...no effect

My reply i.. is that I've...been shipwrecked

Sink my boats...Silly Jane *Once again*

Sink my boats...crash my plane.....................1°

Harmony

You try to be sly, but you're so overt

And you know the main objection

But the passionate pressure that you exert

In the opposite direction

I'm afraid...that it seems...evident

Though you stayed...now it's time...that you went

Can't persuade...me with your...blandishment
Don't

The old maid's...had a bad...accident

Sink my boats...Silly Jane *Once again*

Sink my boats...crash my plane.....................2°

Harmony

'Sink My Boats' lyrics, typed and annotated by Ian Dury

thought the way I came into the piano solo on the end of it was really interesting: that little pick-up on the accent at the beginning. I realized if I was to take that accent and put it on the front of every bar I'd been jamming with Ian I'd have (*hums 'Rhythm Stick' intro*). I went, 'Oh my God,' and called up Ian and said, 'You've got to hear this.' So I bowled down to Kent and practically the moment I got there he hands me this lyric, 'Hit Me With Your Rhythm Stick'. It was the most amazingly succinct piece of writing I've ever seen: no editing required; three verses and a chorus. He said, 'I'll see you in twenty minutes,' and went back into the house. I put some verses in with this amazing groove I had and we were so excited. The Blockheads came down the next day and whilst we were routining it I said to Norman—Mickey Gallagher saw me do this—'How about you do a kind of sixteenth-note bass line, something like (*hums riff*)?' He went, 'How about this?' and developed the line. If a musician plays a crucial part to the development of the song I should say that writer should get a credit. If I was to give Norman or another musician a slice of writing a song it would come out of my portion. Ian would never carve up his lyric. He wanted fifty per cent of the song. I feel wrong about Norman not getting a writing credit.

When you say you had the lyrics and constructed some chords, would the vocal melody line be within your piano riff?

The thing is with Ian he had a very limited vocal ability. I would keep it very simple, almost spoken word; if a melody grew out of that then fantastic. I was putting the changes in the music which gave the appearance that the vocal is moving when in fact it's very simple. In fact with 'Rhythm Stick' he talks the whole thing; he doesn't actually sing one note. After we'd recorded it in the studio I called my mum up and said, 'We've just recorded our first number one.' I knew it, and three months later it actually did. It had all the right elements to make it a hit.

Ian's limited vocal ability allowed you to develop the songs musically?

Yeah, he was sincere and because he was himself it allowed me to be myself. One feature about Ian which I loved about him: he always made me feel confident and he trusted in me musically. Some people I've worked with over the years since that, I haven't felt they trusted me entirely, musically, and as a result I don't give one hundred per cent. If somebody came in here and I'm just trying to service their musical needs and they're not really democratic, the relationship will die and fizzle out. Music has to be a shared joy; it can't just be one person propping up another. Maybe it was easier because Ian wasn't a musician, so to speak. He didn't worry about all the nuances of the music. He wanted it be exciting, challenging, powerful, which is exactly what I wanted to do anyway. Also I was very much aware that he was going to be centre stage when we were performing, so everything had to be about enshrining him. The music had to be the right environment for that lyric.

'Hit Me With Your Rhythm Stick' sold over a million copies and yet was written in twenty minutes: could you always creatively work that fast?

That was a very, very fast song. Sometimes it's an intuitive response. Don't forget I had a lot of stock for the soup, so to speak: it's a killer riff; that was already a major part of the song. Other times it took longer. Often Ian wouldn't have a lyric complete like that.

Was there a George Clinton steal in the song?

Ah, did you spot it? When The Blockheads toured Europe in about '81 we were travelling on a coach. There was a tape of Parliament on and I swear I heard in the background as a backing vocal *hit me with your rhythm stick* on this groove. I went, 'Oh my God,' and I turned round and Ian, who always sat at the back of the coach, just smiled at me again, and I went, 'Ahh,' and shook my head. What do they say: amateurs borrow and professionals steal? Listen, where did he get *sex and drugs and rock and roll* from? Maybe he had heard the slogan, maybe he put those elements together, I don't know. I'll never know really. He was very sharp; he was probably collecting reference points all over the place to fuel his lyrics. Ian used to see albums and singles as being stylistically different. An album is a group of songs that all work together. A single can be a bit flashier, more in your face. What songs would go under that banner? 'Sex & Drugs & Rock & Roll', 'Hit Me With Your Rhythm Stick', 'Reasons To Be Cheerful'. They were conceived as singles: very tight in their structure.

Were you consciously trying to write singles?

Sometimes . . . it's a good question. With *New Boots and Panties!!* all the songs were there to contribute to an album. 'Hit Me With Your Rhythm Stick' was a one-off single; me and Ian jamming and then coming up with this great, great song. We were both doing what we liked doing; just getting into a groove. Ian loved playing drums and loved Afro-American music big time like I did and that's where we kind of met in a way. In some respects I do have a commercial streak in me, which I brought to the table when I was writing with Ian.

On 'Reasons To Be Cheerful' the Latin-American influence is very obvious. Can you remember writing that song?

Yeah, we were doing a couple of gigs in Italy. At one of the venues—the gear had been set up beforehand by the roadies—the lighting rigger, Charlie (*Box-all*) had put one hand on the DJ equipment and one hand on these two metal bars and he'd got this DC electrical shock—not the kind that throws you off; it's the one that makes you grab—and he was getting fried alive. Another

Won't that ~~to~~ could be   (Rock 'n' roll don't mind)
            be   a waste.
ABCDEFGHIJ KLMN OPQRSTUVWXYZ   ~~collars~~
 quarry sorry lorry   dollars swallows
                          barrister   scholars
You could be a ~~lawyer~~ defending ~~thieves~~ and bruisers
I ~~could be a big m.p.~~ with stratagems and poses
You could be a doctor ~~minding~~ helping ~~all the~~ drug abusers
I could be a businessman ~~living~~ off the losers

But I sooner be a person doing rock'n' roll
Doowop rockabilly reggae ~~and~~ soul [write - five figures
~~R and B and~~
I could be glad to be so inclined
~~I could be here~~ rock'n'roll don't mind.

                                       isolation
I could be a ~~pastrel~~ and live in ~~a hole~~
         hermit
I could be a porter at Fulham Broadway Station
You could be a ~~writer~~ with a growing reputation
You could be a parson ~~waiting for~~ salvation
~~I could be a lorry~~   with an interest in

I could be out driving an articulated lorry
You could be a poet and I wouldn't need to worry (more)
You could be a hunter with a most elusive quarry
I could be a spokesman who keeps on saying sorry

You could be a teacher encouraging the scholars
I could be a sergeant in a ~~garrison full~~ squadron full wallahs
You could be a ~~imports bringing in the~~ dollars
I could be   broker ~~filling up~~ manipulating

'What A Waste' lyrics, handwritten by Ian Dury

roadie fortunately saw what was going on and threw himself at Charlie and somehow broke the charge and basically saved his life. Charlie was a big strong lad and was able to take it. We turned up, heard about this and said, 'There's no way we're playing this gig.' The roadies started dismantling all the gear again and put it in the truck. When we went to leave all the local mafia had parked across the exit of the car park where our coach was. A couple of lads got off and moved these cars out of the way. We then, therefore, had a couple of days off in Rome without any gigs. We were in this very nice hotel. Round about ten o'clock one night I was in my room and I'd had a couple of drinks. I remember sitting on a chair not the right way round, sort of straddling, and I started playing this rhythm (taps on table), a tapper's delight sort of thing, and I went, 'Blimey, that's nice,' so I told Ian, 'Hey, check this out.' He was as mad as I was in that respect. He'd love something like that. It's not everyone you can go to at eleven o'clock at night and expect a positive response. So he went, 'Yeah, that's great . . . goodnight.' Next day he calls and says, 'Hey, Chaz, come down to my room, bring your guitar with you.' He had this complete lyric, 'Reasons To Be Cheerful'. He started reciting it and I just started playing the guitar riff that I play on the song. I inserted that rhythm that you hear at the beginning of the song and then he literally said, 'I think we need a pretty bit in the middle. I'd like to give Davey (*Payne*) a squirt for it.' So we wrote a pretty bit in the middle. Needless to say, because Ian wouldn't give up his fifty per cent as writer, I shared my portion with Davey so I got twenty-five per cent of the song even though I kick-started the whole thing.

The rhythm of Ian's delivery was like a precursor to rap.

A lot of people have said that. He wrote in rhyming couplets nearly always. They were well-constructed sentences or phrases that Ian would just do on the beat, and because he was a master of lyric writing they had their own natural rhythm, as you've just pointed out, inherent in the words and in his delivery.

Did that natural rhythm suggest melody and music?

I wouldn't say music as such; it had its own melody because it was quite . . . blunt in some respects. It allowed me to be quite colourful around it.

Did your music have a visual narrative before lyrics were added?

One song comes to mind: 'Inbetweenies'. I'd written the whole shape, every-thing: the arrangement, the structure of the song, and the melody was in the bass line. I took it to him and asked him would he like to write a lyric to it. Ian had a bit of a problem with it because, technically speaking, he had to start on the second beat of the bar and I could tell that rankled with him. It was like I was placing the furniture in the room: he was the furniture. He wasn't used to that; he wanted to be on the beat, possibly thinking he was playing a secondary role to the music. Once he got over that it was a huge step for us because all the other songs up to that point he'd be on beat one.

Had you written the bass line for 'Inbetweenies' with the intention of it being the vocal melody, or did Ian just pick up on it?

Mmm . . . interesting point. I suppose it was just too strong to avoid. It was the central feature. Maybe I *la-la*'d the melody. Often I would do that for him and he would listen to that as he was writing.

As on the chorus of 'I Could Lie' from *Ten More Turnips From The Tip*?

It was never intended to be a *la-la*. He was meant to write something over that. He said, 'That's great, just leave it like that.' That was one of the last songs we wrote together.

Did your process of songwriting collaboration change over time?

Yeah, it did change; every time it was different. Because I've done a lot of gigs in my time, sometimes when I'm writing I picture myself on stage playing and I use that as a kick-start for writing. With 'Dance Little Rude Boy' I imagined myself playing guitar, a monitor in front of my legs, and I'm rocking with a very excited crowd and that's where the whole groove and notion of the piece was born. It was a mental attitude that then determined the rhythm, the earthiness of it. 'Dance Little Rude Boy' had dance written all over it, and Ian picked up on that. On the Blockheads album *Staring Down The Barrel* there's a track called 'George The Human Pigeon': when I first came up with the riff I just imagined Ian stamping his foot, just grooving. Even though Ian wasn't physically around any more, the memory of his spirit, the kind of groove he liked, totally infused . . . that was the kick-start for that piece. His character is within that. Ian's idea of a perfect groove would be about 106 bpm and probably be the sound of a Zulu tribe about to attack whitey as they came over. You couldn't see them, but you could hear this menacing thump. If Ian sat down on a kit that would be his favourite tempo—playing like he was Al Jackson or someone: very solid, simple groove, menacing slightly because really rhythm for Ian was a way for him surging forward through life. It gave him the drive: it was part anger, part resilient; very, very physical. Because Ian was disabled he needed that . . . bit more fuel than the average person because it was that much harder for him to physically walk, to get from A to B, so he really had to make an effort. Rhythms like that were a mirror of the way he tackled life.

How did punk and the scene of 1976/77 influence the way you were writing?

It was coincidental. Ian has this label as the Godfather of Punk and he was the first person, as far as I know, to have a razorblade dangling from his ear. It was way beyond punk. A lot of lyrics in punk are anarchic. Ian's lyrics aren't anarchic; they're humanistic. Every single song that Ian has ever written has humanity in it. He might poke fun at someone but he does it in almost a compassionate way. I don't think punk had that depth. It was more a battle cry and musically it was very unsophisticated, whereas our music had a lot more breadth to it. It meant we could go anywhere, we could do anything. The one thing that I tried to do, if Ian presented me with a lyric, was to write the appropriate musicscape for it, to give it the right environment.

A feature of your songs with Ian is the absence of swearing?

At the time I realized if there was swearing on it we wouldn't get on the radio. It might sound a bit middle-of-the-road, but hey, it's true; you'd do all that work just for it not to be played. The defining moment for a lot of people on *New Boots and Panties!!* was that *arseholes, bastards, fucking cunts and pricks.*

It gets a reaction from anybody.

It does, and it definitely got a reaction from my dad when he heard it; he was more into Frank Sinatra.

Did you refuse those lyrics?

I don't know if I would have actually refused it. Funnily enough Mickey Gallagher has a joke with me now and he once asked Ian, 'How come Chaz never gets the songs with the swearing?' And he said, 'Because he doesn't want them.' It was as simple as that. I wouldn't say I wouldn't write a song that has swearing in it, but a lot of the time you can find equally effective ways of using lyrics. It bothers me sometimes if somebody just swears for the sake of it. Not Ian, but some performers get carried away. I find it inarticulate if they keep on swearing.

Can we talk about Paul McCartney recording 'I'm Partial To Your Abracadabra' for the tribute album *Brand New Boots And Panties*?

It was a fantastic version. I'd like to think he was practising on the way over because he was certainly warmed up when he got to the studio. He sang it up an octave from Ian. Funnily enough 'Abracadabra' was a song we rarely sang live with Ian. He was nervous about his vocal on that. If you've noticed, the more melodic songs Ian just about gets away with it. It's his lyrics and his character that sell it, not his melodic ability, necessarily, but that was the charm of Ian. The other thing about McCartney was he played acoustic and that gave him a musical link with the track, which was great.

Can you explain how your writing partnership was able to write million-selling records and then at the next fail to impact?

(*Long pause*) I think possibly Ian was burnt out. The pressures of being on stage every night, and that wind-up, and the life of sex and drugs and rock 'n' roll did take its toll with Ian. He was addicted to sleeping pills because he was so wound up after a gig, and after we'd finished touring he'd still be on them. Then we did the second album, *Do It Yourself*, and there wasn't enough time for Ian to really think about the lyrics on that. He'd had his whole life to write *New Boots and Panties!!* and then suddenly there was this pressure to write a second album. He was never really happy with it. He felt we put it out too quickly. I think he felt we lost a lot of our core audience because it was so different, more polished, a very hard record to make.

Had the writing process changed?

Yes, we didn't demo it all up front. Most of the time the lyric would shape the song. The more we worked together the more we would just click, do it in different angles. With 'Dance Little Rude Boy' I had all the music written and Ian said, 'Chaz, it's so easy when you do that.' He probably wouldn't have felt like that when we first started writing twenty years beforehand. There's a song I want to talk about to do with structure and how things change: 'Books And Water' from *Ten More Turnips From The Tip*. Ian used to go for a walk every day about '97/'98. I remember one time I was standing with him somewhere outside and he just said, 'Books and water.' Our relationship was such I didn't have to go, 'What?' or 'Why?' I just went, 'Mmm,' and nodded. About a year later I had this idea I wanted to write this piece of music that was drums- and bass-based, jazzy, also to give the Blockheads solos within the structure of the song. Usually you get a play-out and people jam on the end, rarely do you get them actually within the structure of the song, so I thought that would be a great idea. I gave the piece the working title 'Books And Water', which was an interesting image. I went to Ian's place and he looks at my cassette and says, 'Oh blimey, "Books And Water",' and puts it on. He's listening to it and says, 'Oh, no, no, I imagined something much more vulgar than that.' So I felt a bit despondent. He had three verses written out and I said, 'Can I see it? Hang on a moment, Ian, you've written three sixteen-bar verses. I've got three verses in this piece: if you start here, start here and start here it's going to work absolutely perfectly.' He did it and we went, 'Oh my God.' It was the only time we agreed there is a God! It was because of years of me working with him. The fact actually that he couldn't sing in a traditional sense made my job easier. I could rely on him giving a spoken word and that was sufficient. If he put just the slightest melodic change in you're going to hear it. When in doubt, if I saw him really struggling with a melody, I said, 'Just speak it,' and he'd be happy with that, but he'd always try and give it a shot, melodically, before resorting to the spoken word.

Where does talent come from? Is it something you work for or is it inherent?

I think it's passion. It's the divine spirit. It's energy, when you're feeling playful or passionate about something. This thing called talent is you accessing those natural gifts. Is there alchemy involved in it? I'm not sure. It's basically everybody has a gift that's natural to them. That's what makes them idiosyncratic. Maybe because I was lazy reading music I developed my own style. That's what I brought to the table when I met Ian. Ian brought his unique perception and humour and I brought a distillation of my own influences, which was me. Talent is not just the notes you think up, it's how you access information and put things together and how you construct something. The two most enjoyable aspects in life for me is when a lyric and a bit of music suddenly fuse, that is utopia and when you're playing live that's as good as it gets. That moment when you fuse with the audience and you think, 'How come there's all these wars? Wars shouldn't be happening'. You've got this symbiotic relationship going with the audience: they're giving you enthusiasm and you're giving the best you can do musically. That and baba ghanoush, a Lebanese aubergine dish: the three peaks of perfection for me (*laughs*).

Where does melody come from?

I think melody is always there; our antennae are picking it up. For example, 'Ai No Corrida': why did that piece of melody pop into my head? It's probably based on some piece of music I possibly heard, I don't know, and it's one of the biggest-selling songs in my catalogue. I'm just grateful it turned up when it did. There's a lot of music that's been written, there's a lot of music that's going to be written. It's something to do with the rise and fall of our natural emotion. When we speak, when you listen to me talking, there's a melody, there's natural peaks and cadences in a sentence. With a melody you're amplifying that. I think that's why songwriting works so well. That's what I always tried to do with Ian: to make it as natural as possible so there weren't huge leaps in the lyrics unnecessarily, so it stays conversational.

What do you do when you have dry periods?

Worry! It's funny, in between every song I've ever written I suppose that's a dry patch. Sometimes I'll actually do a bit of study. I have records I must listen to: what's Bill Evans the pianist doing on that particular song? Or I might learn some obscure Indian scales. In the past, in my twenties and thirties with Ian, I tended to work on one song and want to get that finished and then move on, all my energy would go into one piece. Now I tend to have three or four on the go, so if I get tired of one I might just put up another song.

Did Ian ever offer you lyrics that you couldn't compose to?

A couple of times: I've still got some lyrics somewhere that I never finished the music for, and a musical at one point—I didn't engage with it. It was based upon conversations with his minder Fred Rowe and his experiences in prison.

Did your friendship with Ian communicate through song? 'Don't Ask Me' seems like him talking to you in a way you wouldn't guy to guy.

You're absolutely right and very perceptive. He wrote that about me; I shouldn't admit it. *Here I stand with a doughnut for a brain.* I used to say things very quickly without thinking; it sometimes would sound like I was really stupid. He thought every now and again I was a doughnut but he ended up singing it himself. If he asked me a question, I'd say, 'Well, don't ask me,' which is a bit of a cop-out, but that's where it started. 'It Ain't Cool' I swear he wrote about me as well. He didn't like the way I challenged him. He was like a big protective wing to little birds who came with their broken wings. That's how I pictured him. They'd come to him for counsel and warmth and encouragement, and I did that. I suppose in a way I was his muse. Ninety-eight per cent of the songs were about other people, characters that he was observing or imagining. Every now and again I'd get on his nerves and I'd find myself featured in a lyric.

'Bed Of Roses' was perhaps another one: *You robbed me of my natural sense of humour and then you nailed my bollocks to the door***?**

Yes, you're absolutely right. *I nail my cojones to the door*—I gave him that expression. It's what Latinos call your balls. I was living, working in LA for six years and started hanging out with this Latino crowd. They had all this slang going down and I remember using that expression and telling Ian when I came back. He loved it. Next thing I'd pissed him off and now it's featured in a song about me. Damn, the guy's a writer, he's going to write about what's on his mind.

One line particularly struck me: *sliding off the scale of least remembrance / Is the way you chose to tell me where to go*—**a tough line to take?**

Repeat that one to me . . . mmm . . . he's obviously feeling abandoned, rejected. I would do that from time to time. He once said to me, 'I will bill this equally as Ian Dury / Chaz Jankel on every banner, on every album, but I want one hundred per cent commitment from you.' I said, 'I can't do that.' You know what it's like if you are rejected or somebody really cares for you and you're not giving them all your time, it can be painful.

There's a tremendous absence of British female songwriters. Do you have any thoughts on why?

I think that's for two reasons. It's been a male-dominated industry and traditionally, women would have to look after the children. It's a natural quality to want to nurture and encourage and that's why they would probably put raising a child way above having a career. Men are more hunter-gatherers by nature. I love good women singers. There have been some great female singer/songwriters. Blokes tend to work with bands. I've written with a lot more girls and woman in my life, like P. P. Arnold. At the moment I'm working with China Soul, David Soul's daughter, and Katie Vogel.

Can we finish with a favourite lyric of Ian's?

The band absolutely loves the line *Cruising down carnality canal in my canoe can I canoodle?* from 'Honeysuckle Highway'. It's brilliant, isn't it? How does he think up this stuff? God knows. Ian liked Noel Coward—he had a great sense of humour. There is a lot of wit in his lyrics. *So place your hard-earned peanuts in my tin / And thank the Creator you're not in the state I'm in . . . As you go by me give me lucky looks / You can read my body but you'll never read my books* ('Spasticus Autisticus'). I wouldn't say it's the most brilliant of all his lyrics but that's the first that came to mind. It's so amazing to think that song was banned in the Year of the Disabled. You talked about talent earlier; I think everybody has got their own gift in one way or another and that's my gift. Ian recognized that. That's why it worked so well. I saw genius in him. As I said earlier, I was looking for a lyricist and boy did I get one! It was like a garden full of surprises.

JOHN LYDON

I want you to know that I hate *you baby / I want you to know I* don't *care*. The song belonged to the Small Faces, with the words and melody of Ian Samwell and Brian Potter. But now the opening stanza had two significant changes: *hate* had replaced *love* and *don't* preceded *care*. The Sex Pistols' version of 'Whatcha Gonna Do About It' summed up the singer's attitude to playing covers: 'Instead of being a victim in songs, you turn yourself into the protagonist.' John Lydon revels in confrontation. His songwriting is an assault on the emotions; he challenges the listener with pointed bluntness. It is a voice that demands a reaction: I think this, where do you stand?

The first of four boys, John Joseph Lydon was born on 31 January 1956. By his twentieth birthday he was to have written two sets of lyrics that impacted on British songwriting irrevocably. *There is no future in England's dreaming.* 'God Save The Queen' could only have come from a writer who cared passionately about his country. Yet a song questioning the role of the monarchy, written from a working-class council flat kitchen table in Finsbury Park, ran against the grain of Seventies musical mysticism. Delivered with supreme venom and articulacy two weeks prior to the Queen's Silver Jubilee in 1977, it earned the Sex Pistols outraged reactions from the public, a ban on national radio, and the label 'cultural degenerates'. Lead singer Johnny Rotten, a nickname given to Lydon by his band mate Steve Jones on account of his 'green' teeth, had already ruffled establishment feathers with 'Anarchy In The UK', the debut single of the Sex Pistols. The fury of the music cut to the quick: *I am an Antichrist / I am an anarchist*. Together, the two singles set out in unequivocal terms Lydon's non-negotiable agenda: Stand up. Be seen. Be counted. His words have continued to speak to those in society who feel marginalized.

Resentment of class plays an important role in British songwriting. Lydon's Irish family history and poor upbringing clearly inform his writing, but his severest condemnation is reserved for injustice and apathy. He has always maintained his right to use explicit language in his lyrics. Virgin Records, on the release of *Never Mind The Bollocks, Here's The Sex Pistols* in November 1977, defended charges of obscenity in the law courts under the Indecent Advertising Act of 1889 and won when the Anglo-Saxon word *bollocks* was deemed not to be offensive.

The Sex Pistols would release only one album and four singles. They played their first gig at St Martin's College of Art in November 1975 and their last in January 1978 at the Winterland Ballroom, San Francisco. As Steve Jones struck the last chord Lydon jibed, 'Ever get the feeling you've been cheated?' Before Virgin signed the band the Pistols cashed in sizeable advances both from EMI and A&M records. But in each case, behaviour perceived to be unacceptable and the growing notoriety of the group prematurely ended the contract. On 1 December 1976 the Sex Pistols replaced Queen on Thames TV's *Today* programme hosted by Bill Grundy. For the ITV network it was a disaster as members of the band and their entourage repeatedly swore on live television and goaded the bemused presenter. The following morning the *Daily Mirror* headline read, 'The Filth and The Fury'. During 1977 the group struggled to record their debut album: Lydon was attacked; bass player Glen Matlock was sacked; Sid Vicious was hired (he fatally overdosed on 2 February 1979); 'God Save The Queen' was blanked out from the listings in the national charts and to this day it is still debated whether it was number one in the week of the Jubilee. In the studio, Roxy Music producer Chris Thomas attempted to capture the essence of Lydon's voice: 'He basically yelled all the way through it. I couldn't understand a word he was singing. I went out there and he said, "You're the one with the track record: you sort it out." I got his trust completely in the end.' What resulted was an album that redefined popular music.

In 1974 nearly three-quarters of school leavers were unemployed. Inflation was soaring, and it was a Great Britain of empty purses and despondency. Lydon joined the newly formed Sex Pistols with the motivation of spite. He'd been spotted on London's King's Road by Bernie Rhodes wearing an 'I hate Pink Floyd' T-shirt. As he mimed to Alice Cooper's 'I'm Eighteen', Jones, Matlock and Paul Cook could not help but be impressed by the flashes of hunchbacked stage charisma displayed before them. A writing partnership of sorts spluttered into action. Matlock and Jones offered chords: rises and falls in simple steps. The cynically titled 'Problem' matched the song's guitar progression, A B C D. The band's manager, Malcolm McLaren, proposed the word *submission* in a list of song titles. Matlock and Lydon traded lines about a submarine mission, deliberately misunderstanding the intended sadomasochistic and bondage innuendo. Later McLaren would be chastised in Lydon's 'Albatross': *you are unbearable / I've seen you up very close*. Songwriting credits cut across all four members of the Pistols. There were Buddy Holly changes, and rudimentary invention from Small Faces and Abba chord shapes: Matlock attributes his 'Pretty Vacant' riff to Benny Andersson, Björn Ulvaeus and Stig Anderson's 'SOS' augmented with a fifth note. The chorus was then assembled taking ideas from Steve Marriott and Ronnie Lane's 'Wham Bam Thank You Man'. It was surprisingly effective. Co-writing credits suited Lydon's philosophy of a group endeavour, both with the Sex Pistols and his ongoing project Public Image Ltd (PiL). Not before 1997 with his album *Psychopath* would the name John Lydon appear as sole writer.

Lydon is an agent provocateur; a voice running contrary to the status quo. His contribution to songwriting rests upon four major elements: lyrics, use of the voice, musical platform and performance. His singing style has no precedent. He uses a minimum of musical notes, compensating with dramatic shifts in pitch. Musicality is found in the natural cadences and tones of his speech. The nearest comparison is perhaps John Lennon's use of Arthur Janov's Primal Scream therapy on his debut solo album, when the former Beatle exposed the anguish of his childhood in musicals howls for his late mother. Lydon, too, howls. 'Death Disco' was written in 1979 for his cancer-ridden mother. On her deathbed she asked her son to compose a song for her. Lydon was distraught because the Church wouldn't administer last rites without a financial contribution. *Silence in your eyes*, he wails. *Watch her slowly die / Saw it in her eyes / Choking on a bed*. It is the desperate cry of a grieving child. By the song's end the writer is silenced: *words cannot express*.

It was inevitable that the music of John Lydon's imagination would match his lyrical style. A natural progression came in the form of Public Image Ltd. Lydon borrowed the title from a Muriel Spark novel, with the added 'Limited' suggesting the group had a temporary future. The 1978 eponymous debut single was recorded by a four-piece: bassist Jah Wobble, ex-Clash guitarist Keith Levene and drummer Jim Walker. Lydon hollered, *I will not be treated as public property*. Playfulness was present, but now Lydon was able to toy with his voice as an instrument outside the music. On occasions when the speech and music rhythmically aligned, a song's impact could be skilfully heightened. It can be heard on the coda of 'Chant': *Mob / War / Kill / Hate*. Elsewhere Lydon elongated words, revelled in repetition and delivered deliberate pauses and silences, stylistically rolled R's and mannered stresses.

In concert, Public Image Ltd are hypnotic. Cyclical grooves provide a platform for oblique guitar lines and tangent effects. Lydon's words allow the listener's imagination to paint its own pictures. Live performance is the fuel of Lydon's creativity. His face and body contort, hunchbacked, staring. The pose comes from spinal meningitis. As a boy, Lydon was hospitalized and missed a year of school. He suffered memory loss and the indignity of not recognizing his parents. On stage, his childhood experiences inform both his music and his performance. Lydon is a law unto himself.

In their early studio encounters PiL would record ad hoc. Limited time forced takes in one and two attempts. The results were bold and dynamic. Their second release, *Metal Box*, was delivered in a metal 16mm film canister. It contained three discs, which played at 45 rpm. *Rolling Stone* magazine regards the album as one of the 500 greatest ever released. Within the music the band's sonic waves predated and inspired the sounds of the Nineties: Massive Attack, The Prodigy, Brendan Lynch's experimentations with Paul Weller, Radiohead, Red Hot Chili Peppers covering 'Poptones'. By contrast, the Sex Pistols had chosen a blitzkrieg pop: heavy and rampaging, the pace of the music measured and confident. Its controlled rage was different from the majority of the emerging punk bands' fast and furious delivery. For many fans and commentators it was a musical ground zero, but for the writers, for John Lydon, there was history: the old informing the new. Lydon's musical influences are as extensive and unpredictable as his music: Kenny Rogers, T. Rex, The Stooges, Can, Hawkwind, Captain Beefheart, dub and reggae. Emotional communication is the linking force. When Miles Davis blew a Bitches Brew of experimental jazz from his trumpet, Lydon listened hard. He absorbed the words of Ted Hughes, Dickens and Shakespeare and acknowledged their influence: '. . . very descriptive, very beautiful and very savage'. Always an avid reader, he adapted the title 'And No Birds Do Sing' from John Keats's poem 'La Belle Dame Sans Merci'.

In the mid-Eighties PiL used the structures of pop music to field their message. In the album *Album*, electronic instrumentation was cleverly manipulated to attract the modern ear. The content was uncompromising, as displays of wealth and conspicuous consumption came under attack from Lydon's social conscience. 'Rise' addressed apartheid in South Africa, with the singer roaring *anger is an energy*, though acknowledging *I could be wrong / I could be right*.

I chatted with John against the rural backdrop of Steve Winwood's Gloucestershire recording studio, where Public Image Ltd were making their first album *This Is PiL* after a hiatus of nearly twenty years. Dressed for the summer sun in long shorts, T-shirt and trainers, John relaxed whilst drinking English tea, his spiked blond hair an instant clue to his occupation and nonconformity. The discussion strayed occasionally during the afternoon, but always provided telling insights: 'There is a bit of a demon in me. I've never learnt to have any brakes and I go way too far. It's like stepping into madness temporarily. This isn't just writing. This is actually how I live my life. That's how I am. If there are seven deadly sins, then there are seven emotions to go with them.' John is a natural dramatist, opposing forces, creating tension, and his words are his weapons. His qualities are great individuality, Englishness, passion and loyalty. He regards imitation as lazy and disrespectful, and he is driven to shake up inertia. During the conversation we were joined by John's manager and friend since their north London schooldays, Rambo. John began the exchange:

When I got kicked out of school I felt cheated so I wanted to get my A Levels. I worked on building sites and at play centres to raise the money. I don't know if they've done me any good but I enjoyed the studying: World War Two history, and geography. Technical drawing was all right until it became too mathematical. That side of my brain doesn't function too well since meningitis. That's probably why I'm not instrument-attached; that side's damaged forever. As soon as there's any counting or four beats to the bar . . . fuck off, I'm in the bar. I call songwriting the lyrics themselves. I don't write music. I don't write musical notes but I can make a tune up. Usually when I put words together I have a melody in mind, but it's not always the melody that ends up on vinyl because you're sharing with other people and sometimes you alter your perception. As soon as a microphone is put in front of you it can change and shift and reshape itself. I hope my songs are accurate. I want them to be little details, slices of my life; to be genuine and truly felt; to represent all the emotions that I like every other human being go through: the things that make us vulnerable and strong. And that means really, really tearing yourself apart—a fucking lot of time.

And you're always prepared to do that?

Oh yeah, 'cause it's ultimately completely rewarding. I learnt at a very early age as a songwriter that the closer you get to your own problems and being able to express them on record, it's so cleansing. You find that you've solved the very problem that was at the root core of something disturbing inside you—really brilliant. In a weird way it's related to scream therapy. It's all just dissipated in different directions. When psychologists get hold of a thing they tend to murder it.

Do you remember the first set of lyrics you wrote?

Yes, I do. It was a song called 'Mandy'. It was about a girl I knew. It was really silly. There was blood on the carpet, blood on the stairs. *Mandy I did it for you*. It's not about murder at all. We had a party round her house. Sid (*Vicious*) invited me. I got so sick on the punch; it was a mixture of Martini, Cinzano Bianco and red wine. I vomited everywhere, particularly the stairs, and bingo! I've lost the original song. We never even rehearsed it. The Pistols died of laughter.

Before you write words down will ideas be circulating in your mind?

Almost constantly, every waking minute of the day, and sometimes actually when I'm deep, darkest REM sleeping. My brain won't stop working and rather than let it eat itself alive . . . I found writing helped me when I was younger. And then songwriting definitely helped me in the Sex Pistols. That was fantastic for me.

Helped you in what way?

I'd never tried singing. I'd avoided singing because I was frightened of being pushed into the school choir, which meant the priests had access to you.

Un-singing went on in my mind. Then, joining the Pistols, not only have I got to find my voice really bloody quickly—because I promised them the moon; I'd waxed lyrical about what great singing I could come up with—but I had to write songs too. I'd never thought of doing that before and I dived in. Lucky for me I learnt to swim very quickly. It's always running in the head. 'God Save The Queen' was running around in my mind for months, long before joining the Sex Pistols; the idea of being angry, of the indifference of the Queen to the population and the aloofness and indifference to us as people. I had to work on building sites to get the money to go to college because I wanted to further my education and yet I was taxed to fuck. Why am I paying for that silly cow who couldn't give a shit about me? Along come the Pistols and just one morning over baked beans I wrote it down in one go on Mum and Dad's kitchen table. A couple of lines were altered later because they just seemed a bit silly and inappropriate. I had lines in there about Persil and Omo washing-up liquid. I can't understand now what the connection was. I remember removing them when we did a rough demo. It's the way I write: I'll spend weeks, months, years, sometimes decades, juxtapositioning a thing in my head and usually when it comes down to writing, it comes down in one fell swoop. It's really good. Something happens up there that I'm not quite aware of and I don't want to discuss too much because if I ever find out what the process is that knowledge might ruin it. It's like I said: songs solve problems. Well, I don't want to solve the problem of songwriting. They're not so much songs as slices of life. They're stories. They're like painting. I'm trying to get as much detail and texture to fill in all the pieces of the jigsaw puzzle so that someone listening and hearing and reviewing the words in their skull will come to accurate conclusions and see what I'm seeing.

What is the process of editing or condensing the outpouring of ideas?

Too many words. It can be a problem. Other subject matters require an intense verbal assault. Some of the songs I've written have so many words it's almost unbearable. 'No Feelings', for instance: I think it's sixteen to eighteen lines where I don't take a breath. Now, live, that's tempting fate. But I managed to do it. I found the knack. And even when we were recording it I thought, 'I'll never be able to sing this live.' I love pushing those boundaries. You can't cut up a verse like that because it would become out of context. It's the monologue that's necessary to paint the proper picture of someone in a state of babbling confusion. The song is from the idea of someone being completely selfish, which I'm not. I like to imagine being in that frame of mind. I'm insulting myself really. That happens a lot.

Do you ever start with a title?

No, never, ever, never. I have real problems with titles. When it came to *Album* album (*laughs*) . . . that's a solution! I'll just give everything one name, but even that tore me up.

So you don't necessarily have a particular theme in mind before you write? It's a collation of thoughts?

A juxtaposition of events that properly honed in can tell me something about myself and about the world I'm in, and hopefully that message can be properly translated to a listener. But an awful lot of the time people take it the wrong way, even my own band members. Glen Matlock quit the Sex Pistols because of 'God Save The Queen'. He hated it. He thought I was singing about fascism and supporting the fascist regime. Fucking idiot! Poor boy, there was no telling him. To this day he thinks you shouldn't use swear words in a song. How else would I describe a song like 'Bodies' without using that kind of language to capture the rage and passion and pain of both sides of the abortion issue?

'Bodies' is one of the most powerful pieces of writing in British music: *Fuck this and fuck that / Fuck it all and fuck her fucking brat / She don't wanna baby that looks like that.*

I wanted to capture the whole scene of the operating table and a baby being dragged out with a coat hanger and the blood and the rage. So rather than being literal in that way I just thought those words absolutely summed it up. It's because I'm uneducated.

Self-educated. You strike me as an educated person, with a lot of intelligence.

I'm an avid reader. I like to analyse other people's thoughts. You can learn a great deal from books, but not everything. The best conversations you can ever have are with drunks in a pub.

Where there's no barrier to thought.

Yeah. When people are quite literally telling you what is what. Fascinating. I love the atmosphere of pubs; everybody loosens up. You really get to grips with things.

Do you carry a notebook to capture phrases or ideas?

No. I wouldn't do that. Urrgh, no. I'm not one of The Clash. I remember Joe Strummer used to sit in front of *The News At Six* and wait for titles and slogans that he could write down. Then he'd rush off and write a song around it: *Sten guns in Knightsbridge* and 'White Riot'. It's all fucking ridiculous. It's too manufactured.

Musically you've pushed boundaries, but lyrically you've virtually always stuck with rhyming couplets. Why is that?

Love it. Love it, just love it. That just seems to be the way my brain works and I'm not going to question it. But not always, like 'Albatross'. I've always loved the minimalistic structure that pop songs have. Pop music is the biggest thrill: *Top of the Pops* kind of hits; the top thirty. I love the simplicity of it. And rhyming words; it's just a shame that a lot of those words that they use may rhyme but they don't make much sense. I've found that I can make sense of that. So maybe they're the tools I use to craft my message with. That might be because I'm writing with a tune in my head that's almost indecipherable. There's always something like a poetic beat going on: one big, huge sonorous rhythm.

I read that when you were first in the Pistols a lack of confidence prevented you presenting your lyrics. Is that still the case?

Oh, yeah. Ha, ha, ha, yeah. Ask the band. They have to fight to snatch them off me. I'm getting over that in the last few years. It's like this: when I try to just show the written word, the message isn't there without the voice. So the bigger picture isn't grasped. I use the line in 'Rise' *the written word is a lie*, because it generally is without the human tone on it; the double entendres just by inflections; the irony just by a mannerism in a tone is vital to the bigger picture. I mean every word. There is absolutely no loose dialogue in any song I ever put together. There are so many bands that quite happily brag that their words are meaningless and think that's an achievement. I find that remarkably disappointing. If that part of the human condition is meaningless, what's the point in padding notes around it? If it starts from nowhere, it's got nowhere to go.

I've often thought that people who don't use an instrument to write with have a distinct way of lyrical scanning . . .

But I do, I have a set of tonsils, two lips, a tongue and some bad teeth. The voice is natural. You must understand that musical instruments are an imitation of the sounds of nature: the wind whistling through the grass. Anything.

Robin Gibb said he could hear melody in ambient sounds like church bells.

I'm dead with him on that one. Absolutely. I'll find in harmonic distortions a melody. I can pick a tune out of a traffic jam, all the different horns. It's there and my mind is clearly telling me it is, but it's almost impossible to repeat; but it somehow comes up in a phrase or a line later. Yes. It's just a way of perceiving how the world works, like painting, which I love.

A painter goes back and corrects: would you, with your work?

No. Live, of course, I'm adapting, reshaping and reforming to fit the exact moment. It's a passionate thing for me. I can't really explain it and I don't want to, other than through the songs.

Have you ever tried to capture what you've painted in lyrics?

Yeah. It's the same thing ultimately. (*Picks up 'Death Disco' single cover.*) I lost this painting. I think I gave it to Paul Cook. It was in beautiful shades of yellow, orange, blue, reds, really gaudy rotting-flesh colours. This is what got me chucked out of my college of further education. It was for my A Level art. The question was 'enveloping forms': you had to offer a theory, a painting. I went on about a mother chewing her baby to death. I called it 'Love Kills'. I draw and paint all the time. This cover (*PiL's first album cover*) we got slagged to fuck. Johnny Rotten's sold out! Is that not taking the piss or what? Look at the face, deliberately beyond meaningless. And at the same time, the eyes are in slightly two different . . . there's so much going on in it. It was an attack on magazine culture. (*Points to* Happy *album cover.*) This I took from Hundert-wasser, a most fantastic Austrian architect and artist. It means hundred waters. I wanted to use his way of approaching life. The stage set at the time was this mad circus. Album covers always reflected what the stage set would look like. (*Selects* Paris Au Printemps *live album.*) That's PiL: me, Keith Levene and Jean-nette Lee as dogs. They went apeshit when I painted this: 'You can't make us look like this,' well, fucking hell!

Do you need certain conditions to write, silence for example?

Yeah, but then again I have written songs on crowded subways. The ideal framework would be absolute dead silence, but after twenty minutes (*laughs*) the TV has to go on. Sometimes I like masses of distortion cluttering up my brain and sift through that. Everything can be an influence. Children don't bother me at all, screaming and running around. One of my favourite jobs was looking after children, before the Pistols. It was the greatest job. Some of them were really problem kids that needed careful attention. They were never a prob-lem with me. Loved, loved making balsa wood aeroplanes and ships with them and things. I've still got a Lego set. I can pull it out and I love playing with it, with anybody.

There is poignant footage of you on Christmas Day 1977 serving cake to the kids of striking miners and firefighters in Huddersfield, and them chucking it back in your face.

Fantastic. The ultimate reward. One of my all-time favourite gigs. Young kids, and we're doing 'Bodies' and they're bursting out with laughter on the *fuck this fuck that* verse. The correct response: not the shock-horror, 'How dare you?' Adults bring their own filthy minds into a thing. They don't quite per-ceive it as a child does. Oh, Johnny's used a naughty word. 'Bodies' was from two different points of view. You'll find that theme runs through a lot of things I write like 'Rise'—*I could be wrong, I could be right*. I'm considering both sides of the argument, always.

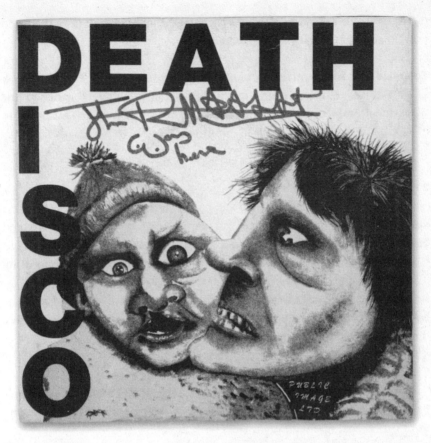

'Death Disco' sleeve artwork by John Lydon

Did some lines from 'Rise' come from South African torture victims: *They put a hot wire to my head / Cos of the things I did and said*?

Yes, and that whole nonsense that was going on out there, but it's applicable to many situations.

Can you feel a song coming on? Can you just sit down and write on a given day?

I could definitely feel building in me the song 'Disappointed'. I love that song from start to finish. It always struck me from the opening line onwards it would be an excellent song. I loved the approach that I took with it. Bury it in studio technology and really enjoy that process—a very worthwhile song. It's about friendship and learning how to forgive. It's about forgiving myself, really. It's very self-analysis, that one.

You freely use everyday phrases in your writing.

No, love them. In fact I've written entire songs made up of clichés and phrases. Generalisms, how they can mean many things and if you shape-shift them slightly . . . You can really achieve something by talking in that clichéd way. Sometimes it's really, really useful.

You once described yourself as a noise structuralist.

I think I was trying to be clever. I know exactly what I meant. It's the same dilemma I faced when I first got my passport. It came to that problem of 'occupation'. I could not think what to call myself. We ended up with *entertainer*.

Are you an entertainer?

Yeah, I think so. I thought long and hard about it and I never liked it. I do now. I think that's very appropriate. I'm many things: I can be quite severe and brutal in language because the songs require that sometimes; other times I'm closer to Les Dawson. I recommend the whole world hears Les Dawson sing 'Feelings'. It's one of the funniest things you'll ever hear; the sheer wit and destruction of that song. To this day, wherever we tour if there's a piano bar in the hotel and a pianist singing I'll run up and quite happily deposit any money they require as long as they do a version of 'Feelings'.

Crafted music negates genuine emotion.

I was thinking there of *Tubular Bells* by Mike Oldfield and 10cc's *Rubber Bullets*. They over-crafted it and killed the passion. Sometimes mistakes can be the most rewarding thing. Again we're back to pop music.

What is good pop music?

Songs that relate directly to you and tell you something about yourself, and it's usually from a youth point of view. Dealing with girls and where you stand in the world. It makes you feel like you're not alone. You can dance to it. Girls like it. It gives you a chance to rub up against them. I jest you not!

Many PiL songs like 'Theme' or 'Poptones' suggest the music and words could be separate entities. 'Religion' was a spoken presentation.

I had the lyrics way before I started PiL. I couldn't get the Pistols interested in shape-shifting it and starting to analyse things in that way. With PiL I kept the backing track on one speaker and the voice on another. You could either listen to them together or separately or individually and I really liked that. It was a very good way of kind of introducing the concept that poetry isn't such a bad thing after all. It's kind of like, 'Hello, boys and girls out there, why aren't you writing songs too?' This is the ideal way of listening to it: first the words without any melody; then the music on its own. And you try to imagine how on earth can that fit with that? Then finally you hear the two things together and it's, 'Oh, ha, ha.' The words need the boisterousness of sound. I choose carefully who I work with. It takes a very long time to find the best palette for your craft.

Are you knowledgeable about how pop songs are crafted in terms of structure?

Of course; sometimes I love verse, chorus, verse, chorus. It's great. It absolutely captures what you're trying to say. Other times you have to go almost jazzbo because there's so many variants in the thing, and in order to express it properly you have to get very complicated with it. It becomes a different force, but a necessary one. You can't say no to any way of doing the thing. You've got to be wide open to it all. The trouble is, the music press isn't very understanding of that. If I use a pop format for a particular song they love to call me selling out, or copping out, or why aren't I weird any more? Absolutely missing the point. Audiences get it. I got it. Mum and dad got it. My mates get it. But the music journalist doesn't want to get it. They really seem to resent the boundaries I'm pushing and the barriers I break down. I'm really unsafe for them because I ruin their safe, detailed, cosseted opinion of things. The talentless will always be there with the meat hooks and cleavers.

When you're writing do you think, this could be a verse, this could be a chorus, perhaps a middle eight?

Sometimes yeah, sometimes no. I loved making the *Flowers of Romance* album. I'd just got out of jail in Mountjoy in Ireland for attacking two policemen's fists with my face. I had no band. Keith Levene was having his mental anxiety problems. You could politely call it a chemical imbalance. Martin (*Atkins*) the drummer was going off to tour. I got him to put down some rough drumming patterns and then started splicing them up and came up with 'Four Enclosed Walls', which is a song I love. Love what it does to people. It really, really, really pushes some boundaries and it shouldn't. That's the joy of that song. It's quite innocent. It manages to offend. Why?—because I sing *Allah*. That infuriates a lot of people. Clearly where it was the most understood, so far in any time when I've ever played it, was in Israel last year: 6,000 Jews singing *Allah* in Tel Aviv. I thought that did more for world peace than any of them arsehole demonstrators.

Did you perform 'Belsen Was A Gas'?

No, never thought of it.

Did you have any part in the writing of that song?

Yeah, all of it. I credited Sid with it for a laugh. It's an absurd song. It's over the top. It's an ironical song. It's so completely, clearly not pro that at all. Yet again, there we go. I credited Sid because I wanted him in the Pistols. I think originally Sid came up with the title, something like 'Belsen Was A Gag'. *Gas* came in because of a T. Rex song, 'Life's A Gas'. It's one of my favourite pop singles. Although it sounds nothing like it, it's how I connect things.

Can you remember writing 'This Is Not A Love Song'?

That came in bits and drabs and pieces. It was odd that Paul McCartney a year later came out with 'This Is a Love Song' (*laughs*).

Do you write beyond songs?

I write. There's some that can't possibly be put to music. They're bordering into a poetry world or a written-word world and don't require a bedrock of music. There's one we're using on this album (*This Is PiL*). It's more like a poem. We had a piece of music that the lads put together which isn't music. It's like anti-music. There's no real pattern in it. There's drones and tones and I just talked this piece over it and it worked really well. It's done in a completely unpretentious way and if that manages to offend anyone, great (*laughs*). If people are going to go out of their way to be offended or insulted by anything I do then at least I've given them something to live for.

Do you reject many ideas?

Ha, all the time: reams, bucketloads. I rip them up. There's no need for them. If I'm going to start collecting bits of notes what chance am I giving myself to write any in the future? That would be just really lazy and stupid. When a project's done, anything that's left over goes in the shredder. It's all about that one specific moment in time. It's done, move on. I write constantly. Sometimes I'll use refrains and lines from one song in another song and find them both equally appropriate. But they're delivered in completely different context. The meaning is completely different. Same words, same sentence, but mind-numbingly, brilliantly, rewardingly differently used.

The obvious one is the use of *no future* in 'Acid Drops'.

Oh, thank you, yes, fantastic fun. I found that so rewarding. 'Acid Drops' is about censorship. I love that song to death. There's quite a few songs I've written that I really love to hear back. They still fill me with great joy. I like every word in that song; the refrain of *no future* in the end which is all about censorship. And the censorship that 'God Save The Queen' went through and all that nonsense I thought was very appropriate. They could have stifled us out of existence way back then. I then wouldn't have been able to write 'Acid Drops' because I wouldn't be in the business. So it's a kind of thank you to the Sex Pistols. And of course it's ironic because I clearly have a future.

You can look to the future when you're confident, **as you wrote in 'Dog'.**

And all mankind is innocent and we can all do without judgement: that's a theme I'm using on this album: innocence and judgement.

Do you try and tie an overall theme to a record?

Not deliberately so. It's all part of the same thing, from the first record I ever made to the very last, whenever that will be; I don't separate them. It's all part of my life. It's like good and bad memories: I don't want to lose any memory. That definitely goes back to meningitis, when I did lose my memory. It took some four years to remember the full picture of who I really was. By that time I'd become a better person so I didn't need to go back to being anyone. I liked finding that out about myself. That I was able to move on and be myself quite naturally, without knowing who myself was.

My mum had tuberculosis when she was eight and missed a year at school. She always felt she had to prove herself because she was behind; the stupid girl at the back of the class.

That's exactly what happened to me. I missed a year at school. Dummy-Dumb-Dumb was my nickname. And that was given to me by a nun.

Thank you very much.

Thank you very much. But look what it did. It made me strive harder to achieve. I didn't want to be like Dummy-Dumb-Dumb. The irony being that I could read and write at four. My mum would always put books in front of me. I loved drawing. I loved the shapes of letters and that naturally led to, 'What's that, Mum?' 'How does that work with that, Mum?' And she would answer every question. Imagine losing all of that and then it coming back to you later. It breaks your heart. Breaks your heart. The point I'm trying to make, before we drift here, is that starting school at five and already being able to read and write, so therefore way ahead of any other kid in the class, was really uncomfortable. The nuns didn't like that because on top of that I was left-handed and that was the sign of the Devil to the Catholic Church. Then at seven: meningitis; gone for a year. Back at eight and I don't know nothing. And still not liked by the nuns: vicious cows they are. I have no resentment to them because I've never written a song about them.

Why, because it would be deep down in you . . . ?

No, it would be right here, straight away.

So why haven't you done it?

Because I don't feel any resentment to them.

Do you have to write with resentment?

No, if it was about them I would think so, but I don't actually resent them at all. I'm kind of like thankful; their nastiness actually helped me achieve something. Priests, on the other hand: now that's a different problem. A nun hating you is water off a duck's back. Brides of Christ, as they used to call themselves. Who else would have them?

Am I right in saying you have stage problems because lights can provoke attacks?

Yes. I'm prone to epilepsy from childhood illnesses: any kind of quick flashing. Afternoons in the summer when the sun's going down through the trees I can go into one and that's swallow the tongue, the whole lot. I have to seal my eyes. And it's the same on stage. I'm oblivious to the end of the stage. I forget where I am. There are no restraints on me. I get off in my universe and I carry on walking and crash. The crew have to put white tape down if there's a pit, something to catch my attention.

Did Chrissie Hynde try to teach you guitar on Clapham Common in the Seventies?

That got nowhere. The left-handed thing is a real bastard. You're playing it the wrong way. I don't know if either is the right way. I can't decide. The answer is bugger off, I don't want to know. I fiddle about on the piano. I can fiddle about on the violin, oddly enough, and sax. On 'Flowers of Romance', that's me. These melodies were in my head and I found out I could play it. I was really chuffed with myself. I generally keep away from instruments.

Why?

I'll get too technical. I'll get too involved in that process. I don't want to compromise what I most love to be doing, which is writing.

As a songwriter I was once interviewed about the greatest song ever written. I chose 'Anarchy in the UK' . . .

I would have said Johnny Cash, 'A Boy Named Sue', a very challenging song.

What were you trying to achieve with 'Anarchy'?

Oh, probably going for shock value. I don't know right off the top of my head. I've never really thought about it. I took great delight driving Glen Matlock crazy. He was just ferociously angry about the rhyme in it: *I am an Antichrist / I am an anarchist.* 'You can't do that.' So in the Pistols that was exactly what I went away and did. And for me it makes my part in the Pistols. I probably wrote it in the rehearsal studio. Trying to get in there and have my space in things. It was very, very difficult; they'd all known each other. They all hung around with each other. They didn't want to know me too much. It was, 'Just put some words to it.'

So it was a reaction to the music?

Yeah, completely, and generally speaking to Steve's guitar, which I loved. I couldn't understand him wanting to give up all the time, saying he couldn't play. It was the greatest sound I ever heard. The New York Dolls was a band that couldn't play, but what a wonderful racket. You don't need to be able to play perfectly. Sometimes not being able to play at all can be a good thing too.

You wrote 'New York' about that scene. Do you write better when you're against something?

No.

Can you write overtly positively?

Oh yeah, there's very much of that going on everywhere in my songs . . . if you bother to look!

When you're angry or against something the pen might flow more easily.

Angry is a complete energy. And it's wonderful. It really is. I recommend it. But don't let it turn to violence. Find an outlet for it and it can be amazingly rewarding. It's a very useful tool. I don't know if it's the driving force in me. I would say completely not. There's many tools out there: all the human emotions. I get angry when I see people oppressed, the disenfranchised. I'm constantly churning up emotions for that. My enemy will always be all political systems. All of them. I support no government or politician anywhere, ever.

When I was considering you as a positive writer I was drawn to the song 'Grave Ride': *No war is worth it, without you / No point in living without you / I know you feel the way I do / It's not a real world without you.*

It's a love song to Nora.

Why was it set in a war context?

It just seems appropriate. I think it was because of that Slovenia thing that was going on at the time. The papers were just full of bloodbaths. I thought it was a neat . . . a proper thing to put in that there are human beings here. It's not just all about the mass murderers. What about the people they're murdering and what it is they're murdering? How much love those fucks killed.

Would you want to write a direct love song without metaphor, simile or analogy?

Then it wouldn't have any purpose, would it. It'd be rather dull if it's not in a proper context.

The context would be a relationship . . .

I'm not going to sing about that one lonely wilted flower there all on its own without mentioning the field it's in and all of its environment. That's how I am; three-sixty degrees of vision. It's much better that way.

Do you remember writing 'Sun'?

Hmmm, there's a fun song. That's absolutely full of good fun (*laughing*). *I miss the car park. I miss the concrete. I miss the rain and sleet. I want my climate, I want remote control. Plenty of water in every single hole. In the sun, sun, sun.* Live, it can be such great fun. And we do it almost acoustically. It's like a folk thing. It becomes really anthemic. Audiences love joining in on it.

Did you play the accordion on it?

No, it's a melodica. No, originally yes, but Lu (*Edmonds*) now plays it that way live. It's a mixture of different accordions, about twenty of them one note at a time, and a Kurzweil keyboard. The drums are actually cardboard boxes. It's impossible to play that record live. It was put together with 'this'll never work' mentality, and it did, and to this day I can't remember how. Everything went into it. The *Psychopath* album I used toilet rolls. I love ambient flutes and Chilean pipes but they didn't have any so we sellotaped rolls together. I found I got the right sounds.

Did you approach writing *Psychopath* differently because it would be in the name of John Lydon?

Yeah, with no restraints. I was approaching it from the music—if you want to call it that—point of view first, and that was an odd thing for me to do. I'd fit the words in later. They would come last. My agenda was an exact upside-down world for me. I didn't know if I'd be able to pull that off or get through that in that way. I think I did. Very pleased with it. I can go that way but I prefer not to. I was focusing in on the discordancy and the harmonic distortions between things and the glory a couple of bum notes can bring in an otherwise perfect pattern when they collide with a few other bum notes somewhere else. Then suddenly there's this wonderful pattern occurring in my head. That's the melody line I want. And the words will just pop right out of the air.

You have a very distinctive approach to melody?

It might be brain damage from meningitis. It's possible. I've not come across anyone who really thinks about it the way I do and I'm really pleased

Sun

v1. S.t in the sun, let nature take me. Lucky for some, that nature hates me. I miss the car park, I miss the concrete, I miss the city, I miss the rain and sleet I want my climate, I want remote control. Plenty of water, in every single hole. I'm never happy with what surrounds me. I like the choices (In the sun (repeat)) The idiot dance, let me dance (repeat).

v2. I'm never happy, with what surrounds me. We're falling apart at the seam. It's never as good as the dream. I like the chorus, and postcard scenery. We're falling apart at the seam. We're falling apart at the seam. (In the sun (repeat)). The idiot dance, let me dance (repeat).

v3. I'm never happy with what surround me. I like the choices and all the scenery. I want my climate, I want remote control. Plenty of water, in every single hole. (In the sun (repeat)). The idiot dance, let me dance (repeat)

In the sun etc....
Good natured etc....

'In The Sun' lyrics, handwritten by John Lydon

about that. It's so disorganized. It doesn't follow what any other person would call logic. When I talk to other people that sing and write songs they have all their own quirks too and it's fascinating. But ultimately it's like . . . if I over-analyse that I might kill it. I might destroy the gift. So I don't want to go there. Once you know exactly how you're doing something then you don't want to do it any more.

I'm surprised more people haven't said that to me.

Sometimes I feel there are not enough words in the world to describe things, and other times when I hear intellectuals I think those cunts have got far too many.

'Tie Me To The Length Of That' has an extraordinary set of words: *I keep these feelings deep inside my body / It's not the union both of us expected / Remember daddy, when you made him hold me? / Safe in his arms, then the bastard dropped me.*

Daddy was very angry, that wasn't how he remembered my birth (*laughs*). My aunt said, 'I remember the day you were born: your father turned up drunk at the hospital and dropped you on the bed.' I remembered that. I thought, 'That'll make a song.' Tell it that way from the child's point of view: a bad baby point of view. That's a bad baby doing that song and it's excellent. It's a sense of fun. It's closer to some psychotic comedy film.

I'm often shocked by what you're prepared to write about because in many respects you delve very deep inside yourself. Not many writers reveal that pain.

Hardly. Maybe when I was young and I repressed all my emotions; that was the pain. This isn't pain now. This is joy. Really. The deepest, darkest hurt and sadness is, oddly enough, in its weird way, proof of your existence, and that's not a bad thing. It doesn't require much. That's what they're all doing: I think I'll go this way. That's being flippant, I know.

Have you achieved the sound on record that's in your mind?

We're in search of that perfectly insane note that absolutely perfectly sums everything up. If I ever hit that note that will be my goodbye card, 'cause I've got there. I've found the clue to the universe in the perfectly most horrible tone. It might be incredibly beautiful. An example of that is on 'Religion' when we do it live now. I'm going up there in the register. I'm reaching some seriously high notes. My range is getting wider and wider and wider the more I work at this. I view myself as fifty-five years young in that respect. I've not had long enough at this to get to where I want to.

(*Laughs.*) There's Johnny at his finest.

What was your involvement in 'World Destruction'?

It was Afrika Bambaataa's song. I put the chorus in and gave it a melody, gave it a theme. I did it as a bit of fun in New York because I liked Bambaataa. From that I got to know Bill Laswell and that led to the *Album* album.

Your guitarist Lu wrote with Kirsty MacColl, but there are few female British writers with notable success . . .

She'd be one of them. Kate Bush. Maddy Prior, she's more a beautiful singer. There's quite a few.

There are few that have achieved the accolades that men do in this country.

Well, they did in punk, and punk did a wonderful thing that it levelled the playing field for women and bands competing. They weren't viewed as just silly girls all wearing matching outfits with bouffants. They took the boys on and many a time beat them. There were some fantastic bands. The Raincoats, X-Ray Spex. Poly Styrene wrote some great lyrics in a really exciting pop way. 'Oh Bondage Up Yours!' was hilarious and deeply sympathetic about a subject that was really quite perverse. She did good. I wouldn't say The Banshees were much cop. They just tended to wait for the newest Stephen King novel.

How would you like your contribution to British songwriting to be viewed?

I'd like to become fantastically pompous about it. I'm quite happy where I am and I couldn't give a fuck. The awards system and the merit system and the chart system and the whole competition of it all is nothing to do with me; never has been, never will. Never thought anything I ever did would stand a chance in this wicked old world of ours. Right from the start of the Pistols . . . loved being in them, didn't like them as people and they didn't like me. But we all loved being whatever it was we were being. But we never ever thought anybody would ever listen to any of it: remarkably freeing, that is. I would recommend that people don't go for the money, honey. It ain't going to win. If you're not enjoying this don't do it. And don't do it just to be a star. God, you can suss those people out so quickly, can't you?

Was there a point from the unknown to the known John Lydon that affected your writing?

It's a tough thing to become instantly Britain's most unpopular, popular person. That's a tough one to try and wriggle out of. You could so easily fall into being a cliché of yourself. There are many people that would love to think that's what happened, but it didn't. But of course the thoughts are there. I'm always riddled with self-doubt. I'm very far from arrogant. That's a word that's wrongly been placed on me; fear and loathing of myself really, and self-doubt and a huge lack of faith in my own capabilities. These are constant problems.

What does the name Johnny Rotten mean to you?

It was a nickname given to me by Steve Jones. I thought it was hilarious. It was because of my teeth.

Whose opinion do you seek/accept when you've finished a song?

Absolutely no one's. It's nice if somebody likes it but if they don't I'm fucking more than determined. Of course I listen, but ultimately the challenge is mine. If others around me think a thing that I'm doing should be something else, they're more than welcome to go and do their something else. It has to be because it's from in here. I can't give my vision of things too well if it's from somebody else's point of view, although I can shape-shift. I can imagine myself inside somebody else's psyche, but not if they're asking me to do that. I can invent characters. 'Pretty Vacant', that's an invention of a song. I'm inventing a character that's trying to explain himself. It's from a yobbo point of view. I'm not a yobbo, but I can be.

How far do you step into that character idea?

Quite a lot. It's not theatrical but it's definitely kind of theatre, but it's real. I know the framework and the mindset of each song. I want to absolutely portray it accurately. I don't have much of a problem doing that. The words lead me quite brilliantly back to where I came from when I first wrote the thing. 'Pretty Vacant' was a generalization. I suppose I was imagining myself as a Slade character, Noddy Holder—serious. That's how I viewed the song: *we're so pretty.*

It's astonishing 'Pretty Vacant' escaped the censors.

Va-cunt: yes, I got away with it holding the pause, but the BBC aired it. There was a debate about it. There was a second's delay. They very rarely let me go out live. It's not because I might use naughty words, the F's and C's which I think are valid: it's the content of what I have to say. It's too disturbing. And it should be. You should make people aware. You should wake people up and give them the freedom of thought. You grab the moment and you turn it into a mad opera and everybody goes home laughing. There's no spite or victimization in what I do at all, unless you're a government figure.

I take no quarter / This is my land / I'll never surrender / I'm a warrior. **What were you thinking when you wrote 'Warrior'?**

A lot more now, when we do it live. You said earlier you make records, but performing them live the songs become bigger and wider. It's about standing up and fighting for what's rightfully yours and don't roll over. Basically it's a rebel song. Sometimes you don't know what you're rebelling against, but rebel first and work the rest out later because at least your mind is occupied. It's an anti-war song. I was thinking of Sitting Bull, a Native American point of view; because they didn't stand up and take no quarter they were basically massacred. Every time they tried to make a peace treaty it meant more of them would be murdered; the disenfranchised.

When you're reading, opening yourself to literature, films, does your mind become a songwriter?

Not deliberately, no, but when I come across an excellent point of view the brain goes, Bing! I can use that message in my own life. If it contradicts a thought in myself then I'm more than happy to change for that because that's the better way. You have to be able to change all the way through life. The things you thought at seventeen were very appropriate for you then but not at fifty-five years young, because the world has changed. As in 'This Is Not a Love Song': *I'm adaptable and I like my new role.*

You don't have a record label behind you?

No, we'd love one, but there's many, many reasons why not. Virgin/Warners was poison. Death by committee. They kept me out of business for quite a long time. Thank God for butter!

Has living in Los Angeles altered your writing?

It's the same head looking at different things. I love the landscape of America and I like Americans. I find them very open and friendly, less analytical and spiteful. Here you have to be on your guard all the time; you can't let it down. It's too tensile here. You feel stretched all the time. And that's me! Bye-bye.

MICK JONES

1977. A year marked by violence and unrest in London. It saw a series of bomb attacks by the IRA in the West End, and violent clashes in south London as the National Front marched on the capital's streets. 1977 also saw the release of 'White Riot', the debut single by The Clash. Inspired by the fighting between police and black youths at the Notting Hill Carnival the previous year, 25-year-old lyricist Joe Strummer wrote *Black men gotta lot a problems / But they don't mind throwing a brick*. Strummer and his band mate Paul Simonon had participated in the riot, but after being harangued by a young posse they accepted the unrest was between British Afro-Caribbeans and the police. 'White Riot' was composed as a challenge to white youth to take action in their turn: *Are you going backwards / Or are you going forwards?* In later years Strummer would recognize his clumsy race rhetoric, but the charge was dynamic. The Clash were all about action. The single's B-side was equally explosive. It seemed to proclaim musical heritage extinct: *No Elvis, Beatles, or The Rolling Stones / In 1977.*

The Clash derived strength from simplicity. When Joe Strummer misheard the title of his writing partner's song about his girlfriend: *I'm So Bored With You*, he added *(SA)* to the end of the line. It transformed the song into an attack on American culture. Strummer's natural modulations of speech interlacing with the easy melodies and inventive chord sequences of Mick Jones. Strummer informed the *NME* in 1976: 'Our music is like Jamaican stuff; if they can't hear it, they're not supposed to hear it.' Adenoidal problems slurred his often unintelligible delivery. It was part of the appeal. Strummer and Jones both had limited vocal ranges, which lent a conversational tone to their lyrics: the writers in bare communication with the listener.

Early Clash songs were short bursts of energy: verse, chorus, repeat, end. 'Garageland' declared *The truth is only known by guttersnipes.* The group advocated an 'English Civil War' and *Johnny* and the *new party army* were *coming by bus or underground*. The old order was changing: Marc Bolan died in a car crash in September 1977, whilst in August, at the age of forty-two, Elvis Presley had suffered heart failure. Rock 'n' roll was in free fall. Clash manager and self-styled provocateur Bernie Rhodes commanded his troops to wage war directly: 'Write about what you know'—housing, lack of education, dead-end futures. He distributed reading material about Dadaism, existentialism and social realism. It was a political awakening for the group. 'Last Gang In Town' with its rockabilly rhythms dealt with identity in an age when allegiance to a band could dictate the way people dressed. Now, though, music could provide an ideology. Poetic ambiguity, which had been the mainstay of earlier protest songs, had been dismissed. The Clash broke with tradition and wrote directly in street slang. Their verse was raw and demanding; Jones and Strummer became voices for the forgotten and the disenfranchised of the city.

'You've got to live something to sing about it in a convincing way. It's experience that writes songs. All things in life are lyrics.' John Graham Mellor was born on 21 August 1952 in Ankara, Turkey. His father was a diplomat with the Foreign Office and moved with his family to Egypt, Mexico and Germany before settling near Croydon in 1958. John was educated at a private boarding school but his enthusiasm was for the music of Buddy Holly, The Beatles and The Rolling Stones. He identified with the hobo lifestyle of Woody Guthrie and by his early twenties had discovered his adult identity as Joe Strummer. The 101'ers' frontman was the perfect foil for guitarist Jones and bass player Paul Simonon. It was in Jones's eighteenth-floor council-tower-block window overlooking the Westway that the song 'London's Burning' was completed. Strummer had initiated the idea in silence in his squat while trying not to wake up Palmolive of The Slits. He told Alan Whiting on Radio 1 in 1984 that it was 'a cry of frustration. There is a difference between protest and complaining. A protest song goes a long way, but complaining stops short . . . it's complaining with subtlety and poetry too.' *Face the new religion*. Strummer was attentive to his craft. He told *Melody Maker* four years later: 'I write from line to line. If I get to line four and find I've gone onto another subject completely I have to go back, otherwise it would just be completely indecipherable. It really annoys me, because I write in a flood. I write the sort of thing that comes to you when you're lying in bed thinking.' Strummer was meticulous in his preparations: 'Every man has his own rituals to get you into the right state of consciousness. I like to have four typewriters in a row and then I feel everything is prepared. I like the blank sheet of paper, the physical idea . . . tapping with a typewriter . . . the hammer striking the paper and the characters printing out. That's exciting to me.' Drafts, previously scribbled on any loose paper that came to hand, were now dignified by being punched out on a 1925 Venezuelan typewriter acquired for five pounds on the Portobello Road. He went on to tell Radio 1 listeners, 'I go about it in a showmanship way. I make sure I'm wearing the right clothes, even though there's nobody there. Nice white paper, a decent ashtray and cigarettes. Get all the artefacts there. Feel the tradition of writing.'

Mick Jones, by contrast, is an instinctive musician. He would strengthen Strummer's lyrics with melodic and musical sweetness. Born Michael Geoffrey Jones in Clapham's South London Hospital for Women on 26 June 1955, his first musical memory was from the age of three, of hearing the Life Guards marching down Mitcham High Street. By his teenage years he had moved to west London, and the influence of The Stones, The Faces and Mott The Hoople was driving his musical ambition. His upbringing in multicultural London also lent vitality and breadth to his creative imagination. The Clash fused cosmopolitan rhythms and attitudes into their sound, and by the early Eighties Jones had earned the nickname Whack Attack from his fellow band members, because of his love of hip hop.

Their music embraced a range of influences, from reggae to disco to punk and funk. *London Calling*, released in 1979, is a double album of stunning musical assimilation and originality. Defying genre definition, it marked Jones and Strummer as the New Wave's first great British writing partnership. The title track ambitiously assembled images of *the ice age . . . engines stop running . . . the sun zooming in*. Its author explained the composition to Alan Whiting, as a reaction to the country's fuel crisis: 'I was cheering myself up by putting all these ridiculous things into one basket.' Verses about football mobs filling Soho streets and the near nuclear meltdown at Three Mile Island underwent many revisions before Strummer completed the song's final draft. In 2004, *Rolling Stone* magazine placed 'London Calling' fifteenth in the 500 greatest songs of all time. In the Eighties, the publication had already voted the LP Album of the Decade, and since 2008 it has been honoured in the Grammy Hall of Fame, with worldwide sales exceeding five and a half million.

Strummer increasingly compared his writing to that of past greats like Cole Porter and Hoagy Carmichael: 'I like things I can feel the craft in. What a lot of young writers don't realize is that they're not telescoping their lines enough. What those old writers realized was, that you say one idea and say half of a line and there's no need to reinforce it in the second half of the line and then add extra detail with a whole 'nother two halves of a line. Then you've got two whole lines of a song that a crafty writer would have disposed of in the first half of a line and then gone on.' Strummer urged Radio 1 listeners to study the craftsmanship of Bob Dylan's *Highway 61 Revisited* writing period, '. . . very dense, like a forest. Just as one image hits you another one has risen to take its place.' He added, 'Lyric writing is like boxing: it's no use one punch and then waiting before you bring another punch in. It's like Sugar Ray Leonard combinations, bang, bang, bang. I like it best when there's an idea, a line and a tune all in one, and then you can expand outward and get a song.'

I don't believe in books but I read them all the time / For ciphers to the riddles and reasons to the rhymes. Strummer loved words and news. Songs like 'Midnight Log' (quoted above) and 'The Magnificent Seven', both from the 1980 triple album *Sandinista!*, expertly capture the mundane detail of everyday life, juxtaposing names, places and people: *English pounds and Eskimo pence . . . cops kicking gypsies on the pavement . . . Plato the Greek or Rin Tin Tin.* References crossed continents, global concerns were distilled, and issues zoomed into focus. The stream of consciousness of 'If Music Could Talk': *I am a shaman, a voodoo a shaman . . . the sailor boys have hit Shanghai . . .* captures a near-automatic writing process. Strummer told *Musician* magazine in 1980, 'It's a blur in my mind when I actually write.'

The final Clash album written by Strummer and Jones, *Combat Rock*, was released in 1982; it contained some of the band's greatest work and had immense commercial appeal. Yet in recent years an earlier mix of the record produced by Jones has surfaced, revealing a remarkably unconventional concept. *Rat Patrol From Fort Bragg* offers almost twenty minutes more music, with additional songs and much lengthier alternative takes than the original release. The seventeen-track bootleg shows the scope of Jones's assimilation of American Seventies soul and on-the-pulse hip hop street sounds. Management and band pressure denied the public an experience which would have placed Jones's innovative vision beside those of predecessors Pete Townshend and Ray Davies.

By 1983, Simonon and Strummer claimed that the original idea behind The Clash was being compromised and forced Jones out. By that point, the threesome had been together for six years and had recorded a score of hugely influential singles plus five albums over sixteen sides of vinyl. Strummer told Ann Scanlon in April 1988: 'The Clash were fucked by success. We were singer/songwriters and the better we did our craft the more it removed us from the frame of where we were writing from.' In response to the split, Jones had formed Big Audio Dynamite with a new writing partner, Don Letts. Music was sampled with art, film and literature; machines mixed with guitars; rap delivery with melody.

In 2010, Jones was reunited with Simonon at the invitation of Damon Albarn's Gorillaz. It was a union with significant history: 'It was a wonderful experience. I loved playing with those fantastic musicians. I was like the maître d'; everybody came on, on my side, and I greeted them and positioned them.' The guest list was both eclectic and impressive and included Lou Reed, Neneh Cherry, Shaun Ryder, the Syrian National Orchestra for Arabic Music, Bobby Womack and Yukimi Nagano. Gorillaz' multi-genre engagement represent a continuation of a musical heritage that flows back to Big Audio Dynamite and, further back still, The Clash. In turn, Jones's ingenuity and artistry connects his music to the street sounds of mid-Sixties Jamaica and mid-Seventies New

York. In Manhattan, Grandmaster Flash and DJ Kool Herc took music to the streets via discarded turntables and vinyl transported in the back of their cars. The 'jams' and 'break-beat' were a direct descendant of Prince Buster and Duke Reid's Jamaican mobile methods a decade earlier. Jones and Strummer celebrated that musical history by fusing culturally diverse dance grooves with reggae off-beat and English on-beat. It was a uniquely British interpretation.

In conversation, Jones describes inspiration as a natural source connecting movements between continents. His songwriting is explained as much in the absorption of the surrounding world as in the act of writing. His co-writing partner was in accord. Strummer voices his search in 'The Sound Of The Sinners': *I was looking for that great jazz note that destroyed the walls of Jericho.* On 15 November 2002, at a fire brigade benefit gig in Acton Town Hall, Jones joined Strummer on stage to perform 'Bankrobber', followed by an encore of 'White Riot' and 'London's Burning'. The songwriting pair had avoided reunion for almost thirty years. Just over a month later on 22 December, Joe Strummer died of congenital heart failure. Setting up a meeting with Mick to talk about songwriting involved tricky negotiation, but when we agreed that it would be a fitting tribute to his passed friend the invitation took on a new importance. In an interview with Caroline Coon for *Melody Maker*, Strummer had said, 'If I tell you how I write, when I next do it my words will haunt me and destroy me completely.' Mick was similarly reluctant to analyse the process. A year before our conversation in a Notting Hill pub, I happened to bump into him at the famous 100 Club. When I described the book as a consideration of songwriting craft, Mick deflected my approach with the telling rebuff, 'What a horrible word. Let's just have a beer and enjoy the music!'

Are you a left-handed guitar player but play with your right hand?

No, that's Joe. That's the story—that's why Joe sounds so incredibly unique, because he's a left-handed guy playing a right-handed guitar. His most dextrous hand is his least-used one, hence 'Joe Strummer'. I'm right-handed and play right-handed. Hendrix was left-handed but played a restrung guitar, but Joe's choice was to play it the wrong way round. That's why it sounds like him. Everybody sounds like themselves anyway because when you play guitar it's the accumulation of your own personal experiences which you are expressing. That's why every person who plays an instrument—no matter how bad or good— sounds like them. That's what happens. It's a means of expressing yourself other than just in words; music as well.

Did Joe's playing spark unexpected rhythms as a result?

I don't know if it did consciously but I believe it possibly had a subconscious effect. We played so you could hear both guys playing. I'm playing the off-beat and he was playing the on-beat. I was playing around him but it wasn't conscious. Nothing was conscious as far as the group was concerned. We were just going on basic instinct more than anything, especially in the early days. On things like 'Police And Thieves' I didn't even know what I did. Then I heard it explained by Joe in *Westway to the World* that I was playing the on and he was playing the opposite. So I might have been subconsciously aware, but it was very much about what the others were playing. Everybody's personalities are coming out. Each person is singing the song in their own way. I always like to think that. So I'm always looking at the spaces as well as the actual notes, they are just as important in terms of the feel. That's why my production is very much like. . . . get the people to produce out of themselves, produce something of that nature . . . I try to go for all universal rather than earthly.

How did you know how to write your first song?

I didn't know. As I learnt to play guitar I just started making up my own little songs. That just came. Early on in my career, if you want to call it that, I used to look in the *Melody Maker* adverts for anybody who needed a rhythm guitarist. It was the easiest thing to do. It wasn't any accomplishment and I mostly failed auditions during that time. I spent a couple of years before then asking people because I knew I wanted to do it but I didn't know how I was going to do it. If I saw anybody playing a musical instrument I would say, 'How do you do that?' I was really curious but I never quite got round to it. By seventeen I was playing guitar, but that's relatively late. I first started on Stylophone, to be honest. I was roadie-ing for my school friends' band, trying to be involved. They called me Little Mick, because there were two Micks. I took up the drums, then I took up the bass after that, then I thought: I can handle a couple more strings here, and I went up to guitar. You know when you're playing blackjack and you can go bust? To me it was the perfect twenty-one. I didn't want to go any further. All of the guitarists that I loved: Keith Richards, Mick Ronson, Jimmy Page—the idea of being the guitarist in a band . . . that was the coolest place to be. Songwriting never came into it. When I went to my school careers officer—it's partly how 'Careers Opportunities' came about, but not entirely—they said, 'What do you wanna do?' I said straight away, 'I wanna be in a band.' They said, 'We can't help you there. All we have is the civil service or the armed forces.' Everybody that came out of Strand Boys' Grammar in Brixton went straight into one of those two professions. I was lucky. The school song went *Here's to the school that was born in the Strand, servants of state to be, that's the high hope for me.* It's a very nice song, actually. It had a great impression on me. The music that really made an impression on me was The Beatles and The Stones and The Kinks and The Who and the Small Faces and after that subsequently The Faces. That's like the big five in my life. A big part was also Elvis. My mum had all his records so I came up with that as well. There was that sense of rock 'n' roll. And the other thing I've got to say is show musicals. Lionel Bart especially, who later on in his life and mine we got to sing together in B.A.D.. We did one of his songs, 'Mirror Man', round about the time of *Higher Power*. It was a really rare single. There are such enduring songs from *My Fair Lady*, *South Pacific*, Lerner and Loewe, Rodgers and Hammerstein. That time of big musicals from the early Sixties: Steve Marriott as the Artful Dodger in *Oliver*. The show tunes were important.

What got you writing?

I like a nice tune. I like something that comes . . . the way that they come . . . The best description I would say was how we wrote 'Janie Jones'. I was sitting on the bus going to rehearsals: the number 31 bus from Harrow Road, where I was living in the flats, to Chalk Farm Road, Camden Town. The bus was going (*hums drum rhythm*) and at that time Janie Jones was in the papers . . . always been interested in what's going on around us, everything in fact. Everything is OK to write a song, no matter how small or how big, as long as you don't put anybody down that doesn't deserve to be. It's got to be from the heart. By the time I got to rehearsals it was already there, we just didn't have all the words, we had the chorus and the drum beat.

Robin Gibb explained how 'Jive Talkin'' originated when the Bee Gees were travelling to the recording studio in a car over Brooklyn Bridge, backwards and forwards each day, and picked up on the rhythmic sound.

Really! That's it. It's all there already: all the stuff that's in the world, all the news, the bits of ideas, the music that's going on around us; walk past shops and you hear different bits of music and stuff. It gets into you, but you make it your own. You don't just go, 'Oh, I'll nick that.' But it comes from nowhere, to be honest, if you really want to know what my opinion is. It comes from nowhere and it's really good if you're able to pick it up. And sometimes you're not able to pick it up because you've got so much other stuff, especially when you get older; you've got responsibilities and that can get in the way of picking that stuff up. But it comes from nowhere. It's out there. It's in there, but when you do one bit of music the next bit is in the bit that you did. It's already there. So when you do one bit, the next bit to do is already there and you have to pick it out. And if you pick that out the next bit to do is after that because it's just there already; you just have to fit it in. It's true. That's how I do it, anyway. But I'm a nutcase!

Where does that stuff come from?

It only comes when it comes. If you don't allow it any time to come, it won't come. You have to actually fight for that time. You don't think about that when you're young, you just do it. But later on you realize what happens and what you did. And then you have to manage that. I've seen a couple of things about Dylan just recently and he was saying the same thing. He's so extraordinary it would have to be a separate case. I don't think you can train the original inception of inspiration. It's the mystery of everybody. Having said that, everybody is good at something: it's just if you're lucky enough to find what you're good at. The greatest thing is to be in a band, to go everywhere with a bunch of friends . . . just to make music.

Do you think you've ever written a song that really expresses your true self?
I expect I have; I wouldn't have said what it was in that way. I might look back on it and say, that is really real, but I wouldn't have done it trying to say, this is what I really am. Funnily enough the one that really seemed to capture an essence at the time was 'Lost In The Supermarket', and Joe wrote it.

Did Joe write 'Beyond The Pale' for you?
No, he gave it the once-over. I already had it but he finessed it.

There's a rocker in Vladivostok / Got every side by Jerry Lee / But for accidents of disorder / That guy could well be me.
That's Joe.

I presumed it was about your maternal Jewish–Russian heritage.
It is, but he wrote it for me. Mine was less finessed. That's what I mean by the once-over; we'd go back and come back with something better. Usually better.

Did he do that with you melody-wise?
No, words-wise. The tune was already there, probably.

Did you once say that music is mathematical?
Yes, I did.

What do you mean by that?
It's like a puzzle, and once that puzzle is solved you can go on to do the next puzzle. What I'm saying, basically, is the chord up the end, the E chord, is the same up here after twelve frets. Plus in the A position it's here on the eight fret or something. On the same fret you can do the A again in the D position. So it's like a graph, if you want to figure it out. That doesn't explain how you do a guitar solo, but it does explain . . . Did you know World War One was fought by mathematicians? They thought, if we've got more men that will go over the side than you've got, if we can get that little bit more extra ground, and then they have to get more men in. That's the mathematical thing. This is just a microcosm of the greater . . . of life. This is all that is. It's like the puzzles of life and one of them is music. I don't read music but I'm a natural.

When you're piecing together a song, do you feel it's a puzzle that pre-exists?

No, it comes. You have to be alert. That's always been the way. It just comes from nowhere. I can't make no great claims on it. It's just a blessing to be able to translate it. I believe that it's there. I don't know what other people think when they sit down for songwriting sessions. Other people like Joe also knew that. It's as easy as can be. We never took too long over our songs. If we took too long there was something wrong with it. The quicker the better. Knocking it out like that. It was just great.

If something didn't come quickly, would you just cut it out or would you persevere?

We might, it might be finished later or if it was something great we might force it. It was just easy, in a way. Horrible to say that for other people out there who find it so hard, because it's so hard to come up with a good tune with lyrics, but it was easy. I find it really hard without a good collaborative other person. But I had success with that with Tony James and Don Letts as well since. They were very good songwriting partners; they brought something different to it but obviously not the same as what Joe brought to it.

Would you reluctantly write on your own?

We'd still write on our own sometimes. We ended up writing by post. We put them through the letter box. We didn't like anything by that time. I guess I wasn't sure either. We were going in different directions after a long time. Funnily enough that didn't take too long to resolve and then we all became good friends again. We just never got the group back together again. We worked together on stuff quite a bit. We worked on the second B.A.D. album. We wrote a lot of other songs at that time as well. Three big batches. We didn't use to write one, we'd always write a batch at a time. If we just needed to have the one . . . there was one time . . . One of the things in the *Standard* was the column Career Opportunities. We were in Foscote Mews round the back of the Harrow Road. Joe had a disused ice-cream factory with all the cartons empty all around his squat. We were writing and Paul went, 'What about career opportunities?' And Joe went, 'Just go round the Kentucky and get us some potato croquettes and we'll knock it out.' There was another time that was quite funny: 'We haven't got enough numbers for the first album.' We were at Rehearsal Rehearsal. 'OK, you better go upstairs quickly and knock one up.' We went upstairs and wrote '48 Hours' in about ten minutes flat. Joe always called it hacking or tailoring. He was like, 'We always make it fit,' how to get the melody line to fit with all the words. It was quite amazing how we progressed from this punk band to something altogether different.

Could you describe what the chemistry was between you and Joe when you were writing?

(*Pause*) It was nice . . . if my memory serves me right. At various different points the dynamic would be different. At best it would be him sitting at his typewriter just doing it straight and I'd be sitting here playing guitar on the other side of the table, like a newspaperman . . . just do it like that in afternoons. Just banging it out. That was the best ever, or maybe how we did it at the start; some of the songs I already had then we changed them. Most famously 'I'm So Bored With You' turned into 'I'm So Bored With The USA'. Also 'Scrawled On The Bathroom Wall' turned into 'Gates Of The West'. 'Protex Blue' was pretty much the same as it was, but probably a few bits. What used to happen with some of my stuff is that Joe would give it the once-over. Put some things better, usually. Sometimes he'd give me a lyric and then if it turned out or it looked like this could be a really good tune I might go back to him with the same thing: 'I think you could do a little bit better here.' That's what happened with 'London Calling'. There was a first lyric but it wasn't really . . . it was good, it was interesting, it had enough but it wasn't . . . Very often he'd do the lyric and then he'd put the chorus, he'd do them in hand and put the chorus on the side, so you'd have to know that that was probably going to be the chorus, or the middle eight. The rest was all here. I had to organize it, arrange quite a lot and give it the tune. That was a really important thing. There were two of us. He was really great at lyrics and I was really good at music and arranging. I learnt alongside that, from the start, how to produce. I got into the studio side of things. I watched like a hawk for the first few years. I watched what other people did whenever we were in the studio in the same way as when you were asking how I did music: ask them questions, 'What are you doing?' If I was in a position where I could ask the engineers what was going on I would do. I'd just quietly watch if it was a big producer. We've got a remix of the single 'London Calling' coming out for International Record Day that Bill Price did. I overlooked it. There's a very interesting bit on it where Joe says before the song starts, *Tonight's news will be read by Barry Baker.* He was one of our roadies and that's never been heard. It was on the original tapes. When they were playing the two-inch tapes back there was a quarter of an inch that wasn't on the playing head; all that music you weren't hearing.

I recently got a copy of *Rat Patrol From Fort Bragg* and for the first time *Combat Rock* made sense to me. I'd always loved side one but found side two strangely inaccessible.

The numbers on that album are like little films: 'Sean Flynn', for sure; 'Ghetto Defendant'; 'Car Jamming', too, and the film noir 'Death Is A Star'. They were us going, 'Fucking hell, this is all happening, amazing.' We were at the height of our success in a lot of ways. We were making it in America. It was mind-blowing. It was always about much more than just the end of the street. We weren't parochial in any way. Even from the start you can tell that. We came out of punk, but we became something of our own.

Would you remaster 'Combat Rock' to your original idea?

I don't know about that. It might be possible if they did a special, a commemorative edition.

Do you remember writing 'Beautiful People Are Ugly Too'?

Not so much: *you thought you were the hero of The Fulham Connection II* . . . the other one is 'Idle In Kangaroo Court', but generally known as 'Kill Time'.

With Joe's great line *the B-line C-line A-line free-line hard-line best-line left-line fine-line breaker.*

Yeah, the story of that is another little film. This is the tramp on the bench watching the world go by in Red Lion Square in the West End. He's watching all the people and he sees this beautiful girl walk past: *perhaps I'll flee my bench to chase her*, and he's a tramp sitting on a bench singing the song. I love that. We had a lot of songs like that: little stories, little films. 'Something About England' is like that too, you know, with the conversation between the old tramp and the young, hip guy. Lovely little stories.

When Joe gave you a set of lyrics, did the melody suggest itself from the words?

A lot of the time the tune was already there. I'd look at the lyrics and the tune would come out like a little bouncing ball. I'd look at it . . . (*Hums classic circus melody*) . . . it would come just like that. It was already there. It's what I'm saying. It was there anyway! It's there! (*Sings theme to 'Rawhide'*) *just rope, and roll and brand 'em*. I'd just read it. I'd just read it. Honestly. People don't know if that's possible. There was nothing contrived in anything we ever did, not in terms of the purity of the songwriting. It might have been contrived in terms of the ideology behind it and the way it presented, but nothing at that stage. It was like a mystic art. It's like alchemy. Its own chemistry. That's it. It's all there in the people, each one singing the song individually. So we sing the song in the guitar, in the bass, in the drums and the singing.

With very few and similar chords you've always been able to harness a vast amount of differing melody.

Yeah . . . that definitely comes from the shows, the musicals, the things that we watch all the time on the telly and at Christmas and stuff. It's all about the tune. We were infused with rock 'n' roll bands and the Sixties explosion and this musical sensibility. I'm just a kid from the flats. It's not like I'm from the Royal Academy of Music.

Were you ever blocked by familiar chord movements and changes?

Sometimes I'd try and . . . that's not good enough, is it, because it's just the same? There's a natural law to it somehow. I try other stuff and it's not right because the natural tune is already there telling you what the natural tune is. You can go against it but it's not going to be any good because you have to go with the natural tune. I don't know how other people work but I'm just . . . I don't know . . . I'm just trying to receive . . . get in touch with all the stuff that's going on out there in some way, or let it come to me so that other people can enjoy. It's like an entertainer. You've got to have a tune otherwise you're going to bore everybody. It must be about something. That's really important. It can't be about nothing. That's the difference between things . . . unless you're Seinfeld, in which case you can be about nothing, but that's the content of it.

How complete were your and Joe's ideas before you took them to the band?

Sometimes I had a little tape recorder . . . for instance, 'Complete Control' was pretty much all done. 'London Calling' we had the thing about the lyrics, but also in the music it was a bit more chunky before and I made it smooth, somehow. It was the same chords but the way I did it, I made it so it was a matter of . . . all you had to do was change a little finger for the verses. I didn't have to do anything, it was already there. They were mostly complete, I think. Complete in terms of the idea, anyway. It wasn't like we had to come back . . . sometimes there'd be another bit that usually vanished: the other bit, 'What's that bit doing there?' There's a few examples of that that haven't come out yet. I don't expect they ever will. It was hacking: 'How we gonna . . . we've got to fit this bit in there?' I saw it as tailoring. Joe saw it too like that. Later on we got a little bit more experimental. We stretched out a little bit and then obviously we had to cut it down. It was like the two ideas of 'Casbah': Bernie (*Rhodes*) said, 'Why does everything have to be a raga?' You know, a really long . . . and at the same time, while our manager was saying we need to shorten everything, the ayatollah was saying, 'I don't like rock 'n' roll.' Topper went into the studio; it was amazing. He put the three things down: the piano, the bass and the drums. I did the chorus tune, *Shareef don't like it*, then Joe did the lyrics, but Topper was the main guy.

Was Bernie an influence on your lyric writing?

He told us, write what you know about, and that changed everything, in a way, for us. Up until then it was all a bit . . . Joe was a lot further on, having been in a band that was quite well known, whereas Paul and I were just like kids. We were like, 'Wow, Joe.' That's how we got him, because we thought he was the best guy out there and we were looking for a singer. The Sex Pistols were supporting The 101'ers at the Nashville Rooms and that's where we first met. They were like a squat band at the end of pub rock. He could see the new thing coming and it was to his great credit that he threw everything in for us unknowns, but we did look good!

It is incredible when you hear The 101'ers' 'Keys To Your Heart' that Joe left the band behind to join you and Paul.

Yeah, amazing, but he took that forward. You know that bit in the middle of 'Keys To Your Heart' when he talks? He took that into our stuff. There's loads of live performances where he stretches out and talks and I'm playing mad shit as well. It was really free, like the Grateful Dead or something, believe it or not, more than the Angelic Upstarts; much closer to that in terms of being organic. We were part of the counterculture. It was as important as punk. Punk was the end of the Seventies and that was a very important thing and changed everything, but before then it was a question of the counterculture. After punk everything was different. It only worked in the UK because we were a small island. It didn't really work in America until much later with groups like Green Day and Rancid. That was like their punk. The equivalent music of the streets for me of punk in America was hip hop. We made the global connection between that, which we all see now because we all see what's going on in the world like we couldn't see it before. So we could see a revolution and see oppression. The real revolution is the Internet now. There wasn't going to be another Sex Pistols. The real revolution is being able to see what's going on the other side of the world and being connected and maybe make a difference to that.

That influence and progression in your writing can be heard in songs like 'The Magnificent Seven' or 'Radio Clash'. Was the writing process that generated those ideas different?

Not really, we were still affected in the same way. We were really interested in everything that was going on. We loved the movies. We loved all the music that had come before: the jukebox stuff. We loved the vibe of places, foreign cities. What a great life. It was a lifestyle choice. It was an overall thing. Songwriting's in there, yeah sure, but we made this life decision, a commitment to the life.

Chaz Jankel talked about the intimate scenario of writing with Ian Dury in that they found their whole lives caught up in each other's.

Yeah, you do. We were so close. When you're younger you can afford to be like that. You have no other stuff and as you get older you get families, which is lovely but it changes things somewhat. I don't know if you can have that later, but you have a much better understanding of what it is. It's like the good football managers: they have an encyclopaedic brain of everything, or like Mike

Tyson when he was young studied every fight that had ever come before him. Like that, I studied every group of that period right up until I joined the line.

Would you study the structures of songs?

Not consciously, but it was imbibed in me. I did play along with people's records that I liked. That's how I learnt. After the failed auditions I went back to my bedroom in my nan's flat and spent a year playing all the records and then I came out again and I could play. I couldn't really play before. I could play a bit, because I started to make up my own little ditties that set me on my way. That was just there. That's like a blessing of talent, whatever that is. I had an artistic leaning. I went to art school to meet other musicians because all the people I admired had been and that's how I thought you joined a band . . .

Ray Davies, Pete Townshend . . .

. . . yeah, and John Lennon, but I'd missed that by about half a generation.

Can you describe how a session with Joe would start? You would have known about John Lennon and Paul McCartney sitting opposite each other with guitars.

We did that. When I said about the typewriter and the guitar across the table like this in this place in Lancaster Road where we used to write then, that was three-quarters of the way through everything. He'd give me the lyrics, I'd knock out the tune and the next thing you know Bob's your uncle and that was it.

Did you have a tape recorder to capture your ideas?

Not there, I had a tape recorder at home. There's tapes; amalgams of bits and pieces. Later on I had a studio in the basement of the place I was living when I started doing B.A.D.. 'The Bottom Line' was originally called 'Trans Cash Free Play One' and that was a Joe lyric, but he didn't like it. It was about credit cards. It was looking into the future. It was very prophetic. He was the prophet! A couple of years later he got into the stuff that I was into a couple of years before. Later on he was bloody doing it!

How did you come to write *No. 10 Upping Street* together?

Don Letts met Joe in Wardour Street when we were recording round the corner at St Anne's Court. He said, 'Why don't you come round to the studio?' So he came round and he didn't bloody leave. He built himself a little hut under the piano in the studio; the piano hut.

Like the spliff bunker?

The spliff bunker was different. He'd build himself a bunker out of flight cases and he'd be in there scribbling away like mad while we were recording.

That's why he was so prolific. We'd go in there for a smoke. It would be him and the lighting guy usually. He'd be in there and he'd be adjusting the arc lights, sitting there like Alec Guinness.

Can you explain the difference between Joe's and Don's lyrics?

It's completely different because that same thing applies: it's the culmination of your experiences which you are expressing. Obviously I wouldn't work with somebody if I didn't have empathy with their views. It just comes from up there and goes out straight. And that's it.

When you wrote for Ellen Foley's album, *Spirit Of St Louis* . . .

. . . Joe and I wrote half a dozen specifically for that, some of our nicest stuff, in fact: 'The Death Of The Psychoanalyst Of Salvador Dali', 'Torchlight', 'M.P.H.'. There was some good stuff there. We liked Abba. We had the same promoter in Sweden. Nobody knows that. It was a real secret. We tried to do Abba-esque songs with Ellen. Nobody ever asks Ellen to be on a documentary on us. She was a really good singer. We were doing that and *Sandinista!* and playing on Pearl Harbour's album. All those records were being recorded at the same time by us and our group of friends. It was one of our most prolific albums.

The Clash had a tight relationship with the audience . . .

. . . we were the first group to break down that barrier . . .

. . . would you and Joe write considering the audience . . . ?

No, but we *were* the audience. We were the fans. I was a kid following Mott the Hoople round and they showed me what life could be like. I followed that and did my part and carried on and so did Joe. Not Mott the Hoople, but all his influences. We were beautiful in terms of . . . we all brought something different to it—all four of us.

Viv Albertine says in *The Rise and Fall of The Clash* that there was an 'artistic conflict between Mick and Joe'. Do you recognize what she means?

Yes, I do. If it's one force it's only going to go one way, but we had the possibility of reason . . . we reasoned with each other.

Do you remember writing 'Train In Vain'?

Yeah, I do. We recorded it so late the artwork for *London Calling* had already gone in. It was a personal situation that started it. When we were recording it at Wessex Studios . . . it wasn't about Chrissie Hynde but she was upstairs and there was a window from the pool room where she could look in. I was singing it to Chrissie. It was like an R&B song. We couldn't believe how popular it became, especially in America. That broke us in there. They thought it was a regular R&B song, then they found out it was The Clash. The same goes for 'Magnificent Seven'. When it first came out in the States, WBLS, one of the hip stations, got hold of it and they put Clint Eastwood and Bugs Bunny on top of it and that was the instrumental, bongo mix. It was a wildfire hit all over New York! Everybody was playing this tune and they didn't find out till too late it was this bunch of punks from England. It was so great. A lot of our stuff was by luck. Our first songwriting award was from the American Songwriting Association, signed by Hal David.

Can you tell me how 'Straight To Hell' came about?

I don't know how exactly 'Straight To Hell' came about. The music was interesting because I'm playing a very early Roland synth guitar that usually only produced whale noises. I managed to struggle with it enough that I was getting stringy sounds out of it. A lot of the stuff on *Combat Rock* or *Rat Patrol* for sure sounds like real instruments, but it's guitar. They couldn't persuade me to play proper guitar by that time.

Can you write songs on piano?

Occasionally, possibly. I'm very limited. It's very funny, if you look on the *London Calling* credits it says M. JONES—PIANO, J. STRUMMER—PIANNER. It was quite funny!

Did you play the piano on 'The Card Cheat'?

Yeah, double.

Did you write it on piano?

Not really. It was one of those songs that Joe gave the once-over to in terms of the lyrics. I was infatuated with Phil Spector and so we recorded everything twice along those lines. Our producer Guy Stevens, his great claim was, 'There's only two Phil Spectors in the world and I'm (*Guy's*) one of them.'

My six-year-old daughter Lottie said, 'Please ask the man did he stay or did he go?'

That's very interesting that she should ask that, and I don't know if I've got a straight answer for you. Any time there's a moment of indecision they play 'Should I Stay Or Should Or I Go': if anybody's about to get the sack in football management or government. It's the great song of indecision.

Did you write the song as the listener hears it, with the dead stops and then the double-time chorus?

I was trying to write . . . that is another R&B song . . . maybe there was an idea behind it to write another hit, maybe, I'm not sure. It's possible. It was always pretty much like that: one tempo and then another tempo on the chorus. It's a really simple song. It's an attempt to write a simple song. They say the hardest songs to write are the simple ones, so I thought, I'm going to try and write a simple song! The great thing about The Clash is they turned you on to stuff. I didn't know what Sandinista was before. It's a real thing. Just the way we shared the information we found, our knowledge. It was always about interest in everything but from a humane aspect. Joe taught me that. It's got to have a heart, like the tin man in *The Wizard of Oz*.

When you got together with Joe in 2001 before the release of *Global A Go-Go* . . .

. . . I didn't work on that. We did some songs but he didn't record them with the band. The plan was, Joe would be recording in the daytime with the Mescaleros and I would come in at midnight and work all through the night. You had to drag the gimp in when everyone's gone, then I'd work all night like in a Hammer horror film, then the gimp would go back and then they'd get the real band back in and it would be all fine. If I worked with them they'd be scared I would take over. In the end it didn't work out like that, but I was really quite annoyed. Later on we met at the Proud Gallery; they were doing a Bob Gruen exhibition just after 9/11. Joe was tired and emotional on that night, and I went, 'What happened to the bloody songs?' And he went like this (*Mick whispers in my ear*): 'They're for the next Clash album.' He knew they were too good.

Don Letts said the rule of B.A.D. was, a song had to be there if you took away all the samples.

Yes, if you could play it acoustically and it had still got a good tune . . . we wrote along to beats.

Was 'E = MC²' written that way?

Not sure about that one. We had a studio downstairs in my basement and we used to all meet there. We'd record. B.A.D. recorded so much stuff that never got released.

I heard one the other day: 'Dog In The Satellite'.

That's a Joe one. After *No. 10 Upping Street* we wrote a batch of songs. It's one of the most beautiful songs ever. It's incredible. It mentions Miss Piggy in it. What other song does that?!

How did 'Bankrobber' come about?

'Bankrobber' is an interesting one. I think my dad was a bankrobber's assistant. There was talk of him driving getaway cars. He was a cab driver but he drove for other people. Joe wrote the words. The songs are like folk songs. They've become like traditional songs. A lot of it was based on truth. We made it so everybody could relate to it. It wasn't exactly the truth, for instance in 'Lost In The Supermarket' I didn't have *a hedge in the suburb*. I lived in a council flat. A lot of the time it got mythologized. It's like the sliver of your boiled sweet: in the end that's all that's left. People take things by the myth rather than the truth of it. If it wasn't from personal experience it wouldn't be so believable. Let's say that.

The truth . . .
    . . . is only known by guttersnipes! (*Laughs.*) End of interview.

PAUL WELLER

On 26 November 1982, The Jam released their eighteenth and final single, 'Beat Surrender'. On the record's gatefold cover songwriting muse Gill Price waved a white flag. To a stirring rhythm and soulful vocal, the opening verse announced: *All the things that I care about are packed into one punch*. It served as Paul Weller's fond farewell to the army of dedicated fans who had followed the trio through five years of energy-fuelled guitar pop, lyrics of biting social comment and intense, passionate delivery: *I am yours and will always be beholden to the beat surrender*. Paul Weller remains a songwriter of prolific output. His productivity spans more than four decades, with over seventy singles and twenty albums released. In 2006, *British Hit Singles and Albums* printed a list of the most successful British singer-songwriters in pop history. Paul Weller was listed seventh behind Lennon and McCartney, the Bee Gees, Elton John, Jagger and Richards, David Bowie, and George Michael. The position is a fitting tribute to a songwriter of consistent quality and consummate work ethic.

Weller is governed by a deep-rooted devotion to good musical taste. It is a self-imposed discipline and one that is intensely attractive to his fans. The dedication it inspires can be witnessed at any of his concerts, where legions of fans dressed in neat button-downs and polished loafers pay homage to a tireless firebrand. Jam lyrics spoke directly to teenage anxieties. They defined feelings and attitudes that legitimized disaffection with society and the growing pains of dead-end routines and broken relationships. Weller showed a rare ability to turn familiar surroundings into accessible verse and melodic harmony. A blossoming love affair in 'Wasteland' poetically sets two lovers *probably* holding hands against a desolate backdrop of despair, hopelessness and discarded household objects: *amongst the shit, the dirty linen, the holy Coca-Cola tins*. 'That's Entertainment!', conceived after an evening down the pub, displayed the writer's sharpened economy of wordplay. Its two-chord acoustic verses offer photographic images of urban English life—*a screaming siren . . . paint-splattered walls . . . smelling stale perfume*—backed up with atmospheric detail: *an amateur band rehearse in a nearby yard*. Weller's observations carry an understanding of class and backyard conversations. The voice of his writing is that of his speech, and it is the voice of conviction.

Shortly after the third of four number-one singles and at the height of the band's success, Weller announced that he intended to dissolve The Jam in order to preserve its legacy. This decision, shocking at the time, can be viewed in hindsight as both confident and shrewd, with Weller taking The Jam's future into his own hands. When his albums are completed, his technique is to rip up or burn his lyrical notes in order to free himself of past ideas. He belongs to an era when the music industry demanded that artists make a record each year. It was a pressure, he claims, that 'helped to refine your craft'. Yet Weller treads his own paths in the search for a great new song.

A commitment to finding the right platform for new ideas would lead him to form The Style Council in 1983. Built around the nucleus of Weller, and Hammond organ player Mick Talbot, their new musical vision would expand on a guitar, drum and bass format and allow the influences of jazz, soul and French chanson to flourish. With The Style Council Weller was to enjoy a handful of top-twenty hit singles. The minor to major-seventh exchanges of 'My Ever Changing Moods' blended a ripening emotive delivery with lyrics of touching honesty: *Daylight turns to moonlight and I'm at my best . . . but I'm caught up in a whirlwind and my ever changing moods*. In 1985, *Our Favourite Shop* offered a damning indictment of Margaret Thatcher's premiership. Against the prevailing climate of slick pop production and middle-class prosperity, Weller's writing documented the perceived betrayal of the working class by its government and a society driven by greed and materialism. As a 20-year-old he had told *Melody Maker*, 'The more bitter you are the easier it is to write.' Seven years later *Our Favourite Shop* contained songs of compassion for the unemployed, solidarity with the plight of striking miners and rallying calls to socialism and unity. In the same year, having contributed to Band Aid's 'Do They Know It's Christmas?', The Style Council performed at Live Aid and Weller accepted joint presidency of the United Nation's International Year of Youth. Furthering his political associations, he co-founded Red Wedge with Billy Bragg. Through a series of UK tours first-time voters were targeted in an effort to deny the Conservative government a third term in office. In 'Walls Come Tumbling Down' the message was clear: *You don't have to take this crap / You don't have to sit back and Relax*. Weller's steadfast convictions combined with an injection of 'in-crowd' humour and new technological studio possibilities. The writer's progressive views led to The Style Council's fifth studio album, *Modernism: A New Decade*, being rejected by Polydor Records in 1989.

Its music embraced the emergence of house as a dominant musical force, but it left Weller without a record deal for the first time in twelve years.

John William Weller was born 25 May 1958 in Woking, Surrey, into a working-class household. Within weeks of his birth his mother Anne reassessed her choice of names and unofficially renamed her son Paul. As he grew up, Paul developed a love for the music of The Beatles. When he was twelve he was given a Christmas present of a guitar, which soon became the focus of the boy's obsessive attention. He could be found under the stairs, bashing out his first attempts at writing songs on the family's battered piano. In 1972, rejecting the discipline of academic life, he formed The Jam together with school friend Steve Brookes. The working men's clubs of Woking and Surrey provided the venues for the band to refine their crafted mix of R&B covers and original material. In the early months of 1977, the new line-up of Rick Buckler (drums), Bruce Foxton (bass / vocals), and Weller (guitar / vocals) eventually signed to Polydor. Their debut single was built round an explosive riff and a phrase that its proud 18-year-old author had stamped onto a badge: *In the city there's a thousand things I want to say to you*. The record reached the top forty, placing The Jam alongside groups such as The Clash and the Sex Pistols. Steve Jones pilfered the descending riff of 'In The City' for the introduction of the Pistols' fourth single, 'Holidays In The Sun'. Weller had in turn cribbed the title from the B-side of The Who's 1966 single, 'I'm A Boy'. The clothing and style of Pete Townshend's band held great sway with The Jam as they sidestepped the fashions of the King's Road and went for a sharp-suited look—an image mocked by Joe Strummer in '(White Man) In Hammersmith Palais'. Weller admired the political rhetoric of The Clash's frontman and was greatly influenced by his call to 'write with meaning'. He focused The Jam on offering a modernist interpretation of the past.

In 1978, *All Mod Cons*, The Jam's third album, combined acutely honed social observation with melodies of enduring quality. The inclusion of 'David Watts' was a telling link to the influence of Ray Davies on Weller's writing, shown in the perceptive detail of 'Down In The Tube Station At Midnight'. What started as a continuous prose outpouring was then refined into a three-minute drama. The narrator recounts a violent attack taking place on the London Underground as the victim uses all his senses to take stock of his final moments: *they smelled of pubs and Wormwood Scrubs and too many right wing meetings*. The four-chord ascension of G, B minor, C and D major skilfully balances the details of the fallen man's last moments, from '*Jesus Saves*' graffiti to British Rail posters advertising *a cheap holiday*. Weller recalls this songwriting breakthrough as a reflection both of his own personality and of his love of mod culture. An affinity with mod fashions, inherent look and sound has informed his entire career. When in the mid-Nineties Weller's fervent voice for disaffected youth was championed by the likes of Oasis and Blur, the media awarded him the telling title of 'The Modfather'. Weller had become a significant figure in the British songwriting tradition

The re-emergence of Paul Weller as a solo artist began slowly. 'Into Tomorrow' was delivered *into the mists of time and space* after a two-year struggle to reawaken his writing muse and self-belief. He was composing at home from 'self-imposed exile' on an Ovation guitar, creating songs from 'top to bottom'. He had bought the instrument in 1980 and has written the majority of his songs on it since. As Weller's confidence grew a wave of critical re-evaluation and public affection greeted his new releases. 1995's top-ten hit 'The Changingman' had been inspired by a small doll so named by his daughter. Its opening doubt, *Is happiness real, or am I so jaded?* spoke of the writer's need to question and shake up the status quo, and the song's success consigned his wilderness years to a distant memory. In a twenty-year solo career Weller has continued to explore unfamiliar territory. His determination to pursue a diversity of genres has produced a trail of critically acclaimed albums throughout the Nineties and 2000s. Weller's hardcore following has long helped sustain his presence at the top end of the charts. Although The Jam was the start of his journey, it was by no means the end point. In 2010, his abrasiveness was still compelling: *get ya face out the Facebook and turn off your phone . . . we're gonna wake up the nation.* 'Green', the opening track from 2012's *Sonik Kicks*, was approached as a sound-poem and many of the album's lyrics were initiated in automatic writing sessions before being shaped by an editing process. This approach allowed for random juxtapositions on the lyric sheet; although connected to a broader overall sense, lines carried individual meaning. In his fifties, Weller has drastically re-evaluated his songwriting methods and has clearly developed through collaboration. His work shows a range of influences, from Lou Reed's electronic instrumental composition *Metal Machine Music* to David Bowie's Seventies explorations, while 'Song For Alice' from *22 Dreams* is a direct tribute to the late Alice Coltrane, much admired by Weller. Indeed, the songwriter has never disguised his pilfering from the past. The Jam's second number one 'Start' famously utilized the bass riff from The Beatles' 'Taxman'; 'Boy About Town' subtly borrowed from the commercially unsuccessful Kinks wonder 'Sitting In The Midday Sun', whilst the melodic appropriation of Eddie Floyd's 'Big Bird' provided a rousing chorus to 1993's summer hit 'Sunflower'.

His popularity in recent years has been both an acknowledgement of Weller's past successes and a celebration of his ability to adapt to a changing musical environment. In 2008, prime minister David Cameron declared on Radio 4 that his favourite song was 'The Eton Rifles', adding, 'Inevitably, I was one, in the corps. It meant a lot, some of those early Jam albums we used to listen to. I don't see why the Left should be the only ones allowed to listen to protest songs.' Weller responded, 'Which part of it doesn't he get?' Written in

Selsey Bill in his family's holiday caravan, the 1979 top-five hit showed Weller's intense pride in his class roots and background. The song was inspired by a story of Eton College boys jeering at unemployed protestors marching through Slough on a Right To Work demonstration: *What chance have you got against a tie and a crest? . . . we were no match for their untamed wit.*

Weller has consistently explored themes of spirituality, romance, home and escapism. He shuns self-indulgence, and whilst songs may start with personal reflection, they invariably progress to wider issues. 'Porcelain Gods' addressed fame and paranoia with emotional honesty: *how disappointed I was to turn out after all—just a porcelain god—that shatters when it falls.* The relationship between artist and audience plays an important role in his music. As a young man, Weller was always quick to dismiss the heroic status that fans and commentators were eager to bestow upon him. He was just a kid off the street, and in his maturer years is still sharply alert to the fickle nature of fame and celebrity, as expressed in 'Woodcutter's Son': *there's a silence when I enter and a murmur when I leave / I can see their jealous faces / I can feel the ice they breathe.* The album on which it appeared in 1995, *Stanley Road*, became Weller's first solo number-one album and is cited by its creator as the peak of his writing capabilities. Beautifully dressed by pop artist Peter Blake, it featured such songs as 'You Do Something To Me', 'Broken Stones' and 'Wings Of Speed', all demonstrating a rich vein of songwriting maturity.

Weller has never been short of musical honours. Alongside three Best Male Solo Artist awards in 1995, 1996 and 2009, in 2006 he accepted a further Brit Award for Outstanding Contribution to Music. Pointedly, in the same year he declined a CBE in the Queen's Birthday Honours list. By the time Paul and I chatted in an outside plot of his studio Black Barn in the parish of Ripley, *22 Dreams* had become his fifth solo number-one album and he was working on the early stages of its successor, *Wake Up The Nation*. Once dubbed 'spokesman for a generation', Paul Weller had passed his fiftieth year and only two days earlier had buried his father and enigmatic manager John Weller. Discussion of The Kinks kick-started the conversation before Paul quietly began to address the uncomfortable process of analysing songwriting.

In 'Science' you sing *grab a piece in the air / try an' make it sing.* Is that a way of describing how melody is found?

Yeah, melody and words, writing in general. A lot of time that's what writing is: picking up what's floating in the air. Generally speaking it's more luck than judgement, I think. You seize on something and just capture it or it comes to you: some words, a couplet, a title, a theme and then a melody. People always ask me how I write: no idea, it's just something that's in me. It seems the most difficult, insurmountable thing to do until you're doing it and then it seems so natural, just like walking or breathing.

Does melody come complete?

Fragments come to me and then after, once I've got the idea, I will run with it and work it and possibly see where the melody should go to. Initially it's something that just happens like that. I think writing's a bit of a waiting game: you have to wait for the inspiration. I'll sit down some days and not necessarily try to write but absentmindedly play guitar or piano and maybe out of that something will come to me. Intuition, I don't know what to call it.

How do you know when it's time to write?

Sometimes I get a feeling, an inkling of some kind, a physical sensation that you think, 'I'm going to write,' but I can't say it happens every day or every week. I couldn't say why that should be or what causes it. They're great, those times, because you know you're going to come away with something when you sit down. You might even get two or three things out of that feeling. It's the same with lyrics: some days or nights I'll just sit down and I'll fucking write away and get two, three or four pieces, or just a verse or a couplet which I'll use as a cornerstone for something else and work on at a later date or improve upon. It's almost like it's unconscious, because you don't have to think too much and it's flowing through you and onto the page. They're the really great, inspirational moments. I write some songs by just making stupid sounds playing along to some chords and waiting for words to form.

When you're in that consciousness, do you think of song structures?

No, because it's more like a prose thing and then sometimes you might have to go back and edit those words to make them fit rhythmically into a musical piece. Often they read more like a poem or a prose poem.

Would 'God' be an example of that?

Yeah, that was never intended as a sung lyric but it worked in that instance. I'm working over the next two days on a poem I wrote called 'Trees' about people getting older. It's more like a prose poem and I'm sure when we come to do the music for it I'll have to edit some of the words to make it rhythmically fit.

Do you ever hear a song before you begin to write it?

Sometimes, yeah, but not in its entirety: a chorus, the start of a verse, a riff, a fragment of something. I might even have it in my head and sing it for days or weeks and then I'll start writing or working on it. It's always hard to talk about songwriting because it's always the same but it's always different. There have been those tunes I've sat down and written top to bottom with a guitar, melody and the words all at the same time, but probably more times I've just got bits and pieces. I'm forever writing bits down on a scrap of paper, whatever it might be, and putting them in my pocket or in a bag and keeping them until I feel I'm ready to work on it, but there's obviously something there, even a fragment, for me to want to hang on to it. So I would say the majority of my songs are written over a length of time.

Do you also carry melody around in the same way before words are written?

Yeah, I have no way of writing it down. I'll store it in my head until I have time to come down and record it. I'm lucky enough to have my own studio so I can demo, obviously, but I don't have anything at home I can record on.

Really, not even a simple tape recorder?

No, nothing at all; if it's good enough it'll always come back to me. It might be buzzing round for days or weeks and when I can be bothered to I'll sit down with a guitar and find the chords to go with the melody in my head—even that I don't do these days very much. I think you get lazier the older you get, in those terms anyway. The days of waking up out of my sleep and thinking, 'I've got to get up and write this down,' I can't be arsed. I just think, 'I'll wait till the morning and it'll come back to me,' or it won't, whatever it may be. I haven't got lazy in terms of wanting to write the best thing I can possibly do. I still don't take it for granted. I used to have a real thing when I was younger; if I didn't write for weeks or months it would just fucking freak me out. I'd just be, 'Right, it's all over. I'm washed up.' Whereas these days, I've lived long enough to know it just comes in cycles and you go through a period of time when you're not creative and you don't write, and other times when you can't stop it pouring out of you. It will always come round again if you're patient and care enough about it.

When did the ability to wait between songs change for you?

Probably only in the last six or seven years. If I go through two or three years without writing, which I have done recently, it doesn't upset me, doesn't make me think it's all over or I've dried up. It's just I know it's not my time at that moment.

Before, would you have forced it?

Yeah, I'd be pulling my hair out thinking, 'What am I going to do?' That's just a lesson you learn in life. You don't ever really stop being creative if you're a creative person, the process slows down. When you're younger you have all these different experiences all the time; everything is a new sensation. You still have those things but they just get slower, that's all.

Is it easier to write when you're younger because the book is open as such: you're laying down your ideas for the first time?

Yeah, it is easier because it's all brand new and fresh; even if it's things that have gone before musically, they are still new to you. It's like the whole thing with a lot of young people being into Eighties music now, it seems really odd to me. I remember it first time round and it was fucking rubbish but for them it's brand new. You have the sense you're writing in this weird void, there's a sense of innocence because there's no rules and parameters of what you should or shouldn't write; it's all open to you. It's easy to lose that but I don't think I have done, to be honest. I know that sounds a bit arrogant.

When you're finding chords for a new song are you reminded of previously trodden ground?

Yeah, but it's inevitable when you've written so many songs; you can't avoid it, really. You're always looking to do something different, you've just got to shake it up every now and again. At the moment we're working on a new album (*Wake Up The Nation*) which is a totally different way of writing for me because I haven't written the music as such. Simon Dine who's producing the record has been coming up with backing tracks and I've been writing in the studio on the spot. So for instance he'll give me a CD of ten ideas and I'll play it for a few weeks without writing anything down and just take it all in. Then I'll come in here and work on it spontaneously; sing over the top of the backing track, maybe changing some of the chords and music. On previous albums I'd normally come to the table with pretty much finished songs: a verse, a bridge, a chorus, 'We'll go to the solo here,' the middle eight or whatever it may be.

Similar to what Brendan Lynch would have done on 'The Changingman', in that case borrowing from ELO's '10538 Overture'.

That was all down to Brendan. I told them. 'If we get sued, man, it's all down to him. We'll take it out of his fucking royalties.'

'Down In The Tube Station At Midnight' revealed your sophistication and depth as a songwriter. Can you describe the evolution of that song and your changing ability to hone in on the small and the particular?

That started as a long prose-poem thing, like a short story in a way. It came from my insecurity and paranoia at being in London. I didn't have any music for it. I was in two minds whether to do it. I was coaxed and talked into it by Vic Smith, our producer at the time. He was saying, 'This is really good, you should try and set it to music.' The attention to the details is part of the person I am anyway, but it's also bound up in the mod ethos which is predominantly all about attention to detail. We were talking about English songwriters: it's picking up on the mundane, the everyday things and putting them into a different setting, the very, very ordinary feelings, emotions or details that, once in a song, you hear them in a different way. Without sounding too poncey or pretentious I was thinking about pop artists as well, where they took the everyday objects and made them into art. I don't think it's that dissimilar.

What was the appeal in chronicling the mundane?

It's a very English thing, the way we all like to moan about the weather or we like a cup of tea or a particular fucking biscuit and all that nonsense, but it's us. It's our identity, isn't it?

'Saturday Kids' and 'That's Entertainment!' are songs that touch people's experiences very deeply but with an apparent simplicity. Was that difficult to achieve?

It was easy for me because that's just who I was. I was a very simple person; there isn't any great intellect behind it. It was the simplicity that people connected with: a 20-year-old kid or young man writing how I saw and felt it and connecting with other 20-year-old young people. I didn't have to sit down and deliberate too much on it, put it that way.

'22 Dreams' and 'Wings of Speed' both start with the hook line, potentially disabling the role of the chorus. Is that melodically a greater challenge?

It's a different form of song because you don't get the build-up of the bridge into the chorus, the whole song's a chorus, or a verse, depending upon which way you look at it. I just follow my nose and take it where the music's taking me. If the song's got an actual, definite chorus you feel it building up, it's an intuitive thing; it's never anything I think about too much. I'll think about musical changes, like if I change to a minor chord there it will have a certain dramatic effect, or a major chord here will feel like a lift.

As in 'A Town Called Malice', which for such an upbeat song drops to a minor chord on the verse after the introduction. The flirtation between the major and minor chords is very effective.

It is effective, yeah. That's just born out of me growing up on The Beatles and Motown, because they use all those kind of mechanisms. It's part of your tools of the trade.

You've said in the past about the importance of the *Beatles Songbook*: how much was it plundered for ideas?

Oh yeah, fucking as much as we could, really. Even now, after all these years, there's still certain chord changes I'll use which directly come from the Fabs. If a song's in a major chord and then all of a sudden it will be in the same key but drop to a minor change, that's really dramatic and that all comes from the Beatles book.

Would you consult the book if you were stuck on an idea now?

I don't need to now because it's so much a part of me, so much inside of me, and forty-plus years later I'm still listening to The Beatles. It's only when talking to you like this that I think, that's come from that. Playing D minor seventh to G minor seventh, the chords for 'Things We Said Today', is such a dramatic great change: dead simple, but it's got such a great sound to it. Fuck knows how many times I've used those chords and they still sound great. You can still get something out of them.

Reading your lyrics is often like opening a diary: 'My Ever Changing Moods', 'I Should Have Been There To Inspire You', 'Time Passes', 'Love-less', 'Invisible'; there's great solitary introspection and emotional vulnerability. Do you regard songwriting as a confession box?

Not entirely. There's definitely that cathartic thing about writing like you were talking about Billy (*Bragg*) before. Sometimes there are things you really want to say or get off your chest that you can't necessarily articulate in everyday life, but you can in songwriting. Some of my songs are definitely biographical, but probably a very small percentage of them, to be honest. Even if they start off with a thread of it I might still run with it or take it somewhere else. I don't live an interesting enough life to write about it all the time. I don't really care about those records that just talk about themselves, that whole singer-songwriter thing from the Seventies: fucking hell, give it a break, fucking cheer up, d'you know what I mean? You've got to be careful with that sort of thing. It's important to be honest and reflect how you feel but it's also important to try and include the people that listen to your record, to make it open enough for them to go, 'Fuck me, I felt that as well; I'm going through this,' or, 'I felt that last year,' otherwise you're just writing for yourself. You might as well just fucking stay at home and do it. If you think you've written a great song you want to communicate it to other people; you play it to your friends first and try and turn them on, and then an audience. That why we're all doing it; that's why I'm doing it.

Many of your songs, like 'Brand New Start' or 'It Just Came To Pieces In My Hand' suggest an emotional fragility, a fallibility. How do you gain your own confidence to write?

(*Pause.*) Well, again, a lot of those things you wouldn't say in everyday conversation; you'd maybe want to, but you can on a page. You're being honest and putting all these ideas down, but there's still a shield because you're doing it in the form of a song or on a record, or hiding behind a guitar or piano or whatever it may be. So in a way it's easier to be that bare because of the context. If I sat down with somebody and said, 'Fucking hell, last week . . .' and spilled my heart out, which I do sometimes, but you can't do it too many places or you wouldn't have any friends. You can do it on record and have loads of friends. It's amazing. It's a good job!

At what stage do you enjoy the process of writing?

Going back to what I said earlier, once you've really grabbed this thing: you've got the idea and think, 'OK, I know where this is going now.' I can sort of see it unfold in front of me: that's when I really enjoy it because it's creative and exciting. You get halfway through the song and there's another little twist; it's unlimited. The only limitation is what you put on yourself. If you keep an open mind you can go anywhere with it. I'm still in love with the challenge of trying to condense however grand the ideas might be into this three-and-a-half-minute pop song. It's challenging and something special when you pull it off. I'll always be in love with that. It's a product of me growing up in the Sixties. You only had that time to do your thing in; there's something fantastic in that. When you think of all the twists and changes in 'Good Vibrations' in just over three minutes—it's incredible. To fit all those grand ideas into this short amount of time. That's when I really get the buzz of writing and feel like I'm really getting somewhere. If I'm really excited about something I've just written I want to play it, even if it's down the phone to somebody or the first available person: 'Come an' hear this, come an' hear this.' It isn't just ego. It's me really wanting to communicate this thing I've managed to communicate with myself and want to push it to other people as well.

When did you first write a song perfectly suited to your voice?

'In The City' I thought suited my voice. It was a lot more crude and raw but that was because I was only eighteen. My voice has obviously changed over the years. In the last five years I feel really, really comfortable with it, much more than ever before. I don't really have to think too much any more, I just open my mouth and it happens. I seem to have more range, more strength and stronger tone. I've always liked it but I just really love singing now. I get something different from it now because I'm able to control it more.

Has that changed the melodies you write?

I don't think it's affected the writing, it's just I'm able to do the things in my head. I could hear them years ago but I could never get to them. It's funny when I hear some of The Style Council records; I really like the songs but some of the vocals make me cringe. I could sing it so much fucking better now. That's always easy to say with hindsight, isn't it?

Dedicated audiences come with an idea of what they expect of you; has that ever restricted your writing?

No, I know what you're talking about, but it hasn't. Even if at times it's dumbfounded my audience or they don't like it, that's just the way it is. I don't think you should ever be shackled or hemmed in by other people's expectation; that's the death of creativity. Sometimes the changes aren't good or particularly productive, but nevertheless they're the changes you have to go through to get to somewhere else. It's just part of the process if you want to continue doing it and improving. I was quite surprised by the reaction to *22 Dreams*— people seemed to really love that record, despite its indulgent sides. At the time I wasn't thinking whether people would like it; I was purely doing it for myself in a very, very selfish way. You can never tell, you could do the same record at another point in time and people would hate it. There's no real logic to it.

'Start' was a fantastic summation of the pop song and the artist–listener relationship: *If we communicate for two minutes only it will be enough / For knowing that someone in this world feels as desperate as me.* **Has the decline of the single affected your approach to songwriting?**

It hasn't personally, because I'll always be rooted in the music of the Sixties, that's the first thing that I heard. That will always be my benchmark of a good song; to be able to put it into this short space of time. The death of the single is a shame; it's potentially the death of another art form.

Can we talk about your political awakening in the Eighties? *Our Favourite Shop* **was lyrically a very direct, dogmatic and socially aware album: did that create a greater challenge to find melody?**

Yeah, it was, nearly all those songs I would have started with the lyrics first. 'Internationalists' definitely; 'Walls Come Tumbling Down' I'm not too sure. I was writing as a definite reaction to what was going on around me. It worked on *Our Favourite Shop* but there's other stuff where it definitely didn't work: too much emphasis on lyrics, and melody taking a back seat, which is never good. The great stuff is when both work at the same time: the melody's really strong but the words are special as well, saying something. *Confessions Of A Pop Group* which was a few years later, there were some great songs, but a few things was me trying to push a fucking square shape into a round hole.

What was your belief in lyrical communication at that time?

It was a political awakening for me, for someone who had no political background whatsoever. My parents were totally atheist and apolitical, that's putting it mildly. I never thought about politics and I've gone back to that. I've gone full circle. But the early Eighties, the rise of Thatcher and the breakdown of a lot of things like society and community, whether trade unions or local communities, the loss of individualism and a sense of having no control over our lives or say in our country or our future . . . It was born out of being aware for the first time and reading more—I never read any books at school—becoming educated and discovering politics and socialism. You couldn't fail to be moved or react when you saw those pitched battles with the miners and the cops, '83, '84 time. It was a reaction to all that was going on.

As opposed to being a commentator you were speaking directly to the listener.

Yeah, a certain revolutionary spirit, it was of the time. Things were much more extreme then; it wasn't this kind of blandness you've got in politics now where everyone seems the same. You were either for this thing or against it; there was no sitting on the fence. In some ways it was probably easier to write and react against something when it was that extreme. I'd find it really hard to write any political song these days because what's the difference between Tony Blair and David Cameron?—even their policies are the same. To write anything political now would just be me probably writing the same thing I fucking wrote twenty-five years ago. It'd be pretty depressing, like we haven't moved on at all.

By the time of 'Savages' in 2005 the inspiration behind the writing was often ambiguous.

It was written about a town in Russia (*Beslan, North Ossetia–Alania*) where these Muslim extremists had taken over a school and shot people and children indiscriminately. I just thought we couldn't get much lower as human beings really, whatever your fucking cause is or not. I wouldn't say it's any kind of political song really; it's just a reaction to a very specific thing. *As the children run to mothers, you put bullets in their backs.* It's about terrorism generally, and that includes Bush and Blair's warplanes dropping fucking bombs on Afghanistan and Iraq as well; terrorism on a global scale. I didn't intend it to be ambiguous.

Can you write in any environment?

Pretty much anywhere, really: on the road, at home, obviously. In The Jam I used to have a small flat in Pimlico and I would write in a small recess by the front door. I always carry a pen—not always paper—'cause you never know.

How does the use of drugs or alcohol influence your writing?

Alcohol certainly has a part to play in a lot of songwriting for me. I don't necessarily mean to be fucking arseholed, but that free-flowing thing is definitely instrumental after I've had a few drinks; but it's not exclusive to that. You're not really conscious of what you're doing; you're just writing it down as it comes to you. 'Porcelain Gods' was a drugs song; it's got that certain foreboding sense to it. Drugs or drink are not important enough issues to be incorporated in my work, but it manifests itself in some ways, certainly around *Stanley Road* time. At a certain level my mind just goes into a different sort of gear, a flowing free-form. When I've got too drunk and I've written, in the morning I can't decipher my writing. I know there are great lines in there but I just can't read it, so it's a bit of a fucker. I can make out the odd word that would be fucking great if only I could read it.

Why do you keep writing?

It's what I do in life. I never really question it. I just accept it's part of me and what I'm meant to do on this planet. I always have done and I guess I always will do. I never intended to be writing and playing music when I was fifty. When I was eighteen I would have been shocked and horrified, but then I wouldn't have expected to get to fifty anyway. Every time it's still a challenge. I'm not saying the records are always great but it's never a drag. Very few records have been a chore: maybe one or two where I've had to think, I've got to do this. I enjoy it more now than ever. Maybe that's not true, but there's less pressure to physically deliver a record. The only pressure is one that's inside me: that I still want to be the best, or the best I can be. I can't imagine a time when I wouldn't want to write. It's a catharsis of a kind. It's who I am.

When you said 'you're meant to do it', is there a greater thing that casts you as a songwriter?

You've got to be careful when you talk about this, it's like saying, 'I've been fucking chosen by God to write songs on the planet.' Whatever name you care to put to it, I just know I'm meant to do this. There's absolutely no reason why a little, very mediocre kid from Woking could still be writing songs that turn people on. I don't feel I've been specially chosen or blessed by the Big One or the Great Spirit. I don't even think about that, I don't go any further; I just know intuitively that's how it's supposed to be. I've still got the same interests, I've still got the right reasoning behind it all: I want to make music and communicate that to other people. After all these years that still shows in the music. I can't imagine that really changing. I'm not one to rest on my laurels. I've seen a lot of other writers from older generations who've done that, who have burnt very, very brightly at the time but then burnt out and repeated the same formula. I guess I've got them to learn from as well. Without naming names, they were pioneers; it was the first time they set down the fucking match for us. You've got to be conscious of what you're doing, of always changing, trying to adapt and trying to move forward—which is difficult; it's easier said than done.

Can I read some lyrics and titles and get your thoughts on them? Do you recall writing 'You Do Something To Me'?

It came about while I was working on *Wild Wood* at the Manor in Oxford. There was some sheet music on a grand piano there. I couldn't read the music, obviously, but I could read the chord symbols above it; either an old standard or a classical thing. It had certain chord changes in it that I nicked, or appropriated, should I say, and that kick-started the song. I was just playing the chords as they were written and I thought, 'They're nice.'

What is the difference writing on the piano as opposed to guitar?

I'm not that conscious when I pick up the guitar. I naturally always play D or G or something like that. Whereas on the piano, obviously I know what the notes are, but because I'm not a proper pianist I just play chords, whatever they might be. I can throw up some nice harmonic sounds, stuff I would never think about doing on the guitar, which again can lead on to a song.

Rows and rows of disused milk floats stand dying in the dairy yard / And a hundred lonely housewives clutch empty milk bottles to their hearts, **from 'A Town Called Malice'.**

It's that cheeky thing: while the other is away the milkman will be banging on your wives, all that silly sort of English nonsense, really, just funny things, the everyday but exaggerated. The dairy yard was the one in Woking in my mind, a lot of suburban images: *playground kids and creaking swings, lost laughter in the breeze*, all that stuff. The let-up was the last line of each verse: *I'd sooner put some joy back in*.

'Wild Wood' has a beguiling, intimate, understated arrangement.

I was trying to write a modern folk song in a very traditional way, like a round; the same four chords and the only dynamic doesn't come from a chord change, but from the playing or the voice which takes it up and down.

Go to church do the people from the area, all shapes and classes sit and pray together, for here they are all one, for God created all men equal.

The whole song is a comment or piss-take, whatever way you look at it, me being flippant about the class system. It keeps coming back to *the man in the corner shop*: the person underneath who's jealous because he thinks he's making all the money, but the man in the corner shop's struggling and the boss in the factory also gets his cigarettes from the corner shop. So it becomes a central focus people come back to, but then they're all equal in the eyes of the Lord, the church.

'Ghosts of Dachau' is a poignant song about love in the unlikely setting of a Nazi death camp: ***the crab lice bite, the typhoid smells and I'm still here, handsome in rags, a trouserless man waiting helpless for dignity.***

It came about from this book by a Polish writer, Tadeusz Borowski, *This Way For The Gas, Ladies and Gentlemen*, about the experiences in Auschwitz and other concentration camps. In amongst all this fucking degradation and disgraceful human behaviour there were still people having love affairs. There's a bit in the book where he describes a guy who's lost his trousers. He's walking around semi-naked because there was nothing else to put on, all those kind of images. Whether it sounds right to say but life still carried on, in a strange way, in those camps. I thought it was unbelievable, whether it was a strength or a stupidity of human behaviour; whichever way you look at it I thought was fascinating.

'From the Floorboards Up' felt like a reclaiming of the emerging guitar scene in the 2000s.

Me and Whitey (*Steve White*) always used to say, 'On a good night the energy comes from underneath our feet and travels up.' It was about playing live, the whole communion thing you get going at a gig on a good night and this invisible energy comes from somewhere. It seems to start on the stage, on the boards itself, and just comes up and out of you and into the people and becomes this cycle. I wrote it in the middle of a tour, so that live energy was going on. Wrote it in one night and the next day after soundcheck—we had a little portable tape recorder thing—we demoed it there and then in one of the dressing rooms; Whitey on a little makeshift kit. Pretty much that demo was it: the arrangement, the stops, everything. It started off with me playing that Wilko Johnson sort of thing. It was also influenced by bands like The Rakes at the time, that sort of spiky thing they were doing. Post-Libertines time, it was all right to play the guitar again, it renewed interest in it for me anyway.

'Peacock Suit' has clever lyrical interplay around Nemesis and Narcissus: *I'm Nemesis in a muddle / In a mirror I look / Like a streak of sheet lightning / In my rattlesnake shoes.*

Yeah, I like all that taking Greek mythology and classic images and putting them in the local high street. I'm not sure the character in the song is meant to be me; maybe it was at the time, I don't know. It's kind of confident 'cause I was a bit of a wanker as well; he's in love with himself which is probably me, actually, somebody preening themselves in a shop window. *Narcissus in a puddle*: he's not looking into a pool or anything classical, just a street puddle.

'Boy About Town' is a rare example of you writing confident, strident lyrics.

I never look into it that deeply. I just write whatever I feel, really. All those comedians like Tony Hancock who tried to work out what the funniest thing was: it's just funny, don't worry or think about it, just be. I take that approach to music and writing: if I analysed it too much it would do my head in. It's explaining the unexplainable often when you talk about writing and music.

Does the success of number-one records affect your writing?

'Going Underground' was our first number one: obviously we were pleased about it but there was a part of me that was, 'Fucking hell, where do you go after being that high?' It was all right, as it turned out, because we had a few more after that. It's a mixture: it's exciting but really scary and the expectations from people as well ... *22 Dreams* was number one last year: it's great to have a number-one album, of course it is, but there's other records that I'm really proud of that haven't made it. It's just nice when people like what you're doing; it's nice to have a pat on the back. With *All Mod Cons* we got great reviews and it did really well for us and that was really good for me because it made me take myself more seriously as a writer. I thought I got really stuck in after that and *Setting Sons* followed on from that. So sometimes success can be a really good thing; it's an encouraging thing, people like what you're doing and that can push you to greater things.

Did your songwriting approach change between The Jam and The Style Council?

The songs changed and the musical setting was different but I don't think the process of writing has ever changed. I still sat at home with an acoustic guitar and bashed out ideas and wrote down reams and reams of lyrics. Some got used and some didn't.

What was the genesis of 'Into Tomorrow'?

I think it started off with the riff. Me and Brendan put that together with samples and I just jammed the idea out when I had my old Solid Bond Studios. Similar to what I'm doing here, I suppose. I already had some words but I wasn't really thinking if they'd be a song or not; they just happened to fit.

You wrote a word-piece in the early Nineties: *My name is Larson! Larson! And I don't give a fuck. I'm as hard as nails I am, and I hate everyone.* Do you have a need to write beyond songs?

Sometimes, yeah. I wrote that because we were on tour in Germany and I just saw some big, tough, invincible kid striding down the street and I made up this story. When I was younger I used to write a lot more poetry, or whatever you're supposed to call it. I used to do a little fanzine for a while which I put my poems in. If I do it at all these days I try to incorporate them into what I'm writing at the time; sometimes it's impossible to. I don't do it for any other reason than I want to at that time, not to show anyone or for use of any kind. 'Larson' was only used because we did a book. I was writing an awful lot at that time, just at random, really.

'You're the Best Thing'?

That's just me writing a song. It's not really about anyone or anything particularly. That came about because the first two chords are so sweet. It's got to work if you've got a chord sequence like that.

'Broken Stones'?

Me and my son, when he was little, were on a beach and he was asking me where all the pebbles came from. I told him we were all part of one rock before and we all got smashed down in time and splintered and sent around the earth. I don't know if that's true or not; scientifically, but that was my explanation to him anyway. But even if it wasn't true, as a metaphor for us as a human race, human spirit, that we all come from one source and we just got splintered and sent round the world, there was a sense of spirituality that we're all seeking to get back to that core again or get back home. So that spiritual element I married to the gospel accordion chords in it. It's like an old gospel or spiritual tune to me.

Like 'Wings of Speed', which has one of your most enticing melodies?

Yeah, that came again out of the chord sequence, constantly playing the sequence over and over for weeks, months even, until the song formed. I was on holiday in Los Angeles with my son. There was a piano in the hotel and I just kept going to it, driving me fucking mad, going over and over it until it formed. I had all the verses but it took forever to get a middle eight for it. We left a space in the demo or recording until I found something to fit it. I think I wrote it the night before, one of those things you improvise. I always liked the middle eight because it jumps out of the key and goes into a different key. I thought that was cool, and then it comes back again. I've used that sort of device a few times. I can't think of anything specifically—a Beatle-ism maybe; you're in the key of C but all of a sudden you're in the key of E flat, but then you find a way of getting back to it.

'Headstart For Happiness' has similar unexpected chord movement.

I was getting into jazz around that time, not in any big way, studying it all, but finding different jazz chords on the guitar.

'Ghosts': *There's more inside you that you haven't shown.*

That started with the minimalist riff high up on the neck. It's very sparse. The idea in the words was for people to see their own potential.

'Pretty Green'.

Me writing about consumerism and being on tour in America. That phrase was on a game show, the host talking about money as 'pretty green'. I thought it was a great title.

Did you like the Mark Ronson version with Santogold?

It made me think of those old Eighties hip hop skipping songs, with the girl singing it. I thought it was all right. It's kind of like a nursery rhyme; it's got this sing-song thing to it. It's dead simple, just like two chords or something. There's quite a lot of songs on the *Sound Affects* album where I was really trying to get to the bare bones: musically, as few chords as possible and lyrically, just shaving it down, having something very direct, almost like you come in mid-conversation and then you go out again.

A Gang of Four influence?

Yeah, definitely. Wire, people like that. I liked the sort of angular pop they were doing.

'Wings of Speed' was inspired when you saw John William Waterhouse's _The Lady of Shallot_ at Tate Britain. Do you use art for inspiration: would you have been looking at the painting and thinking of lyrical ideas?

Not that literally, but it's being inspired and moved by whatever the art form. There's lots of different dimensions to songs. 'Wings of Speed', the inspiration came from the painting, the mood I caught from it, but it's also about splitting up with my wife at the time and feeling removed from her and my children and even becoming a different person. But there's also the musical side where I wanted to write elements of gospel in it, but also an old English hymn as well. Often songs are a mixture of lots of different influences, whether they are musical, lyrical or inspired by other people's work. There's never just one dimension, not in a really good song, anyway. There's lots of different sides to them, even if they're just personal things which no one ever gets to hear or see. They mean something to me.

STING

'I became obsessed with my hometown and its history, images of boats and the sea, and my childhood in the shadow of the shipyards,' Sting wrote in *Lyrics*, reflecting on the loss of his father Ernie to cancer in 1989. He was still grieving for the death of his mother two years earlier. After a reflective trip back to the docklands of his Tyneside home, the boy who'd watched the world from his bedroom window expressed his grief by recording a new set of songs. He was now forty years old, and *Rolling Stone* and British magazines declared *The Soul Cages* his greatest solo work. He was back in familiar territory and once again top of the charts.

Between the rows of houses and Gordon Matthew Sumner's childhood home in Wallsend lay the shipyard. Mighty vessels were constructed here and on completion launched onto the River Tyne. Sting is quoted as saying, 'Growing up in the shadow of a ship gives you a sense that you're destined to be a traveller.' His mother Audrey was herself a pianist, and Sting recalls in his autobiography that his earliest musical memory was 'sitting at her feet as she played'. He was fascinated by how the black marks on the sheet music could be translated into such beautiful sounds. As he watched his mother's shoes on the pedals 'rising and falling with their rhythmic counterpoint', he fell under music's spell.

Sting passed the eleven-plus and gained a place at St Cuthbert's Grammar School, Newcastle, in 1962. When an uncle emigrated to Canada in the same year he left behind an old acoustic guitar. With five shillings begged from his mother, Sting bought *First Steps In Guitar Playing* by Jeffrey Sisley. It taught him to tune the instrument and how to play his first chords. It was the year of The Beatles' 'Love Me Do'. Sting obsessively studied their music and soon progressed to the attractions of Bob Dylan and jazz. At the age of fourteen he wanted to be James Taylor. A year later he learnt every note of Eric Clapton's guitar parts on John Mayall's *Blues Breakers* record. He listened to a wide range of music: rock 'n' roll 78s from his parents' record collection, the big-band sounds of the Dorsey Brothers and Benny Goodman, the show songs of Rodgers and Hammerstein and Leonard Bernstein. He taught himself how to play and learnt basic music theory. His ability to read a score was put to the test when he played bass for the Newcastle Big Band. Meanwhile, dead-end jobs paid the bills. He worked as a labourer, a bus conductor, and a tax-office clerk. By 1972 he was a schoolteacher by day and gigging at night.

It was his wasp-like black-and-yellow sweater that provoked Phoenix Jazzmen bandleader Gordon Solomon to dub his new bass player Sting. The name would come to be associated with an immensely successful solo career, but first Sting was to play his part in a dynamic new trio who would become known the world over. The Police had been the brainchild of drummer Stewart Copeland, the son of a CIA operative. His progressive rock band Curved Air had broken up in the mid-Seventies as punk gained popularity in London, and Copeland wanted in on the cutting-edge movement. After he saw Sting at a Last Exit gig the pair were introduced, and together with Corsican guitarist Henri Padovani they recorded a debut single, 'Fall Out', in early 1977, on a borrowed budget of £150. Four thousand records were pressed and established The Police as recording artists. Veteran guitarist Andy Summers was thirty-four when he joined the group that spring, swiftly displacing Padovani. Summers' new position coincided with the emergence of reggae as the street sound of the capital, and The Police tried fusing it into rock and found that it worked. Copeland suggested using Sting's bass guitar to accent the second beat of the bar in syncopation with his kick drum. In 'Roxanne', descending chords from G minor, originally conceived in a bossa nova rhythm, worked dramatically with the technique. Other songs followed: 'So Lonely', 'Can't Stand Losing You', and the distinctive rhythm of The Police was born—although the resulting trio of singles all faded without significant impact on the market. It was an inauspicious start for relatively mature musicians who had already spent over a decade earning money on the club circuit. The Police toured America with XTC as unknowns, carrying their own guitars and booking cheap flights on Freddie Laker's budget airline. After months of determination, The Police's debut album *Outlandos D'Amour* broke into the US top thirty. It was the beginning of an extraordinary upturn in recognition. By 1979, songs written by Sting had sold over five million copies. 'Don't Stand So Close To Me' sold half a million alone and was the biggest-selling single of 1980. In later years fellow Geordie Mark Knopfler (ironically also a teacher prior to musical success) would invite Sting to contribute to Dire Straits' transatlantic hit 'Money For Nothing'. Sting sang background vocals with the words *I want my MTV* to the melody of 'Don't Stand So Close To Me'. He was credited as co-writer of the song.

Britain's initial indifference towards The Police was soon forgotten as a succession of records streamed into the charts: 'Message In A Bottle', 'Walking On The Moon', 'De Do Do Do, De Da Da Da', 'Invisible Sun', 'Every Little Thing

She Does Is Magic', 'Wrapped Around Your Finger'. After a string of number ones and memorable melodies, Sting produced 'Every Breath You Take'. It was a defining moment in the songwriter's career. While staying at Ian Fleming's former home, Goldeneye, Sting recalls waking in the middle of the night and within ten minutes sketching the idea at a piano. Harmonically simple, the song is built around two circular parts and a haunting opening verse: *Every breath you take / [And] every move you make . . . I'll be watching you.* The song's construction is that of a standard pop ballad and congruent with the familiar four-chord structure of Ben E. King, Jerry Leiber and Mike Stoller's 'Stand By Me'. The song topped the charts worldwide and became America's biggest-selling single of 1983. And then The Police split.

The theme of forbidden love runs through much of Sting's work. The opening stanza of 'Don't Stand So Close To Me'—*young teacher, the subject of schoolgirl fantasy*—goes on to play cleverly with the eroticism of a girl *half his age* waiting at a *wet bus stop*. A view of prostitutes from a Paris hotel window and the name of the heroine of Edmond Rostand's play *Cyrano de Bergerac* provided the inspiration for 'Roxanne'. 'Mad About You' drew on the Old Testament Book of Samuel and King David's lust for Bathsheba. The verse establishes itself in Jerusalem and we are told of *an ancient king* and *another's wife*. Sting will often take a real or literary subject as a starting point for his songs, before adding his own personal interpretation. The lyrical development informs the musical structure. Opening verses will typically establish the subject and setting of the narrative. Middle eights invert and shift the lyrical perspective, whilst the chorus anchors and connects the song's thematic whole. The protagonist of 'I'm So Happy I Can't Stop Crying' is grieving for his broken marriage and the loss of his children. In the third verse, he begins to take comfort from gazing up at the stars and his new resolution is represented by a slide half-tone step up on a pedal steel guitar. Musically and spiritually, the song has evolved. It is typical of Sting's technique. His writing shows a strength in narrative which helps draw in the listener.

Sting has a luxuriant imagination that allows him, as an adult, to access the fancy of a child. In 'Stolen Car (Take Me Dancing)', a thief imagines, from the atmosphere within a car's interior, the lives of the owners of the vehicle he steals. The romantic 'Shape Of My Heart' is lent complexity by the metaphor of a card game, and 'I Hung My Head' is a tragic ballad based on Sting's childhood memories of Westerns. Melancholic writing would come to the fore in Sting's solo years. It could be glimpsed in his work with The Police in the symbolism of 'King Of Pain' or the regretful tone of 'The Bed's Too Big Without You', but a line from a song written to a late friend's piece of music, 'Song For Kenny's Dienda', expressed the mature writer's feelings: *How like a song or a sad melody / To linger long after it's gone.* Literary influence pervades his writing, from Homer, T. S. Eliot and William of Wykeham (*manners maketh man*) to William Blake (*dark-satanic mills*) and sonnets of Shakespeare (*my mistress' eyes are nothing like the sun*). Happy to cross-fertilize ideas, he is a keen explorer of possibility.

Politically, Sting uses metaphor to reach beyond a specific situation. In 1987, 'They Dance Alone' attacked General Pinochet's military regime in Chile, but the wider subject of the song was collective suffering. It has enabled this and many of Sting's other songs to travel freely across contentious borders. To celebrate the fortieth anniversary of the Declaration of Human Rights, Sting toured the world, sharing stages with Bruce Springsteen, Peter Gabriel, Youssou N'Dour and Tracy Chapman. *Confronted by this latest atrocity* was the axis line of 'Driven To Tears', and it was Sting, perhaps with a little irony, who sang Bob Geldof's lyric *the bitter sting of tears* on 'Do They Know It's Christmas?', the 1984 Band Aid record to raise money to relieve Ethiopia's famine. Never afraid to show his interest in political and global issues, Sting has had a long association with humanitarian causes.

The Police at the Locarno, Bristol, March 1978 by Lawrence Impey

With *The Dream Of The Blue Turtles* in 1985, he took a new direction, inviting virtuoso jazz musicians into the world of mainstream Western pop. Sting wanted a conversation between instruments, a debate between forms. The content was rich and textured, and the limitation of a fixed band was overthrown. Successive albums have called on a range of styles and instrumentation, from flamenco and folk to hip hop and the Elizabethan lute. In 2009, Sting's Symphonicity world tour involved the Royal Philharmonic Orchestra, as his back catalogue was re-imagined with classical arrangement.

The success of The Police will always be seen as Sting's greatest legacy and much to the surprise of their fans the band reformed in 2007 for a world tour; it would became the third-highest-grossing concert tour of all time. Yet Sting has always been a working musician, and his solo career is a continuation of his first teenage endeavours in music. Thirty years after the initial break-up of The Police, Sting's songwriting style remains a synthesis of infectious melodic ideas and considered lyrics. Many of his songs have seeped into the musical consciousness. 'Fields of Gold' was released in 1993 with relatively little impact, but has since come to be considered a classic, perhaps in part because of Eva Cassidy's interpretation. The samba-influenced 'Fragile', originally released in 1987, was featured in the 1992 Academy Award–winning documentary *The Panama Deception*. The song later became a symbol of hope in the aftermath of 9/11. Sting's nylon-string guitar arrangement is a studied balance between minor and minor seventh chords. After an unadorned four-note introduction the verse and chorus are beautifully finger-picked to allow bass notes and arpeggios to harmonize a plaintive vocal melody.

Gordon Sumner was dressed in khaki trousers, a plain T-shirt and Converse sneakers when I met him at the King Charles Hotel in Munich, forty-one years to the day after Neil Armstrong walked on the moon. He was coming to the end of an eighteen-month world tour. We sat across a table strewn with LPs in a quiet room with blinds shutting out the afternoon sunshine. Sting spoke softly, but with self-assurance.

We're here to try and capture your songwriting mindset.

If you can do that you're a better man than I am. I rarely see these things. I don't think I actually own them. I'm not really into memorabilia. I don't collect things. Music is very much now. I listened to them too many times when I was mixing and making them; I don't really want to listen again. I'm always surprised when I hear them by accident in a shop or a bar or something.

So before the current tour you didn't listen back to the arrangements on record?

I knew. We're trying to recreate something from the template, but it's evolved.

I understand you use the 'work-back' method: using titles as your starting point.

Yes, it's a reverse process. You begin with a refrain. It usually ends up as hook line or a chorus line that people will sing in the shower or when they're cleaning windows. You start there and you do that by free association. Normally I write the music first. It doesn't matter if it's a tune or a series of chords or something that intrigues me: the time signature, a cadence or where a chord moves. That will fascinate me. I'll construct a song entirely without lyrics. My theory is that music, when it's structured correctly, has a narrative. It's an abstract narrative but it's nonetheless a story: beginning, a bridge, a key change, coda. That's a narrative. So it's my job to translate that narrative into something that people will recognize as a story. Most of my songs are written that way, although some songs might begin as a lyric, or the lyric and the music come together. Most of them are written as a translation of the narrative of the music. Then I take the music away when it's finished. I put it in an iPod and go for a walk and I free-associate and usually come back with something that I can recognize as an end point of the story. Then I say, 'So how do I get to that?' For example, I wrote a song called 'I Hung My Head' which was covered by Johnny Cash. I had this very strange time signature. It's in 9/8: a bar of five and a bar of four. It started with a walk in the country thinking, 'What is the song about, what is this narrative telling me?' It's a kind of Western. It sounded like a horse, a lame horse, the rhythm of it was strange. I had this refrain in my head, *I hung my head*, but what does that mean? Why would that be? What sort of person would say that? What kind of situation would he be in? So I write the story backwards. It ends up there's a guy who's out one morning, he borrows his brother's rifle, he's practising and he sees someone in the distance and he shoots them by accident. He runs away, he gets tried, he gets executed for murder—that's the story.

Are you aware of synaesthesia? Andy Partridge explains how hearing music creates images in his mind.

I haven't seen Andy for years. We used to tour together in the early days. Is it a disease?

A positive disease!

I wish I understood it. It just comes to you. You pluck it out of the air and you recognize it has potency. It can go somewhere.

Is there difficulty forming the opening verse to the narrative when you are working backwards?

You can start a song with a wonderful first line, but where do you go? I write quatrains that way. I write the last line of the quatrain because that's the clinch. You finish a line; you have to rhyme it with line two. Line two is easy if you've got line four. The first line is fine, but the two and four are what's important. This is a very clinical way of songwriting; I know it sounds that way, but it's a craft. You learn how to do it.

Predominantly you employ rhyming couplets: what is the attraction?

I don't think it's unusual. I'm famous for using couplets that are perhaps a bit dodgy. It's called feminine rhyme and it's used for humorous purposes. I'm famously lambasted for rhyming *shake and cough* with *Nabokov*, which amuses the hell out of me. It's funny. You can get away with it. I use a rhyming diction-ary, not because I need to but to make sure I've exhausted all the possibilities of a rhyme. Generally I have the only rhyme that can be possible, but I like to make sure there isn't a better rhyme. If you use this method, starting with the fourth line of a quatrain: what is line two . . . ah . . . *moon* rhymes with *June*, shit! Rhyme is a mysterious force. Rhyme can lead you like a story. Words will drag you along like a fishing line. There are only a limited number of words that rhyme with each other. There are only a limited number of notes on the scale. So you're working within limitations in the English language.

I ask because musically you've challenged yourself in a variety of directions, yet lyrically you've honed yourself to a template.

What are the alternatives?

Not to rhyme?

I like it. Rhyming does something therapeutic for the song structure. For example, you can write a song about a situation: in the first verse and the chorus you set up this situation; in the second verse you reiterate that situation. Then you get to the bridge. Bridges always interest me because it is a doorway into another key, perhaps, or a change of viewpoint, or in the best cases both together. So you have this hypothetical situation of a guy trapped in a mindset of this love affair that he can't get out of. The bridge allows the character and the music and the story to shift slightly to see a different viewpoint. Ideally it goes into a key change: 'Ah, there is light at the end of the tunnel, my life isn't so hopeless after all.' So that is good therapy for the listener, the character in the song, and for the writer. Rhyming also helps that. Order is something we impose on the universe. We feel better when we order the world. We feel more comfortable and able to cope when there's order out of disorder. The reality of the world is the opposite: disorder and chaos. As human beings we try to make meaning out of chaos.

What are your thoughts about story resolution for yourself and the audience?

It's not always important to resolve a key or a narrative. Sometimes it suits your purpose to leave that hanging, a suspended chord or a story without a comment; just a slice of life. I've done that. In many ways the most satisfying thing is to resolve, go back to the major key. I'm not saying there are any hard and fast rules here at all.

Do you find subject matters find you as much as you find them? I'm think-ing of the albums *Nothing Like The Sun* and *The Soul Cages*, reflecting the illnesses and passing of your mother and father?

My parents I try to avoid more than anything, and yet they kept coming round. My creative landscape is really formed by my parents and my upbringing.

Even as a 59-year-old man I'm still trying to resolve what happened to me when I was eight, so my songwriting would of course reflect that, not by intention but because I have no choice. Last night I sang about my father and he's there; his presence is with me. It's comforting and it's also disturbing. You invite these entities into your life that aren't in the climate any more.

Is their presence there when you're writing?

Yeah, in a way it's a long extravagant process of mourning the dead when you invite them into your creative life. They're your teachers. Your parents were there before you in every sense and so you look to them for guidance even when they're gone.

Does that scare you when you're writing; does it drag you into areas that you wouldn't emotionally want to be pulled to?

It doesn't scare me. They're not comfortable feelings, a lot of them. That's the price you pay as an artist. You're forced to deal with issues that people would put on the back burner. I'm not ungrateful for it. It's wonderful to have that.

Would you say you react to life as much as a writer as a human?

I don't structure my life to coincide with inspiration, if that's what you're saying. I don't manufacture situations which I think will be creatively useful to me. That is a method. You can create chaos and mayhem and heartbreak as a way of stimulating creative juices. I don't want to do that. I want to live a calm, quiet, balanced life. I'm not inviting mayhem but mayhem comes anyway.

In given situations, would you recognize writing potential or does it come as an afterthought?

It would be an afterthought. It would be very cynical of me to go through a family crisis or any kind of crisis and think, 'Mmm, this is good: 9/11, whoopee; the plague!' When you look back you may think, what is my reaction to that? How can I express that? How can I make sense of it? How can I have a useful viewpoint that other people would find interesting? I don't go through life looking for inspiration. I really don't. It either comes to you or it doesn't. It's like fishing: sometimes the fish will catch the line, sometimes it doesn't. Generally it doesn't.

Many years ago I heard Michael Stipe say he wouldn't write a love song and therefore his greatest challenge was to write one. What are your thoughts on the use of the word *love* in your songwriting? Interestingly, in 'Love Is The Seventh Wave' the use of the word is withheld until the end of the song.

It's an easy word to say, love. It's shorthand for something that's very complex. There's a huge spectrum of meaning within the word love. What is love, from lust to devotion to worship? It's not something I'm very conscious of. I wasn't aware that I used the word love a lot.

Let's talk about process. Do you practise daily?

I play every day, a couple of pieces that I'm working on. I'll do a bit of Bach. I keep the muscle going. A lot of songwriting is what I call finger-fishing, you just play—Oh, what's that? A flattened fifth, that's interesting'—rather than actually composing. I don't think we compose so much as we just find things. Collate them. I put the hours in every day and occasionally something will arrest my attention. I'll make a note of it and then go back to it and add to it a different fragment from another day or another day beyond that and think, 'Mm, I must do some work on that.' It comes less and less easy as I get older. I think because there are more filters on the work. As you get older the critic gets more and more powerful and smarter and has a forensic memory and says, 'Oh no, you've done that before,' or 'Somebody else has done that before,' or 'That's not quite as good as that.' You get all of these barriers to the creative child which is what you're really trying to nourish. When you're younger that creative child is very strong. Whatever you try is fine. But as you get older and wiser the child gets buried. So your job is to try and stimulate that child as much as you can. It's largely an unconscious process. You have to get into a state where you just allow things to come through. Which begs the question: are you writing anything or is it being written for you in some other, collective unconscious? I don't know the answer to that. Often I think you write good stuff . . . it's kind of religious, but when you're in a state of grace, when you're not trying to do anything. You have no agenda. You have no end in mind. You have no care what happens next. You're just in that moment and then things just come to you. It's rare but I try as much as possible to get in that state. True freedom is not caring what happens next. There are certain jobs where that would be dangerous, but in songwriting it's OK.

Within your practice do you play scales, use a metronome? How strict are you?

I play the odd scale. When I'm singing I practise with Jo Lawry. We'll do tenths, thirteenths. It's using the mind to warm the voice up.

I was struck last night by how strong your voice still is. Often singers lose their range or depth as they get older.

It's a bit stronger now. It's athleticism more than anything. I've done thousands of gigs; you're supposed to get better. It's a kind of yoga, singing. It's good for you.

You lost your hearing mid-range in the mid-Nineties. Has it affected your writing?

What? I wonder if it does. I have no idea. One of my ears is definitely low. If somebody's talking in a car, in a front seat away from me, I can't really hear what they're saying, spoken range. When I'm mixing a track I say, 'I can't hear the tambourine.' They say, 'Are you kidding, it's way up.' Maybe I'm hearing what's in my head more than what I'm audibly hearing.

How is writing a song affected by the instrument you're using?

It's interesting to change your instrument because you can play a major chord followed by a relative minor on the guitar and it's no revelation. Play that on an accordion and the same cadence will suddenly sound interesting to you. If you're completely adept at something then you tend to be in that rut. Being a beginner on an instrument is also useful. You stick something in your hand that you're unfamiliar or slightly at odds with—like the lute, which is close to a guitar but different, and complex enough to really mess you up—it will put you in that strange territory of not being in your comfort zone, and that position can be stimulating and very fruitful.

Was 'Spirits In The Material World' written on a Casio keyboard?

Yeah, a cluster of chords, and we used it on the record. It cost about thirty quid.

May we pick up on the idea of motion when you are writing? In your book *Lyrics* you recount writing The Police's first record shouting ideas whilst you were driving. Similarly, 'Murder By Numbers' and 'Shape Of My Heart' have come from movement.

I think it orders the mind in many ways, that binary left right, left right. It calms the mind. I've built a labyrinth in my house in Wiltshire—sixty, seventy feet across. It goes in a big circle. This design (*shows inner picture on* Songs From The Labyrinth *album*). It looks like the brain: four quadrants of the brain. It takes about twenty minutes to get to the centre and I swear to God, whatever might be troubling you, by the middle you will have changed your viewpoint because you're constantly shifting left to right and round. It's an interesting meditation tool. I can't just sit at a table and write. I need to walk.

How do you remember your ideas? If you're on a long journey, can you hold on to them?

Yeah, if I have a good one I'll keep repeating it. The majority of my songs are written on the hoof. I like forward momentum; it's become an addiction to me. I find it very difficult to sit still.

Aptly, I understand you wrote 'Walking On The Moon' in a Munich hotel with the original words *walking in the room*.

I did . . . *walking round the room* (*laughs*). I do remember waking up in Munich, it's amazing you know that, and I had that bass riff in my head (*hums bass line*) and I started walking round the room. You can't have *walking round the room*! *Walking on the moon* seemed a useful metaphor for being in love, that feeling of lightness, of just being able to walk on air. It's an old idea. So from that refrain I just worked backwards, so 1969: *giant steps are what you take*, one giant step for mankind . . . It's not meant to be serious.

Is touring conducive to writing?

Well, that's interesting; the paradox is I don't write when I'm touring unless I have to. I like the tour to be over. I like to have one place I can sit and orbit. I go home and I have a little garden shed. I'll set out for two hours, go for a per-ambulation and then come back and write something down and then go off again. Have a bite to eat. When I'm being creative I need a place to call home, otherwise you're just spiralling off.

I stumbled across a featurette, *The Police in Montserrat*, in which you demonstrate to Jools Holland how you wrote 'Message In A Bottle'. You had a tape recorder and a drum box and you are seen recording the four-chord sequence D minor 9, A minor, B and F sharp major and then building harmony to mumbled words. Is that typical of your process?

Typical of the time, yes; is that unusual? I think most people . . . it's a process that is ongoing. I'm demoing the whole time. I record ideas, go for a walk, build something on top of what you've got. Studios are great writing tools. Just put an idea down, put anything down, and then try and make sense of it. I wrote 'Message In A Bottle' on the guitar. Again, it's modal. It's a series of ninth chords. The melody is folky . . . I don't know. I was very influenced as child by church music. I used to sing Gregorian chants and plainsong as an altar boy. I think a lot of my melodies might reflect that love and early exposure to that stark, melodic narrative. 'Message In A Bottle' reflects that too.

Are the original strokes a song's backbone? You've said of 'A Thousand Years' you locked yourself away for days to crack it.

I recognized that was an important song for me. I had the melody and really had to work hard to find it because it's very repetitive. It's just two notes. I think it was a good three days of thinking, drinking, not eating and putting myself through the mill to finish the song. I think it paid off. I like that song very much. It's an important song to me and it has the word love in it!

Which begs the question, when do you know when to reject ideas?

I don't finish anything I don't think is worth pursuing.

Three days is going some. There must have been some nugget you believed in.

I believed in that melody, then the way it went into the chorus I found very uplifting. I was just finding the right set of images and rhyming to make sense of it. For me it was a very weighty idea. The idea of many lives, of reincarnation, what does it mean? What would give that idea continuity? What is the point of having thousands of lives? Why bother unless it was held together by something important? And love being the only thing that makes this idea coherent; the fact that I still love is important to my philosophy. I knew there was a nugget, as you call it, there. I was willing to put the time and the effort in. It was a great moment to finish that song. 'Ah, that's what this is about': how many lives I've led, successful or not, and what kind of a life I've led; I've been led to this by a belief in love. I suppose in a sense that's kind of religious, although I don't subscribe to any religion. I'm quite religious in my own sweet way.

Did you have the melody of 'We Work The Black Seam' for ten years?

Maybe more. I wrote the melody in Newcastle. Then during the miners' strike—a part of my community I come from was coalminers—I felt inspired to write a defence of community. It was an argument about community versus economic theory. Whole communities were dispensed with because of some economic theory by Mrs Thatcher. It's kind of a hymn, more than anything, based on miners' hymns, folk modes.

Had you tried to put words to it in the past?

Yes, but there wasn't anything substantial. It was finished, but there was no real place for it. It was just something in my head. I wrote that in a car driving to school when I was teaching, in the morning traffic—a lunatic singing at the top of his voice in a Citroën 2CV.

A device you often use is re-employing words in other songs. *Every breath you take, every cake you bake, every leg you break* **appears in 'Love Is The Seventh Wave', and** *Do I have to tell the story of a thousand rainy days since we first met? It's a big enough umbrella but it's always me that ends up getting wet* **pops up in many places: 'O My God', 'Seven Days' . . .**

I'm trying to humorously point out that this is of course a modular system. All of this can be rearranged and those little modules can work in almost any order in any way you like. I think that's an important admission to make about music. It's very, very pliable. The songs are not this sort of sacred, written-in-stone 'That's it, that's it.' You can take bits out. We collate pop songs. So I try and do that using my own stuff. I'm always borrowing: from myself, from poetry,

Message in a Bottle

Just a castaway, an island lost at sea,
Another lonely day, no one here but me.
More loneliness than any man could bear,
Rescue me before I fall into despair.

I'll send an S.O.S. To the world
I'll send an S.O.S to the world.
I hope that someone gets my
Message in a Bottle.

A year has passed since I wrote my note
I should have known this right from the start
Only hope can keep me together
Love can mend your life
But love can break your heart.

I'll send an S.O.S. to the world
I hope that someone gets my
Message in a bottle.

I walked out this morning I don't believe
what I saw,
A hundred billion bottles washed up on the shore.
Seems I'm not alone in being alone
A hundred billion castaways looking for a home.

I'll send an S.O.S. to the World
I'll send an S.O.S To the world
I hope that someone gets my
Message in a Bottle.

'Message in a Bottle' lyrics, handwritten by Sting

from literature. It's like enlightened stealing. I have no shame about that. Everything fits in everything else. There's no originality at all. I really don't believe there is. If any originality exists it's in the interpretation of existing tropes, of existing riffs. It's like folk music.

We all have the same tools but none of us use them in the same way.

I can't claim any originality. I don't need to. It's a strange idea and linked probably to the publishing industry, which is quite a modern invention. Music has existed for thousands of years without copyright and that idea is actually coming to an end too. It's been short. We gather stuff around and then we mix it up and say, 'That's ours, that's mine.' I've made a very good living out of it.

More than collations, are songs in some way already out there, beyond . . .

I hope so. Songs are found, in some strange ether.

Lee Mavers is convinced he is a conduit to songs from the ether.

I agree . . . There's a danger of grandiosity in that statement, but we don't really write songs. They pre-exist. We find them like an archaeologist. It's my experience . . . it feels that way. Even though I've put the work in and I've done the graft they seem like they're already there. The best songs are that way. That's paradoxical. What a great privilege, some great fucking songwriter out there!

Do you recall writing 'Every Little Thing She Does Is Magic'?

I wrote that when I first moved to London in 1975. I was struggling to make a living. I used auditions in clubs just to stand up as a singer. I did an audition at the Zanzibar in Covent Garden. I sang 'Every Little Thing She Does Is Magic' and the guy said, 'We need commercial hit songs. We don't need this kind of stuff.'

You held that song back for so long, but the demo from the mid-Seventies clearly reveals its hit potential.

It wasn't appropriate for The Police's first few records. It was later I had the courage to say, 'Let's try this,' expanding what we do. It was done with a great deal of resistance from the other two. It's very much piano based and bigger than a three-piece but it was clearly a hit. I originally wrote it on guitar. We put The Police on as an afterthought.

When were you first aware of creating original melody? You'll question that.

I will question that. I had tunes in my head that perhaps I hadn't heard, but were related to tunes I'd heard. I didn't invent music, but I was exposed to music from a very early age. I recognized if somebody could write a tune then I could write something similar with a few changes that interested me. I wrote songs . . . I had things in my head as a young child that I would play with, improvise. I'd walk to school and have the tunes in my head linked to some sort of fantasy about being a musician. Where I got this idea I don't know. My mother was a piano player and I'd sit and listen to her play. I'm sure I was inspired to live in that world of music. I was left to my own devices a lot so music was my play area. It's where I got solace.

Where does melody come from and how do you develop a melodic idea?

I'm fortunate that the instrument that I have at my disposal, my voice, has a wide range, probably wider than most people. I'm not saying that with any hubris. Having that landscape to work in, my melodies can soar or they can swoop. Singers with a narrower range, neither is better or worse, but the band width of the melodic content is limited. I like songs that soar. I'm developing the lower ranges of my voice as I get older. The instrument you are given dictates the kind of melody you write. Singing high helps to get across the noise of drums or PA. Most rock singing is pretty high. Brian Johnson of AC/DC has a high voice because he has to get across that level of noise.

Do you physicalize melody on an instrument to develop it?

I sing it. I'll experiment a lot with the chords and the structure underneath it. It takes hard work putting the jigsaw together. I know when I've found it: 'Oh, that's the melody I'm looking for.' You have an ideal in your head that you can't quite define but then just by working it materializes. Once you've defined and recorded it and you start performing it then you're constantly modifying it night after night, little incremental changes to it that interest you, nothing particularly radical or even noticeable to your average listener. I sing 'Roxanne' every night; there's always a little inflection that is new or a possibility that opens it out. It's not my job to reproduce a record that was made thirty years ago. I use that and I respect that, but it's only a template. It's that jazz mentality. You use the head of the song just as a starting point.

The words *if I ever lose my faith in you* arrived from a nine-syllable melody.

Again, that came to me walking. I know exactly where I was when I had that melody (*hums melody*). Yeah, it's nine. Once I got that then I wrote the song backwards from that. I was looking for the end point that would trigger the lyric. I had the song, all the harmony and melody written. Many of my song titles or refrains are multi-syllabic: 'Don't Stand So Close To Me', 'When The World Is Running Down You Make The Best Of What's Still Around'. Is that unusual? I don't know.

'Fortress Around Your Heart' has a challenging melodic verse until its more open chorus. It's an intriguing relationship. Was that difficult to write?

It was written in the studio. I like the tension: you're not quite sure where the verse is going, and nor was I, then to go on to something that resolves very grandly into this big anthemic chorus . . . it only works because you've been in this strange place. I do these things by instinct, I don't do them by design. I'm not a trained musician. I'm working in the dark a lot of the time. We all get to the same place. You don't have to study at a conservatory to be a musician.

There's a moment in the film *Bring On The Night* where you are rehearsing and asking the backing vocalists to sing a more English harmony. Is Englishness important in your music?

Well, I'm English. I have a great investment in my musical heritage: folk music. We're largely working in an American idiom based on blues and jazz. Popular music is an American idea. To have some Englishness to the stuff is very important to me. I'm not the first writer to bring Englishness into pop music. I think the world respects our music, knows of it.

Damon Albarn told me he often uses time signatures as a catalyst to generate ideas. Your songs 'Straight To My Heart' and 'Seven Days' are in 5/8.

The interesting thing about time signatures is if you're playing in a compound time you can make the most banal melody interesting. Change 'Mary Had A Little Lamb' into an odd time signature and suddenly it's interesting to my ear. A song like 'Straight To My Heart' (*hums*), it's a nursery rhyme, it's actually Harold Arlen's *hallelujah, come on get happy*: that's a pretty good song. You change that into 7/8 time, that interests me. That makes it worth carrying on. So time signatures are an interesting puzzle I like to solve. How do I make that strange little jerk of a rhythm coherent to a listener? How do I make that pop music? People who listen to pop music generally only use one half of their brain: the part of the brain that analyses thirds and fifths, simple harmony, simple time signatures. More complex intervals like sixths and elevenths and thirteenths are dealt with by another side of the brain and most people haven't opened that side of the brain. So they hear jazz and they go, 'Urggh, that's not music,' or they hear 11/8 time: 'There's something wrong,' because the part of the brain that analyses those things hasn't been switched on. You need exposure to different kinds of music to have the whole range at your disposal. Musicians are lucky because that's what we do for a living. We expose ourselves to more difficult music in order to make sense of it and bring it back. I make pop music, but I like complex music. I'll get much more from listening to Schnittke, an extreme violin quartet, than I will from Radio One. There's not much to learn from Radio One for me. I hear the archetype that it's based on. I hear it very simply. I know what it is. My preference is to listen to music that challenges me because I'm learning more.

How do you taper that boundless creativity to commercial success?

How d'you bring that idea into this world? That's my job. Although my interests are fairly esoteric, what I've managed to put together has largely coincided with popular taste over thirty-five years. I don't think I'm compromising. I know what will work in little doses. I'm very fond of flattened fifths and people might hear that in pop music and go, 'What is that?' In 'When We Dance' (*hums melody*) that last note sets up a tremor, a vibration, but that's what's interesting in the song, that little thing. I'm not setting myself up as an avant-garde composer at all. I take those ideas and make them hearable. You could say that Schoenberg is important for people to hear as a reflection of twentieth-century mindset, but it's not getting across to that many people. Pop music, on the other hand, gets through to millions of people. If you want to have a message you need to tailor it to most people's abilities to hear it.

Where do you stand in your sense of social responsibility? Many of your songs have addressed world issues: 'Born In The 50's'; 'Russians'; 'They Dance Alone'.

I don't think it's necessary to be a musician to have any social responsibility or conscience at all. You can be completely out of that and still make great music. Speaking personally, I think I have citizen's rights and therefore citizen's responsibilities, so when I'm asked about a serious issue I'll try and give a congruent answer or if I feel I have a useful metaphor to express a situation I will do that. I'm not in that business of propaganda or just writing about issues for the sake of it. It has to be art for me. I'm not a journalist.

Had writing for a three-piece affected you by the last Police album *Synchronicity*?

I was a songwriter before I was in The Police. When you're in a band like The Police it does limit your songwriting to those three primary colours. It's a good discipline to have, but you look forward to the day when you don't have that limitation and you just have a huge palette of colours to paint with, which is what *Symphonicities* was about. But then it's good to go back to that limitation. Sometimes art thrives within limitation. At that point in my career I could have anything I wanted: a gamelan orchestra! We're talking about styles. If I wanted to write a country song or a torch ballad The Police wouldn't have been a vehicle for that. It worked. It forced me to be very concise in my writing. Then I wanted the opposite freedom, to do whatever I chose to do.

At night a candle's brighter than the sun.

That's from 'An Englishman In New York'. That line doesn't sound a particularly original idea to me. I wrote that in New York about Quentin Crisp, who'd become a friend of mine. It's about standing out from the crowd and being courageous about who you are, which of course Quentin famously was. *Be yourself no matter what they say*: it's something I hope to subscribe to in my courageous moments. I'm not claiming any originality.

For all those born beneath an angry star / Lest we forget how fragile we are: beautiful lyrics from 'Fragile'.

Thank you. Again, one of those lyrics that took a long time to conjure up; I had the melody and the arrangement done. I went for long walks on the island of Montserrat during the monsoon and it rained and it rained and it fucking rained. I'd go out and get completely drenched and of course *on and on the rain will fall (laughs) like tears from a star*. They're nice lyrics. They were hard ones and then very obvious once I'd done them. Of course that's what this song is about.

'Fields of Gold' has an expressive archaic lyric: *so she took her love for to gaze awhile upon the fields of barley.*

I'm using poetic licence to alter syntax. I wanted to create a timeless idea that the song could have been written in the sixteenth century. One of the lines is very reminiscent of Edgar Allan Poe's 'Tamerlane'. It's full of old tropes, I don't think particularly original. *Will you stay with me, will you be my love*: you could find that in some old songbook.

What gives the song its originality to you?

The way the chords move, me singing it. Some of my most successful songs don't sound original at all to me. 'Every Breath You Take': again it's the relative minor and kind of nursery-rhyme and rhyming-dictionary rhymes, but there's something darkly ambiguous about it. It's both romantic and threatening at the same time. That's its power. I wrote the refrain *every breath you take* then worked backwards from that. Then once I'd written and performed it I realized there was something dark about it. My intention might have been to write a romantic song, something seductive and enveloping and warm. Then I realized that actually another side of my personality was involved too, which is about control and jealousy, and that's its power. It was written at a difficult time in my life.

Did Richard Bach's aphorism inspire 'If You Love Somebody Set Them Free'? 'If they come back they're yours; if they don't they never were.'

Probably. Again, I'm not claiming that was particularly mine. It was appropriate to my thinking at the time. It was an antidote to 'Every Breath You Take' . . . let's use this idea and build a song around it.

I see you've sent my letters back and my LP records and they're all scratched.

It doesn't rhyme. It's supposed to be funny.

Did it come from a moment in your life?

I've only been jilted once, but boy, did it hurt.

If blood will flow
When flesh and steel are one,
Dying in the colour
Of the evening Sun,
Tomorrow's rain
Will wash the stains away
But something in our minds
Will always stay.
Perhaps this final act was meant
To clinch a lifetime's argument
That nothing comes from violence
And nothing ever could.
For all those born beneath
an angry star
Lest we forget how fragile we are

On and On the rain will fall
Like tears from a star
On and On the rain will say
How fragile we are.

'Fragile' lyrics, handwritten by Sting

'Can't Stand Losing You', like many Police songs, shifted rhythmically between verse and chorus. At what point would those changes infiltrate the songwriting?

It came in the arranging stage. That song was written many years previous. We had this idea of going back and forth between heavy rhythmic and rock and something a little more free. It was something we did well. We could all play well enough to pull that off. It became one of our signatures.

Do you ever imagine yourself as another artist to initiate an idea? 'Inside' is very reminiscent of Stevie Wonder's 'Do Yourself a Favour' and 'All This Time' very Paul Simon.

OK! 'Inside' . . . interesting, I'll take that as a good thing. Both artists hugely influential in my listening life. Paul lyrically, certainly, and Stevie definitely musically, but I don't do that. Their influence is strong like a lot of artists. I wouldn't say, 'What would Paul do?' No, I'm always thinking what would Sting do? One of my mantras is that surprise is important. You need a surprise every sixteen bars. Surprise the listener with a chord change or something happening in the song that captures the ear. That's how I listen to music. You can predict what is going to happen and when that prediction is confounded I'm really interested. Also in the choices of what I do in my career. I want people to be not quite sure what I'm going to do next. I think that's paid off. My courage to tackle different stuff has never been in question; the wisdom of it may be moot. I will try things.

'Invisible Sun' has a wonderful riff leading into the chorus.

I was working on a little tape recorder and played that bass riff. I was living in Connemara in Ireland at the time. It's odd, I watch these orchestral musicians practising these little riffs that just came out of my head. You've got these oboe players playing these lines and they're playing as if it's some god-given composed music. And it was just me. I get a little chuckle off it.

That's what vinyl posterity presents . . .

And success: vinyl confirms in people's psyche that that's a piece of music. Then you have orchestral versions of this stuff, but it's just some kid playing with a guitar.

Do you have a theory as to why so few female writers in Britain achieve success equivalent to males?

I think that's changed within the past five years: more and more female artists are taking precedence over males in the pop charts. I think it's to do with historical male prejudice. I did some work on Robert and Clara Schumann. Everybody knows Robert Schumann and his work but nobody knows Clara

Schumann, who was equally as good, because she was a woman. We treated women badly. They were downtrodden. I would never say women are less good at songwriting. I actually believe women are a far superior breed.

What do you think your contribution to British songwriting has been, or how would you like it be thought of?

I don't have the need to define myself in that way. I have no idea. I just did my job. I did the best I could. I'm not looking for a place in history. Not interested. Music is now. It's tomorrow night in Lyon: getting through the show without fucking up.

The Police at Wembley Arena, 20 October 2007 by Lawrence Impey

ANDY PARTRIDGE

What do you call that noise that you put on? This is pop.

It started purely as tongue-in-cheek *White Music*: quirky, youthful three-minute songs. But as Andy Partridge's music developed artistically, commercial success began to elude his band XTC. The creative highpoints were undermined by mental-health problems, addiction to prescription drugs and diminishing sales returns.

'Please Help Me', Partridge's first song, written at the age of fifteen, was an early cry for comfort. When three years earlier his mother had been admitted to a mental hospital, the shaken boy was prescribed Valium to calm his troubled response. Increasing dependence on the drug, and the effects of its subsequent withdrawal, ultimately contributed to his own breakdown in 1982. Just as XTC were enjoying their first headlining American tour to promote the critically successful double album *English Settlement*, the lead singer succumbed to record industry pressures, stage fright and a desperate dislike of the cycle of record making and touring. The life of a working musician had become too much to endure: 'If I'm going to do that, I might as well shovel shit for a living.' Beyond a handful of television shows and radio promotions, Partridge abruptly ended the band's years of live performance.

In the early days of punk, a highly stylized vocal with Buddy Holly–affected hiccups accompanied by short, fast chords, welcomed XTC to the British charts. Through the Eighties, Partridge's writing flourished. His English roots lent a unique flavour to his lyrics. '1000 Umbrellas' asked, *How can you smile and forecast weather's getting better if you never let a girl rain all over you?* In the earlier 'Statue of Liberty' Partridge had disclosed *and in my fantasy I still sail beneath your skirt*. His unique lyrical imagination brought recognition from the American buying public. But in the Nineties, a five-year recording hiatus, prompted by Partridge striking in protest and frustration at his treatment by his record label, nearly ended the band's career. A final, delightful

DANIEL RACHEL

two-set release in 1999, the *Apple Venus* recordings, was a fitting reminder of a relatively neglected musical talent.

When I explained to Andy that this book sought to understand the mind-set and approach of great British songwriters, he responded with characteristic charm, 'How are you going to describe a little twittering bird flying in very small circles (*mimics a bird's whistle*)—that sound—in print?' This is an enduring theme. Whilst the romantic in 'No Language In Our Lungs' struggles with the inadequacy of speech: *I would have made this instrumental but the words got in the way*, it is, ironically, Partridge's flair for language that breathes life into his writing. Though he chose early lyrics for the effect of their sound over any clear meaning, this was rapidly overtaken by wordplay and metaphor: *1000 umbrellas* are *upturned* to catch tears; the pedals are pushed on the *season cycle*; and in 'River Of Orchids', a diatribe against the motor vehicle, there is the wonderfully absurd chorus, *I heard the dandelions roar in Piccadilly Circus.*

To maintain freshness a writer must overcome the familiarity of chords and attempt to maintain a mystique. It may be found in irregular tunings or by reworking the structures of other people's writing. Partridge talks about deconstructing the songs of Bacharach and David. He cites Ray Davies as the master and proclaims The Kinks' 'Autumn Almanac' the Holy Grail of English writing. The influence of The Beatles and Brian Wilson lends further magic to his compositions. The melodic approach of 'Pale And Precious' showed a precise understanding of the song construction of The Beach Boys. The same knowledge of West Coast harmony can be heard in 'Wrapped In Grey'. The song grew from a three-note waltz pattern that caught Partridge's attention when he used a Proteus keyboard set to incorporate a piano and string sound. The song's unusual structure flirted with the positioning of the chorus, offering a bridge section heard once only before calls to *Awaken you dreamers adrift in your beds*. Partridge's piano playing was good enough to generate ideas, but not sufficiently developed to record in the studio. Dave Gregory, who would play the composer's parts, explained to MySpace/xtcfans website in 2008 the process adopted for 'Rook'. 'He'd added an extra note to a basic piano sample, tuned one fourth above the root key. By using just two fingers of his right hand, and his left index finger, he plotted out a simple four-chord sequence, each chord comprising six notes in stacked fourths. This became the main theme of the verses. For the chorus sections he constructed four more tone clusters, battering the keyboard like a bongo drum and taking the time signature into a very modern 18/16.'

Partridge's insight into the methods of other songwriters took a strange turn when XTC developed an alter ego, The Dukes Of Stratosphear. They released a mini-album on April Fool's Day 1985 and later a full-length album, in which the musical impostors paid homage to the psychedelic music of the late

Sixties. Using masks to hide their identity had been a feature of a previous XTC album, *Mummer*. The title reflected a West Country tradition whereby local tradesmen taking part in a play would assume disguises in order to distance themselves from the audience. For the group, The Dukes of Stratosphear's songs provided a childlike licence to inhabit their favourite artists. Partridge adopted the pseudonym Sir John Johns and was reunited with XTC's first producer Swami Anand Nagam (John Leckie). The rules of engagement were declared. Songs had to have 1967 / 1968 psychedelic credentials, there would be only two takes of each tune, and wherever possible the equipment used had to be authentic. A sceptical Virgin Records forwarded £5,000 for the project, and after a resolute two days in the studio, £1,000 was returned: project complete. Sales of the mystery music, boosted by the possibility that the songs were gems recovered from ancient vaults, surpassed those of both previous XTC releases.

If there's one thing I don't believe in it's you. Partridge has never shied from controversial subject matter. In 1986, 'Dear God' was written in indignation after he had leafed through a book in a local shop which had asked children to write letters to their Maker. His song tried to articulate an individual's right to see the troubles of the world and question the existence of God. Bible-Belt America reacted with outrage, and the adverse publicity propelled 'Dear God' into the national consciousness. Likewise, 'Books Are Burning', from 1992's *Nonsuch*, was written in response to the fatwa issued against Booker Prize-winning author Salman Rushdie on the publication of *The Satanic Verses*. Partridge's defence of literature recalled the poignant words of Heinrich Heine: 'Whenever books are burned men also, in the end, are burned.'

Sustained commercial success has eluded Partridge, but his quality and ability is undeniable. As he confidently and yet self-consciously asserts, 'At certain points, I thought I was slightly better than the major artists that I admired when I was younger.' When *Mojo* magazine voted 'Chalkhills And Children' one of the top fifty best British tracks ever, it recognized a song that rejected the rock 'n' roll lifestyle and planted itself firmly in the inspirational landscape of his adopted county, Wiltshire. The floating visitor to strange lands, escaping *fame's fickle fire*, is anchored by the ancient soil *bringing me back to earth / Eternally and ever Ermine Street*.

Andrew John Partridge was born on 11 November 1953. His father was indeed 'in the Andrew' and also a multi-talented musician who had played guitar in a skiffle band. Navy life meant that the family lived in Malta until Andy was two, after which he was raised on the Penhill council estate, Swindon. The family home had a piano, but Andy had to rely on a neighbourhood friend to come over with records and the accompanying player. Inspired by seeing The Monkees on television, the schoolboy dreamt of becoming a pop star, and experimented with a second-hand reel-to-reel tape recorder. Despite being unable to play, as a teenager he took his father's acoustic guitar to school

for its magnetic female appeal: *I used to stand proud like a sphinx / In a noble immovable state.* Lacking self-confidence when it came to pursuing girls, Partridge found that his relationships with the opposite sex at least provided plenty of material for his lyrics. In 'Snowman' he wrote, *People will always be tempted to wipe their feet on anything with 'welcome' written on it.* Elsewhere the top-twenty-bound 'Sgt. Rock (Is Going To Help Me)' had the writer looking to a brave and handsome comic book hero for confidence: *if only I could be tough like him then I could win my own small battle of the sexes.*

After two albums and five singles, XTC's first significant showing in the UK charts came from a song written by the group's bass player, Colin Moulding. The secondary writer was slower out of the blocks, but by *Drums And Wires* in 1979 his contribution, 'Making Plans For Nigel', was comfortably in the top twenty. The song, about corporations and British Steel in particular, struck gold when within months of its release steelworkers went on strike in defiance of the Chancellor of the Exchequer, Nigel Lawson. Two decades later, Robbie Williams was to revive the Steve Lillywhite / Hugh Padgham production at the height of the Brit Pop jamboree. Moulding has continued to write for XTC and has great melodic flair, but remains overshadowed by Partridge.

The paths of Moulding and Partridge first crossed in the early Seventies. Andy's further education had lasted eighteen months before he joined and formed a succession of unsuccessful and quickly abandoned groups. As Star Park he supported Thin Lizzy in May 1973. Four years of rejections followed, before in 1977 Partridge and his group settled with Richard Branson's independent record label, Virgin. Further name and line-up changes had seen Helium Kidz become XTC. Partridge came up with their name after phonetically writing down a line spoken in a film by the actor and singer Jimmy Durante, who on finding the lost chord exclaimed, 'Dat's it! I'm in ecstasy!'

Such is Andy's avoidance of unknown situations that we agreed to carry out our conversation over the telephone. Any hint of admiration was quickly deflected: 'Stop it, my head's expanding; I'm never going to be able to get out of the room. Please, no more praise.' This was a very genuine appeal, but in print it's essential to acknowledge certain of Partridge's achievements. As a producer, he has worked with the likes of Blur, The Lilac Time and Peter Blegvad, who described him as 'a master of song structure'. He has guested on many other artists' records, including Joan Armatrading, Thomas Dolby and Ryuichi Sakamoto. In the early Eighties, Brian Eno almost joined and produced XTC, but ultimately decided against it because he sincerely believed the band had enough great ideas of their own. 'The Disappointed', a song originally inspired by Argentina's Mothers of the Disappeared, was nominated for an Ivor Novello Award after former Specials frontman Terry Hall had rejected a rough cassette version, albeit with unfinished lyrics. In 1992,

XTC's wonderfully upbeat portrayal of a modern-day messiah, 'The Ballad Of Peter Pumpkinhead', was covered by Crash Test Dummies and featured in the film *Dumb And Dumber*. Dennis Fano manufactured a range of guitars, Fano's Partridge, inspired by Andy's daughter's three-quarter classical, the guitar with which he regularly writes. And in 2013 Last Shadow Puppet Miles Kane wrote a batch of songs with Partridge for his second solo album: 'He'd always be doing things like showing me chords that I never would have thought of using, or ways of writing. Every time we met up, we'd nail another song. I think he's a genius.'

You once said, 'Most good music is either written out of extreme depression or extreme joy.'

Yeah, I think so, that's the engine. All the musical influences, all of the books you read, all the dinners you ate, all the arguments you had, all the films you saw, all the pavements you trod, the embarrassing flares you wore, the awful haircuts, the pimples, everything you did in your life, that went into your sensory inputs: suddenly a situation of extreme joy or extreme misery will bang the cork out of the keg and suddenly bluurggh, out comes a load of stuff. I've found the most stuff comes out when I'm really down or I'm really feeling up.

And you're happy to share those emotions with other people?

I find it very difficult sharing emotions with other people. Now I realize I do the classic songwriter trick: every time I talk about *she*, or *them*, or *they*, or *him*, or *her*, or *those* or even *me*, I'm talking about me. You put masks of being all these other actors on and then I can do it. Putting the mask on is the only way I can stand naked. I can't stand naked and say, 'Here I am, this is what I think and this is what my feelings are on said subject.'

Are you truthful with yourself at the point of writing before disguising it in the lyrical form?

It's a hesitancy and a fear of knowingly pulling too much of yourself out. You self-delude.

What is the fear?

Of . . . just . . . being too human. You're human with a capital H. Oh, the humanity, the degradation: 'Why's he telling us all this?' But if I can disguise it with a mask I feel safer. I can be naked as long as my face is covered up.

Have you ever revealed more than you intended to in song?

Yeah, at the time, but I'm usually aware of it and pathetically fight half-heartedly not to do that song. For example, 'Your Dictionary' or 'I Can't Own

Her' on *Apple Venus 1*; both of those. Maybe I'm exposing myself too much as a softie here or it's too personal or something: 'Maybe we shouldn't record these songs, chaps,' or 'Mr Producer, we don't need to do these songs; we've got some better ones than these.'

'Your Dictionary' was evidently a great release of emotion. *S-H-I-T, is that how you spelt me in your dictionary?*

It's straightforward anger. Almost the second I'd finished writing the song I thought to myself, 'I feel better about that situation now and we don't necessarily have to record it, but dammit, I should demo it because it's not a bad song, and maybe it'll make a B-side if we're lucky or it'll creep out somewhere or I can use parts of it to build a better song.' You're always doing that, building these dodgy Mad Max vehicles out of junk. You might think it's really not rolling along very well but I can cut the back bit off and use that in another song or cut that bit off and turn it on its head and change the key and use that in another tune.

There's a stinging lyric in the first verse: *Black on black, a guidebook for the blind.*

What sort of guidebook would a blind person need? There wouldn't be any pictures in it. It'd just be black and they'd print it in black ink because you wouldn't need to see it; you wouldn't be able to see it. It was one of those self-defeating, self-loathing things, you know.

Whilst writing 'Rook' and 'This World Over' I understand the process made you cry, and 'River Of Orchids' had you dancing round the room. You must place incredible emotional investment into your songs.

You've done your homework. What happens is you sometimes surprise yourself. You're digging around in your guts and you pull up an idea, a concept or a thought and it just comes flopping out like some big, wriggly, wet fish. 'Oh my goodness, where was that hiding, whoa!', 'That is so sad, what made me bring that up?' I've been known to blub like an idiot. While making the demo of 'This World Over' I kept stopping to blub; it was stupid. 'I hope nobody knows I'm doing this and can see me in some weird, super-villain lairs somewhere, see me in the back bedroom here sat on the mattress of the spare room and blubbing into my four-track cassette machine.' Sometimes you do go real deep down, scrimmaging around like a lucky dip. Your psyche is this barrel of bran . . . 'There's something!' I've paid my sixpence: I'm going to hoick it out, but it's not till you've got it out in the open and pull the wrapping paper off: 'Ah, it's a hand grenade. I've pulled out a really uncomfortable personal feeling,' or 'Wow, that's really jolly, I do feel that great.' You can hoick out all sorts of stuff that you're not always expecting to.

Your door
Your windows
Your attic full of paintings

ROOK ROOK
Read ~~gaze~~ from your book
Who murders who and where is the treasure hid?
CROW CROW
Spill all you know
Is ~~that~~ my name on the bell?

ROOK ROOK
Gaze ~~read~~ in the brook can be
If there's a ~~secret~~ am I a part of it
CROW CROW
O please wait, don't go ~~have to know~~ before I'll let go, say
Is ~~that~~ my name on the bell?

See the semaphore from the washing lines

BEAT your waxen wings
Soar up high bove the washing lines
Chimneys whisper you four confessions

Soar up high ~~above barking sheets~~
~~on their washing lines~~
Break the code of the whispering
Chimneys and traffic signs
What's the message that's
written under
the base of clouds
Plant eternal, I know you know
So don't blurt out loud

ROOK ROOK
By hook of my crook
I'll make you tell me
What this whole twist's about
CROW CROW
Why cant you show
If thats my name on the bell

On the winds of night
~~Fast asleep~~ I
fly too
Above field any stream
My head bursting with knowledge
Till I wake from the dream
If I die and I find that I had a soul
Inside that
Promise me you'll take it up on its final
ride.

No more water
Clean the shore
Help the poor
Humanosaurus.

'Rook' lyrics, handwritten by Andy Partridge

How did you initiate writing 'River Of Orchids'?

That's a classic example of one of the things I find inspiring quite a lot, which is repetition. I sometimes will set up a pattern, played or programmed, and I'll just let it run, just kind of lose myself to the trance of repetition and start literally speaking in tongues. Singing anything, let this stuff out. That's the process of sticking your virtual hand down your virtual throat into the bran barrel and pulling up anything that your hand can grasp. I can do that quite easily if there's a repetitive pattern. I seem to get into another place. I've done it all the way through my songwriting career, everything from 'Battery Brides' to 'Stupidly Happy' or working on repeat patterns like with Colin's song, 'Day In Day Out'.

With 'Seagulls Screaming' you sketched the images before the words came. How considered are your lyrical ideas ahead of committing to the page?

I'm a little bit synaesthetic: it means when you hear sounds you see colours and pictures as well. The act of sitting at a mellotron, which we'd bought for the previous album *Mummer*; I volunteered to look after the monster. I started to mess around with it on some setting of mixed brass and strings. I started to pump away on this clustery three-note chord. I thought it sounded like fog and a little bit of a carousel about it, and wait, the fog is by the sea. So immediately it threw me to a foggy day, maybe near a funfair, and because it's foggy that suggests it's winter, so maybe it's closed down. You're making a stage set in your head. That happens all the time. That's where songs come from.

Do you frantically write ideas down, or think them through first?

Two ways of doing it: either the song comes from the stage setting suggested by the chords and/or the melody, usually the chords. Chords like sixths always suggested Donald Campbell's speed car, Bluebird. Don't ask me why. 1950s idea of super-fast futuristic cars. I blunder into chords (*plays guitar chord*) and think, 'Wow, what does that sound like? A thick piece of rusty cloth,' or (*plays another chord*) 'It sounds earthy.' I don't necessarily know the name of the chords I play. I was never taught an instrument and I never learnt to read or anything like that. You can blunder on a chord and it's almost like having a can of paint: a silver can; you don't know what colour it is, then you take the lid off and throw it at the backdrop. Suddenly it's made this kind of colourful, drippy pattern that looks a bit like . . . that chord would suggest: splat. It's like being in a Parisian pavement cafe.

At what point do you decide the meaning of a song?

Usually when the chords are coming out. I'm searching to explain the setting. With 'Seagulls Screaming Kiss Her, Kiss Her', just the act of playing those two chords suggested all those images. Then you start to dig in, fleshing out the stage setting. 'I need some side panels, what am I going to have? What do you have at the seaside? Buoys, lifebelts hanging up on the railings, and, oh yeah, they always look like the black and white minstrels' mouths gaping, sort of *Mammy*.' You find yourself describing to yourself the rest of the scenery. It becomes the lyric. The other way to write is where you subconsciously write gibberish words and phrases down and then pillage it later. It either forms a poem which can become a lyric, or you go through this garbage not knowing what you've written, and it will suggest a lyric. Neither way is always successful but that way is more frustrating because then you have the script before the stage setting. I find it's possibly easier to have the stage setting first, and then the actor describing this stage set becomes the lyric.

How do you regard the role of rhyme?

Rhyme is just another way of neatening the package, causing more rhythm, tension and release. It's like, where do you fold and put the Sellotape? Well, that's a rhyme point. I've left too much paper this end and not enough that end so I'm going to have to make these folds and turns and tuck that under and put two bits of tape on, so I need a rhyme there to hold that down. It's the process of neatening things up and finding where the song should push–pull. I love internal rhymes. You're pulling forwards and suddenly you're knocked back and then pulled sideways, then forwards again for a bit more, then sideways because it's part of the pattern. I like that sensation: the tension and release inside a line. If it's just at the end it's like Hallmark cards.

Your use of wordplay is very inventive, for example from 'I'd Like That':
I wouldn't Hector if you'd be Helen of Troy.

Yes, keeping on about something and this hero. I fucked that one up terribly. Isn't it Paris and Helen? I got the wrong historical couple. I don't check my facts. I love etymology. To me every word has at least two meanings, if not more. Blue never just meant blue: it's the colour and also blowing something.

Does it slow down the writing process, trying to use double meanings and wordplay, or is it very natural?

Sometimes I don't try to, it just bursts out in a bit of a mangled-up . . . I was a very late reader at junior school, one of the last few kids in the year to read. I had to be held back in class and have special lessons after school. I felt very special at the time. I didn't realize the other kids were probably pissing themselves with laughter that I was backward or something. I hated reading. I felt intimidated right up until I left school. Obviously I read the books I had to for homework but they usually bored the arse off me: *Prester John*, *Lorna Doone* and crap like that. It wasn't until I left school, when I wasn't being forced to read, that I became a voracious reader. It was an initial fear and confusion with words, and then from fifteen onwards the floodgates opened and I was filling my head with as many words as I could. The combination of the drought and the cloudburst had made a word storm in my head.

Your spoken language is full of metaphor like your lyrical writing.

It is, totally. A metaphor's only a mask. What's a meta for? (*Laughs.*)

What are your thoughts and approach to the structure of songs? 'No Thugs In Our House' is set in three acts with four characters, whereas other songs are very playful with form.

Songs have to push the envelope. I'm thinking what I like in other people's. They have to have surprising structures and elements. All the best things in life have that. If you're reading a book you think, 'What a great twist.' If you're looking at a piece of architecture it's got to feel balanced, but it's got to have enough detail that you can go back to it every day and see something new in that detail, but it's also got to have a pleasing symmetry to it.

Do you write with that consciousness or is it that once there are component parts you can begin to juggle them around?

It affects how it gets written. I'm lucky enough the more I wrote I developed the ability to step back from the song. Like a piece of architecture: 'Is that pleasing me back here, from a distance?', 'Does it feel symmetrical enough?' or, if it's pleasingly differently, lopsided, does it have some pivotal point in the middle where all the fractions are different values, does each side actually balance up where you put the *fulcrum*? and that's immensely important. I don't like lopsided things for the sake of lopsidedness. I'm a frustrated architect, I think.

Did you deconstruct Bacharach and David songs to discover their formula?

Sure, and I did it with The Beatles and half-heartedly with Jagger and Richards, who I thought were really good until they could afford drugs, then The Stones become shit after about 1970. That's the usual hothouse period of any creative person: a run of about five years of the real white-light stuff, the real phosphorus-burning enough to weld you to the table intensity. But at some point in the late Eighties I thought, 'Why do I like a lot of Bacharach and David?' I include David because he's always left out of the equation. Hal David's lyrics are deceptively simple but they encompass all the world's emotions in the simplest everyday language. I don't know how he does it; it's really difficult to do. I thought, 'Why do I like these songwriters or writing teams so much, they must have a formula? Let me look for the aural patterns and signatures of these great writers and try and break them down.'

What did you discover?

I discovered Bacharach and David seemed to have this shape—not a verse or a chorus—which I called the Vorus. I listened to about three albums' worth of their stuff, usually by other people, and made charts of symbols for each song: when there's a verse there's a triangle, when it's a chorus it'll be a square, when it's a ramp section an isosceles triangle, an intro a circle. There were a few shapes I couldn't decide what they were. Is that a verse or a chorus? I found that almost all of the big Bacharach and David hits start off with the title line, *Pow!* right in your nose. Then they have a kind of a set-up of after that, then the title line again and then they have a rhyme completion to the set-up line. Title line, one; two, a comment on that; three, title line again; and four, a rhyming tie-up comment to rhyme with number two. Then it'll be widdle, widdle, widdle, back to title line, and that I thought it's like a chorus with changing lines in between and therefore it's a Vorus. I started to hear Vorus shapes in other things: 'Yesterday' by McCartney.

What did you write after that applying the theory—presumably you tried?

I just wanted to know how they did it. It wasn't a case of 'I'll steal that.' I'm just one of these people that have to know how something functions. I'm not keen to go back to songs; it's a bit like a dog returning to his vomit. When you've recorded something and got rid of it, why d'you want to go back and poke in your own faeces?

When you're writing, do you ever take away the instrument to define the melody line?

I always used to say that a great song sounds good with one instrument and one voice, but a really great song sounds good with just the melody.

Do you test your own songs to see if it works?

Yeah, there are sort of rules: if the chord base is very simple, placid or non-moving the horizon is kind of flattish; the melody can really swoop and soar over that in lots of quite big leaps. So the movement is in the melody. You can be the little swallow zooming and zipping around the abbey. If the movement is in the chords, the melody can be much more linear and flat. If you do busy chord movement and busy melody you've got to really, really be careful because that's too much information in a kind of J. S. Bach sort of way and you're going to be colliding with yourself.

So you explore the melody with the chords as your base?

You know that you can leap and flail and be like some kind of circus performer. The safety net is the chords, knowing that if you fall it doesn't matter because the chord is going to catch you. You're only writing the song until you get it right. You can go up that ladder and jump off and flail around as much as you like until you perfect your routine, but it's the act of you just jumping. You just grab it and go. It doesn't have to be the right notes; sometimes the wrong notes are much more stimulating.

Does melody ever come to you away from an instrument?

Rarely. I've got the safety net of the chords and therefore I can jump and I can be more adventurous.

Alan Bennett recently spoke of an internal voice when he's writing that posed questions and filtered his taste. Can you relate to that?

Oh, totally and utterly. There's me talking about basic ground rules, but really you have to forget all that and make a complete and utter twat of yourself. If no one's watching that's completely fine. I'll stand in my socks spinning around with a little acoustic guitar just singing gibberish, hoping to pull something out. Then if you do, Mister Editor comes in the room and says, 'Oh, let's see what you've got?' You're like a teacher coming in. You've done your drawing and your little essay: 'Oh, I like that line; that's bad, that's bad, that's a nice word . . .' It's a real schizophrenic thing, 'cause you've got to be the complete shameless child to create. You know there's going to be a lot of rubbish in there, and then you have to pull the child head off and put the editor head on to shape it up and turn it into an acceptable piece of architecture. The editor doesn't create: he just wields the axe and chops it about. The trouble is, I think the editor has grown too powerful and it's stopping me creating.

Why do you think that has happened?

Partly because I'm afraid of repetition, repeating what I've already done: do I really want to write 'Easter Theatre Two'? I seem to be doing that a lot at the moment. 'Right, stop,' the editor's saying. 'Stop that: sounds like something from *English Settlement* years ago.' Oh, the editor's going to stop that. Before you know it the editor is setting up the barriers and wielding the big axe. You haven't allowed the child to come into the room, puke up everywhere, throw paints and pull out all this stuff and make a mess.

Was it different at the front end of your writing in the late Seventies and Eighties?

Yeah, I was learning to make a mess and in the same process learning to say, 'OK, I've made enough mess, now bring the editor in.' You learn to be these two people, but if one takes more control than the other you'll never get anything created.

A major feature of your work is the combination of the experimental with the conventional within one song.

It's essential. I have to surprise myself. When I sit and play the guitar I make a mental note not to play anything I've ever played before.

You're purposely being illogical?

I'm trying to trip myself up to let the kid back in the room. If you sit and play the guitar with your editor head on you'll just play old Hendrix and Black Sabbath riffs: 'Oh, how did that Free number go?', 'Listen, that's a Beatles tune,' all the stuff you heard as a kid, you'll go nowhere. You'll just be repeating the same old crap round and round, but if you say, 'OK, I'm going to play something I've never played before, doesn't matter how odd it is,' and just leap in you will find . . . 'Ooh, that's good, what's that chord? I've no idea.'

Many of your verses have unusual and unexpected developments before releasing often very beautiful melody in chorus parts, particularly songs like 'Ugly Underneath' or 'Pretty Girls'. Are you consciously playing with that form?

It's conscious that I want to surprise myself. I like material of other people's that is surprising, whether it's the way that Captain Beefheart's music would be arranged for two guitars, a bass and a drum, that was so dense and thick and alien-sounding using so many wrong chords or wrong lines that crash in against one another: I was really excited by that, or the first few times I heard 'Strawberry Fields Forever'; it was like the sound of some incredible jewel from Mars. I couldn't imagine how you made a sound and a structure like that. Unfortunately I know now and it seems to have killed a lot of the magic. That's the frustrating thing of becoming a surgeon with music: you want to know how something works, you've got to kill it and cut it up. You want to know what pipe goes where . . . 'Oh, I see, that pipe goes round the back. I thought it went round the front.' It's like wondering whether a gynaecologist has a great sex life. That's the act of killing.

Are you aware of having a grounding of Englishness in your music?

Yeah, I gently despise international-sounding people, specifically English people that do their darndest to play music that seems to come from some mythical country in the middle of the Atlantic, and it's not Atlantis. It's like an English theme park that Disney have built where everybody talks in DJ mid-Atlantic English and the music playing on the tannoy system is probably by The Police or some of the Genesis singles. I find it slightly offensive that people seem to be in denial or ashamed of where they are from.

What defines your Englishness in the writing?

I didn't always have it. When I first started writing songs, of course I wanted to sound like all the people I could hear on record, of which ninety-nine per

THE DISAPPOINTED
ALL SHUFFLE ROUND IN CIRCLES
THEIR PLACARDS LOOK THE SAME
WITH THE PHOTOS AND THE NAMES
OF THE ONES WHO BROKE THEIR HEARTS

THE DISAPPOINTED
ALL CONGREGATE AT MY HOUSE
~~WHERE~~ ~~THEIR~~ ~~SOBBING VOICES SING~~ WHERE THEIR VOICES SOB WITH GRIEF
WHAT THEY WANT ME TO BE ~~WILL~~ CHIEF
OF THE ~~TRIBE~~ WITH BROKEN HEARTS
        TRIBE

THE DISAPPOINTED
WILL ~~ALL~~ BEAR ME ON THEIR SHOULDERS
~~TO A DARKENED UNDERWORLD~~ TO A DARK AND SECRET LAND
AWAY ~~SMILE~~ ~~ALL~~ ~~SCATTER~~ ~~LOST~~ FROM SUCH A GIRL   WHERE A SOMBRE MARCHING BAND
~~FOR~~ ~~WHO~~ COURSNESS BREAK MY HEART   PLAYS A TUNE FOR BROKEN HEARTS
WHERE SHE

ONCE I HAD NO SYMPATHY ~~COMPLETE~~
FOR THOSE DESTROYED AND ~~THOSE~~ IN LOVE
SEEMS   ~~LEFT~~ THROWN AWAY
~~COMPLETE~~ TO YOUR RING UPON MY FINGER
SIGNIFIES THAT I'VE THE ~~LEADER~~ OF:....
        BECOME   SPOKESMAN

THE DISAPPOINTED ~~ARE~~
ARE ~~MARCHING~~ PILGRIMS IN THEIR MILLIONS
~~ALL CLAMOURING TO SEE~~ ~~THE RING OF~~ ~~AND BUY~~ ~~WHERE~~ SPILLING FROM THE BUS
A MONUMENT ~~TO~~ ~~ME~~ ~~FOR~~ US
        TO
MADE OF BITS OF BROKEN HEART

THE DISAPPOINTED
ARE GROWING EVERY SECOND
AS WE'RE FILLING UP THE GLOBE
HERE WITH SCEPTRE CROWN AND ROBE
I'M THE KING OF BROKEN HEARTS

'The Disappointed' lyrics, handwritten by Andy Partridge

cent of them had an American accent, so I thought that's how you had to sing. Then as you get older you think, 'This is wrong, I don't have an American accent so why am I singing in one? Why don't I sing in my Wiltshire burr, I have one of those?' It's the act of knowing and being more truthful with yourself. Weirdly, when I think I'm being English people think I'm being other than. For example, with 'Green Man', to me that is rooted more in a pagan English, folksy, drone tradition, yet every reviewer that ever talked about it says it's Middle Eastern; you can literally smell the Baghdad bazaar. I thought it was a cross between Vaughan Williams and some thousand-year-old druid with his finger in his ear.

Does Swindon shape the sound of your work?

Yes, because I can see those chalkhills out of the bedroom or attic window upstairs. I can see the trees. I walk the dog in the park where you can see carpets of daisies or in the summer be getting the idea that you're drowning in flowers. It's enormously influential in its mundanity, in its everyday. It's a Victorian park here, it's a wet alleyway there, it's a load of cars choking up a length of tarmac there. It's some people you know and their funny small-town manners. I don't know about dusty Californian highways. I don't know about denim-clad hippies, chicks laid across the bonnet of your Buick '57. I don't know about this accepted rock language. It doesn't speak to me.

When The Dukes Of Stratosphear presented their tribute to English psychedelic music, did writing free a creativity otherwise suppressed?

Oh yeah, and funnily enough I read recently Paul McCartney said The Beatles were stuck and the act of saying they were another band, Sgt. Pepper's Lonely Hearts Club Band, suddenly gave them a burst of creativity where they didn't have to be The Beatles any more.

The act of tricking yourself.

Yes. The Dukes was a combination . . . everything you do, your history branches off. All those funny little branches of decisions, times and consequences of what might have been if I'd said yes to that one and no to that one and vice versa. All the bands I loved when I was a schoolboy, when I really opened up to music, there were records like 'See Emily Play' in the charts, the Small Faces singles like 'Lazy Sunday' or 'My White Bicycle' by Tomorrow: still pop singles but with the then still fashionable psychedelic edge. I thought, when I grow up I'm going to be in a band just like Syd Barrett's Pink Floyd or the Small Faces, doing *Ogden's Nut Gone Flake* type stuff. Then of course history puts you off all these different tangents and you find yourself all grown-up and in a group thinking, 'Hang on a minute, this isn't actually the group I wanted to be in when I was a schoolboy. What would it be like if we bent history around you to actually be the kind of band that I wanted to be in when I was thirteen?' I thought that was a bit of mischievous fun to do. Also we didn't have to be ourselves and what everybody was expecting from XTC. It's that mask thing: if you put on some fancy dress and a mask you can behave much more outrageously. The Dukes was really a fancy dress party that we could go to, pretend to be other people and say and do different things. And lo and behold, it was very freeing.

The conundrum being, would songwriters love the songs they write if they were not the creator?

A lot of songwriters have done that; The Beach Boys made that album *Carl And The Passions* where they got to be the mythical doo-wop band that they probably wanted to be when they were thirteen. Roy Wood did Eddy and the Falcons, a kind of rock 'n' roll group; Frank Zappa and the Mothers of Invention as Ruben And The Jets, a really greasy doo-wop group. There's probably dozens more examples in the arts of people doing stuff pseudonymously. I had a phase of loving science fiction. Kurt Vonnegut wrote about this cheesy sci-fi writer called Kilgore Trout who appears in several of his books. He then wrote a book as Kilgore Trout in the style of the crappy sci-fi that Trout would have written. That's his Dukes Of Stratosphear.

Is the lack of recognition financially and artistically a contributing factor in your approach to writing?

It's poisonous. Erica said to me the other night, 'There's a lot of disappointment in you.' I just had to say, 'Yes, there is.' I feel that for thirty years—this is going to sound horrible because it's all self-trumpet-blowy shit—I was maybe as good as or slightly better in some cases than the major artists that I admired when I was younger. At certain points I've been slightly better than Ray Davies or Lennon and McCartney or Bacharach and David. Not generally maybe, and not in terms of sales and recognition, but I think I've strived for an artistry that . . . it's that thing you hear; you must kill them.

When you don't get that acknowledgement, how does it affect you when you come to write the next batch of songs?

For a long time it was the huge battery in my back; it's what keeps you going. You write what you believe is a great album's worth of material and then nobody buys the bugger. Then I thought, 'Oh my God, I have to write better, it's got to go up. It's got to be better words, better melody, better chord structures, better emotional content, better everything: better, better, better.' So you make an album that you believe is 300 per cent better: still no bastard buys it. So then you think, 'Right, the next one.' We were constantly ignored, and painfully, the most in England, our own spot, not so much in America or Japan. I don't know why the Japanese loved us so much in the Nineties; it's not even their language, what are they getting from it? My power pack was that constant failure; jolted me with a million volts.

The observation has been made that few artists consistently improve with successive records as is the case with your career.

There are very few artists that I can think of where the graph went up. Most artists, the graph went *kerpow!* Then the line nosedives over successive albums, singles and career. Ninety-nine per cent of bands and artists do that. I know that we got better, but it is rare. I am somewhat embarrassed by the first couple of albums which are very juvenile, but then are they any more juvenile than some of the Merseybeat shit that came out?

Do you consider the audience when you are writing?

Occasionally in the early days but not much, in fact I had the totally wrong attitude to the audience. I used to see it as a battle and it's not, because generally they love you. They want to love you and adore you and like what you're doing. I used to go out on stage and think, 'Right, you fuckers, I'm going to fuck you up real good (*laughs*). You think you're gonna dance to this? You ain't. You think you're going to get my songs quickly? No, you're not. You think you're going to go home and go, "Yeah, I know what chords he's playing," you've got another think coming.'

Why have you never written with Colin?

I've often thought about this. We tried to at one time, but a lot of it was due to Colin starting under my wing. The first few things he ever wrote were like bad surrogate Andy songs until he found his own voice. Colin's strength was his melodies. He's much more melodically (*laughs*) acceptable than I am, much more traditionally melodic. The weak points in Colin were his words. I would say to him, 'This is a really weak rhyme, there's a much better line if you would say . . .' and he'd look at you, 'Yeah, I'll consider that,' and he'd never change it; or you'd contribute something: 'If you went to this chord here, it'd get you there so much quicker.' 'All right, I'll bear it in mind,' and it would never change.

Can you recall writing 'Chalkhills And Children'?

Vaguely, yes, it's like remembering a colour or a shape of a spark. It was to do with having a synthesizer. I'm a really crappy keyboard player. Before I knew how to work a sequencer, if I found a good chord I've been known to make a cardboard hand in the shape of that chord. You hold the keys, when you find all the notes, then run in the house and hold your hand over a bit of cardboard and draw round it in that shape, then write on it, 'That noisy song' or whatever. You take the cardboard hand out to the shed studio and hover it over the keyboard: 'Oh, it's those notes.' Another system I had was writing the notes on the keys and drawing diagrams of keys in a sketchbook and writing number '1' on a certain key and '1' on another, meaning that was the first chord, then '2' on another and that became the second chord. I couldn't write music so I had to find my own ways. But the initial thing behind 'Chalkhills And Children' was with this synthesizer. I thought, 'Is there a function instead of playing one note at a time, can I make it play two notes?' There was: you could split the sound into two voices. So I held down C and bent the other sound that was being triggered up or down to a G or an F and it made, to my mind, a very pagan-sounding, droney thing which suggested hills. When you held these very simple three-note chords down they became very complex six-note chords because you had two notes for every key. I was just lazily holding down these very simple chords and then I came up with that pattern (*hums*) which was the main melody, but also the harmonic melody because it's two notes. I've never analysed what the tuning is. It's something simple: you add a G into a C, it's like a fifth or a fourth, I can't remember. Just messing about with this multi-tuned keyboard these simple chords sounded like floating and flying above green hills, like the ones around here, the Marlborough Downs. The synaesthesia kicked in and because it's an organ-y kind of tone—to me organs suggest floating because of their placidity—there you are floating in a dream state. Again, I was describing the scenery coming from the sound. Why am I floating above green hills? Because . . . and before you know it you have a lyric.

Did 'Dear God' come out of McCartney's 'Rocky Raccoon' picking style?

(*Laughs*) Not totally, no. My nickname at Swindon Art College was Rocky because 'Rocky Raccoon' was the only song I could play through at the time.

Not Rocky for your punching strengths then.

Exactly (*laughs*). I was so skinny at the time I wouldn't wear short-sleeved shirts; my arms were like a knot in a piece of fishing line. I was the youngest one in the class, fifteen, and everybody else was a lot older than me. They made a special exemption because they said I was artistically talented. There was a degree of bullying; they'd stand me on the desk and say, 'Play that song, come on, play it, Rocky.' But did 'Dear God' come from 'Rocky Raccoon'? Possibly. Sometimes you're dicking around trying to work out a song and you find one of your own. That's how 'Books Are Burning' came about. I was trying to find the chord structure to The Beach Boys' 'I Get Around'. (*Plays guitar.*) From the G, *I get around, round, get around I get ar . . .* What's the next chord? Ten minutes later: 'Wow, what is that chord? It's like an E7 but it's got an A flat on the bottom. Wow, that's a great chord. I never knew that one existed,' and that gave birth to 'Books Are Burning'.

Going back to 'Dear God', how often do you accomplish what you set out to do, lyrically?

For me that was a complete failure, which is why when Virgin said the album's too long, what are you going to lose, I asked for 'Dear God' to be removed from the original running order. I wanted to write a song about the point in my life where I was wrestling with the definitive concept that there isn't a God. But I thought, how can I do it in a creative way other than it sounding like a kiddie tantrum: (*squeaky voice*) 'There is no God, there is no God'? I remember being in W. H. Smith in Swindon and seeing those books of children's letters to God which are so fucking offensive, making poor little kids . . . that's how religion survives; it gets beaten into kids until they are scared shitless. If no kid was exposed to religion until they were twenty-one, religions would die out overnight. It jumps from parent down into child and the child gets scared stiff and believes that's the way it's got to be, and they put that into their kids. These children's letters to God were called *Dear God*. I thought, that is one sick concept, a really cynical little ploy telling him all goofy, cutesy things, but if you were going to write to God you would start the letter, Dear God; but wait a minute, there isn't a God, so how do you write a letter to someone that doesn't exist? So just the paradox started to hurt my brain. 'Well, this might be a great way of putting my wrestling with being an atheist into a form I can handle. How do you write a letter to someone that doesn't exist and telling them, yet questioning . . .' Ah, it's even difficult to explain.

Do you remember writing 'Senses Working Overtime'?

Yes, because that's one of those songs coming from bits of car chopped and hacked up. It was about two or three bits of song put together. At that point I got the use of living above an abandoned shop on a Victorian street called Kingshill Road. My brand-new wife at the time, her parents owned a little sign-making business. They took over these premises and we got to use a couple of rooms for free. I was living on about twenty-five pounds a week. One of the rooms had nothing in it because we couldn't afford furniture: bare floorboards which I painted black and the rest of the room was white, so it was very stark. I found being in such an empty space was quite inspiring to fill with your own sonic pictures. I'd stand there staring out of the window or at the black wooden floor with a guitar, just trying to pull stuff out. I thought, 'I'm going to write a single. How do you write a single? What's the most moronic thing I can think of? I know, Manfred Mann's "5–4–3–2–1". Fuckin' hell, that is *so* moronic,' so obviously that was a hit because before it even gets to you people know what the next lyric is going to be: after 5 it's going to be 4; the next lyric is going to be 3. Instantly moronically acceptable. 'So why don't I use that as a basis and sing *one, two, three, four, five*?' I've got the chorus: *one, two, three, four, five*. 'Five what? What's five? Five days of the week?' Five senses was the only thing I could think of. So I started to write *one, two, three, four, five senses*. 'What are they doing? They're *working*,' so you have sensory input. 'Wow, they're working *overtime*. Good phrase. Working, working overtime, *senses working overtime*. OK, got it.' So I've got *one, two, three, four, five senses working overtime*. It's got to be instant: it's got to go crunch, crunch, crunch. I thought, 'Well, I can't start with that.' So I was dicking around: what else do I have in the key of E, and I made a mistake and accidentally stumbled on this dissonant-sounding E flat because I wasn't looking. 'That's a nice chord. What if I swapped my fingers to the polar opposite where they are now? That's a nice movement, that sounds like some medieval serf ploughing.' Do you know what I mean? Like a little picture on an illustrated bible. The serf with a cow pulling the plough, and that's the music you'd hear: those two chords going round, so that became the verse shape. Then I started singing: what would your medieval serf be singing as he's ploughing? Let's describe the scene. I've already got the pictures, let me tell you what I'm seeing: *Hey, hey, the clouds are whey, there's straw for the donkeys and the innocents can all sleep safely.* You're singing about the clouds and the earth. Then I wanted a way of getting from that to my *one, two, three, four, five* backwards Manfred Mann bit. I had a song already that had an A and A suspended and then went up to B and B suspended, very Pete Townshend actually. A song I liked the chord changes but wasn't working called 'The Wonderment', so I thought, 'Yeah, I'll bolt that bit in there from the B suspended.' It was a perfect set-up to go up to the E.

Brilliant! How do you store all your ideas?

I used to do it either in my head or on a cassette or both. I still do that now. There's loads of cassettes over by the fireplace with the last five years' worth of ideas; something like four hundred bits of songs in there that I've never taken anywhere.

Do you regularly go back to pillage for ideas?

Yeah, I would have done in the past but in the last five years I think the editor has got too important. Also it's that personal thing that I don't want to repeat myself, so I want to look for new territory. I've been much more fired up by things that are for me out of the accepted zone. I'm very excited at the moment: I'm just putting the finishing touches to an album of electronic, I won't say electronic *music* because it's not even music in the accepted form; it's just sounds.

The conceptualist Michael Landy has been asking fellow artists to bin their creative failures. Would you have donated 'Sgt. Rock (Is Going To Help Me)', having once said you'd gladly erase it from XTC's history?

Lyrically, in hindsight, yeah, because I thought they were really stupid and banal. I really liked the Marvel Comics artist Jack Kirby and for years and years I had wanted to write a song about Sgt. Fury, then lo and behold Alex Harvey came out with 'Give My Regards To Sergeant Fury'. 'Oh no, the bugger. I've been robbed!' So I thought I'd write about the competition, DC's wartime hero Sgt. Rock, drawn by another artist I admired called Joe Kubert. I wrote about this nerd, basically me really, who didn't have success with women and perhaps this macho hero could show him the way. It's got quite an interesting groove and chord changes, but the lyrics I find a little embarrassing. I did get some hate mail from feminist groups who wanted to string me up by the balls for writing a song that advocates beating women, which it doesn't.

'Pale And Precious' shows your precise understanding of the construction of Brian Wilson's melodic and musical approach.

That was meant to be a Cornish pastiche, better-tasting than the conventional pastiche of everything that Brian Wilson wrote. 'How can I say thank you in a song? It's got to sort of sound a bit like everything from the *Smile* or *Smiley Smile* album and sort of everything from their early career, the surfer kids thing.' It was an attempt to do an identikit Brian with Carl singing, but my Carl voice isn't very good. I was better at Mike Love . . . he's got Mike Hate on the other hand!

'Respectable Street' had quite a few lyrical concessions for the single: *proposition* replaced *sex position*, *abortion* was changed to *absorption*. Why?

Oh, that was such an ironic story: usually Virgin would pick the most banal songs as singles and inevitably the ones I was least proud of, which would cut me inside. You'd deliver *White Music* and they'd pick 'This Is Pop', which is the crassest thing on there, or *Drums And Wires* and they'd pick 'Life Begins At The Hop', not my song but the crassest one on there. But they warmed the cockles of my heart and said 'Respectable Street': finally a lyric with a bit of grit, a track with a bit of spunk in it. 'This will be great . . . but we want you to change the lyrics because there's no way the radio are going to play it with words like *abortion* and *contraception*.' 'Oh yeah, I knew there'd be a catch.' But I thought half a spunky song with a half-gritty lyric is better than none so I agreed to rewrite the lyrics to get rid of certain words that Virgin found offensive. So *contraception* became *child prevention*, *abortion* became *absorption*, which I thought was a lot filthier; seemed to suggest sanitary protection to me. *Retching* became *stretching over the fence*, and fuck me, the radio still wouldn't play it. I was told years later by a BBC employee they were really upset by the phrase *Sony Entertainment Centre*. The same reason Ray Davies had to change *Coca-Cola* to *cherry cola*; it was an advertising brand. How frustrating is that!

Todd Rundgren's input had a profound effect on 'The Man Who Sailed Around His Soul'. Is there an argument an arranger should have a co-credit for artistically interpreting a songwriter's vision?

That's my favourite lyric. Possibly; it's difficult because Todd was the first and only person that had a big musical input in an album that we did. Todd sat down and said, 'How do you see this song being done?' I said, because of the lyrical content and the title alone, 'The Man Who . . .'—the very phrase suggested a spy film: the spy who came in from the cold, the spy who haunted himself— 'I'd love a cod John Barry-type arrangement.' Also because of the psychotherapeutic nature of the lyric in general, about finding and discovering all that you are, the decaying reality of what you are, and accepting it and being OK with it: that had a real beatnik coffee thing to it, so, 'We should do it with a John-Barry-does-spy-music but with a beatnik finger-clicking coffee thing, maybe an upright bass?' With this input he literally went away overnight and came back with it arranged just in the style that I'd asked for. He did a great job, but should an arranger be given credit? I guess it's down to how much they put in it. Then again, usually either the band would just play my demos how they'd been put together, or in the earlier days, pre-demos; I'd just describe what I want from them and they'd chip in at rehearsals and we'd push it and pull it until we had what felt right. I had no musical training: it's no good me saying, 'I want sevenths and fourths and give me a diminished on the turnaround.' I can't do that. 'I want it more fidgety. You're not yellow enough.' I'd speak in those sorts of terms.

Do you have an opinion on why there are so few women in the history of British songwriting?

It's in the history of anything creative: there are not that many famous painters, cooks or sculptors; generally it's men using it as a substitute for childbirth. Women can have babies, they can create the ultimate brilliant thing: a human being. Because men can't do that they've got to have surrogate creativity. He can make a picture of a human being or a sculpture or describe a human being in a book or their traits in a song, but woman don't need to do that so much because they can just make the real thing; they're too busy creating life and we've got to make do with second best.

The implication being that women aren't creative when they don't want to have children.

I don't think it's so much about holding women down, because surely the arts is a freer set of worlds than anywhere else.

What effect has not touring had on your writing?

Made me get much better.

A band that tours gets immediate reaction to what they're doing from an audience; where do you . . .

. . . They're not applauding you; they're applauding each other like fucking chimps because they recognize the intro. The gig's not about the artist: it's about all those people being together, exciting each other. I never liked live gigs very much. I had to stop playing live because I was coming unwound after thirteen years of Valium addiction. I stopped suddenly, having no concept of withdrawal, and my brain literally started to melt. Trouble is, I was coming unwound on stage as well. I didn't know anything about panic attacks at the time, or withdrawal, or about the symptoms of that, and I thought I was going insane. Move over Syd Barrett, here I come, this has driven me to nuttiness; I've got to slow down. But thank goodness, in my naivety, when I did stop I'm glad, because our material, or my songs particularly, got a lot better, because I had the time to make them better. *English Settlement* was the first record I mentally decided I didn't want to take on the road. 'Let's stop touring, please. Let's take a break.' Whereas before, the material was all snatched literally in a few weeks: 'OK lads, we've finished the tour and you've got three weeks off . . .' 'Oh, great.' '. . . in which you, Andy and Colin, have to write the next album, and then after three weeks we start rehearsals and then after two weeks' rehearsals you're making the next album.' So we had really narrow gaps to squeeze this stuff out. You were getting little desperate ideas on the road, in the back of vans, and trying to jot them on napkins or hotel notepaper. You'd finish a tour, be exhausted, get up the next day jet-lagged and completely empty and have to start gazing at a blank notebook trying to squeeze it out, knowing you had three weeks to write the album in. But when I put a stop to that it was like, 'Now I'm not rushed for time I can make these lyrics better. I'm not happy with this part of the song. I'm going to put it aside, come back to it in a week or a month's time and see if I can get it any better.' The material suddenly got much more widescreen and colourful; before it was pretty monochromatic or like dual-tone. That was start of us becoming multi-coloured, as opposed to *Multi-coloured* fucking *Swap Shop*.

CHRIS DIFFORD
AND GLENN TILBROOK

In 1973, Chris Difford passed over the lyrics to his song 'Hotel Woman' and Glenn Tilbrook wrote a melody. Although never formalized, an unspoken deal on the division of songwriting duties had been brokered and is still intact some forty years later. The new associates shared a flat in Crooms Hill, Greenwich. Difford climbed the stairs from his basement room and left a sheet of words beside the morning milk for Tilbrook to collect in his slippers. His new partner would then invent a melody and find chord progressions. A call to Difford from the top of the stairs would signal a listening session. When Squeeze first floundered as a band after four albums, a combined solo work, Difford & Tilbrook, was delivered by the warring frontmen. The lyricist wrote, *Love's crashing waves upon the rocks is seen by some, by you it's not*. The melodist retorted, 'There are a lot of different Chrises and I know some of them.'

It all began with an 18-year-old Chris Henry Difford stealing fifty pence from his mum's purse and posting an advert in a sweet shop in Blackheath: 'Guitarist wanted for band with record deal and tour. Influences: The Kinks, Small Faces, Lou Reed and Glenn Miller.' Many weeks later the first and only reply came from a local hippy, Glenn Martin Tilbrook. He was three years younger than Difford and had been expelled from school for having long hair. He had played piano and guitar since the age of seven. The duo began to practise and play ska, Motown and Jimi Hendrix records in Difford's bedroom. Chris was considering a career in the law, but his hopes were abruptly ended when he stole from his employer's safe.

Petty theft and unsavoury underworld characters began to infiltrate Difford's imagination, reflecting the company he and Tilbrook were keeping and the surroundings they inhabited. They began to fill their writing with the imagery and sounds of their neighbourhood. Minute details and habits were observed. 'Vicky Verky' was peopled with personalities from the pub across the road: *With her hair up in his fingers, the fish and chips smell lingers.* 'It's like writing a book,' Difford explained. 'You really have to know the characters you're writing about.' 'Cigarette Of A Single Man' was inspired by watching a lonely and depressed-looking chap in the local Hope and Crown. The fag became an allegory for a friend, but also 'an inanimate object without emotional needs'. As the pair sought out the seamier side of life, sketches of south London friends, acquaintances and criminality lent their songs an authentic voice: *The Deptford had a beano to Southend for the night / With forty crates of lager, to see the Southend lights.* Verses were packed with rhyme and metaphor; the everyday references of 'Cool For Cats' tugged at the imagination, from the *likely lads who swear like how's your father* to *the Sweeney doing ninety.* Difford focused on small characteristics. It led to great similes such as *the skin on his face like a well-worn saddle,* from 'Melody Motel'. On the album *Play,* 'Letting Go' chillingly embraces rising minor melody notes with a lyricism poised with tension: *she plaits her hair / I bite my nails / We balance love on the scales.*

Difford's verses always furthered the narrative, invariably beginning with the subject *she, they* or *you,* keeping the story moving with character development. He wrote in block capitals with blue ink, centring his verse on lined A4 paper. The ideas were succinct and neatly structured with concluding storylines. 'Up The Junction' was an impressive piece of lyrical invention written when Difford was stranded in a motel on the outskirts of New Orleans: the girl from Clapham Common who *stayed in by the telly*; the boyfriend who *bought the girl some flowers* and always *put away a tenner.* By mid-song the couple *make evenings by the fire and little kicks inside her.* In the fifth verse she has given birth, but by the sixth, *mother's with a soldier* and the narrator's drinking has become *a proper stinging.* The song ends with the enduring hook *I'm really up the junction.* Like Paul Weller before him, Difford found inspiration in the BBC's *Wednesday Play,* but he was also paying tribute to Nell Dunn's 1963 novel *Up the Junction,* with its depiction of sexual encounters, births and deaths, and its colloquial dialogue. Difford's contemporary reading of working-class survival in south London drew on the seamless storytelling of folk music. As the writer reveals, both Shirley Collins and Bob Dylan's 'Who Killed Davey Moore?' were primary influences. Tilbrook had Dylan's 'Positively Fourth Street' in mind when he wrote the melody to 'Up the Junction', playing against the darkness of Difford's lyric with musical brightness so that the breakdown of the couple's relationship comes as a shock. It was a clever juxtaposition, and one often repeated. Where Difford veered down, Tilbrook lifted up: the negativity of 'Hourglass' is jubilantly enriched with a rapid chorus delivery; 'Third Rail' pushes along Sixties country-pop tracks to collide with emotional buffers; 'Everything In The World' see-saws between major and minor chord play. Tilbrook constructed optimism out of pessimism. His partner had attempted suicide as a teenager, his self-esteem damaged by his excessive consumption of drink and drugs. The two chemicals raced through the song sheets. Squeeze was labelled as the birds and booze band.

Chris Difford's early experience of the opposite sex was far from positive. Perhaps not surprisingly, an element of misogyny can be seen in his early writing. 'Out Of Control' was a list of male sexual desires. The 'it' of 'It's So Dirty' was a deliberately objectified female figure. The media lambasted the songwriter, and the criticism seemed to have a profound effect. Songs began to emerge from Squeeze that recognized the independence and strength of women: 'Man For All Seasons', 'Woman At The Top', 'Woman's World'. 'She Doesn't Have To Shave' is possibly the only song by a man to directly address menstruation.

Difford has been keen to confront lyrical taboos. On many occasions the topic was domestic abuse: love *driven to violence* in 'Jolly Comes Home', or the male as victim in 'No Place Like Home'. His subject matter spans domesticity, nesting, boredom, infidelity and masturbation. As his writing reached out beyond his immediate circle of friends and acquaintances, so maturity gave vigour to his craft. Reserve may be an English trait, yet songwriting encourages an exchange of confidence with the listener. Difford expresses genuine sentiment in conversational language. *It's funny how the missus always looks the bleeding same*: 'Cool For Cats' had been rehearsed with a different set of lyrics before Tilbrook suggested a rewrite. At Difford's home that evening *The Benny Hill Show* was on television, and the flat metre of the comic's delivery inspired the writer. The set was turned off and twelve verses poured out, subsequently captured on a cassette recorder. It became A&M Records' biggest-selling UK single ever, racking up over half a million sales. The title was taken from the 1956 TV series *Cool For Cats*, in which presenter Kent Walton reviewed the nation's new releases. In 'Labelled With Love', Difford depicts a GI bride at the end of her life where *the past has been bottled and labelled with love*. With Tilbrook's melody fitting snugly across a D major vocal scale, the song tells a story of marriage and motherhood overtaken by the bottle and the booze.

While Difford's lyrics, borderlining between reality and fiction, were the content of the songs, the sound of Squeeze was Tilbrook. His skill lay in taking the everyday Englishness of his companion's words and delivering smooth, continuous melody. A hallmark of Tilbrook's songwriting is a prolific use of chords. 'King George Street' has an array of changes. 'Piccadilly' bustles with movement and lifts, reserving its repeated vocal hook until the end coda. 'If I Didn't Love You' came with a stuck vocal groove: *If I, If I, If I, If I, If I* suggested by the line *the record jumps on a scratch*, complemented and underpinned by a Roy Orbison-styled three-chord trick. Tilbrook has always been happy to let other writers infiltrate his music. The diversity of his listening constantly pushed Squeeze into new musical domains. There is the major/minor chord flirtation, reminiscent of The Beatles' 'Things We Said Today' in 'Is That Love' or 'Daphne', and the spirit of Frank Sinatra in the brooding 'When The Hangover Strikes'. Where Difford often drew from the metre and rhythm of Ian Dury, Elvis Costello or Brinsley Schwarz, Tilbrook explored the combinations of opposing musical genres. 'Black Coffee In Bed' is delivered with the voice of American soul to a country metre; 'Slap And Tickle' makes use of the Germanic electronica Kraftwerk sound, utilizing sequencers and a Minimoog; 'I've Returned' pushes an Attractions-shaped arrangement to a dramatic dead stop to focus on the filling melody line: *you've thrown my jigsaw all over the floor*. The one-bar tacet highlighted Difford's unconventional turn of phrase and emphasized the writers' musical differences; even their trademark harmonies were seated an octave apart.

Tilbrook's writing complements the drama of songs with varied musical moods. 'Pulling Mussels (From the Shell)' takes the simplicity of Difford's postcard-verse impressions of holidaying in Margate and cuts across the lyric with chord tension rooted in A minor. As a musical tribute to the American group The Tubes, the chorus is then resolved with a grandiose major lift. Written in the back of a van, the single would sell over a half a million copies. Tilbrook is a great believer in challenging the ear with the unfamiliar. He began 'Hourglass' by feeding a succession of unknown chords into a drum machine. 'Tempted' took a good week to crack. The first two lines were the starting and then the sticking point. After Tilbrook recorded his vocal, producer Elvis Costello somewhat surprisingly suggested that new recruit and former Roxy Music and Ace keyboard player Paul Carrack should sing the lead. Nevertheless, the song was a huge radio hit in America, where record label stickers on its accompanying album, *Sweets From A Stranger*, declared Difford and Tilbrook 'the new Lennon and McCartney'.

A 2008 Ivor Novello Award for Outstanding Contribution to British Music more appropriately recognized Difford and Tilbrook's songwriting individuality. They continue to write, record and tour, but predominantly for solo albums. After a fourteen-year hiatus the couple, who have now been together longer than they have been with their respective wives, entered 2013 with a new Squeeze EP, *Packet Of Four*, and a succession of reunion tour dates behind and ahead of them. Chris Difford was living in Brighton when we met. He was impeccably dressed for a quaint English tea shop rendezvous and littered the conversation with deadpan asides. We reconvened a week later in a Bloomsbury gentlemen's club where we once again picked at his songwriting habits. Prior to both meetings, Glenn Tilbrook shared his reflections in the sanctuary of his Greenwich recording studio, 45 RPM. It has been the home to solo records and Squeeze releases since 1993. Glenn was relaxed, but challenged to find appropriate words to analyse his natural vocation. At the end he revealed it was one of the best exchanges he had ever given. The revelations are an intriguing insight into the inner workings of a musician's mind. He also referred me to an interview he'd given to Dan Ehrlich for *London Calling*, MIAATV. There is no better way to give a 500-word history of Difford and Tilbrook's career:

'1973, met Chris. 1974, Squeeze formed. We played together for a couple of years and wrote up to a thousand songs in our bedrooms which was a very creative time for both Chris and I. 1974, met Miles Copeland. 1975, toured supporting some of his bands: Curved Air, Renaissance, Climax Blues Band. 1976, started doing pub gigs. They were great. We played a lot: twice, three times a week, every week for a year. That meant we got our chops together. 1977, made first independent EP, *Packet Of Three*. Great. Got us onto the pub circuit. We gradually played around London and then around the country. Signed to A&M Records. 1978, our first album and chart hit, 'Take Me I'm Yours', in the UK; worldwide not so good. 1979, *Cool For Cats* LP: 'Up The Junction', 'Slap And Tickle', 'Cool For Cats'; you name it, they were there. Great success in the UK, not so good elsewhere, except for Australia, Egypt and Ireland. 1980, we released *Argybargy*. More success in America this time, coming on strong on the East Coast; West Coast lagging behind a bit; Midwest couldn't give a fuck. Then 1981 saw the tumultuous *East Side Story* album. That was a great deal of a step forward for us. America, we toured supporting Elvis Costello And The Attractions. Suddenly our audiences rocketed up—coming in their thousands to see us. It was a heady day for us, or two. 1982, *Sweets From A Stranger*; suddenly we were headlining Madison Square Garden. Europe—not much. Australia— we'd been forgotten about. 1983, all got too much and we split up. Stayed at home. I had a bit of a heroin habit and looked at my toes for about a year. 1984

'Harri Kakoulli diary entry, 1975

I got married and that was good. 1985, Squeeze got back together after the solo *Difford & Tilbrook* album which we don't talk about much these days, but it was an interesting excursion. *Cosi Fan Tutti Frutti* was a bit of a weird record; we didn't all play together at the same time, therefore not playing to our strengths. 1986 we toured. 1987, whoaah! *Babylon And On*, our biggest success in the States: 500,000 sales—not a lot by industry standards, but it wasn't bad. 1988, we toured. 1989, *Frank*. We were surely going to go to greater heights. Unfortunately our record label, A&M, was sold and we were dropped. Bit of a disappointment. In 1990 toured and supported Fleetwood Mac. Bit of a bummer. 1991, signed to Warner Brothers. Brilliant! New dawn. Fantastic! Released *Play*—dropped. 1992, toured. 1993, signed back to A&M and we released *Some Fantastic Place*, one of my favourite Squeeze albums. Didn't sell—dropped. In the UK, 1994, toured. 1995, released *Ridiculous*, which was Squeeze's last official big-label album. Sick of the process, didn't like it any more.'

CHRIS DIFFORD

Did you come from a musical household?

There are no musicians in the Difford family. I am the breakout artist. I first realized music because my brothers would play it on our stereogram: Bo Diddley, The Rolling Stones, The Hollies, The Beatles. My mother was into The Bachelors, Matt Monro and Irish music, being from an Irish family. I was fascinated by it. It became something that flowed through me in a spiritual kind of way. I have a photograph of my first record player, a Bush mono, and the three records leant against it are 'Make It Easy On Yourself' by The Walker Brothers, *The Sound Of Music* and *With The Beatles*. When I was about twelve or thirteen I bought a beautiful pear-shaped Vox Wyman bass from a friend of mine. I thought an instrument with four strings would be easier than one with six. Then I played in a couple of school bands.

When did you begin to write?

I was writing poetry at school, pretend places in my head. I had a really good English teacher who saw some of the stuff I was writing and inspired me to write songs. He played a Bob Dylan album, *Highway 61 Revisited*. I saw the potential of lyrics and music but didn't really understand it. A friend's parents used to take me on a Sunday to a folk pub down in Kent and I used to sit and listen. It was very odd because I was a skinhead, beating people up and finding solitude in poetry and writing about it. My writing didn't get defined until I'd met Glenn. It wasn't until the two of us discussed what songwriting was for us and started to absorb what was around us musically that it really started to take shape. We listened to a lot of the same music and both liked to watch Judy Garland musicals on a Sunday. Music was the only thing I wanted to explore, and girls of course, and to do that I really needed to get away from the council estate and the gangs and meet up with people that were like-minded.

Is there a distinction to be made between poetry and lyric writing?

They're pretty similar, really, but getting together with Glenn and deciding verses were verses, choruses are choruses and these are middle eights, made you write in a certain way.

Do you write with musical structures in mind?

Writing with Glenn I do. I write CH over the top of what I call a chorus and M8 over the middle eight.

Are the suggestions historically honoured by Glenn?

Yeah, pretty much, but when I'm writing on my own I leave it more free-form. I write reams of stuff and sort it out later.

Do you need certain environments in which to write?

Being a writer allows you to live in a bit of a fantasy world. Everybody that I know suffers because I'm sometimes in that world and they don't know whether it's real or it's fantasy. It's quite a nice place to be in. The trick is to have your head in the clouds but your feet on the ground, and that's quite hard because you have to be very, very tall.

In *Squeeze: Song By Song* you said, 'There's a fine line between songwriting and reality.' What did you mean?

You can use a lyric to disguise a message you're trying to send somebody who might be listening to the song. For instance, if I was in the courting stage of a relationship, a bit shy and didn't know how to ask a girl out, I might write it in a lyric form. Play it on a guitar in a Shakespearian fashion outside of her window and hope that she drops her knickers!

Love's crashing waves upon the rocks is seen by some, by you it's not.

It was really a tough time around the *Difford & Tilbrook* album. We weren't communicating very well. It's always a tough time for us both; we're not exactly the greatest communicators.

'Tempted' was written in the back of a cab on a cigarette packet.

On the back of a Woodbine box, travelling from Blackheath to Heathrow Airport. It was a list of all the passing images out of the window. The germ of the idea can happen anywhere. I had one on the train coming up today. I wrote it in my book and I'll see what happens to it later when I get home.

Did you believe in any kind of spiritual channelling of ideas?

Yes, definitely. Getting ideas together is a bit like building a nest. When I watch birds flying from tree to tree with twigs they are kind of like lines of songs; you collect them all together to eventually make the nest out of them. The channelling normally takes place when I sit at my desk and try and open up . . . give myself over to whatever's out there and tune in to it. More and more, as I get older, I love meditation: it's a really great place to be. If you can hold yourself open and see what happens you'll be surprised. It's like pulling the walls open and letting air in: it's amazing; see what's being brought to the nest. I tend to have lived with an idea and then there's an instinctive outpouring.

How disciplined are you?

If I've got empty days I'll be disciplined and work all day. I really enjoy it. Lyric writing is a bit like developing photographs: you write the idea down, put it in the tray and it starts to develop, then you go for a cup of tea, come back and have a look at it and say, 'Actually, I don't believe that, it doesn't work,' and you move on to the next lyric. There's a lot of chaff involved in lyric writing, a lot of stuff that gets hacked away. I remember Ray Davies saying that out of a hundred songs that he writes probably only five of them are any good. I totally agree with him, if he still believes that philosophy.

When an idea first arrives, do you try and complete it?

I try not to pore over lyrics; they're either spot on or not quite or they're crap. When they're crap I never come back to them. If they're almost spot on, then I'll come back and look at it. Some I have a feeling that it's really good, so I leave it and never read it until it becomes a song. 'Some Fantastic Place' was like that: didn't bother reading it twice, just wrote it, gave it to Glenn and that was that.

'Some Fantastic Place' is regarded by both you and Glenn as one of your greatest achievements.

It was really written from the heart. Our best friend died, the lady that brought Glenn and I together in many ways. She was Glenn's girlfriend and died of cancer seventeen years ago. To remember her I sat down and channelled some thoughts about her and put pen to paper and didn't stop till I'd finished. I know it came the same from him; he put it in front of him, wrote the music and that was that. The really cool thing about that song is the really intricate solo and middle eight. Glenn lifted that from a very early song while Maxine was alive. It was a very clever move on Glenn's part.

As you write, do you word-associate to inform the next line?

There was more of that around the time of *East Side Story*, when we were working with Elvis Costello. He's the king of wordplay. Going up before him every day with a new song, I was really on call. Songs like 'Woman's World' and 'Someone Else's Heart' were playing on words, and 'When The Hangover Strikes' from the next album, *Sweets From A Stranger*, a favourite song of mine from that period.

Setting out all your lyrics chronologically reads like a diary of a life. Do you recognize patterns of development?

They've become more personal, especially me being a solo artist. I think they've matured, on the whole, but the stories are still the same. There are only five stories in the world, they say, and I've written about them all, about 500 times. It's very difficult to find a unique take on a relationship or a situation. It really is. For instance, on my last album I wrote about what it was like being overweight and going down the gym, in 'Fat As A Fiddle'. I don't know many songs about that, apart from Olivia Newton-John's 'Let's Get Physical'. I wrote another song about vasectomy reversal, and there are no other songs about that that I know of. I'm forever prodding around looking for different avenues to write. I don't want to keep wearing the same dress to the same ball. I want to be able to show off a bit.

Do you have any thoughts on resolution in lyric writing?

I don't really mind either way. In some ways, how can they resolve, because the characters carry on? I live with a lot of the characters I write about, so they continue into other songs. They weave between different states. I had a lot of imaginary friends when I was a kid and they're still there. They come to all my concerts!

Do you write linearly? I ask that knowing the line *Singles remind me of kisses, albums remind me of plans* came first for 'If I Didn't Love You' but sits in the second verse.

That's one of my favourite lines. It came from an image. I can see it now, being in a single bed in my first flat trying to chat up a girl and putting on Todd Rundgren's album because it was the longest on one side, so I could get my hand down her bra. If I come up with an idea, a lyric or one line that I think is particularly good, I wait for the right moment to put it in a song.

'Black Coffee In Bed' opens with *There's a stain on my notebook* and 'Is That Love' begins *You've left my ring by the soap*. Do lyrical ideas infiltrate your everyday thoughts?

Yes, images that burn themselves into lyrics. It's a bit like blotting paper: it blots up the images. If they're interesting enough I can use them in some way.

'Is That Love' was about the domestic situation I was in at the time. We'd just got married, the whole nesting thing had been taken care of and now we were just man and wife. The ring was by the soap, the beds were being made. It had become very mundane: is that love? The finger was being pointed at the individual.

Elvis Costello said of you, 'He's such a craftsman in terms of metre and rhythm, much more so than I am.' Is that ability instinctive or studied?

Instinctive, that's just the way I am. I've recently been listening to Jay-Z and Black Eyed Peas and trying to figure out if I could still write in that metre. It's quite a short metre, but lots of it. Some people don't want long lines. When I'm writing with Paul Carrack he doesn't want lyrics that allude to salad or beetroot or ironing boards, but if I give those words to Glenn then he can use them because he's very good at that.

Glenn Tilbrook and Chris Difford, Greenwich Baths Rehearsal Rooms,
1975 by Lawrence Impey

You've written words for many artists. Do you vary your style and vocabulary accordingly?

Definitely, you have to be like a tailor: you've got to assess people, ask them what they want from a song and understand what fits them well. With Paul I really get into his space and time and think about what he can sing. The sitting and understanding is like . . . before a therapist can give you any feedback they need to listen. I wrote an album like that with Matt Deighton. He came to my house for a number of weeks and I listened to his story about his family life and what was going on and just gradually wrote the whole for him, about his life. Writing with Marti Pellow, there are certain words that sound ridiculous in his mouth, like marbles; they just don't fit. They say that people with great voices can sing the telephone book, well, they can't. They can only sing bits of the telephone book that are relevant to them.

Elton John said that he would sometimes have to edit Bernie Taupin's words. Would you expect Glenn to sing exactly what you had written?

That used to be the way. He's a lyricist himself now, so I would have to learn not to be so conscious of my part in the song and not to be selfish with it. Before, if somebody would say something I'd feel hurt but say, 'Oh yeah, that's great,' but inside I'm going, 'Fucking arsehole.' I use to sulk if he didn't do what I'd given him.

She used to do a topless down at the Surrey Docks / With tassels on her whatsits she did a t'riffic job. **Your writing style is unmistakably English.**

It was very natural; that was the life I was living when I wrote 'It's Not Cricket'. I'd witnessed those images. I used to work down the docks with my brother. At lunchtime on a Friday everybody would get their wage packet and we'd go into this smelly pub and watch girls get their tops off. As a young boy it was a shifty education and a smelly one too. We also courted the criminal underworld, and some of the characters I wrote about we were drinking with in various pubs we'd frequent in Greenwich and Deptford. They loved having us around because we were the local pop stars. They bigged it up whenever we turned up: the lights would go down, the door would be bolted and we would be given Tequila Sunrises till they were coming out of our ears. They were amazing times, really good fun; somebody would get hit over the back of the head with a fire extinguisher and be dragged out the back door. All those ideas and phrases were filtering through, in the blotting-paper sense.

Your lyrics are packed with a seemingly very natural use of your humour.

It's part of me to supply lyrics that have that kind of bent to them. It's the way I write: I don't have to go very far, it's there most of the time, I'm lucky to say. It used to be a very dark process, writing lyrics, but it's not like that any more; it's much more open and friendly. When I was drinking, being an arse, most of my lyrics were written in a hangover or when I was pissed. I came up with some killer things, but now I don't have that part of me to worry about. It's just a different kind of me, I suppose.

Can drink and drugs enhance a writer's creativity?

I'm not against it; it's not me but I wouldn't say more creative. The *Play* album: 'Letting Go'; 'The Truth'; 'Walk In A Straight Line'—I'm so proud of all those lyrics but they were written in a very dark place, behind closed curtains in a sort of nocturnal world. Glenn was at his wits' end, he'd be saying, 'Have you got any happy songs?' and that really pissed me off 'cause I didn't have any. My days didn't differ really: I'd get up, nurse my head and then by four o'clock be back on the drink again, so there would be very little time to not be either coming down or coming up. They inspired lots of great images. I don't knock any of it. The experience was again just part of me and now being part of me is not to be like that.

You've addressed many social taboos in your lyrics. What was your motivation to tackle the female menstrual cycle?

I happened to be living with somebody whose cycle . . . you could visually see the change in her mood. It struck me because it really was painful, not just for her mentally but for anybody who was within six feet of her. 'She Doesn't Have To Shave' is a very flippant lyric, actually.

You've always been able to turn your hand to masturbation songs.

That's a good line. It's an intriguing part of life; it's not talked about as something that everybody has done or does do. It's quite interesting there aren't any songs about women masturbating—but now I'll do one!

Male sexuality is also very evident in your solo work: 'Julian And Sandy', 'Cowboys Are My Weakness' and even understanding the unlikely third point of view in an affair, in 'The Other Man In My Life'.

I don't think there's ever been a really great gay album and I want to write one, but from a straight person's point of view. I may be way off beam doing that, but it's part of society. Men have really intense relationships with each other but are also very domestic. Often one plays the motherly role and one the father role. Sometimes there's more devotion and love in two men.

Domestic violence is a recurrent theme throughout your songs, in which you often and intriguingly take the female perspective.

The early lyrics for Squeeze were steeped in sexism because I didn't really know any better, I guess. As you get older and your accent starts changing and you live on the posher side of Blackheath and you start listening to Radio Four instead of Radio One, you get more tuned in to what's going on in life. I still feel really sad how alcoholism and drug addiction really wrecks family life, in every instance. I'm careful to take on board the feelings of characters like that and it's normally the women that need to be sung about, although men can be downtrodden too. Men have become much more feminine in the last twenty, thirty years. Their masculinity's been taken away by the female partners. It's just an observation. There is a song in there which I shall now write about down-trodden men that climb in Superman outfits to the top of Big Ben and say, 'I want my children for the weekend.'

What is the handover process of lyrics between you and Glenn?

Traditionally, it was just leave them at the bottom of the stairs, and he would pick them up and start writing music to them. As time grew they became emails, then I built a little website and put all the lyrics up with photographs which only he can see. I've stopped doing that now because I think it was a bit cold. I'd like to get back to writing more with pencil and paper and then photographing what-ever I write, and then send him that.

Would you offer any suggestions or discuss the words with Glenn?

Not really, no. I know Bernie does or he did; he might write a lyric and at the bottom put 'Working In the Coalmine', telling Elton it could be like a Lee Dorsey song. I don't think Glenn would go for that.

How would you hear Glenn's music?

He'd just send me a cassette, or these days a CD or an MP3. Most of the time I'm really delighted with what I hear. I remember when we were doing the *Some Fantastic Place* album getting the demos and going in the car, finding a nice stretch of road, putting the cassette in, listening to it thinking, 'This is great', just driving round and round, really loud; then calling him up and telling him how much I loved it. I always thought whatever he did was always pretty spot on. I've never really questioned what Glenn writes.

'Pulling Mussels (From the Shell)' has each verse told from a different point of view.

I wrote it in New York. It's a story about going on holiday with my friend's parents to Dymchurch and staying in a caravan. It's the imagery from that and being a young kid. I do remember a band playing in the social club that I think, hope, was the Small Faces.

Glenn said you were labelled as great songwriters at that time and felt that the songs became mannered, sometimes self-conscious and slightly self-important.

It affected Glenn much more. I always knew we'd be bigger than The Beatles, so it didn't bother me. I just walked around in circles until I wrote the next song. I don't chase that kind of success. It would be great to do those kinds of records again, but it's never going to happen.

What determined when you sang the lead?

I didn't have an awful lot of confidence, so whenever Glenn said, 'What songs do you want to sing?' I always used to say, 'I don't want to sing any,' which he'd get really pissed off about. He always loved my voice. He's always tried to help me with my confidence but I've always felt in the shadow; now I can give him a run for his money. A lot of people have commented how I sound like Lou Reed. Before I met Glenn I used to just cover his songs: that's where my voice is, in my boots like his. It's a great place to be.

Home is a love that I miss very much / So the past has been bottled and labelled with love: **a tremendously sad song but with wonderfully cinematic images.**

The images came from a Cartier-Bresson photographic book called *Paris*. I was flicking through it and that inspired that song. I've got a lot of photographic books and sometimes they're very useful for imagery.

Did 'Up The Junction' originally have ten-plus verses?

It was quite long. Glenn's got all the original lyrics. It was my attempt to write something like Dylan's 'Who Killed Davey Moore?', although more so; it was inspired by a radio show, folk music hour or something, and there was this wonderful domestic song. It may have been Shirley Collins. I thought, that's amazing, how she's summed up domestic harmony, or disharmony. I thought if folk writers can, then I can write like that. I would be very happy to retire into folk clubs just playing to fifty people every night.

'The Apple Tree' was written after Glenn's request for a political song.

I'm not a political writer, by any stretch of the imagination. 'The Apple Tree' I'm not so keen on the music, it's a little bit alienating. I'm very proud of it lyrically because it sums up my grandparents' garden. They had a wartime shelter and an apple tree's roots had grown through the building. As a kid I thought that was a really interesting thing, that a tree would have grown right through it in its lifetime. It was just a really powerful image.

'If I'm Dead' was changed at an A&R request to 'If It's Love' to make for a better singalong. Similarly, 'The Great Escape' was formerly titled 'Rape'. What are your thoughts on concessions to commerciality?

Around that time we were making a lot of concessions. It was quite painful when record companies would say, 'No, we want this,' or, 'We want it mixed by that person.' To A&R, Squeeze has always been a mistake. It's like going back in the lion's cage because you've left your hat in there; you never want to do that with Squeeze because its strength and weakness is being left alone. In a way that's what ended the band: being A&R'd so viciously. Particularly Glenn turned inward; it really wasn't a very positive move. Every artist's suffered it.

It's an amazing insult to tell an artist how better to write a song.

It's so difficult to tell that to somebody; that's their livelihood, that's the way they do things. It's like going into a shop and saying, 'I don't like the way you make those shoes: do you think you could cut the end off?'

'Maidstone' has a plain, beguiling charm. Do you think simple ideas carry greater resonance?

Possibly. I've never got it why people love that song. I don't. It doesn't really tell a story. What's brilliant is it really captures Maidstone as a place insofar as there's nothing going on.

Songwriters' explanations of their lyrics are often difficult to marry with the words written on the page. 'Last Time Forever' was inspired by an amazing story but in the song the great complexities of the event are substituted by more ambiguous words of regret. Why did you make that decision?

It's a good question; that was a song that got regurgitated from previous records. It had been re-demoed and lyrically had changed a couple of times. I remember reading about an airline pilot who had murdered his wife and dropped her into a lake with concrete round her neck so she wouldn't come up. They discovered her five years after and the rug she was wrapped in had a tag on it from a dry-cleaners. The detective traced it back to the shop and eventually got to the husband who was still using the dry-cleaners. That's a great story to put in a song, but I couldn't elaborate more on it because there just wasn't room within that song, musically speaking.

Cold shoulder like a slaughtered cow in a butcher's fridge: **a most alienating metaphor.**

It's one of my favourite lyrics. That was one of those really amazing times; I was driving home in the country, in the rain, and I saw that image and it started to drip through my imagination. I stopped at a church and I thought, 'I've got to write this down.' The lights were on so I sat at the back and the whole lyric just tipped out. The images were so strong. The alcoholic getting stuck with his head in the cat flap was the image I really wanted to go for.

'Piccadilly' has the memorable image *She hooks up her cupcakes and puts on her jumper.*

I like that line a lot; that's a really good song as well.

Why do you think classic British writing is a male-dominated domain?

Kirsty MacColl, Amy Winehouse and Lily Allen are probably three of the most dominant writers we've had for years. Depends on your taste. I think Cathy Dennis is a fantastic writer, but she's a jobbing writer. Why is it all men?

I don't know. Kate Bush is there. I think the music industry is floating in female songwriters at the moment. You can't go to a club without some woman pouring her heart out over an acoustic guitar: it drives me nuts—it's like, 'Give us a bloke!'

GLENN TILBROOK

What brought you and music together?

The simple answer is that I grew up in a house where records were played. Neither of my parents could play instruments. My mum could sing. My earliest memories are of really loving music and I always wanted to play an instrument. My aunt had a piano, which we got hold of when I was six. I really liked that. I got a guitar when I was seven. It really fascinated me to just sit round and teach myself how to play it. I was quite self-absorbed when I was a kid. I didn't really aspire to be anywhere other than where I was. By the time I was eleven or twelve I could play most of the chords through picking up what I'd heard on record. It's a wonderful time when you're young to listen to music because you don't have any of those taste filters that you develop. All sorts of stuff would go in and settle quite happily with me. Thirteen onwards you develop aversions to types of music because of what you think it is, rather than just being open. I used to get these things called Record Songbooks which had lyrics in. I'd learn to play songs I knew and if there were songs I didn't I'd make up my own tunes to them, so without knowing it that was a forerunner of how I worked with Chris. The first band I was really mad about was The Monkees. They had some gifted writers working for them. I bought *The White Album* when it came out: what a strange record to have as your first Beatles record, the depth and the width of experimentation is astounding.

You once said, 'Writing is about tricking yourself into doing something different.'

(*Laughs.*) Yes, that is true, sometimes. With my keyboard playing I got to a certain level and went no further. I still write more on keyboards than I do on guitar, although I swap between the two. It's the unfamiliarity of a keyboard plus the ability to play around with different bass notes and chords, stuff that I probably couldn't achieve on a guitar. And the thing about tricking yourself is, you don't know where you are with a keyboard and it's always a bit of a magical mystery tour, setting out on an adventure and seeing where you can go. It's like solving a crossword puzzle: it's just really fun. I can play chords really well but that's as far as it goes. It's the sound of the chords. I'm always fascinated with the possibility of where you can go with chord sequences. I never consciously think about it in those terms.

A great hallmark of your songwriting is the prolific use of chords. It gives tremendous movement to the music without compromising the flow of melody. Was 'Tempted' the kind of adventure you're talking about, where the chords are changing every bar?

Yes, very much so, although 'Tempted' is interesting because it wasn't an easy song to write. It took me about a week. I had the first line and then I couldn't figure out where it was going. Songwriting is sometimes about being inspired but more often than not it's about working and getting inspiration from a mistake that you make, or finding something that then inspires you to go on. It's always about putting the time in. It's very rarely about an idea that pops into your head. I worked and worked on 'Tempted' but it doesn't sound like it to me, it flows.

When you use so many chords in a song, do they lead the vocal melody because the movement is happening so rapidly?

When I write music to a lyric the chords and the melody would be coming at the same time, so neither one will dictate to the other. Ninety per cent of the time I'm not thinking about anything. The best way to write music is to try and banish any conscious thought at all and just get to a stage where you are at one with whatever you are doing. However, sometimes there's a conscious thought. You'd swear if you weren't paying attention to the lyrics of 'Is That Love' it was a very upbeat, happy-sounding song. The contrast between the lyrics and the music actually takes one to a third place where you are almost standing outside it and seeing that it's a reflective song, and it is quite depressing but it's OK, which is the result of both of those things working together. It could very easily have been a melancholy song. I would never have analysed it in that way, but that's what I think is going on in that song.

'Up The Junction' has a couple of fantastically deceptive key changes. The song starts in E but after the middle eight the song has a wonderful push: it's unexpectedly down to D and yet the feel is a lift.

It was a very happy accident. It just works, doesn't it? And then when the song goes back into E it feels like you've had a traditional key change and you're back where you started. The technique didn't really enter my head. It flowed that way and it worked. It was a brilliant lyric, a complete story, and I thought my job was to be in the background and to convey the lyric as much as possible. I was trying to be like Bob Dylan: of course it doesn't sound anything like him, but that was my approach in terms of making the lyrics absolute centre stage and the music conceived to deliver the lyric. It wasn't a big tune; it worked out to be very nice but I wasn't thinking of it in the same way as 'Tempted' was a tune.

Up the junction **is famously only sung as the last line of the song, subverting the traditional approach to chorus writing.**

Yes, but I would never think about it in those terms. I would be thinking, 'That works, there's the story, it doesn't need anything else.' When I'm writing I don't think about the structure of the song, really. It should occur naturally, whatever it is. Sometimes you make a chorus out of nothing or you feel it doesn't need a chorus. That whole process is as instinctive as I can possibly get it. I think that's why I don't function well in songwriters' workshops or anything like that.

Earlier you touched on how in many of your songs musical brightness plays opposite to the sentiment of the lyrics.

Chris's lyrics were quite often dark. He went through some very dark patches. If I were to reflect that musically it probably wouldn't be to my taste. The music is a reflection of my personality. I'm generally quite optimistic and happy in my outlook.

Is it difficult to write up-tempo songs?

To consciously write fast songs, I guess it is harder. Having finished a song I like to try to have a bit of time between writing and recording it because then you can take a look at it with fresh ears and try and figure out how you can play about on it. If I do demos I'll sit and listen to them at certain points. It's like a process of osmosis. The time when you're going to be recording you just do it how you feel it, which may be different to the way that you thought it was going to be on the demo. It's not really a process of analysis. As I said before, if I can get away from thinking too consciously about anything that's the best way for me. One of the things it took me quite a while to learn, six albums in or something, was just letting go of how a song is conceived. Sometimes it will be exactly what you thought it would be and other times it won't, and you never know. You could arrange it a different way; you can write a slow song and you can speed it up and it may work better, it may sound like that's the way it's always meant to be.

Do you think there is an English style of melody writing?

It's a process of everything you've ever listened to plus whatever you're listening to at the moment. Everything filters through and what comes out I guess is the essence of me.

Do you ever pursue melody without Chris's words?

I don't really write melodies very often without having some sort of words to go with them. In the times I've been writing by myself I will always do a lyric first and then consider the tune afterwards.

Would you say you sculpture melody?

That's an exact analogy of the way it works because you are trying to look at it from different angles: walk around it, walk out the room, come back. All that stuff is a process of reduction. What I was saying earlier on about music being a reflection of my personality, my least favourite periods of my writing was '82, '83, '84; we went through a bit of a bad patch then. They are also my least happy years in terms of where my head was at and the things that were happening around me. The melodies reflect that. I don't really enjoy an awful lot of the stuff from that time. I find that interesting. I'm glad I'm not there now.

Chris once likened 'Slap And Tickle' to a Dury/Jankel composition, but the difference is your great vocal range. Do you steer melody wanting to use your singing capabilities?

I know what you mean: no, I think it's just a matter of what pops out. There's a song on the album with The Fluffers called 'Best Of Times'. The melody arrived in a strange way for me. I had a complete chord sequence without any idea where it was going with the melody. Having written the words I then just sang randomly to the backing track and what came out was a reflection of the fact that I can sing much higher and harder live than I do on a record, which is a different thing than sitting in a room and creating a melody, where I will probably sing slightly softer. That returns to tricking myself; it was a different way of working for me and a good thing to discover.

When you are creating a song, do you try and get to the end?

Mostly, when I first started out writing and quite a few years after that I would have an idea and try and see it through one way or another. Perversely, now I have a studio and all this stuff around me, I like to go and sit in my bus and work there. There's a song I'd been working on for a couple of days that I put down; it didn't have any lyrics, just a melody. I haven't played it since, which was probably three months ago. I'll go back and I won't remember what it is. It'll be like someone else wrote it. I'll play with it and then take it on to somewhere else. That's another way of tricking myself. Of course I eventually go all the way round the houses to sitting back in front of a piano in the studio, and that then becomes fun and different because of all the different ways I've approached working.

Before you had studio facilities, how did you record your ideas?

The first thing I bought with my first royalty cheque was a four-track recorder and a Minimoog. I stayed with that for the best part of sixteen years. Four tracks is enough to put down an idea. One of the worst things for me was when I got a twenty-four-track studio. I started doing really complicated demos. It was fun, a different way for me, but incredibly time-wasting. I'm now back to doing either really simple demos or no demos at all. Just playing the song to whoever I'm working with and recording that way.

Do you ever imagine yourself to be other musicians when you write?

No. One of the things I'm wary of doing is genre-hopping. That's to do with the style of music and whether you become a sort of parody, whether it's Motown, blues or a Sinatra-type ballad. Those things are fun to imagine but I would almost always try to pull away from the original idea.

Do you consider band arrangements in the songwriting process? For example, there's a wonderful gospel-influenced push after the guitar solo in 'Some Fantastic Place'.

When I wrote 'Some Fantastic Place' I stole the chord sequence from one of mine and Chris's earliest songs, which is where the solo starts and the gospel choir comes in. It was called 'We're In Love'—we never recorded it. I did it because it reminded me of a time when Maxine and I were together, a tip of the hat to that time. It also happened to work beautifully. A ready-made chord sequence waiting to be plucked, and it lifted the song in a really great way, I think.

Do you ever feel trapped in your own writing style?

The only time I ever felt trapped was when Chris and I were called great songwriters. Again, I refer back to '82, '83, '84: quite a lot of our writing got mannered and slightly self-important, self-conscious. Besides that, it's a whole world of possibilities. One of the best things I can do is to sit down and write. Around that period I found it hard to write; this was coming out of a time when I wasn't in a very good space. But I got through that and never really had that problem since.

What I'm learning is that you are incredibly instinctive and shy away from any theory.

I just wasn't interested in theory. It never fired me up because everything I ever learnt was from listening, an entirely internal process that was best if I could bypass thought altogether.

Do drink and drugs affect the writing process, assuming you've encountered that throughout your career?

I certainly have. I went through a stage of smoking a lot of dope around about the third album, and everything was slow. The band, when we were learning the songs, would reinterpret and speed them up, so initially it was quite interesting. Anytime I've leant on those things to try and be creative it does the opposite and clogs me up.

Are you disciplined as a writer?

Yes, I am to the degree that writing is a question of putting time in and not waiting for inspiration. Last night I went to bed and thought of some lyrics, got up and wrote them. I like it when that happens, because I wasn't even thinking about it. You always have to be aware and try and make space to take notice when that sort of thing happens, rather than wait till the morning and it's gone. With writing music it's about sitting down and finding a way. The way that it happens nine times out of ten is by sticking at it.

Do you set hours for yourself?

I used to do ten till six, nine to five, eleven to seven with a leisurely lunch. The more time you put in the more you'll have to play about with, even if it's rubbish. I used to with Squeeze write for a record and then not write until the next time it came around. Then I was just dealing with music. It's like turning over a car that's been in a garage for a year; it may or may not work. You may have to go through a process of writing four songs that you know are horrible to get to the fifth one.

What is the handover process between you and Chris and what are you looking for in a set of lyrics?

In the olden days it was handwritten lyrics, for a while it was typed, and then emailed. Chris is quite a prolific writer and will always give me a batch of lyrics. What I've always tended to do since the very early days is to make a conscious decision not to look at them until I'm sat down with a piano or guitar or something. So my first impression I'm able to translate instantly, rather than read through and think about what I want to work with. You engage with the lyric in some way or other, sometimes from the first line, or maybe I'll read them all the way through. If I get nowhere, after a while I'll flip over and go to the second lyric and see if that works. The lyric inspires the tune.

Does Chris offer comment or explanation with the lyrics?

No, never. 'There's some lyrics, there you are.' The first song we wrote, he just gave me a lyric and we didn't even speak about it. Chris's lyrics were way, way better than mine, so great and fun. I just stopped writing words because I had more musical knowledge; I was happy. Here was a guy who was expressing all these wonderful ideas that I would never have had in the first place but that I could empathize with. So when he gave me a lyric it felt totally natural for me to scurry away and write something to it. That in a way was a blueprint for, and the essence of, our relationship, in that we discussed very little, if at all.

So obviously you wouldn't call Chris to discuss the meaning of his words?

No. Mostly they were pretty clear to me. I know there have been a few songs where a few years later I'd understand what they were about; fortunately not that many. On our first record, *Squeeze*, John Cale, who produced the album, threw out all of the songs that we did have and told us basically to write the album in the studio. He gave us subjects that we would never have written about; it was almost like imagining ourselves into John Cale's head, trying to get what would please him, and in so doing our writing was unlike anything we did subsequent to that. It was harder and tougher, certainly musically, than we became. *Cool For Cats* is more like our first album.

'Hourglass' was an attempt to write together having previously shared a flat. Were you and Chris literally writing in the same room?

We were in the same room but we'd almost always agree to meet up later once we'd got an idea going. I'm not really good at working with other people. The process of writing that I got involved with, being in front of a tape machine or making demos, took me away from that ability to make instant decisions. Particularly when I started working with midi stuff; to have the ability to change something at a later date is an open invitation to daydream. To trust myself not to dot all the i's and cross the t's ahead of the time was really liberating for me, and that's another way of tricking myself into doing something different.

When are Chris's lyrics at their strongest?

It's like that thing you say to aspiring songwriters: always write about what you know; anyone who writes is best served by remembering that. The best of Chris's lyrics always reflect that.

Chaz Jankel said of Ian Dury, 'his words had their own natural rhythm'. Do you recognize that in Chris's words?

Yeah, there's almost always some sort of rhythm to a lyric that you can't help but pick up on. Ian Dury's lyrics are very rhythmic, perhaps more so than Chris's.

Who is the first person you play a completed song to?

With Chris; it would be Chris unless it's to my partner. I might play it to them.

Can I ask about some particular songs and get your memories and thoughts? What happened in that week writing 'Tempted'?

The lyric was obviously brilliant, and when you get one that stands out as being special you want to be extra careful to make sure you get it right. It ran against the grain to spend such a long time on something. Within that week I was good at not losing sight of what it was I was after; although I didn't know what it was, I knew it had to flow. Through banging my head against a wall, finally it emerged. Even then, when I had written it, I thought it was like an ELO power ballad or something really horrific. It was a great tune but the way Squeeze recorded it first was horrible. It wouldn't have been the song it was without the version that we recorded second with Paul (*Carrack*) singing it.

'Jolly Comes Home'.

'Jolly Comes Home' was a really old tune that had been knocking about for twenty years, nearly (*'Love Is A Four Letter Story'*). It was very poppy and it was an inconsequential lyric, shall we say. So Chris rewrote the lyric, this was just when he'd been into rehab. It was a very powerful lyric. Musically it stayed the same but the arrangement, the way that the tune reflected the lyric, changed in a very direct and obvious way, but one that worked, I think.

I was astounded to read that 'Labelled With Love' might have been rejected had it not been for Elvis Costello's intervention.

I went in the obvious direction that the lyric of 'Labelled With Love' was pointing, which was country music. I didn't know what I thought it would be, but it didn't strike me as a Squeeze song or one I would even play for Elvis, who was producing that record. I was trying to find a different song, fast-forwarding on a cassette of my demos, and played a bit of the song. It wasn't the one I wanted to hear but Elvis said, 'Why don't you play that one?' The next thing we were recording it. It was great what Elvis did for us on that record to broaden our horizons.

'Vanity Fair' and 'When The Hangover Strikes' both highlighted your expanding musical vocabulary and maturity.

'Vanity Fair' was very Kate Bush influenced musically, and The Beatles, sort of welded together. There's a good bit of 'She's Leaving Home' in there, retrospectively. 'When The Hangover Strikes'; that's one of the few late-night drunken songs that I've written. I remember coming back from a pub one night and opening the lyric book. The temptation to write a Frank Sinatra-style ballad was too great so I didn't fight it. I'm very proud of that song. It flows. It was quite easy to write, for me.

One of my favourite songs is 'Letting Go'.

I'm very proud of that song, musically. When I demoed it, it had an entirely different chorus. I really liked what I had but Tony Berg (*producer*) said: 'It should go up, it should soar,' and so I rewrote the chorus. Musically it's very Prince-esque. It's a very dark song and it's again exploring the possibility of what you can do with chords and where they go. It fell together quite easily.

Does commercial success play on your mind?

Fortunately that was never a thought for me, I was so far removed from the commercial process. I had this idiot thing thinking that anything we did would be successful, so I was never really bothered whether it was or not because in my mind it was. My last record is a brilliantly successful record in my mind, but actually it's not. It sold eighteen hundred copies or something; it's like a vanity project. The real upside of my personality is that I can judge my stuff away from the commercial glare of whether it's been successful or not. The downside is that I'm deluding myself and I've still got a career.

'Maidstone'.

When I wrote that I thought it was an absolute contender for *Play*, but no one else thought so and it got sidelined. It's a great song. One of the things about it is, the lyric is very unassuming. It's about a night out and going back to sit in a bath . . . and this girl that you vaguely fancy from the pub. It's about nothing but in fact it's a great snapshot. Musically, by the time that we recorded it, it was as a B-side, so we could go out on a limb to do whatever we liked without having the importance of it being a track on your album. It turned out to be what it is: a fantastic song of no consequence.

Do you have any thoughts on the historic scarcity of classic female British writers?

That's a really intriguing question. Whether it's black artists or women, the history of companies standing by them is very short and it's a shameful record. There's Kirsty MacColl. There's a whole crop of women writing now but the process seems to have changed. There's a little bit of sausage-machinery going on whereby everyone will be put in with the same bunch of writers, so people who write with Lily Allen will write for Amy Winehouse or be suggested for Duffy. There's a little group of those writers that operate. Lily Allen is absolutely brilliant. She's got a great ear for detail and I think will go on to develop and develop. I don't think it's for a lack of talent or ability; it's for a lack of foresight.

MADNESS

A pop band for a knave: Madness were disreputable and roguish, the Artful Dodgers of north London. Tonic suits and brogues. Levi's and braces. The music was instant, youthful and life-affirming: surface sheen with polish. But what lay beneath, and what became clear over successive releases, was a depth and talent that would give Madness so much more than the fleeting appeal of a short-lived popular phenomenon.

Madness are amongst the finest exponents of the three-minute song. In the 1980s their hits spent more weeks in the singles chart than those of any other group. Seven members, seven songwriters: a unique mix that allows all the band members to contribute in a variety of combinations. Most ideas come from interchanging pairings where one person's chord movements or demonstration backings are fused with the other's lyrical suggestions. Less frequently, three or four writers pool their talents, and on occasion a song may be written by a single individual. Royalties, traditionally an area of conflict within bands, are split on a simple system. The songwriters equally share fifty per cent, while the remaining half is split seven ways.

At the centre of Madness is the pianist 'Barzo'. Technically Scottish, Michael Wilson Barson left his birthplace, Edinburgh, in April 1958 when he was two weeks old, and was brought up in London. Deadpan in delivery, he is a highly disciplined musician. Barson developed the writing and playing of his companions into the self-defined 'Nutty Sound': rhythm and melody, fun and humour. It was a conscious antidote to the aggression of punk. His keyboard arpeggios chime through the music: simple play around thirds and fifths and chromatic runs conjuring up both the music hall appeal that traces the group's lineage back through The Kinks, and their shared territory of Chalk Farm, Camden and Kentish Town.

The music of Madness is a soundtrack for London. Their aim has always been to capture the heart and spirit of the capital and create a musical tribute to the nature of being a Londoner. The early LPs *One Step Beyond* and *Absolutely* conjured up the experiences of youth in the city. Later, *The Rise & Fall* collected together songs in a range of musical styles which reflected nostalgia for childhood memories. The ninth studio album, *The Liberty Of Norton Folgate*, delivered in 2009, had the band mapping the streets of 'The Good People of Lud' from *Pimlico to Morden, from Muswell Hill to Bow*, weaving a vivid tapestry of characters past and present. This was not a concept album, however, but the band's celebration of London as a living organism.

From his onstage position behind his Vox Continental, Barson can scan the rhythm section of drummer Daniel 'Woody' Woodgate and bassist Mark 'Bedders' Bedford; to the side, guitarist and founding member C. J. 'Chrissy Boy' Foreman; opposite, saxophonist Lee 'Kix' Thompson. To the centre, sometime trumpeter, dancer and vocalist 'Chas Smash', and completing the line-up, frontman 'Suggs'.

Graham McPherson was born on 13 January 1961 in Hastings, Sussex. Frequent moves during his childhood took the young lad around the UK before he arrived in London at the age of eleven. Suggs is loath to be defined as a songwriter. He explains how craft and the understanding of formulas are anathema to his instinctive and natural approach. Yet his lyrical compass and his handling of colloquial speech give him an astute and colourful take on contemporary life. His skill lies in moulding the deceptively simple everyday observations of the ordinary and dull in a voice which is both affectionate and clear-sighted. 'Baggy Trousers' was tailored from a list of school reminiscences, written in Thompson's flat on the Caledonian Road. As the school bell rings, three chords descend chromatically whilst *all the teachers in the pub* are to be found *passing round the ready rub*. The verses then invert the opening sequence of B, B flat and A flat with an additional F major chord. Foreman and Barson's arrangement fixes on a three-verse chorus structure but deviously upsets the system with a diatonic harmonica solo mid-song, underscored by the minor chords of E, D and B. Whereas Suggs explains the struggle to free his lyrical imagination, he regards 'Kix' as the benchmark of writing within the band: the songwriter who can get his ideas down successfully.

Lee Jay Thompson (born in London, 5 October 1957) fulfils the role of band enigma: a hugely gifted songwriter who initially struggled to understand that the instrument's B flat tuning was a tone below standard concert pitch. In a memorable rehearsal sequence in the Madness biopic, *Take It Or Leave It*, the untutored musician is berated by Barson for playing Fats Domino's 'I'm Walkin'' out of key. His leap to providing the burps and squeaks of 'Cardiac Arrest' and the cultivated beams of light in 'Rainbows' are testament to the patience of six fellow untrained professionals. As a wordsmith, 'Kix' offered Madness storytelling with English imagery and offbeat narrative, and as with

Suggs, the influence of Ian Dury resonates stylistically and verbally in his songs. The *new recruit* of 'Land Of Hope And Glory' with his two teenage years *given to this stand to attention life* is assailed by the packed lines of drilled instruction until the welcome call of *lights out* ends the number. The chart-topping 'House Of Fun' celebrates coming of age in a chemist's shop with the self-conscious request, *A pack of party hats with the coloured tips.*

Cathal Joseph Patrick Smyth (born 14 January 1959) began his Madness career as a bass player. The band subtly demoted the upstart to drums and then showed him the door. Finally the boy cracked. Leaping on stage, he proclaimed down Suggs's microphone *Don't watch that, watch this / This is the heavy, heavy monster sound . . . One Step Beyond.* 'Chas' then danced on stage, capturing the exact mood of the moment. It brought together stage and crowd, and Madness was complete. Within three years the same skinhead-shaved pretender shared an Ivor Novello Award for 'Our House' after fitting his words to Foreman's chiefly minor-chord-led backing. He wrote *The kids are playing up, downstairs.* It is a magnificent piece, and at the Queen's Diamond Jubilee Concert in June 2012 the band chose to perform the song on the roof of Buckingham Palace while images of less affluent homes were projected onto the royal residence.

'Our House' is packed with the tricks of the band's trade, particularly key changes. There are three in the outro. Earlier ingenuity takes one chorus down a tone and a half from D to B major before lifting back up to a second verse starting in C to suggest a new change. Other songs move by half-steps and lend a distinctive feature. Often half or extra bars are added, providing a productive quirkiness. In structure, song patterns reveal further Madness chicanery. 'One Step Beyond', 'Night Boat To Cairo' and 'The Prince' are characterized by long instrumentals, opening the song, or coming after an introductory verse but daringly before the first chorus. For a band that prides itself on infectious melody and instant appeal, the writers are frugal with refrains. The chorus of 'Bed And Breakfast Man' teases the audience before finally arriving in the fading bars. The song rotates in a cyclical groove with short instrumental hooks positioned between the rigid metres of each verse: *Of course he had to be fed / I had to give him a bed / He used to kip on my sofa / They used to call him a loafer.* It should have been a single. 'My Girl', a tale of repressed emotion, offers the lyrical hook and title merely to identify the opening of each verse. Barson's grandiose five-chord introduction is played over six bars, switching between common and 2/4 time. These are audacious statements in the world of Top Ten pop, but lend weight to the songs. In 2000, Madness were presented with an Ivor Novello Award in recognition of their Outstanding Song Collection.

Manipulating their recordings are the production team of Clive Langer and Alan Winstanley. Just as George Martin was for The Beatles, the duo are key to the magic of Madness. Over a thirty-year working relationship, Winstanley has generally engineered, allowing Langer to produce with skill and precision.

KEEP MO
SAMANTHA
TAKE IT OR LEAVE
M·CAINE
MAD NOT MAD
GREY DAY
MY GAL
TOMORROW'S DAY
HSE OF FUN
4 BF
YESTERDAYS MAN
BLUE SKIN.
NIGHT BOAT
TIME
IT MUST BE
BURNING BOATS
SHUT UP
UNCLE SAM
EMBO.
COMPETE
OUR HSE.

1) SWEETEST GAL. MADNES
2) COLDEST DAY. ONE STEP.

Ticket and set list from Madness
concert, Birmingham Odeon, 30 October 1985

'Cardiac Arrest' grooves to a heartbeat; 'Driving In My Car' has a childlike accompaniment of beeps and squeaks from the automobile. Space and soundscapes are never wasted.

The story of Madness begins in 1976 with Thompson, Barson and Foreman; three primary school friends augmenting their love of R&B, ska and Roxy Music with a swing-door policy on musicians and a belief in work, rest and play. Foreman flippantly pulled out Prince Buster's song title from their set-list, and The Invaders became Madness. Then Jerry Dammers, whose Coventry-based Specials shared their love of Jamaican rhythms, met the band on the London pub circuit. Madness signed a one-single deal with Dammers' new Midlands-based label, 2 Tone Records, which specialized in a hybrid of ska, punk and reggae-influenced music. The label helped to launch the careers of other signings: The Beat, The Selecter and The Bodysnatchers. Soon afterwards Madness switched labels to the independent Stiff, negotiating an agreement which gave them considerable creative freedom.

Part one of the group's adventure is a story of instant success and a relentless procession of chart hits. A Motown backbeat cushioned the brutal story of an unwanted mixed-race child in Barson and Thompson's 'Embarrassment'. The instrumental 'The Return Of The Los Palmas 7' had the solitary lyric *Waiter!* with Woodgate and Bedford this time contributing rhythm to Barson's piano melody. Suggs gave meaning to Foreman's music for 'Shut Up', in which a housebreaker caught in the act insists on his innocence. Smyth took inspiration from gospel and, with a little help from McPherson, offered up 'Wings Of A Dove', missing a second number one spot by one place. The stream of hits seemed unstoppable. Then in 1983, Barson quit. The songwriting remained strong, but Barson's style of melody was missed. New musical directions ran contrary to public perception of the band, and the curtain closed on the act two years later.

Part two of the Madness story is a triumphant return to performance. In 1992 the band staged a reunion concert, Madstock, in London's Finsbury Park, bringing together the original line-up for the first time since 1984.

Part three has all seven original members recording together again for an album, *Wonderful*, in 1999. 'Johnny The Horse' takes *his battered bones and his broken dreams to Regents Park at sunset* and the band sings, *Can you remember his name?* inviting the choral pantomime response *Whoa!* The album also featured the Barson / Thompson collaboration 'Lovestruck'. With typical Madness polish Suggs's top line was mimicked by the piano, harmonizing his vocal and lending melodic timbre to the song's appeal. Following the enthusiastic reception of Madstock, the concert was repeated and toured over the following years. Then in 2009 a career-defining album, *The Liberty Of Norton Folgate*, was released. Suggs singles out the title track as his greatest contribution to popular song. It is an ambitious ten-minute voyage through east London's history via a myriad of communities all linked by *a needle and thread* and the *hand stitches of time*. The song is a bravura mix of waltz and two-step time-signature variation, tempo leaps, key changes, spoken-word narration, elegant turns of phrase and music hall humour.

My conversations with Suggs and Barson were conducted in a threadbare east London studio between overdubs for *The Liberty Of Norton Folgate*. Suggs was adding percussion and Barson piano to a remix version of 'Forever Young', shepherded by Lily Allen's producers. There was a new maturity in the expression, but the signature Madness sound remained undiminished. After a swift recce of the dingy adjacent rehearsal rooms, Mike settled on a sofa in the studio's anteroom. Loafers shining and the top button of his Ben Sherman loosened, he thumbed through his band's picture discs, gatefold singles and double album sleeves, agreeing to chat more for every Guinness served. Madness's unofficial musical director found it tough to articulate what came so naturally to him as a musician. Earlier, taking a break in an upper-room bar, Suggs had seemed bashful, if not nervous, at the task in hand, reserved in making eye contact, and evidently uncomfortable with the label of classic songwriter. Still blessed with youthful looks, he perched on the couch's edge. As he wound his way down the staircase back into the studio, he turned and remarked half jokingly, 'Explaining songwriting is like trying to catch a butterfly in a suitcase . . .' After the extraordinary upturn in Madness's career in the wake of the album *The Liberty Of Norton Folgate* and its successor *Oui Oui Si Si Ja Ja Da Da* I caught up with a 57-year-old Chris Foreman at his home in Brighton. The conversation is a fascinating insight into the complexities of group songwriting and the space seven individual artists have negotiated for over thirty years.

SUGGS

The more you know about music and how songs are constructed, the more confusing it becomes. I wrote a song called 'All I Knew': it goes, *I can never know what I then knew in a million years / I can never know what I used to in a million tears*. Our drummer John Hasler who, God bless him, left the band: I saw him writing songs. I thought, 'Fuck me, if he can write songs I certainly can.' I was writing ideas down and trying to convey something of what I was feeling and it was being put to music. The idea of being a songwriter was something that never occurred to me.

What gave you the confidence to keep writing?
I wrote 'Baggy Trousers' pretty early on, which was a good start. In that context I used to really like Ian Dury and I noticed quite a lot of his songs were

just lists of things. That was a list of things I felt about going to school that I then managed to make rhyme and into the format of what could be sung as a pop song. I didn't set out to do that. Then I came up with the idea of the chorus because Pink Floyd had written that song *Teacher, leave them kids alone* ('Another Brick In The Wall'). I remembered how put-upon the teachers were at my school so I decided to make the chorus *Oh what fun we had, but at the time it seemed so bad* to try and put both sides of that coin. I suppose there was some innate guilt that I'd let myself down at school and it wasn't the teachers' fault any more than it was my fault that the school was so rubbish.

Similarly, 'Shut Up' understands theft from a policeman's perspective.

Yeah, true, true, true, because I knew a lot of people who were concerned with petty crime. It was a vaguely glamorous thing to be involved with as a kid. Then you thought of all the lives it affected and the coppers themselves. I thought about them chasing after petty criminals. It went on for a few more verses that never made it onto the finished record. I think they were about the policeman and his family and him running around after these burglars and then at the end they both meet up in the courtroom with this copper saying, 'Shut up.' I kept the word as a title for the song. It's petty criminals bemoaning their lot, and the chorus turnaround *because I'll be gone and you'll forget* and at the end *because I'll be gone and I'll forget that what you give is what you get*. I was concerned with those things. I remember reading something Neil Tennant said: 'Pathos is a mixture of happiness and sadness'—I instinctively felt that from the beginning. I liked lyrics that would be both, that were bittersweet. Often we'd have songs that would have a happy lyric but the music would be sad or vice versa.

So you were writing prose without considering the song?

Definitely starting off writing abstract prose; I'd think of a subject and everything I could about it, write it down as completely unconnected thoughts, then think about whether or not I could make the lines rhyme.

'One Better Day' was a song of great pathos. Was that written after visiting America and your return to Camden Town?

Yeah, I remember feeling quite good but also a bit disturbed. Camden was a pretty dreary place then; it wasn't anything as colourful as it is now, just a lot of homeless people. Arlington House had at least two thousand people staying there. At that point they were just like little cells. Come midday there'd be two thousand souls wandering the streets of Camden. It was interesting but it was also sad. The idea of that song was when you'd hear people say, 'Oh, he's seen better days,' like when you see a guy in a suit looking a bit tatty. I thought, 'What was that one better day?' Then I had the idea that he would meet this other homeless person that happened to be a woman—and they fell in love. Between them they could engender *one* better day as people who had, supposedly, seen better days.

A love song about a bag lady falling in love. Where does that identification with misfits come from?

I have an affinity for that, for sure. If we were to leave here and I saw someone sitting on a park bench or somebody going to the Ritz, I'd rather sit on a park bench. I go to the Ritz and I don't mind drinking champagne but I don't mind sitting on a park bench with people drinking cans of cider, either. I feel it's like a kind of a greed that I like to see it all, from the bottom to the top. I've had the great fortune in my life to be able to do that but I should say it's much more interesting to write about people whose lives have gone unrecorded. There's lots of great books, of course: George Orwell; *The Grass Arena*, about all the people that kipped in Mornington Crescent; *In Camden Town* by David Thomson, written in a diary form. He spent a lot of time with those characters from Arlington House. If you went to any of the pubs in Camden in those days you'd see a guy who still had a tatty naval uniform. People that had just come out of some what you would have thought was a permanent line of working for the government, or for whatever reason they'd fallen off the rails and just literally in a matter of a couple of months they were going down a path of lunacy and drunkenness. Let's be frank, my life was very disparate and had no stability, so that's maybe why I identify with those people.

Was '(Waiting For) The Ghost Train' the first song you wrote on a piano?

It was very much three fingers. I was trying to write—they call it native American now—a Red Indian *dum, dum, dum* (*drums rhythm on table*). I had the intention of writing about South Africa and what was happening there.

A straw headed woman and a barrel chested man / A pocket full of posies with a hat brim full of sand / Waiting for the train that never comes.

Did I write that as a sort of surreal collection of images? I don't know exactly, somewhere in between. I could see this downbeat Transvaal couple waiting at a railway station for a train that was going to come and change their society, full of ghosts and skeletons and all the downtrodden.

Do you keep the rails of meaning in place when you are writing or do you allow your imagination free rein?

Like I said, I was almost averse to the idea of songwriting because once you decide you are writing a song you almost feel like you've got to apply some kind of restrictions. I try not to even think of whether I'm writing a song or a bit of poetry or something that will just end up on the floor. It's a fabulous process and obviously I got to know it more as I got older. I don't really like to think what the process is. When people talk about being lyricists I immediately want to run away. I don't know why, maybe it's a sort of snobbery; that's not what I'm doing. I'm trying to engender some sort of feeling for something that is important to me, if I can express it. It's not necessarily the lyric, even; it's the way I sing it, it's the way I feel about it. The writing of the words are just one part of the process for me. That's why I have long periods when I don't write a song at all; I have no interest in writing songs, I don't want to make my craft any better. The craft of songwriting, as far as I can make out: you just listen and get obsessed by other people's music and try to rip bits off, then trying to apply that spontaneous moment to the next time you write a song. Each time I've written a song it's because of some peculiar combination of coincidences. I was in a pub on the corner and they put 'Our House' on the jukebox. I was thinking about the whole thing: the tambourine, the idea we were trying to do something a bit Motown-y. We were going to do a concept album about London and then Cathal was the only one who wrote any words. We had this really fantastic string part, then we got to the chorus and there's no strings because we put the chorus in after. Clive Langer said, 'We've got to have some sort of chorus,' so we wrote this quite prosaic *Our house in the middle of our street*, which I thought was a bit boring, but actually because the song was so melodic and fabulous it really worked. It was totally outside of the idea of crafting in any way. You get to that point and you think, 'I'd prefer something else to happen now,' not, 'What did they do on "Reach Out, I'll Be There"?' We had the string arranger Dave Bedford and it was great; all we said was, 'We want it to be English Motown.' We didn't give any examples of what that might be, but ironically we ended up with that. But to deconstruct it all the time and try and work out what it is to be a songwriter is just too boring. I'd rather do the other things that I do, which is make radio programmes or go on the television. To actually focus my time on being a songwriter is not the be-all and end-all of my life. I'm very fortunate to have achieved what I have as a songwriter, if I can be called such, but I certainly don't . . . I know that the great songwriters do and they struggle for weeks, days, months and years on end. To me it debases whatever it is you do get when you write a great song, which is a sort of spontaneous outburst of something.

How do you inhabit the words of other writers in Madness? Lee writes very idiosyncratic lyrics.

Lee, I genuinely say, is one of the great—I wouldn't say lyricist—writers of words for pop music. Lee does inhabit a very particular world. They're his lyrics, but I can inhabit them. I edit them sometimes for the better, sometimes for the worse, to make me feel like I understand more about what he's trying to say. 'Lovestruck' is one of my favourite songs that we've written, which Lee wrote the words to. I didn't edit but I moved some of the lines around to make me understand a bit more, because they're very dark, often, what Lee writes about.

Is it more difficult to write a melody for other band members' words?

Now for sure, that's an interesting thing. You definitely write differently when you are writing words to music. When you are presented with music you get a more spontaneous notion . . . like this new track 'Forever Young'. I had the tune first. I tried to get rid of it because I knew it was . . . not clichéd, but I knew *stay forever young*. You said it was Bob Dylan and I know I've heard it a few times in pop records, but I just couldn't get rid of it and no matter what I tried to sing in place of that I couldn't. Whereas when you're writing the words without music you can obviously get rid of whatever you want. But once you get stuck with a melody and a phrasing to someone else's music, then you are stuck with it and you have to go with it. 'Yesterday's Men' was exactly like that. The songs that I write where the music comes first are definitely more simplistic lyrically. You are being tailored to the rhythm and the melody that's in your head. I tried to make it more complicated, emotionally, but I just couldn't.

Can you account for where melody comes from?

Melody's something else, that's a really bizarre thing. Some people can work on it and listen to a bit of Bach and think, 'Will that fit on there?' But if you're just listening to a backing track with some chords and a melody comes into your mind, it seems to me, nine times out of ten, you can't improve on that. First time it comes then you have to say, 'That's it.'

'Rise And Fall' reflects upon the changes in Liverpool from your time there as a child.

An abstract memory of going back to Liverpool. Songs like that, I could have been so much more specific. It's very ambiguous. They'd knocked a lot of the old Georgian streets down with the idea of developing them, which eventually they did. I had a distant memory of a different kind of community, or the bits I remembered were just wasteland. I didn't want to be totally dismissive of what they were trying to do, but I was also thinking, 'It isn't great the way it is now.' Like the 'Baggy Trousers' thing: *Oh what fun we had, and did it really turn out bad?*—not making it a totally negative statement.

Thematically similar to 'Disappear', inspired by Alexandra Palace?

It was indeed. The same sort of thing; they burnt it down. I missed it and it was a shame, but they built it up again. The Specials were writing very specifically political songs. I could never be that specific. They were playing a tuba and we were playing a trumpet . . . theirs was more deeply resonating but you could still hear ours from a distance! I always felt something for the idea . . . to look at the other side of the coin somehow.

Later you allied yourselves to causes like Greenpeace and became more politically literate?

Exactly, 'Yesterday's Men' and all that. We were basically socialists. We were just thick kids when we started, we were so young. It was a great privilege to have met The Specials and they really taught us a lot about the world, with me certainly. It's the old story of political with a capital 'P' or political with a small 'p'. 'Embarrassment' which Lee wrote is just as political as anyone's written, but it wasn't 'have you got a racist friend?' It was, I've got someone racist in my family.

The cleverness of 'Embarrassment' was a catchy melody which then inspired you to . . .

. . . think a little bit about what you're saying. It's also having faith in your own notion that you can change people's ideas; I never really thought that you could. Then I saw what happened with 2 Tone and it all did change. We've got some songs on *The Liberty Of Norton Folgate* that are pretty enlightened, I hope so anyway.

'The Liberty Of Norton Folgate' is a fantastic piece of writing, breaking new territory for you as a writer.

I had this idea about immigration. My family was Scottish, Cathal's were Irish: all these things even within our own band. I found out about this thing called the Liberty of Norton Folgate. They had an area for two or three hundred years outside the city walls that newcomers would come and gather before they came into the city proper. Before that Shoreditch itself was a point of entry to get into Bishopsgate, into the city. It was a rubbish tip originally. When the wall came down and the city expanded Norton Folgate managed to keep its own liberty, as they called it, and that seemed a rather inspiring thing. We had some music that sounded a bit Bangladeshi and Cathal had some nice music that sounded a bit Jewish-y and we made this whole story of Shoreditch from then until now. It ends up with *in the beginning there was a fear of the immigrant* and we were singing away and I thought that's what Cathal had said, but he was singing something completely different. I thought that was a great way of saying without the immigrant there wouldn't be such a thing as London. So to try and explain the complexity of London I tried to write a song about one small area. I read Peter Ackroyd's biography of London. He keeps talking about how you get a certain area that keeps its own identity, regardless of changing hands. Shoreditch and Brick Lane, the French Huguenots came—the Protestants, the silk weavers—the Jews came with their tailoring, the Bangladeshis with their leather. That sewing machine has been going for eight hundred years and it's still got the same character even though it's changed culturally. Total cultural change is what makes London the fascinating fucking place it is—when you get a bit older and realize—but for every passing generation it's scary as it changes.

The use of words and introduction of characters at the beginning of the song contrast immensely with a later verbal exchange over a dodgy DVD: *'Only a fiver!!' 'Ow much?' 'Alright, two for eight quid. Ee-yar, ee-yar. Look, I'm givin' it away. Givin' it away!'*

I'd written the middle section first, which was my memories of Petticoat Lane, the old store holders: 'All right missus, no, no, no.' The first bit was trying to engender some of the feeling of the Jewish thing, *the hand stitches of time, the gutters filled with gold*, sort of subtle. There's some Victoriana which I like a lot, *Mr Truman's beer factory*, and then at the end *you're a part of everything, you see*, but you're also *a part of everything you see*. I think I did all right with that, and with the help of the rest of the band. If I never make another song, I'd be happy that that was my last one.

Did you write it as continuous prose, as you described before?

All the lyrics first, but they took about four years to write. I had pages and pages and pages of stuff I wanted to incorporate. It's three or four songs put together. I just had all the information. Then I worked out what bit would fit each metre and then I started to hone it all down just from raw prose. Sometimes no metre, sometimes there are passages of music where I just talk because I felt like I didn't want it to be like a song as such. Cathal came with this little tune for the first bit and that dictated the rhythm for *a little bit of this, would you like a bit of that*, like klezmer music, traditional Jewish folk music. Then I had the cockney bit in the middle with the *aw missus, no moody DVDs*. The rest was free-form: *once round Arnold Circus and up through Petticoat Lane* to where *the people stared out of the upstairs windows because we are living like kings and these days will last forever*. All these abstract bits of what I felt would be atmospheric. Then to round it all up with a big fucking crescendo at the end *cos in the Liberty of Norton Folgate / Walking wild and free / and in your second-hand coat, happy just to float*. I'd get to a certain point and think, 'Fuck, what was that book I remember, *Dan Leno and the Limehouse Golem* or something?' Dan Leno was the first music hall artist and the Limehouse Golem was a fictional character made up by the Jewish community to scare people into behaving properly. It was supposed to be made out of dust that could just arise. It's like someone has a very untidy room; I'm writing a song and I've got a million ideas all written down. I can remember where they all are when I need to know something or find a word. I've got books and books of this stuff. I can be a library of my own, but once it's done then that's it and I don't want to ever think about it again. It's about fourteen minutes long. It's a pretty remarkable piece of work.

MIKE BARSON

Clive Langer suggested Thunderclap Newman was an early influence on your playing?

Clive has always been very instrumental in making Madness records and he likes the piano as well. It's often been the teamwork of me and him. He would often bring in little bits of music and say, 'What about this?' which would inspire you in a certain way. There was a bit of discordant piano on 'Something In The Air' as I recall it, and then I did the solo on 'My Girl' which was sort of coming out of that. I wasn't a big fan of Thunderclap Newman.

The sound of another record to inspire something new. I understand 'My Girl' came from listening to Elvis Costello's 'Watching The Detectives'.

That's right, sometimes you hear a sound or a song and that inspires you. I liked that chord progression. On 'My Girl' it's D flat minor going down to A. They had C to A minor and we changed it a semitone. I like those moody minor / major key changes. I don't know if I was trying to get it exactly the same; maybe I was. Nowadays I think it doesn't really matter. You think, 'Oh, what about that song?' It gives you a bit of inspiration to get you up and running, as it were. It doesn't matter if it sounds like it at the end of the day because when you are inspired it makes all the difference. On 'Bed And Breakfast Man' I was trying to get Smokey Robinson's 'Tears Of A Clown' (*hums the bass lines of both*)—sort of similar, although they sound miles apart. Nobody would say, 'Oh bloody hell, "Bed And Breakfast Man" sounds like "Tears Of A Clown".' Everything, any sort of human endeavour, has got such a history behind it. Somebody makes the first fridge and it's like Fort Knox and then somebody makes a smaller one. It's all about refining and building on other stuff. In music you get inspired by other people's music. Earlier we were talking about the Funk Brothers and the bass-playing and somebody says, 'Oh that's great,' and then you want to do the same, but interpreting it in your way and doing something more with it. There's copying and there's bringing something original to it so it's not sad and ripping off. When Mr McPherson and I worked together solo for a while it all got a bit unpleasant and I got less and less inspired, then it's all, 'That's no good,' and you can't do anything. When we were working with Clive and Alan on 7 in the Bahamas all their minds were on going to this bloody casino on Paradise Island. If nobody's listening and saying, 'Yeah, it sounds great,' and you're playing away and they're all looking the other way, discussing—if you're a bit sensitive to that, it's not easy. When you have a good atmosphere it brings it out of you. That spark just kind of comes.

What was your process adding melody to other people's lyrics?

When I wrote 'Embarrassment' I had just the lyrics and Lee's bad spelling and grammar. I would just use bits that worked. I prefer to write the melody as well but sometimes he'd come up with one and I think it could have been better. You get a feeling of what fits and what's right and you work through it slowly and methodically. You get a good bit on a good bit on a good bit. It's sort of a question of concentration. There is the habitual part of your mind which is repetitive and another part when you are inspired which fits the parts together more naturally. Not all, 'Whoa' and suddenly it all comes automatically.

As with many Madness songs, 'Embarrassment' has an unconventional structure disguised by an immensely catchy melody, and the hook line *You're an embarrassment* is not heard until late in the song.

Writing choruses has always been tricky. I remember playing it with the words and thinking 'That sounds nice,' and just going along and it came together. Sometimes it's through the history of writing, then other times people saying, 'It's got to have a chorus.' It can be a bit limiting. It's like record companies wanting to hit people with the big strong songs at the beginning of albums and then slowly all the shit ones at the end; that's not what I like when I listen to an album. It's like theories coming out of fear. You have to follow the feeling of what you like. Once you start thinking what the punters are going to buy you're going off already; you know best somehow. You work your way along: 'What would I like to hear now, what would be interesting?' Like 'Bohemian Rhapsody' just meanders on and on and God knows what's happening, but it's interesting. That idea of verse, verse, chorus and that sort of structure I don't think you have to follow.

'Night Boat To Cairo' opens with a very long instrumental, which was very daring for a new band.

(*Laughs.*) It was supposed to be an instrumental and then Suggs bloody got hold of it and wrote all those dodgy lyrics. At that time, particularly, I really had a strong idea of what worked and what didn't. That long instrumental at the beginning just sounded great to me. The guitar sound I was never overly mad about. It was based on a lot of songs we were listening to as teenagers, like (*sings*) *Hoots Mon, there's a moose loose* (*Lord Rockingham's XI*), all those instrumental records. That's the litmus test: if it comes together nice and you think it sounds good, that's it.

How do you decide what key you write in?

Usually Suggs's capacity: you want to get it so he can sing it with a brightness, although these days he's into singing a bit lower. I'm not sure that works always. You work out his highest note in the song and that's the key so he can get up there. Often you'd write a song and then go into rehearsals and change the key to fit his vocals in. When I got professional, at one point when we were very busy, I knew what his highest note was so then I would write a song with a melody or change it whilst I was writing. I used to be of the opinion that the key didn't matter: it does a bit and in some ways it doesn't. It just gives a bit more oomph sometimes on the bass: you want to go down to an E and if you change the key you have to go up to an E. Generally we would change keys without too much problem, apart from learning to play it in a different key, which could be a bit tricky sometimes.

Did you use to write lyrics in a Morris 1000 delivery van?

Yeah, that's true. I had a little notebook with me while I was driving around. Sometimes it's when you're not trying hard that things come, you're doing something else.

What are you looking for when you write or work on a set of lyrics?

When I was younger, sixteen, seventeen, eighteen, I used to write songs to an Elvis Presley songbook I had. Some of the songs I didn't know and I would just use the words as something to hang the song on. I had a lot of those songbooks: a Motown one, Elton John, Carole King. When I wrote 'Going To The Top' I had one line that I really liked and then all the words just came. I recorded a demo of it which I was pretty pleased with, but once again without a bloody chorus. It was all tits up just meandering on in its own way, then Clive Langer got involved: 'Oh, it's got to have a chorus,' so he made us stick that bit in, *Na, na, na*, with no singing on it. It was supposed to be a chorus and I just couldn't write anything for it after that, it's like I'd done it. It opens up and then it's like the book closes and you can't get in there and mess around with it. When you try too hard or listen to a song too much it becomes solid and loses that opening for change. When you're first writing it's like a blank page in a book: it can go anywhere, everything is possible, but after a while if you've got the words and the tune down and you rehearse it with a band then it's more difficult to open up and change. Like 'Prospects' that Suggs wrote: it didn't have a chorus. The verse was brilliant; it really sounded pukka to me, a really solid song, but Clive was, 'Oh, it needs another bit.' The extra bit that got written wasn't as good as the verses were.

A great example of that was 'Chemist Façade' which became 'House Of Fun'.

We'd recorded the song without the *welcome to the house of fun* chorus and Dave Robinson (*Stiff Records*) came in saying, 'It's missing something here, boys. It needs a chorus.' Suggs said, 'I've got this little bit,' and Chris had a couple of chords and we stuck them in and it worked.

Does the band often come together around the piano to write?

Often used to happen. I used to be the only one that could really play an instrument in the beginning. Often Clive would say, like on 'Our House', 'It needs another bit.' He would make suggestions and I would play chords that I think might work and then somebody would come up with something else and we'd fit it together. Anyone could do that, I don't know if it's particularly unique; it's just that I play the piano. I suppose there is a little bit of skill in fitting it together. You've got a melody on the right hand and then you fit the chord. I'm quite good at making up melodies.

Are vocal melodies suggested by the chords?

Sort of, yeah. Usually I play it on the piano and then sing it after, chip out a melody, but rhythm is not my forte. Suggs has really good rhythm. On 'House Of Fun' I was playing all the harmonies on the piano so Suggs could sing them, because his could be rough. In the end we kept them all in, this three-part piano underneath the vocal.

Can you write melody without a piano?

Not so well. With the piano I would do something more intricate than I would just do with the ear. If I was just trying to sing it would be a lot more basic. When you can actually see it then you can pick out the third, the fifth or the root. Mentally you might not be able to imagine it but when you start hitting it you might find something that's more difficult. There's a mathematical aspect to it; it's a combination of what it sounds like and then knowing there's the chord and if I hit that note . . . and then playing around with what you know is going to fit.

I understand the inspiration for 'Tomorrow's (Just Another Day)' began with Cathal whistling a melody to you at the piano?

Yeah, Cathal came up with that melody, but we wrote the song together. Cathal is more hands-on: you play the piano and he starts singing, writing whilst he goes along. (*Sings chorus.*) *Tomorrow's just another day I hear them say*, I remember him making up that bit. I would play a couple of chords and it'd be like, 'Ooh, I like that, oh yeah, do that.' It's all different variations of how we write songs. I made up the tune for the solo. I don't know where I got it from; it sounded like it came from somewhere else. It's funny, when we did 'Embarrassment' in rehearsal I had these chords that I thought sounded so much like another song. I thought it was crap because it was so unoriginal. We started playing it and everybody was perking up. I'd discarded it as being

copied from somewhere or other, the first couple of chords maybe, but then
after that I wrote all the verses which were different, made it a valid thing.

Are you disciplined, do you put time aside to write?

No, not really, that would be quite good. When we were really successful
and making a load of money out of it, then there was really a point to writing,
well, financially, you know. Then I was really writing a lot but not really happy
with it. We'd be sitting around: 'What are we gonna do?' so I'd start playing
the piano. I'm a pretty undisciplined person, which I'm not happy with anyway. It was just a pastime but when we were really successful I didn't like doing
it too much. I wasn't doing anything else, just constantly writing. I found it
difficult to have a balance.

Did listening to the radio for ideas become an obsession?

Yeah, I'd be thinking, 'I like that, I like that': not obsessive, good in some
sort of ways. I just didn't want to be twenty-four seven thinking about writing
songs. There was a time it got a bit unpleasant because I was thinking about
nothing but writing and the connection of financial rewards. The enjoyment of
it, the life and the joy of music, was going out of it. It was more like a job. Instead of enjoying the radio whilst doing something else it was like, 'Hold on,
don't miss that, don't miss that'—it's like you're trying to get something all the
time. That's why I stopped the band. When I was younger I used to enjoy music
just for its own sake, but then it became my work and then it became something
I could profit from. It all became a bit much. I wanted to enjoy music again and
get back to being a listener.

**Did the succession of hits affect you, as a composer trying to write the next
big one?**

Yeah, definitely, it gets harder. We were always trying to be different in the
music we were making and not retrace our footsteps. We boxed ourselves into
a corner: 'Oh, can't do that, done that.' At a certain point there was nothing left
that we could do, that's what it felt like. We were always trying to do different
styles, like calypso on 7, the rhythm on 'Mrs Hutchinson'. I played a vibes solo
on this song, a harmonica on another. Being interesting is about what you've
done before or what's current; it's dependent on what's floating around in
people's noggins at that time. Sounding repetitive at one moment in history is
going to be different at another: it's always changing. These days it feels more
open what you can do. There's different periods in music when it gets really
narrow to when it opens up so there's only one type of music that people listen
to, like everyone's doing punk rock and no one's listening to heavy metal or
prog rock, and then another time when everybody's doing completely different
things.

Do you feel constrained as a writer by current fashions?

Sometimes, it depends; when something first appears it's new. There's one side where people get inspired and they progress by using what's gone before, but there's another aspect of people that they start copying, they want to make money. They're thinking, 'If I do what he did, he made a million pounds; maybe I could make a million pounds?' It loses the spark and starts getting boring.

The lyrics of 'Mrs Hutchinson' suggest you were writing from personal experience: *There's been some complications, she's very near the brink / I have to tell you, it's my duty to speak / Your mother will not last a week.*

That happened to my mum. I was pretty pissed off with doctors and the National Health. This doctor pulled me and my brother into a room and said, 'Your mum's not going to make it.' Then he went to my mum, 'Ooh hello, Mrs Barson, it's going to be fine,' whilst he's saying to us she's going to kick it. It was completely wrong. She had something else in the end. Talking about death was a taboo then. I wrote the song quite a bit later, once my mum got the green light. I didn't have a plan to write on that subject, it just came. Suggs takes a subject that he will write about. I'm not so good with that, and Lee, if you tell him to write about something, he'll write about something else. It's that not knowing what you're going to do, having a blank page and filling it up with something or other.

'Lovestruck' was a return to the classic Madness sound after the band reformed.

That's a good one: *lagging in deepest Tottenham.* I wrote the music. It's like a David Bowie song, thinking about it now . . . *Hunky Dory*, I think, the resonance of something off that. Originally it was quite different. I was in Holland and Lee came over to stay for a week or so. We wrote 'Lovestruck' and 'Drip Fed Fred': that was a pretty fruitful trip. He wrote the words and melody in the back room of my studio on the boat I was living on then.

Did you work independently?

Lee said, 'Maybe we could make some music together?' I had a couple of little ideas and before he came I put together 'Lovestruck' and then I got the 'Drip Fed Fred' backing track, which was quite simple. So I had it all set up, the music, the channels: 'Here's your microphone, I'm going to have dinner now.' When I came back he'd more or less written the whole of 'Drip Fed Fred'. He'd been in there, had the headphones on, gone into one and got really inspired. I was just bowled over: 'This is fucking great.' All these different bits he had, he came up with loads of stuff. That's what I mean when you really get into it; he puts on the headphones and he's gone into another planet. The funny thing was we recorded it and Ian Dury was staying in Amsterdam; he was doing a

'Driving In My Car' makes hilarious use of rhyming couplets: *Last week it went round the clock, I also had a little knock / I dented somebody's fender, he learnt not to park on a bender.* **Does the rhyme or the reason come first?**

I would write the first line, *I bought it in Primrose Hill,* and be thinking what rhymes with *hill,* and maybe there would be a few variations.

You're trying to keep the meaning of the song as opposed to letting the rhyme determine its direction?

It can be both: sometimes there's a coherence that makes something good. It might throw you on a tangent that something rhymes and then you try to write to that. When you get into that space where there aren't any rules, that's when it becomes enjoyable. When it becomes enjoyable it becomes enjoyable for others as well, which is a golden rule. If you don't really like it, how can you expect somebody else to? To an extent you're writing for yourself: if you're really happy with it that often pans out well. We're all receivers as well as givers and writers as well as listeners. Like the radio: you're writing something but also I'm somebody that listens to the radio.

Was 'Driving In My Car' a euphemism for sex? That was the talk at my school when the record was released.

No, it wasn't about sex, but at that time there weren't many people writing about simple things like driving in your car. You know: rolling your window down, the little joys of life, simple pleasures. Ian Dury brought that quality, the enjoyment of the mundane.

Was Jerry Dammers an influence on your writing? The major / minor changes in 'Never Ask Twice' are very reminiscent of his feel and playing style.

When you said Jerry Dammers, I thought of 'Never Ask Twice'. We got that change from one of his songs (*hums 'Pearl's Café'*). We were sitting in Eric's in Liverpool as they were soundchecking. I don't know if they had lyrics but they were playing it as an instrumental. We picked up a lot from The Specials and songs like 'International Jet Set'.

Suggs wrote some great offbeat words for it: *Please observe my continental alligator skin line shoulder bag / I've covered it in stickers from far and wide / And stuffed it full of suits and matching ties.*

Yeah, I like the lyrics, he did a good job on that. I found what he wrote on 'Night Boat To Cairo' a bit trite, but that one gave it an exotic sort of something.

Madness and The Specials became linked together by the 2 Tone movement; were you conscious of writing differently from them?

When we first started there was no history; you're just two two-bob bands. Sometimes we'd be looking up to them and other times we'd be thinking, 'We don't want to be like The fucking Specials,' because their popularity had waned or something.

Suggs was talking about the cynicism of The Specials in contrast to Madness's lighter, more common touch.

It was natural, I think. It obviously says something about Madness that things came together like that. Not being too self-conscious is a thing about the band, for sure, and maybe The Specials were more precious about it. So they were like, 'It's got to have the right tune with the right words . . . oh, this doesn't work . . . it's got to be . . .' With us lot somebody would stick something with something and then somebody would start dancing and enjoying it and that would be that—we would go along with it.

Was 'Grey Day' inspired by Roxy Music's 'Bogus Man'?

Somehow or other, I'm not sure how. I listened to 'Bogus Man' recently; we recorded a version of that for the *Dangermen* album, I think, but it got stuck somewhere. It could have been pretty good. I was inspired by that, if not too closely then on a sort of feeling, vibe sort of level. When we did that song Lee had a space echo machine with a tape on it. He brought it into rehearsals and everyone was, 'Wow!' So we started messing around with it. The song never sounded as good as that time; it had a different rhythm. Somewhere along the way we lost it and the song got dropped. Later we did it again in a harder style, a meaner sound; it changed and went through a progression.

What was the vision of 'That Nutty Sound'?

Lee came in one day with a Levi jacket and he'd done it with bleach and put 'That Nutty Sound' on the back with all musical notes and stuff. Lee would come up with this and somebody would come up with that and I'd say, 'Whoa, we could put all this together, guys: this is a way of doing it.' I was somebody who could collate everything. There were all these different elements in the band of music that we liked: ska, reggae, Motown. Lee had this circus idea, something a bit nutty, and we would know what he meant: something sounding a bit discordant, a bit weird. We all listened to music together, so if somebody suggested something it would fit a general taste of the band; we had the same references.

Has there ever been a part of your songwriting that doesn't belong to Madness?

Yeah, they end up on cassettes in the bottom of a drawer somewhere. Maybe you have dreams of somebody recording it one day. During this album

I was going through a lot of stuff that I'd written in that ten-year period we weren't together—everybody went over their old songs.

Were you writing for pleasure after leaving the band and moving to Holland?

No, I was always thinking they could be used. If I want to do something for pleasure then I don't necessarily have to write a song. I'm not just going to spontaneously write a song for myself. These days I get more enjoyment out of the process. Before I left the band I was thinking it's practical: only doing it because at the end you're making a living from it. There's got to be a purpose to it. That's one of the mainstays: you want to make good music that's going to last with a certain quality, but if nobody ever listens to it, if it never gets on an album and stays in your cupboard, that's going to lessen the enjoyment.

Do you have any thoughts on why there are so few classic British female writers?

I've never considered that. I don't know, macho England, women at home with the kids maybe? If you don't have one to start the ball rolling there's no inspiration for others to follow. British bands have always been a bloke's thing. In the Sixties you would often get a girl singer; she would be the legs and the short skirt but with blokes behind it writing. It's a strange one.

CHRIS FOREMAN

Looking through all the songwriting credits on Madness singles it made me realize that you are the B-side king!

Oh, yeah.

You have predominantly collaborated with Suggs?

Suggs and Lee, mainly, and also Cathal. I remember when the band started, like a lot of bands, we did covers: rock 'n' roll songs, Motown and reggae. John Hasler wrote our first song, which was called 'Mistakes'. It was like, 'Ah, you can write your own songs.' It was a real moment. We dropped all the Motown and rock 'n' roll but kept the reggae, because no one else was doing that sort of Bluebeat stuff in 1978. Then Lee wrote 'The Prince' and Mike wrote 'My Girl' and I thought, 'Well, they can write all the songs; they're really good at it.' I wrote my first song when I was living in a council flat with my wife and kid in Chalk Farm and Suggs came round and I said, 'I've got a tune, a few chords,' and we wrote 'In The Middle Of The Night' in my kid's bedroom. It was like an epiphany: 'Oh yeah, that's how you write a song.' 'Not so hard at all, really.' So generally I might have a tune in my head and then try and work it out on the guitar and I'd write some chords down and go to rehearsals.

Did you then work out the next part of the song together with the band?

If you go back to when we first started, you'd have the musicians in the band, as it were: Mike, Bedders, myself and Woody. Lee would think up brass parts at home. We would work on the songs daily. It would centre around the piano because Mike was a very good musician and I'd go, 'I've got these chords.' We would work the songs into shape and record them onto cassettes and then a lot of the time Lee or Suggs would take them home and start writing lyrics. So it wasn't really done initially all in the same room. Then we would all go through them again with the lyrics and then maybe change them about again. Then Clive would come in and we would play them to him. He would sort out the good and not-so-good songs, and they'd either eventually become B-sides or not go any further. That didn't often happen because we also had weeded them out ourselves. Later on, Cathal would also start to come up with lyrics as well. So it became established that Lee, Cathal and Suggs, and Mike would write most of the lyrics. Now in the twenty-first century, because it's organized a lot more, people do incredible demos on computers using Logic and turn up with really well-worked-out stuff.

Is that how you work?

I always wrote using a guitar until 'Yesterday's Men'. It's funny, Mike left the band and everybody started playing keyboards. I borrowed a little Casio with a drum machine in it that could add bass lines automatically as you played the chords. I did a demo of 'Yesterday's Men' which was later released on the 12-inch version of the single. There's nothing technically brilliant about that song. I was playing these chords thinking, 'This sounds great,' then I transposed them to a guitar and thought, 'Oh, it's just B and B flat,' but I never would have written that song on a guitar. It's hard to explain. It's just the inversions, the way you play chords on a piano.

Perhaps similar to 'Baggy Trousers', which has unusual chord changes for a guitar: F to A flat to B flat?

No, that I wrote on the guitar—I had this tune in my head. Very often I have an idea of how I want the song to sound and it often doesn't come out like that at all by the time we've all worked on it. It's usually because probably my initial idea wasn't all that good anyway. 'Baggy Trousers' was supposed to be more like a rock song, actually: y'know, more power chords. It turned out brilliantly when we did it in a ska style. When we'd written it I thought it was good, but I thought at the time, 'It's not a single. It hasn't got a chorus.' It had *oh what fun we had*, but I didn't think it was that commercial, but it was incredibly successful.

I remember them saying, 'We need another bit,' and I said, 'How about this? What about these chords?' (*Hums the instrumental melody of 'Baggy Trousers'.*) Sort of like a little bridge. I hate to use the ska thing, but we'd go, 'We'll do it in that style—we'll ska it up a bit,' put an off-beat on it. The first two albums there's a lot of songs like that. By the third album we experimented a lot more with different rhythms. Mike did a lot of that. I remember 'Tomorrow's Dream'. He's pretty good at getting ideas across because musically he's more capable. I'd just say, 'Can we play it like Chuck Berry, in this sort of style?'

How did the band decide the method for dividing royalties?

That's one of those things clouded in the mists of time. I always thought it was John Hasler. Dave Robinson said it was him. Lots of people say it was their idea. I think the actual formula we all worked out where fifty per cent of the song goes to the writer and the other fifty goes between all seven of the band, so the writer gets half plus a seventh, seems the fairest split.

With a song like 'Our House', for example, does it still feel like your song after the lyrics and melodies have been added?

'Our House' is a sort of a band thing, I suppose, in a way. I had these chords and the middle eight, and the odd lead line—maybe before we went into the studio, I'm not sure—but it didn't have much of a rhythm. Going back to the art of songwriting, Dave Robinson gave everyone in the band these little cassette recorders. They were a camouflage colour. They were brilliant. They had a drum machine built in and you could record two tracks on them, and that's what I wrote 'Our House' on. It was a strange device, and then Cathal came up with the lyrics, of course. So we did it a bit like a Motown style, you know, because sometimes you say, 'How are we going to do this song?' I came up with the idea for the solo in the studio. Every song we did Thommo was always doing a solo, so I thought I'd get in there. It's a very simple solo. I think I even somehow managed to do a harmony. I don't have that kind of musical knowledge. Suggs and Cathal can work harmonies out instinctively and Mike can do it in a musical way by knowing root notes and fifths. I don't know any of that and I'm quite glad that I don't in some ways, because very often I might go in to record something and I don't really have a clue what I'm going to do. I know the actual chords of the song, obviously.

'Our House' received an Ivor Novello Award for songwriting.

It's really funny. Chas and I just thought, 'Oh, we won't win,' so we didn't go. Our manager accepted it on our behalf. We were all in the studio writing a new album at the time.

When do ideas come to you?

I like coming up with ideas spontaneously. We just recorded a song called 'How Can I Tell You' and there's a guitar riff which I thought up in the studio.

I read that the guitar idea for 'The Hunchback Of Torriano' came to you whilst riding on a bicycle.

That's right, yeah. I loved that song. I put a whole lot into it, with the main riff and other parts. But then there are some songs of mine that other people have put a lot into as well. That's why we split the publishing that way: Suggs or Cathal can do great vocal harmonies or lead melodies and really change the feel of a song, Mike does loads of really great stuff, Thommo does some great brass parts, and Bedders and Woody equal Paul and Ringo!

Do tunes come to you at random times or can you be disciplined with your creativity?

That's definitely a discipline that I used to have. I used to spend so much time every day just going through stuff and refining it and tweaking it. That is one thing about working with a computer: they'll remember it forever! You can go back to something you did ten years ago: 'Oh, that's quite good, that.' I'll walk down the street and some tune might come to me and so you'll hum it into the mobile phone. Some of us have got stockpiles of half-finished songs. That's why the last two albums had so many songs on them.

Before phones, how long could you hold onto an idea?

That's a really good question: quite a while, a couple of weeks. You think of a tune and then you write down the chords, then you're sort of all right. On *The Rise & Fall* there's a song called 'Madness (Is All In The Mind)'. I'd just moved to Finchley and I was in my house and I had every bit of that song worked out in my head. I had an acoustic guitar and I had two cassette machines: a home stereo one and a little one. They ran at different speeds. I got the little one and recorded a guitar part then I played it back on the other one at a different speed, detuned the guitar by about a semitone, and played along with it—very crude overdubbing. I kept on doing it, maybe eight times. I thought that was technically quite an achievement so I was able to say to the band, 'Here you are: vocals, guitar parts, solo etc.' Obviously these days everybody sends people MP3s, or they turn up with them. You think it's all over, and then you get an MP3 from Chas with some great songs on it. Lee and Suggs are not really that well versed in technology. Barzo and Woody's stuff is technically brilliant: vocals, the lot. Mine are a bit rough and ready, whereas Suggs or Thommo will still now, in the year 2013, turn up with a cassette.

Do your backing track demos have vocal melody lines?

Not really, unless I'd written the lyrics, but I don't write many. I find it quite difficult. Plus the bar is set quite high with the other lyricists in the band. Sometimes I'll write a tune and it's very well developed and there's sort of melodies and keyboard lines and the person that writes the lyrics uses them as a melody line. We did a song called 'Deolali' which I wrote with Lee, and the *man of steel* chorus was a melody line I had played. I really liked it. It nearly got on *Oui Oui Si Si Ja Ja Da Da* but I thought the song needed a little bit more work.

What is the process, choosing which songs make a Madness record?

Blimey, that's a big argument. Me, I'd like to put twenty-five songs on, but some of the band think, 'Well, that's one's not too good,' but then you're starting to really judge each other's . . . There are great albums like *London Calling* or *The White Album* with a ridiculous amount of songs on, but they're all good. It's like having some closure. I write songs for people to hear them and enjoy them; if they buy millions of them then that's great. But with the last two albums, I realized we don't make money from doing albums any more. It's become an expensive process, which is partly our fault. You don't sell enough to cover the cost of them, even though *Oui Oui* has already sold in excess of 100,000 copies, which is brilliant. On the last album there was a kind of committee, which wasn't the band, to select the track listing. They came up with a list of songs that I didn't necessarily agree with, but I thought, we're doing a special edition so all the songs will eventually get released, so I wasn't really worried about it. The only time when we have less songs on albums is when we haven't got enough good songs.

Would the instrumental 'Don't Look Back' which backed 'House Of Fun' be an example of a backing track that would have found melody and lyrics had somebody hooked on to it?

Well, I had written some lyrics for that, but they were unfinished. Yeah, a lot of my songs ended up on B-sides. Y'know, they were songs that basically weren't good enough to get on an album, but we didn't want to do throwaway B-sides either.

Like 'Shadow On My House' which backed 'It Must Be Love'.

That's a favourite one. I wrote the lyrics for that one. That came out pretty much how I wanted it to—with a country feel.

Also 'That's The Way To Do It' on the B-side of 'The Return Of The Los Palmas 7'.

Oh yeah, blimey, I'd forgotten that. That was good as well: it ended up again, musically, as I intended it.

'Shut Up' is very inventive in the mechanics of the writing, where the verse is in two parts divided by a clever key change. Was the song originally around ten minutes?

No, that is a bit of a myth. There was another verse where Suggs said *shut up*. There wasn't another massive piece; it was just that the song was too long. I've got these certain templates, especially when I did my other band Crunch! with Lee: I'd do verse, verse, chorus and then a solo, which is often the first verse three tones up. I always feel you have to have some kind of middle eight or solo, just out of interest. 'Shut Up', I really wanted it to be in the style of Slade, which funnily enough in the video I randomly ended up with Dave Hill's Super Yob guitar. Clive said, 'We need another bit,' and I came out with the spaghetti Western bit and then he said, 'That's really good, you should do a whole song like that.' So I wrote 'Town With No Name', which was on the B-side. I actually wrote that tune on the piano. I was just playing some notes and I thought, 'That sounds good.' I don't think I came up with the entire song, but some of it. I just picked out some moody notes. If I have a tune these days I play it on the piano and then I take my time and think, 'Oh yeah, this chord goes with that note.' I basically know the names of some chords on the piano. This is where computers are so brilliant because they can tell you the chords and notes. I can quite confidently now write out the chords of things for the band and some of them are weird, diminished sevenths. That's where Mike's great because he knows the name of all those weird chords. Generally I use bass, piano, and organ; I don't go too mad. Some songs I've used samples. Actually, the other day I heard the drums at the beginning of 'My Sharona' and thought they'd be good to sample.

The story goes with 'House Of Fun' that Dave Robinson heard the original version 'Chemist Façade' and gave the band two hours to come up with a chorus.

It wasn't that. It was definitely not as if we recorded it and then as we came out, Dave Robinson marched us straight back into the studio to record the chorus. The idea was always to write 'an extra bit', which we did, but a while later. We went to Basing Street Studios in west London and I said, 'I've got these chords,' and we were playing it and playing it. I remember I went round to the chip shop and when I came back Suggs had written the chorus lyrics. So Suggs and I wrote the chorus. The song had been recorded on 24-track and I don't know how, but they spliced the new chorus into the song. Suggs sings, *"elcome to the house of fun*; the *w* is missing. Our brilliant engineer Alan Winstanley had to get it exactly in time.

The chorus chords have the classic Madness trick of a key-change lift within a few bars, but then after *Welcome to the lion's den* it returns to its original key.

I just had that chord sequence in my mind for 'House Of Fun'. It was a song I was working on. As I said before, that sort of thing has come up in other songs where the band or Clive will go, 'You need another bit,' and I'd go, 'Oh yeah, hold on,' 'cause I always have little bits of tunes lying around in my head. The last major time I did that was on 'Simple Equation' from the Madness musical *Our House*. I came up with this little riff and when the musical finally appeared on the West End stage they used it for the theme of the father. People thought the musical was about us, which it wasn't, by the way. It was another very good story altogether.

It's amazing that seven feisty lads who met at school and as teenagers are still together after thirty years.

I genuinely say I really enjoy it when we all get into a rehearsal room and somebody's got an idea for a song and you do it and it all starts gelling. That and the actual recording process are the bits I like most.

'Deceives The Eye' is the only Madness song with a Bedford / Foreman credit.

Yeah, yeah. Mark wrote the music and I wrote the lyrics. That was a shoplifting one from my own, er . . . personal experiences.

Like 'Razzle In My Pocket' by Ian Dury.

Yes, same theme, except he gets away with the *Razzle* in his pocket. I didn't. I can't remember much about writing that, or going home with a cassette of it. I can remember writing the lyrics. I might have got together with Mark, I can't remember.

Can you write music to somebody else's words?

No. That's what Mike can do quite easily. Whereas luckily I've got Suggs and Lee who I'll send them music and they'll come up with lyrics. Otherwise I'd be right snookered! Cathal these days is a sort of one-man writing machine. He does it all.

You co-wrote 'Uncle Sam'?

Lee wrote most of that, the tune as well. I was never happy rhythmically with a lot of the *Mad Not Mad* album: 'Burning The Boats' and 'Uncle Sam', for example. 'Yesterday's Men' was good. It was a strange time: Mike had left the band; there was a lot of confusion; we had a lot of drum programming going on. I don't remember rehearsing it a lot. It was one of those albums where a lot of it was done in the studio.

'Cardiac Arrest' has a lovely symmetry in the verse chords.

That was quite a funny, strange song. A lot of that was worked out in the rehearsal room. I think I had a bit of an idea of how it should be played, maybe a rough idea.

Do you play the guitar at home?

I never really play the guitar at home these days. I've got a piano down-stairs which I don't play much. If I start doing a bit of music—I've got a little keyboard—say I might write a song, I might think up guitar bits for it, or if somebody's sent me a song. I wasn't there when they rehearsed the early Nor-ton Folgate stuff, so I went over the early backing tracks at home to have ideas ready for when I went into the studio, instead of thinking them all up when I got there: early stuff like 'Bingo' and the 'Norton Folgate' song itself. I needed to know the basic chords.

Did you write 'La Luna' with a Cuban feel?

No, I didn't. I wanted it to be kind of Russian. There is a version on the *Oui Oui* special edition that is in the style I wanted it to be. I was never quite that happy when we played it live. I was always thinking when we mixed it we could change it. We were going to Mexico for the first time to do this gig and Cathal said, 'Why don't we get a mariachi band on some of the songs?' 'Great idea!' and that song seemed to lend itself to that idea, but by the time we found a band to do it (*Mariachi El Bronx*) they were from LA—brilliant parts, though.

ANNIE LENNOX

'I carried the bomb internally for years waiting for the explosion.'

Summer 2012. Annie Lennox is reading at Aberdeen Art Gallery to introduce her touring exhibition, The House of Annie Lennox. When she was a child, she reveals, her piano teacher had threatened to put an explosive device under her seat to make her practise. The young Annie was mesmerized by the 'sound-scapes of Bach, Mozart and Debussy' that drifted from the elegant fingers of her tutor, but found her studies a bore, preferring to 'wish away' her mistakes. Having begun piano lessons as a seven-year-old, and then taken up the flute four years later, she reacted against the discipline of classical music, finding it a world of rules and regulation. Her earliest musical memories are of singing herself to sleep and of picking out television themes on a toy piano. As a school-girl, Annie entered music festivals and played in a local orchestra and a mili-tary band. At seventeen, as described in 'Legend In My Living Room', she *ran away from home to be with all the pretty people*. She accepted a place at the Royal Academy of Music in London to study the flute, but by her third year felt that its staid atmosphere and formal teaching had stifled her natural expres-sion. Days before her finals she dropped out.

'I have been intrigued with the poetic power of "words" ever since I can remember: symbolism, metaphor, and the magical transformations that can occur when you combine the sounds and shapes of language in unexpected ways.' In her website autobiography, Lennox further reveals the emotional ex-amination that permeates her work: 'We use words to communicate, to de-scribe, and to express something that cannot be easily accessed . . . something from a deeper part of our psyche. I cover all kinds of ground . . . Love (Eros and agape), loss, grief, rage, despair, joy, hope, longing, jealousy, confusion, anguish, ecstasy, harmony, gratitude, peace. These words are my soul talking.' It is a conversation of candid self-analysis and exposes a writer closely involved with primal response. On the page, Lennox's lyrics are simple and direct. They call for intense musical delivery. Her voice has the cry and longing of gospel, both in its melodic range and in its hunger to reach a higher spiritual plain. 'There Must Be An Angel (Playing With My Heart)' requires her vocal to pitch a bottom G before leaping twelve whole tones to hit top D for the middle eight: *I must be hallucinating / Watching angels celebrating.* The singer's contralto range lets melodies play over three and a half octaves. Its natural ease, its *sprezzatura*, lends many vocal ideas the element of surprise while still allowing them to feel natural within the flow of a song. Conversely, 'Here Comes The Rain Again' restricts the opening melody to a dominating single note. Its isolating theme sets up *rain* as a metaphor for depression. The second line takes up the word *falling* to retain a thematic link whilst imitating water's natural movement. The downward spiral *Raining in my head like a tragedy / Tearing me apart like a new emotion* is skilfully introduced by Lennox's songwriting collaborator, Dave Stewart, who furnishes an A minor chord with an added B natural in the song's introduction. The suspended, melancholic mood is lightened by a vocal lift and accompanying shift to F major to support the positive suggestion *So baby talk to me like lovers do* in the bridge between the first and second verses. 'Here Comes The Rain Again' was composed in the Mayflower Hotel, New York, on a newly bought Casio keyboard, after a row between the two writers. Looking out of the hotel window, Lennox spontaneously sang the title line in response to Stewart's riff and the darkening city skyline. 'That was all we needed,' the guitarist wrote in *The Dave Stewart Songbook: The Stories Behind The Songs*, 'like with a lot of our songs; you only need to start with that one line, and that one atmosphere, that one note, or that intro melody. And the rest of it was like a puzzle where we needed to just fill in the missing pieces.' In 1984, with a score written by Michael Kamen complete with dramatic orchestral flourishes and pizzicato strings—a clear precursor to the arrangements of the Pet Shop Boys—the song rounded off a year of solid chart success and reached the top ten on both sides of the Atlantic. It earned the composers their first Ivor Novello Award for Best New Songwriters of the Year.

Lennox discovered her vocal talent singing along to Stevie Wonder's 1972 Motown release *Talking Book*. She identifies the record as one conceived from both instinct and intellect, and it made a profound impression on her. Significantly, although she had devoted her teenage years to the formal theory of music, her voice played no part in her studies and so was a tool to explore without instruction. Lennox was then introduced to a second much-celebrated record, *Ladies Of The Canyon*. Joni Mitchell was a rare example of a female artist who composed and performed her own compositions. Her sound acted as a catalyst to Lennox's first creative endeavours, and with the aid of a huge wooden harmonium she soon amassed a collection of ideas. It was these twenty or thirty compositions that she invited Stewart to hear at a Camden flat in 1976. The pair made an immediate connection. They were both disillusioned musicians who had lingered on the outer edges of the music business with little satisfaction and scant reward. They fell in love, and Stewart described their relationship in the French phrase *folie à deux*—meaning a shared delusion or mental disorder affecting two people living in close association. For the next thirteen years they were inseparable.

Eurhythmics is a form of dance that originated at the beginning of the twentieth century, concentrating on music and rhythm. It was developed by the Swiss composer Émile Jaques Dalcroze, with a focus on non-intellectual bodily engagement. At school in Aberdeen, Lennox had taken classes using the method to 'encourage musical expression through movement'. Dropping the *h* from the original Greek word, Lennox and Stewart came up with the name Eurythmics, a hybrid of *Euro* and *rhythmic*. It matched what would become their defining sound: a European synthesized style mixed with soulful vocal melody. The duo would be about the celebration of deliberate juxtapositions: warm and cold, male and female, synthetic and natural. The appearance of their second long-player *Sweet Dreams (Are Made Of This)* in 1983 was an assured musical statement. It invited the listener into a sparse, synthetic landscape, littered with percussive intrigue. Lennox's voice was intimate and central in the sound spectrum. Her delivery invariably utilized mid-pitch melody and was harmonized by octave falsetto harmonies. The voice is further plied for textured effect, most notably on the stunning 'Love Is A Stranger', in which Lennox contrasts the beauty of love with obsessional and destructive impulses. The verse opens, *Love is a stranger in an open car / To tempt you in and drive you far away*, sung over a clinical synthesized rhythm supplied by a rare and expensive Movement MCS Percussion Computer.

The impact of the Eurythmics was immediate. It followed six years of struggle for the pair, first as The Catch and then The Tourists, despite the high-flying success of the singles 'I Only Want To Be With You' and 'So Good To Be Back Home Again'. But now, and for the first time, Lennox and Stewart wrote the songs. The division of duties was blurred. Both were highly accomplished musicians and both had a flair for melodic ingenuity. Their collaborative relationship brought together two extremely talented individuals to produce a third, unique, musical entity. Credits were split evenly, although on some later records the switching of the leading name—either Stewart or Lennox—gave a clue to the dominant creative force. When the duo parted in 1990, after eight studio albums, it was Lennox who was first to establish and deliver her lone writing credentials. *Diva* shone with solo confidence and redefined the singer with titles such as 'Why', 'Little Bird' and 'Walking On Broken Glass'. Though the solo route is always more difficult for a non-vocalist musician, Stewart has nonetheless co-written over the last twenty-five years with a glittering array of names including Bob Dylan, Bryan Ferry and Mick Jagger. In 1999, Lennox and Stewart recorded together again after a decade apart, and the record-buying public duly lapped up the tenth Eurythmics album, *Peace*. A return to solo projects followed, and Lennox has continued to display her maturing ideas, fusing modern production techniques with naked lyrical honesty.

The House of Annie Lennox is an invitation to enter the creative shelter of Lennox's complex persona. Extravagant costumes, masks and awards line the glass displays. The central focus of the exhibition is a life-size doll's house. Inside are a functional wooden chair and a modest writing desk. To the left, a set of books that include *Schott's Original Miscellany*, the poetic works of Robert Burns, a book of English lyrics, *The Art of Seduction* by Robert Greene, *Simone Weil: An Anthology*, *I Don't Know How She Does It* by Allison Pearson, and a hardback edition of *Jigsaw Art*. A table lamp lights a sunken glass display presenting handwritten lyrics, musically notated vocal lines and scrawled notes for an impending video shoot. In a side drawer a page of unlined paper is filled with four columns of rhyme schemes, each with its own underlined heading: *Take: ache, break . . . Give: live, forgive . . .* Another drawer contains an original draft of 'Thorn In My Side'. It is written in blue ink and block capitals on a white-paged jotter pad. There is much direct accusation in the original draft which Lennox later distilled into two short verses and a chorus command to *run away from you*. The emotional outpouring includes phrases such as *two-faced lies* and *hypocrite's curse*. Ringed at the bottom of the A5 sheet is the damning assertion: *I'LL NEVER BE YOUR FRIEND. (YOU'LL ALWAYS BE MY ENEMY.)* Released in the summer of 1986, 'Thorn In My Side' would be the Eurythmics' ninth and final British top-ten single. The despair of the lyrics is lifted by the hope in the melodies, and this contrast between bitter words and joyful music underscored the changing dynamic between Lennox and Stewart. In the writing and recording process there was little need for verbal communication; familiarity was a double-edged sword, born of compatibility, but perhaps masking growing discontent. Whilst Lennox laboured over her lyrics, Stewart was challenging himself to write classic pop songs. His three-chord acoustic picking was as reminiscent of the style of Johnny Marr as of the mid-Sixties-era Beatles. Before recording the album *Be Yourself Tonight*, Stewart sat with an acoustic guitar on his lap over breakfast one morning in the search for a 'killer R&B riff'. It was a conscious departure from the electronic sound that identified previous Eurythmics records. 'When we started putting it down the song had a lot of energy and inspired Annie to come up with the great lyric "Would I Lie To You?" and a melody with very odd answering harmonies: *Now would I say something that wasn't true?'* Stewart expands in his *Songbook*, 'These harmonies are very unusual and Annie is a genius at working them out very quickly in her head. The song started to be a fusion between Stax-type R&B and Eurythmics.' On their seventh album, *Revenge*, 'Missionary Man' was conceived in a similar manner. The song had been assembled after Bob Dylan had visited Stewart's house and ad-libbed to versions of the band's backing tracks whilst Lennox hastily scribbled down poetic inspirations.

The Eurythmics' success neatly coincided with the increasing dominance of music television. MTV provided the opportunity to use image as a means of escaping categorization, but also to channel the language of pictures as an extension of writing themes. In the same period Kate Bush had emerged as an exceptional songwriting talent after her debut single 'Wuthering Heights' topped the charts in February 1978. But whereas Bush became increasingly sequestered from the music industry as she explored, experimented and presented radical challenges to pop music expectation, Lennox cemented her writing in visual imagery and particularly in video communication. Inspired by the stage presence and ambiguity of conceptual artists Gilbert and George, both Stewart and Lennox were fitted at Burton for men's suits. For Lennox it was a battle against traditional perceptions of women by means of a public search for her own identity. The impact was immense. Messages of androgyny, power and sexuality that equally baffled, charmed and offended viewers sent the Eurythmics' singles to the top of the music charts in the UK and the US. The arresting and unpredictable imagery of Lennox was a huge factor in their domination of Eighties pop. It would take the titanic imagination of Madonna coupled with her blatant sexuality to measure up to the unique image that Lennox presented for more than a decade. Both artists represent pop icons defined as much by their image as by their musical output.

There would have been no hint of such a future when Ann Lennox was born at 11.30 p.m. on Christmas Day 1954 at Fonthill Hospital, Aberdeen. Despite her working-class upbringing, Ann was educated at the city's prestigious High School for Girls. It was her first experience of institutionalized conformity, which in her adult life would increasingly grate against a naturally impulsive creativity. When she was thirteen her poem 'The Visitor' was published in the school magazine. It offered the teenager a first taste of recognition. At home, money was tight and as a result Lennox never owned a hi-fi record player. A love for The Beatles, The Stones, The Kinks and Motown came from Friday night dances and the radio. Yet despite adolescent years that veered between belonging and insecurity, her final school report simply read, 'an undoubted talent in music'. To date, eight Brits and four Grammy and Ivor Novello Awards reflect the extent of her songwriting achievements. She has had eighty million record sales worldwide. In *The Guinness Book of Hit Singles 2006*, music historian Stuart Devoy assessed over 27,000 hit songwriting credits. Less than a quarter were British, and of the three female entries Annie Lennox was the sole representative for the UK.

In the past decade she has increasingly devoted her time to home, motherhood and humanitarian work, and in 2011 she was awarded an OBE for her services to charity. Her official website announces, 'Several years ago I personally witnessed Nelson Mandela standing in front of his former prison cell on Robben Island, addressing the world's press. His message was that the pandemic of HIV/AIDS in Africa was, in fact, a genocide. Since that time I resolved to do as much as I can to bring attention to the crisis.' In 2007, she invited twenty-three internationally acclaimed female artists to collaborate with her in the recording of her composition 'Sing'.

Lennox's resistance to *the paparazzi pester and Fleet Street fickle fester* of pop was a high hurdle to vault in securing her contribution to this book. To protect her privacy and in view of the many demands on her time, Annie chose to contribute via a formalized written question-and-answer interaction.

Why are you a songwriter?

I think it's just something I've been drawn towards intuitively. Singing is a great experience, but writing and performing your own songs is a deep and powerful means of self-expression. I started writing when I was about nineteen as I was simply fascinated by the effects of words, melodic line, phrasing, nuance, chord progressions, and all the magical things that go into the alchemy of the process.

Does songwriting come naturally to you?

I'm very familiar with the intriguing pull that leads me to sitting down at a piano and exploring whatever comes. It's instinctive. When I've felt inspired or particularly melancholic I'd write out my thoughts and feelings in notebook pages. There's a certain catharsis in that process.

Do your songs begin with a meaning or a developed idea?

Not very often. In my universe songs have usually started with threads of ideas, some sketches of chord progressions, and a melody to follow.

In the exhibition The House of Annie Lennox there are some early drafts of your initial ideas. Does rhyme control the narrative direction of a song?

Absolutely . . . It's a kind of associative thing. You never know what you're going to find.

Do you use rhyming dictionaries?

Dictionaries and thesauruses can be useful tools . . . Whatever rocks your boat!

Can you describe your editing process?

Word by word. Line by line . . . after an initial outpouring. Lots of overview and revisiting.

Do you value taking breaks?

Lots of breaks . . . Going out for coffee and sandwiches . . . Lying down . . . Getting up again . . . Lots of repeating lines and phrases over and over until they finally find their true nature. I work on my laptop, cutting and pasting.

Suggs said: 'The songs that I write where the music comes first are definitely more simplistic lyrically. You are being tailored to the rhythm and the melody that's in your head.' Can you relate to this thought?

I haven't actually ever analysed it that much, but I know what he means about having to try to fit something around a structure that's already been laid out.

Do you try to write words or use vowels to complement your singing voice?

Hard to say what comes first . . . I think it's just something that comes naturally . . . there's no strict formula or regime about it in my view.

Would you say your voice led the melody or the melody led your voice?

Some people think of their voice as an instrument, and that being the case, your voice has certain potentials and certain limitations which all contribute to its character. The most important thing is that you 'find' your authenticity. You can't be anyone else other than yourself. You have to create your own sound and style, and be completely at ease with it. I would say that melody comes first, and the voice finds its own best way to communicate with the world.

Where does melody come from? Can you describe how you might develop a melodic vocal idea?

Melody is a human sound, produced by sustained breath combined with the vibration between two tiny vocal cords . . . It's like the expression of your 'soul', as opposed to your 'talking' voice. It's a mystical/multi-dimensional sound that can shift your mood and make you cry or dance, or become deeply inspired.

How do you approach writing choruses?

With huge trepidation!

Do you have a preferred time or place or any rituals when you write?

Not really . . . You just have to capture the ideas as they come. That's why notebooks and pens at the side of the bed or in your bag come in very handy. I would always have to go to the piano to start the serious process, though, as that's where the ideas start to get fleshed out.

Can you be creative at will; do you sense inspiration arriving, or can you try too hard to force it?

Well, a lot of alcohol and narcotics have been imbibed by a lot of people in the pursuit of the muse . . . Whatever works but doesn't damage you is fine by me.

The author Ian McEwan has described how three or four times a year he finds a flow of writing divorced from the world and how he can become totally absorbed by it for up to ninety minutes. Can you describe the space or state of mind you inhabit when you write?

It's not 'describable', really . . . I'd answer this question with another question . . . 'What does it feel like to play with sand?' You're just 'in the moment' of attention and connection.

Imagery has played an integral role in your song delivery; do you write music with visual pictures in mind?

The visual pictures, or landscapes, seem to come more in the recording process; they really help to capture mood or atmosphere where words don't cut it.

Is your emotional state a determining factor in directing the attitude of your writing?

Unquestionably, but it doesn't help to be sobbing your heart out in the studio. I think you have to simply feel inspired and 'fascinatingly charged'.

As a solo artist you have had lengthy periods without releasing records: does the need to write leave you or perhaps encourage creative self-doubt?

Right now I've become drawn to gardening!

Can you put into words the creative force between you and Dave and the significance of a male/female writing dynamic?

To be frank, I think that the results of our collaboration should speak for themselves. But having said that, I think we both shared a particular creative understanding that drove us throughout our explorative journey together. At the time we used to describe it as having two complementary pieces of a jigsaw puzzle.

Did you have territories of writing as your relationship with Dave developed?

I wouldn't really like to think of them as 'territories', but I wrote the lyrics and Dave would work as a kind of mentor/editor in that department. Sometimes I'd write ninety per cent of a complete song . . . like 'Sisters Are Doin' It

For Themselves', or 'There Must Be An Angel (Playing With My Heart)', where Dave would have great input in terms of structure and form, and at other times we'd start a song from scratch and both put ideas in, like 'Sweet Dreams', or 'Here Comes The Rain Again'. He was definitely in charge of the technical side of the recording process, as he's incredibly au fait with cutting-edge technology, so he was more of the 'producer' in that sense, but I also had a part to play in production ideas in a more organic way. We always shared everything fifty-fifty, as that was how we saw our partnership.

What was the importance of Dave as an editor to your ideas?
I think it's always great to have someone to bounce ideas off both ways. Dave has a super-fast mind and is a lightning-speed worker, whereas I was always the more introspective/shadow side, and in that way I think we complemented each other very well at the time. I had a mixture of lack of trust in my abilities combined with an absolute certainty and confidence that always got me through everything in the end. Dave and I were foils for each other. We were a male and female version of the Three Musketeers, with the sum of both our parts adding up to more than two.

Is creativity sourced differently by writing a song straight to tape in the studio?
I don't know . . . I've never really done it!

Is there a song that you have written in which you perfectly expressed yourself artistically?
One or two, perhaps, but at the end of the day it all boils down to opinion, and I'm not really in a position to describe anything I've done as 'perfect', even though perfection's what you always strive for!

Can you recall the creative inspiration behind 'Butterfly Music'?
I just wanted to improvise freely on piano with no time signature restraints or click tracks. What came through is a certain quality of atmosphere that's almost meditative in its nature . . . transient . . . then falling still . . . somewhat elusive but delicate, tranquil and alluring in a way that makes your brain sort of 'shift' into a different space.

What were you trying to say with the song 'Why'?
It's basically about the point we humans inevitably come to when we realize that the knots and twists in relationships simply can't be untangled, and we're left dangling with a massive question mark with no apparent resolution. Why? Why? Why? Haven't we all asked that question of ourselves and the universe?

Your exhibition revealed that 'Thorn In My Side' had a undergone a signifi-cant rewriting of the lyrics.

That was work in progress! Rage, fury . . . revenge . . . regret . . . What can I tell you?

'Savage' has the wonderful line, *Everything is fiction / All cynic to the bone.*

It's a pastiche, like a Quentin Tarantino film . . . about fakery, superficiality and the darker side of human behaviour.

'You Have Placed A Chill In My Heart'.

Despair at the human condition . . . to be frankly frank.

'Cold'.

Beauty, melancholia, unrequited love and longing . . .

'I Need A Man' demonstrated the great dynamic range in your voice. When does the persona for a vocal idea arrive?

At 6.35 on Platform 7, on the train headed for Sutton Coldfield! The title could easily have been completed with 'Like A Fish Needs A Bicycle' . . . but the pitiful thing is that it was (and wasn't) true at the same time . . . Irony, sir . . . Irony!

Why do you think the last fifty years of British performance/songwriting has been dominated by men?

I suppose it's simply a reflection of the gender bias that's dominated the world for centuries in terms of what a woman can or can't do. When I first had the glimmer of an idea that I wanted to write songs, in the very early Seventies, there were very few female singer-songwriters around at the time—Joni Mitchell and Carole King are the two that spring to mind. All the female art-ists who influenced and inspired me were incredible singers and performers, but not necessarily songwriters per se. I used to feel somewhat patronized when interviewers would ask me what it felt like to be a 'female' singer-songwriter. I'd usually have to point out that I actually didn't know the differ-ence, because I was just being myself. Things have been evolving significantly since then . . . but there's still so much more to be done in terms of gender equality and parity in every walk of life.

BILLY BRAGG

Billy Bragg's public emergence as a songwriter coincided with the Conservative Party's 1983 landslide victory and subsequent second term in office. Whilst the country succumbed to Margaret Thatcher's vision of a classless society and individualism, Bragg's music reflected the spirit of the struggling worker and the challenges previously laid down by The Clash. In 'To Have And To Have Not' he sang, *Just because you're better than me doesn't mean I'm lazy / Just because you're going forwards doesn't mean I'm going backwards*. Bragg took up a political stance. His writing asserted what he stood for. It took issue with Thatcherite dogma and openly sided with the unions, the teachers and the miners. Bragg was sharp, focused and compelling. His commitment to socialist ideology was resolute, but he delivered it with disarming humour.

Bragg's 1983 debut album *Life's A Riot With Spy Vs Spy* was recorded in three afternoons and played at 45 rpm. It consisted of one voice backed by one guitar. Seven tracks played in sixteen minutes. Side two opens with a Fifties-style Eddie Cochran guitar chug and chord movement recalling Simon & Garfunkel's 'The Sound Of Silence'. 'A New England' was an immediate and enduring fan favourite in which the protagonist ruefully explains: *I don't want to change the world / I'm not looking for a new England / I'm just looking for another girl*. Bragg's presentation utilizes guitar playing to maximum percussive effect: dampening chords for playful dynamics, single bass notes on the lower strings, or riffs played on higher strings inbuilt to fit open-shaped chords. Often billed as The One-Man Clash, the Bard of Barking carried his punk ethos openly. He was musically direct but verbally dexterous. Intros might be just one bar or simply start in immediately on the vocal. Bragg offered slimline songs free of all excess fat and unnecessary additives. No solos. No middle eights, often no identifiable chorus. 'Lovers Town Revisited' has two melodic verses before playing out with a newly introduced E minor coda. In eighty seconds the mini-album finale is packed with images of tension-fuelled evenings and *big blokes on the door*. As the *ladies in the cloakroom* ignore the narrator and *fighting in the dance halls* erupts, Bragg's succinct four-chord drama is abruptly concluded with him running away over an echoing G major. Bragg's singing voice is his natural one, complete with Essex plunging vowels and estuary stretches. He is an acquired and addictive taste, and like Bob Dylan no natural singer, but nonetheless has a voice full of style and character.

In 1984, Bragg supported striking miners as pitched battles broke out between their communities and the police. 'Between The Wars', written and recorded at the height of the conflict, showed a compassionate understanding of the dispossessed and exposed Bragg as an ally of the common man and an opponent of Thatcherism: *I kept the faith and I kept voting, not for the iron fist but for the helping hand / For theirs is a land with a wall around it and mine is a faith in my fellow man.*

'Between The Wars' is a folk song of the modern age, delivered with the simple union of electric guitar and a one-take vocal. It became Bragg's first chart hit and stood as a radical challenge to the fashionable pop bands of the mid-Eighties. The lavish outfits and Savile Row tailoring of Wham!, Spandau Ballet and Duran Duran contrasted sharply with Bragg's Dockers, turn-ups and Fred Perry cents. There followed a sister release, 'Days Like These', in which Thatcherism was bluntly and skilfully critiqued by the determined songwriter.

During Margaret Thatcher's second term of office Bragg was to be found not only trying to bring together the left-wing pop community under the socialist banner of Red Wedge, but releasing his third and greatest album, *Talking With The Taxman About Poetry*. It was the songwriter's defining year. As Red Wedge targeted first-time voters, declaring themselves 'for the Labour Party but not of the Labour Party', Bragg was joined on stages across the country by the likes of Paul Weller, The Smiths and Madness. At the same time, Bragg was expanding his ability to evoke common experiences with poetic capability. *Talking With The Taxman* carries images of *unknown soldiers, monkey trials on TV, the Human Zoo, thoughts of Chairman Mao* and marriage sacrifices at the altar. The album opened triumphantly with the great song of sexual politics. 'Greetings To The New Brunette' chimed with the guitars of Johnny Marr and the harmonies of Kirsty MacColl and offered a succinct three-minute pop song packed with melodic invention, wit and pathos: *How can you lie there and think of England when you don't even know who's in the team?* The achingly beautifully 'Levi Stubbs' Tears' placed the song's protagonist in a mobile home, injured by her husband's abuse and finding solace in tapes of The Four Tops and the security of the Motor City's best writers: *Norman Whitfield and Barrett Strong are here to make right everything that's wrong.*

Born Stephen William Bragg on 20 December 1957 in Barking, east London, Billy left school at sixteen with one O level in English and formed his first band, Riff Raff. The punk-inspired four-piece released one album including the debut single 'I Wanna Be A Cosmonaut', written by Bragg. In 1981, the disillusioned punk joined the army to drive tanks, but after ninety days bought himself out, reflecting in hindsight, 'The best £150 I will spend in my life.' He began performing with the nom de plume Spy vs. Spy. Then, by claiming to be a TV repair man, Bragg managed to gain access to the offices of Charisma Records. After fumbling behind the broken television set he declared his deception to Peter Jenner and handed over his demo tape. Jenner liked it, and Bragg got a record deal.

A decade later, Labour failed to win over the electorate at a fourth successive attempt, and Bragg disappeared from the music headlines dismayed. Re-emerging in the mid-Nineties, he avowed in *William Bloke* a redefined *socialism of the heart*. The youthful explosions of energy had been replaced by a powerful strain of romantic writing and domesticity: *I steal a kiss from you in the supermarket / I walk you down the aisle / You fill my basket*. There was political re-examination: *I used to want to plant bombs at the Last Night of the Proms*, and poignant reflections of fatherhood: *My son and I stand beneath the great night sky*. Bragg's work is a continued evaluation of socialism in the modern world. Songs demand of the listener: 'Which side are you on?' They flirt between first- and third-person dialogue. On *Brewing Up With Billy Bragg*, 'The Saturday Boy' cemented another fan classic into Bragg's expanding canon. It is a recollection of unrequited love in the school classroom, about a girl *not old enough to shave her legs*. Depth, brevity and the common touch are the cornerstones of Bragg's work. The melancholy of 'The Myth of Trust' is one of his many politics of romance songs, set *in the land of Cain* and creating images of *flushing babies down the drain, Elizabethan girls* and the *forbidden apple* of erotic temptation.

Performing 'Take Down The Union Jack' on *Top of the Pops* nearly twenty years after his debut appearance, whilst a gaggle of teenage girls swayed to a live electric guitar, Bragg passionately sang about a nation's need to redefine its Englishness. As a mature artist he has subtly shifted from the hard left stance of his Eighties writing, but shows no signs of mellowing and is still keen to explore politics and pop as a combined force. The single's accompanying album, *England, Half English*, addressed notions of national identity, the working week, globalization and the Internet. By 2013 the 55-year-old activist argued it was the turn of young blood to rally against the governing coalition. Instead, Bragg offered *Tooth and Nail*, an album of self-reflection and household politics. He wrote in 'Handyman Blues', *I know it looks like I'm just reading the paper / But these ideas I'll turn to gold dust later*.

It is ironic that Bragg will be remembered as much for his political affiliations as for his musical collaboration with the American hobo Woody Guthrie. At the invitation of the folk singer's daughter Nora, Bragg was granted unique licence to explore over two thousand of her late father's unused lyrics. The results were a remarkable piece of songwriting time travel. Released over two volumes, the albums stand amongst Bragg's most endearing works. They contain a beguiling set of songs covering a catholic range of musical styles, with expressive use of sounds and instrumentation. The ambition and risks of such an undertaking are obvious: the challenge of giving relevance to words as much as fifty years old; the demands for an English melody writer of working with American vocabulary; making Dust Bowl lyricism relevant to the Nineties; and collaborating with an unfamiliar cast of musicians in Jeff Tweedy and Wilco. Bragg may have been leaning over a poet's precipice, but *Mermaid Avenue* was extremely well received on its release in 1998 and would receive a Grammy nomination for Best Contemporary Folk Album.

When this conversation took place, Billy had just completed a year touring the world to promote the album *Mr Love And Justice*. The final show of the tour was a sold-out performance at London's Shepherd's Bush Empire. Between songs, Bragg emphasized the need for his audience to *keep faith* with their left-wing political persuasion and unfashionable belief in New Labour. Witnessing The Clash perform in 1978 at a Rock against Racism demonstration had ignited in Bragg a lifetime's belief that music, whilst not capable of changing the world, can transform people's perception of it. In Bragg's kingdom, melodies serve as by-products to communication: *it takes a mess of courage to go against the grain . . . I keep faith / I keep faith in you.*

Accusations of champagne socialism are often slung at left-wing artists who find success, but as a closing note it is worth recording Bragg's commitment to

Red Wedge at the Birmingham Odeon,
27 January 1986

fairness about monetary reward. On signing to Go! Discs in 1983 he waived his record company advance in exchange for a tin of 1965 Beatles talcum powder and the complete *Motown Chartbusters*. The young artist was also allocated a percentage share of the company in an attempt to give a cooperative feel to the label. Years later, when the independent syndicate was bought out by PolyGram, surprised employees of the business benefited from a dividend of over one million pounds. Ill at ease with profiting from his good fortune, Bragg had altruistically donated his share to a trust fund for present and future Go! Discs workers.

I'm going to take you back to a quote from 1985.

Oh fucking hell, that's always a worry.

On the *South Bank Show* you said, 'Politics is life. Good music should reflect life and society.' It suggests a maxim for your career.

Some songwriters choose to write only love songs but I choose to occasionally look out the window at the world and try to reflect that, trying to offer people different perspectives. Smokey Robinson gave me different perspectives about my emotional state, made me feel like I wasn't the only person. You know that feeling people say, 'It feels like they're reading my mail': a song can make you feel like you're not the only person in the world who's ever felt this pain. Just as you can do that about relationships, so you can do that about what's going on the world.

Smokey Robinson's influence is evident in much of your writing.

Yeah, the thing that Smokey most influenced was the shape of his songs. If you look at 'Tracks Of My Tears', rather than content, the simplicity of it: it's only three chords; and the immensity of the production. Succinct is not a great word to use about a song . . . his songwriting is very economical. He doesn't need to tell you more than you need to know and what he does tell you is incredibly insightful. I'm a less-is-more man when it comes to lyrics and guitar playing.

Did you learn about the structure of songs from other records?

If you listen to them you just think, 'How do they do that?' Some people want to ride motorbikes and some people want to know how they work. I guess I just want to take off the gearbox.

Paul Weller said he used to appropriate structures from a Beatles songbook or from Motown records.

I don't do so much of that. I think this is a very common method, in fact I use this when I do songwriting workshops: taking a song you're very familiar with, you really love, and writing a lyric to that. The path is already there;

you've got to lay your own patio, your own pattern on the path. So you're not starting with a blank piece of paper. No songwriter becomes a songwriter by sitting down one day with a blank piece of paper and writing a song.

Have you used that method outside of writing workshops by building on another's song and making it your own?

That's how I learnt to write songs. I spent a long time writing in the style of other people before I could put my finger on and say this was the first proper Billy Bragg song. I was writing from when I was about twelve. I wrote a poem at school like everybody else does; I think I just did it for homework, and then the teacher sent a letter home to my parents asking if I'd copied this from anywhere in the house. We had books but not poetry. I eventually got to read my poem out on Essex Radio. I thought, 'This is good. This is pretty cool. Write a poem, get on the radio, it makes me stand out from everybody else.' Before I could play guitar I started writing songs in notebooks and keeping the tune in my head, mostly in the style of Bob Dylan or Smokey Robinson. When I was sixteen the kid next door taught me how to play guitar and that really helped. Around the age of nineteen onwards I was in a band doing gigs.

Do you remember the first song that you wrote where you found your own voice?

It was one of the Riff Raff songs, 'Richard': that's why I ended up putting it on the first album. I thought, this is a song you can't really say, 'OK, there's a bit of Jackson Browne, a bit of Elvis Costello or The Clash.'

Was that a clicking point, a path that you could follow to achieve originality?

More kind of like . . . I'm out now. I'm out on my own. I've finished my apprenticeship and now I'm a songwriter. I'm writing Billy Bragg songs. Not to say I don't still write songs that are heavily influenced by other people: I do, but I also write Billy Bragg songs that are stand-alone rather than being a copy or a modification. You are the sum of your influences, ultimately. Originality is the accumulation of all your influences and then adding a bit of yourself, and the more of yourself that you can get in there the further you will go to touching other people.

Is there a pattern in your approach to writing?

There is no single way to write a song. They're like mountains, every one is different. When you get close . . . you might find one and you're there, another one you're stuck on it for a year because you can't work out where to go but you know it's a good one . . . you're not getting off. Some songs, they all come in one go just like that; others I get the chorus and I know what the song is going to be about but I just have to shade in what I want. Other times I get an incredible tune and I write three or four different verses and I know none of them are going to work. I write the entire song . . . 'This ain't the lyric,' and then eventually I write the lyric and start playing it.

You're happy to go back and re-edit, refine.

Sure, particularly when you play a song to somebody and they don't really get what it's about; you better go back and have another look at that.

An example would be 'A Nurse's Life Is Full Of Woe', which became 'Little Time Bomb'.

What happened there, I got the phrase *a nurse's life is full of woe* which I kind of liked, and I would have sat down with a guitar and bashed out a tune that fitted around that. Using that phrase as a piece of grit I would then construct everything else around that, including the tune. But when I couldn't write a song that convincingly conveyed that idea—and I couldn't—I still had a tune. Take the tune off, then use that as a way of forming an idea around it; use that as an anchor. That's just a way, that's not the way. There's a great poem by Rudyard Kipling, 'In The Neolithic Age'; the chorus is, the punchline is, *There are nine and sixty ways of constructing tribal lays,* (medieval term for song) / *And every single one of them is right!* There is no one way to write a song. It's like saying, 'How do you have a conversation?' You don't know when you start it how you're going to do it, where it's going to go, how it's going to pick up. All you know is that subsequently it made sense and that it can be communicated to other people.

How would you pursue melody?

Ah . . . I don't really pursue melody. I'm not a great musician. Melody to me is all a matter of what works and sounds good. For instance, 'St Swithin's Day': I've no idea what those chords are; all I do is just walk my fingers across the bottom three chords while strumming.

Is vocal melody dictated by what you are playing on the guitar?

In that case, yeah, because I undoubtedly came up with those nice chord phrases before and then put the lyrics around that. Sometimes you just come out with a nice guitar phrase. 'Tank Park Salute': I would have had the melody for that before. Other times you've got an idea and you're trying to hammer out a way of putting that idea across. Melody has never been to me a matter of huge importance. I know a good one when I hear one. I love a hook but it's not something I've ever fretted over. Whereas lyrics: I've been lying on the floor in the studio control room writing lyrics on the last day of mixing. On the last album, *Mr Love And Justice*, when we'd finished the recording of the music, half the tracks I hadn't written any lyrics for at all. I didn't even know what the songs were going to be about. I just had ideas, really good ones, and we just went into the studio, me and the band, and we worked them up into a shape. One morning I got in the shower and out of absolutely nowhere into my head popped this phrase, *Johnny Carcinogenic*. Got out the shower, dried myself off and went for a walk; an hour later I'd written that song. That was a little nugget of thought; that little pun on Johnny Carson just gave me enough purchase on the mountain to get to the top. Instead of being on an ice face where I didn't really know where I was, I suddenly got my little fingernail in there and thought, 'Hang on a minute,' and reached the next bit, got to the top and was able to finish the song. Having written a song it's an idea that's worth putting on a record, because it says something that hasn't been said before.

How disciplined are you as a writer?

I'm not very disciplined about writing. I tend now to just write when I need songs. Whereas in the old days, twenty-five years ago, the energy and the excitement of fame, I was firing them off all the time. There's songs going all the time. I've got half a dozen knocking about but they don't really fit the balance of the set.

What changed from that youthful exuberance: firing out songs, and the need to pick up a guitar and write?

Nobody's desperately waiting for the next Billy Bragg single, are they? After about ten years, after *Don't Try This At Home*. It's not like people have given up on me; they haven't. I'm not competing every week for radio plays, so the pressure isn't on me. I'm not doing a radio or Peel session every three or four months and I need new songs. Whereas when I was younger there was that pressure and that was my edge. Having said that, in Dublin last week at the soundcheck, just fucking around with the guitars, I definitely came up with two usable riffs and Grant (*Showbiz*) taped them. He'll send me a tape at the end of the tour and over the next six months I'll sit down with those, piss around with them and probably write something. So the process is still going on but I'm not so constantly engaged in it. It's something I can come and go from whereas before it was gung-ho: writing on trains, people would say something to me. My theory about how songwriters are different is that our intuition is more tuned than other people; we tune into ideas and vibes. I was in the zone for *Mr Love And Justice*; I was thinking about it constantly and eventually it delivered. I'd tuned into my intuition: my muse to be able to write six songs in five days, half the album.

What fired up the passion to write lots of songs when you were younger?

Because I was Billy Bragg all of a sudden. I just wanted to get shagged and it seemed to be a good way of going about it. As you get older you don't have that desperate urgency. If I was terminally ill maybe that urgency would come back. Woody Guthrie clearly knew he was dying and that's why he was writing six songs a day. This urge to write doesn't go away, it reasserts itself; before it was compulsive. Part of the reason why I joined the army after Riff Raff was to ultimately confound this ridiculous idea that I could ever be a singer-songwriter. It was like, 'Fuck it. I'm going to press an eject button on this pretend life kidding myself I could have a job in the music industry.' As soon as I got to Catterick, where I did my basic training, I started writing songs: they wouldn't leave me alone and I got ideas every day. I saw shit and I was writing notes: 'Oh, fuck this, this is fucking stupid.' I didn't like it, anyway, so when I bought myself out I thought, 'One last go, then. I'll tell you what we'll do. I'll do it solo with an electric guitar so it'll be so scary I'll never want to go there again if I fuck up.' It was like a last kamikaze attempt: fix bayonet and just charge the machine guns, and it fucking worked, thank God.

Do you subscribe to the idea that songs are already out there and as a writer you are compelled to catch them?

It's not like that. They're not out there. The songs are in here. Some people believe they pick them out of the ether; I'm not sure about that. I do think the creative urge is a compulsive one; it's whether you're in control of it or it's in control of you. Back in the day it was in control of me and now I'm in control of it. The other night I felt as energized as I did twenty-five years ago: I don't feel any less excited about what I'm doing. I'm just a bit more measured with it now. I don't think I could keep the pace up before. Also I felt for a while that if I wasn't writing songs and doing gigs I didn't really exist. I don't really feel that any more. I think I exist now; I'm not worried about ceasing to exist.

What are your thoughts about a set of lyrics standing apart from the music?

The only stuff I write now that has to stand up in its own right is poems to my missus. They are stand-alone poetry so they have to work rhythmically and be focused. Songs are integral to the tune. I know lots of songs that would stand alone as poems: *Take me disappearing through the smoke rings of my mind / Down the foggy ruins of time, far past the frozen leaves / The haunted, frightened trees out to the windy beach / Far from the twisted reach of crazy sorrow.* That's Dylan, we can leave poetry to him. We are poets, we're poets with guitars. Yevtushenko used to perform his poetry to thousands of people in Russia. If that had been tried over here maybe I wouldn't have bothered with the guitar business. In the end poets do get shagged, but poets with Telecasters get shagged more.

Do you recall writing 'Levi Stubbs' Tears'?

I had been on a cross-channel ferry with Andy Kershaw. He had been talking incessantly and would not shut up. I thought, the only way I can make him stop talking is if I write a song. 'Ah, sorry, mate, I can feel an idea coming on,' so he went to have a smoke on the deck and I wrote 'Levi Stubbs' Tears'. I used the riff originally on 'I Won't Talk About It', which I recorded during the *Brewing Up* sessions. Its genesis would be buying the Burns guitar and being able to make that big, high, shredding treble noise: those clanging chimes, and wanting to use them in some way. Grant says to me sometimes, 'You're making a fucking awful noise in "Levi Stubbs' Tears".' I say, 'Grant, it's meant to be the sound of the world falling apart. It's not meant to be a pristine bit of music. Her world is falling apart: listen to the effing lyrics.' So I wanted something hard-edged in the sound and the Burns really gave me that percussive sound. As a musician I really think of the guitar as a percussive instrument; the melody is my voice and the light and shade is the play between the two. Dynamics is very important when you play solo. If I'm playing with an acoustic I can hear what it'll sound like with an electric in my head. I don't tend to plug in at home—too noisy. I could have written 'Levi Stubbs' Tears' on an acoustic. I'm often writing late at night and everyone's in bed so I have to sing softly, like Smokey Robinson.

Your use of metaphor to convey the common touch is a wonderful mainstay throughout your career. In 'The Boy Done Good': *You weren't that kind of a bird that likes her studs covered in mud* **and in 'Goalhanger':** *like trying to knock in a nail with an inflatable hammer / In the game of life . . .*

. . . *he's just a dreadful goalhanger.* I know, I am a total sucker for a metaphor. I'm always trying in my live show to use a bit of self-effacing humour to leaven some of the heavier shit I've got to say. I've done gigs with bands that are all political and it's as boring as hell. It's like, 'Come on, guys, lighten up.' I like artists whose lyrics are a bit knowing, that they know they're doing a daft job; they don't take themselves so seriously.

'Sexuality' would be an example of that.

Yeah, it should be a joyous song. Bands like Oasis who take themselves so seriously just switch me off. You've got to remember I was writing at the time The Smiths were, so Morrissey's warped *joie de vivre* in his lyrics I always found very enticing; I was always trying to get a bit of that in as well, and Johnny's melodies. Before, I was trying to compete with Elvis Costello, which is a waste of time: you'll kill yourself, that's a mountain you'll never get to the top of. I'd rather have less words, leave space, leave people hanging on a phrase, just chuck a phrase up there . . . use the guitar to rise and push the phrase right up above the rest of the song. In a song like 'Valentine's Day Is Over', *Brutality and the economy are related now, I understand*: these kinds of lines I try to highlight.

Also from that song, *Don't come round reminding me again how brittle bone is,* **writing from . . .**

. . . a female perspective, as was 'Mr Love And Justice'. Sometimes you have to inhabit a character in order to give more weight to what you are saying. At the Vancouver Folk Festival one year I got into an argument with some woman about 'Valentine's Day Is Over'. Their argument was, I would never know what it was like to be a victim of male violence. I totally agreed but said, 'I am not writing this song for other women. There are plenty of women writing songs about this issue for other women to relate to. I'm writing this for other men, as a man saying, 'This is not acceptable,' so that other men will hear this and think, 'What is going on in this song is not right.' I think it's worth trying to articulate those kinds of things whilst both at the same time accepting that from my perspective, it will always be one step removed from the reality of someone who's actually felt or been a victim of it. I never went to the Falklands but I have been in a foxhole in the dark and I know how scary it is. It's imagination that we're working with here and we have to inhabit that. It's like 'Between The Wars': I don't think it would have been so effective if it had just been purely about the politics and economics of that period. It's that man trying to keep his family together, keeping the faith, keeping voting and things not happening the way he wants. It's more possible to identify with him as an individual, rather than just as a general précis of the economic situation of the mid-1980s.

Can you remember writing 'Between The Wars'?

Oh yeah, I'll never forget it. I lived in a house in south London that we couldn't afford to heat and I got the idea. There's bits of the 'Ode To Joy' in there and bits of . . . might be 'Land Of Hope And Glory': not bits, references somewhere. The only place where it was warm was the bathroom because that was where the boiler was. I was about a verse and a half in when the woman I was living with wanted to use the bathroom. I was like, 'Fuckaaarggh,' so we had a screaming exchange and I ended up writing the last verse on Wimbledon Common in a huff.

There's so much compassion in that song and there you are in an . . .

. . . argument, exactly. It's just one of those things, two young people. I think we were house-sitting for a year and we couldn't afford to heat the house in winter, so it was a little bit harsh.

Did you take your guitar with you out onto the Common?

No, no, no. The tune must have been knocking about for a bit. Sometimes the tune might come when you haven't got a guitar. One time we were driving down to the south of Spain overnight in the van and a lyric started forming in my head. I didn't have a guitar and these ideas and metaphors were coming, *the wasted sea*, *the bulldog breed*: 'Fucking hell, this is really good.' The guitars were in the back, so I borrowed somebody else's song and wrote the whole lyric to 'Desolation Row'. When I finally got a guitar I wrote 'The Few' with the same metre and scan as that tune. Later I did the Fleah Festival the same day as Bob Dylan and sang it with his melody. I'm always fond of putting in a little quote if I've mischievously stolen something: a little marker, a nod. *At night the baby brotherhood and the inner city crew* is a paraphrase of a line from 'Desolation Row'. 'Ideology', the tune is stolen from 'The Chimes Of Freedom'—in fact to the extent that someone once came up to me and said, 'You'll never guess what? I saw Bruce Springsteen the other night; he's stolen your song "Ideology" and called it "The Chimes Of Freedom".' I said, 'Really, the bastard (*laughing*) . . . we need to have a chat!'

In 'Ideology' you sing, *(We) expect a little more back for their taxes / Like school books and beds in hospitals*. Is it hard as a political songwriter to offer solutions?

Yeah, *and peace in our bloody time*, but I would think of it more as a suggestion rather than a solution, *and all they get is politicians grinding axes*. I would argue that's not a solution, that's the way it was.

If not a solution you're saying, 'This is the problem, this is what we need.' Dylan wouldn't do that?

Dylan isn't really a political songwriter. If you want to talk about political songwriters you've got to look at people like Phil Ochs. Dylan is the songwriter's songwriter, the greatest songwriter, but he's a man of many parts. You choose your own Dylan from the great variety that he's offered us: the Woody Guthrie impersonator; the old blues man; there's a Bob Dylan who's The Beatles; a Dylan who's a country singer; a Rimbaud; a great protest singer. But was he a political singer? I don't think so. You've got to be very careful of writing songs like 'Blowin' In The Wind'. They sound really nice but they don't actually say shit, do they?

'Waiting For The Great Leap Forward' is asking the questions.

'Great Leap Forward' is my post-Red Wedge song where I've been there, I've done that and this is my conclusion. Can you mix pop and politics in a way that actually changes the world? Well, my experience is no, but it's still worth having a go, ain't it? What you can do, which I've come to understand, is you can give people that other perspective. You can give them another view of the world that they may then be able to take away and build on, and that's worth trying and having a go. That was my experience as a fan of The Clash; they gave me another perspective which I then built on. Subsequently I came to see them as a band that didn't really walk it like they talked it; that didn't really engage, and that was their mistake, and that's why I felt duty bound to engage in Red Wedge: to build on the mistakes that they made. I'd like to think the next generation of political songwriters will build on the mistakes we've made, because that's how you stop keep making the same fucking mistakes.

I recently read Margaret Thatcher's *The Downing Street Years*.

Oh yeah.

The overriding theme was her hatred of and desire to crush socialism at all costs. Those looking to Billy Bragg as a challenging songwriting voice of the post-Thatcher era found a redefined *socialism of the heart*. Was it a vindication of her dogma?

You have to understand between *Don't Try This At Home* and *William Bloke*, Thatcher went, the Berlin Wall had come down, the Soviet Union disappeared, I became someone's dad. Any single one of those things would have forced me to change the way I addressed issues of socialism. All of them together, you can't carry on. I would have been a museum piece if I hadn't moved on and recognized that the ideological language of Marxism was, frankly, dead. It's not on the first album, it's barely on the second and it's all there on the third because of the miners' strike. I haven't changed my ideals; I'm just looking for a new way of articulating them. *Socialism of the heart*, to me, is compassion: to want to live in a compassionate society, rather than socialism of the head which is classical Marxism. We are in a situation where if we can no longer talk in the language of Marxism we have the opportunity to create a new language for socialism that isn't tainted by Stalinism and totalitarianism. It's very fortunate we live in this period. Now we're in the tailspin of individualism, there's opportunities to come up with these notions of how we talk about a compassionate society, a collective expression of society's will. I think poets are in the front line of that discussion; better it be poets than academics, in my experience.

Does songwriting fulfil a need to archive your life?

I religiously kept a diary as a kid from sixteen up to *Taxman*. If you're going to reflect life, you're going to reflect the life you're having. I can't reflect your life; I don't know what you do.

Workers Playtime had many heart-rending songs almost placing honesty beyond any commercial design.

That's my great bust-up album. I still want to be Smokey Robinson; I'm trying to write songs that make people cry. That's my job, to get some sort of emotion out of the audience. You're in a situation so you have the landscape of that and then clearly you're going to write a song. The chances are a figure that walks through in the song is going to be the landscape you find yourself in.

'The Short Answer' revealed that honesty: *Between Marx and marzipan in the dictionary there was Mary / Between the deep blue sea and the devil that was me.*

I've always tried to be honest about my own complicity in the phase of relationships I'm in. *I hate the arsehole I become whenever I'm with you:* I was that person. It's not, you're fucked up and I'm perfect, it doesn't work like that. Someone like Springsteen writes in cinemascope: vast screen, fast writing and

'Born In The USA', whereas I'm looking more at the detail, perhaps more European. I wouldn't say Bergman, maybe it's as characterful as Mike Leigh, Ken Loach maybe. It's more actually the detail that defines the characters. *I'm celebrating my love for you with a pint of beer and a new tattoo:* you kind of know who that bloke is. He's not some swish fellow that went to university. He's clearly confused by the new sexual politics. There's a bit in the middle of 'Greetings To The New Brunette' where it's clear he's not totally comfortable with being in love with a very intelligent political woman. *Your sexual politics has left me all of a muddle.* This is someone who's come from a traditional working-class background who's dealing with a modern relationship, still having the residue of a sexist attitude that he grew up with. You can write loads of material about people being socially awkward but being politically awkward in the Eighties, getting the sexual politics right, the angle of the approach to a relationship.

Was 'Tank Park Salute' a song of catharsis for you?

Before I wrote that song I had never spoken to anybody about my father dying, not even my brother. I didn't set out to write it. I had the tune. I had the whole shape of the song but I was writing a lyric about something completely different. I wrote that line *I closed my eyes and when I looked your name was in the memorial book.* It opened a floodgate and there it all was. Again, it was another one sitting: Bang! And I looked at it on the paper and I thought, 'I don't know about that. If I sing this song to people I'll have to talk about it. People will come up to me and say, "It's a real shame", "Sorry about your Dad" . . . phew.' I went to the rehearsal studio and played it to Cara (*Tivey*), my piano player. At the end of it she said, 'Wow, that's about your dad, isn't it?' I thought, 'This works, I can do this, this is a good song. This is something I've got to do for my own sake.' People come up to me and say, 'Your song helped me.' I'm like, 'It helped me, never mind you.'

What does *Tank Park Salute* mean?

My dad was in a tank regiment in the army. There has to be in a song that revealing, that personal—and this is the song that exemplifies this idea—you've got to reach as deeply inside of you as you can, be as honest as you can, if you want to write a song that touches the majority of people. Although we all have different experiences the way we feel inside can be similar. In a song that naked and that personal there has to be one small shred that's between me and my dad, and that's what *Tank Park Salute* is.

***You were so tall / How could you fall?* says so much about a child and his father.**

It's a very, very precious song to me because it does to me what Smokey Robinson songs do. *Pale moon in a sunny sky*, that's the best line, that metaphor 'in the midst of life we are in death', that kind of idea; that's the reality. I am inordinately proud of that song but also inordinately in awe of it as a thing. I've seen hard men shudder at the prospect of me playing it. It's good that we're talking about this at length because it really gets to the nub of what songs can do both to the listener and the writer. Songs shouldn't just be something that you just knock off; it should be something that you invest your deepest emotion in. If you wanted a classic Billy Bragg song 'Tank Park Salute' would be right at the top with 'Levi Stubbs' Tears'. It fascinates me how it works, how something so simple can have such an effect. Through songwriting you can say the things to your loved ones that you can't say over the dinner table. As a kid me and mum didn't speak about it and we both regret it dreadfully.

I used to want to plant bombs at the Last Night of the Proms but now you'll find me with the baby in the bathroom—the poetics of the mundane?

It is, but incredibly important. That used to be the centre of my life, now this is. I'm sending out a signal that there is another reality; politics isn't the be-all and end-all.

Does marriage and domestic happiness change songwriting?

Parenthood has to change everything or you're not doing it properly. It forces you to recalibrate things, but if you're asking me if a pram in the corridor is a hindrance or a help, I would say if your songwriting is as easily swayed by a change of circumstance as that you're clearly a one-trick pony. The real job is to reflect the world as you see it, and parenthood gives you a whole new set of fresh perspectives. Shouldn't it be an emotional sabbatical from the old you: let you see the old you in a different light, where you were to where you are. Surely great art is about perspective. So your sudden change of perspective and your immersion in parenthood and a steady relationship should put what you did before into a starker contrast. Being in a happy relationship should not in any way challenge your songwriting ability. There is so much cynicism at the moment it's really important to come and really step beyond just metaphorical calls to arms and really be specific. People know 'I Keep Faith' is about Juliet; a love song for the person I love, but at the same time it's a call to arms. That's my idea of a good song; it can do both those jobs. The best songs are the ones that are both political and personal. *Brutality and the economy are related now, I understand* is a prime example from 'Valentine's Day is Over', in which the economic situation is shaping their relationship in a negative sense. It's about being unemployed and the pressure that we are put under: the bailiffs coming round; having to travel and look for work. But the thing about songs is people have their own meanings and you can't disavow them; it's as valid as mine.

What were you looking for in the lyrics of Woody Guthrie?

Mermaid Avenue was a breeze. I was just picking tunes off the tree: sit down with the lyric, play a song; if it didn't work, turn the page over, try the next one. Initially I chose the songs that I thought were great. I played the first little batch of them at a tiny little fan club gig. I had a couple of new songs and a couple of the Woody ones; one of them was 'All You Fascists Are Bound To Lose', and talking to them after it became clear to me they couldn't tell if I'd written the new songs or Woody had, and that really bothered me. I went back to the songs and realized I'd chosen Billy Bragg songs, and that's when I realized I needed Wilco. I needed someone else in there to choose 'California Stars' and those kind of things I wouldn't have chosen. There's so much stuff in there you can find the songs you wish you had written. Going back in again and finding 'Ingrid Bergman' and 'My Flying Saucer' was a revelation.

Did the experience affect how you wrote thereafter?

Yeah, yeah, yeah, that experience might have been the catalyst for my realization that my true enemy was cynicism, because Woody never wrote a cynical song. He never wrote a song that put people down. That was part of my understanding that this is the real enemy of all of us who want to make a better world—our own cynicism. If I want to be empowering, encouraging, inspiring people I need to be addressing this issue, because there's so much of it about. I'm as prone to it as anybody else.

In 'England, Half English' you wrote, *Those three lions on your shirt, they never sprang from England's dirt / Them lions are half English and I'm half English too.* For many people the three lions are the personification of what it means to be English.

Well, they are English, but they didn't come from England. They're Norman lions. How ridiculous to have an animal that's never been seen in your country as your symbol. That wasn't much after 'Three Lions': you have to draw people's attention to the details, the origin of symbolism.

Is it harder when your audience has grown older to challenge their viewpoint?

Particularly with that song: that was the first time I tried to address the issue of national identity, and my audience weren't really ready for that. One guy, who I considered was a fellow traveller, said to me of the pay-off line: *Oh my country, oh my country, what a beautiful country you are*, 'You're being ironic, yeah?' and I said, 'Sorry, man, I'm not. I do love my country: it's beautiful. I don't love it in a way that I think all other are countries are shit, but it is my own.' The only justification I have for writing a song is that I feel that I have something to say that everyone else isn't saying, that I have a perspective that might help add to the issue. I never did come to a conclusion about what Englishness was but I was willing to explore that territory to my satisfaction.

Who was 'William Bloke'?

'William Bloke' is trying to evoke the sort of person who would climb to the top of Primrose Hill to watch the sunset wearing an England football shirt.

How would you differentiate English songwriting from American?

Mmm . . . Americans tend to write in cinemascope: wide-open spaces, mind-expanding poetry. The British tend to write with more characterization and detail, more kitchen sink. Those aspects of British songwriting that I admire are looking at detail and examining it closely, drawing a conclusion from that rather than the sort of broad lyrics of 'This Land Is Your Land'.

In the great tradition of classic British songwriting, how would you account for the lack of women songwriters?

I can't. There are some brilliant women songwriters: Sandy Denny, Eliza Carthy, P. J. Harvey. Maybe it's something to do with our culture. If you think of women at the moment: Duffy, someone else is writing her songs. With girl groups, they hook up with someone who does the writing for them. Maybe there are not enough models like Laura Nyro: there has never been a songwriter that has approached songs and lyrics in the way she has. I don't think there is any reason why there shouldn't be but you're absolutely right to draw attention to the fact that there aren't.

Take the M for Me and the Y for You out of family and it all falls through . . . I've got friends who are telling me they're living in clover but lose the C for commitment and the L for love and it's over.

I misspelled *family* when I was typing something on a laptop. I dropped the *M* and it said *faily*: 'Oh, that's interesting.' So I took the *Y* off. 'Mmm . . . if you take the *M* and the *Y* out of *family* it becomes *fail*. I wonder if there's a metaphor in there?' So once you get to there you start looking at other things. But the best one for me is *Let's pull the Y off of yours and put it on the fire and make them our problems baby*. A very simple idea; it doesn't really go anywhere other than what it says on the tin, but it works.

How can you lie there and think of England when you don't even know who's in the team?

That's just one of those little scenes where you're taking a classic, a cliché, I suppose, that people are familiar with: *lie back and think of England*, and subverting it. That's one of the things I get the most delight out of. You're a craftsman

A New England

15/8/79

I loved the words you wrote me
But that was bloody yesterday,
I cant survive on what you send
Every time you need a friend
I saw two shooting stars last night
I wished on them but they were only satallites
It dont count if you wish on space hardware
I wish I wish I wish you'dd care

So, hang your pictures in the hall
One the ceiling on the wall
And be thankful for what youve got
Prey God Bless the Electric Clock

My jean were full of strange ideas
My mind was set despite the fears
But other things got in the way
I never asked those girls to stay

I love you then as I love you still
Though I put you on a pedistal & put you on the pill
I dont feel sad about letting you go
I just feel bad about letting you know
So hang you pictures on the wall
Dont look over your shoulder at all
Just be thankful for what youve got
~~God Bless the landlord & God Bless the clock~~
And sing God Bless the Electric clock

I dont want to change the world
Im not looking for a new England
Im looking for another girl

and you're writing a song but you do want to put a little bit of embellishment on it, you can't resist. Having said that, when I wrote 'Something Happened' off the last album it was one of those tunes where I had the tune and no lyrics. I went off on a walk and wrote two statements: *Do you know what love is? Love is when you willingly place someone else's priorities above your own.* Do you know what lust is? Lust is when you actively force your own priorities on someone else. *I just wrote them down and I walked and I walked and I walked, and I thought, 'That's it, that is what you wanted to say and you've said it, don't fuck about.' Sometimes you see those things that an artist does where it's just a few lines and you fill in the bits. Leaving the audience to do that is sometimes worth doing.*

I was twenty-one years when I wrote this song. I'm twenty-two now but I won't be for long—a line taken from Paul Simon's 'Leaves That Are Green'.

When I wrote that song I didn't realize it was going to be number seven in the charts one day, but it's such a lovely line. I wanted people to know that I was a fan of Paul Simon. I was twenty-two when I wrote that song. It was exactly where I was. It's just one of those things that I fired off. I didn't think, 'Here's the song that's going to define me as a songwriter, that most people know, that's going to be the one that finishes my sold-out London shows with everyone fucking singing it.' I was living in more or less a squat in East Northamptonshire, walked back from the pub, looked up and saw these two satellites flying over side by side, came home with the metaphor and wrote 'A New England' around it.

Take down the Union Jack, it clashes with the sunset, and put it in the attic with the emperor's old clothes.

The opening was a steal from Philip Sassoon, a guy at the tail-end of the British Empire. He said something like, 'The reason they take down the Union Jack each night is because it clashes dreadfully with the sunset,' something arch like that. I read that line and thought, that's too good a line. It just stayed in my mind really bugging me: 'Come on, babe,' like a little bit of grit. 'Get out of my head,' and eventually I was forced to sit down and write the song.

The song is balanced with the common touch at the end: What could be more British than here's a picture of my bum?

Exactly: *here's a picture of my bum . . . Gilbert and George are taking the piss*. People said to me, 'Is that a St George reference?', 'No, fucking hell, man!'

In the end it took me a dictionary to find out the meaning of unrequited / While she was giving herself for free / At a party to which I was never invited, from 'The Saturday Boy'.

I didn't realize it then, but this was the great unrequited love affair of my life. It's only subsequently I found that out, is what I'm trying to say there. I never got invited to those parties at all, and I did used to phone her up and her mum did used to say she was in the bath, and I knew she wasn't. Nobody can have that many baths a night.

The temptation to take the precious things we have apart to see how they work must be resisted, for they never fit together again.

That's absolutely true; if you dig a hole the dirt never goes back into the hole, for some reason. Sometimes you can spend too much time analysing relationships, picking up problems, opening up things that ultimately you might get some momentary sense of vindication from, but they're not in the long run going to help the relationship. Commitment to a relationship has to overcome that urge to go back and to continually kick at the same bruise.

Then one day it happened, she cut her hair and I stopped loving her.

(*Laughing*.) The fucking thing had to end somehow. The pay-off is an illustration of the fact that for all of the great weight I had invested in it, as you can see from the song, it really wasn't that important. It was as ephemeral as a haircut. I don't sing that any more, as you heard the other night . . .

Billy Bragg at Berry Street Studio, London, July 1984 by Nicki Rodgerson

. . . then one day it happened, she voted Tory and I stopped loving her. **From** '**Richard**': *How can I go on when every alpha particle hides a neon nucleus . . . our titanic love affair sails on the morning tide.*

I was in the process of writing that round Jayne's house whilst watching Nottingham Forest in the European Cup Final and Richard was there and Neil, who also gets a mention. He was talking about . . . it's actually not right. I had to change it to fit: *every alpha particle doesn't hide a neon nucleus*; it's actually something else but it didn't sound so good. That's what I meant earlier about a Billy Bragg song: I had let go of meaning and worrying about literalism and I was being impressionistic: it just fits. Would Jackson Browne do this? Would Elvis Costello do this? Would Bob Dylan do this? I don't care: Billy Bragg is going to do it. That was the freedom that I felt, that was the celebration in 'Richard'. It's not about Richard and Jayne getting together; it was about me finishing my apprenticeship and becoming a proper singer-songwriter. It feels both free and empowered to put any line in; give me any piece of clay and I'll make it into something. It's my job to be poetic. I am a poet. You go back and look at these lines later and you think, 'Why is that line in there? It just fits.' I remember Johnny Marr laughing when I sang him the final lyrics of 'Sexuality': *I look like Robert De Niro / I drive a Mitsubishi Zero.* I said, 'Well, it rhymes.' I think he was used to working with a higher class of songwriter!

JOHNNY MARR

Oh Manchester, so much to answer for: so decreed Morrissey in 'Suffer Little Children', judging his city's culpability in the Moors Murders. But Lancashire has had a distinguished history of popular music, having been home to artists ranging from George Formby to the Buzzcocks, with such varied talents as Ewan MacColl, Herman's Hermits, Wayne Fontana and the Mindbenders, Freddie and the Dreamers, Georgie Fame, Graham Nash and Mark E. Smith along the way. In the 1980s, Manchester was to produce a pair of songwriters with an original and uniquely modern take on their craft: Steven Morrissey and Johnny Marr.

Johnny Marr openly acknowledged the influence of the landmark pop singles of the Sixties. He told Keith Richards that 'Bigmouth Strikes Again' was his 'Jumpin' Jack Flash'; its insistent four-chord double-time riff propelled the song's acoustic rhythm and percussive momentum. Marr specialized in using a range of different guitars and tones to create complex arrangements. He is an exact musician making precise choices, always aiming to serve the song beyond his own technical capability. Arpeggios animate intricate melodies through chord-based progressions and shapes, and he excels in poignant passing notes and melancholic shifts. His debut recordings favoured the use of a Rickenbacker 360 twelve-string and a 1954 Fender Telecaster guitar borrowed from producer and former Roxy Music bass player John Porter. The instruments were at first tuned at F sharp major, an open tone up from its standard setting, before Marr opted to use a capo to accommodate a natural bass sound and a vocalist's lower register. In their turn, the chiming treble waves lent an instantly identifiable sound to the group.

The songs came from the soul of north-west England. The writing captured the flavour of their environment and created a sound that redefined the possibilities of guitar and vocal parlante. These second-generation Mancunian–Irish songwriters inhabited an imaginative landscape of travelling fairgrounds and gritty film realism. The drive behind this richly organic creation was The Smiths.

Johnny Marr's right forearm is tattooed with the Motown motif, 45RPM, reflecting the music he heard while growing up, but his catholic tastes cover a far broader church of influence. He is an inventive composer who engineers ambitious works from limited machinery. 'Panic' mimicked the famous chords of Marc Bolan's 'Metal Guru'; open guitar tuning inspired the jumps and changes in 'You Just Haven't Earned It Yet, Baby'; for 'The Headmaster Ritual' Marr imagined his left hand playing in the style of Joni Mitchell ('as a punk rocker in MC5') and his right welding together elements of George Harrison and Dave Davies of The Kinks; while the American rhythms of Bo Diddley and Scotty Moore anchored the frantic rockabilly of 'Shakespeare's Sister' and 'Vicar In A Tutu'. The stories of the past were being revived, with contemporary interpretation. Marr wrote complete, pictorial musical statements. Beneath his infectious melodies he wove songs in cyclical, hypnotic grooves. 'What Difference Does It Make?' is driven by a beguiling multi-layered guitar pattern, and, like 'The Boy With The Thorn In His Side', it makes intriguing listening independently of Morrissey's added textures. The inventive combinations in 'The Queen Is Dead' marked another advance in Marr's stylistic oeuvre as he imagined MC5 again but this time rampaging through The Velvet Underground's 'I Can't Stand It'. Song scenarios were often inspired by acts of random association. Marr's role was to offer whole, fully realized pieces before his partner sewed words and vocal melody into their fabric. While Marr was consciously reacting against Seventies singer-songwriter introversion and rock band self-indulgences, his collaborator was stretching the boundaries of writing matter.

John Martin Maher was born on 31 October 1963, later adopting the spelling *Marr* for his name to avoid confusion with his Buzzcocks namesake. He grew up in Wythenshawe in an Irish Catholic household, yet his childhood featured the modern influences of fashion and the exploding beat music of the day. Marr's extended family all lived within two streets, and long hot summers were spent in his parents' native Kildare. It was there that Johnny would hear his uncle playing guitar and singing traditional songs, ballads, and—crucially—contemporary pop. Back home, he would practise devoutly, playing guitar on the bus to school with dreams of making it big. He was keen to expand his musical knowledge, and the range of influences absorbed in his youth can be heard in the music written as an adult. The musical minimalism of the British punk scene was bypassed in favour of New Yorkers like Patti Smith, Television, Talking Heads and Blondie. There was a mid-teen flirtation with soul, disco and funk, and evergreen favourites like Rory Gallagher, Keith Richards and Nils Lofgren were also regularly played. Marr needed a lyricist, and after falling in and out of a few local bands he found himself at the door of an undiscovered wordsmith.

Steven Patrick Morrissey was the son of a librarian. He read voraciously and cherished ambitions of becoming a music journalist. Before meeting Marr he was writing poetic lyrics, but without an instrumental accompaniment the ideas were nebulous. In May 1982, Marr stepped over the threshold of Morrissey's semi-detached Stretford council house, prophesying that they would be 'the next Leiber and Stoller'. Johnny had been watching a borrowed video of the Brill Building writers. Morrissey was four years older than Marr and impressed the visitor with a life-size cut-out of James Dean and an Elvis Presley poster on his bedroom wall. Reconvening days later at Marr's rented room in Bowden, the quick-witted lyricist stunned the cocky guitarist with his typed words for 'Suffer Little Children' and 'The Hand That Rocks The Cradle'. After their previous encounter Marr had struggled to find a suitable arrangement to Morrissey's 'Don't Blow Your Own Horn', but now rested the new pages on his lap and with the author's nodded approval mustered a flow of chords. Within five years the songwriting partnership would spawn over seventy songs, five albums and fourteen hit singles.

Morrissey wrote in the confinement and safety of his own private space, and his songbook is one of bewildering beauty and unconventional lyrical approach. Ideas stand their intellectual ground without being dumbed down. Morrissey's delivery was accessible yet enigmatic. His yelps and falsetto leaps distracted from an underdeveloped voice stretching just beyond an octave in range. Typically, the music led his lyricism. Marr would often write songs in sets of three. Having been sent a cassette of his partner's ideas, Morrissey would then marry his contribution to the music in isolation, often working over a couple of days. In the early years the four-piece would then expand the song in rehearsal, trimming extra verses and links, adding key changes and rhythmic pattern variations. Later, songs would be rehearsed and recorded by Marr, Mike Joyce (drums) and Andy Rourke (bass) without the knowledge of how Morrissey's melody or verse might shape them. The chemistry of individuals is the unrecognized component in songwriting. The rhythm section created a compelling sound, and what Morrissey added defined the group. He has a unique skill with words and the use of voice. As a child he was obsessed with vocal melody, learning from his beloved seven-inch singles. He stretched the possibility of song with his words and derived strength from honesty, expressing emotions commonly bound by social convention. He could be majestic and then suddenly mocking in devastating moves of the pen. Morrissey understood the spell that enchants the nation, from Shakespeare to *Coronation Street*, and could swiftly turn a dark mood with rapier wit and wisdom. He called upon the British ability to laugh in the face of adversity, and though he sang of unhappiness, loneliness, violence and death, it was never self-pitying. Metaphors were used sparingly, and even the personal *I* of the first two albums gave way to a third-person standpoint. Morrissey was drawn to the morose humour of George Formby: they shared a deadpan domestic tone. He was rarely gender-specific and drew on writers like Elizabeth Smart and his beloved Oscar Wilde. *I dreamt about you last night and I fell out of bed twice* was appropriated from the Shelagh Delaney play *A Taste Of Honey*. Morrissey devoured film and it indelibly marked his writing imagination. *A jumped-up pantry boy who doesn't know his place* was first spoken by Laurence Olivier to Michael Caine in the film version of *Sleuth*. The references built bridges between the writer and his audience. He ironically quipped in the deliberately misspelt 'Cemetry Gates': *If you must write prose and poems / The words you use should be your own*. Uncommon phrases and jarring words, alien to pop, issued from Morrissey's pen: 'Shoplifters Of The World Unite', 'Bigmouth Strikes Again', 'The Boy With The Thorn In His Side', 'Meat Is Murder'. British music, unlike the nation's literature, art, or theatrical heritage, is still in its infancy, but our cultural past is a celebration of variety: high- and lowbrow nestling cheek by jowl. Morrissey reflects this tradition. His lyricism combines humour with pathos, the mundane with the profound.

The Smiths were the alternative musical soundtrack of English Eighties pop. Their faith in the bass, drum and guitar combination was a reaction against the mainstream taste for synthesizers and surface sheen. The group remained fiercely autonomous. They found a home in late-night radio and had unprecedented independent success. On 8 December 2010, Kerry McCarthy, Labour MP for Bristol East, spoke in Westminster in a debate over university tuition fees. She addressed David Cameron, citing The Smiths as the archetypal student band: 'Both Morrissey and Johnny Marr have banned him from liking them. If he was to win tomorrow night's vote, what songs does he think students will be listening to: "Miserable Lie", "I Don't Owe You Anything", "Heaven Knows I'm Miserable Now"?' The prime minister countered with the suggestion of 'This Charming Man' and 'William, It Was Really Nothing'. Morrissey and Marr may have aspired to represent the marginalized, but their music clearly crossed social divides.

While both Morrissey and Marr found success beyond The Smiths and independent from one another, neither has captured the indefinable quality they had as a partnership. Together they had a unique alchemy, and they created a style and sound unheard in popular music. The darkness of Morrissey's thought was often lifted by Marr's light spirits; the dominant three chords of 'Girlfriend In A Coma', a song of grave introspection, is remedied by a deliberate juxtaposition of tragic and comic moods in the music. The more complex acoustic gaiety of 'Please, Please Let Me Get What I Want' is shaped by sparse vocals speaking of hope and desire. Many Smiths songs were completed in around two minutes, with backing vocals applied frugally if at all, and guitar solos kept to a minimum. 'How Soon Is Now?' was Marr's creative touchstone, featuring guitar suspense and overdubbed tremolo effects. His original demo was labelled 'Swamp' before Morrissey added words to the group's edited initial fifteen-minute jam: *I am human and I need to be loved.* President of Sire Records Seymour Stein proclaimed the recording the '"Stairway To Heaven" of the Eighties'.

In 1987, Marr left The Smiths, with a fourth studio album, *Strangeways, Here We Come*, recorded but as yet unreleased. He went on to make contributions to the music of Billy Bragg, Bryan Ferry, Talking Heads and Kirsty MacColl, in addition to spells as guitarist for The Pretenders and The The. With Bernard Sumner of Joy Division and later New Order he formed the band Electronic, which proved to be a refuge and an opportunity to explore music beyond the guitar. It was a highly successful venture. Their 1989 debut single 'Getting Away With It' sold in excess of 350,000 records in the USA. 'Get The Message' and the album on which the song appeared, *Electronic*, also had input from Chris Lowe and Neil Tennant. It was an impressive piece of work, bringing together four musical minds and amalgamating electronic pop with guitar dance to confound expectations. Marr's association with Pet Shop Boys continued when he added shining touches to *Behaviour* and later *Release*. He was allowing his creativity free rein. Beth Orton, Ian McCulloch, Liam Gallagher, Bert Jansch, Modest Mouse and The Cribs have all benefited from his talent. In 2013 he released his debut solo album, *The Messenger*, to considerable praise and a position in the top ten.

Within two miles of Morrissey's King's Road home and the site of his fateful meeting with Johnny Marr is L. S. Lowry's birthplace. The words the painter spoke about his matchstick people: 'Natural figures would have broken the spell of it, so I made my figures half unreal,' would have readily applied to the intentions of The Smiths. On my walk to meet Johnny in the heart of Manchester, the evidence of his legacy was everywhere: a photographic exhibition, posters advertising tribute bands, and shops offering Smiths records and T-shirts. Johnny was dressed in black, with painted nails and a turned-up coat collar. On seeing his vast catalogue of music laid out before him he politely asked if he could take some photographs on his phone, clearly appreciating the care and attention given to their display:

'In songwriting there is no right and wrong. If there was, it would be pretty boring: everybody would be copyrighting the right side. You've got to respect and like the mystery of it. It's very easy to get into the idea of formulas and systems. Almost everybody on *The X Factor* sings a ballad: a slow, quiet bit to set the song up, about fourteen seconds; a bridge with a little build and then into the chorus at a minute. I went through a period where every record I heard on the radio followed a certain kind of pattern, where things kicked in and devices were used at exactly the maximum commercial point. Aside from that idea being utterly crass, I'm not entirely sure that it even succeeds. I don't think humans react to music in such a Pavlovian manner. There are so many wildcard examples of commercial music over the years that betray that idea of a system and break all the rules.'

I started listening to records in a certain way that was almost analytical. My parents used to say that I didn't so much listen to records, I studied them. I got that directly from my mother. One of the strongest memories from my childhood was her and my dad's sister, who were both very young at the time, breathlessly rushing into the house having bought the Everly Brothers' record 'Walk Right Back' and watching them play it fifteen times in a row stood up at the record player. I observed the glee and the joy that they got from watching this thing go round and discussing it. From that day on I just joined in. Up until her late twenties my mum used to do her own charts every week. She'd be sat by the radio going, 'T. Rex have gone down: I was sure that was going to go up to number fourteen,' or, 'Bryan Ferry's dropped down eleven places.' They weren't musicians but here was a culture of records and obsessive observation about songs that rubbed off. I started to clock things like breakdowns and what fade-outs were about. Production, songwriting and devices to make records were all a part of the same thing and have stuck with me. There's a distinction between a record and a song. A song was a 45. That's a whole discussion in itself: is a song the words backed up by some music or is it part of a whole thing?

Often the line between songwriting and arrangement can be blurred. 'Greetings To The New Brunette' is heavily defined by your playing but credited solely to Billy Bragg, whereas 'Sexuality' is a co-write.

Billy is a good example. His words are very important and stand alone from the music in the way poetry can. The song is from the album *Talking To The Taxman About Poetry*, which is probably something he did. My part was as accompanist and musician; using the guitar as a way of adding colour. I guess I was following his melody, really. 'Sexuality', you're right to say, is completely different. That was written by the two of us when I heard him singing the word *sexuality* with that five-note tune and this reggae skank, for want of a better word, on the one chord of G. So I said, 'Sing that onto a cassette and let me finish it?' I tried to turn it into a record and along the way I didn't notice it was a song. I was just trying to come up with a tune. The end result was what I was thinking about. I had the production in mind when I was coming up with the chords, like the middle eight (*singing*) *I'm sure that everybody knows how much my body hates me*: I thought it needed a Patsy Cline bit. When I was producing him I was saying, 'Make him more Patsy Cline,' which just shows how completely abstract musicians can be. In the studio I had a complete backing track done. I was quite nervous. I thought, he's either going to hate it or hear a hit, which is what happened. What some people call arrangement: playing your instrument, the flutes come in there, or that's the way the bass part goes; that's instrumentation. The structure of chorus, bridge, verse, breakdown, whatever it may be: those building blocks in a linear way, is the arrangement. I'm very lucky because I get to work with all different types of approaches. Writing a song as a member of Modest Mouse, stood in a room with five other guys all with different agendas trying to pull something out of the sky is different from the way I would sit down with Kirsty MacColl or Neil Finn.

Can you sense inspiration arriving?

When you're already writing, sitting down plonking around or absent-mindedly doing something, it sneaks up on you and kind of starts to fall under your fingers. The other side of it is that it kind of can happen and you scurry around going, 'I've got this really strong feeling, I need a guitar.' I get into these slightly introspective moods where it's time to try and turn it into some music.

A physical sensation that needs to be channelled?

Turned into something, yeah . . . I don't put myself under any pressure if it's going to be any good or pay the rent or please a critic or do anything other than be channelled into something creative. There's another kind of mode whereby if you feel like over a period of a few days that you've got some idea and you want to write a song, you kind of have to get really quiet and need to set up a scenario where you make yourself almost bored. Particularly in this day and age where there are so many distractions. I used to write a lot of songs when I was younger just for something to do. Passive entertainment, whether it's sitting watching television or listening to crappy radio or whatever, just didn't have enough gravity. I had a real serious drive to make music, a massive passion and joy for it, but there was also this feeling of dissatisfaction just in the way I felt: some kind of hole that needed to be filled up, like a nag. Not necessarily a negative thing. It could be a beautiful kind of nagging. At twelve or thirteen I'd be doing something and not be satisfied with it, so I'd have to go and sit in the corner of my bedroom and play guitar for a few hours and out of that would come a song.

Can you force inspiration or do you need given circumstances?

Some of the best eureka moments have happened while I've been in the trenches with my sleeves rolled up trying to make another one work. For example, 'Forbidden City' by Electronic poured out whilst I was working on some other kind of clever, more abstract-y electronic thing that I'd been doing for a few days with machines. I was really trying to structure and craft something that I was determined to wrestle into submission. In a gap in the proceedings when something had crashed I heard this entire tune. I said to Owen Morris, the engineer, 'Put a DAT in right now, hit record,' stuck a microphone in the room and played the whole melody from start to finish. It kind of dropped on me like an existing song. One of my favourite ever Electronic songs, 'Get The Message', happened in a similar way. I was sat messing around working on a different song. I'd built this makeshift studio set-up in a bedroom. It was a beautiful summer afternoon and I was working on my own. The breeze was coming through this half-open window and this thing just snuck up on me. I'd stopped to have a cigarette or something and I heard this bass line and groove and played what I heard. I put a loop underneath it and literally twenty minutes later it was all done.

How would you begin to explain that?

This idea that you're in the supermarket and a number-one song comes and you write it on the back of a soap box sounds really good when it comes from the Brill Building; at a traffic light and they heard this amazing Shirelles song and wrote it on the back of a cig packet. That's never happened to me. Where does inspiration come from? You have to be in there doing the donkey work for the real gems to drop in on you. It doesn't happen just walking down the street. If you walk around expecting some divine thing to happen and go in the studio and switch the gear on, you're going to be waiting around for a long time. There is a lot of craft to songwriting and that's a totally valid and fun thing too. You have to write some stuff that doesn't work or is only OK. In terms of a spiritual aspect to it, that's where I thought the word inspiration comes from: in spirit. I assumed it was some sort of connection that bypassed the critical faculties, bypassed your analytical mind, came from something beyond that was pure. Like when a song comes to you in a dream: I always thought it would be absolutely genius because it was untainted and unfettered. The ones I've remembered I don't think have ever been any good. If I look at a painting I like it, it's saying something to me on an emotional level and entirely bypasses the intellectual level. I'm feeling that same emotional aspect that was put in it by the artist. That's one of the reasons why some of The Smiths' music is so popular, because there was so much emotion in the making and writing of it. If you play a regular member of the public who's not interested in the machinations of record making or songwriting two songs and one is a 'good, well-structured clever song with all the dynamics' but is recorded in a passionless way, and you play something that's got a lot of emotion and passion—it's got to have some melody—they'll go for the one with passion in it. 'The Boy Done Good' (*Billy Bragg*), I heard the tune a few times away from the guitar (*hums riff*): is that not like every late-Sixties and early-Seventies record you ever played rolled into one? If it isn't, it's a really good approximation of what you would have liked on the radio when you were a kid. I put the guitar into a tuning and said, 'Hang on a minute, I've got a tune here.' It was puzzling because I was just stood there without an instrument. 'Vivid' by Electronic was the same: I heard the whole song in my mind before I put it down: the harmonica part, the vocal melody. It's worth developing an idea conceptually before you pick up an instrument because then you know what you're going for. If you know it's good in your mind then you know it's going to work on guitar.

When I listen to your music it's notable for its lack of aggression. It's very positive and at the risk of sounding corny there's a lot of love, suggesting a positive, highly emotional writer.

That's very interesting to me. I like that idea. Maybe because of the working-class environment I grew up in: you have to get the other side of you out that you weren't really allowed to display, not in my family but growing up on a council estate. I was very, very quiet and not insensitive. I'm glad I've still got that. That's what being artistic's all about. There was a lot of love in The Smiths for the situation; being in the band, having a guitar in my hand and being who I am, having a partner, having my mates but being alive. When we were writing and recording those songs we were living that. I was walking three foot high off the ground. The idea of the band being miserable or me hating it or wanting to leave all the time is completely wrong. Where better to hear the evidence of that than in the music? It was super, super joyful and super up. I like that feeling when you're hearing music, that the tune tells you it's sad but the feeling tells you it's completely opposite. That's what Kirsty (*MacColl*) always asked me to do: 'Write one of those songs that you don't know whether it's happy or sad, at the same time.' You don't know how to feel about it; you just want to hear it over and over again.

You hear that in Kirsty's 'Children Of The Revolution'.

That's the kind of thing I'm talking about when I look for that top line. That's really sad, but how can I make it really, really sad but in a way that makes you want to hear it several times. I don't know what attracts me to that because it does feel up. A musicologist would tell you that it's very melancholic. The biggest example of that would be 'Last Night I Dreamt That Somebody Loved Me' off the last Smiths album, which is much more dramatic. It's swimming in this gorgeous melancholy. There's a big difference between melancholia and depression. Melancholia is a valid human emotion that can fill you up and be positive, where depression is just a void.

Is there validity in using drink or drugs to tap into inspiration?

Absolutely, but most humans are just gluttons and want to keep going back to the well. I include myself in that. You have to really know what you're doing. I don't mean that in a dramatic way, because if you're not careful you can just end up playing the chord of E for twenty-five minutes and thinking it's good. It's great for grooves and getting immersed on an emotional and rhythmical plain, whether it's Massive Attack or Miles Davis. You want to stay mobile. You want to avoid emotional peaks too much because it starts to feel hysterical, but is that cool or is it boring? There's a place for it, but I don't want too much drama every few seconds in my music. What I'm best at is some chords and some tunes and with some impact. Trying to tune into the mood of the room happened a couple of times. You can't do that if you're hungover or fucked up. You have to be sure of your instincts and feeling pretty clear and you're on it. 'People Is Places Is People' (*Modest Mouse*) was written when we were packing the gear up. We'd written eighteen songs for the album and were about to start recording in a different city the next day. All the guys were standing around talking and smoking and I just got this feeling in the room, and almost as an experiment said, 'I think everybody's feeling something like this.' I just went (*hums riff*) and we got on it and got really excited. That was a time when six people wrote together, a song in fifteen minutes. 'Whale Song', that's largely instrumental. I did it in the same way. We were meant to be working on something else more upbeat and I got a hunch about the feeling of suspension in the room and started playing this riff and chord progression that was very atmospheric. This might all be bullshit, they might just be good catchy riffs, but if it works it works. I love that idea of tuning into the atmosphere of the room.

How do you remember your ideas?

I always put stuff down on cassette. One of the problems these days; it's so easy to record every little idea that you can tend to record ideas before they're that great. But more importantly it's very easy to dismiss these ideas, because they're easy to lose. Easy come, easy go. It's so easy to put fifteen different riffs down . . . some great riff can just be one of fifteen riffs. If I'm playing the guitar, if something holds my attention for a few minutes I'll put that down on my phone or on a little digital recorder. The Cribs record 'We Share The Same Skies', I played that riff just before I went to bed and thought, this might have something about it. Because Gary Jarman lives in Portland too, I was able to go round to a band mate's the next day and say, 'What do you think of this?' and get that immediate reaction. When you're in a band you set the wheels in motion working with other people and then it becomes something that the two of us are playing. Gary got behind the drums and started jamming it, then it becomes nearly a Cribs song and it doesn't just stay on your iPhone. You have to be aware of all these things that are going on. It's important to fix any weaknesses or leaks in the boat. Be aware of the effect technology, your lifestyle and your environment are having on your writing. Don't be blindly walking around and turn round two years later and say, 'I should have done things differently.' Maybe that comes with getting older and knowing yourself. In my teens, because I got so bored of people being stoned and playing that one chord, I just thought, 'Tomorrow when I go up to rehearsal somebody better have some chord changes.' I got used to writing entire backing tracks on my own, whether they had drums on or not. Just a start and an end point and a middle bit, as music. I always liked the idea of collaboration and other people pulling things around. I didn't necessarily want to write all the music myself, it just turned out that way. Then when The Smiths formed and I got a partner who just wanted to write the words and the vocals entirely—that was perfect. So I started writing instrumental songs.

I understand the inspiration for 'Hand In Glove' necessitated calling at Morrissey's house without an invitation.

I was round at my parents' house and I'd moved my cassette player to where I was living. There was this little guitar that Andy (*Rourke*) had given me and I'd given to my little brother. I played the riff and immediately knew it was a song. Angie had her parents' little Volkswagen outside; she'd just passed her test, and we drove to Morrissey's and by the time she'd driven there she'd said about five times, 'Make it sound like Iggy.' So I went from these clipped kind of funky chords to this big open thing. She was absolutely right. I've still got this three-track cassette recorder which is a kind of an anomaly; it's two-track and you can bounce it down, and we wrote all the early Smiths stuff on that.

Do melodies lead you or are they woven out of chord shapes?

Chords are so rich and say so much and the contrast between a few different chord changes is that a lot of things just jump out. It's like the stained-glass window analogy: I see my approach to the guitar and the record as this big circular thing with different colours in it. Playing the guitar, whether it's six- or twelve-string, I was always looking to do my stuff in that very big background in preparation for somebody coming along and singing over the top. For the longest time I didn't need to find my way into vocal melodies because of people like Kirsty, Matt Johnson, Bernard Sumner and Morrissey, of course.

Having found some chords that you like, at what point do you leave behind the key or the next natural progression?

Straight away. If I play three chords that I like I can hear something in the mid-range, something in the top, and some melodic movement. I don't hear the chords as a block. The chords almost become choral, like the way a choir works. I hear the voicing in the chords. You hear ascension, falling lines and rising lines. Particularly big twelve-strings in drones and tunings give you this amazing potential for different voicing and tunes.

Glenn Tilbrook spoke of tricking himself by using different tunings to avoid familiarity.

That's what I meant by mystery. There's a massive temptation to want to know how things work, to get where you want to be. Many, many people know plenty of devices; certain chord progressions will create certain set-ups and moods. But mystery and tricking yourself not only makes it fun but brings a quality to it. There's a magic in that and unexpected things happen and it's followed emotionally then rather than intellectually, and that's very important. That's one of the reasons I like putting the guitar in tunings. I'm using my ears and feelings rather than my brain. I know what will happen when I put a D minor next to an F: I'll go to an A minor and I know exactly what will happen if I hit a B flat. But if I'm in a tuning that I've made up I might play that chord change and think that's it's never been invented before, whereas if I explain it, it sounds a little unappealing. It bypasses that circuitry. I would never have played the chords to 'Cemetry Gates' in regular concert tuning because it's essentially G, C and D. I very rarely wrote in G—although 'This Charming Man' was in G—because I'd decided it was a key that never really resonated with how I felt, but the tuning I didn't know, so I didn't have that judgement. My partner said, 'What's that, that's great?' and I said, 'Really?' It was also intentional because the songs up to then were in a lot of minor keys: A minor, E minor, C sharp minor, which I use a lot because the guitar reacts very well to it. The Cribs' 'We Share The Same Skies' sounded really good to my ears in that key, and 'Bigmouth Strikes Again' too. On the rare occasions I've shown people some tricks on the guitar I put a capo on the fourth fret and show them A minor. There's something about the architecture of the guitar and the scale length that makes it react very well to that position.

'Bigmouth Strikes Again' has just one opening verse, which is unusual for a pop song. Was the shape of the song your vision or was it determined by Morrissey's vocal decisions?

Both of us had absolute unshakeable faith that what the other person was doing was right, whether we heard it or not. Alongside that, unshakeable faith in what we were doing individually. In that example, it didn't need to go anywhere else. Maybe that's an example of the drugs working. It would have got too conceptual, too conceived, too thought out and just too fucking crafted had I put some clever bit in there. It'd have been bottling it. Sometimes it's cooler just to let it go, let it fly. 'Rusholme Ruffians' is an extreme example of that. It's just the same cycle. The same point being made round and round and round ad infinitum. It would have been the easiest thing in the world to add a device to break it up. I wanted it to be insistent. It felt like being insistent. It gets really emotional in places and you want more of that. You want the writer to stick to his guns.

Many of your songs are cyclical, finding a motif and building out from it as opposed to more linear progressions through traditional structures.

That's for sure: I don't like classicism too much, believe it or not. There's a danger of sitting back and saying, I'd like to be able to do things as well as they were done in the Fifties or the Sixties, and obviously I've taken a lot of inspiration from those periods: the skill of the Brill Building writers, Burt Bacharach, and we all love The Beatles, blah, blah, blah, but I like that I came out of Manchester in 1982 and like to keep a little bit of that about me. I was in a Rough Trade band. It was the start of indie music: Josef K; Cabaret Voltaire; The Birthday Party: all of these things arrived when I was about to escape. I don't want to work off any classic template.

Do keys have different characters and personalities? 'What Difference Does It Make?' was recorded in three different keys.

That's right; Bernard Sumner and I used to get into this a lot. We were writing essentially in the studio and not in rehearsal rooms or soundchecks and aware of the pitfalls there might be: do we need to jack the tempo up? Keywise, where are we trying to pitch this? The golden rule is, it's got to make the singer sound as best as possible. 'Forbidden City', the original key of D was the right key for it but we did try a bunch of different ones. They hit you in different places, they mean different things. We are talking about soundwaves and vibrations, after all. The key of D will resonate in a different place than the key of G. Sorry to be cosmic, but that's what it is. The key of D major is very strident, confident and robust. However, because it was one of the first chords that me and my mates learnt and everyone could play it, I decided at the age of twelve that it wasn't for me. You have all these stupid ideas that you need to shake off. 'Get The Message' is in D. I very rarely wrote a Smiths song in D.

Can you write as if you are another artist or by imagining musicians in other scenarios?

I'd love to be able to do that. I tried a few times at the piano to write a Burt Bacharach song. When it got to the fourth chord I just had to put one of my stupid B flat major sevenths in there: 'I've made it sound like me again.' I told Neil Tennant this and he said that was a good thing, it meant I had soul. I like that idea. He meant if you're somebody that is able to resist putting yourself into it, then it's a somewhat cold exercise. I like the idea of rock music that hits you in the heart with poignancy. A really rollicking rock tune with a romantic quality to it is the mother lode. Conveniently, I've got that in 'We Share The Same Skies'.

So many of your songs are barely over two minutes. What is a classic single trying to achieve?

It's trying to be fully engaging: whether it pulls you with dramatic sadness or harmonic and melodic quality or just musical intrigue, something that hooks you. Roxy Music singles used to do it for me, or some Sparks records: some unpredictability. For some people it's the emotion in the lyrics; a story or a narrative. When I write songs I'm just trying to write a record that I would like, would like to play.

Not writing words, does your music have stories or images?

Not so much images; certainly story. Things unfold; things will peak and then go round a corner and come back to something. It might sound grand but I think it happens instinctively, which goes back to loving pop singles when I was younger. I like to get things wrapped up in three and a half or four minutes generally because that was my passion, 45s. That's what I do best.

The marriage between your music and Morrissey's words is so fluent it's incredible they were not conceived together.

That is proof that despite the differences in our personalities there were emotions underneath that we both share and understand about each other, whether we like it or not. Luckily we found each other and were able to put it to music. We helped each other realize our dreams and escape our situations and have success. But we also found someone that we could both match and play emotional snap with. We were both romantics.

Did your music change when you became familiar with Morrissey's personality?

Not the way I composed or the technique, we both expressed things ... there's a lot of our relationship in those songs. That's not to say the words are about our relationship, but the feeling in the recordings and some of the songs are a product of our relationship because we were so wrapped up in each other.

Did you ever write together?

Once, which was 'Half A Person': that was incredibly uncanny. The morning we were supposed to do the B-side he said, 'What are we going to do?' I picked up the guitar and said, 'Maybe it should go like this?' and he hummed the melody whilst I found some chords. It was done in like four minutes. We did it that one time because the tape was rolling in the next room and we hadn't come up with something. It was just a necessity. We'd decided, very unexpectedly for us, impulsively, to do an A-side which was going to be 'You Just Haven't Earned It Yet, Baby'. We wrote and recorded that in twenty-four hours. That tied us up. I put it down and the band learnt it, he took the cassette away and the next morning all the words were written. We were pretty prolific.

How important was his reaction to your music; how did you present your ideas?

I'd bring a cassette round to his house, which was the main thing, or, because we were always working, either in the studio or at gigs. I knew he'd be waiting for me . . . my riffs would be around. When I put 'Bigmouth' on a cassette for him it was that riff I'd been playing at the soundcheck for the past two weeks. 'Last Night I Dreamt', for example, was something I played in the hotel room in Scotland one morning. When I got on the tour bus I had an acoustic guitar there and he and I sat at the back. I was playing this riff round and round for about twelve minutes, just saying, 'Check this out, check this out, check this out.' So when we came to record it on the last album it was something he was familiar with. Sometimes I'd stick it through the letter box and split, with a little card saying, 'Check this out, check this out, check this out!' He'd digest it and call me back a couple of hours later and say, 'It's a single,' or 'It's a triumph,' or 'It's so great I even switched *Coronation Street* off.'

Did you ever have to rewrite?

No, never, everything worked. We were coming from the same place. He did his bit in The Smiths and I did my bit. That's what it was. There was an unquestionable thing about it. Even though we got a certain kind of success quickly, we'd been in the trenches together when there was just me and him and the wrong bass player, or EMI turning us down, or people making quips. The two of us were very hardworking; all four of the band were, obviously. Andy Rourke and I had a really strong history, because we were friends from school. Me and Morrissey knocked on a lot of doors and tried out musicians and did a lot of graft getting the band together. We had a bond, a lot of people forget that; maybe he and I forget that sometimes. One of the great things about that partnership was that I had no idea what he was going to do. Again to use a painting analogy, I'd done this intricate background that could be complete in itself, but then someone came along and did this utterly brilliant thing in the foreground that was very often coming from a different . . . was unexpected.

Did he ever share ideas with you before going into the studio?

No, no, we never needed to do that. He had no device to play. He would never record his vocals on a cassette. He'd just have them in his mind. We were too impatient. We'd just write a song and go in the studio days later, which is such a great thing. However, in the early days, because we were a poor lowly street band, we'd hear it in rehearsal. We'd almost always write in groups of three: the A-side, the B-side and the extra track specifically for a single. We decided when we first got together, before we even knew anyone would go for it, that we'd do that, and that came true, because we admired some T. Rex singles that had two songs on the other side.

Could you sit down and write a single?

I did do that a few times: 'Panic', 'Girlfriend In A Coma', probably 'Heaven Knows I'm Miserable Now', 'Walking Down Madison', 'Dashboard' with

Modest Mouse. With 'This Charming Man' I didn't know it was going to be a single, but I wrote it with that intention just because it was too early in our career to say what was going to be a single. I wrote it as an answer to Aztec Camera being on the radio. I'm not a competitive person at all, but Roddy (*Frame*) was the same age as me and on the same label. He was on the radio and we weren't. I got out of bed and thought, we're not going to get anywhere playing these A minor chords: better write something in G. We also needed something for the John Peel show. When we did the session everybody said, 'That's the single.'

It's quite extraordinary, just tapping into creativity, and makes sense of how The Smiths produced so many classic singles in a short amount of time.

It's nice of you to say so, but it's great when it works. I was very, very lucky. I was in a band that was on fire. With 'Walking Down Madison' Kirsty was saying, 'Write me a single,' and she knew that the two of us wanted to break away from what we'd done on *Kite*, which was quite Smiths-y guitar pop. We wanted to do something a little more of the time, more dance based. Obviously if I was able to do it more I would have done. It hasn't really occurred to me that's what I'd been able to do. Like other songwriters, I'm trying to write a really big hit and they're fairly elusive.

Why do you think your prolific success predominantly came early in your career?

It's to do with circumstances and what band you find yourself in. I really was happy not to be in a four-piece guitar group for the longest time. Until The Cribs came along I thought that was one of the least attractive things to do. I just built my own studio and fucked around a lot, which was something that I always wanted to do. Something I feel fortunate to have done. I don't always want to be in a rock group, as simple as that, but I'm always playing guitar and recording backing tracks. For a long time I did that at that same time as bringing up two kids; it's what I wanted to do. Electronic, Bernard and I really took our time making three albums. That took the middle part of my career, so far. We took too long, but that was a really fantastic period.

Did you write differently with Bernard?

Bernard and I wrote in three different ways. One was that I'd write a backing track and he would sing on it and then contribute to the music: some top lines and sounds, which he did on 'Get The Message', 'Idiot Country' and 'Feel Every Beat'. Other times he would come up with most of the music which was more electronic and I'd play guitar or a lot of keyboards, which is something I'd been dying to do for years. Who better to do it with than my favourite electronic musician? The third way we would write would be head to head, two guitars thrashing it out. We did that a lot: 'Like No Other', 'Late At Night', 'Prodigal Son' and 'Flicker'. 'For You', we sat down to write a single.

Would one of you come with an idea to kick-start the process?

Yeah, like I've got a verse: 'What d'you think of this chord change? Let's go there,' which is how The Cribs write, but with four of us in the room. Sometimes we'd bring it down and kick a song around for half an hour or an hour, then you get to a certain place and say, 'OK, what does this mean?' The Cribs' writing process was how I thought it'd pan out when I was a teenager: get in a room in front of your band with three other guys that you think are great and songs appear.

Do you hear vocal melodies?

Yeah, but I've always been so fortunate to work with singers like Isaac Brock and obviously Morrissey who are so distinctive and strong in their own direction. I just love them doing it. With Bernard, he'd encourage me to come up with melodies. I learnt a lot from him. 'Vivid' is my vocal melody; he bent a couple of places to make it sound (a) more like him and (b) better. Similarly with 'Forbidden City': that was really an achievement for me, having put out a lot of records before that, even though I was still only very young. It got in the top twenty. It was like a new box to tick.

Did you write with Lee Mavers?

Lee and I jammed together for three days. It was fascinating and frustrating. Frustrating for the same reason that anybody who's worked with Lee will tell you: he still wanted to make that first La's album, maybe he still wants to make it now. He's an amazing musician and a very likeable person; I respect him, of course. Me and him playing 'Pinball Wizard' is pretty interesting.

When Morrissey offered lyrics or suggestions of a theme, did it creatively change your approach to writing the music?

Yeah, it did. 'Rusholme Ruffians' is a good example of the oddity that we had in common. Only a very brief discussion was needed where Morrissey said we should do something about the fair. I immediately took to the idea of a mid-Sixties Elvis Presley song, which I'm assuming made sense to him when I said it because when we were both children and went to the fair in the mid-Sixties, you'd be hearing an Elvis Presley song. Someone else might not have got that. When you're inspired you don't question your instincts.

Can you recall the origins of 'How Soon is Now?'?

'How Soon is Now?' is one of the biggest concepts I had away from the guitar; something swampy and fairly modular, for once not having chord changes

coming at you straight away. I'd made a mental note that I liked Gun Club's
version of 'Run Through The Jungle', which is ironic because I don't like
Creedence Clearwater Revival at all. The idea of The Smiths doing a song like
that was such a challenge, but if you're trying to be innovative that's what happens: something that makes sense to you doesn't make sense to somebody else.
In the context of the other songs it was like playing on what could be described
as a groove because I'd already written two other songs that weekend. I was
thinking that I could cut loose a little bit. I didn't know what key it would be in
but I knew that it would go up four tones and what the progression should be:
I, III, IV, because we'd not done that yet.

Were the tremolo and slide figure part of the original demo?

It wasn't actually a slide, but the two-note figure was in there, done in a different way. The tremolo wasn't. When we came to do it we made it more intense by using the slide and putting some other notes in with a harmonizer
and putting the guitar into a tuning. It's essentially the two parts that you hear,
one a rhythm and the other one with the two-note part dropped on top of it in
a much more primitive form. I'd written the music to 'William It Was Really
Nothing' on a mattress in the back of a van travelling down to London, came
up with the riff and put it all together. I had a Portastudio in my flat in Earls
Court and put it down with a couple of overdubs. Like I said, we wrote in
threes, therefore the third track I wanted it to contrast with 'William' which
was short and fast. For a few weeks before I had this idea of writing something
quite romantic that reminded me of my childhood in Manchester that needed
somewhat of an Irish flavour in there as well, which became 'Please, Please Let
Me Get What I Want'. I was in London, eighteen, nineteen; I'd moved away
from my city and was feeling quite romantic about it. I had this concept of a
romantic, wistful, yearning, looking-back-into-music song. So I started to play
in 3/4 or 6/8 waltz time. I just followed that for a morning and put it down, got
swept up in that wistful, sentimental atmosphere. It reminded me of a Del
Shannon melody that the folks used to have on a record. I just held the atmosphere of that track: not exactly a copy, just a vibe of that tune.

**There's a certain similarity between 'How Soon Is Now?' and 'Shoplifters Of
The World Unite'. Were you inspired by yourself?**

No. I always hated that idea, recycling. Some people are good at it; I feel it's
cheating, lazy. Andy once said I was trying to recreate that but he was actually
wrong, it just happened to be the mode I was in and the same key. It was purely
coincidental; that's a thing I like. It's very important in songwriting for a song
to take on a life of its own, but sometimes it goes somewhere it shouldn't. That's
why I say it's great if you can really hold a concept in your mind and map it out
before you start putting too many bits in there.

Do you place value on ideas that come quickly?

The best stuff comes really quickly, but I always liked the backing track to 'Feel Every Beat' by Electronic, and that was crafted. It's a track as opposed to a song. 'Headmaster Ritual' was a mixture of craft and inspiration. Without craft it wouldn't have happened. I had these different, unfinished bits and had to apply myself to make it work: 'How am I going to fit that bit onto this bit? I'll have to change the key of that and I'll have to change the end chord of that, but do these bits work together? It'd be good if they could. Well, how am I going to make that happen, because that's almost like a different song?' That craft is not dry; it's fun and almost inspiring in itself. It's one of my favourite things I've ever done.

'You Just Haven't Earned It Yet, Baby' seems more obvious as a cut-and-paste song.

I did get stuck on a bit on that. It's all right, it turned out OK.

What inspired the introduction for 'Last Night I Dreamt That Somebody Loved Me'?

Me or Morrissey had the idea to put a dramatic intro on the front. They were chords I'd been kicking around on the piano, probably at a much faster tempo, but they worked really slowed down. I already knew from that main riff that I'd played on the bus that that was the song. It didn't need a middle eight or another bit. It was one of those rare things that come along where the song can just be the one thing over and over again and what happens to it is dependent on the vocal melody and the dynamics of the singer. You don't need to do a left turn or U-turn or any turn: you just go down the road. I really like songs when they do that; it's quite unusual. The singer has to be really inspired and to be able to move somewhere melodically.

What does writing on an acoustic guitar change?

It becomes a lot more chordal on the acoustic. You tend to strum a little more unless you're doing a lot of picking. Because I like a fairly clean sound I'm able to strum big chords on electric, but it is different. With electric it's good to have a drummer around. On acoustic you become too laid-back, a little troubadour-y. Ironically I'm an aggressive acoustic player and a more gentle electric player. I got it the wrong way round.

What are your feelings towards 'There Is A Light', which was written on acoustic guitar?

To be honest it was just a normal song when I was writing the music for it, just something I liked. I wasn't running around knocking over things. What

Morrissey brought to it really made it magic and in turn inspired me to put the string parts on it and the little flutes; it really upped my feeling for it. He really took that to another place. The music in it is very beautiful, but initially I thought it'd be a track four, side two, which it might be, I can't remember. (*Looks at* Queen Is Dead *sleeve.*) Oh, it is, I was right!

The clean guitar sound on early Smiths records is often attributed to the influence of African Highlife.

It's purely the time I came out of. At the end of punk rock, what's become known as post-punk started. Distorted guitars were out, they'd been done. I didn't particularly play a Rickenbacker because I loved the Sixties so much. You either went with a choppy, clean, funky sound and style like David Byrne had done or Edwyn Collins was exploring in Orange Juice to get away from the rockism, which I did a little, or if you were trying to write a lot of chord-y songs, as I was, you needed a clean sound. In that movement that could be a position of adversity, and lack of choice is actually a good thing. It was a great time: people looked and dressed in a very sparse way. A lot of punk rock was still about adorning: whether it was about safety pins or studded belts, the Pistols or The Ramones, leather jackets, stuff hanging off you. After that it was a much more austere style, and that applied to the music and thinking too. That informed a lot of my guitar style. Bending notes, solos, long songs and even a lot of reverbs were out. Artistic style in fanzines, clothes and music; you really tried not to be rockist. I wanted to play to my strengths, but you want to be of the times and be your mates' favourite band. It's very, very important your mates like what you do. The trick is to have some very discerning mates.

The Smiths created a style and sound unique in British music but it was often infused with American railroad rhythms.

I was trying to draw on American music in a way that had been forgotten. I'm into writing with rhythms that are very infectious but don't have any traces of James Brown in because I wanted my band to be different. A very deliberate and keen interest in finding rhythms that other bands around me were not using, that I liked hearing my parents play: Eddie Cochran; Elvis Presley; and because I was such a Stones nut, Bo Diddley. I always was obsessed by that beat. 'Nowhere Fast' has that rockabilly rhythm and 'Shakespeare's Sister' was written entirely from that rhythm; some idea of a fucked-up Johnny Cash on drugs. It sounds half like that.

Also the opening to 'Girlfriend In A Coma'.

That was me with the headphones on warming up. I just liked the feel of it. 'Girlfriend In A Coma' was ten per cent of me trying to be Trojan.

The harmony between Morrissey's vocal melody and your guitar beautifully intertwine.

Musically, I wrote that song specifically for my friend and writing partner. Obviously I was trying to write a single, but I just wanted him to like it. He and I had this love of 'Young, Gifted And Black' by Bob and Marcia. It was just a kind of wink to my friend. I did that a few times.

Your contribution to Talking Heads' '(Nothing But) Flowers' lent a defining character to an infectious song.

Interestingly enough, when I first heard that it wasn't really a song, it was a track: Tina's (*Weymouth*) bass line and Chris's (*Frantz*) drum groove and some percussion, but no clearly defined chords. I listened to the track and for the first time I started to panic somewhat because I couldn't imagine coming up with something. I usually have a few ideas immediately. I asked for them to play it again, and again, and again. I thought to myself, 'Oh shit, I'm not hearing anything.' I said to (*the producer*) Steve Lillywhite, 'I need to go for a walk.' I went round Paris for half an hour and was thinking, 'This is it now, Johnny boy: you've got nothing, where are you now?' It occurred to me the reason I was having a problem getting into the track: there was no harmony, no chords. So I quite meekly asked for permission to put some chord changes in there. There might have been something going on the verse but not on the main part where I played. I put some big ringing chords on which I later took off. Then I put the twelve-string on and came up with that riff that went over the top of it. I always regarded my contribution as a guest player. That was what I was invited to do. 'Cool Water' was even more of a modal drown. David (*Byrne*) and me got into building the song in an abstract way with the twelve-string electric in a tuning. I was just strumming along trying to find melodies and sections within that. I never felt like that was songwriting.

'Back To The Old House' exemplifies your one-man symphony style.

Thank you. That happened by accident, it's totally natural. I was just trying to get something right: I can hear that I'm reaching for something that perhaps I didn't get. All I can say is, honestly, it's not hard. The emotional quality in it I can now see is an individual thing and is personal. Some guitar players react to some of the moves and think it's quite accomplished, but mostly people are reacting to something pretty or beautiful. I look at it in a bigger picture: how lucky I am to communicate something to somebody else without using words.

Like the emotion in the opening of Billy Bragg's 'Walk Away Renee (Version)'. The second chord resonates with an emotional pull.

That's what I hear in music and that's why I will never tire of it. Occasionally I'm asked about my seemingly endless enthusiasm for music and records, but it's about a quality that it puts into the world and my world. It's way beyond culture. If it was enthusiasm for pop culture I really ought to have grown out of that by now, but it's about evoking emotions that we feel as humans and surely that's never going to go away. I want to be a person with a life, interacting in the world. I'm a songwriter and guitarist first and foremost and I always have been; that's my identity that defines my self-worth, not success. These things sound grand and it's easy to theorize, but real life gets in the way.

NEIL TENNANT
AND CHRIS LOWE

> She's made you some kind of laughing stock because you dance to disco and you don't like rock.

Pet Shop Boys are a mass of contradictions. Neil Tennant and Chris Lowe are the first songwriters in this work who have theatrically challenged the conventions of rock and pop presentation. Their sound, whilst firmly rooted in classic British songwriting, has essentially relied upon electronic instruments, yet they have absorbed a range of influences which are reflected in their music. They are an incongruous mixture of contemporary mainstream and creative originality.

Lowe developed as a musician without any thought of songwriting. Tennant declared as a teenager that he would become a pop star, but struggled with the image of the Seventies singer-songwriter, and then punk. In 1983, now writing for the teen magazine *Smash Hits*, he managed to turn to his advantage a trip to New York, ostensibly to interview The Police. Both Tennant and Lowe were great admirers of American producer Bobby Orlando. Tennant engineered a lunch date with him and handed over a demo cassette containing the future hits 'It's A Sin, It's Not A Crime' and 'Opportunities'. Orlando was impressed. With Chris still a student at Liverpool University, the producer recorded the boys' first single, 'West End Girls', at a time when the popularity of synthesizer duos was supposedly in decline.

To the uninitiated, Pet Shop Boys' hard electronic sound and dry vocal delivery in the early part of their career seemed to emanate coldness, a music without warmth. Fans, however, knew that it veiled charged emotion and a deep resonance of song. Tennant and Lowe's backgrounds subtly inform their music. Neil is open about his knowledge of Stephen Sondheim's songbook and his love of Richard Rodgers, and likes to use lots of chords. Chris, by contrast, veers towards simplicity. 'Paninaro', a song about an Italian youth cult, employs just three chords, reduced to only one in the middle section. Ironically, on this, his first vocal outing, Chris is sampled from a radio show declaring, *I don't like rock music . . . but what I do like I love passionately.* Neil is a more suggestive writer, who rarely reveals his inner thoughts. His ambiguity leads you to ideas, but is ultimately tantalizing: as he wrote in 'Why Don't We Live Together?' *The woman in me shouts out / The man in me just smiles.* This has widened Pet Shop Boys' appeal without limiting them to a gay audience. Neil came out in 1994. Musically, the duo is more overtly camp. 'New York City Boy' is clearly indebted to the Village People hit 'Go West', recorded by the Pet Shop Boys in 1993. The success of the cover version was significant in raising the duo's political profile. Not only had the Berlin Wall recently been dismantled and the Iron Curtain parted, but AIDS was sweeping through the gay community. These themes were reflected in the cover version. Meanwhile, 'Go West' achieved unexpected popularity amongst football fans when the Highbury faithful adopted the melody to chant *1–0 to the Arsenal.*

Christopher Sean Lowe was born on 4 October 1959 in Lancashire. He grew up within earshot of the screams and shouts from Blackpool Pleasure Beach. The seasonal thrill of the rides coloured his outlook from the moment he could walk. While dance-pop will always be the centre of Pet Shop Boys' art, it has not been the limit of their ambition. They are always keen to give their voice a theatrical context. They visualize songs on stage. After making their debut stage appearance in Brixton in 1984 singing and playing over tapes, Neil and Chris refused to tour. The traditional industry pattern of recording followed by live promotion was not on the duo's agenda until five years into their partnership. Then, judging rock concerts to be stale and predictable, they enlisted film director Derek Jarman to create a spectacle, and musicians were banished from the stage. It wasn't until 2002 that Pet Shop Boys presented themselves as a band with the tie-in *Release*, an album grounded in bass, drum and guitars. Two years later, the boys composed a soundtrack to Sergei Eisenstein's innovative silent film of 1925, *Battleship Potemkin*, which was projected and performed in Trafalgar Square in front of an estimated audience of 20,000. A decade on they premiered at Sadler's Wells the award-winning ballet score *The Most Incredible Thing*, inspired by a Hans Christian Andersen short story. These are remarkable achievements for a synth-pop duo. The musical language of Tennant and Lowe has an instantly recognizable sound, but in the boys' fourth decade of writing it is increasingly organic as it takes on new challenges. They wrote the songs for 'Closer To Heaven', staged at the Arts Theatre in London's West End, which invigorated musical theatre with its innovative and contemporary pop sound. And in 2004 'It's A Sin' even found its way onto the Lyttelton stage at the National Theatre when it was performed by a character in Alan Bennett's play *The History Boys*.

Twenty-three years earlier, Neil Francis Tennant assumed he had missed the boat. Born on 10 July 1954 in North Shields, Northumberland, he had journeyed through both school and failing bands, and was now taking a degree in history at the Polytechnic of North London. Needing a lead to make his synthesizer work, the 27-year-old Tennant ventured out to the King's Road, and in the shop got talking to another customer. Chris Lowe was a student taking a year out in London with the intention of later studying architecture. He was five years younger. They talked about music and they connected. Chris knew some boys who worked in an Ealing pet shop and a name was born as the pair imagined themselves as a glamorous stateside hip hop group. They began to collaborate. Chris told Neil, 'Make the words more sexy.' Neil responded with passionate lyrics expressing the excitement of London. For two years they wrote and recorded in thrice-weekly sessions many songs that would form the basis of their debut album *Please* and its 1987 follow-up, *Actually*. Neil continued to work, first at Marvel Comics and then at *Smash Hits*. He left the magazine in 1985 to concentrate on his musical career. 'West End Girls' at first faltered outside the top 100. Re-released a year later, the song shot to number one in the UK, USA, Canada, Finland, Hong Kong, Ireland, Israel, New Zealand and Norway, selling one and a half million copies, receiving an Ivor Novello Award and later being voted by Radio 2 listeners the best song of the ten years 1985–95. The award stands on a shelf next to an array of other prestigious marks of recognition. They include a Brit and an Ivor Novello Award for Outstanding Contribution to British Music, at which Elton John commented, 'Neil and Chris's songs I think are incredibly underrated . . . the ability to write great personal lyrics with great melodies is a very hard task.' There is also a World Arts Award presented by the former Soviet president Mikhail Gorbachev in 2003, 'for their extraordinary dedication to art, their social engagement and their unique contribution to popular music as well as their overall patronage of the arts'. In America, the Pet Shop Boys have been listed as the fourth most successful dance act behind Madonna, Janet Jackson and Donna Summer.

Pop music comes from simplicity, and, like Ray Davies, Tennant delights in un-pop vocabulary. He favours everyday, conversational words, titles like 'What Have I Done To Deserve This?', 'I Wouldn't Normally Do This Kind Of Thing', 'I Don't Know What You Want But I Can't Give It Any More'. It is the speech you might hear on the high street. In 1998, Neil coordinated a tribute album for charity: *Twentieth-Century Blues: The Songs of Noel Coward*. The British songwriter and playwright's influence on popular music was demonstrated by the calibre of artists who agreed to reinterpret his songs, including Paul McCartney, Elton John, Marianne Faithfull, Bryan Ferry and Damon Albarn. Noel Coward's writing resonates in the wit of Neil Tennant. Tennant is an heir to the tradition, writing funny songs with social comment and romance from a distorted perspective. 'I Get Along' imagined the relationship between Tony Blair and Peter Mandelson. 'I'm With Stupid' partnered Blair with George W. Bush. The single 'Opportunities (Let's Make Lots Of Money)' reflected the greed endemic in Eighties Britain. 'So Hard' carried the gem:

We've both given up smoking because it's fatal / So whose matches are those?
'Left To My Own Devices' depicts romance at the flat end of inspiration: *Maybe if you're with me we'll do some shopping.* 'Suburbia' offered *Mother's got a hairdo to be done / She says they're too old for the toys*, words that could easily have been written by Madness. In 2008, Suggs and Cathal from Madness performed their hit 'My Girl' on stage with the Pet Shop Boys. By coincidence the two bands share similar songwriting techniques, employing half-tone key changes in choruses and focusing vocal melodies as piano parts. Both Tennant and Suggs adopted a parlante delivery, though of different styles. Tennant's lyrical melancholy and feyness are effective because Pet Shop Boys handle familiar ingredients with contradictory dynamics. As Neil says, 'We are mundane every-day life with dramatic music.'

Pet Shop Boys' music is grandiose. It is a concoction of hard and soft forces: four-beats-to-the-bar bass drum patterns; double-time percussion; moving driving rhythm; epic filmic panoramic backdrops. The music charts the changing nature of dance-club fashions: Euro-pop and synthpop, Italian disco, house, indie dance, rave, techno. The marriage between Neil's lyrical intelligence and Chris's progressive vigour has sustained the duo for over thirty years, mixing genres to complement and expand the pop palette.

In 2013, Pet Shop Boys released their thirteenth studio album, *Electric*, continuing their playful use of single-word titles. Previously the dance remixes

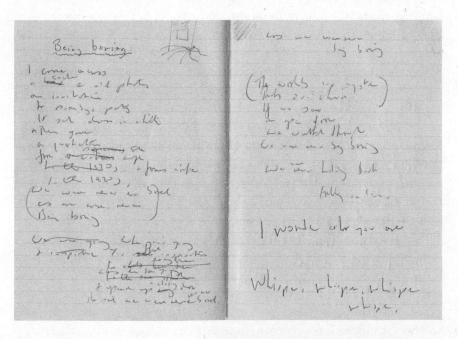

'Being Boring' lyrics, handwritten by Neil Tennant

within *Introspective* had clocked a career best of four and a half million sales, yet two years later in 1990, 'Being Boring' from the album *Behaviour* became their least successful single in six years. Over time the song has been widely recognized as a Pet Shop Boy classic. The title was inspired by a party invitation extended to Tennant quoting Zelda Fitzgerald: 'She was never bored, mainly because she was never boring.' The theme of the loss of abandonment is spread across three verses, each set in different decades. The writer's aspirations feature in the first, *When you're young you find inspiration / In anyone who's ever gone / And opened up a closing door*; the second shows Tennant's move to London *with a haversack and some trepidation*; and finally the passing of a friend: *All the people I was kissing / Some are here and some are missing / In the nineteen-nineties.* Tennant's handwritten lyrics are a rare glimpse into the original ideas that would go on to form the body of the song whilst also revealing rejected ideas and unused possibilities: *I wonder who you are . . . Whisper, whisper, whisper, whisper.* A further aspect of Tennant and Lowe's writing, as suggested earlier, has been the reinvention of other people's songs. Pet Shop Boys' third number one was originally a hit for Elvis Presley. 'Always On My Mind' was transposed into a modern environment with stunning assurance. Ironically, 'Go West' had in its turn appropriated part of Pachelbel's *Canon in D Major.* The classical piece has been assimilated by many British songwriters, from Pete Townshend and David Bowie to The Beatles' recording of 'In My Life', and Oasis's 'Whatever'. For an electronic outfit, Pet Shop Boys happily blend sources that confuse and confound expectation. In 1991 the pair produced a cover version of U2's 'Where The Streets Have No Name', cleverly melded with Frankie Valli's 'Can't Take My Eyes Off You'. The Irish band responded with amused bewilderment, 'What have we done to deserve this?

Pet Shop Boys have had fruitful collaborations with a range of artists, including Kylie Minogue, Shirley Bassey, Robbie Williams and Tina Turner. At Lowe's suggestion, Tennant 'cut up' words from 'Space Oddity' for a remix single version of David Bowie and Brian Eno's 'Hallo Spaceboy'. The collaboration was performed at the Brit Awards in 1996 with Bowie and Tennant trading vocal lines. The measure of Tennant and Lowe's writing ability is reflected in the talent they attract. Within four years of their debut recording they had written most of the songs for Liza Minnelli and Dusty Springfield's albums, with both artists celebrating a return to the top ten.

Spending a couple of hours with the pair in their west London office was riotously funny. Neil, resplendent in a long-sleeve polka-dot shirt, jeans and black boots, strikes an assured and confident figure. Chris has something of Tony Hancock and Walter Matthau about him, and is relaxed in dress and attitude. They have an obvious rapport, talking over, repeating and finishing one another's sentences. It poses many problems in transcription. Where their conversation overlapped I have marked the interjection by a slash (/). Neil and Chris's ability to feed off each other's thought trains provides an insight into their musical compatibility and warm friendship.

Are you a trained musician, Chris?

Chris: Trained! I've had piano lessons. Let's put it like that.

Neil: How many years?

Chris: Oh, quite a few years, and trombone lessons and drums in the school band as well.

Did you take grades?

Chris: Yes, what was it? Seven? Never quite got to the end of anything . . . (*Laughs.*) Architecture, music . . .

Neil: Well, grade seven's pretty good. There's only eight, isn't there?

Chris: . . . stopped before the end . . . wouldn't want to complete anything. I might not have gone as far with the drums. Maybe that was six. There were two piano teachers in Blackpool. Started about ten, or younger. The trombone I started to learn after that. The piano lessons were only an hour once a week and then you were meant to practise, but I didn't like having to do that bit.

Neil: I can't imagine you playing scales.

Chris: D'you know what? I could probably still just about do them. When you're young you're quite nimble . . . I'll now do three octaves! Your fingers do start to go quite quickly with the practice.

Neil: D'you know I used to play the cello at school?

Chris: Neil is a classically trained musician.

Neil: I'm a classical musician and singer.

Chris: And he's had singing lessons!

What prompted taking singing lessons?

Neil: We'd released the first version of 'West End Girls' and we were getting very serious about it. I thought my voice was too weak. EMI suggested it.

Chris: I think that everybody should have singing lessons / not just for the actual quality of the singing, but for the voice. So many people sing incorrectly and their voice goes because they sing from their throat.

Neil: So do I. / Not their diaphragm. It's quite good to have singing lessons because you think about singing. I only ever sang in the Pet Shop Boys because there was no one else going to. When we started to feel reasonably serious about it we used to occasionally have discussions about getting a singer. I didn't regard myself . . . even though I sang in Dust.

Chris: What we need now is a rapper, of course. (*Laughs.*)

Neil: I was also the rapper at that point.

What persuaded you that you were right for the Pet Shop Boys?

Neil: There was no one else.

Chris: Also you'd sung anyway.

Neil: I'd sung anyway. Then we made a record so it was all too late by then. That was it. I was evidently the singer.

Did you continue with the lessons?

Neil: I had the lessons throughout 1985.

Chris: Were they like having piano lessons? Were you stood in front of a music stand?

Neil: Well, you sat.

Chris: You sat!

Neil: With a straight back.

Chris: With a music stand; with words and music notes?

Neil: You've got to breathe (*sings scale*). *Una furtiva lagrima.*

Chris: I can see why they wanted to take it further. That's your natural musical form. You're wasted in pop, Neil.

Neil: My singing teacher said I shouldn't do pop music—she was very ahead of her time—I should sing baroque opera because I had the perfect voice for it. She was absolutely right because in the mid-Eighties a boom started—which was regarded as obscure—in baroque opera. Unfortunately I didn't like it. I said, 'I want to sing Puccini.' She said, 'It's not right . . .' I said, 'Well, I want to sing it anyway!' We settled on the famous aria from *Tosca*.

Did you play an instrument other than the cello?

Neil: I got a guitar when I was twelve years old and I taught myself to play from *Bert Weedon's Play In A Day*—one of the most influential music books ever published in Britain: Brian May, Eric Clapton, they all started with it. Then I had one or two guitar lessons, but when I got there it was folk I could already play really. So I only went twice. We had a piano; my sister had piano lessons and I taught myself to play guitar chords on the piano. I noticed in your questions here you've got, Neil: more chord based. That's why . . . it's because I taught myself. We used to have Beatles sheet music which my sister might buy. She used to get annoyed 'cause I could play it quicker. Susan would be playing it properly whereas I'd just be going, 'Oh yeah, E minor, A minor.' Then at St Cuthbert's . . . where I was told just the other day that in the music room there's a picture of me; there's also a picture of Sting, obviously; he was three years above me . . . I played the cello because if you had music lessons you could go to the music room in the lunch break rather than hang around the playground. For the first two years I studied quite hard, and then I lost interest in the sixth form.

Did you take grades?

Neil: No. I never did grades. I was in the school orchestra. I think I was always studying for grade three. At the same time I had my folk group Dust which is where I really / started writing songs.

Chris: *My* folk group. Was it very much *me* and *my* band? / Ah! (*Laughs.*)

Neil: No! / Actually I had two groups and then I had my folk group and we split up due to musical differences.

Chris: Beautiful South split up recently due to 'musical similarities', which I thought was good.

Am I right to make the assumption that your interests in music are quite diverse with just slim similarities?

Neil: I don't know that it is that diverse. What would you say?

Chris: When we met there was quite a big overlap, mainly David Bowie.

Neil: Also when we met there was an explosion of synthpop, so Soft Cell, Human League, OMD. We both agreed on that.

Chris: Yeah.

Neil: I remember being shocked that Chris liked 'Body Talk' by Imagination.

Chris: I was more overtly pop and disco. Neil probably liked it as well but would never admit to something like that in his circle of friends, I'd imagine. It's still a great record. (*Laughs.*)

Neil: It's not my favourite one by them. We used to watch *Top of the Pops*. I used to go round a friend's house.

Chris: Actually disco wasn't accepted in a lot of circles.

Neil: Well, disco was the same time as punk and New Wave. I loved *Saturday Night Fever*, by the way. The disco music I didn't like was . . . when it became . . . when you're younger you have far more prejudices about music.

I was shocked to learn you liked The Clash and Elvis Costello and had a New Wave influence.

Neil: That was my major influence.

Which is not obviously sensed in Pet Shop Boys writing.

Neil: No, it's not. Well, even now there's Clash records . . . no one can deny that 'London Calling' is a wonderful record, or 'Bankrobber'. I'd personally gone on a trajectory in terms of songwriting before I met Chris, from my folk group to being a singer-songwriter literally just writing songs for myself. When I first came to London I had three auditions with music publishing companies including Rockit Records. I was very much an early Seventies singer-songwriter. Then of course punk came along. I was trying to play a punk style on the acoustic guitar. I wasn't really getting very far with that.

Did Chris's influence change the way you approached writing songs?

Neil: Totally, because we started writing together. I was immediately struck that Chris knew about . . . I'd never considered the existence of a bass line before. I just thought about the chords and melody and words. Even though in the songs I'd written before I met Chris they would have had different rhythms. That was all instinctive and I'd never have thought about it.

Do the two of you sit in a room and write together or do you bring individual ideas?

Chris: When we started writing together . . . actually, we need to go back further. When I was young I used to sit at the piano rather than practising for the lesson, and play for hours. No thought of any song or song structure. Extemporizing, is that what you call it? I suppose what you'd be doing would be expressing feeling through the piano: normally frustration and anger.

Neil: A good starting point; same as punk, in fact.

Chris: Maybe the odd bit of beauty here and there. That was my tradition. I never thought of even putting anything down. Just for the pleasure of it, really. When we met there was this explosion of electronic music and there was also Bobby Orlando. So there was this fantastic minimal electronic stuff with a lot of energy. And that was what really excited us and started us writing. Wasn't it, or was that later?

Neil: That was a little bit later. I bought a Korg MS10 monophonic synthesizer.

Chris: Which is great 'cause you only play one line at a time.

Neil: And so Chris used to play that and I used to play the acoustic guitar. And there was a record I really liked, although it wasn't a hit, by Pete Shelley, called 'Homosapien'. It was produced by Martin Rushent who did the Human League *Dare*. It wasn't a template and Chris probably didn't even know the record at that time. I liked the combination of the electronic synthesizer and the chords on the guitar. And of course that was all that we had, and a really crap cassette recorder.

While Chris was playing the chords were you playing single notes to find bass or vocal melody lines?

Neil: Sort of everything.

Chris: I can only remember doing one song on that. There was a song by Bobby O. (*hums riff*): *the best part of breaking up is when you're making up* (*Roni Griffith*). I just wanted to emulate this one song. There's not a lot you can do / with the Korg keyboard. It's not even an octave long: one and a half?

Neil: We didn't really get very far. It must be an octave. We have a virtual one now in the computer. It's a good sound. We sort of had a few ideas because it was too limiting and totally random. D'you remember it had a template you put over it and you marked . . . ? It couldn't quite do Donna Summer. I've got these early cassettes where we are doing things like that. My recollection, the big breakthrough was that Chris went to Blackpool for the weekend and came back and gave me a cassette, and it was the entire mute backing track, just on piano, for what became 'Jealousy'—including, by the way, the piano solo. I then played that on my cassette player. I had my little *Smash Hits* recording thing by this point for interviews. I sang live over Chris's backing tape the lyrics for 'Jealousy'. That was the first song we ever wrote / properly and that ultimately never changed.

Chris: Properly. / When did we do 'Na Na Na Na Nah'?

Neil: Having written 'Jealousy', and I think we'd also written that really funny song about *I was walking down the high street*. We hadn't written 'Budadudadubadudum'.

Chris: When did we write that, then?

Neil: At Ray Roberts'. I was using part of my redundancy money from when I left Macdonald Educational Publishers and we'd booked the studio for a four-hour session at £30 an hour. We started to write that song then and there.

Chris: We wrote three songs that day.

When you create a backing track, is your mind thinking in terms of structure?

Chris: Well, 'Jealousy', that's unusual. You see, after having met Neil I was obviously thinking songs. Before I'd never thought of writing in terms of songs: verses, choruses. I wouldn't have seen the point to it, or writing pop songs even. It's definitely a song. It's a backing track to a song.

Neil: 'Jealousy' is the instrumental of the whole song, start to finish.

Chris: So that would have been something new, for me to think like that at that point. I've got so used to verse, chorus, verse, chorus, middle bit, now. It's second nature. Sometimes we'll discuss what's the verse and what's the chorus? That's quite common within the Pets. I will think, 'This section is obviously the chorus,' and Neil will go, 'That's the verse,' or 'It's the bridge.'

Neil: This is while the song is being written. This is even when it's got a melody or lyrics on top of it.

Chris: There might be a structure in the songwriting process, but it might be wrong. It might be changed. We even fly in bits from other songs occasionally. It's all quite amorphous.

Does your understanding of song structure come from dissecting other people's records or is it instinctive?

Chris: Mostly it's instinctive, but there are odd occasions when we've listened to a record by for instance Stock, Aitken and Waterman and thought, 'Wow, that's really interesting how they've gone up a semitone into the chorus. We'll have a go at it.'

'Being Boring' for example.

Neil: Being a specific example, yes.

When you're composing how does the instrument—piano, keyboards, guitar—affect your approach or thinking?

Chris: We do use those three methods. Obviously the guitar's Neil, and the piano.

Neil: You don't really write on the piano any more. He can't remember it.

Chris: I don't like to write on the piano because I can forget what I've done. It occurred to me when I was young: wouldn't it be fantastic if there was a machine that could notate everything you've just done, and how great would that look as well. But that computer didn't exist back then. You can print and see the notation, which is fantastic. I'll use a piano sound on a keyboard rather than use an actual piano simply because I don't want to forget what I've written, because you just press record when you're doing it. Neil can remember things far better than I can . . .

Neil: Less than I used to.

Chris: . . . which is why the computer is a godsend, because sometimes you remember it wrong. And you've lost that great . . . sometimes there's something very simple that's good about something and it's so subtle and your memory has glossed over the good bit and you think, what was that good point?

Neil: The first time I learnt that was when we wrote 'What Have I Done To Deserve This?' with Allee Willis, who our manager Tom Watkins knew and brought us together to write this song. She had a Dictaphone, just like Xenomania actually, and she sang her bit and she kept singing it in there for that precise reason: that there was a nuance that might get lost. I personally had never thought of a melody being so subtle as that way. For instance, writing with Chris, he would say, 'No, you sang that better last time.' To my simplified thinking I couldn't really work out what the difference was. Then you play it back: 'Oh OK, yeah.' I remember thinking how right Allee Willis was. When she sang *Since you went I've been hanging around / I've been wondering why I'm feeling down* she had to go back to the first time she'd sung it 'cause she knew she'd done it better, and she was right. I also remember thinking, 'Wow, I'd never have written those lyrics, it's too banal,' but reluctantly admitting it puts across the idea well, and learning from that as well that you don't always have to try and sound like W. B. Yeats—that you can just say the obvious thing.

Chris: Going back. The way that Neil would play the piano would be chords. I would play the piano instinctively with a melody and chords or individual notes. I wouldn't think in terms of chords. Neil would say, 'What chord's that?' and I would have to say, 'It's a B, an F sharp, an A, a D sharp and a G.' Then Neil would say, 'Oh yes, it's a . . .' So we play the piano differently.

Neil: You think in terms of the lines.

Which immediately opens possibility because presumably if you play a C chord on the guitar your thought process will then be F and G within the key and probably the relative minor?

Chris: I often go for the look of the notes on the keyboard.

Neil: So do I. There's a song on the new album (*Elysium*) that's mostly written on the guitar, but in recent years I haven't and the reason is I know everything on the guitar, like you just said. Whereas even though I know every chord shape, as it were, on the piano, you can still just think, 'I've never thought of doing that before.' I did something the other day at home and I thought, 'Oh, I've never thought of doing that before.' It's more flexible, the keyboard, because the shapes are just easier.

Chris: Writing with a computer and keyboard also your imagination is triggered by sounds as well, so it can become far more abstract. Quite often you can play a sound on a computer and you don't know what the note is. You might be playing an A but it might not be playing an A. Then you're layering things up so you're not thinking traditionally at all. You might be developing a lot of single-line parts. You're not thinking in chords at all.

Neil: My brain simply doesn't work like that.

Chris: It's just a case of what sounds good on top of it. Do one thing, put something else on top, something else. You might start with the drums, so there's lots of different ways of working.

How collaborative is the process, or do you develop ideas independently?

Chris: We quite often develop stuff ourselves and then take it as far as we can, then the other person comes in. Sometimes you've got a great idea but you can't really finish it or you haven't got a chorus for it. That's the great thing with two; you don't get stuck.

Neil: In a studio situation now, if we were writing in this room, Chris would be over there writing something on the keyboard doing lines: drums or percussion things. I'd be sitting flicking through my computer thinking, 'I haven't got any sort of idea what will go with that.' Then I'll say, 'Oh, I've got an idea, that's the chorus.' And I'll sing some quite moronic thing and maybe double-track it and put a harmony on it. Then you're going somewhere. Sometimes you can't think of anything. Recently Chris wrote a piece of music that sounds like—well, we're calling it 'Baltic Beats'. In fact, we're calling it . . . what are we calling it? / 'Balkan Beats'. Don't say Baltic.

Chris: Balkan. Don't say Baltic, people will think we don't know what we're talking about. (*Laughing.*)

Neil: So somebody we know said, 'Oh, it's Baltic Beats.' / And we said, 'No, it's Balkan.' 'Yeah, Baltic.' 'No, Baltics are in the north. Balkans are the south.' So it was like an 'Oh, whatever,' thing. Anyway, Chris wrote a / and I was slightly flummoxed by this piece of music . . .

Chris: Which is very unusual because I have no idea where that came from.

Neil: . . . and came up with something which followed one of the lines in it, but there were too many notes in it so we dumped it for a while.

Chris: We thought, 'It's going to have to be an instrumental.'

Neil: Then ages later I remembered this funny poem I started to write called 'Hell', about all these dictators sitting in hell bitching about each other, and it suddenly occurred it could go with Chris's 'Balkan' piece.

Chris: At that stage there wasn't a chorus and you said, 'I need a chorus,' and I was like, 'Oh God, we need a chorus, more chords . . . back upstairs . . . write a chorus . . . / it's got to fit in.'

Neil: And it's got to fit in.

When you're creating ideas are you always recording / or do you wait until you have an idea first?

Neil: Yes.

Chris: No. It goes straight into the computer. That's how we write. Neil might come with a fully formed chord progression and song, maybe missing a middle bit or something. Neil will then sit down and put the chords into the computer. We've both got these little gorgeous Yamaha pianos at home which we managed to blag for quite a good price.

Neil: I record on my phone.

Chris: Is that how you remember it?

Neil: Yes. I do the Allee Willis thing: I think, 'I'm going to forget that in a minute,' so I record it, listen back and I think, 'That's better if I do that.' Then I wipe the previous one and build it up like that.

What about using a sample as a starting point, for example Aretha Franklin with 'Decadence'?

Chris: It's very rare.

Neil: An overall comment: we're impressed by your research; all of your noted examples are broadly speaking exceptions to the rule. We did start 'Decadence' with 'I Say A Little Prayer For You'. I think that's the only time we've ever done that.

Chris: We never got round to mastering the Akai sampler.

Neil: We couldn't be arsed.

Chris: We couldn't be bothered. Too complicated. Our programmer showed us how to do it and I had pages of notes and I thought, 'I can't be bothered with this. It's getting in the way.'

Neil: It's got to flow, otherwise it comes to a grinding halt.

Chris: We've used sampled sounds but they've only ever been a sound. Also it's a minefield of copyright.

Neil: What it did was, it gave the rhythm: if you think of (*sings*) *the morning*

I wake up . . . dec-a-dence. Otherwise it has no relationship to it, unless it's got the same key. Likewise your classical examples: there are only those three examples. We only did that because 'Go West' was Pachelbel's *Canon*. We thought, 'Oh right, what else could we do?' 'Moonlight' Sonata, I knew the chords, so we did 'Delusions of Grandeur'. I'd forgotten 'Red Letter Day' was Beethoven's Ninth, which I can't even see now.

Chris: 'Red Letter Day' was Beethoven's Ninth? Who says that?

These are suggestions I've picked up in previous interviews which I wanted to qualify.

Chris: That's news to me. That's just coincidence.

Neil: No. We were having a go . . . we wrote these songs at the same time at Rocky Lane . . . we probably drifted away from it, we were definitely thinking . . . (*Hums 'Ode To Joy'*.)

Chris: I don't like Beethoven's Ninth. It's very, very unlikely that 'Ode To Joy' would appear in a Pet Shop Boys song deliberately. As my famous quote, 'You can tell he was deaf when he wrote it.' (*Laughs.*)

Neil: What's the third one?

'All Over the World': Tchaikovsky *The Nutcracker* Suite progression.

Neil: That went into it when it was / yeah.

Chris: We were doing another song and I just went (*shouts riff*) over it, not in the same key or anything. Just aaargh . . . then of course it sounded quite good. It was literally a moment of frustration.

Neil: I thought it sounded great (*laughing*). We've invented a new way of writing recently which is Elton John and Bernie Taupin. In fact we did it ten years ago for the first time, where I write the lyrics and give them to Chris. It was the last song on *Release* actually, one of my favourite songs we've ever written called 'You Choose'. But having said that, we've done it a handful of times.

Chris: Actually, a new thing we've just done is that we have a fully formed song with lyrics and music and then decide to change all the music, keep the lyrics and rewrite the melody, which we've done on the new album.

Why would you do that?

Chris: When the lyrics are humorous and the music is upbeat it can . . . if you take the funny lyrics and add some melancholy music it completely changes the whole feel of the thing.

Neil: In fact it gives the humour pathos. We've got this song, I don't know if it's going on the album yet, called 'Your Early Stuff' and it mainly consists of what taxi drivers have said to me. Like, 'I suppose you've more or less retired now?' and he was driving me to *Top of the Pops* at the time. Originally we had a sort of humorous . . . it was a bit naff . . .

Chris: It wasn't really humorous, it was . . .

Neil: Upbeat. Then Chris rewrote the music and suddenly it became rather wistful. Rather than being sarcastic it made the whole thing sound as if the taxi drivers are probably correct, which gives a sadness about the whole thing.

Did you do that with 'Discoteca' as well?

Neil: No, we wrote 'Discoteca' in New York. We always wanted it to be a single so we recorded it. It's been released in a faster version, then another version with some different backing-vocal ideas. Sometimes when you write a song with very, very dense chords it's very difficult to pin it down. Our interest in recording 'It's Alright' was because the song always sounded unfinished. We thought, we're going to nail this song. We worked with it on and off for eight months. In fact, the single version of it, Trevor Horn pretty much did the backing track with a programmer while we were making Liza Minnelli's album. We'd driven ourselves mad with it. 'Discoteca' is like that, some big huge thing— if only you could release it. So it was never a single.

How long will you work with an idea before you reject it?

Chris: Stuff goes into storage, doesn't it? Sometimes something that has been rejected and you think, 'That's just rubbish,' can sound good ten years later. We very rarely—although it does happen—delete the file.

Neil: Very, very rarely. For instance, writing the ballet, Chris and I did some songwriting in 2003 at his house. I always remember melodies. I kept dragging out things mostly Chris had written: some very nice melodies but I never came up with any words for them.

Chris: Perfect for a ballet.

Neil: I like ballets. No lyrics. We often have good melodies. When you get a really strong romantic melody sometimes all I can think of is the most sentimental tosh, and I don't like it then. So it's quite difficult when you've got a very, very defined melody to put words to it, which is the opposite of . . . Elton John doesn't give Bernie Taupin music for him to write the words to. But we have occasionally done that. 'Can You Forgive Her?' was a total Chris Lowe backing track that I wrote the words to, to fit the melody line. It's quite tough doing that.

How do you develop melody lines?

Neil: Physicalize it, normally. Chris will put a melody down on a hideous trumpet sound.

Chris: Always a horrible brass sound. There are very few things that cut through that you can clearly hear.

Neil: Which makes it sound like the Black Dyke Mills Brass Band playing, so it has an incredible sad, tragic pathos and it's like a Hovis advert. I like putting it down on what's sampled: Voices 1 on the emulator immediately turns into the Vienna Boys' Choir. But what we realized quite a few years ago: it's good to sing something, even if it's just rubbish. But I don't like singing something that's not good 'cause I get it in my head and can't get rid of it.

It's quite unusual for writers to physicalize melody.

Neil: I realized from my singing lessons. For instance, our song 'Suburbia': to this day I'm never totally sure what the melody line I'm meant to sing is. I sing it now different, more accurately than I do on the record.

Chris: That melody was written on the piano / . . . you've probably improved it.

Neil: I know it was, but I've bent it a bit. That was before I had singing lessons. But what the singing teacher made me aware is, you should know what the melody is. For instance, when you do a cover version, you realize your rough approximation of melody is not what it's like at all. Again, that Allee Willis thing: it's details that make it interesting and so when we have a new melody I like to have it defined, or if Chris has written a melody I like him to sing it and then I've got to learn it. Chris and I have different melodic senses / instincts.

Chris: Different phrasing, definitely.

Neil: Another thing, Chris will play a melody and I will sing my version of it which then I realize has more got notes than his, but broadly speaking . . . / in there.

Chris: . . . sometimes we'll leave my piano melody in there. In 'Suburbia' there are two melodies nearly the same. Now we would take out the guide. If you listen, the vocal and the lead line slightly clash.

Like imperfect double-tracking.

Chris: Yeah, it is. We often have an instrument playing the vocal line.

Neil: I think once the melody goes in with a relatively attractive sound . . .

Chris: It tends to stay there.

Neil: . . . everyone gets used to it and it becomes part of the backing track even though it is almost always slightly different from the vocal line. But then that gives it a sort of harmonic richness. Sometimes you forget it's there. If you take it out, it's amazing: there's this incredible gap left.

Once the melody is defined, do you strictly honour it when writing the words?

Neil: Now we are more likely to strictly honour the melody, more than we used to.

Chris: When Neil's got the melody fixed it tends to stay exactly the same in perpetuity, which is fantastic because having worked with other singers on a few occasions they sing the same line differently every time. Hence Neil's double-tracking / is really easy to do because it's always the same.

Neil: I always double-track because I like the sound of it. I don't like my voice exposed.

When you're writing words, if the syllables don't match the melody presumably you change the word?

Neil: I'd probably change the melody to fit the syllables, or we might change the melody. The last song we were doing we were going through 'cause I didn't want to change the words. As time's gone on we've got more musical. When we started we were more punk. You were saying you can't hear the punk in the Pet Shop Boys. Actually, *I've got the brains, you've got the looks / Let's make lots of money* is a total punk song, more or less; a three- or four-chord song with that sort of punk attitude: the sarcasm, saying something you're not meant to say. Those kinds of songs are just kind of luck because it's very catchy, very simple.

The immediate sound of Pet Shop Boys is very far from punk. Perhaps 'The Truck Driver And His Mate' reveals your influences more.

Neil: We also have a sort of song which is totally reacting to what's going on at the time. 'The Truck Driver And His Mate' was written at the height of Oasis, although it doesn't sound remotely like Oasis. When you were writing it, you said, 'Make it sound like Oasis.'

Chris: You might think, 'I'll have a go at that,' and of course it sounds nothing like it. We're obviously so bad at it. It doesn't happen often, but when we do . . . I don't even know how we started that . . .

Neil: We had a guitar sample thing and you were trying to make it sound like Oasis.

Do you use other writers' songbooks for inspiration?

Neil: I had a little phase on the piano where I bought the Stephen Sondheim songbook. The nearest influence song would be 'So Sorry, I Said' . . . /

Chris: I thought it was 'Sho Shorry, I Shaid'.

Neil: . . . pretty much an exception to the rule. Following the guitar chords you get some great chord changes. There's a chord I learnt from Stephen Sondheim which I put in things all the time because I really like it, which is F minor seven with a B flat bass. You could do that in any key, of course. If you're playing in E flat rather than playing B seven you play F minor seven with a B flat bass; it's got this very rich showbiz . . . / 'Send In The Clowns', I love that song. I always wanted to sing that song.

Chris: Isn't it rich.

Can you sense creativity arriving / or can you tap into it and just write?

Neil: Yes . . . oh no, you can sense creativity has arrived. Sometimes you do feel (*dramatic pose*) 'I've got to write,' 'I've got to get to a piano,' 'I've an amazing . . . Oh my God.'

Chris: I know that I can always sit down at a piano and play something. I don't like to think about that, just in case after this interview . . . that was the last time. (*Laughs*.) Whether it's good or not is another matter. The hard thing is coming up with things to sing about / you don't. I would find that impossible.

Neil: I don't have that problem at all. I had two ideas for lyrics yesterday.

What is the sense of creativity arriving?

Neil: We just get this frisson: you can feel that you've got an idea. I remember the way 'West End Girls' was written. I wrote a rap with no music in the style of 'The Message' by Grandmaster Flash. Went into the studio in Camden and performed it to Chris. Then we wrote a piece of music which I have on cassette somewhere. It went hysterical at the end. It was a bit punky, actually!

I've set up a recurring theme here.

Chris: Yes, we're rebranding ourselves as punk rockers. File under punk.

Neil: We've always seen ourselves in the tradition of punk and Bowie rather than the singer-songwriter thing, which is what I had come from. So we wrote this backing track with me playing piano and Chris playing a bass line and a top line.

Chris: All I remember was it coming together in New York, and Bobby O., who I thought would do everything, said, 'Well, go in and play it.' 'Play it? We haven't come to you for us to play it.'

Neil: That's by the way typical of Chris, to have reluctance to get involved in the studio. Anyway, one night lying in my little studio flat off the King's Road I suddenly thought of the rap. It was an incredible feeling. I've probably over-exaggerated this because I know what happened to the song. Originally it was just spoken: *in a west end town in a dead end world, east end boys with . . .* Suddenly I realized (*sings line*). I didn't even record it. I just remembered it. When we went in to Bobby O. and he said, 'Play something,' Chris started actually to play (*hums bass line*) and I started. We had a keyboard each, stood there in the studio.

Chris: One take, he didn't even let us correct it.

Neil: Bobby likes mistakes. I said, 'Oh, by the way, you know that rap: it works over this.' Chris was really panicky. Bobby O. immediately liked it. Doesn't sound remotely like one of his records; it's got some pretty lush major seventh chords and stretches. He programmed the drums.

Chris: Which were, for fact finders, a 'Billie Jean' pattern and David Bowie's 'Let's Dance' drums / everything on the emulator.

Neil: Samples. He put it in the LinnDrum first. The Bowie samples were put in manually. Then I said, 'I'll do this thing; I think it might be quite good.' I went on the microphone, did the rap and went into the singing bit. I remember the assistant said, 'Your voice is so easy to listen to.'

Chris: The engineer on that was the bloke who made 'Popcorn'.

Neil: Steve Jerome, he was called. I remember that evening lying on the floor of my flat listening to the cassette and thinking, it's amazing you can do that: a frisson of creativity; a little magical moment when you think you've written something good. Funnily enough when I came back to *Smash Hits* after that New York trip we'd recorded four songs. I played the office three of them because I was embarrassed by the one I'd rapped on.

Chris: Didn't Boy George say something similar, that he was embarrassed by 'Do You Really Want To Hurt Me?'—'That's not going to be a single.'

Neil: Too personal. I remember when we released the album *Behaviour* feeling horrified that journalists from *Melody Maker* listened to these songs.

Chris: What about 'Love Is A Catastrophe', your sister?

Neil: My sister came and saw the lyrics and burst into tears . . . well, she went very quiet.

Chris: That must be very difficult, when you're putting yourself, feelings into a song, / exposing yourself.

Neil: Very difficult. I try and distance myself a bit from . . . also you don't have enough personal emotions all the time. Nowadays there's an idea common across all media forms that the best art form is if it's really emotional.

Chris: Or personal.

Neil: It's really personal, really emotional. Actually I think that's bullshit.

Chris: We were saying before about P. J. Harvey winning the Mercury. That is not her. / It's not ego music. It's not being personal.

Neil: It's not ego music. She's female, a woman singer and songwriter singing about the First World War. It's not totally to my taste but I admire that. So much music is ego.

When you're putting words together do you have a thematic idea in mind?

Neil: Sometimes you do get a hooky idea in your head if Chris is playing the keyboard.

Chris: Actually, 'Shopping' came around like that. We spent a lot of time in the Eighties shopping. / We were always going, we're S-H-O-P . . .

Neil: We were always buying clothes for TV shows; we didn't have a stylist then. We were walking down New Bond Street, to my knowledge. Then we thought we better write it as a song.

'Shopping' was a title Paul Weller used as the B-side to 'Beat Surrender'.

Chris: Was it?

Neil: But no one remembers it (*laughter*), including me. 'Beat Surrender' is quite a good song. Normally I will have a title and a strong title suggests a theme; for instance, I had the title 'Rent' beforehand because I thought it sounded so punk! It sounds so uncompromising; it sounds like it's about rent boys. There was also a lot going on about rent at the time. It's a hard word: rent.

And so we would write a romantic song called 'Rent'. I had the line *I love you; you pay my rent* which I thought was intriguing because I wasn't quite sure what it meant. Nowadays I'd be reluctant to have that line because I wouldn't like *I love you; you pay*: I wouldn't have the two 'you's. I cringe when I hear the record now because I hate the way I go *I love you-oo; you pay my* . . . I would never do that now. I sing *I love you; you pay my rent*.

Chris: A big issue with the Pet Shop Boys is where the words fall onto the music. So you don't put the emphasis on the wrong part of any word. The Manic Street Preachers . . .

Neil: Who I've discussed it with now. I was having a laugh with the singer.

Chris: The classic being *a design f-or life*. The emphasis is on *a* and there's two syllables on the word *for*. It should be *a design, for life*. But they've had to fit it to the music. So it's simply wrong. We were thinking of doing a whole album of songs where the song is incorrect and correcting it.

Correct and incorrect are fascinating words to use in music.

Chris: You / wouldn't say it like that.

Neil: It's not that. Emphasis. I remember years ago when I was kid reading an interview with Frank Sinatra and he said that phrasing and singing should be like speaking because then you put across the meaning. In a way it's not that difficult, it's pretty blatantly bloody obvious to me. Also in the 1960s I read an interview with John Lennon about writing 'Strawberry Fields Forever'. He was trying to write it like speech. It has that *er* in it. *I think er no, I mean er yes.* Well, no one in songwriting to that point had put *er* in, although everyone says it all the time. I thought, 'Yeah, if I was going to write songs that's what I would do.' Singing nowadays has moved closer to opera singing, where it's about taking the sound and using it as a springboard for vocal operatics. I've got literally no time for that whatsoever. It started with Whitney and then Mariah Carey. Nowadays there's a lot of singing, to my ears, that sounds totally insincere, although it's supposed to sound totally emotional. If you listen to 'Your Song' by Elton John, he sings it in a sensitive and relatively matter-of-fact way; puts across the lyric. Ellie Goulding's version is about her voice. It sounds insincere. It sounds like ego. That song's got lyrics I don't like in it, but the way it goes into the chorus, *I hope you don't mind*, is so beautiful. She sings in that heavy breathing and that weird vaguely Celtic accent they all sing in. We'll quite often talk about the accent everybody sings in. We think it comes from The Cranberries—who possibly even got it from Sinead O'Connor, who actually doesn't sing in an inflective way (*affects accent*): *Do you have to let it linger* kind of thing that's gone right the way through pop music; this weird voice that people put on. I always prefer people who sing naturally. Suggs sings like conversation. Of course it requires skill in songwriting. The Manic Street Preachers' song 'A Design For Life'; it's a very powerful track but it didn't quite deliver the lyric.

Although in a way that's their style; the lyrics and the melody fight, in a way, which is a sort of a punky thing. Anyway, it's obviously worked for them. That's what we don't do. People will say, 'I like the way you can hear the lyrics,' about our music, which sounds like a very small compliment. But actually it's true; most of the time you can hear the lyrics. They are phrased like real conversation.

How do you develop the themes of your writing? Sting talked about the importance of walking and motion.

Neil: Exercise gives oxygen to your brain. I quite often play the demo, the melody, and then go for a run. Some of the words just accrue to the melody in your head without you even doing much. If it's got an insidious melody it will collect words of its own accord, which may then of course be rubbish; the classic idea being *scrambled egg* for 'Yesterday'. When Chris wrote the music for what became 'Can You Forgive her?' I was walking back from Charing Cross Station when I lived in Chelsea and I thought of the first line . . .

Chris: Laughing to yourself.

Neil: . . . I can remember even now turning the corner into my road and thinking *She's made you some kind of laughing stock because you dance to disco and you don't like rock*, and then literally burst out laughing. I couldn't wait to get home to write them down in case I forgot them. There is something about the rhythm of walking. I like walking through cities by myself because you get ideas.

Do you carry a notebook?

Neil: I put them in my iPhone now. In the 'Can You Forgive Her?' days I didn't have a mobile phone then, so I had to remember it and write it down when I got home. Pre-phone I didn't have a book. I'd have to remember them. I'd have to keep repeating them. It would drive me mad because it's very easy to forget. I have actually forgotten song ideas before, unfortunately.

Do you ever assume the style or character of other writers, for example Morrissey, in 'Miserabilism'?

Neil: Playing a role. In writing the lyrics for 'Rent' I was imagining myself being a woman. I always find political scandals a good source for songs. At the time Edward Kennedy had a mistress in a shared apartment in New York. That song was written from the point of view of that woman: whether it was a love affair, whether it was a sex thing. What her motive is, how she feels about it now. That's why there's no conjunction, because it's ambivalent whether she loves him or not. So I was imagining I was this person and that's quite common. Also I take experiences from people I know. I put people I know's experiences into song lyrics.

You write being them or commenting on them?

Neil: Being them.

Neil: It's a very theatrical approach. It's probably not as rigorously thought through as if I was a playwright. I'm writing a song lyric. 'Getting Away With It': we were in Manchester with Johnny Marr (*laughs*). I was sort of pretending I was Morrissey. I didn't tell them that at the time. I had the idea for a song called that already. It was in my list of titles.

Do you have a long list?

Neil: No, it comes and goes. Often I'll look at it and think, 'That's rubbish.' I delete them and start again. The good ones will probably come back again.

On a recent BBC documentary about songwriting Guy Chambers and Rufus Wainwright have a conversation about subject matter before they start writing. Would the two of you discuss a song's meaning?

Chris: Very rare. We did agree on something once about how when you're older you can be invisible, but you'd had that idea already.

Neil: But we did it 'cause you'd had it as well. Sometimes I write lyrics for songs that I think Chris will like.

Chris: And then I like them. (*Laughs.*) / Oh yeah . . . yes.

Neil: Chris likes what I call happy clappy. He likes the hands in the air, ecstatic. I do too, actually.

Did you want the words to 'How Can You Expect To Be Taken Seriously?' to be nastier?

Chris: I did what? I / don't remember that at all. Did we both come up with the idea of 'Bet She's Not Your Girlfriend'?

Neil: I think you did, actually. I'd forgotten that until I read it in your notes. Oh, we certainly came up with that, when we were drunk.

I thought that chorus was very different for you, quite Michael Jacksonish.

Neil: It's got a Michael Jackson rhythm track . . . we haven't sat down and tried to be . . . ! But I know what you mean. It's got a 'Wanna Be Startin' Something' . . . (*Sings.*) *Whisper round the town 'cause you're my friend and that's the end.* Chris wrote the rhythm track for that. It was about George Michael.

Chris: And Kathy Yeung. We should perform that on our next tour. That's quite a punk song.

Neil: Although then having had that idea, the song is about me going out with a very beautiful girl at school. All the guys couldn't believe I was going out with her.

Chris: Which you weren't, or were you? / Back of the net! There you are, everyone. Yes, I was actually.

Neil: I was going out with her.

Do you read Neil's lyrics before he records them?

Chris: If I've been presented with lyrics to put a melody to I'll obviously study them, but no. First time I'll often hear them is when Neil goes to the microphone and sings them.

Like Morrissey with The Smiths.

Chris: Johnny Marr's interesting because he'll say similarly Morrissey will come in at a very strange moment in the backing track. Morrissey will have interpreted the structure of the song completely differently to Johnny. Morrissey will come in halfway through the introduction, then the chorus will be during a bridge and Johnny will be astounded by what's happening.

Neil: Morrissey has always written over completely recorded backing tracks. I have done that occasionally, but it's the exception rather than the rule. When you are presented with a backing track, as a singer you can think, 'I'm not singing on the downbeat, it's too obvious.' You want to.

My thought has always been, Morrissey doesn't play an instrument so his melodies don't necessarily fall in with chord movements.

Neil: Oh, I think you're right. Morrissey is a very good example of someone who does the conversation thing, but also plays with the vowel sounds. If he sings *You're the one for me, fatty* he doesn't emphasize *for*; you emphasize *you're, me, fatty*.

Chris: 'The Last Of the Famous International Playboys'. (*They both sing line stressing famous and international playboys*). It's exactly spot on.

Neil: Any songwriter has got to be really conscious where they place melody. Madonna, who in my opinion writes quite a lot of banal lyrics, but she's a mistress of banal lyrics because she gets sound. She knows how important the vowel sounds are in a song and drops them in the right place.

Chris: Like *ring, ring, ring* ('Hung Up'): she makes that sound great, doesn't she?

Neil: Think of (*sings*): *Every little thing that you say or do I'm hung up waiting for you-oo.* Every key bit is a vowel sound. I couldn't sing that. I'd be saying, grammatically it's all over the place! But as an ecstatic disco song she's delivered the vowel sounds, hitting the key notes of the melody. It's a kind of a chant as well. (*Sings.*) *Get into the groove.* It's vowel sounds all the way through: *ee, oo, oo ee-ee.* She totally gets that. I assume it's instinctive and probably because she's a dancer. Madonna is someone for whom a melody comes from choreography, which is a very interesting way of thinking.

How careful are you at the writing stage that words will sing well?

Neil: I don't think my talent as a lyric writer . . . we don't quite do that Madonna thing, do we?

Chris: No, but I think we should start right now. / We are in the studio next week. We'll start with the vowel sounds.

Neil: I think we'd like to. My classical singing teacher made an impact on our music because she pointed out the best sound to sing is (*sings*) *ah*. It's a big sound. Worst sound to sing is *ii*.

Chris: Horrible.

Neil: *Oo* is good as well. There's a little bit of a tendency for me to nudge things in that direction because it opens out the voice.

But you use very particular English words from everyday conversation which ordinarily might not suggest musicality.

Neil: That's a thing of trying to bring in, which I think Morrissey does as well, words which you haven't seen in songs. Then maybe it works or doesn't work; you might scrap the idea.

***Sybarite* in 'Casanova In Hell', for example.**

Neil: 'Casanova In Hell' was written while we were writing a song. So the two things were written together. You started writing it on the piano. Then we changed the melody slightly to give it a . . . it was slightly more lyrical at the beginning.

Chris: One of the great things when this works is, I might be doing something on the keyboard and at the same time Neil is coming up with the lyrics and a melody and they finish at the same time.

Neil: That was pretty much what happened.

Chris: So by the time it's all done here Neil says, 'Right, I can put the vocal on,' and you think, 'Wow, that was great.'

And you can hear one another?

Chris: No, Neil's writing it on a piece of paper or doing it in his head.

Neil: That song, I was just doing melody (*hums it*); there's this insidious note on the end. On every line I tried to put something slightly . . . *The boy is . . . naked. The girl is . . . naked. Her sharp . . . perception, he couldn't get an . . .* yes, I'm going to sing it in a pop song . . . *erection.*

Chris: That didn't make it, did it, into the final . . . we couldn't have been working with Brian Higgins. He / would have had that word removed. We'd have had a meeting. 'Conference!' Can you run down? (*Much hilarity.*)

Neil: Yes, my mother was horrified. 'Conference!' 'I'm just looking at the lyrics, Neil. What's this erection?' I did take out of my own volition the reference to masturbation. I thought, 'We don't need to hear about that.'

Rufus Wainwright's interpretation is very memorable.

Neil: He sings it so well. I thought, 'Why don't we write an album and Rufus just sings it?'

With a song like 'Casanova', do you research ideas?

Neil: No, I have another lyric writing scheme which is to read a book and condense the book into a song. I read a short story by Arthur Koestler, a Viennese novelist. I had an idea for a song title, 'Casanova In Hell', and what it would be like if he couldn't shag any more, because it was so much of his life. And of course that's what did happen at the end of his life. He was exiled in this castle in the Czech Republic and he was a librarian. So he started to write his memoirs as revenge on the situation. There's a song we wrote in the same period of time called 'The Resurrectionist' which I happen to really like, which all of our fans think should be on the album. I'd read this book called *The Italian Boy*. It's about the people who used to dig up graves and sell the bodies. They were called resurrectionists. There's quite a few historical songs: 'My October Symphony' was all about Shostakovich. With the song for *Scandal*, 'Nothing Has Been Proved', I'd written the lyrics before I knew Chris. I'd read this book about Stephen Ward, Christine Keeler's pimp. It's rather a sad story because broadly speaking he was innocent and he ends up killing himself because he's going to go down. Then we wrote new music for it. But that's a whole story.

'Nothing Has Been Proved' only uses first names.

Neil: I liked that as well. I was thinking of the newspaper coverage: Christine Keeler was so famous; was just Keeler, and Mandy Rice-Davies was Mandy. All that happened: *Mandy's in the papers 'cause she tried to go to Spain*, which she did, and they brought her back from the airport. *Stephen's in his dressing gown*. Amazingly, Lucky Gordon, who's mentioned in *Christine's fallen out with Lucky, Johnny's got a gun*, worked in Sarm West Studios. We tried to get him to come in and say (*Jamaican accent*), 'It's a scandal, it's such a scandal,' which would have sounded great. Like it's a shame we didn't get Frank Sinatra to sing 'So Sorry, I Said' with Liza.

Did coming out affect your writing?

Neil: It affected me in a way, because before that I used to like to tease the audience.

Chris: It's more fun when you can have fun with / it. It's not about rent boys.

Neil: To say *I love you; you pay my rent*. It's not about rent boys, actually, but it's where the idea came from. 'Can You Forgive Her?' which is a bit like 'Bet She's Not Your Girlfriend': that theme; everyone's realized he's gay, apart from the guy singing the song. The girlfriend's realized. It's like a farce, really. I like the plots of farces. Then after I came out I wrote my least favourite lyric of the Pet Shop Boys' catalogue, which is the song 'Metamorphosis', which embarrasses me now. If you heard the original demo it's really fantastic, but we never really nailed it. We had this thing, *you grow up and experience this—a total metamorphosis*, which is a good line, and I thought, 'Oh, I'll make it about being gay.' Now it makes me cringe, which I'm happy to say not many of our songs do. It's like a modern song where people think the song is a diary. Lily Allen is good at doing it. But sometimes you wonder where the art has gone. Or if it's just like *thank you, you're a wanker*. Some people can go too far the other way. And that's like that: it's a bit me, me, me. Brian Higgins went off our records: he thought they became too personal. I sort of knew what he meant. He meant 'Being Boring', which is totally autobiographical but is a success as a song, but 'Metamorphosis' is ultimately failing. But that must be down to the artistry as well as the music and the production.

Do you remember writing 'Left To My Own Devices'?

Neil: It started off as an instrumental.

Chris: That started off as more of a Motown song. (*Hums bass riff.*) The chords I did on my baby grand in my front room. That's how I always remember the chords, because it was played on a piano, not into the computer. Then we took it to Trevor (*Horn*) and Steve Lipson. When we went into the studio Lipo had done this whole house backing track which we can't really take credit for.

Neil: I went into the Abbey Road demo studio by myself to record the vocal, having had the idea of the spoken bit. And that vocal is on the record. We added the middle bit when we were with Trevor; we didn't have that originally. I remember the engineer at Abbey Road being really not into it. It's like, 'He's just talking.' I was deliberately making it super conversational. It doesn't have a rap rhythm really, and then a sung chorus. It's been a constant theme of our songs to have mundane everyday life with dramatic music. It seems to me to be what life is: people have normal routine but under the surface there are incredible emotions and jealousies and heartbreak and ambition and hatred and anger and unrequited love and passion going on, and that's represented by the music.

Is there an influence from 'E = MC²' in 'West End Girls'?

Neil: It's the other way round. They nicked the chord change. Blue Weaver worked with Big Audio Dynamite and said they nicked the backing track from 'West End Girls', but as a sort of revenge in 'E = MC²' there's a sample from *Performance*: something like *Who d'you think you are, jack the lad?* so I took the song title.

What are your thoughts on being a writing partnership?

Neil: When I watched that songwriting programme that you referred to before I was pleased that Chris and I write together. But we don't write together in that modern songwriting way, where the song is . . .

Chris: . . . done by committee.

Neil: Yeah, what doesn't seem to come through is originality. The idea of the song is assumed in advance: 'It's a gorgeous tear-inducing ballad,' 'It's a song where I diss my boyfriend,' 'It's a song where I'm an empowered woman.' They're all sort of a cliché.

Chris: Watching that programme, Guy Chambers would put on a Sly and the Family Stone record—we would never start like that: 'My idea of an anthem is this'; put it on, then try and do it. It's against everything we . . .

What's really come across in conversation with the two of you is an integrity to your musical spirit.

Neil: But our musical spirit interests us. We like it.

It's all you've got, really.

Neil: Yeah. We can hear a lot of contemporary pop records but I don't ever think, I want to be that. It might just be an age thing. I used to think, 'I want to be The Beatles,' 'I want to be David Bowie,' 'I want to be Holland-Dozier-Holland and write all those amazing fucking songs,' 'I want to be Brian Wilson,' 'I want to be Marc Bolan.'

Isn't this to do with age and connection with music?

Neil: The problem is, is it? Because the last person we wanted to be, albeit briefly, was Eminem. We loved Eminem on the first and second album. That's why we wrote a song about him.

'The Night I Fell In Love'.

Neil: Yeah. That was taking Eminem's songwriting procedure, because he said he's not homophobic.

Chris: Then in that case you won't mind being portrayed as a gay, will you?

Neil: I'm just playing a character. The character happens to be a gay Eminem. There's a great moment when they played that to Dr Dre on MTV. He said, 'He's gonna fuckin' kill them.'

Chris: We did actually get mentioned.

Neil: He did a song called 'Can I Bitch'.

Chris: But it didn't appear on an album, which is a real shame. It would have been such a thrill to be namechecked.

Neil: He comments on me and says he raps in his normal voice. I thought, 'Well ye–es!' The English bring out the beauty of mundane. Eminem does mundane. He's one of the few American superstars to have done humour.

LEE MAVERS

The melody chord unwinds me / The rhythm of life unties me /
Brushing the hands of time away.

'Timeless Melody' belongs to an exclusive collection of works: one album and a throng of B-sides, radio sessions and live performances—it barely adds up to twenty-five songs. It is the smallest pool of writing by any artist in this book. But there is no doubt that Lee Mavers has been blessed with an unparalleled talent. His hoarded songs have an outstanding quality and appeal. The problem is that he disowns all recorded versions of them.

Mavers may well be the least known name in this collection. The key to his identity is the band, The La's, and their infectiously successful 1988 song 'There She Goes'. So why the commercial silence? Mavers continues to write, but refuses to publicly release any of his new creations. It is an extraordinary stance that has now lasted for almost twenty-five years. Managers, musicians and friends with whom Mavers has shared his new songs have privately marvelled at them.

Lee Mavers follows a narrow tradition of British songwriting renegades: artists who have mystified audiences by withdrawing from the public arena and restricting access to their exceptional catalogues. Cat Stevens ceased recording at the end of the Seventies to get closer to his transcendent beliefs. Syd Barrett discovered hallucinogenic drugs a decade earlier and never recovered. At a similar time, Peter Green was also seduced by LSD and later diagnosed with schizophrenia. His writing for Fleetwood Mac and his seductive interpretation of the blues was lost for most of the Seventies. Nick Drake, another writer at the turn of the Sixties, recorded three albums then began to suffer from depression amidst a bewildering lack of mainstream acceptance. He too withdrew from live performance and died from an overdose of anti-depressants at the age of twenty-six. The common thread amongst all these composers is the urge to turn their backs on the expectations and demands of the music industry, whether in pursuit of artistic independence or simply in reaction to the pressures it creates. The journey from a song's conception to the public's ear is an arduous and complex one, and it seems to be one that Lee Mavers no longer wishes to make.

He's alive and living in purgatory. The words of 'Son Of A Gun' suggest a troubled mind and a damning sentence passed: *He was burned by the twentieth century / Now he's doing time in the back of his mind.* Mavers stresses that his artistic role is as 'a medium' whereby melody and song pass through him. The act of songwriting is in itself a therapeutic release. 'Feelin'' declares: *Thank God for that feelin' / Oh my lord I can't take no more.* In 'Failure', on the other hand, the writer is *wrapped in chains,* while 'Looking Glass', mostly composed on the writer's twenty-fourth birthday, examines the role of fate and redemption: *Look into the past / We can't live without it / We can't live within it.* The delicacy of the arrangement rests upon a restrained vocal locked into the chords of A, F sharp minor and D, released over the bridging D major to minor and grounding A. It's one of Mavers' most ambitious songs and, at seven minutes, more than double the length of his standards. The songs of The La's are succinct and tightly structured, driven by a raw vocal honesty; powerful but tender. Harmonies weave through the lead vocal with its Liverpudlian tones. Mavers' blended percussive acoustic guitar is amplified by spacious bass lines; two-note bars are reminiscent of Paul McCartney's early style. The use of chords is very Fifties, regular, rhythmic; the three-chord trick Buddy Holly-esque. There are middle-eight switches to minor chords, and ghosts of the past drift through the writing: a touch of the Stones in 'Doledrum'; a nod to The Kinks in 'Clean Prophet': *take me, take me, take me.*

Lee Anthony Mavers was born in Huyton, Merseyside, on 2 August 1962, two months before The Beatles' debut single 'Love Me Do' was released. 'We had one music lesson at school when I was seven. We had a piece of a xylophone each and waited half an hour for our bit to come round and probably forgot. Music wasn't on the curriculum.' By the time Lee entered secondary school, Liverpool was reeling from strikes and rising unemployment. His memory of his schooling is dismissive: 'You educate yourself. Your education on the streets beats one in school.' His response is the message of 'I.O.U.': *On the street for knowledge you must eat your porridge / I'll feed you—you'll feed me.* Life on Merseyside in the early Eighties saw rioting on the streets, fuelled by central government's dismantling of the city's industry and commerce. Government papers released under the thirty-year rule reveal the Chancellor of the time, Geoffrey Howe, proposing 'managed decline' for Liverpool. Mavers' urge to escape from 'Doledrum' came from a fear of stagnation and a realization of his inherent talent. The La's' debut single 'Way Out', in October 1987, urged the writer to move on: *Give me your hammer to shatter the dream.* Similarly, 'I.O.U.' spoke of physical and mental pulls and traps, inspiring the call to *get up a fuss and shout.* The song's snare shuffle is locked to a tight acoustic that typifies Mavers' guitar playing. The rhythm is in the guitar. The approach is thoroughly Liverpudlian and also reminiscent of the skiffle style popularized in the Fifties by the Glaswegian-born Lonnie Donegan. Liverpool was at the heart of the post-war musical developments. With the merchant navy employing large numbers of local men, the north-west was quickly flooded with rare rock 'n' roll and blues singles from America. British musicians imitated the songs, often improvising rough instruments from household objects, and a new craze was born. Four decades on, the raw unadulterated sound of skiffle was at the heart of The La's' imagination.

The La's was the invention of Mike Badger. Before taking over the role of songwriter and lead vocalist for the band, Mavers joined as its bass player. The duo wrote and worked together for two years, during which time a recruit from the Liverpool Musicians' Resource Centre, John Power, became a mainstay of the line-up. In July 1987, now minus Badger, The La's were signed by Go! Discs, but the first recordings failed to capture the sound that Mavers had in mind. A succession of producers strove to satisfy the fourpiece, including John Leckie, Bob Andrews, Jeremy Allom and Mike Hedges. Three singles were released without notable impact. Finally, Steve Lillywhite was given the job by the label of compiling session material for an album with the working title *Dole Pay Me So Far La*. On its release in September 1990 as simply *The La's* it was dismissed and disowned by its songwriter.

Consequent singles releases shot The La's into the charts, with the band suddenly exposed to industry pressure. Dissolution was inevitable. The group, which had employed over thirty members, barely limped into 1992. Apart from brief live reunions in 1995 and 2005, The La's remain silent. Mavers' attempts to find kindred spirits amongst other musicians have made little impression and in some cases resulted in duplicitous behaviour: bootlegs of new songs, to the horror of their writer, have been circulated, revealing half-ideas and private developments. Mavers is cornered by the very people who love his music. He is rightly suspicious of publishers, record companies and Internet users, who have all made public unfinished songs. There is a plethora of La's product on the market, none of which has been sanctioned by its creator.

In the summer of 2011, Mavers performed a secret ten-date acoustic tour under the implausible name Lee Rude And The Velcro Underpants. He was accompanied by a local musician on bass: 'Me and Gary are a force. It's taken twenty-five years, but the record will be understood as a necessary path to now. Once that four-piece is there we will be a force that no one will be able to touch.' In a conversation the following year, Mavers described the gigs to me as the best of his life, but rued the end of the group's short-lived collaboration as a consequence of financial politics. The preceding silent years have provided ample time for myth-making amongst musicians and the music press. There is the apocryphal tale of Mavers rejecting a mixing desk because it did not have authentic Sixties dust on it, or his supposed plan to write material on an outbound cruise ship before recording the tracks inbound. Mavers has scant time for such stories.

A week after Mavers' secret acoustic dates we met at his home. Talk of songwriting was postponed until his children had been taxied to their Saturday activities. As we journeyed across Liverpool in Lee's Mini Cooper, past Penny Lane and the graveyard with Eleanor Rigby's headstone, the driver's Beatle melodies filled the car. It was an educational trip through local history past and present. Before talking about songwriting, Lee explained his world view. Amongst many other topics he referred to the Japanese scientist Dr Masaru Emoto and the science of Cymatics. He detailed his research into the molecular structure of water, explaining how it shapes and reacts to sound. 'He worked out that you can put water in a bottle and put a label on it saying "Love" facing inwards and it will react, and one saying "Hate" and it will react in a bad way. It's not even the sound, it's the intent.' Lee's enlightenment came when he

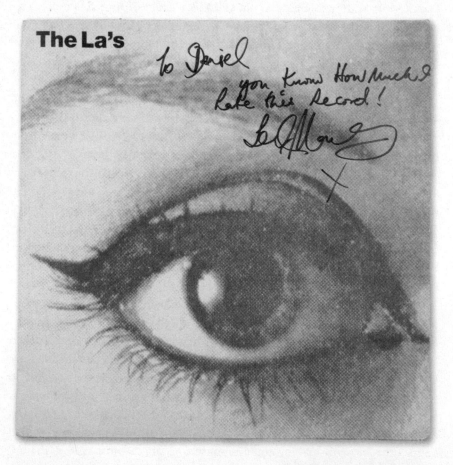

The La's album artwork by Ryan Art

realized water's dominant presence in the universe and in the human body. He talked too about John D. Rockefeller's and later Joseph Goebbels' promotion of concert pitch to the British Standards Institute: 'It's through him and them that it's become a standard today. It's too tense, it's wrong. It's anti-musical. Vibrationally, it turns music upside down.' Mavers' guitar is tuned by ear to the third harmonic, a remembrance of the whistling sound heard in the flow pipe from his childhood bath. 'Wind pitch. It's like a light within the music to me. It's the music of the spheres. It's what holds the planets up. It's that mathematical time and space thing. It's around semitone, quarter tone.'

Once back in his kitchen Lee rustled up a full English breakfast for his eldest son, dressed in trainers, jeans and a tracksuit top. Everton mugs of tea were filled and roll-ups administered. A Spanish guitar was brought in from the hall and over the afternoon Lee played snatches of songs, Hendrix riffs, Chuck Berry extracts, and used the instrument to illustrate many of his own compositions. As the afternoon light faded I asked him to play a new song.

Once he had confirmed that the batteries had been taken out of my recording device Lee sang a beautiful, soulful melody, the verse mainly changing between two chords with movement near the neck of the guitar. It had all the charm of a classic La's composition. He followed with an older song, 'Who Knows', to make the point of how 'melody will find its natural time', and in doing so evoked his vintage classic: *The melody always finds me / Whenever the thought reminds me.*

You wrote in 'Feelin'', *I get the feelin' I am responding to a call*. What was your meaning?

Dunno. I just follow the melody. I don't stand by every word I've ever written. I'm not a diary. But again, I'm not jumping away from it either. Half the time the words write themselves, just like the melodies do. You see them. Like when I came across 'There She Goes'. It's such a musical equation I wonder how any other idiot never spotted it.

The equation being what?

There's about four different melodies going on. (*On guitar plays two scales segueing into opening of song.*) It's like scales. (*Sings.*) *There she goes, there she goes again*. It's always been there, before man, all of these things that we fall upon, and not just music. People who invent things, they don't. They come across a natural—what people term as—phenomena, but it's not, it's just a natural occurrence.

Does melody come from finding notes on the guitar first?

In that case, yeah. I didn't try to sing with it; I just heard a contra melody and heard all the rest of them and just joined in with it because it's already going on. I don't invent anything. No one does, unless you work with the 'pop industry'.

It's the way you then use those combinations of notes.

No one invents melody. Everyone just sees what's there. The scales are already there, otherwise it wouldn't make any sense to people. No one invents nuttin'. It's already there. The information within the notes themselves, it's like mathematical information on a level that's deeper than language can grasp. You can fart and hear melody. Birds singing. What instrument are they using? The voice: that's the first instrument. Probably drums next: the ribcage. Two ribs on the ribcage or whatever. Language, what we're talking in now, is not music; it's just nonsense. We're lucky we've got the willingness to understand each other; these noises that are coming out of our mouths. They really wouldn't make sense to an animal or someone else from a foreign country. Whereas music does; there's the language. Music is the language. I'm not talking about what people play with guitars and stuff like that. I'm talking about melody is informational on a level that is so deep.

If music is our natural communication that has evolved from birdsong, what are you trying to communicate?

I'm just moved to it. It's like autism. It's just lovely in this day and age people are entertained by it.

Do you write melody to communicate a feeling within yourself?

No, it's communicated through me and it comes out in music. I think if it's turning me on it must be turning someone else on. I'm not trying to make a living out of it, although I have. I didn't condone that record that went out but it's bought me a house and allowed me to bring my family up and all of that. And if it hadn't I'd be scrapping around like every other chicken.

What makes you want to write a song?

I don't. I don't sit and write anything. It comes to me. It comes through me and I come out with it. You can write stuff after the fact, but it all just comes out.

When you say 'comes to you' . . . are you talking about phrases?

Phrases and things like that stick until you realize, 'Oh, there's a structure,' and blah, blah, blah. When I was about twenty-one I thought, 'What am I going to do here?' All me mates were driving cars and had a job. I'd been the soft lad; always going for a laugh and everything. But in the end I was on foot everywhere. I thought, 'Shit, this is the time you should be thinking about your future. Everyone's sorted out. Shit. I'm only good at music, really.' So one thing led to another and rather than playing the bass, which I did in other bands, I ended up coming out with it and then realizing, 'Hey, you're onto something here,' and it just grew itself. And out of that has come a living. It's not why I was doing it. It serves two purposes: you get a living out of it and you're doing what you really want to do. In the past I haven't enjoyed it because playing with bad players who reduce the music to less than the magic it is that turns me on, I don't want to do. Don't forget the record came out as a record company composition. I didn't even recognize those tunes. They've still got life because nobody recognizes them. They're completely different.

When is your music at its purest, just you, an instrument and your voice?

Music is pure; I just join in with an instrument or a voice. It's going on already. It's not manufactured.

I don't get the 'joining in' idea.

Here y'are (*la's descending scale*). I just waited and joined in with it. It's already going on, otherwise if I didn't join in with it I'd be off-beat, off-time and off-key. There is a structure to the universe.

You have a wonderful ability to form melody in unique ways. What does that make you?

A facilitator, a conduit, a medium.

A medium implies there's something . . .

. . . there first. A priest is a medium. A witch doctor is a medium. A shaman is a medium to something that is already there: the true spirit of life, which is being veiled by what I've been talking about; de-education.

Were you chosen to be a musician?

I think everyone's musical. Take the music out of football. Take the music out of any occasion or any time of life. So I can think of nuttin' more important to be doing. Yeah, you're correct. I have chosen to be a musician. And I suppose I was chosen to be a musician, if music be the word. Magic and music: there's two letters' difference. The muse is in the music, not in the magic. Amuse is opposite of *a muse*: amusement.

Why did you choose to put that medium into the traditional format of the two- or three-minute song?

I don't know. Who can say, we are creatures that move in predestined grooves. We don't really control anything.

Can you explain why your recorded output ceased pretty much twenty-five years ago? Have you written since?

I've got lots of stuff but I haven't been once bitten, and twice shy. Meaning I don't do business with crooks.

Then why not, in the old tradition of a troubadour, just go and play wherever?

What did we do on Sunday; there's your answer.

Do you not want to share your music?

I can go and sing them songs but there's a lot of harmony and juxtaposed melodies which are missing, which take the beauty away. So it becomes pretty uninteresting for me. So if I'm uninterested I don't think anyone else is going to be that interested watching some fellow who's disinterested on stage, wondering what he's doing there. Music is a shared experience, not just between a musician and an audience. I'm not like a fuckin' one-man band, although I can do a pretty good job of that. I'm part of an orchestra and I choose to be a part of teamwork. I live to be part of a team.

Do you hear musical parts when you write?

One sets off the other; you can't see that line without seeing what it's attached to. (*Illustrates with two pieces of paper.*) It's down to taste to go, 'You can leave that bit out there,' but that is the archetype of them bits. The archetype, it sets the rest up—minimal. I just like the four-piece; three instruments and voices. The first La's were me and Mick Badger. He had some ideas but it was more poetry, and I had music to back him. He was a driven force, much like myself, and together some magic came out of that. John Power was a bass player that Mick picked up on a musical job scheme. He was a good aider and abetter. When Badger walked from the band the magic died. You're as good as the team you play in. Poor players can bring the music down so it's like what you hear on the record.

How often do you write?

I don't sit and write.

When was the last time you had a completed song, a new one?

It can be decades in between. I don't care to do it. If something comes along . . . then I'll do it. I've got plenty of tunes that can rub shoulders and live with anything.

What was the last song that you wrote?

'Gimme the Blues' and 'Stop'.

When was that?

A few years back.

Would you ever sit down and try and write a song?

No, never, ever.

You've never picked up the guitar and thought, I'll write today?

Yeah, I've done that when I've been buzzin', but I don't think, 'I'll write a song today.' You've got these things going through your life, your head: your music; your heart; these rhythms; these phrases and snatches that you hear that recur until they stamp themselves in you and you find you're doing stuff without realizing it. Then you look at it afterwards and go, 'Wow, that's something,' and there's one and there's another one. It's just like seeing an equation. Have you noticed the words and the music cannot be pulled apart in their sense and attitude?

Johnny Marr talks about how over a period of time he will sense the need to write a song.

That's the same as me, but I don't sit down and write a song. I think that's manufactured. What's the word I'm looking for . . . not fabricated . . . contrived. It is already contrived when I see it.

Your songs have very strong structures that suggest you've applied the mechanics of writing at some point.

I can't write or read music. No one's ever showed me anything except, 'Why are you playing it all on one string? Have you noticed after the fifth fret it all starts again?' And I went, 'Oh . . . yeah.' Then seeing a chord on a Ramones picture: Johnny Ramone playing a barre chord, then I worked out when you go past the nut it's an open E, and I understood what a fret was, and how to minor / major. All that I just worked out myself when I was fifteen, just from being grounded and kept in from been naughty. There was a guitar in the corner of the room. I got one when I was eleven 'cause I seen Beatles films: 'I wanna guitar,' but it never got played.

How did you learn chords; did you have books?

No, I didn't know they were D and G. I've got my own way of playing things.

How did you learn other people's songs?

I remember saying, 'We've got to throw "Jumpin' Jack Flash" in,' so I listened to the tape. I've got a sense where the lowest note would be. I can look at something, listen to a few bars and go, 'There's your lowest E,' so I know what key I'm in.

What was the first song that you wrote?

'Clean Prophet': I heard Noel Character doing it. He ripped that off, didn't he? (*Hums opening Oasis part.*)

'The Importance Of Being Idle'.

The importance of being honest. I'll tell you another one. I remember waking up in the car, tripping somewhere, and on the radio: *Some might say we'll find a brighter day*—that chord change, I'm going, 'That's boss, that.' Then months later it dawned on me why it was boss. (*Plays 'Who Knows'.*) *Who knows what tomorrow knows, who knows what tomorrow knows, who knows?* (*Switches to Oasis song.*) Where else have you heard that succession of chords? Not even in classical music. And the other one is—(*plays opening chords of 'Wonderwall'*). Andy MacDonald, the record company boss, phoned me up one day; this was years ago when I was on the smack: 'Johnny Marr wants to meet you.' Within twenty minutes of the phone going down this BMW is on the path and he took me to his mansion house in Manchester. He took me down to the basement studio and puts a guitar in my hand. (*Plays chords.*) 'She Came Down' (*then plays 'Wonderwall'*)—same chord sequence, different rhythm.

Noel might argue 'I Can't Sleep' borrows in a similar way from The Who's 'I Can't Explain'. (*I play the opening chords.*)
No, that's something else. He might argue, but I'd say they're from the same stable and completely different tunes. 'I Can't Explain' is from the same stable as another Kit Lambert song. What about—(*sings The Kinks' 'You Really Got Me'*)? Another one from the same stable, and this is a better one: *I was lookin' thru my window, I was lookin' thru my eyes / There's a big black car coming get off the street outside—come in. / Go into a pipe dream no one listens anyway. / When I say I'm so sad about, I'm not so glad about / I'm so mad—I can't sleep tonight.* And his is (*sings and plays 'I Can't Explain'*). Two completely different songs.

Songwriters give new character to what is already there. We've all got the same notes, same chords. It's interpretation that takes it somewhere else.
Like the blues men, they're all doing the same thing.

When you put together your ideas, do you feel like you're in a creative moment?
No, I just see a beginning and an end: 'Oh, there's the intro'—it's already going on. 'Oh, there's an outro'—it's already going on. The piece just fashions itself.

Would you write words separately?
No, they all come at once, or they can come most and I'll just fill in the bits.

Do you fill in away from the instrument with a piece of paper?
No, I just think about it and realize it. Play it through my head.

And consider what your song wants to say?
I'm not particularly looking to say anything, but I'm glad if it does. And if it does it's not me that's the muse, but I'm fully behind the muse.

The songs have thematic similarities and narratives; is that intentional?
Such as?

It seems to me you're trying to chase away something in your mind, something that's holding or trapping you.
I don't know. I was twenty-two when I wrote those words. What a 20-year-old knows is natural, without thinking. And what a 49-year-old knows is all that and more. He knows how to do it and he knows why. When's it's natural it

might just be firing through you, like when you neck a trip or whatever and you know something's coming to you. You can allow it to guide you. But there is no substitute for experience. Experience will show you what you were doing wrong and therefore what you were doing right. You don't learn anything without making mistakes. My mistakes in the past were being too trusting of people and thinking, 'Hey, this is God-given.' Everyone is good. My knowledge now is that it's self-given. It's also what's given comes through a muse as well. You're not born with it. You're born with the ability, everyone is, but you develop it over time. If you don't develop it, it doesn't develop, so it stays as nothing. Most people don't do anything for fear of ridicule. What's ridicule coming from people you wouldn't give the time of day, because they are ridiculous?

How did you come to write 'Failure'?

I wrote that on a trip. I had the tune (*segues Bob Dylan's melody 'The Lonesome Death Of Hattie Carroll' into 'Failure'*): *William Zanzinger killed poor Hattie Carroll—No, you can't throw failure over your shoulder. If you don't look after you're going to look back. If you don't hurry forward* . . . so it's just like streaming words with a pen there, tripping. And then a year later I was just messing around (*sings 'Failure'*). Things happen just like that. Like 'Callin' All', I had the words for a year, found the music a year later. It's when you recognize the metre is the same as something. I went to bed and I had a pen and pad under my pillow, because I had some book out of the library when I was about twenty-one and it said, 'A good thing to do is . . .' so I did it. When I was drifting off to sleep I seen these clouds rolling on these hills and I thought *a cloud came swirling round the hills from high above the valley spills* and then I seen that black-and-white with the palm trees. You know the hurricanes in the Sixties, Fifties in Hawaii—this was the Eighties so you know the footage that was around. *A battered street a tattered coast a wind it gathered like a ghost*, and then *with heavy cart I worked the land for weathered heart and withered hand*. I'd seen that Constable picture in me head with that fellow, *weathered heart and withered hand, yet still the cane comes beating down on me. I've wandered along the beaten path*: that's Wordsworth. When I looked at it the next morning it was all across each other and I had to decipher it. So I had that. But I had from a trip six months before . . . loads came out of that one stream: *There was once a boy of life who lived upon a knife . . . love is all the world will fall . . . I'm not scared to die, God help me . . . To swim the endless sea of tragedy*: that's how it opens, so from a ream of stuff. So when I got so far I'd go, let's have a look: Bang! Metre perfect. Bang! It's written itself, hasn't it?

Were you writing thinking of song, or just enjoying the words?

Don't forget, what am I good at? It's that age, better throw myself into music, and I started writing stuff. I was thinking about things and seeing models and archetypes. Much the way everybody does: 'I want one of them, I want one of them.' But pretty early on going, 'What you've got here is one on its own.' Just let it go, let it come out as it comes out. It doesn't matter what styles you're borrowing from. As you say, your blues etc. We've got the same blocks and put them together our way, like everyone does.

Can I ask you about 'I Am The Key' and its repeated pattern?

I only got so far with it. I thought, I can't really say any more with that one so it's finished. You know, 'Something I Said' and 'Tears In The Rain' and all the stuff that's been put out was actually sitting round the table showing the lads: very slow and very stoned, half the speed of what them songs are, and the record company have slyly snuck them out so they get the publishing. They're not finished. They're not even a quarter finished.

Why did you not play new songs the other night?

I won't touch the new songs until they're out. You can't fart on stage without watching it straight away on the web. The world's full of grasses with camera phones.

Do you rewrite songs or borrow from yourself? I've heard two versions of 'Tears In The Rain', both with different words.

No, usually it comes. I'll get as far as I do and when I wanna get round to finishing a song, I do. Like 'There She Goes'; I had the verses, then I had to sit down and write the middle eight. All the new stuff you haven't heard, it's mostly unfinished. There's about five tunes that are finished. What is on the tapes and bootlegs, whatever form, they're a million miles away from the true form, and that album is. You realize why they had to stop it? Because no one could have competed with it.

How do you feel when you hear 'There She Goes'? It's played so often.

I hated it at first. It was embarrassing. But I've lived through all that. I don't mind. Sometimes it does surprise me because it sounds better, but then there's that many different mixes out there. For instance, 'Way Out', we were told we were doing demos. Next thing it was brought out as a single. It's poor, very slow and sloppy. There's no animation.

Like many, I love the La's album but it's a great sadness to understand that the creator was appalled by the way he had been represented.

Well put. I couldn't put it more succinctly and true myself. I was appalled by the way it was represented, so I just went to ground. That record that was stuck out by Go! Discs, it's terrible. It's awful, but I'm not hurt in the slightest. My pride's all intact. Everyone's got to have pride, but not at other people's expense. But there was nothing but shame. It was embarrassing. They didn't understand it, and then looking at me like I'm some sort of crank and paying homage to this Syd Barrett, Shaun Ryder I'm binned in with. All the Sixties dust crap. It's a load of bollocks. Cornish pasties to get a bass drum sound. Just like all the Syd Barrett shit. Great, I'm a crank. Thanks for giving me that card: I'll play it every time. Everything's brilliant. I couldn't have invented it.

Is your mind as free writing when you're straight from drugs?

I'm a father now. I haven't done any of that for decades. I'm not walking around thinking I'm some kind of writer. I'm just a fellow that's got four kids and just living and observing as anyone could anyway and it forms itself into droplets . . . makes songs . . . sometimes.

Do you understand the meaning of all the words you've written?

Not really, no. Some I could tell you totally what I mean; others I think, 'What the hell was I meaning there?' It's written itself. I don't think it's gobble-degook. I think it's powerful stuff.

If only the word could see me I'd promise I'd send the word away.

I was just trying to up the melody, just getting something in there to get to the chorus. Nuttin' really. It sounds vain. I hate that line.

We went to the same schools and all learned the same rules of lament.

What else could I mean than what I said? We all know the score together. I don't know; it just formed itself, poetry.

Can I ask for a theory from you as to why there are so few successful female songwriters in this country?

I can't think of anyone really. There is from America. Yet nobody leaps out, certainly no one in the last twenty or thirty years; men or women. When was the last reactionary movement in music? It's all controlled. It's like Blue Peter look after it. Anyone who's got any sense or self-respect, any sensibility, would stay away from it. This is the real stuff. It's not an act like they are an act. Every now and again you get something that is real, like when The Ramones first came out.

Are you proud of any songs that you've recorded?

All the songs I love. All the records, no. But there is 'Over' on the back of one of the singles, which is just a tape recording of the band playing it. It moves right and sounds like The La's. Not even 'There She Goes' (*sings and claps to demonstrate how it should be*). It's not like that on the record. 'Son Of A Gun' on *Lost La's* came near, but not that version.

What's let you down? Is it the players or the microphones capturing what you're doing?

Everything at once: me being so addled in the head with all the drugs and not really knowing, really believing that I was with good people who wanted the right thing. I was only playing the guitar, singing and writing the songs. Not the bass and the guitar and the drums; in the end I had to. That's what I did. When I come off the gear I got my desk and learned how to play everything and just went like that: bang, bang, bang. I can prove what you were fuckin' doing wrong. So I know what I'm doing. I didn't have the knowledge and background to know all of that back then. If I did I'd have just fuckin' chased 'em. I wouldn't have entertained them in the same place. But you think people are going to grow together.

Could you make a La's album playing everything yourself?

Yeah. It's a big effort. Music is a shared experience. If that's the way it be then that's the way it be. I'm quite happy, come what may. If it's not going to happen it's not going to happen. I don't want to be a star anyway.

Are you frustrated people just don't hear your songs? There's talk of a couple of gems: 'The Human Race', 'Raindance'.

No, not really. I haven't played them to the record company. If I had they'd be out. Even if I'd just played it like I am here, to you. Paranoid and suspicious: fuckin' right to be . . . with experience. I don't show anything until it's right. I do not trust people. You know what paranoid means, by the way? Someone who has the ability to connect seemingly unconnected events. Just capable of joining the dots, that's all. So yeah, I am. I've joined them all.

I understand that, but where does that leave you as the origin of this creativity?

In control.

Yes, but it's trapped in you?

No. Not all.

Do you not have a desire to share what you've got?

Yeah, and I have a great patience that it will happen in the correct way. I'm not interested in doing it in the wrong way. Is that driven enough for you? As will be proven; everything that has ever happened in my life has been correct.

I'm astounded by your patience.

You've got no choice in the matter. I've got no choice in the matter. You're only as good as the team you're in. I'm only interested in sharing this experience with people who can share it. And now I've found someone to make it really work and three and four have got to step into that without stopping that working. If they can't enhance it then do not make it worse in any way.

How often do you get into the studio?

I was in there yesterday. I've sort of swerved it for the last three years because there was no one to play with. I was bored with it. I was waiting for the right time.

Does music motivate you on a day-to-day level?

It used to a lot more. I don't know if that's age or just the fact that music is shit. All the good stuff is all before the mid-Seventies. I've heard it all. I can hear it playing in my head anytime I want.

What was the first record you bought?

'Wig-Wam Bam' by The Sweet when I was nine, just for the intro. It was boss.

What was the first band you got into?

The Stranglers.

And instrument?

I got my dad to buy me one for my birthday. His mate had moved into a house and found a Fender Precision in the loft. I got it for sixty quid. It was from 1962. My first guitar was £50; a Gretsch Anniversary 1958. I was into punk. I really loved The Ramones; first two albums. Too many Union Jacks in the Pistols and The Clash. You can tell when something is establishment while pretending to be anti-establishment, and when something is real. The ones that are real always get the rough ride.

Which British songwriters do you like? Lennon and McCartney?

Theodor Adorno was reported to have written 'Yesterday'. *Revolver*'s good. *Rubber Soul* is awful. Some of them key changes are sick. I do like the silver-suited Beatles, 'Twist And Shout' and 'I Wanna Hold Your Hand'; style which you wouldn't have had without Roy Orbison, who I absolutely adore. His voice is beautiful. Bob Dylan, too. I appreciate Buddy Holly without loving it to bits. I had Bo Diddley's first album; the rest was garbage.

Can you remember writing 'Looking Glass'?

I'd written the chorus at Christmas in my bedroom. I'd come out of hospi-tal because I had a cyst on my arse. I had one of them polo mint things you've got to sit on, sponge. I had a couple of mics when I was starting to write and I came out with *I've seen everybody* and *so the story goes*. Six months later it was my birthday, me and my mate Cammy and Black Pyramid trips. We just went off onto our own things in this room and all these words flew at me, the verses: *tell me where I'm going . . . tell me where I'm bound?* About three months later I knocked them together. The verses were in G when I put them to music and the chorus was in A, but it didn't lose anything to put it all up to A. There's no single format. I suppose what you're looking for is a recipe. There is no recipe. You're born knowing what things should taste like or you haven't got a clue and have to eat what you're served. (*Sings 'Looking Glass'.*) *Tell me where I'm going, tell me where I'm bound?/ Turn the pages over, turn the world around. / Open up the broken door for all lost will be found, / Walk into the empty room but never make a sound. / Oh tell me where I'm going, tell me why I'm bound / To tear the pages open, turn the world around . . .*

That sounds brilliant.

I was rushing that: *The past it never says it, it never makes a sound. / Whispered ways were chosen, echoes will be found.* That's the time we're in now.

Were you trying to escape lyrically? Did you have a sad upbringing?

Not all. It was more to do with prospects of being on the dole and no life. It was *get on the bus*, get out of this and working for the state.

What did you do at sixteen after school?

I was on the dole while working, played in different bands from eighteen, arsing around until twenty-one when it hit me hard.

Did Thatcherism hit you hard?

Being of working class and not being a worker, no. It allowed me to work when I wanted. No boundaries to cut across diagonally or as the crow flies; anywhere I wanted unbothered by anyone, because everyone was fuckin' on their arse. For an artist it was a very fertile time. Depends what your art is, though. Basically I was a dole-ite bouncing around, getting wrecked, having the time of my life, banging birds and playing my music, coming out with my ideas. Feeling I was on a mission, gifted and driven. Then we got signed up after a year.

'Doledrum' addressed the situation?

We were on an InterRailing holiday in 1983. Six weeks: pair of jeans, T-shirt and a haversack, passport, sleeping bag and dole in your pocket, kipping on the trains and the beaches. Spain, Italy. We bumped into these Mancs and one of them said, 'What's wrong with him?' 'Oh, he's in the doldrums.' I said, 'What's that?' He was pissed off. 'It means when a ship's at sea and there's no wind and it can't go anywhere.' So I just logged it in my head. So when I was coming out with this tune, 'Don't Go Down to London,' I'd just been down to London to work on Cannon Row police station painting massive sash windows. It was like painting the Queen's wedding coach. Three days to do four windows. Me mate messed up and this fellow threw us off-site. So were starving in London, two weeks in a heatwave, walking the streets, waiting for the dole to be switched on for the B&B. This was when I realized, 'What d'you wanna do?' I did a lot of thinking. I started to write then. My mate was going on about poetry, fancied himself as an artist, into Jim Morrison. I looked out of the window. There was a little gap and all I could see was sky and this seagull. *Oh seagull watching weather, you're so clever I can see. Oh seagull, you forever will endeavour to be free.* Get that, you can write! I thought yeah, you're good at words. So I started to write my own songs. I was a bass player then, so as I'm writing them I'm starting to learn the guitar. I knew the odd G and barre chord. You put your hands on things and go, 'Wow,' and things form themselves. I'm totally self-taught but informed by good music. Good enough to have the taste to know what's what.

When are you happiest making music?

Not very often. When I see an equation, play a tune and go, 'Wow, wow,' and then have me dreams for a bit. They all wake up again. Go and put it down on tape and after a while you get fed up playing by yourself. It's like being Pelé and there isn't a team to play football with. I was resigned to a fate . . . it was just a waste. If this is what the creator wants, then so be it. What can I say? I've got used to that. Life's being very full and enjoyable anyway. Sure enough it always comes knocking back though, but after six months you realize you've got nowhere people and the guitar goes back in the box.

DAMON ALBARN

A London television studio. Channel 4's *The White Room*, 13 March 1995. Two songwriters are seated. Ray Davies, now in his fourth decade of writing, the benchmark of musical character narrative, and beside him Damon Albarn of Blur, twenty-seven years old. The duo perform The Kinks' classic 'Waterloo Sunset' and then an impromptu round of Blur's *ohrwurm* 'Parklife'. It was a moment that brought together two very different musicians both of whose work draws on a long songwriting tradition and is defiantly British in identity. By 1997, Albarn would have reinvented Blur and he would go on to greet the new millennium with the experimentalism of Gorillaz. A decade on, after a number of further musical experiments, Albarn is a liberated artistic force driven to explore music regardless of expectation or convention, and evidenced in his debut solo album 'Everyday Robots', released in spring 2014.

The songwriter's ambition owes much to his musical upbringing. Home life in the Albarn family was bohemian: theatrical, musical, relaxed. His mother was a set designer for Joan Littlewood's Stratford East theatre company. His father ran an art gallery and managed Soft Machine. Ten years after Damon's birth on 23 March 1968, in Whitechapel Hospital, Leytonstone, the family moved to Colchester, Essex. Armed with huge self-confidence, Damon explored at Stanway Comprehensive School his twin affections for music and theatre. He had an early love affair with the writings of Kurt Weill and Bertolt Brecht (as a student he performed with the Berliner Ensemble) and was further influenced by Eric Satie and Vaughan Williams. One of his early compositions won a heat in the nationwide Young Composer of the Year competition. At school, he showed theatrical aspirations and regularly starred in musicals and rock operas, though equally happy performing or backstage. At sixteen he chose East 15 drama school to further his ambitions. This rejection of music for a dramatic career lasted a year. A series of forays into solo, duo and band scenarios was less than successful but resulted in a deal to use studio downtime. It provided the catalyst for Blur's formation. Having enrolled on a part-time music course at Goldsmiths College in south London, and whilst holding down a job at Le Croissant at Euston Station, Damon by night developed and honed his writing skills. As musicians came and went, a nucleus formed around his old school friend and guitarist Graham Coxon, bassist Alex James and drummer Dave Rowntree. Within a year of the band's first rehearsal, their debut single 'She's So High' entered the top fifty and made *NME* Single of the Week in October 1990.

It was a false dawn, and the reaction when the band toured the United States in 1992 was one of indifference. Blur's chief songwriter found solace in alcohol, homesick for English ritual and simplicity. His new songs reacted against the Americanization of British culture, with social comment bolstered by the band's bright pop delivery and traditional arrangements. Albarn's awakening played out in Blur's second album, *Modern Life Is Rubbish*. It contained a defiant songwriting stance against record-company economics and current taste. Sub-pop grunge in the wake of Nirvana's 'Smells Like Teen Spirit' was dictating the direction of guitar music and leaving British-sounding groups marginalized. Yet a month after Kurt Cobain committed suicide, a new Albarn song emerged that effectively redefined the musical landscape.

'Girls and Boys' was built around a four-chord turnaround bridging the worlds of alternative and mainstream pop. The crossover appeal lay not only in Albarn's lyrical tongue-twister *Girls who are boys who like boys to be girls who do boys like they're girls who do girls like they're boys* but in the music's unrestrained fusion of guitars locked to a 120-beats-per-minute dance rhythm. There followed a Pet Shop Boys remix solidifying the union of Eighties electronica and Nineties six-stringed accessibility. The lineage of 'Girls and Boys' can be traced back through the Eighties bass rhythms of Duran Duran and the melody of David Bowie's 'It's No Game' to the Seventies wordplay of Roxy Music's 'Editions Of You': *and boys will be boys will be boys*. A distant echo from the past was the verbal dexterity of George Formby: *if women like them like men like those, why don't women like me?* Blur's impressive trilogy of albums between 1993 and 1995 clearly benefited from the environment created by earlier English songwriters: Madness, The Specials, XTC, Syd Barrett, Steve Marriott and Ronnie Lane. The records were a celebratory mix of impressions from childhood, Sixties sensibility and music hall joviality. Traces of the Small Faces hummed through 'Sunday Sunday' as Blur conjured up weekend inertia and a war veteran's nostalgia: *the England he knew is no more*. Notably, the singles' B-sides revived old-time standards: 'Let's All Go Down The Strand' and 'Daisy Bell'. But Damon Albarn was more than a mere imitator. His modernism came from the connection with a common root of songwriting inspiration: the response to immediate surroundings. In 2011, looking out of his studio window he saw British wartime planes fly past en route to mark William and Kate's royal wedding. Moments later the aircraft were pictures on his television screen, inspiring the opening lyrics for 'The Marvelous Dream': *Hurricane spitting tornado / Growl over London today / Brought some God fire to the stay*. Replete with recorders and flutes, the Elizabethan atmosphere plays cunningly with vocal time variations and a homage to songwriting four hundred years old.

Attention to suburban detail characterizes a rich vein of British lyricism and, combined with tight structures and melodic richness, it complements Albarn's concise storytelling. In 'Parklife' the *habitual voyeur* oversees the rituals of *so many people* as they all go *hand in hand through their parklife* routines. The verses were voiced by Phil Daniels in a deft move to appease the actor when Albarn failed to deliver lyrics for Daniels' intended contribution to 'The Debt Collector'. Both songs appeared on the quadruple platinum album *Parklife*, which went on to spend over ninety weeks in the British charts. Nevertheless, Albarn was in emotional free fall, pensively revealing *Blow, blow me out / I am so sad, I don't know why*. 'Country House' was one of the decade's most memorable songs. Its verses vaulted lyrically through a series of internal rhymes: *Balzac* with *Prozac, morning glory* with *Jackanory*. Appearing in August 1995, it coincided with the release of 'Some Might Say' by the nation's other much-loved group, Oasis. The public and the media feverishly projected a head-to-head rivalry onto the bands while fiercely championing their favourites. It was north versus south, working class versus middle class, philistine versus art. The debate gripped the country and the two acts became national news. The hysteria was nonsense, but nonetheless significant. Not since the Sex Pistols' damnation after the Bill Grundy affair had British guitar music been such public property. Blur celebrated their first number one single and an Ivor Novello Songwriting Award shared with Noel Gallagher. Almost twenty years later the two lead singers shared a stage at the Royal Albert Hall to sing Albarn's 'Tender' to a jubilant, if not shocked, audience. With Paul Weller on drums, the occasion firmly laid to rest the petty differences of the Nineties.

'Country House' appeared on the presciently named *The Great Escape*, which, although it matched the success of previous albums, also unmasked a writer suffering from panic attacks. Despite the upbeat melodies, these were not happy songs. Dysfunctional misfit characters, viewed without sympathy and often with open hostility, led the listener to question the writer's lack of warmth. Albarn's lyrics obsessed over the sexual activity of others in seaside-postcard style. The chorus of 'Stereotypes' was typical: *Wife swapping is the future*. The phrase had revolved around the writer's mind months before the track was completed. Albarn articulated his songwriting dilemma to the music press: 'I've got to divorce myself from writing songs that have that semi-detached quality and go for shopping centres . . . reach that Britannia Book Club level. Y'know, take your trousers down at the Brits and then come back with an album that competes with Garth Brooks but is intelligent.'

Lyric writing does not come easily to Albarn. From his first recordings he has resisted the task. Talking to *NME* in 1991, he remarked, 'I don't like using more than ten words in a song.' Reflecting back to *Q* magazine a decade later he confessed: 'I was an appalling lyricist: lazy, conceited, and woolly.' During the rehearsals for 2011's opera *Dr Dee*, director Rufus Norris was caught between frustration and fascination as he observed Albarn's technique of making sounds to suggest the possibility of words. The director's own contributions were rejected as lyrics finally emerged at the eleventh hour. As Albarn matured, emotional disclosure infiltrated his writing, often born from periods of inner turmoil. In 2003, 'Out Of Time' was delivered with a beguiling sensitivity: *you've been so busy lately that you haven't found the time.* Albarn's notebook for the song displays an ad hoc jumble of handwritten phrases and doodles. The page captures the creativity of random thoughts and associations written without reserve. (At a later stage Albarn then types up his ideas into a logical format over several drafts.) 'No Distance Left To Run' was an admission of a failed relationship, handled beautifully in voice and words. Captured for the accompanying video whilst awaking from sleep, the writer proffered its meaning: 'It's a warning . . . and a gentle reminder.' Pervasive melancholia, in Albarn's twenties masked by youthful exuberance, has increasingly revealed itself in his thirties and forties. The simple strains of his voice accompanied by an acoustic guitar invite listeners to appreciate his natural, pensive tone. 'On Melancholy Hill' has a simple arrangement and great honesty. Stephen Street, producer of five Blur albums, believes 1997's number one 'Beetlebum' was 'the moment Damon defined his voice'. More significantly, the songwriter had turned his back on purely commercial directions in favour of greater artistic sincerity.

Gorillaz is a collaborative partnership with animator Jamie Hewlett. The project was born from a one-page draft manifesto that set out to dissociate music from the cult of celebrity. It was the birth of virtual pop. Gorillaz' live debut in March 2001 was performed behind a screen of graphic projections soundtracked by a mixed palette of genres. Hip hop, rap, sampled loops: all helped to define the radical musical departure. *It's a sweet sensation over the dub* are the first words sung on the band's eponymous debut album. Albarn was escaping his perceived creative mould. Arrangements and song structures were freed of limitations. The top-five hit 'Clint Eastwood' grooves lazily between two bass notes and a drum loop. Its instrumentation is sparse apart from occasional effects or accented beats and a plaintive melodica reminiscent of film Westerns. Albarn sings one repeated chorus, with a rap taking the place of a traditional verse and ambiguity of meaning surrendering to the overall sense of the idea.

Gorillaz' four studio albums show a songwriter at ease with experimentation. *Demon Days*, released in 2005, is the pinnacle of Albarn's creative ability. A variety of keyboards, drum machines and rhythms are integrated into a range of pop music references: rock, reggae, orchestral strings, gospel and guest contributions. Prior to its release Albarn financed a double-page advert in the *NME* headlined NO WAR ON IRAQ. The record expressed his opposition to invasion: 'I really wanted to create a piece that was a provocative reflection on the world I see out there. How bleak it is.' In the mid-Nineties Albarn had been pursued by the then Leader of the Opposition, Tony Blair (as were Noel Gallagher and Jarvis Cocker). An invitation was extended to exchange views at his Westminster office. But by the time of New Labour's euphoric landslide victory in the 1997 general election, pop-Britannia allegiance had slid off Blair's political radar. Now, his foreign policy was governed by 9/11. The new world order divided the nation. Over one million citizens, including Albarn, marched through London opposing British troop deployment against Saddam Hussein. Albarn's song titles indicated precisely his lyrical focus: 'Last Living Souls', 'Kids With Guns', 'Every Planet We Reach Is Dead', 'All Alone'. Addressing the global view, 'Hong Kong' questioned: Is the rise of an Eastern sun gonna be good for everyone? Across *Demon Days*, Albarn's personal terrors battled with a conscious political agenda: *So hard for a good soul to survive / You can't even trust the air you breathe.* Five years later, *Plastic Beach* picked up the environmental baton. The abundance of world recording artists responding lyrically to the writer's inviting concept was remarkable: Snoop Dogg, Mos Def, De La Soul, Mark E. Smith, and Lou Reed.

In his mid-forties, Albarn's drive to be immersed in and challenged by music making has never been stronger. In various guises his songs have sold in the millions. The first three Gorillaz releases have achieved over sixteen million sales alone. Albarn thrives on the unknown. He holds the challenge of discovering new musical possibilities in greater esteem than what he regards as the often imperfect final products. In 2007, a one-off project, *The Good, The Bad And The Queen*, brought together the rhythmic combination of Clash bass player Paul Simonon and Nigerian Afro-beat drummer Tony Allen. The ensuing release was one of Albarn's greatest works: London's gothic, supernatural quality captured by a musical soundtrack evocative of the prose of the city's biographer, Peter Ackroyd.

I met Damon in mid-production as he was composing songs about the life of Dr John Dee, the mathematician, polymath and advisor to Elizabeth I, for the Manchester Festival and Cultural Olympiad at the English National Opera. Four years previously his score *Monkey: Journey To The West* had provided the soundtrack to a Chinese modern opera. Damon is an artist pushing increasingly the possibilities of his songwriting. There have been soundtrack collaborations with classical composers Michael Nyman and Einar Örn Benediktsson and an award-winning album co-written and produced for Bobby Womack. Africa Express, in 2006, encouraged cross-cultural fertilization between African and Western music in the wake of Live 8. Six years later a customized train travelled around the UK with eighty Western and African musicians aboard conducting workshops and impromptu performances. *Mali Music* was recorded in aid of Oxfam. A choral piece was performed on a Greenpeace boat on the River Thames as a protest against the government's plans to replace Trident nuclear missiles. In 2003, the *Beagle 2* spacecraft, bound for the surface of Mars, carried a sequence of nine notes composed by Blur. The ill-fated mission coincided with the demise of the band, yet as Damon points out, a reformed group and tour in 2009 culminated in a huge display of audience affection at the summer's Glastonbury Festival.

Outside the French windows on the top floor of Damon's west London studio, the sun shone and commuters rattled past on the city overground. Whilst we talked he sipped from a pint glass of nettle tea. Sporting a ragged beard and a worn leather jacket, Damon presents a hobo image. His speaking voice reveals teen years spent in Colchester and his subsequent return to hometown London. We sat opposite one another with records spanning his career as far back as his debut single spread on the floor between us. Amused to note some missing releases, Damon pondered and searched for his trains of thought. In one telling exchange, he explained his reluctance to share some elements of his creative ability. Like many writers, he fears that the natural process may be damaged by being articulated.

You're currently working on the opera *Dr Dee*?

It's a really interesting thing we're doing. It gives me an excuse to write the most English music I've ever written. It's going right back to *Modern Life Is Rubbish* but taking it a lot further.

In 1991 you said, 'The trick of pop music is to rip off as many people as possible, but choose the right people.'

(*Laughs.*) Rip off! When did I say that? . . .'91 . . . well I was full of fucking . . . rip off . . . rip off . . . my command of the English language has slightly improved over the years. I'm not quite as flippant about stuff. Rip off . . . did I really say that? In my day there was no formal education for songwriting. Now there's all these academies. The people that come out of them are very adept. They've got a bit of understanding of how the business works. They must have some sort of psychological training, because they seem a lot less likely to do rash things. I'm in two minds about the whole pop music as a career. How can you define creativity? You can define success. Creativity is a series of mistakes. It's not about success. Success can come out of creativity, but there will never be success in creativity . . . guaranteed. You can guarantee success, but you can't call it creative all the time. I don't know whether we have better pop music now or worse. What do you think?

I think you're always tied to what you connected with as a child.

Yes, but now there's no cause and effect. Taking for example Adele: it's an organization. It's a fantastic young singer in the middle and well-managed creative behind. I suppose it's always been the same. It's more transparent now because of all these light entertainment processes we're subjected to showing us exactly how you take somebody off the street and turn them into a pop star.

Do you await inspiration or is writing a compulsion; do you write daily?

I work from ten to five, five days a week.

Have you always?

Since I got my first studio. This is my second studio. I had a much smaller one over the other side of Ladbroke Grove. I always write every day anyway, but with four-tracks and stuff . . . now I have a huge great four-track . . . a four-storey-track.

Is the intention to always create something within those hours?

Oh yeah, that's what I do. I don't have a set routine. With *Dr Dee* it's been . . . you set yourself certain parameters. I started off just becoming comfortable in traditional modes, especially *Mixolydian*. Medieval music was built on modes, so I've been listening to that music for the last year. Just getting to the point where I can be instinctive about it. I can write music, but it's very slow. I like to be able to listen because I've grown up in that culture of always recording everything I do on a four-track or a tape recorder or a seventy-two-track and listening, and then I get my perspective. I've been writing the whole piece on my own for the first three or four months. Just recording everything and making the sounds through strange means and medieval instruments, trying to get the tonality and understand what's going on. So the process this year has been different from the year preceding which was starting with drum machines and Gorillaz-type stuff, which is different from *The Good, The Bad And The Queen*, or Blur which is very simple song ideas on guitars and then you work with a band. Some things start very hermetic in the sense I keep it all very internal, how I see the bigger picture. Sometimes I'll just record four bars and then that's it and I'll move on knowing that it will develop into something much bigger. It's just a reference. Some days I'm just sketching. Sometimes I'm being a bit more detailed. Towards the end of each process it gets really specific. *Rocket Juice & The Moon* started with just Flea (*Red Hot Chili Peppers*), Tony Allen and myself sitting in a room: one synth, drums and bass doing a whole album of live grooves and then building it up from there. Later Erykah Badu came in and laid down some vocals. *Mali Music* was a totally different process: travelling around Mali with a tape recorder recording everything in a particular period of time and then going back and using Pro Tools; chop it all up and make music out of it. I'm doing another record like that after John Dee in the Congo. I'm taking young producers out to Kinshasa and then up to Goma where the civil war is. Similar sort of process: everyone goes there with laptops and tape recorders and we meet at the end of each day and do a sort of sound clash. Try and make an album in eight days. Within all of those disparate processes the common thread is turning up and just getting on with it. I see myself in terms of a farmer. I get up in the morning and I do my work. Sometimes it's putting seeds in. Sometimes it's husbandry. Sometimes it's praying for good weather. Anything that becomes your life is affected by seasonal and emotional circumstance. For example, I've got a studio on the second floor that looks out there, that I've done a lot of writing over the years in. I've got those trees there and the chapel. In the winter my outlook is different from the summer. That's the nice thing about doing it every day. There's such an inbuilt variety in the calendar. You no longer see it like, 'Oh, I'm going to work, where's my inspiration coming from?' because it's there every day. You don't have to search too far.

Do you carry a notebook?

I always start a notebook for everything and I'm very intense with my ideas for the first couple of months and then . . . I've never finished a notebook. There's always about a third of it left which is just virgin and never filled. Maybe one day I'll go back through my books and give them all an epilogue.

With 'Chemical World' and 'For Tomorrow' the record company asked you to come up with a single. Do you have the ability to create something that has a capacity to be popular?

Yes . . . well, that's not possible. You can definitely set course for something that's maybe simpler and easier for people to identify with immediately.

How do you develop vocal melody?

If it's on a guitar I fiddle around until I've got something I'm enjoying playing and I just let it happen. Melody can come from anything . . . one comes to my head and I put it on my phone. Because I've done it with such regularity for so long, it is like second nature writing melody. It's the thing I find most natural. It's the other stuff that's hard.

Are your melodies always suited to your vocal range ability as they develop?

Yeah, because I'm singing it. It's always in the right key; that's the hardest thing writing for other people's voices in *Dr Dee*. I've got twelve other voices to write for and because all my melody tends to come from an emotional response to whatever it is I'm playing, it is trial and error. I keep doing this stuff and then get the person in, because we've got rehearsals down the road. And then it's not quite right or they can't articulate it the way I do, so it doesn't sound right to me. At the moment I just do it every day, so some days are good and some days are not so good.

Do melodies vary depending on which instrument you're writing with?

Yeah, I started off on the piano because that's what I grew up playing. In the early days of Blur it was too rich harmonically and didn't have the feeling that a bunch of young lads playing together needed. So I taught myself very, very basic guitar and I haven't got any better in twenty years. I've kept it at that very naïve stage, purposely simple. My piano playing has definitely developed. I do write on the piano but it's a very different feeling that comes out. It's generally more sentimental on the piano than the guitar.

Do you have favourite keys that you gravitate towards?

(Fast Show *accent*.) I've been mostly playing in the key of D for the last six months. John Dee: D. It's also the most popular key of the Renaissance; also, funnily enough, in Africa, and as I've got some African musicians it's really good because modally their instruments like the kora is happiest in D. D is a very universal key. But I've written in most keys really. D, C, around that area. A lot of minor as well.

You distinctively mix a lot of out-of-key chords within songs.

The longer you spend in that world, the further you can move around. I'd like to think I know the relationship between most chords and the intervals and what happens. It's just familiarity with your work.

Does familiarity breed limitation, touching on why you limit your guitar-playing capacity?

No, because as soon as I hear myself doing anything I've done before I just do something else. I go the other way or I just go below or above. I can't bear repeating myself. I've always felt . . . it's about where you end up and the great thing is the process from that first point to that end point. Everything you're doing in between is in some way an experiment that wasn't quite right. I never feel I've done anything that is completely perfect. As soon as I've finished something I think, that's shit, right, I better start again.

You once said, 'You have to go into the wilderness to get really good ideas.'

What, literally! . . . I get my backpack and my ration of biscuits and chocolate and head out to Willesden. I refuse to be categorized. As you've probably gathered, my mind goes all over the place. I get into the world that I'm in at the time very deeply. The wilderness, figuratively, is I go into places I'm unfamiliar with. Yeah, definitely. You get totally absorbed in something and then you really think you're there and then something hits you in the face and you realize you haven't . . . you've only just scratched the most minute part of the surface. That's why I'm very happy that this is my job, this is my life. It's impossible to own it. It's so fluid and mysterious to me still.

When you write words, how far will you go before you edit your initial stream?

I always allow a first thing to come out. Sometimes it has a few great words in it and then a load of rubbish. The words come at the same time as the melody, always.

Are you recording that?

Yeah. I get a few lines that the metre is just perfect. It's just the luck of the draw if something makes sense that comes out of my mouth. If I left everything on my first draft a lot of it would sound like I'm speaking in tongues. I like that. That's why I very rarely listen to English-language music, because I find immersion prohibitive if I understand it too well. It needs to be somehow alien, then I can just let myself go. Maybe that's just a hang-up I have. It's not that I don't like great lyrics and poetry. I aspire to that all the time. I find that a lot harder than making music, a lot harder. I'm getting to the point now with *Dr Dee* where I've got to really nail the words. Everyone's starting to go, 'Well, come on, what's this actually about?' There's a lot of *urhghghgh* at the moment.

Is 'Rockit' a good example of that?

'Rockit': *blah, blah, blah, blah, blah*. That's just a first take, done, finished, no thought. That's just, 'Right, I've got to do this and just do it straight.' (*Animated.*) I like it. I just made it up as I went along. It kind of works . . . sometimes it does. Like 'Green Fields' I actually wrote for Marianne Faithfull. It was in a little basement studio on the Goldhawk Road. I was with Alex James and her. It was very late at night. I literally sat down at the piano and wrote the whole song perfectly, just off. If that happened every time there'd be twice as many records as this.

Similarly with 'Song 2' I understand the words just came out, but you tried to rewrite them.

My version of 'Song 2' was about a third slower and Graham sped that up. It's definitely better the way it ended. Although to be honest we had to do a few B-sides: 'Oh, here's one I've got' . . . you know. The words were what I sang, but what I sing you can sort of make out what I'm saying and then I try and articulate it. That's how I work. I do something really quickly and then I have to go and listen to it and go, 'Was I really saying that?' On *Demon Days*, bless him, Brian: Danger Mouse, he wanted to keep the metre of what I'd babbled. He actually sat down and painstakingly made sense of everything that I'd written, which was an act of love, I think. It'd be perfect for me to have someone who was constantly around who had a poetic sensibility but could work out my speaking in tongues stuff. It'd be a great partnership: it'd be my Tim Rice, but it just wouldn't be like that.

I tend to go with the sound of the words. It's important to have some kind of direction. All of these records definitely have a mood to them, some very specifically like *The Good, The Bad And The Queen* and *13*, that's a very specific record, and *Modern Life Is Rubbish*. This is the record where I really changed. This is where the gobbledegook started (*picks up* The Great Escape *CD*), after this the gobbledegook really kicked in. Up until here, all these three (*picks up* Modern Life *and* Parklife *CDs*), they're all very thought-out, third-person narrative stuff. We'd made this under extreme pressure. Suddenly something quite enormous had happened to us and to British music at the time. We'd gone from being an indie band into being a stadium band almost in six months. We were doing this when the Brits were happening and all that tabloid stuff. We were enjoying it. It was a lot of hangovers. I got a little too over-analytical about what I was doing. After that there was a real change and then it started to get a lot more abstract. It came back to focus again with this record (*The Good, The Bad and The Queen*); that had a real . . .

It's quite a big gap . . .

Yeah, there's a lot of stuff in between.

Had you lost the ability to focus?

No, I just wanted to do other stuff. I wasn't interested in doing songs about *he* and *she* and *us*, just seeing what else . . . being much more oblique, in a way.

I'm interested by your relationship with Ray Davies's music. At the time you described 'One Born Every Minute' as 'The Kinks song Ray never wrote', and with 'End Of A Century', said 'I got my Kinks book out for that one.'

I studied Ray Davies, in the sense I really listened to it and understood . . . worked out what was going on.

To understand writing patterns?

No, it was just a feeling, and once you get into that mood: the descending bass line . . . It was something I felt very comfortable with. In a way, the more you explore your musical heritage, in the sense of your cultural identity, you realize what makes stuff unique is the individual's interpretation of something that is actually already there. There's very strong elements of folk in what Ray does and there's very strong elements of folk in what I do. He chose to really mine that area a lot more . . . for me it was a period. But then again, I do keep coming back to it; there was a big departure until *The Good, The Bad And The Queen*. But now *Dr Dee* is the most English piece I've ever done. It's so English, it's just ridiculously English. It's coming right back to my roots.

Is it important to reflect Englishness in your writing?

I love it, but I just can't do it all the time. I need to stand back and go away and do other stuff. This (*pointing at Gorillaz records*) is sort of hip hop but also a lot of dance influence. It's not very English at all, in fact. But it's just as much a part of me as that. I love singing about where I live. I love this place. You can't express it all at once. I express a bit of it, then I go away and then I come back and focus on another bit and get really obsessed with that. Then get that out of my system and wait until another part grabs me.

When did your writing start drawing from within yourself?

I've done that ever since the beginning really. I try not to get too self-conscious about what I'm doing. I just get on with it. This is what this farmer . . . I'm a nine-to-five musician. Obviously, I can't quite control it like that. There are nights . . . when Erykah Badu . . . she was supposed to come at five in the evening. She didn't turn up till twelve-thirty and we didn't leave until five, half-five, six in the morning. Obviously it's not perfect. I like being with my family at weekends and during the school holidays. Obviously if an idea comes to me during those periods of not-work, then I won't be obstructive to it. I'll sneak away in between roasting the potatoes and satisfy my compulsion and put it away again. I don't do anything else. I'm completely obsessed by it. There has to be some discipline otherwise I would do it all the time. I don't ever get tired of making music. If I didn't have any family . . . God knows . . . it would never stop.

Was 'No Distance Left To Run' a difficult song to write?

Yeah, that whole record (13) was not easy to write. I hope I don't have to write another album like that again. I just felt fucking miserable. It's a miserable record but it does have 'Tender' on it, which is the opposite of that. It's incredibly uplifting, as we realized at Glastonbury. It was extraordinary: to come out of something dark and dismal to be such a celebration. It's interesting, something's life . . . You never know how long it's going to last. The fact that it's even lasted nearly ten years is great. Music doesn't last forever. Some music lasts a lot longer than others. You can't put a shelf life on a piece of music. Look at The Beatles, how long that lasted. It's a strange alchemy for the things that last. You can't actually put your finger on it. It goes back to 'Chemical World' and 'For Tomorrow': can you try and make a hit? No, you can't, but you can concentrate on certain specific aspects. I thought 'Out Of Time' would be an absolute killer and it wasn't. It doesn't always work. But then some things take a lot longer to settle. The point is, even though at this point, twenty-two years in, I have no idea how to write a hit single. I genuinely don't. I may never write another hit single. A little secret corner of my heart would like that. I'm sure Paul McCartney secretly feels the same way . . . just one more.

Who is a soundboard, barometer to your work?

Who do I play my stuff to? My mates. They've had to put up with far too many late nights listening to my demos over the years. My daughter is my harshest critic. Absolutely brutal.

Kids have a great melodic sense.

Yeah, but then I hear her liking stuff which I just think is whack. They know what they like, that's for sure. They're far more confident in their choices than adults. They cut through a lot of the artifice and just go, 'That's really good.'

Let's talk about some specific songs that you've written: the incredibly infectious 'Clint Eastwood', *I ain't happy, I'm feeling glad / I got sunshine in a bag / I'm useless, but not for long / The future is coming on.*

You're asking me to discuss two things I'm not particularly comfortable with. Which are: what you meant by what you said, and two, what do you think your contribution had been? Although you haven't asked the second one, that will come. But you're asking the first difficult question. Well . . . what do you think it means?

You're not getting away with that . . . I have no idea, but it makes me feel good.

Yeah . . . the funny thing is, on this last world bloody tour I did with Gorillaz I definitely got the sense that people were singing *I ain't happy, I'm feeling sad.* I'd never ever sing that. That's just not me. The truth is, people just like a catchy tune. It's so different what I was actually saying: I'm not happy, but I'm glad . . . that . . . whatever it is that I've got in my bag (*laughs*). I'm not sad, but I'm not happy. I'm glad. The mood of the thing is entirely different if you take it . . . but I could hear 20,000 people a night in America singing *I'm feeling sad . . . yeah!* I suppose it doesn't matter because the overall mood is the same. If you've noticed, I haven't answered your question.

You have kind of.

Kind of. Yeah.

It's intriguing talking to songwriters and discovering what is and what is not comfortable territory. If that's a private space for you that's fine.

Yeah, it is, it has to be. I have some quite mad thought processes when I'm writing and if I articulated them on paper I'd feel like I'd let some of that tension go. I think it's important to maintain some of that confusion in my head, you know.

How collaborative was your writing with Graham, for example, 'Tender'?

When he had something it would be something he would slot in. In that case *Oh my baby.* He had a little demo with that on. It was in the same key, I think. So we put them together and they felt very natural.

Would you ever write together in the same room?

No. We'd arrange and change things together. He didn't write in anywhere near the volume I wrote. But not sitting down together. But it was definitely collaborative because songs transformed with his interpretation. But the initial thing generally was done privately on both sides.

My daughters have spent weeks trying to sing the chorus of 'Girls And Boys' without the music on but they get stuck in the tongue-twisting words. We saw Graham in Regents Park and he sang it to Lottie perfectly.

I don't know if I can do it. I tend to just go with the flow whenever I sing that song. That was a proper demo, just keyboard (*mimes; finger-thumb 1st / 5th oscillation*). That was easy. It came really quickly, virtually just one go.

What were you trying to achieve lyrically?

Those first lines came to me in Magaluf, but it wasn't as easy as *Greece*: oh 'cause that was *police*, fuck it, it's Spain; you mean *following the herd down to Magaluf.* The spirit is the same. The whole of that period was looking at the way . . . it's mad the way that *Modern Life Is Rubbish* and *Parklife*, the perception of them was a celebration of all things English, but actually it was a lament to the loss of . . . the transitional period of our culture into what we have now, which is a fully Americanized system.

A recurring Ray Davies theme.

Absolutely, that's why I completely . . . did you ever see us singing 'Waterloo Sunset'? . . . I sound like I'm just there with him, the harmony . . . With Ray Davies and David Bowie I felt very close to them both. They were the people that I related to the most and put on a pedestal and considered to be . . . If stuff during that period, if I felt remotely like Ray Davies or David Bowie, emotionally for me, I was quite excited about it.

Did you deconstruct Bowie songs . . . ?

Deconstruct constantly. I've been deconstructing Dufay and Perrichon and Janequin, Renaissance composers . . . you do that all the time.

Are you classically trained?

Badly, yeah. I did most of my grades on piano. I played in youth orchestras. I got somewhere between grade six and eight.

Shall we say seven?

No, it wasn't as simple as that, but I was never good at exams. I played violin up until grade five or six.

I noticed at a Gorillaz gig recently you had scored music on your piano. You rarely see that with rock and pop musicians.

Are you sure they weren't just some words I'd forgotten? I do work with scores but my reading is not good. I'm much better just learning everything. You have to get to a point where you can play with your eyes closed. You have to really, really let music become that completely transcendental thing, whatever it may be. You have to be blind. I'm really looking forward to doing Amadou and Mariam's gig at the Manchester International Festival. They're playing completely blind. The whole audience is in pitch darkness so that everyone listens to it as how they hear it.

Did you write 'Parklife' as prose or was it in metre for singing, as such?

I had (*sings riff*) and the chorus. I think I wrote it as prose. It sounded really weird to me when I did it. Graham and I had a childhood obsession with *Meantime* and *Quadrophenia* so we just chanced it and contacted Phil Daniels. It was so natural and immediate when he did it. It was fantastic.

You performed 'Essex Dogs' at the Poetry Olympics in 1996: *From this town, the English army grind their teeth into glass.* Do you often write away from song?

I needed to say all of those things. It was about Colchester. Then Michael Horovitz asked me if I'd present it in a more poetry-friendly way. I wasn't trying to say this is poetry. It was just the most word-y thing I had.

Another line from that song reminded me of Terry Hall: *the smell of puke and piss on your stilettos.*

Yes, exactly, very close.

The musicality of Jerry Dammers is very evident in your work, particularly in Gorillaz.

Yeah, absolutely. There wouldn't have been Gorillaz without Fun Boy Three or The Specials or Big Audio Dynamite, and obviously De La Soul and Tribe Called Quest.

Do you use other musicians from your musical past as a starting point for your ideas? For example 'Slow Country'; was that born out of 'Ghost Town'?

It's got a similar sound in the background. Did I sample 'Ghost Town' (*quietly*) in a way no one could ever hear it? I can't remember. It's definitely got that atmosphere about it.

'To The End' has five bars in the verse, which is quite unusual. Do you think in terms . . . ?

. . . I think more and more in what would be perceived as strange time signatures. The next pop record I make, which is a very loose term; if you're talking about how do ideas start, well, I have an idea to make a record where there is no 4/4 ever in it and see if I can make that pop. Especially with what I'm doing at the moment; it's all in seven, eleven and thirteen and nine.

Time signature as a conscious starting point?

Yes, as a conscious starting point because that's all you need, is a starting point. I don't want to spend the rest of my life writing pleasant, charming English ditties, or doing hip hop / Specials-influenced tunes where someone sings a cool infectious melody and then someone does a rap. But all these things are areas which I've really enjoyed . . . and I probably won't make another record in Mandarin.

What are you trying to achieve as a songwriter? What drives you to make these changes, to go beyond where you are comfortable?

I love the whole mystery, as you say, going out into the wilderness and becoming at one . . . with my wilderness (*laughs*). It's an enormous amount of joy and energy from just the very idea that I just can get up in the morning and go anywhere in my head.

Can music be conquered?

No, I'm not trying to conquer it. I just scatter myself every day amongst its magnificence.

Did 9/11 affect you as a songwriter?

Yes, it definitely made me sober up a bit . . . realize that I had a family and I needed to become a little less self-absorbed.

And the influence for *Demon Days* came from that.

Yes, both of those albums. It was a difficult one for Jamie, *Plastic Beach*. It was about recycling and rubbish. It's not the sexiest of subject matters but I'm glad I made a record dedicated to those sorts of ideas.

Did you influence how the guests wrote on those records?

With *Plastic Beach* you've just got to meditate on plastic and rubbish. Like Lou Reed met me in the morning at the studio. We talked over it. He got in a cab, went uptown, did something, came back downtown, got out the cab and did the thing. He'd written it in the cab journey up and down; a very Lou Reed, New York thing to do. I love collaborating with people. It makes my job a lot less lonely. But then again I need to have a healthy dose of loneliness and a good old shot of melancholy, once in a while. That's the fuel of music.

Up on melancholy hill / There's a plastic tree / Are you here with me?

It doesn't get worse (*laughs loud*). That's as sad as it gets . . . There's no life then left . . . a tree made of plastic . . . And humanity, which is bound to become extinct under a plastic tree. It's annoying, that song; I don't think I quite got it right. When I sing it just me on the guitar it's one of the best songs I've ever written, but I slightly overcooked it on the record.

Why do you think there are so few female writers in this country?

There's loads of very musical women out there. It's the selfish gene . . . of the man, maybe. I'm not qualifying that. That's it.

Do you remember the first song that you wrote?

My mum's got a lot of these early demos still. I started in exactly the key I'm still in: depressing, miserable, melancholic, with just a little glimpse of hope. It was something about nuclear power stations and acid rain. I also remember getting the twelve-inch of the Human League's 'The Lebanon' and using my dad's record player, my cassette player and then having another cassette player and mixing one of his Arabic albums over the top of that. I was trying to do stuff like that (*Gorillaz*) right back then, very, very crudely.

Why did you start writing?

I used to get into trouble with my dad. He was aware that I would be playing Mozart or Schumann and it would suddenly become a lot simpler; the arrogance of youth. I was very distracted from my classical studies and very interested in just letting it out.

Am I right in saying you didn't buy many records?

I listen to music all the time and I have a lot of records. I definitely have bought more records in the last ten tears than the previous twenty. It's strange if you make music all the time . . . I don't listen to records over and over again. Maybe once or twice, really listen to it, and then I need something new.

The opposite of an artist like Paul Weller whose collection continually inspires his career?

It's in his DNA. I've never been anything. It'd be nice when I drop off this mortal coil, a pleasant sense of one's worth, if there was some kind of thread through the whole thing.

Could you define that thread?

Joy in mystery.

NOEL GALLAGHER

All my people right here right now.

Oasis songs urge you to sing at the top of your voice—and loud. For the spectator at an Oasis concert the sensation is one of collective belonging. Witnessing this shared singalong experience at Knebworth in 1996 was extraordinary. Over two nights a quarter of a million people, at the biggest UK gig ever, united in their passion for the songs of a former Inspiral Carpets guitar roadie. From the opening line of 'Wonderwall': *Today is gonna be the day that they're gonna throw it back to you*, the crowd took over. Not another word was needed from the stage until the song's end.

The songwriting of Noel Gallagher had stolen a country's imagination, and not since The Jam had a band been so at one with its audience. The atmosphere was electric. At the turn of the Nineties, The Stone Roses, The La's and Paul Weller's renewed passion for British pop and pastoral heritage were refuelling the popularity of the electric guitar and songs in a British classic tradition. Oasis was a band burning with attitude and, alongside Blur, they offered a much-needed home-grown alternative to the popularity of Nirvana and grunge rock.

Born 29 May 1967 in a council house in the Longsight area of Manchester to Irish parents, Noel Thomas David was the Gallaghers' second son. He was not suited to the conformity of school life, and his early teenage years were marred by petty theft offences and burglaries. It was deemed uncool to be seen in your bedroom playing the guitar, so Noel kept his hobby quiet from friends. School and home life was fraught, particularly coping with a violent father, and Noel developed a stammer because of the beatings he received. He found a release in music and the use of readily available drugs: glue sniffing, mushrooms, spliff. As he overcame self-doubt and a natural shyness, Noel's songwriting soon developed from the innocent wit of early compositions like 'Badge': *and on your badge it says wear a badge* to the dominant theme of escapism which would define the first Oasis album.

Released in September 1994, *Definitely Maybe* was a set of eleven tracks written over a two-year period by an uninhibited, classic bedroom-bound writer motivated simply to produce songs for his band and his mates to hear. As Gallagher faced his mid-twenties he depicted a Manchester drained of hope. His writing expressed a desire to flee a city broken by a decade of Thatcherism. These were songs written without commercial pressure. They were full of optimism and freedom, but always asking: *is it worth the aggravation / To find yourself a job when there's nothing worth working for?*

Serendipity would play its part, and the above lyric from the top-ten hit 'Cigarettes And Alcohol' was accurate in the sense that Gallagher needed direction for the newly demoed Oasis. He handed a tape to a fellow gig goer, Ian, who turned out to be the brother of Johnny Marr. The Smiths songwriter listened and wanted to help. Marr and Gallagher came from similar Mancunian–Irish upbringings, and a mutual respect developed between them on a guitar-shopping expedition to Doncaster. The time and support invested by Marr lent great credibility to the unknown five-piece. Johnny gave Noel a 1960 sunburst Gibson Les Paul formerly owned by Pete Townshend, an instrument which immediately inspired Gallagher to write 'Slide Away' about his then girlfriend Louise Jones. Far from being the traditionally symbolic 'baton passing' in recognition of a new musical succession, however, the gift was in fact an attempt by Marr to ensure that Gallagher wouldn't spend so much time on stage tuning up. The instrument itself soon met its demise crashing over the head of a stage invader at an Oasis gig in Newcastle. Marr generously replaced it with a Black Les Paul which he had previously used to record one of Gallagher's favourite albums, *The Queen Is Dead*. The guitar remained intact for Marr to contribute a solo on '(Probably) All In The Mind' from the 2002 release *Heathen Chemistry*.

The music of Oasis impacted with a wall-of-sound energy reminiscent of the Sex Pistols and the melodic appeal of Sixties bands. Gallagher prides himself on transparently creating a melting pot of homages to earlier songwriters, shaped by and combined with his own distinctive talent. As a listener, it is easy to hear a George Harrison riff here, a John Lennon lyric there or a Paul McCartney melody everywhere, but they are designer wallpaper to Gallagher's bricks and mortar. His working-class upbringing infused his songs with simple, infectious melody and positive words of universal appeal: *together we'll fly*; *I wanna talk tonight 'bout how you saved my life*; *tonight I'm a rock 'n' roll star*. He would famously dedicate his songs to the man who buys the *Daily Mail* and twenty Bensons every day. Yet the songwriter considered by George Martin to be the finest of his generation reveals his struggle to write these anthemic, decade-defining words. At the heart of his creativity is a constant battle with lyrical inspiration, summed up in 'Cast No Shadow': *bound with all the weight of all the words he tried to say*. Keith Richards figured, 'You don't go after the songs, the songs find you,' and Gallagher concurs: 'The best songs pour out of you.' His words are often shaped by getting the first line right and he will readily make use of a rhyming dictionary. Oasis's debut single 'Supersonic' from April 1994 declared: *I need to be myself / I can't be no one else*. Gallagher writes honestly and easily, without the irony of many of his peers. The vocabulary speaks directly to his audience with accessible words, while the melody provokes an instinctive reaction which needs no analysis.

It was Noel's brother Liam who was behind the formation of Oasis. Five years younger than Noel, Liam Gallagher was the band's lead singer and the epitome of Manchester cool. Soon after their debut gig in August 1991, Noel was invited to come down to a rehearsal. He played a selection of his songs, amongst them 'Live Forever'. The anthem had been written whilst Noel was working for a firm subcontracted to British Gas. After an accident at work resulted in him breaking bones in his foot, Noel's return from sick leave found him posted in the storeroom: a hideout where he could compose songs on his acoustic guitar. He has often related how on finishing the final chord a feeling passed over him that his songwriting credentials now stood head and shoulders above his hometown rivals. The verse of 'Live Forever' is sung over six notes. The chorus introduces an E minor chord and suspends the melody to a reduced three tones. It is the occasional vocal push to G that tugs emotionally, until a falsetto voice pushes up to a top B ahead of a floating F major seventh chord, embracing the sentiment *you and I are gonna live forever*. The song made an immediate impact, and Oasis celebrated their first top-ten success in August 1994.

Just fifteen months earlier on the last day of May, chance had brought the head of Creation Records, Alan McGee, to King Tut's Wah Wah Hut in Glasgow. After witnessing a four-song, fifteen-minute set, he instantly offered a record deal to the band's songwriter. After extensive touring and Radio 1 backing, the enormous self-confidence of the Gallagher brothers paid dividends. Recorded for a meagre £75,000, *Definitely Maybe* became the fastest-selling debut album of all time, achieving over three million sales. A startling public affection for Oasis arose, shown both in the charts and in media coverage. Noel's new songwriting reflected the group's changing fortunes. From writing on the dole he was now a wealthy man addressing an acquired fan base of millions and coming to terms with newfound popularity: *You gotta roll with it*; *I took a walk with my fame*; *Where were you while we were getting high?* In 1995 (*What's the Story*) *Morning Glory?* hit number one in seven countries. Its twenty million purchases placed it fourth in the bestselling UK albums ever; a feat not surpassed until *21* by Adele in 2013.

Easy-listening band Mike Flowers Pops released a cover version of 'Wonderwall' which reached number two in the Christmas charts. By the summer of 1996, the original had breached the American top ten—it marked Oasis's finest stateside achievement. Like 'Live Forever', the chorus of 'Wonderwall' is distinguished by its introduction of a new active chord after a verse movement of four.

The song lifts as the vocalist speculates: *maybe you're the one that's gonna save me*. Two years later, Gallagher revived the chord sequence in 'D'You Know What I Mean?' and gave Oasis a third number-one single. His lyrics typically surrender to the onslaught of two guitars, bass and drum, but detached from the soaring solos and pounding rhythms, many of the songs reveal an introspective writer laying down his abilities in the barest of forms: guitar and voice. The directness of 'Going Nowhere' or 'Talk Tonight' acts as an emotional pull on an intimate plain. 'Half The World Away' inverted the chords of Hal David and Burt Bacharach's 'This Guy's In Love With You' with charming two-verse, two-chorus simplicity: *if I could leave this spirit I'll find me a hole and I'll live in it*. Asked in the mid-Nineties if he considered himself a romantic writer, with touching embarrassment, Gallagher refused to answer. The lyrics speak for themselves: 'Stand By Me' cries, *There is one thing I can never give you / My heart can never be a home*. In 2005, 'Let There Be Love' lamented: *Who kicked a hole in the sky so the heavens would cry over me?* By Gallagher's mid-thirties, his faith in the power of love was plainly expressed in 'She Is Love' as he defends an old heart from wounding words: *your wings begin to unfold*.

'If I have seen further, it is by standing on the shoulders of giants.' The words of the seventeenth-century scientist Sir Isaac Newton can be found inscribed on the edge of some British two-pound coins. Noel Gallagher appropriated the quote, albeit with a singular 'shoulder', for the first Oasis album of the third millennium. The band's weight carriers had been dispensed with, and by 1999 only Noel and Liam remained as the principal members of a new line-up. The chart-topping run of Oasis would continue, but now writing duties were shared out between group members. The quality and development of Noel's writing continued to equal and often surpass his youthful offerings. The three-chord 'Mucky Fingers' tipped a hat to The Velvet Underground with a relentless piano drive. 'Sunday Morning Call', 'Little By Little' and 'Lyla' all provided new stadium anthems. 'The Importance Of Being Idle' stretched out with a combination of minor chords and major sevenths to back a beguiling verse falsetto. 'Force of Nature' exemplified Gallagher's incisive turn of phrase: *You look like a faded picture / I see the cracks freezing on your skin*. The decade's end brought about Oasis's curtain call and the inception of Gallagher's solo career. In 2008 the last Oasis album, *Dig Out Your Soul*, featured six of Noel's tracks with God, angels, devils and a myriad of biblical references sprinkled across the lyric sheet. Dance-influenced groove bonded with traditional writing, and number ones duly followed. The Brits honoured Oasis with an Outstanding Lifetime Achievement award as their popularity in the UK and even more in the States reached staggering proportions. In 2013, Noel was presented with an Ivor Novello Award for his Outstanding Song Collection. In Britain they are the fifth most successful singles band of all time behind The Beatles, Queen, Abba and The Rolling Stones.

The rise of Oasis had been astonishing. During 2000, they played to 1.2 million people across twenty-three countries. Seven years before, the five working-class lads from Manchester were gaining notoriety as a support band with an uncompromising sound. Before leaving the stage, the group would speed through a thrash cover of The Beatles' psychedelic classic 'I Am The Walrus'. Oasis scaled breathtaking heights, but as in all Greek tragedies, the downfall was inevitable. After a major altercation between the two warring brothers, Noel Gallagher left the group in August 2009.

My conversation with Noel in the band's offices in Marylebone, central London, took place two months after the Oasis split. Noel was relaxed, candid, extremely funny and very much at ease with discussing any dimension of his songwriting. As an explanation for leaving Oasis, the band's leader cited an inability to be in the same room as Liam a moment longer. The following year, Noel Gallagher's High Flying Birds would be conceived away from the beady eye of his younger brother. Behind them lay a decade and a half of national media attention, more often than not with scant regard for the group's life blood, the music.

Tell me about the last song that you wrote?

Wow. I wrote it in a hotel room in Peru, in Lima. Obviously it's not been released yet. Somebody asked me to write a song for a film; consequentially the song got rejected but luckily enough it's great. I was fifty-fifty when I gave it to them: 'Fuck, it's really good that,' so I was glad when they knocked it back.

Can you write anywhere?

I tend to write more on the road because (a) I've always got a guitar with me; (b) I've always got shitloads of time, sitting round and doing fuck all; and (c) I've got my entire record collection in an iPod, so I'm sitting round listening to music a lot. You might listen to something and a chord might spark something off; you pick the guitar up and off you go. The thing that sparked off this song was a track on the Doves album called 'Jetstream'. I don't know when the last time I sat down and listened to an album was. If I've got music on at home I'm either in the shower, tidying up or doing something. If a new album comes out, the Arctic Monkeys for instance, I listen to it once and then stick it in a pile. Then when I go away that's when I listen to them the most, because you get more than five minutes: other than that there's kids running round the house and your missus and all that.

How was that different when you were in your twenties?

The only difference was I used to listen to music a lot, 'cause I was on the dole. Being on tour, apart from the gig, is really like being on the dole, but you're just in different cities in the world. I used to sit in my flat on Whitby

Street in Manchester staring out of the window listening to The Beatles, writing songs. Now I do it in expensive hotel rooms 'round the world.

How long can you go without writing?

Oh, fuckin' ten months. I don't chase it any more, doesn't bother me in the
slightest. It only really dawns on me when I'm out with Weller. He'll say, 'Have
you written any songs recently?' and I'll say, 'Actually no, I haven't.' He'll say,
'When was the last time you wrote?' and I'll say, 'Oh fuck, nine months ago.'
We'll have an argument about that or something or other and he'll say, 'Get
your fuckin' finger out, you lazy . . .'—all that. From when I joined Oasis to
when we became a real big, fuck-off band—when you fall into that cycle of
album, tour, a year off, so it's once every three years—I was on a mission. All
that *Definitely Maybe*, *Morning Glory* and *Be Here Now* stuff was all written
while I was on the dole. After that other shit gets in the way, like going on tour
for a year and a half. It slows down a bit. It comes with age, kids: you don't get
the time to devote to it any more.

**It's quite remarkable you had so many songs written ahead of the band's
success, and then withholding songs like 'All Around The World', 'Stand By
Me' and even planning 'Whatever' as the sixth or seventh single.**

I had all the chords, all the arrangements, all the melodies; just bits of little
lyrics to fill in. I only actually wrote one new song for *Morning Glory*: 'Some
Might Say', in a flat I was renting in Chiswick. There's another two albums'
worth of stuff before we even got signed that I actually found a bootleg CD of.
I think you can only get it in Japan: about sixteen tunes from 1991 to 1994.
They're all shit, but they're there all the same.

Was it then more difficult to write songs with your new status?

Well yeah, I was writing those songs for me and I didn't give a shit who
heard them. If we'd do a gig we'd play to ten people, and then you become a big
band playing stadiums. Then you start to second-guess yourself: 'These have
got to be played in a stadium.' You kind of think, 'The room in which I write
these songs dictates what song I'm writing.' For instance, I wouldn't write a
song on a sitar; playing that to 60,000 people, they'd walk out. You're in this
big band and you've got a lot of equipment; you just try to utilize it all. That's
where most of the *Be Here Now* stuff came from. It's like, 'Fuckin' hell, man, we
can afford whatever we want: let's get twelve fuckin' string sections in.'

Do you write imagining the audience?

No, I wrote 'Rock 'n' Roll Star' before I was in the band and 'Columbia' before I was in Oasis. I wrote 'Live Forever' while I was still a roadie with the Inspiral Carpets. I could play the guitar and I was into music so the next logical

'step is to write songs. I was never careerist about it, like, 'I'm going to be a song-writer.' I was just doing it for me. Then I joined the band and it was like, 'Wow, there's an outlet for this.' All the songs I'd written were on a cheap, shitty guitar. I remember the first rehearsal with Oasis; I walked in going, 'Right, you play that and you play that and I'll play this.' Then when it all kicked in, it fuckin' blew my head off: 'Wow, it all works.' I got addicted to that for two years. From the minute I joined Oasis it was like a kaleidoscope: my brain with all these ideas. I was writing all the time. I was on a mission. It becomes a profession, it's differ-ent then. You start off writing songs that you're not sure who's going to hear them. Then when I tried to write the next batch of songs you're like, 'We've got twenty million fans in the world.' Then your records become eagerly anticipated and then you start going, '. . . umm . . . I might just go to the pub today.'

Did that mindset affect your writing?

You try not to let it, but . . . it took some of the joy out of it. For instance, a song like 'Digsy's Dinner' which is about going to somebody's house for lasa-gne—you write a song like that now and the *Guardian* or the music papers would destroy you. You can only write songs like that when you are free of any inhibitions. You're writing it for a laugh. I wrote that song because my mate was called Digsy, just to make him laugh. Every time I played it to him he'd piss himself laughing. Next thing it ends up on the album because everybody's going, 'It's brilliant.' 'Oh, is it?' It was a piss-take. When we were in the studio doing *Morning Glory* nobody at the record label had heard any of the songs: Alan McGee, Marcus, our manager, the band even. I had them all at home written, knowing they were all going to work: 'Champagne Supernova', 'Wonder-wall'. You fast-forward two years, and I remember being in this very room putting on 'D'You Know What I Mean?' There must have been twenty people from all over the world: Sony representatives, radio pluggers saying, 'This is going to be the first single.' It starts off with a minute of feedback and you could see people like this . . . It was kind of symptomatic of that whole record; it couldn't live up to the hype, the expectations. The minute the song kicked in I was thinking, 'I'm not sure this is any fucking good.' It certainly didn't war-rant all these people. People had flown in from Japan just to listen to it. I don't know if they were expecting 'Hey Jude' or something. I was a fucking drug addict by that point, I couldn't be arsed being there. That's the extremes it went to: it's somewhere in the middle now.

Do you get a chord sequence going to kick-start a song?

It's always followed the same path. I write a full song with chords and mel-ody. I arrange it all, work it all out and sit there until the words come along. I wouldn't have three chords and a melody and take it to a producer and say, 'Can we do something with that?' When I go into the studio it's done. I don't fuck about when I get in there. If I have four chords that I like I'll work on that—there won't be any words—until I've bashed it into a tune. I'll do a middle eight, work on the rhythm, the phrasing of how the rhythm of the words will be. Then I'll play it and play it until some words come along, and nine out of ten they don't. I've got about six albums' worth of stuff. It's a nightmare. Words just don't fall out of the sky for me. It's really frustrating sometimes. I've also got a book that I keep that's got shitloads of words. You think of sentences or lines but you can never get them into a song once you've written them. Just random nonsense, I guess.

When you have a chord sequence, are you making sounds to form the melody?

I sing words but I couldn't tell you what they are. I've tried to sit down and sing it into a mic from a distance and then try and think, 'What do they sound like I'm saying?' But that doesn't work for me either because I know I'm just talking gibberish; I don't believe in it and if I don't believe in it I can't make anybody else believe in it. I just sing shapes, not actual words, and that becomes frustrating because you get so used to the phrasing of the words. It kind of becomes a puzzle in the air and only the words with certain shapes will fit that thing. I've got a tune going round at the minute and it's fuckin' great, but for the life of me I can't get . . . once I get a first line I'm generally all right. I struggle with it. But the good songs are the ones that you just pick up and go, ba, ba, ba: 'Fuckin' hell, there you go, look at that; brilliant, let's go to the pub.'

Do you then write the words without an instrument, just pen and paper?

It depends on where I am. I write a lot on my mobile phone, like I'm sending a text. I've got reams of words in there. Usually when I sit down to write, turn the telly off, pad and all that . . . nothing happens. It comes to me at random times. For instance, I've had a song called 'Mile High Moon'; I had the title nine years ago, the song and the backing track. I've sat down to try and write that song a dozen times. One day I'm in the back of a car going from my house, across the road, up to visit a girlfriend's friend in Harlesden, and all of a sudden I'm sitting just thinking and there it is: appears out of nowhere, and why I don't fuckin' know.

Like Keith Richards says, 'You don't go after the songs, the songs find you.'

I learnt that a long time ago: not to go looking for it. If you go looking for it they're the songs or the words that don't really mean anything. It's not natural for me to say to my missus, 'I'm going out to the country to write an album.' That's what happened with *Be Here Now*. I had all the music but not the words. It came to the point we were starting in two weeks, so I went to some Caribbean island and I thought I'd do it all in two weeks. I listen to those words now and cringe. I was heavily into drugs at that point and didn't give a fuck. I did the demos while I was away and when I got back I played them to everyone in the studio thinking somebody might have said . . . but everybody went, 'It's fucking amazing.' I was like, 'Wow, this is a piece of piss.' It was the worst thing that could have happened to me. I thought, 'It can't be that easy.'

When the band needed a first single you just went into a room and wrote 'Supersonic'.

That just appeared. We were doing 'Bring It On Down' because Creation wanted it as the first single and it was just fuckin' rubbish. Instead of scrapping the session somebody said, 'Just go and write a song.' I had the chords and that, it was just magic, and I've never done it since. It was amazing, that night. I wrote the whole song in less than half an hour, recorded it and mixed it that night, played it to Creation and that was it—fuckin' hell great.

Do you give value to the speed at which a song is written?

There are exceptions to the rule, but generally speaking the quicker they come the better they are. Lots of people say that; it's true of most of mine. That said, I worked a lot on 'Rock 'n' Roll Star' and that's equally as good as 'Supersonic'. 'Let There Be Love' took nine years to finally finish off. It's not a rule that's set in stone.

Do you have to write many to get a good one?

The more you write the better songs you write. You just have to get the shit ones out of the way. Everybody's got shit songs in them.

Are you disciplined: do you write every day?

I've got to say I'm inherently, generically . . . it's been proven that I'm a lazy bastard. I don't mean this to sound like I'm a smug twat, but once I'd felt in my own brain . . . not that I'd made it or done it . . . it's like I said, I don't chase it. If somebody said to me that after the next song you'll never write again I could look at all that there and think it's better than most people. I could look at half of the songs on that Albert Hall CD, and they're all B-sides, and think it's better than most people. I'm not, 'I must write something.' If it comes it comes, if it doesn't it doesn't. It's not that I'm not arsed, I'm switched on for when it arrives. I'm not standing out on the fuckin' runway waiting for the aliens to appear going, 'Come on,' 'cause it never happens, does it.

You have written an enormous number of B-sides that could easily have been used for another two albums. Do you write differently if you know the song is to back a single?

When we first started there was that thing of three B-sides on a single, which ruined a lot of bands. Now you've only got to write one track a year. I'd really like to be twenty-two tomorrow and starting off. On the *Masterplan* album every B-side is a single. We'd be twice as big now than we were then, we'd smash it. All the B-sides for the *Definitely Maybe* and *Morning Glory* singles should have been the third album. That was when I was at my peak as a song-writer. I was young, single, living out of an Adidas holdall, just had two guitars, wasn't rich, wasn't really famous; I was really, really into it then. If I had just been a bit cleverer when I wrote 'Half The World Away', 'Talk Tonight' or 'The Masterplan'; it beggars belief I put them out as B-sides. I got so much mileage out of those songs: 'Acquiesce', 'Listen Up', 'Rockin' Chair'. At the time every-body was just going, 'Great.' Nobody was going, 'Hold on a minute.' To answer the question, I didn't have a different mindset: I wish I did. I wish I'd have thought, 'I'm writing a B-side here so I should experiment a little bit,' and doing some quirky nonsense.

Do you think in traditional structures when you are writing?

I only listen to music derived or from the Sixties. I'm not interested in jazz or hip hop or whatever's going round at the minute; indie shit. I don't loathe it but I don't listen to it. My education as a songwriter was from listening to The Kinks and The Who and The Beatles. I don't listen to avant-garde landscapes and think, 'I could do that.' I'm not a fan of Brian Eno. It's Ray Davies, John Lennon and Pete Townshend for me.

Where would that education take you? Was it listening and absorbing or thinking, 'What's Ray Davies doing here?'

No, I'm not that clever. I would play along at home to 'Dead End Street' and 'Waterloo Sunset', but that's it. I taught myself to play the guitar; it's just a tool for me to write songs. I'm not a great guitarist. I don't study it. It frustrates me some-times. I'll never be the super session guy: I can do sessions for Oasis. It would take all the magic out of it to break down 'I Am The Walrus' to its basic compo-nents. I listen to it and go, 'It's fucking amazing; why is it amazing? I don't know, it just is.' That's why I find journalists such joyless fucking idiots. They have to break music down and pull it apart until there's nothing left, until they know it all; they analyse it down until it's bland nonsense. They don't listen to music like the rest of us. I had the Red and Blue Beatle songbooks like the two albums. I actually found the Blue one easier to get into than the early stuff; those chords are mental. I used to have this with Gem (*Archer*)—who I used to be in Oasis with—a lot; we'd be playing around with Beatle covers in the dressing room and he'd go, 'You're doing that chord wrong, it's this one.' It's like, 'So what, I'm sing-ing it for me; I'm not in a Beatles cover band.' It's like the bit at the end of 'I Am The Walrus'; we only just nailed it on the last tour, we used to do a different end-ing. People used to say, 'You know it's not the right ending,' it's like, 'Yes, but it's near enough.' I'm not a studier of music, I'm a listener.

In 'The Masterplan' the bridge line *Say it loud and sing it proud* is repeated after the first solo, but instead of going back to the chorus it sets up another verse hanging like a soap-opera ending.

That's the first time I've noticed that, to be honest. It's like I don't know why there's the little clap in 'Half A World Away'—that's a bit odd. I write songs purely by feel. Like the drums coming in on 'Wonderwall': people were going, 'Why have they come in there, it's an eighth of a bar too early?' 'What's an eighth of a bar?' I struggle to understand other people's perceptions. It comes in there because to me that's where it sounds right to. 'That's wrong.' I'm like, 'Wrong to who? How can it be wrong?'

Do you demo a song once it's written?

I used to do these fabulous demos and you'd take them into the studio always trying to recreate them, but you'd never really get close to it and it'd be really frustrating. When you get in the studio there's a lot more scope for everybody to throw their ideas in. I'd come in with these demos and they'd be done and I'd be thinking, 'What am I in a fucking band for?—I'm doing it all myself.' Now I've gone back to basics: just stick a mic out and play it acoustically, be out in a couple of hours. But I don't write a song and then go to a studio the next day. I wait till I've got three or four, like a full day's work or two. I know that if I've got four, two will be usable. If you go in with two, you might come out with nothing because they both might be shit. You get there and think, it sounds right in my head but it's not coming across, somehow. They work sat at home on the couch but when you start singing it doesn't sound as good. Yesterday I got to my mate's studio in Clapham and did four. Two you'll never hear; you listen back to 'em and go, 'Nah, it's not having it.' Now I've got nothing left in the bank. I'm a blank canvas again, which is a good thing. Usually I would stockpile these songs for months and months and have like twenty, but then you never know where to start.

You're a left-handed guitarist that plays right-handed; does that restrict your rhythm playing?

I don't know. I ended playing lead in Oasis because no one else would do it, but I'm a far better rhythm guitarist than anyone I know. I'd never heard of a left-handed guitar; I'd always seen Jimi Hendrix playing it upside down. When I first started playing the guitar I didn't know what the rules were. My dad had some old battered acoustic in the house and I just picked it up. It felt as natural as I guess a guitar can when you pick it up for the first time; it didn't restrict me in any way. Many years later when I ended up in secondary school there were instruments somewhere and the music teacher said, 'You won't be able to play that 'cause you're left-handed' and I said, 'No, I can play it.' Not play it—I could play a Joy Division bass line. He was saying, 'You'd find a left-handed guitar easier.' I was like, 'What, never heard of it.' We used to bunk off school and hang out in the music shop A1 in Manchester; I got a left-handed guitar and it felt the most ridiculous thing I'd ever picked up in my life, but funnily enough I play piano left-handed. All the bass notes feel alien to me. It would be better if I was playing the rhythm down here and the lead up there, but they refuse to make left-handed pianos. They're like some little fascist organization; they won't remake the frame. I tried to get one made for years. I wanted a left-handed white baby grand. You can do it on a mini-keyboard and transpose the keys the other way round, but it's shit. I'd love to have a left-handed piano to see people walk in your house and go, 'What!'

How did you teach yourself guitar?

The first musical notes was playing along to Joy Division bass lines on the top string, like 'Love Will Tear Us Apart' and all those great songs. Then you get a few years older and you start smoking spliff and then somebody knows a guy—you're always round somebody's house or flat—and he showed me a chord: 'Wow, E,' and he was going, 'And you can move it anywhere on the neck,' and that was fuckin' mind-blowing. You just pick it up little by little. I still see other guitarists on the telly and think, 'What's he doing there?' I've never been that driven to learn all the chords. I don't know what half of them are, to be honest. It's only since Gem joined Oasis; he knew what all the chords were called: E flat and suspended major ninth. I couldn't get my head round it. It's like the songwriting: I picked it up and it felt good to do those things and that was it. Again, I'm not interested in breaking it down.

You get a phenomenal number of songs out of a few chords, often using sus4's and add9th's, I believe.

One of the most amazing things that ever happened to me as a songwriter was around *Definitely Maybe*; somebody bought me a capo. I'd never seen one: 'What does that do?' I remember writing 'Wonderwall' immediately. They said, 'Put it anywhere on the neck.' 'Wow, that's amazing.' I wrote loads off that. Something that sounds fat and horrible down the neck can sound plaintive and melodic up the neck.

What can you recall of writing 'Wonderwall'?

Its original title was 'Wishing Stone'. We played the Cathouse in Glasgow, where it says on the record we recorded 'I Am The Walrus', but that's actually from a Sony conference we played; but that night we played with The Verve I ended up with this capo. I met some girl and we went back to my hotel room and she had this stone in her pocket that she insisted I had. You meet these kinds of divvy birds all over the place. I thought it was a great title and the song came out of that. I don't recall where I was when I wrote the lyrics. It was called

'Wishing Stone' for ages until we were listening to *Wonderwall Music* by George Harrison and it was like, 'Brilliant, I've got a Beatles connection!'

I've often wondered if there was a nod to Weller's 'Has My Fire Really Gone Out?' in that *fire in your heart is out* lyric.
Actually, a couple of people said that at the time.

No love songs to Paul, then.
No, I've ripped a few of his off but never written a song about him. He'd think I was a cunt, anyway.

Do you find a difference writing on acoustic or electric guitar?
I find it really limiting writing on an electric. You can write rock 'n' roll on acoustic guitars. The way I play electric guitar is fucking loud, so if I'm writing on electric it usually ends up as 'Shock Of The Lightning'; saying that, I wrote that on an acoustic guitar. I would never sit at home with an electric guitar; you'd just end up riffing all the time. The best songs come acoustically. I always find if it works on an acoustic guitar you've nailed it; you can only fuck it up after that. If you listen to 'Listen Up', for example, I wrote that on acoustic but recorded it on an electric guitar. My point is it works both ways. At the time I was into grungy, sleazy rock music. Whereas 'Supersonic' I wrote in the studio with electric guitar. You can't play it on an acoustic guitar—it wasn't written in that mindset.

I find that quite surprising because your back catalogue is so up and positive, but coming from an acoustic guitar you'd expect more introspection.
The words are always dictated by the melody. Because I'm first-generation Irish there's always a melancholy, but a kind of uplifting sadness. 'Some Might Say' is quite a sad melancholy lyric but the sound of it is so euphoric, and the melody, it's like everything's going to be all right. That's the Irish in me. The melody for 'Digsy's Dinner' could not be about somebody leaving you. It could only be about going to your mate's for tea.

How influential was Irish music for you? Did you have family sing-arounds?
I recall doing it when I was small. Your aunties and uncles used to always say, 'Go up there and sing us a song.' I've never done it publicly; it was always someone's house. My dad was a country and western DJ. He had tons of Irish music. The rebel songs I used to like, because they're really chest-beating but melancholy too. U2 have the same thing: 'One' is a really kind of sad song, but it's not. It's really uplifting; powerful words, but it has a real down-vibe to it. It's the same as 'With Or Without You' or 'Pride', most of *The Joshua Tree* there's a duality to the words. Gospel music is what it is, because it's quite euphoric but it's all about redemption. There's a little bit of that in my stuff, I think.

Who do you write music for?

Me. There was a bit in the middle where you're writing it for the fans: 'How's this going to sound at Wembley Stadium?' The bit at the beginning, everything up to *Be Here Now*, was done for me. *Be Here Now* to *Don't Believe The Truth* was done for the fans. I was a bit lost at the time. I was in a bit of a state of . . . not couldn't be arsed, but didn't have any inspiration. I was just writing songs for the sake of it because that's what we do. If we're not in the studio and not touring, are we a band any more? So it's like, 'I'll write some songs, then.' That period is reflected in the songs themselves: not really my best. There's some good stuff in there. It picks up again from *Don't Believe The Truth* to the last album. Now it's for me it's great not having the added pressure of being in a big rock band that's going to sell out Wembley Stadium for three nights. It's like, 'Right, I'm starting again,' in a sense. I write songs and we'll see what they sound like when I've finished them, 'cause I don't know what's going to happen in the next five years.

There's an often-used quote where you said you wrote 'for the man who buys the *Daily Mail* and twenty Bensons every day' . . .

I meant that at the time. I consider myself as an average man in the street who's been blessed with a talent to write songs. I don't write songs for people in the fucking *Observer* or the *Guardian*, or people at the *NME* or in *Mojo* magazine. I'm not bothered about pushing the envelope. I'm not fucking arsed about trying out new forms of music. I wanted everybody to like Oasis, not just some people in Oxford, a few people in Hull and a couple of people in Glasgow. I was into being fucking extremely popular. I'm glad I'm not too clever when it comes to writing music. I write from the heart, I don't write from the brain. I think a lot of music now is from the brain. A lot of music doesn't move me because you think, 'They've sat in a room for six months and that's the best they could come up with?' Things should fuckin' happen, bang! Radiohead, for instance, who I actually like: there's endless debates about what kind of record they're going to make. Write a song, that's what you want to do first; worry about the rest of it later. That was always our rule in Oasis. Every time we'd start going into the studio people would be, 'So what happens next?' 'We decide the concept after it's finished. We write the songs first, that's the main thing, and then when it's finished we'll tell you what kind of album we've made.' Other than that, there's no point talking about it.

Did you consider Liam's voice when you were writing?

Only towards the end: in the beginning, no. I knew he could sing it. The last couple of albums his range had shortened a little bit, he couldn't sing falsetto any more—'Oh right, I'll be singing that one.' Every time I would do a demo . . . explain it in simple terms . . . I would have to move the capo down a couple of frets to accommodate Liam's voice. I would always sing in a high register. I'll let you into a secret about that: I realized early on when I sat at home, I'd get to the end of a song to myself and think, 'This singing malarkey is brilliant, it's like taking drugs.' So I would write songs where the melody would always have to be at the top, on the verge of shouting it, because when people sing along in stadiums or en masse in arenas, when you're singing and shouting at the top of your voice; that's like taking drugs. That's why we're such a fucking great live band. If you go and see Radiohead and sing 'Karma Police' you're not getting anything from that. With a song with Liam we would always try and edge it up so he's at the top of his range. If he's singing at the top of his range . . . we're not professional singers . . . everybody else was singing at the top of their range, and the melodies were catchy and the words were easily accessible: it's like you're at a rally.

Daniel Lanois used to say a similar thing to Bono. You write very anthemic songs: did watching Manchester City at Maine Road as a kid play an influential part?

There's two main things: one is being of Irish descent and the other is going to a lot of football matches from a very an early age and listening to those chants (*sings*): *la la la lalala la ci-ty*—that's 'Hey Jude'! Those songs that transferred themselves from the pop charts to the terraces, that's where it's at. I'm not going to bullshit you and think I was seven stood at Maine Road going, 'That's where it's at.' I've got to say U2 were a big influence on me when I was writing. They're Irish and have got the fist-punching thing with added religion. I'm not religious, mine is a bit more working-class euphoria than spiritual. They're amazing. They're the most loathed band in England; other musicians fucking hate them, but secretly they all want to be in them . . . when that show comes to town. *Achtung Baby*, 'Beautiful Day' and stuff, it's fucking great. I remember doing an interview with the *NME*, a round-table kind of thing. There was Jarvis Cocker, that bird from Elastica, some cunt from Therapy? doing a round-up of the year's singles. They started going on about U2 and there was shock horror from these indie kids. I was going, 'U2 are fucking brilliant, the biggest band in the world. If you don't want to be in the biggest band in the world you're a fucking idiot. Where are you playing tonight? Sorry? What's the capacity of that? 900. Do you know where they're playing tonight? In a fucking stadium somewhere and it's 900,000. So thank you very much.'

You have an honourable reputation for plundering from the past.

I don't give a fuck, that's what it's there for. I never said I was inventing anything. I'm a lover of music. If I nicked guitar riffs here and there I'd have thought the songwriter would be quite fucking pleased. The guitar riff in 'Supersonic' is a bit George Harrison but I wasn't expecting anybody not to notice. I saw it as when you would read interviews with The Jam and they'd always accuse Weller of the same thing. Then he'd mention these bands and you'd go, 'I'm going to go and find that, 'cause if he's into it I'm going to be fuckin' into it.' People would say, 'It's just Beatles this and Beatles that.' There were kids all over the country starting bands because of that, because they were going to buy Beatles records because they'd never heard of them before.

It's undoubtedly a love and a tip of the hat to the past, but is it a substitute for a lack of inspiration?

I guess it's so ingrained in my musical life: Oasis were basically a cross between The Beatles and the Sex Pistols. They were the two main loves of my life when I was growing up. I'll put it to you this way: when Radiohead in the middle of 'Karma Police' dropped that bit in of 'Sexy Sadie', to all the people down here that's fucking brilliant, but when I do it I'm accused of some kind of plagiarism. It's not important to me. The Beatles are in my DNA, and the Sex Pistols and The Kinks and The Who, for that matter. If bits of their songs find their way into mine, great; they're well within their rights to sue me and I'm not arsed. I've been in here listening to Radio 1 and thought, 'That sounds a bit like one of mine,' but it's like, fair play, man. That's what music is. You're supposed to inspire the next generation. The Beatles were finished before Oasis came along anyway.

You were once asked but refused to answer this question. Do you recognize the romantic writer in yourself?

I remember that question. Yes, I am romantic. My missus would sit and scoff at this. I can only be romantic when I'm writing songs. I've written lots of love songs. I'm fucking shit at remembering birthdays and all that malarkey, buying cards and flowers: absolutely rubbish. There's a romance in all music, isn't there? If you're a mod band you're romanticizing the Sixties. If you're a metal band you're romanticizing the Eighties, Def Leppard and all that shite, or you're romanticizing The Velvet Underground or something. I'm a total fan of music. If we're talking about romance in the terms it's written in the dictionary, then yeah, of course. Being in love is a great thing to write about.

You recognize beauty in simple things, like the weather.

Oh yeah, for five years I was obsessed with the rain. It was raining a lot.

Or *shining*.

Well, there was sunshine after the rain. Somebody pointed that out to me at the end of the Nineties and said, 'It's been raining a lot in your music for the last five years.' It's like, 'I'm from Manchester. It rains. I'm from up north.'

Is it a default when you're stuck for ideas: *rain, shine*?

I'm not one of the world's great thinkers. Damon Albarn said this once in an interview: he can 'see four black dudes playing cards in a pub in Notting

THE DEATH OF YOU AND ME.

High-tide Summer in the city, the kids are looking Pretty
But isn't it a pity that the Sunshine
Is followed by thunder with thoughts of going under?
And is it any wonder why the sea's

Been calling out to me I seem to spend my whole life running
from people who would be the death of you and me
And i can feel the storm clouds Sucking up my soul

Hard times life is getting faster and no-one has the answer
I try to face the day down in a new way
At the bottom of a bottle is every mans apostle
lets run away together you and me

forever we'd be free - free to spend our whole lives running
from people who would be the death of you and me
'cause i can feel the storm clouds suckin up my soul

Let's run away to sea forever we'd be free
free to spend our whole lives running
from people who would be the death of you and me
'cause i can feel the storm clouds coming
And watching my t.v. (or is it watching me??)
I see another new day dawning
Its rising over me with my mortality
And i can feel the storm clouds sucking up my Soul

'The Death of You and Me' lyrics, handwritten by Noel Gallagher

Hill and write a symphony about it'. I could see the same four black dudes and to me it's just four black dudes playing cards. It's just how you perceive things in life. I'm not a great reader of books; I'm not a great art lover. What I know is street life and street talk and football and drugs. I was probably the only song-writer in the entire world that hasn't written a song about 9/11. Why would you put that to music? It would be a very short song. This is wrong, full stop. Musi-cally it just doesn't interest me in the slightest. If somebody gave me fifty mil-lion pounds right now and gave me a subject to write a song about, I'd still be here nine months later. It goes back to what we were saying: it has to just fuck-ing happen. I remember once watching a programme; Elton John said he could write a song about anything and they gave him the instructions how to assemble a Hoover or something and he wrote that song. I sat there thinking, 'That's ludi-crous.' I'd hate to be that kind of . . . sit and write a song about ice cream: it's not going to happen. Some Scouser in a band said to me once—I was asking him about a song he wrote—'I was walking down the street, la, and there was an empty can on the pavement and I kicked it and it rolled in a rhythmic way and I just started singing this song.' I was like, 'What, that's fucking nuts. What are you on about, you mad cunt?' I would have thought every songwriter would have a different way of perceiving world events or the day's weather or what they see on the news or how their girlfriend is being or how much they love their children, blah, blah, blah—whatever moves you to write songs.

It's unusual for you to write very personally. Did having an abusive father contribute to your reluctance to reveal yourself in song?

All the songs that I like, they're not written by songwriters pulling the scabs off themselves. All John Lennon's shit about his mother; I'm not interested in it, doesn't mean anything to me. All these songs about personal torment, how can it? How can 'Mother' mean anything to anybody apart from John Lennon? It can't, because he's singing it about his mother, not mine. That's just my perception of it. It's never come out in my music 'cause (a) it's nobody's fucking business; and (b) it doesn't make for great music. For instance, 'Waterloo Sunset'; the sun setting at Waterloo Station belongs to everybody. The abusive father I had belongs to me. I really wouldn't want to share that or put it into a song. Why waste that three minutes when you could be writing about the sun coming up in the morning?

Other songwriters have said that to be able to write simply you have to dig deep into yourself, but you've said you find it difficult to write lyrics . . .

It's a nightmare.

. . . is it because you're not prepared to look right in at yourself? I may be way off beam here.

No, it's not that. It's difficult for me because I haven't got a lot to say.

THE ART OF NOISE

But you're a great talker.

If I was to write a song about all the things I have an opinion on you wouldn't be here interviewing me. I'd be like the guy in Placebo.

Lots of writers in your record collection have written about themselves.

Johnny Rotten was never singing about Johnny Rotten, was he? He was singing about us. The Specials were singing about us. The Jam were singing about us—that's what I felt, and if they weren't I never read it anywhere that they were. If you were to write a really personal album you'd have to talk about it. What would be the point writing about it? It's like going to the gym and being so toned up; you're going to have take your top off at some point because what would be the point of hiding it behind all those leather jackets? Robbie Williams, for instance; everything is about how fucked up he is, how could it appeal to anybody else? Rap music is all about the rapper's struggle, how he came from the street and ended up in the boardroom. Good for you; doesn't mean anything to me. You're not talking about anything I can relate to, because you're talking about yourself. There are lines all over the place that are personal to me, like the line about the wishing stone; that girl was a real girl, but it could be about your girlfriend or your mam. That's the beauty of it.

Can I ask you for your thoughts about some lyrics and songs you've written? *Cast your words away upon the waves / Sail them home with acquiesce on a ship of hope today / And as they fall upon the shore, tell them not to fear no more.*

I was stoned writing that, for starters . . . I wrote that in a hotel room in Japan. I've still got the sheet of paper in there that says The Roppongi Prince on it. I'd had the title for 'The Masterplan' for ages. Don't know where it came from, just thought it was a great title . . . What does that mean? Fuck knows. The word *acquiesce* is in there because we had a song called 'Acquiesce'. I guess it's saying that words . . . is it . . . I was going to say that words are really powerful, but I'm not a believer in that. I believe actions speak louder than words. I'm not sure what that means, to be honest; you've picked a really vague one.

You found your God in a paperback / You get your history from the Union Jack, from 'Mucky Fingers'.

The Gideon's Bible, you see that a lot in American hotels in paperback. American culture and its history come from England. That song came directly out of 'I'm Waiting For The Man'; it was on in the dressing room one night really loud. Gem's not into The Velvet Underground and I said, 'You mean you're not into that?' and he went, 'That's fucking brilliant,' and I said, 'The rest of it is fucking amazing; what are you talking about?' and he said, 'No, I'm not having it.' The very next thing that came on the iPod was Bob Dylan. We started

DON'T LOOK BACK IN ANGER . .

SLIP INSIDE

(1) ~~TAKE A WALK IN~~ THE EYE OF YOUR MIND

DON'T YOU KNOW YOU MIGHT FIND

A BETTER PLACE TO PLAY

YOU SAID YOU'D ONCE NEVER BEEN

ALL THE THINGS THAT YOU'VE SEEN

ARE GONNA FADE AWAY

BRIDGE

START THE REVOLUTION FROM YOUR BED

THEY SAY THE BRAINS YOU HAVE WENT TO YOUR HEAD

STEP OUTSIDE THE SUMMERTIMES IN BLOOM

STAND UP BESIDE THE FIREPLACE

TAKE THAT LOOK FROM OFF YOUR FACE

COS YOU AINT EVER GONNA BURN MY HEART OUT

CHORUS

So SALLY CAN WAIT, SHE KNOWS ITS TOO LATE, AS WE'RE WALKING ON BY

MY SOUL SLIDES AWAY, BUT DON'T LOOK BACK IN ANGER I HEAR YOU SAY

(2) TAKE ME TO THE PLACE WHERE YOU GO

~~WHERE~~ NO-BODY KNOWS IF ITS NIGHT OR DAY

~~AND~~ PLEASE DON'T PUT YOUR LIFE IN THE HANDS

OF A ROCKN ROLL BAND

WHO'LL THROW IT ALL AWAY

REPEAT BRIDE + CHORUS .

'Don't Look Back In Anger' lyrics, handwritten by Noel Gallagher having a drunken conversation about crossing Bob Dylan with The Velvet Underground, and he can play the harmonica. I said, 'I'm going to write that tune tomorrow.' Again I wrote the tune and then waited for the words to come along. The song's not really about anything, but that line is specifically about American culture and how it's very prevalent in our society at that moment, everything about it annoys me. But I like Americans, funnily enough, and I like America. I love going there, it's a brilliant place, but the shit they export around the world is mind-numbingly awful. Hate it, can't stand it.

'Don't Look Back In Anger'.

I wrote it in Paris. The words I don't remember. Liam came up with the word *Sally*. I was doing it at a soundcheck. I was singing *so* . . . didn't have that word, I was saying something but I don't know what. He came up and said, 'Who's Sally?' and I went, 'What do you mean?' and he said, 'Who's *so Sally can wait?*' and I went, 'Fucking genius.' (*Noel points at the tape recorder.*) 'You're not having any money for that, by the way.' Somebody gave me really early on when I went to the States a cassette of John Lennon speaking into a tape recorder about his memoirs. He was going to write a book before he was shot, apparently, and one of his lines was *the brains I had went to my head.* I'll have that, thank you very much. The opening was a bit like 'Imagine'. It sounds like it's about a girl who's lost something, she's leaving home, she's going off to . . .

Stand up beside the fireplace take that look from off your face.

My mam always used to say that to us. St Patrick's Day, she would always take a picture of us and send it back home to my grandma in Ireland. It would always be by the fireplace. It was just a council house with a little gas fire. She would say, 'Stand up there beside the fireplace while I take a picture of you.' A lot of that first album, a lot of childhood stuff is in there, like nursery rhymes. (*Sings.*) *I'll be you and you'll be me* is from the programme *Stop, Look and Listen*. We used to be at school and you'd have a class when they'd play TV. It was like *Sesame Street* but an English version. That stayed with me for years until I wrote 'She's Electric'.

We'll see things they'll never see.

That's about when you've got a best friend; it could be a girlfriend. I had a mate in Manchester called Rob Rodgers; he worked in a butcher's. He used to have a scooter and we used to go on rallies. We'd drive to Skegness in the pouring rain just to sleep in a bus shelter and come back again. We were both seventeen at the time and just left school. He had a job and I didn't and he bought a scooter on HP. We'd get dressed up in our mod gear and go on scooter rallies. I remember our mate saying, 'What do you do when you get there?' 'Hang around outside chippies with about 10,000 other people, sleep in bus shelters, get pissed, go to a disco and come back again.' He was like, 'You fuckin' pair of idiots.' It was like a thing between me and him; they don't get it, we get it.

The falsetto on the line *live forever* **is sung over an Fsus2 chord according to the Oasis songbook. Was that you exploring unusual shapes?**

I don't play barre chords if I can help it. I always find a way to play with the strings resonating. (*Demonstrates position on his hand.*) The F is like C with two fingers; I don't know what it is, it just happened naturally. Being on the dole was a great thing. I had a girlfriend who was out from eight in the morning till six at night. That's ten hours a day sitting round smoking weed, playing the guitar. All day to fanny about going (*whispers*), 'Wow, listen to that,' for hours, one chord: 'That is fucking outrageous.' Then you'd say, 'Listen to this—it's the lost chord,' and people would say, 'Oh, F suspended major seventh,' and you'd go, 'Oh, fuck off, no, I've invented a chord; it's N, N major.'

Some might say they don't believe in heaven / Go and tell it to the man who lives in hell.

Social comment, there. I'm not religious and I'm not spiritual, I don't think. I guess it maybe was directed at myself. Poor people tend to be exploited by religion a lot. The poorest people in the world have got God—that's all they've got. Fat Westerners like us: 'What you talking about? Money's where it's at, man.' I guess it's the idea of heaven is what keeps the poor going. The rest of us don't see God on a daily basis, do we?

You have a propensity for Ringo-esque incongruities: *Slowly walking down the hall / faster than a cannonball*, **from 'Champagne Supernova' and** *True perfection has to be imperfect*, **from 'Little By Little'.**

Slowly walking down the hall is from either *Chigley* or *Trumpton*. Which is the one with the train? I wasn't watching it at the time, but I remember as a kid the phone ringing and the guy walking really slowly down the hall for ages. This is going to sound bizarre, but it's about that and a train in American mythology called the Wabash Cannonball which is a really fast train. *True perfection has to be imperfect* is a Buddhist saying I read in a book. I like that, because everything that's beautiful slightly has to have an imperfection to it or else it's just a blank canvas. Nothing is perfect, the way I see it. There's another one in 'Force Of Nature': *if what you seek is the wise man's treasure it's buried beneath your feet.* That means that whatever you seek is all around you anyway.

'Little By Little' is very typical of many of your songs: starting low and then climbing melodically.

The chorus always has to be right up there. If I remember correctly, that was one of the songs that I had the chorus for ages and could never get out of it, then I went to that chord and went, 'Oh.' The chord in the verse is a bit Pink Floyd and then it goes into the terrace anthem. So it wasn't a conscious decision to start off low; it just happened. When I first played that demo people were like . . . I was a bit unsure about it. To pull it off live is quite weird because it's really low to sing it down there and you've got to be a bit of a crooner almost. People are always shouting for it at gigs.

The tone in your voice is very beautiful, reminiscent of a version you sang of Bacharach's . . .

. . . 'This Guy's In Love With You'—I'll tell you a funny story about that. For years I listened to that song and it blew me away. I thought it was called 'The Sky's In Love With You'—that's as psychedelic as fuck. I thought it was the most cosmic thing of all time.

Do you have any thoughts on why there are so few classic female British songwriters?

I think that's about to change. All business rules were set up during the war and the Fifties and Sixties. Women's role was in the kitchen. So women pop stars were fronts for songwriting teams. There seems to be powerful women in the music business at the moment like Madonna, not that I like any of it, and edgy characters like Amy Winehouse. It's not Bananarama any more. As for why that is, there's a very simple reason: birds get pregnant. Guys can go off and be rock, pop stars, whatever you want, forever. Chicks eventually get up the duff and have to take nine months off and that's the end of that.

But it doesn't affect American female stars.

I don't know why that is, why is that? That comes from the soul background: Aretha Franklin and The Supremes, it's in their culture. We didn't have it in ours; it was Cliff and The Beatles. If you think of Odetta, the blues lot, there were really strong female characters before rock 'n' roll came along. A lot of it's to do with the movies as well. The film industry had female stars, Bette Davis and all that, way, way before there were any female British stars. It's just in their culture.

JARVIS COCKER

I never said I was deep—'I may have this phrase inscribed on my tombstone.'

In 2011, Jarvis Cocker published his first book of lyrics, *Mother, Brother, Lover*. It can be categorized as neither poetry nor prose, and the introduction begins with Cocker stating, 'I never intended to be a lyricist.' The role was thrust upon him by default. Jarvis Cocker was still at school when in 1978 he founded Arabacus Pulp. Since the band was not yet competent enough to play cover versions, all the members turned to the frontman for words to fit their instrumental compositions. For the 14-year-old boy the task was reminiscent of doing homework, and he often left it to the eleventh hour. The habit followed him into adulthood. Words were often hastily scribbled out while an expectant band or producer waited for the final piece of the jigsaw to be presented. For *Different Class*—the album that would commercially define his band (now simply Pulp)—he completed eight sets of lyrics over two nights sitting in his sister's kitchen with a bottle of brandy brought back by his mother from a holiday in Spain. Needing a justification for his modus operandi, Cocker reasoned that 'maybe words weren't that important to a song's success'. A little like John Lennon, who would listen to the sound rather than the sense of a record, Cocker questioned how much listeners actually absorbed the content of the words. For him (and indeed myself), the aural experience of music is always greater than the subject. This gave him licence to play: lyrics could be fun. Inner sleeves of Pulp releases carried the simple instruction: 'NB. Please do not read the lyrics whilst listening to the recordings.' On record sleeves the words were set in blocks of continuous prose to underline their 'neutral and unimposing' status. It was in stark contrast to verse: 'Lyrics are not poetry: they are words to songs.' Cocker argues that his prose exists only because there is music for them to belong to. They are written with the knowledge of their intended placement; it is the experience of hearing them within their musical framework that determines their meaning and value.

In 2008, Cocker gave a talk at the Brighton Festival questioning the role of lyrics in popular music, under the title 'Jarvis On Song—Saying The Unsayable'. Using PowerPoint presentation, he projected an equation to illustrate the interdependent relationship of words and music:

Music +
Lyrics +
Performance
= *Dynamite*

His lecture, presented over two hours, examined a history of lyrical misunderstanding and controversy, including the concept of a 'rhyme whore—someone who will do anything for a rhyme'. As early as the seventeenth century, the poet John Milton, in his introduction to *Paradise Lost*, had put the case for blank verse, arguing that the striving for rhyme 'set off wretched matter and lame metre'. He felt that rhyming verse was 'of no true musical delight'. Cocker crafts internal rhyme and wordplay within sentences, often ending with feminine couplets, where the rhyming words end on unstressed syllables. This is in contrast with the predictable rhyme on a single stressed syllable at the end of a line, referred to as masculine.

Cocker is a writer of fine detailed observation and revels in the study of the everyday. He inhabits the 'behind-the-net-curtain' world of Ray Davies and Ian Dury and portrays it with the gritty filmic vision of Mike Leigh or Shane Meadows. His interest in creatively feeding back the familiar through song was further focused in 1985 by a six-week stay in hospital. Cocker had sustained injuries to his wrist, ankle and pelvis after falling twenty feet from a window in a misjudged attempt to impress a girl. He got into conversation with a miner in an adjacent bed and heard stories about life down the pit and the devastating effects in South Yorkshire of the 1984–85 strike. It was to have a profound impact on his approach to writing and mark a change in his attitude towards the glamour of the pop star lifestyle. He told Sky Arts, 'I realized that there was more material in looking down at the ground than up at the stars.' It was a wily play on Oscar Wilde's famous quip, 'We are all in the gutter, but some of us are looking at the stars,' but now Cocker embraced the practical and the mundane as a creative resource. In 'Love Is Blind' he mused, *instead of walking around with eyes glued to the sky I turn them down to the ground.* There was renewed focus on physical detail: *In the morning it was all still there the spilled milk and dog turds, in that grey ashtray morning light.* '97 Lovers' is a sensitive song that speaks of *lovers twisted out of shape* and female hearts smashed *on the floor.* Its memorable verse was inspired by a conversation with his Aunt Rita: *I know a woman with a picture of Roger Moore in a short towel and dressing gown pinned to her bedroom wall.* He told *Vox* magazine, 'Reality wasn't this grey lump of concrete after all. It's been my personal thing ever since . . . to try and be specific.'

Jarvis Branson Cocker was born on 19 September 1963. He is a month older than Johnny Marr. Both artists made their recording debuts as 20-year-olds, but whereas The Smiths made an immediate impact, Cocker's journey to recognition would take a further twelve years, by which time he would be thirty-two. Yet Cocker seemed less than comfortable with the idolization of pop stars. At the 1996 Brit Awards Michael Jackson gave a performance of 'Earth Song' in celebration of his newly bestowed title, Artist of a Generation. Cocker watched from the side of the stage as the 'King of Pop' was surrounded by adoring young children. In the light of the recent child sex abuse allegations against the American singer, it was an image Cocker found distasteful. On impulse he invaded the stage mid-song, gave the V-sign, wriggled his bottom, and exposed his belly button to the audience. In a later statement he bluntly explained his protest: 'Michael Jackson sees himself as some Christlike figure with the power of healing.' His actions divided opinion in the media, but amongst his peers Cocker became something of a national hero. Noel Gallagher suggested he should be awarded an MBE and declared, 'Jarvis Cocker is a star.'

In 1988, Cocker had left Sheffield to take up a place at St Martin's College of Art to study film and video. His new life in Central London was to be another key influence on his writing. The cosmopolitan capital pulsated with hope and possibility. The breadth of culture on view was in stark contrast to his provincial upbringing in the suburbs of Intake. Still attached to Yorkshire, if not in body then at least in mind, Cocker began to appreciate his hometown with a sharper focus. Not wanting the steel town to fade from his memory, he began to write about it with vivid detail: *The sun rose from behind the gasometers at 6.30 a.m., crept through the gap in your curtains and caressed your bare feet poking from beneath the floral sheets.* 'Sheffield: Sex City', released in 1992, was written in a single outpouring on the first hot day of summer, 'lying in Hyde Park'. In the autumn of 2011 Cocker revisited his secondary school to lead a session on songwriting. He explained to the gathered pupils his desire to write about his life in Sheffield: 'All those kind of normal things, suddenly they weren't normal any more because I wasn't seeing them every day.' He added that what might appear dull and boring, 'to somebody else will seem exotic'. It was the same school hall where Pulp had made their debut appearance during a lunch hour in the spring of 1983. As a schoolboy Cocker had dreamed of pop stardom, and flanked with four other friends would strut around pretending to be in a band. He told *Select* magazine at the height of his success, 'It just made it seem more interesting when you were walking down the corridor.'

Cocker's musical career neatly divides into three stages: ten years without recognition, ten years as a commercial success and a third act as a solo artist and fringe national treasure. The success of pop's perpetual outsider masks a bewildering history of record company machinations, band line-up changes, and mainstream rejection. Through the barren years Cocker presided over twenty different members of Pulp, enjoyed the prestige of a John Peel session before ever making a record, deferred a place at Liverpool University to study English, and masterminded his eventual triumph from the unlikely setting of a rehearsal room in the attic above a pottery shop. Speaking to Radio 1 in 1998, he reflected on his quiet resilience in the face of adversity: 'Crocodiles can slow their heartbeat to three times a minute if they're conserving energy, and that's kind of like what we were doing. But we weren't actually dead; we just looked like we were.' The band truly came alive at Glastonbury in 1995 when Pulp were invited to replace The Stone Roses in the Saturday-evening slot after the Mancunians' guitarist, John Squire, suffered a bicycle accident. The under-studies' performance would go down in festival history and win Pulp a place in the hearts of music fans. Cocker told the audience about the will to make things happen: 'If a lanky get like me can do it, and us lot, then you can do it too.' Capturing the mood, Pulp then performed 'Common People'. The song had been written in a flat in Ladbroke Grove on a second-hand Casio keyboard purchased from the Music and Video Exchange in Notting Hill, where Cocker used to work filing cassettes. The first bass note on the instrument is C, which he repeatedly thumped with the middle finger of his left hand. He then moved up a fifth to G and then one tone down to F for what would become the chorus, *live like common people*; with his right hand he picked out a melody line using his index finger. The rudimentary approach to instrumentation was a con-scious admission of musical limitation, but it also, crucially, left space for the band to fill with individual interpretation. The song's title and theme was in-spired by a passing comment made by Pulp bass player Steve Mackey in re-sponse to Cocker's riff, 'That sounds like Fanfare for the Common Man.' Enthused, the lyricist recounted the tale of a student at his college, with subtle poetic licence. The wealthy Greek girl existed, but in verse Cocker switched the unrequited attraction from him to her. In reality he had wanted to have sex with the girl but was put off by her admission of wanting to live in Hackney and *sleep with common people*. Chris Thomas, producer of the Sex Pistols and Roxy Music, crafted the record in the studio and the song became a defining single of the Nineties, setting Pulp alongside Blur and Oasis. It was followed by the similarly successful 'Sorted For E's And Wizz'. Cocker explained the song's origin on stage at Glastonbury: '[It's] a phrase that a girl I met in Sheffield once told me. And she went to see The Stone Roses at Spike Island and I said, "What do you remember about it?" and she said, "Well, I just remember all these blokes walking around saying is everybody sorted for E's and wizz?"' The song is an example of how the writer's rhythm guitar playing follows the metre of his verse to match the evolving narrative. After the opening rhythmic two-chord verse, D minor is introduced alongside F and G major to act as a bridge for Cocker to chart the effects of taking MDMA and amphetamine sulphate. From it, *feeling alright* in the *middle of the night*, two hangover chords, A minor and B flat major, are then struck to welcome the morning *come down*. The band then dramatically reassert the song's major chord, C, and set in motion a second verse. 'Common People' having being denied a number one by a song from the television actors Robson and Jerome, was followed by 'Sorted For E's And Wizz', coupled with 'Mis-Shapes', which also scored a number two, behind Simply Red.

Cocker's first attempts at writing lyrics coincided with his sexual awakening. He viewed it as both an outlet for his frustrations and an opportunity to catalogue his feelings. At first he turned to his record collection for answers but was disappointed by pop's sanitized picture of romance. Cocker wanted to hear about sexual experiences with 'all the awkward bits and the fumblings'. In *Mother, Brother, Lover* he outlined the blueprint for his songwriting, as the pairing of '"inappropriate" subject matter to fairly conventional "pop" song structures'. He cited David Bowie and Mark E. Smith as both having an 'ability to tackle thought-provoking subject matter in song'. His forthright sexual expression was a forerunner of Lily Allen's outspoken lyrics a decade later. Cocker told *Vox* magazine in 1995, 'What struck me was how sexless pop music had become.' His lyrics peel back the layers of sexual encounters to reveal stained sheets and messy aftermaths. *On a pink quilted eiderdown*, the narrator of 'Acrylic Afternoons' admits, *I want to pull your knickers down*, whilst in 'I Spy' the writer imagined *a blue plaque above the place I first ever touched a girl's chest*. In 'Babies' Cocker describes listening outside the room to the noises of his girlfriend's sister and *some kid called David from the garage up the road*. In the second verse he takes to hiding in the wardrobe, only to be discovered in the fourth, confessing, *I had to get it on*. As the music climaxes Cocker delivers the song's killer punchline: *I only went with her 'cos she looks like you—My God!* The origin of 'Babies' came from the band's drummer, Nick Banks. During a rehearsal break he picked up the singer's acoustic guitar and played an open A chord with all three fingers positioned one string higher, inadvertently strumming D major seventh. The suspended chord was then resolved with the more standard G major. The sound sparked Cocker's imagination, perhaps reminding him of the first song he ever wrote as a teenager, which shared the same two-chord sequence—'Shakespeare Rock'.

Cocker has a uniquely conversational tone in song delivery. He speaks directly to the listener with candid observations and revealing private thoughts. It is akin to being read extracts from a diary entry or overhearing a private telephone conversation. Musical trope has a distinguished history in pop recordings. It can be heard as recently as Gorillaz' 'Fire Coming Out Of The Monkey's Head' narrated by Dennis Hopper, or as far back as The Shangri-Las, or Elvis Presley reciting from *As You Like It* in 'Are You Lonesome Tonight?' When discussing his natural propensity for narrative, Cocker insists 'a skill is really just a disability in disguise'. His use of spoken word often arises from a failure to find suitable melody. Spoken interludes are littered throughout his work. 'Wickerman', like many Cocker compositions, owes a great debt to the delivery and inventive craftsmanship of Lou Reed. The piece was adapted from an article written for *World of Interiors* before Cocker delivered the song without melody over eight minutes of atmospheric backing. 'David's Last Summer' sandwiches spoken word between melodic choruses. 'Inside Susan: A Story In Three Parts' follows the protagonist 'from puberty' through to 'wild teen years' and then 'her eventual marriage and settling down somewhere on the outskirts of London'. The success of this style rests upon an array of varied emotional expression, musings and dramatic release, with Cocker happily breaking between the first person and a narrator's point of view. It is the musical equivalent of speaking directly to camera, or a theatrical aside. 'You're A Nightmare' describes *rolling empty tin cans down the stairs* with the confidential comment, *don't you love that sound?* Cocker frequently spices his songs with *oh*'s, *alright*'s and *yeah*'s, and his parlante delivery recalls the idiosyncrasies of Suggs, Neil Tennant and the great English songwriter Noel Coward.

As a Christmas gift to fans in 2012, Pulp issued their first record in over ten years. It followed a year of world touring and a decade pursuing individual projects. Cocker had carefully established himself not only as a solo recording artist, but also a BBC radio presenter. His award-winning Radio 4 series *Wireless Nights* allowed him to piece together strange and unusual stories told by ordinary people. It was a natural thematic extension to his songwriting interests. Jarvis had just finished recording a new episode in Calais, near to his current home, and his early-hours finish prompted us to conduct our conversation over the telephone:

'I haven't written a song for about two years, so it's a bogus thing to talk about.'

Why is that?

Well. Pulp got back together for a bit. So there was a lot of stuff to be done, actually relearning old songs and trying to perform them in a convincing way. You can't just trot a song out. You have to inhabit it and live it a bit for it to come across as convincing. So there was that. Also I don't really like writing songs when I'm in a happy relationship, because then when you write a song you generally spoil it, or the way that I write and do things it's sometimes like that. To write a song you have to step outside a relationship or outside a situation and pass comment on it, and once you do that you're removing yourself from it, so I try to stop myself from being like that.

Yeah, I used to try and just write about things that had happened at least five years ago. That was my safety valve, and also changing people's names. My way of writing is not very imaginative. It's more just reporting things, really. So you have to be careful with that because obviously then you're using other people as your raw material and you could see that as a little exploitative. You have to be careful with that. As I say, I have a kind of problem exploiting personal relationships for material, but it's the only way I can write, see. So it's a bit of a Catch-22 situation.

Hence the five-year rule.

Well, it wasn't really a rule but I tried it and sometimes it would work a bit, y'know, 'cause hopefully after five years people have forgotten or lost interest.

Only to be reminded in cruel print.

Well, that's the problem, yeah.

When do you begin to consider melody?

Melody's the first thing that I consider, really. I generally have two ways of writing songs. There's the way sitting at home strumming a guitar or having a go on a piano or something. Or if we're rehearsing as a band, we'll have a go at improvising, and I'll kind of moan over the top and try and come up with a vocal melody. That's usually the starting point for all the songs. It's very, very rare that there will be a lyrical thing first. Sometimes a phrase may just spontaneously pop out because it seems to scan with what you're having a go at doing at the time. But maybe due to laziness I will wait until I've got what I think is a convincing or compelling vocal melody. And make sure that you tape that, so you remember it, and then try and write some lyrics or find some words that will fit with it. I do write words down on an almost daily basis. I always have a notebook with me. And when I've got some songs that could be interesting then I will look through the notebook and see if I could adapt some of those words to make them fit with melodies I've come up with. The melody is very important for me.

How do you build upon a melodic idea once you have the initial inspiration?

I can't write down music, or anything like that, and I'm not much of an instrumentalist either. My guitar playing or piano playing will always be just block chords which I then try and fit something over the top. So that's why it's so important to actually record something. Once it's recorded I will then listen back to stuff. I find that then your brain just naturally starts doing work on it. Some songs you'll write, you have a go and think, 'That's OK,' then you listen back to it and say, 'Actually that's rubbish,' and then other things will stick. If something sticks in your mind that usually means there's something to it. And then it can be quite irritating because then you'll find it playing over and over in your head and you'll try and refine it: 'Well, that bit's OK, but that's bit's a bit boring,' or 'That bit reminds me too much of another song.' A test of whether it's any good or not is if you keep coming back to it in such a way that it starts to drive you mad a little bit, then you know there's something to work with. You find almost subconsciously you work on it.

In 'The Birds In Your Garden' you wrote *they taught me the words to this song,* **which reflects the belief of many songwriters and commentators that birdsong is the origin of melody.**

It's funny because I was speaking to David Attenborough about this on my radio show. He did a programme called *Song of the Earth* and it's really interesting because he's looking at where human music-making comes from and whether the animal kingdom can give us some clues as to where it comes from. He believes, and there is some scientific evidence for this, that the human larynx is so complex, much more complex that it needs to be for just speech. So many people believe we were making sounds before we were saying words. So a variety of calls would have developed. So really the roots of melody would be territorial calls or mating calls. They looked at some examples, some bird that lives in some reeds in Scandinavia or somewhere, and the way the male gets a mate is by a complicated song with a lot of different syllables, the equivalent of a complicated tune or involved melody. Maybe that's part of it, that at some long-distant point in time the structure of a melody, or the way it would stick in someone's head, maybe that was the tool for attracting a mate. I find that quite dispiriting because I'd like to think that we'd evolved beyond that. It seems kind of depressing that it's all just about territory, eating or having sex. I'd like to think there was something more. It's funny that music is one of those things that is held up as an example of the fact that man has developed beyond the animal kingdom where life is just those basic instincts. It's like the fact that we can make beautiful symphonies or things that transport us to a loftier, spiritual place. But maybe that's not right, maybe it's just the same thing and it does all come down to the basics of the animal kingdom. I've always wanted to escape that.

When you're formulating melodies, do the sounds suggest lyrics to you?

Yeah, sometimes, because it will have syllables that are metred so then you will think of words that will fit. That's like a trick, really. That's often where I think songwriters can really fall down, is when they mess around with syntax and syllables in order to make it fit with the melody that they've come up with. I think you've got to keep the rhythm of the words as near as possible to how they would be if you spoke them, so it fits. That can be quite a trick, really, and it's hard, and sometimes you end up changing the melody a bit because once you put words to it . . . you don't want to mangle it too much, but people do all the time and that's what drives me mad when I listen to songs.

That's very similar to how the Pet Shop Boys explain spoken word fitting to melody.

People will add certain words to syllables like (*sings*) *to-night* and *all right*, y'know, *du-du*. They just add bits on and it drives me insane. Gary Barlow does it a lot. He's a bit of a serial offender. Melodically some of his songs are OK, but the way he brutally shoehorns the words on top is a bit much.

There was a transition in your writing to uplifting melody in the early Nineties. I am keen to identify what makes or controls better melody.

I would be keen to know that as well. I'm sure you've had that from a lot of other songwriters. A melody is a very kind of nebulous thing. I find that is really what you chase after when you write a song. Once you've got the melody there . . . you can improve a song a bit if you write some good words, but the song will still be pretty good even if you can't come up with words that are that great. So that's always the kind of Holy Grail of songwriting, I think, is to think of a melody that is affecting in some way. And that's a difficult thing, to say why something is an affecting or an attractive melody. As we say, it may be rooted in some kind of very pre-verbal thing in human nature. So it's a hard thing to analyse. I know that people have come out with computer programs, and things like that, that supposedly tell why music has certain effects, but I don't want to believe it's mechanical. I prefer to think of it as being something that's beyond that. It was probably allowing yourself to have a bit of pleasure in it. The situation of when we were in the group in the Eighties . . . I'd left school and was living in some kind of abject poverty and it was all I had, was the group, and therefore I was trying too hard. I was too uptight . . . that is part of it, you have to allow yourself to be a bit of a conduit through which ideas come and tunes come. And to do that maybe sometimes you just have to be relaxed and maybe, dare I say it, slightly happy to just allow it to happen. Rather than say, 'No, this is significant, this really means a lot.' I don't like listening to any music that I've made anyway, but the stuff that we did in the Eighties I just find unlistenable, just embarrassing. It's the sound of somebody trying much too hard. It's just painful.

Separations **and then** ***His 'n' Hers*** **marked a clear advance in your writing. Did you have a belief you could be significant as a writer before those break-throughs?**

For some reason, I always had quite a lot of self-belief and sometimes I find that quite astounding because I didn't have much to base that on. But I did, for some reason. It's very useful to have blind self-belief. It's a kind of weird self-belief because also a lot of the songs are about inadequacy, or the way you feel you can't measure up to how everybody else is going to be. It's a weird feeling of superiority. But I still had it, misguided though it might have been. That kind of misguided self-belief can go a long way.

Was the self-belief in being able to write songs as successful as they became?
I did want to have some success, I guess, but that wasn't the driving force.

I didn't mean commercial success, more a sense you could write in a manner beyond where you were at the time?
I didn't know that, but the way that songwriting works . . . that groping after something . . . it's almost like a leap of faith, to believe it's there to be caught. So it's also like a faith in yourself that you can achieve something, but you don't know how exactly how to do it. That's the thing that's very enticing and exciting about making music: no matter how long you do it for you don't really know where it comes from, but then it's also the thing that makes it very, very frustrating. Sometimes you'd like to establish a way of working, a modus operandi, and do it, but I don't believe that that's possible. So when it's not working it's very, very frustrating because it's hard to work out exactly why.

Do you cross a border after becoming a successful writer? Is there a sense of having to better yourself with every next song that you write?
Well, you have to make sure that you're not repeating yourself, yeah definitely. You might end up saying kind of the same thing, or you might end up writing about similar kinds of subject matters because you have to write about emotional subject matters, but hopefully as you move through life your view of the same things changes anyway. That fact that you're altering as you move through life alters what you produce. Probably what you're wanting to make . . . generally people get quieter as they get older, don't they? I guess you crave a bit of peace and stability.

Do you mean as a person or a musician?
As a musician; people try to make, I certainly feel more attracted to quieter, subtler music nowadays.

That's ironic because as a solo artist, particularly with the last album *Further Complications* and also *Relaxed Muscle*, the music is getting heavier.
Yeah, it's true, but that's like getting things . . . what I'd think of as getting antisocial impulses out; trying to neutralize them by putting them into music.

Am I right to say with the album *Different Class* that the band set out to write twelve pop songs where each one could be a single?

That could be true! It was written very quickly, that record, because we'd forced Island's hand a little bit by making them release 'Common People' as a single before we'd recorded an album. Usually what people do is go into a studio, record fifteen songs, and then see which one seems to be the best; release that one as a single, and then the ones that didn't turn out so well, have those as B-sides and then that's it, you're done. But we'd written that song and felt that it had to come out. It felt like it had captured some kind of feeling that was in the air at the time and we were scared if we took too long that moment would pass. So that was a big success and then that put a big pressure on us to actually have a record to follow that up. So it was done very quickly, which in the end was the best thing that could have happened, really, 'cause you just kind of get on with it. Maybe at some point we thought everything could be a single.

I was intrigued by the idea that as you sat with an instrument you were consciously trying to channel writing towards a single mode, as opposed to whatever creativity happened to come out.

Well, it was, and it was written in a state of nervous excitement and also from a different position because 'Common People' had been a success. So finally we knew that actually people were going to listen to whatever we did. That was a lot different to releasing stuff on an indie label in the mid-Eighties where no one was going to listen. It was like screaming into the darkness. Knowing that you had people's ears, to some extent, we wanted to make sure we didn't blow that opportunity, and make the most of it. So the subject matter of some of the songs, like the first song on the record, 'Mis-Shapes', would have been really ridiculous if we hadn't been successful. *Brothers, Sisters, can't you see? The future's owned by you and me* would be a silly thing if you were only selling a hundred records. But being a chart-topping band we could say that. So it was an attempt to write music that reacted to that situation and hopefully did something interesting with it. The unfortunate thing about that whole scene they called Britpop was that it just fizzled out into ego gratification, really. It seemed for one brief, flickery second it could have been something more.

Recently I was shown a notebook of Joe Strummer's which contained all his notes and reworkings for *London Calling*. The song itself was formed over many pages from an accumulation of notes and divergent possibilities. Are the notes and ideas you referred to earlier similarly used to arrive at a set of lyrics?

Yeah, I'll generally have a lot of notebooks and then when it comes to the time when I can't put off writing the words to the songs any more—usually the day before you go in to record them—then I'll get all the notebooks out and I'll maybe treat myself to a big jotter or ring-bound folder. And I'll go through the notebooks and the first thing will be to sift out good things from bad things and start putting them in the back of the jotter and then see what I've got and then read through those edited highlights. Sometimes you combine lines from different notebooks, other times a couple of lines will set off an idea for a whole song and you'll just try to add to that. Then I try to marry the words to the songs to see which ones will be appropriate. It's just trial and error, really. You can think it looks great on paper but you have to sing it to see whether it convinces you. And whether it convinces you or not is again a kind of nebulous thing. It's not always the best lyrics that do it. It's just whether it feels right when you're singing it. I always used to get really nervous about going in and singing proper words in front of the group for the first time. Often that would actually be in the studio, which would be even more embarrassing 'cause they could actually hear them then. If you're in a rehearsal room then they can't really hear what you're singing anyway, so it's not that bad. For instance, the first time we played 'Common People' was at the Reading Festival in 1994. I think there's a recording of it. I was up trying to finish the words off the night before, and had kind of forgotten quite a few of them during the actual performance of the song, but you can tell it's kind of there and some bits got changed. You kind of know when you sing it in front of the band, but when you sing it on stage then you really feel it straight away and sometimes that's very unpleasant, because if a song doesn't work you generally know after about twenty seconds and you've got to go through the rigmarole of finishing it, five minutes or whatever, and then you feel really embarrassed. It hasn't happened that often, but there have been a few songs that have been played once or twice and then just binned because they just don't work. You feel like a fraud singing them. That's just a very personal taste kind of thing. Sometimes words on paper look really stupid but sound fine when you sing them. The one I really remember was that song 'Bad Cover Version'. When I wrote the end bit, *like an own-brand box of cornflakes he's going to let you down, my friend* I thought that was pathetic, but when I sang it, it was fine. It's a tough one.

You have said you find it fun 'to look for profundity' in the everyday, and that 'Auschwitz to Ipswich' was an 'irresistible phrase' you heard in conversation, and in 'Big Julie' you quote from the writer Carson McCullers. It suggests writing consumes your everyday thoughts.

I'm always on the lookout for stuff. Since I've been doing a radio show it's been quite an interesting thing and I've wondered about that sometimes because in a way that's coming to music from a different end; that's coming to it as a listener and appreciator, and that's been interesting. But I've been constantly on my guard to make sure that it hasn't changed my attitude to music. I don't want to become just a consumer of it and not a producer of it. But if an idea pops into my head—it's usually just a phrase or a couple of words—I can't help but write it down. Sometimes it's just like two words; I'll see if I can find an example. I'm going to find my notebook out of my jacket. See if I've written anything particularly stupid down recently . . . The last thing I had written down is *house clearances*. That's not really . . . I think what I was thinking there was . . . your possessions are really significant to you and maybe if you live with somebody and you had all their possessions if they'd died . . . here's one: *discounted tomato ketchup . . . gave money to a busker playing pan pipes . . . can bubble wrap be recycled?* That probably wouldn't end up in a song. So that stuff goes in there and then I'll just see if anything makes me laugh. Often it is laughing. I often find when you come up with a good tune I'll get excited and it makes me laugh. When you get that feeling that a song is going to work and the words combine. That's really the best bit of songwriting, I think. It's not finished yet, but you can see it if you can work out the bits.

You've written about the 'haphazard nature of memory' informing an 'original voice'. So it's not something that can be consciously crafted?

Not really, I don't think that you can . . . it's what sticks in your mind and what doesn't . . . Often for me it's negative things: I'll be talking to my sister and not remember a family event of major significance, but then I'll have a really clear memory of a television programme I once watched when I was twelve. I'll kind of be appalled by that, especially when it's childhood memories, when you really weren't that conscious of trying to remember. So you have to recognize that, and if you do recognize that, even though you might not be that happy with it, you can learn to use it or adapt your voice and it can be your style. You can work on that. What you're trying to access when you're writing songs is something to do with the core of you, and that doesn't change that much as you grow up, and dare I say mature. You do learn things about how to make songs and how to write words. It's not like you make rules, but you do learn tricks. It would be dishonest to say that you don't, but they're just cosmetic bits. I don't like to know how it works, really.

To keep the romance.

Yeah.

The line *pudgy twelve-year-olds in Union Jack shorts addicted to coffee whiteners and frankfurters* has appeared in three of your songs, 'Catcliffe Shakedown', 'Modern Marriage' and 'Wickerman', which reminded me again of Carson McCullers, whose phrases would often reappear in short stories until they found the right home.

That was a phrase . . . I think we were all bored on the tour bus one day so we all decided we all had to write a phrase down or something. Maybe we were trying to write a song collectively and I liked that so I kept it. But I kept putting it in these songs that didn't make the grade. It was kind of like a filler that was always trying to get in there and eventually it felt right in 'Wickerman'. I've got a lot of lines that have been around for five or ten years, maybe.

Do you ever see images in your mind's eye when you write?

Sometimes; if a song is about a specific person then I'll try and think about that person. But that doesn't always work that well.

'Mis-Shapes' and 'Weeds' share a common outsider theme. Are you conscious of finding the right framing device or story angle when you revisit a song?

Like you say, you can end up covering the same themes, but hopefully you do something a bit different with them, but I'm not always that aware of it. I wrote 'Weeds' cycling along a towpath on the River Lea. I was also fascinated by weeds where they'd been concreted over and not meant to grow back. We had a lot of trouble recording that song. I don't think we ever quite got it right, really. We'd recorded it and it came to the chorus. For a long time the chorus started with the two words *Oh but*. You can't have a chorus that starts *Oh but*. Yawn. It ended up being *We are weeds*.

Is it difficult to be an observer once you've become the observed?

Yeah, it makes you become self-conscious and then you might begin to look at yourself as well.

Do you have a preferred time, place, or ritual of writing?

No, I wish I did. I envy other songwriters who have that. I'm sure if you establish that routine and go and sit there you will eventually do it. I'm a bit disappointed in myself that I've never managed to establish that level of discipline for myself. It would be better for all concerned if I could avoid leaving it to the last moment, 'cause I do enjoy the process of writing. If anything I tend to write late at night.

Do you have a special type of notebook you always use?

No. I buy a different notepad each time 'cause otherwise you get confused. If you use the same notebook then you'll always be picking the wrong one up. So I vary the colour. It's got to be able to fit in your inside pocket so you carry it with you at all times. I've managed to avoid any kinds of superstitions in that respect. I don't have a favourite pen.

Does the size of the page determine the length of lyrics you write?

Yeah, I'll try and fill a page up, whatever size that is. So often there'll be a lot of words crunched up towards the bottom to make sure it all fits. Generally it's quite small, or other times my writing will be very big to fill up a page.

Have your writing habits changed over the years, particularly thinking
about technological advances?

I do have a phone that's got a recording device on it, or I might use Note-pad, but I don't like using that because I forget there's stuff on there. I used to leave myself voicemail messages. If I had an idea and you're in the rehearsal room you can't really record a phrase so I'd put the phone on the piano or whatever and record it. Sometimes I'd leave myself late-night recorded messages. They used to delete them after a fortnight. There was one particular one I'd recorded on the piano and kind of forgot about it and then I was away for a week and a half. When I came back it had been deleted. I rang up the phone company to ask them to access my voice messages 'cause I knew it was a really good song idea, but they wouldn't help. I said, 'Look, I bet if I'd been killed and they had a police investigation into my murder you'd be able to look through my voicemail records. So it must exist somewhere.' She said, 'Yeah, but you've not been killed.' So I lost it forever and maybe it was the greatest song ever.

If only you'd known somebody at *News of the World*.

Yeah, I could have got a journalist to hack into my account to find the song.

What are your thoughts on drinking as an inspirational force?

Yeah, drinking has helped me in the past, but it's very volatile. It happened when we did *Different Class*: I wrote a lot of stuff in a one-night session aided by a lot of Spanish brandy. It wasn't like I came up with all the songs in one night. I'd got lots of envelopes and things like that with ideas on and put it all together in one night, but then I tried it again a few months later and I fell asleep. It can help . . .

. . . as with 'This Is Hardcore'?

Well, that's the example I always give. In the case of that song I had the title but I had absolutely no idea what it was going to be about . . . pornography, y'know, but . . . it was a big title to live up to. So I got drunk and then I woke up the next morning and I had written something, even though it was very hard to read. I could kind of decipher it so I wrote it out a bit more neatly. I had a vague idea of where it was supposed to fit melodically, because that song's got lots of different bits, but I didn't really know. So the only way to approach recording the demo of the song was to repeat the same process, so to get blind drunk again and then sing it. I sang it last as well . . and most of the melody came from that session. I would hate to quote that as an example because that really is a one-off situation. It's never happened with any other songs. I wouldn't recommend it as a way to work.

Was that typical that you had a title? Do you have lists of them?

Sometimes a phrase will suggest itself and I'll think, 'That's a good title,' so then I'll have a clue what the song's going to be about.

I was fascinated to read about Pulp that the band would assume characters to abstract scenarios. Nick Banks suggested it might be 'Animals . . . deep in a forest,' or 'Let's do a jazz funk song,' and then the band would jam around that idea.

We never got anything any good out of that, though. It was fun to pretend to be an elf or something. We used to record everything on cassette. I've got about 500 cassettes in my loft in London. I keep thinking, one day I'm going to listen to those and I'm going to find these lost gems. I did actually try and do it once. I got onto side two of the first cassette and it got chewed up in the cassette player, so I chucked the cassette at the wall and it broke. So that was the end of that process, but what I'd heard up to that point wasn't amazing. It was probably all right to do at the time, and maybe there is something on there and I will get round to listening to those 500 cassettes one day. I can't bring myself to throw them away. That's a lot of work.

If you were employing that device up to the last album there must have been something in it sparking creativity.

We would just try lots of different things. You've got to vary your approach. If you just do the same thing every time . . . so sometimes you'd change instrument. So I can't play the piano but I've written songs on it. If you play the guitar a lot your hands seem to get used to going to certain places and it gets boring. So then you can tune the guitar a bit weirdly and that will take you somewhere else. Buy a new keyboard that makes a weird sound. Often musicians will do that; a new piece of equipment will start some new ideas. Another one we would do a lot would be everybody swap instruments, so sometimes I would even end up playing the drums. You knew for a fact that nothing good was ever going to come out of that, with me on the drums. But it was funny to play the drums for twenty minutes until everybody got sick of me being too loud. Actually the one time when that worked was 'Babies': we were trying to play stuff and getting bored; Nick was playing the guitar but because he doesn't really play the guitar he didn't really like to do chords properly. So he came up with the chord sequence in the verse which is this D major seventh to an E which I think was him trying to play an A but he played it on the wrong strings. I heard that and thought, that's really good, do that again. That was the start of that song. The rest of it came from that once we got the verse going. It suggested where it would go after that.

Would you ever approach writing with the style of another songwriter in mind? You can hear The Velvet Underground in 'Glory Days' or Roxy Music in 'Homewrecker!', for example.

Not really; generally speaking I'll see that as a negative thing. Like if you write something and you think, 'That's OK,' then suddenly you think, 'Oh

God, that's the melody from "Take On Me" by a-ha'—actually I wouldn't mind that. That wouldn't be so bad. You know when you've kind of ripped off somebody else's tune. I don't like that. I haven't really got the technical ability to do that anyway.

Are the conditions of where you try and write important?

Volume makes a big difference. I tend to like to go places where you can shut the door and then you make as much noise as possible and nobody can hear you. If I think that people can overhear me, again it's that self-conscious thing, I can't do it. So I have to know it's soundproofed. To sing convincingly I think you have to be singing towards the top of your range because then it's got some kind of urgency to it. But to do that it's obviously got to be loud 'cause if you're just shouting over an acoustic guitar . . . so amplification does make a difference. That's why I really started using Casio keyboards and things like that, because you can press a button and it's got like drums and a bass line and some chords playing. So it's like a band playing straight off. So you can just set it going and then try and do something over the top of that and it will make you write something with a bit more energy to it. Otherwise, if you're always just strumming an acoustic guitar in a bedroom you're always going to write pretty low-key songs and usually probably singing it a lower register as well. On stage you often find that a song doesn't happen because . . . I found that with that song 'A Little Soul': that song was never played live before it was recorded. The recorded version is OK, but when we came to play it, when it came to the middle bit, it was just super flat. There was no dynamic to it. So when I sing it now I go up an octave for the bit in the middle and then it works. If we'd played that song live before we'd recorded it that would have become really apparent to me and obviously we would have recorded it that way. In the studio you're singing into a microphone and it's amplified and you think, 'Oh yeah, that sounds OK.' You don't realize you're not actually singing it out enough for it to work as well as it could work. With a couple of songs on tour we've moved them up. Usually when bands go out and play in their later life they transpose songs down. Generally speaking, as you get older you get less able to reach the higher notes. We moved 'Helped The Aged' down two notes because that was always too high (*sings*): *funny how it all falls away*—super hard to do. 'Party Hard' we moved up two notes. 'Trees' we had a go moving up. 'Bad Cover Version': I always had a problem there. I really liked that song and really like the chorus, but the first verse doesn't really grab you, so I found myself singing the first couple of lines up an octave. You're singing the same words and it's got the same chords behind it, but I think for the voice to grab you and for it to feel involving you should be making an effort. Not too much, not painful effort, but just feel like it's . . . because then it's like unconsciously you think, 'Oh yeah, that person actually is bothered about what they're singing, because they're actually busting a gut to get there and sing that note.'

Do you recall the creative moment when 'Heavy Weather' first emerged?

That song, I was trying to become neutral. I was trying to become Switzerland. I'd left England and I was married and I was trying to be a proper person. I was trying to write a song that other people could sing. It's a kind of vague-ish song. I like the tune of it. Lyrically I find that song a bit weak now. It's trying to be too neutral. It's trying to be too much like this classic song that another person could sing. In the end I don't think I'm very good at doing that.

Would the musical inspiration have been the hammer-on the A string on the second fret that forms the G chord?

Yeah, I like that. That's what I found interesting about that song. I liked the idea of having something with irregular bar counts. So that was the interest of the (*hums two notes A to B*). Then everybody had to look at each other and go 1–2–3–4–5–6 (*hums two notes again*). I realized I had to do something like that because it was so conventional in chord structure. A friend, the guy who I did the Relaxed Muscle record with, Jason (*Buckle*), he used to do all these demos of ideas and send me them to see if we could come up with some more songs. One of them had all this thunderstorm sound on it. I didn't really like the music that he'd done, but I liked the idea of something with a thunderstorm, so it started from that. Then I just tried to add something that could go over that. So I always knew that there was that storm sound on it.

You had many attempts to incorporate 'Tell Her You Love Her' by Stanley Myers and Hal Shaper into a song.

I'd had that *Otley* soundtrack album for years. I always thought that riff would be great for a song. I first tried using it when I did a thing for Nick Cave's Meltdown in 1999—this Harry Smith folk song archive thing, which I think I got the wrong end of the stick. I thought you were supposed to take that as a starting point and write something of your own. That was an attempted response to the 'Boll Weevil' song that's on there. I did a song called 'Cockroach Conversation' which was about when I was living in Camberwell. It was quite infested with cockroaches in this flat. Once, one was walking around the edge of a pan that I was trying to make some food in. I was just hoping it wouldn't fall in, because then I wouldn't be able to eat the food and I didn't have any money to buy any more. Any road, so that was a semi-improvised thing with that loop going off in the background all the time, but it didn't really develop into a proper song. And then we kept coming back to it and it never getting anywhere. Then we were in the midst of doing the *We Love Life* record with Scott Walker and we didn't have quite enough songs, so we went back and did a bit of writing towards the end of that record and that's when I managed to actually get something to fit with it. I was very pleased. Again, 'Trees' is a song that we've never been able to play it live very successfully. I think the recorded version works really well and is probably one of my favourites on that record, but live it never really convinced me.

You wrote the lyrics for the album *We Love Life* **at the demo stage for the first time.**

Yeah, I was probably trying to be a bit efficient. We had so many goes at recording that record. We started it in summer 1999 and then abandoned it a couple of times. So it took a real long time.

I read that you dreamt 'The Last Day Of The Miners' Strike' as a John Lennon song.

Yeah, usually when you dream a song, that's really awful. Again talking about recording things on your phone, I've got a few things where you wake up in the middle of the night and think, 'This-is-fucking-amazing.' It's often like I'm listening to a song in a dream and thinking, 'Shit, this is so good I wish I'd written this,' and then you suddenly think, 'Oh yeah, this is a dream. I am writing it in my mind now,' and then you can sometimes force yourself to wake up and I'll run and get my phone and then I'll start humming into it thinking, 'Oh yeah, I've got it down, I've got it down.' Then you listen to it the next morning and it's just like *uuugghaagguugh*, this random, completely unintelligible grunting and groaning, 'cause you do it when you're still basically asleep. So that's a very rare example where something actually did end up being useful. But in my dream, this thing of *the last day of the miners' strike was the Magna Carta in this part of town*—it wasn't really that appropriate because the Magna Carta was written by the feudal lords that reined in the power of the king. That's not what the miners' strike was at all, really—but it scanned, so I stuck with it. That was basically the bit that came from the dream; I had the title and that bit and I had to write the rest around it.

I chatted to Chris Thomas and he said that you 'write every note', referring to Pulp arrangements.

That's nice of him to say that, but I don't think that's really true. I play a lot of things on the record. I don't just play the guitar and sing. I play keyboard bits and things like that as well. But I don't write all the bits. Generally speaking everybody's got their parts and sometimes I'll suggest bits. I love overdubbing, I'm sure he told you that. I've tried to take a more frugal approach to song recording nowadays, but in those days I had the attitude if a studio had 48-tracks that meant you *had* to use all forty-eight tracks, otherwise you were wasting tracks. So those Pulp records are very dense. That's how we got to where we were going for it to reach this terminal density which somehow the sheer weight of it made it convincing.

Did the inspiration for 'Don't Let Him Waste Your Time' come from the riff?

That was a rare example where the melody came into my head. The riff is copied from a Dion track that he did with Phil Spector called 'Only You Know'.

Alex Turner has said he would like that song played at his funeral.

I really liked that riff, so I had it in my head. Then I was filling a bath, my son had only just been born so I was getting ready to bathe him, and the melody just came to me and I knew that it would fit over that riff. And I think even the words *don't let him waste your time* came to me. So the whole chorus stuck in my head. At that time I was trying to convince myself to stop writing songs.

Why?

I thought I'd done it enough and should do something else (*chuckles*). So I didn't record it. I thought it'd go away. But then it was quite a good tune so it actually lived on without being recorded. Then because it kept going round in my head, then eventually I just recorded it 'cause then at least maybe I'll stop thinking about it, because it was beginning to drive me a bit mad.

Nancy Sinatra did a wonderful version of it, but she wasn't the reason for the song being written?

No, I'd come up with that tune, sat on it and tried to ignore it. And then she got in touch asking for songs and I thought, 'Maybe this is a way of doing it. If I give her that song that's great, because that means I don't have to do it.' So it might be a way of still writing songs but without me having to actually go through the rigmarole of doing them. So I did that, but then in the process of it I realized . . . I really liked the versions that she did of them, but I wanted to do my own. She did two songs, that and 'Baby's Coming Back To Me'. I realized I was attached to them, so although I thought I'd been really clever and found a way of escaping the trap of self-expression, I actually hadn't.

Were the chromatic notes from C through to G on 'Sliding Through Life On Charm' the musical starting point of that song?

That was a Casio one, definitely. I'd borrowed Mark Webber's big, massive Casio keyboard, which we still use on stage now, because it had some different pre-sets on it. It had this rock pre-set which I was particularly fond of and I was always messing about with. 'I Spy' was also written using that, because it's really just the same chords as 'Common People' but minor. And 'Sliding Through Life On Charm' again is basically those same three chords, but as you pointed out—you said chromatic, I don't know—the notes are a bit more unusual. I don't think I wrote it at exactly the same time as 'I Spy' and 'Common People' but it had been around for a while and I thought it was too similar to those two songs for us to do. So when I bumped into Marianne Faithfull and she said, 'Write me a song,' I said, 'Well, give me a title, then,' and she gave me that title and I just remembered that song and recycled that to give to her. It made me finish it off and write some words for it and try and formalize the melody of it.

What were you thinking when you wrote *everybody wants to kiss my snatch / to go where God knows who has been before*?

She'd got this biography out which hadn't been out that long at the time, called *Faithfull*. I read through that and underlined bits, and I'd always liked 'Why D'Ya Do It' off *Broken English*. I was trying to do something in that style, trying to write a song that had that kind of feel to it. So I thought, well, if you're going to do that, if you're going to try and write something that's not that dissimilar, why don't you make it clear to people that you know that's what you're doing by actually quoting from the song that you're basically ripping off? (*Laughs*.)

You wrote three songs for the Harry Potter film *The Goblet of Fire*: **'Do The Hippogriff', 'Magic Works', and 'This Is The Night'. How did you approach those compositions?**

I think they'd approached a few people. Jason and I again had a song that we'd never finished that we just recycled and then they liked it. So then we got the job of writing a couple more. They were for a very specific thing and they were songs that were played by this fictional band at a school party. We knew there had to be one really up-tempo song, and one—what is often referred to as the erection section, the slow dance at the end of the night—a romantic one, and then something else that would just be around in the background. So they were very much written to a brief, which for me again at that time—which wasn't that long after writing the songs for Nancy Sinatra—this way of attempting to write stuff without getting too emotionally involved in it was a real relief: to have a brief and feel that what you were writing was useful in some way to someone else. That it was helping to move forward a story or a dramatic moment in a film. I really liked that, the fact that it fulfilled a function.

And you were not inhibited by the enormity of the success of *Harry Potter*?

No, the sad thing about that was the group was meant to be called The Weird Sisters because that was what they were called in the book, but there was a slightly lezzy Canadian folk group who kicked up a fuss and tried to sue the film company saying that they'd stolen the name from them. So even though that was ridiculous and eventually that got thrown out of court, the film company cut down the amount the band was in the film. At one time they were talking about doing a whole album of songs and I thought that might have been funny, to have a go at that, but because of the threat of legal action, in the film the group aren't referred to as The Weird Sisters, they are referred to as the group with no name. It's a pity.

Did J. K. Rowling have to approve your lyrics?

I didn't have any dealings with her. I guess they must have been run by her at some point. Strange thought, but I was not present.

In 'Disco 2000' would the Stones-like two-chord riff have been the starting point for the song?

Yes, it was. We were messing about. That was off *Different Class* and so we were really trying to quickly write songs. That may have been me messing about on Candida's (*Doyle's*) keyboard when she wasn't looking and thinking, 'Oh, that's funny to have that.' It was played on the keyboard first (*hums riff*) and then we realized it sounded better on guitar. Sometimes that happens: at first you don't actually take something seriously for a bit, and then we kept playing it, and if you keep being drawn back to something and keep playing it then that probably means it's all right. I suppose that's probably the most conventional, commercial pop song we ever wrote. It's quite a catchy one, that one.

How did the words and theme follow?

The phrase 'Disco 2000' I liked. We'd done a party when I was at art college and I'd done some slides on very early computer technology that said Disco 2000 on them. That idea when I was a kid, the year 2000 seemed the most futuristic thing ever. The year 2000 was looming and it had seemed mind-blowing to me as a kid that I'd be alive in the year 2000 and we would be in space and I'd be there and wasn't that incredible. It was very naive to think that now. It was 1995 and the millennium was only five years away and I thought, This is a very upfront song: what subject could go with that? It seemed to me that a lot of people of my generation had that feeling and maybe you would have that thing of saying when you left school, 'We'll never forget each other and we'll all meet up in the year 2000.' I guess a lot of people made pacts and it never happened. In the case of the fountain that I wrote about in that song, Sheffield Council didn't help by actually removing it in 1998. So it physically couldn't happen even if people had remembered to do it. Then it was memories of a true story of a girl who was born at the same time as me, and my mum was in the same maternity ward as hers and we ended up going to the same school.

When you were putting the words together, did you have a tape of the backing track to fit them to?

No; because we'd played it a lot of times I knew how it went. I don't think I would have had a tape. I would just kind of know it by then and would just try

and get the words to fit it. The bit about the woodchip wallpaper kind of
fetishized a lot of the things that were around me as a kid. I was always fascinated by woodchip wallpaper. I wanted to have that as merchandizing on this
last tour that we had, sell rolls of it. We even considered having the whole stage
done in woodchip, but I was outvoted on that one.

**More's the shame. A final thought: there have been few really successful
British performing female songwriters. Do you have any thoughts as to why?**

No, I wouldn't know that at all. I don't think there's any reason why that
should be. Have you got any thoughts, since you've been speaking to people?

**There have been thoughts around traditional expectations of women; some
have talked about maternal instincts that prevent women following careers;
others have spoken of the sea change currently happening; or that in America there isn't the same scenario, but largely it has baffled people.**

Maybe it goes back to the start of our conversation, if all human music
making is an extension of this ancient primal thing. All those things of sexual
display are usually done by the male attempting to find a mate. So maybe it's a
leftover from that. It's still the men prancing around shaking their tail feathers
around attempting to impress girls. And girls are too mature to get involved in
all that.

LILY ALLEN

You must be joking me if you think you'll be poking me. In 2010 Lily Allen's work was included in an exhibition at the British Library about the evolution of the English language, ranging from Anglo-Saxon literature to the cockney rhythms of 21st-century popular song. Lily Allen is a female voice without compromise or historical precedent. In a songwriting tradition where it is rare for women to address sexual topics directly, Allen's bold stance is a revelation. Crushing comic put-downs and blatant scorn for male weakness are key ingredients in her songbook. The cutting candour of her lyrics refuses to pander to writing stereotypes. Allen exposes female moods, desires and disappointments with casual ease. She seems to be simply reaching out as if in conversation with friends or family, the lyrical honesty often masked by a light musical veneer.

In November 2005, two months after signing a record deal, Allen opened a MySpace account: lilymusic was to have a profound impact on the relationship between an artist and her fan base. Allen engaged in direct communication with her social networking Friends, writing daily blogs and sending out mixtapes. The format had found favour with DJs in the 1990s as a natural successor to cassette compilations. Lily Allen persuaded Polygram to fund her mixtape as she worked towards her first release. Each CD was hand painted and individually numbered. The Internet was proving to be the essential source of pop music interaction. As of Christmas 2004, downloaded tracks were outselling physical singles for the first time in British music history. 'Crazy' by Gnarls Barkley became the first song to top the singles chart on the basis of downloads alone. Online purchases accounted for an additional thirty million sales. Meanwhile in Sheffield, the Arctic Monkeys were giving away free demos at their gigs. Devoted fans then circulated the recordings online. When their debut single 'I Bet You Look Good On The Dancefloor' was released in October 2005 on Domino Records it shot straight to number one. The music industry had undergone a quiet riot. The means of production, distribution and exchange was suddenly in the hands of the creators.

In time, Lily Allen albums would invite customers to download 'track stems' enabling fans to remix drum, bass or vocal takes to their own satisfaction. The flirtation between official and unlawful circulation of music was increasingly challenging the market. In 2008, when the International Federation of the Phonographic Industry released figures declaring that over forty billion music files had been downloaded illegally, Allen blogged in response, 'I want to make it clear that file-sharing is not alright. And I want the industry and the artists that have made it, to look at how we can help those artists that are still struggling to break through in the file-sharing age.' The debate was global and Billy Bragg focused the argument, placing responsibility on Internet service providers. The speed of technological advance was incredible. Songs could be written, recorded and released within hours. When Allen's producers Future Cut had a final day in the studio, they playfully mixed an old reggae track with 'Window Shopper' by 50 Cent. Allen employed her acerbic wit updating the lyrics to fit the rhythm and metre of Curtis James Jackson III's rap, with references to *KY just to ease up the friction* and *leaks in your colostomy bag*. Three hours later 'Nan You're A Window Shopper' was on lilymusic, with almost instantaneous reaction and comment firing back. It was nothing short of a musical revolution. By the summer of 2006 the demand for an official Lily Allen single was at breaking point. In April a 500 limited-edition run of 'LDN' had been issued to appease online demand. Allen's website had seen traffic of over a million downloads and her Friend count was nearing 25,000. Despite the demise in the same year of *Smash Hits* and *Top of the Pops*, music was still very much a cutting-edge phenomenon.

Allen was clearly in the vanguard of the new order, but because she is not an instrumentalist she needs to work with musical collaborators to unlock her writing and melodic talents. Finding the right production team to inspire her imagination is crucial to her success. She had a brief relationship with London Records, but in 2002 the label let her go. She had been signed on the strength of her work with her father Keith, who had written folk songs for her, but the recordings were not released. Allen was then picked up for a development deal by Regal, a division of EMI. Incredibly, her £25,000 advance would be recouped within ten days of her debut album release. *Alright, Still* would go on to sell in excess of two and a half million copies, receive five Brit nominations and enter the American *Billboard* top twenty. The masterminds behind the unpredicted success were Darren Lewis and Tunde Babalola. Billed as Future Cut, the drum and bass production duo negotiated the delicate balance between studio production and Allen's natural gifts. Together they built ideas from samples, raiding the extensive record collections of both parties. With a loop in place, the singer would then free-associate at the microphone to generate melodic and lyrical designs. Improvisation has remained Allen's trusted outlet for creating instant sketches. The first complete song she ever wrote rested upon Jackie Mittoo's 1969 rocksteady keyboard instrumental 'Free Soul'. The resulting song, 'Smile', would become the lead track of *Alright, Still,* and by the end of 2006 it was listed as the UK's eleventh-bestselling single. The record launched Allen's career across Europe and would eventually achieve over half a million sales in America.

Lily Rose Beatrice Allen was born 2 May 1985 in Hammersmith Hospital. She had an unconventional upbringing, abandoning her education at the age of fifteen after attending thirteen different schools. Her first positive musical step came when a schoolteacher happened to overhear her singing 'Wonderwall'. That teacher, Rachel Santesso, was to become a mentor to Allen, and on the liner notes of *Alright, Still* was specially thanked 'for discovering my voice'. While still a teen-ager, Allen persuaded her mother to allow her an extended stay in Ibiza. After she had spent a month dealing drugs and partying, a chance meeting with George Lamb was to transform her life. The future BBC DJ had faith in the wayward teen-ager and undertook her management. Aged barely sixteen, Allen began to channel her energy into becoming a pop star. It would take six years to achieve her aim, during which time she worked as a florist and took various jobs in bars and restau-rants. Always a heavy dope smoker, she struggled to find security and happiness. Following cognitive behavioural therapy to address her anger, at eighteen she took an overdose after splitting up with her first serious boyfriend. She would later self-harm and undergo a four-week residency at the Priory clinic. Allen's parents had separated when she was four, and the underlying effects of the break-up have gov-erned her subsequent relationships and invited much candid songwriting about her family. From an early age she had moved in a world of show business and well-known faces. Her mother is the BAFTA-winning film producer Alison Owen, and her father the actor Keith Allen. Joe Strummer was one of a number of famous family friends and was known to Lily as Uncle Joe. The former Clash frontman would lend his adopted god-daughter records from his eclectic collection. The exposure to Jamaican dancehall and reggae, British punk and New Orleans jazz would play alongside her own leanings towards Blossom Dearie, Ella Fitzgerald, The Slits, Wreckless Eric and the more current Prince and Eminem. In 2009, her connection with The Clash led to an invitation from Mick Jones to contribute vocals on 'Straight To Hell' for the charity recording *War Child Heroes*.

Allen is a product of her environment. She writes from direct experience. Her flair for storytelling lends her writing a natural energy and authenticity. 'LDN' (a text-spelling of the city's name) offers a ride through the city by bike. The lilting brass pop, lifted from 'Reggae Merengue' by Tommy McCook And The Super-sonics, with its sun-in-the-sky chorus, shadows the lyrical verses of *pimps, crack whores* and street crime; its photographic observation factually exposes London's everyday narratives: *the sights that I'm seeing are priceless.* The words are deliv-ered with honesty, simplicity and precision. The lover in 'Never Gonna Happen' recoils at her scorned partner's desperate tones, but then confesses *it's weeks since I've been laid.* 'Not Big' teases a dismissed boyfriend for not being well endowed after spending *ages giving head* and being left *lying in the wet patch in the middle of the bed.* The modernized country rhythms of 'It's Not Fair' build to the accusation *you never make me scream.* It is astonishing to learn that her talent for words only reveals itself in the security of the studio. Allen hoards observations in her imagination until the final moment when the recording red light goes on.

Seven different producer/songwriting teams were involved in the making of *Alright, Still.* While Regal tussled with the retail value of a 20-year-old star with obvious pop sheen attributes, there followed a search for suitable artists to collaborate with Allen. Time spent with Gonzales, Bjorn from Peter, Bjorn and John, and even Damon Albarn produced no results. The songwriter's need for an external creative energy to draw out her own individualism was eventually found in a trip to Los Angeles and collaboration with the English-born producer Mark Ronson, whose work with Amy Winehouse had generated the hugely successful and influential *Back To Black* album. Allen's work with him resulted in the song 'Littlest Things', with incorporated elements from the soundtrack to the film *Emmanuelle.* Intriguingly, a later writing session was unproductive, as Allen reveals in conversation.

Allen's songwriting process hinges upon creating hooks and finding vocal and melodic lynchpins. 'Knock 'Em Out' displays a hilarious blend of rap and melody, with one-line put-downs designed to deter male suitors building to the mention of *herpes, syphilis* and finally *I've got to go my house is on fire!* Sessions for Allen's second album began in a rented cottage in the Cotswolds. *It's Not Me, It's You* was a more focused collection. Allen worked with Greg Kurstin, who had co-written three tracks on *Alright, Still.* The subsequent *Paris Live Sessions* bear witness to the strength of the partnership's songwriting match. Simply accompanied by acoustic guitar and piano, a handful of their songs are transformed by their minimalist presentation. They also reflected a rewarding organic approach to creating song. Kurstin would play chord combinations on guitar or piano with the vocalist directing with simple stop, start instruction. If an idea occurred it would be sung over the top, with words ad-libbed. An initial week and a half session resulted in six songs. The producer realized that Allen's speed and instinct was her greatest gift. If she liked an idea, Kurstin would loop the chords, allowing Allen to conjure fitting melody and words before the producer built up the track on a laptop from the resulting contribution. It was a set-up that included both acoustic instruments, analogue synthesizers and a MIDI controller. In 2010, Allen and Kurstin were named Songwriters of the Year at the Ivor Novello Awards and 'The Fear' picked up the award for best song musically and lyrically. The words recognized an unhealthy pop culture where Allen was becoming increasingly uncomfortable.

In 2009 the season's annual Mercury nominations included the largest female presence in the prize's seventeen-year history. Allen declared it the Year of The Girl. Florence Welch, Lisa Hannigan, Elly Jackson of La Roux, and Natasha

Khan from Bat For Lashes all watched as the industry award was presented to the London-born rapper Speech Debelle. The charts were flooded with women songwriters: Amy Winehouse, Adele, Little Boots, Estelle and P. J. Harvey. Yet thanks to Dame Vera Lynn and television discovery Susan Boyle, it was mature artists whose records topped the year's end sales. Their success marked a change of attitude in the music industry, as it was proved that older artists could deliver as readily as younger ones and that women were capable of writing their own material, even if sometimes still with the aid of production teams. Meanwhile 'Puppet On A String', a Eurovision Song Contest-winning entry for Sandie Shaw in 1967, had provided the musical backdrop for Lily Allen's 'Alfie', the closing track of *Alright, Still*. This sampling of an earlier popular favourite for reuse in a very different type of music was bringing British songwriting full circle.

Lily and I met in her west London office. It was her first official conversation about music since she had posted a shocking blog two years earlier entitled 'It's Not Alright'. It read, 'Just so you know, I have not renegotiated my record contract and have no plans to make another record.' After playing her final shows in June 2010 in Manchester and London, the 25-year-old retreated to her country home. Her name has constantly featured in the tabloid press ever since, as much for her personal life as for her venture into fashion with the Soho boutique Lucy In Disguise. As we chatted, Lily was seated at a computer desk in front of a wall adorned with platinum discs. Dressed down in a light-blue floral dress and black cardigan, with hair tied back, she was disarmingly natural and open. Ethel Mary, her five-month-old daughter, was tired and the loving mother was happy to have her sit on her lap between sleeps in the adjoining studio. Lily's retiring blog had included the phrase, 'I do however remain a fan of new music . . .' and it was very welcome news that, after a two-year hiatus, the artist was returning to the studio to begin work on what became her second UK number-one album, *Sheezus*.

I'm really thrilled you're going to be in the book.

I thought it was a joke.

Why?

I thought I was being set up.

Why did you start writing and when?

I always wanted to be a singer. Earlier on in my career I used to sing other people's songs or what other people gave me to sing. Then I had this manager called George Lamb and he said, probably because he was financially driven, 'You should start writing yourself.' I was terrified of the prospect because I'd never done it before. I went up to Manchester to work with these two guys called Future Cut—Darren and Tunde—and I just kind of started really. I just sort of made it up as I went along. I was absolutely terrified. I didn't know what I was doing. I don't study other people's music. I'm not really very knowledgeable. All I know is what I'd heard on the radio growing up. I hadn't really thought about it before. I remember the first proper song that I wrote was 'Smile', which was my first single. I remember writing the verse and the chorus and then them going, 'OK, we just need a middle eight,' and I was like, 'I don't know what that is.' So I had to run out of the studio and call my manager. I was so embarrassed. (*Laughing.*)

How was it described to you?

He said it's that piddly bit in the middle that's not the verse and not the chorus but kind of links the two. I was like, 'OK.' So that's why on 'Smile' it's just *la, la, la*.

Did that prompt you to want . . .

. . . to keep writing?

. . . or to understand structures?

No, I've never really . . . I've just kind of done what . . . classic sort of radio songs really, to be honest. At the beginning I was just doing what other people did, so, 'How long does a song last on the radio? Three and half minutes: OK, so we'll divide that up into three choruses and two verses and a middle eight and it kind of fits,' you know. It's only as things have progressed further that I've had the confidence to do my own thing a little bit more. Now I'm doing this musical for *Bridget Jones's Diary* and that's a completely different thing I'm doing with pop songs. I don't really live by rules in my life or my work.

Would you say songwriting comes naturally to you?

No, I wouldn't. I find it really difficult. I get really nervous before I go in for writing sessions. I never write unless I'm in the studio.

I find that extraordinary.

Really?

Do you not collect any thoughts?

Sometimes I'll be talking about something . . . usually some kind of contradictory conversation comes up and I'll think, 'That's quite funny. I could turn that into a song,' but more often than not I forget it. Sometimes I do think during everyday life, 'Oh, that would make an interesting subject matter,' but I never write it down. I should. (*Laughs.*)

I find listening to your records there is such a breadth and succinctness of ideas. I assumed they came from threads of collected thoughts.

It's strange. (*Laughs.*) I do wish that I did think about it more. I've just started writing again, a new record for myself, and I'm struggling to come up with things to write about. So I should probably start carrying a notebook around, writing down all my ideas as they come into my head.

Is the difficulty that you are forcing yourself in a given moment . . . ?

I suppose maybe at previous times in my life I've been doing so much; I've been out and about . . . a colourful social life . . . I was struggling. Whereas now I am struggling but with things . . . I don't know if I could write a story about my baby being tube fed. I don't think anybody would find it interesting. I live quite a reclusive life nowadays. I live in a nice big house in the countryside. I'm not going out to clubs. I'm not getting into altercations with people. I'm in love . . . before I wasn't. I was looking for it. So it's quite hard. It's just going to be a little harder.

It's a transition, presumably, or how to recalibrate your mind.

Exactly. I wrote three songs last week and they're good but I feel they might be slightly one-dimensional. There isn't a bittersweet aspect to it like there has been with my previous stuff.

When you say you've written a song, what is that to you? You've written a set of lyrics?

No, I've put down three songs; recorded three songs. I write and record at the same time, basically in collaboration with Greg Kurstin.

Do you only write if you are with Greg?

The reason I'm writing with him is because I have been so out of practice that I'm a bit nervous of going in with other people. I need to be in that musical environment in order to write. I need to be inspired by what I'm hearing, so it does need to be a collaboration. With Greg what we do is we sit around a piano, and he plays different chord progressions, and something will remind me of a feeling that I've felt recently and that turns into a song.

Does the location make a difference to your writing mindset?

Yes, big time, or it definitely did before; I don't know if it does now. I've always grown up in London, in a big city, and I'm very easily distracted. So I have to leave London to write, whether it be in another country or just in the country from London. I really enjoy the process of writing songs but I get frustrated if I haven't accomplished something very quickly. So if something doesn't come very naturally I find it hard to push myself. That's when I might start thinking, 'What am I going to make for dinner? I better go to Sainsbury's and pick up those chicken breasts.' Do you know what I mean? I'm suddenly not thinking about the task at hand.

When do titles come into your writing?

D'you know what, they never do. It's weird, isn't it? Last week I wrote these three songs and Sam (*Cooper—husband*) said, 'What are they called?' and I just find titles so insignificant. I don't know, just usually whatever's the most prominent words in the chorus or . . .

You've never worked the other way round, where you've thought of a title . . .

No, never, because I find that way of writing—I'm sure other people do it and successfully—means that things become a little bit throwaway and clichéd all of a sudden, if you're writing a song around one phrase.

What makes you decide the subject of a song?

Usually just the music.

When you are writing lyrics do you have an editing process?

People usually laugh when I've said this before. I say it always in my sessions: whatever doesn't make me feel sick usually stays (*laughs*), if that makes any sense. I find so often you listen to mindless drivel that's on the radio and you just think, 'How unimaginative that chorus hook is, or just predictable lyrics.' What I try and do is something that sounds different or sounds like an original idea. As soon as you've used a crap metaphor in a song it just becomes rubbish.

Do you write line by line?

Yeah. Sometimes I write line by line. Sometimes I'll start off with the first line of the first verse and then I'll really struggle with the rest of it. Then I'll think, 'Where's the rest of this song going as a story?' and then I'll write the last line of the last verse and then try and join the dots. Also I don't like getting three-quarters of a way through the song and realizing I've only got two bars left and I've got so much more to say. So you've got to try and figure it out.

Wonderful rhyming couplets dominate your songs in 'LDN': *Tesco / al fresco;* **'Everything's Just Wonderful':** *weight loss / Kate Moss;* **'Him':** *Caucasian / tax evasion.* **Do you find rhyme leads your thoughts?**

Yeah, definitely, but weirdly, because my mum and dad always used to sing stupid songs to me when I was little. My mum is a big couplets fan; that's her thing. She sings this song to Ethel: *You're a little trouper, you're a star, You're a little trouper, you're a star, You're a little trouper, you're a star, You're Ethel Merry Cooper, yes you are* (*laughs*). She'd always just do about silly objects: what you're wearing or what you're having for dinner. Maybe I was always trying to second-guess where she was going with the end of her songs. I've probably inherited it from her (*laughs*).

Would you use a rhyming dictionary?

I hadn't done before, but on *Bridget Jones's Diary* I've been writing with this other girl, Karen Poole, and she showed me RhymeZone, which is an online dictionary which I've started using. They're quite good things aren't they? I didn't know they existed before.

Do you get the first line rhyme . . .

. . . and then the second one . . . yeah, I think so . . . although sometimes you just really can't find a rhyme for something and then you'd have to rethink everything. That's really annoying. When you've got seven out of eight and you can't find number eight and you've got to go back and start again.

You've done that?

Yeah, loads of times. That's so infuriating. I can't recall any one in particular, but it's definitely happened.

Do you have melodic ideas playing in your mind to help write the words?

Well no, usually with Greg he'll come up with the chords and I'll come up with the melody of the top line of what I'm singing first and then I'll try and scan in what I want to say in that first line, and that just leaves the rest of it.

Then you go away from the music to write the words.

No, it all happens at the same time.

I'm confused. When you're doing the top line you haven't written any words at that point, so you're on the mic . . .

. . . not even on the mic, I'll just be there *la de da*-ing. Then sometimes one word or one phrase to do with the idea that I'm thinking of will jump into my mind and that will lead the rest of the song. It's definitely a laborious way of working. That's also why I stick with Greg, because I'm too scared that other people will just be like, 'For fuck's sake come on,' because it does mean it takes a little more time. I think a lot of people go into these sessions and they've got millions of ideas and they just kind of stand around a microphone and shout them out and see what works. I'm a little more meticulous than that. I can be sitting there for eight hours before I've even stood in front of a microphone. I like to have a whole verse and a whole chorus ready in my head to go before I go anywhere near a microphone.

So the trust that you place in Greg to make you feel relaxed and allow time is enormous?

Yeah, and I don't know if anybody else would do it. There's a mutual respect there. What he does is really amazing and he's very clever. Also he finds what I do interesting or more interesting than a lot of other people that he has to work with. So he's willing to put that time aside because generally something good comes out of it.

Can you get beyond being apologetic for taking time or things not flowing?

No, but time is a really interesting thing. I find that when I book a writing session I hate just having a week or five days because I immediately feel then there's pressure to deliver something after those five days are up. If I've got three weeks I feel a lot freer. Usually Greg will have to come over here to England. So when someone's got on a plane, left their family behind, come to England and you haven't got anything even to do at that point you're just like, 'Oh shit, I hope something comes.' And then by day three, if you haven't got anything great you might as well not do day four and day five. Whereas if you've got twenty-one days to do it all then I feel a lot more confident and comfortable.

Do you feel creative when you haven't booked studio time or a writing session is not in the pipeline?

Yeah . . . yeah I do . . . I don't know . . . honestly, it's all a confidence thing with me. I feel like I need someone holding my hand to do it, that's all.

I've picked up on that. It's an undercurrent of you as an artist.

I find it really nerve-racking. When I get up there to do my first verse to show what I've been working on, whether it's been twenty minutes or four hours, I do feel quite anxious.

What do you feel you're being judged on?

Whether it sounds silly; whether I'm good; whether I'm worth all of this fuss. I feel a little bit like a fraud and that I'm just about to get discovered.

Does all this help or hinder? (*Pointing to discs and awards on wall.*) **At one stage in your life you're writing and nobody's heard of Lily Allen, then suddenly your name is everywhere.**

This is a sort of joke really. I'm never really here. I wish now, when I'm writing this, didn't exist, because I feel like I've got something to live up to. I don't know if it has helped really. (*Laughs.*) That's a really big question.

Are you a songwriter when you're not in the studio?

No. I'm an observer of people and life. That's my thing: people-watching. I'm so fascinated by human interaction and how people get on and why we do what we do. I try and take that fascination and put it into my music, for sure. When I'm genuinely fascinated by it I'm not doing it for the songwriting. I just use the songwriting as a vehicle for my fascination. (*Laughs.*)

THE ART OF NOISE

When you wrote 'The Fear' I read you had seen a small girl in a country village dressed inappropriately for her age with her mum, and that you'd imagined her in five years wanting to be on *The X Factor*.

It was Moreton-in-Marsh and we'd literally been out to get some breakfast, me and Greg, and I'd seen this little girl and just thought, 'Hmm.' Then we started writing a song and it happened right then.

I believe that you have pushed the frontiers of female lyricism, particularly talking about male inadequacies. Do you feel that?

Not really, I just felt like that at the time. I was pretty angry at one particular guy and I wanted to direct my anger somewhere. I wasn't really thinking about the effect that might have on other people. Even the effect that it would have on him, because even to this day he doesn't know it's about him. No, I don't feel like I was pushing any boundaries at all.

And in your choice of language and expression? I don't think a female had written like that before. Were you aware of that?

No. I lived with my mother and my brother and my sister, but I was so defined as a young person by the time that I spent with my father and his friends. I only ever really got to hang out with my dad when it was a social occasion with his friends. So I was always surrounded by young obnoxious males and I guess that's probably where that language comes from, or those means of expression. Does that make any sense?

It comes across as language that you've naturally acquired as opposed to copying from somewhere else. There's an abundance of expletives.

See, I didn't even realize that. I remember going on Amazon and you know you can read the comments of people: they review your records, and the amount of parents that would be so up in arms about the amount of swearing. I'd be like, 'Really, do I swear that much?' I didn't really notice.

The last few weeks at home with my three girls under ten has had me diving to kill the sound on the record player.

Can't you get an unadulterated version of it, or not?

You can't do that: it would be like having a sanitized Sex Pistols—it'd be horrible.

Exactly! I do swear a lot. My husband says to me, 'You've got to stop swearing, it's so unladylike.' I just don't realize it. I do it in front of the wrong people. When we were getting married the vicar would come over and I'd have dropped the milk on the floor: 'Oh, for fuck's sake . . .'

By the time of your second album there must have been a lot of commercial pressure put upon you?

Yes, there was. I'm quite antagonistic in that way and my record company probably did allude to the fact that it should be a little more palatable. My reaction to that was to probably swear more.

With 'Fuck You' the melody is so infectious but there's not a chance it's going to make daytime radio. The Blockheads had the same resistance from Ian Dury but he was very much, 'This is how I write.'

Well, that's the same. I know that there isn't an unadulterated version of the album because I remember the singer Jamelia had done an interview saying, 'I love Lily Allen but I can't play her records for my kids. I wish she'd do this version.' I remember saying, 'If you don't want your kids to listen to swearwords then don't put my album on.' I'm not going to make a record that's not got . . . because that's not the record.

How have you overcome your experiences of writing block?

Greg says my way of dealing with it was to literally go out and get absolutely smashed. I'd come back and feel so awful that something would come from somewhere. I've not had it for long periods of time. I've had it intermittently. But yeah, it's horrible when it happens.

It strikes me you place incredible demands on yourself to write in booked writing periods; having to conjure ideas in the studio with nothing prepared or to lean on, despite your active life influences.

It sounds so ridiculous when you put it like that. The other thing is to write as I'm going along feels a little bit like homework . . . in a weird way, and I was terrible at doing homework when I was at school.

But homework implies something you don't want to do.

But I suppose writing is in a way confronting myself and my feelings, and maybe that isn't something I want to do, unless I'm writing.

Because you're so honest with yourself, is it a form of therapy?

It's very cathartic, for sure.

Do you find yourself pulling in on yourself with thoughts and feel the need for restraint?

I didn't before, but now I do. I think that because I'd become a public figure or public property in a lot of ways, I know with the next record that I do . . . everybody knows what's been going on in my life. I lost a child and it was such a massive experience. I've had to come through that and it would feel wrong to ignore that on a record, but at the same time people don't know me for serious stuff. But I feel the last few years of my life have been incredibly serious years. They haven't been going out and getting high and having fights with other people or whatever. It's been quite a dark period, but I'm not going to write dark serious songs. I think they've got to have a touch of darkness but also a funny side to them as well.

Are your melody ideas always suited to your vocal range?

No, quite often I'll sing things in and Greg will then have to go back and change the key completely. Does that make sense? Your inside voice is very different to your outside voice so I write a lot of stuff in a different key in my head. Then when I stand in front of a microphone I think, 'Fuck, I can't sing this.'

So your internal ideas are beyond your capability?

Yeah.

You've got a limited range . . . within an octave?

Hmm-mm . . . I've never actually studied it.

Is that frustrating?

You know what: I have got quite a good range. I just don't like the sound of it when it goes to other places. I studied voice. I got my grade seven. I also did music theory and got to grade five. You have to get to a certain point in theory in order to go further on and study voice. I also did jazz improvisation competitions when I was younger. It's just making it up as you go along, basically: somebody playing the piano and you're literally improvising and scatting to chords. There was an afterschool course, one to one with my teacher. She would take me to jazz improvisation events around the county. I find weirdly enough it's something to do with me singing in an English accent that limits my range . . .

. . . because the vowel sounds are ugly compared to Italian in classical training.

Yeah, sometimes I do think, 'Fucking hell, why don't I just sing in an American accent, where you can link the sounds a little bit better?'—it's a lot easier. I think people would be a little bit frustrated.

And it would take away from your strength. So there's quite a technical mind at play.

There was a while ago. It's not really there any more. I stopped studying that stuff when I was fifteen or sixteen. I left school at sixteen.

Did you take grades on piano and trumpet?

Three or four in piano, and trumpet. I didn't do it for very long.

On the documentary of your USA 2007 tour you're seen learning the guitar. Have you progressed; can you write with it?

A little bit. It's more to do with the coordination. I can't play guitar and sing at the same time. So no, is the simple answer. I can play chords and then stop and go, 'This will sound nice over that.' My husband plays, we've got guitars everywhere around the house, but it's not stuff I'd take into the studio. I probably should, but that's the homework thing again. (*Laughs.*)

How do you further melodic ideas? Is it instinct?

It's totally to do with instinct. Occasionally I can work things out on the piano and sometimes Greg will show me how to do things on the guitar, or where I am on the guitar. Then I can kind of piddle away.

So you'd physicalize the notes that you're singing to see what you're doing?

Yeah.

How do you build up a song's melody, is it bit by bit?

Yeah. I do a verse or sometimes start with a chorus, depending on what Greg's playing. We'll both go, 'Does that sound more like a verse or a chorus?' We'll just decide that we like one snippet of chord changes. We usually finish off that section and then find another piece of music that links in with the first piece and then I'll write another top line to go over the top of that.

Have you ever written a melodic idea from start to finish?

No, it's all a little bit music-by-numbers. Is it really different to most people?

Yes, I think it is. But then . . . there are elements that aren't. Everybody's got their unique way of doing things. The great theme I hope that will emerge in the book is that nobody can tell you how to write a song. Nobody can ultimately write like Lily Allen because that has come from within you. That's the same with all artists. The similarities are irrelevant. A great song is a great song despite the process that engineered it. Do you ever write new melodies over existing ideas? You once said that you 'rewrite stuff that's similar.' I wondered about 'Alfie' borrowing from 'Puppet On A String' or 'Cheryl Tweedy' and The Specials' 'Friday Night, Saturday Morning'.

Those were both definitely the reference points that we started with, but I don't think they were written over exactly the same . . . I don't even know if they are exactly the same, to be honest. Quite often if we're feeling lost, or on this record I've just started, I'd listen to hundreds and hundreds of records and start compiling a reference mood board, so to speak. Then I'd give it to Greg. Then he'll come over and we'll start playing things. I don't know why I bother doing that, but I do . . . it's if I want an aesthetic feel or sound to something. With the last record I played Greg a lot of Keane songs. I love Keane. I wanted that bigger ethereal sound. That was definitely the starting point. It's not where the record ended up going.

I hear that on (*hums melody*).
'Everyone's At It'.

I hear a lot of influences in your music, particularly from your mixtapes, yet if on the whole you're not creating the music it's intriguing that those elements are within it.
We do talk about our reference points and he knows what I want.

Where do the harmony ideas come from?
Interestingly enough, sometimes Greg works out some harmonies, but usually I stand in front of the microphone and make them up. That's probably about my jazz impro influence coming out, because I just stand there and whatever sounds like it fits.

Do you imagine the sound of a song you want to make before the collaboration process?
Yes, I might do, but it never turns out like that. (*Laughs.*) I've always felt like doing what I want but the reality of what I can bring to something usually limits where we can go, to be honest.

We've talked about the chemistry between you and Greg. Why didn't the collaboration work with Damon Albarn?
I find him a little bit too irritating.

It's to do with a personality match before you can make music together?
I have to like the person in order to work with them or I have to think that they believe in me. I don't think I felt that with him. We'd known each other through my dad but in that particular session we didn't gel. I didn't feel a mutual respect there. (*Looking at my notes.*) I didn't work with Cathy Dennis. Now, Mark Ronson it did work with: 'Littlest Things'. Actually I was thinking about working with him the other day. On 'Oh My God', the Kaiser Chiefs one that he did, Mark was really good at bringing me out of myself. I remember him saying, 'Just sing on this one, just do whatever you want—just let yourself go,' and I did. He said, 'I didn't know you could sing like that,' and it

just made me feel really good. I don't usually listen to that good feedback from people. I'm just so kind of hooked on the bad stuff. But actually when you're in such close proximity to someone and they're looking you in the eyes and going, 'That was good,' then you're (*childish voice*), 'OK, shall we go again, then?'

You've also spent time with Mark that hasn't been productive: why is that?
Actually when Amy, God bless her, was around . . . Winehouse, obviously; when Mark and I worked on that second session for the second album together, it was in the studio that he'd been working with her in. I very much felt like her ghost was there. She wasn't actually dead yet, but I felt so untalented in comparison to her. What I was probably feeling was, 'Fuck, Mark's been here for two weeks with her and she's probably been brilliant and amazing and now he's sat here with shit old me.' I couldn't do anything. I don't think he knew that was how I felt. Usually if I can do at least one verse or a chorus as a starting point you can move on from there. I didn't even give him that. That's also quite an interesting point: when Greg and I worked on the last album there's only one song out of all fifteen songs that we did that didn't make it onto the record or B-side. I never do that thing of writing a big amount of stuff and choosing the best. I don't finish a song unless I'm pretty sure it's going to make it onto a record.

If you get a certain way into something . . .
. . . and it doesn't feel like it's working, then I'm not going to finish it.

Does that mean scrapping the lyrical idea or the whole thing?
Everything.

You don't go back and try and rewrite a new melody or new words?
No.

What if Greg thinks it's great?
It doesn't matter. Sometimes he might be able to convince me by promising if we just keep going . . . then I might do it. But if I feel like he's lying . . . (*laughs*) and actually it's really bad, then I'm like, 'No, I'm going home!'

From your earliest interviews you were very set on the idea of a short career in music before giving it up for home and family.
I was a different person then to the person I am now. Slightly more naive and maybe not accepting of the things I've achieved. I definitely had that idea of wanting to stop and give up and move to the country and have a family. I've done that and I do still want to be there, but I need to do something.

When did you feel the need to return to music?

I think when Ethel started getting ill and I felt such a powerlessness over it. There's only so much tube feeding . . . if you're not able to do things the natural way and breastfeed and be at one . . . We've bonded and I love her more than anything in the world, but the frustration of having to put food into a baby via a tube. Something about it made me just go, 'You know what, I need to get out there and do something with my time.'

There hadn't been creative urges since your last session?

No. I think that's because I've been so concentrated on wanting to have a baby, and then I lost a baby. Those months add up after a while. I might have had creative urges but they were very quickly forgotten about, although I have been writing *Bridget Jones*, but that's different, that's not writing for myself because I found it so easy—embarrassingly so.

Why was that?

I think because you're given a subject matter and you're given a direction, almost, and it's easy then. I've been writing all the songs with Greg for all of the different characters.

What remit are you given for each song?

We're not, really. Basically you look at the musical as a whole. They say, 'We want this amount of songs for this character, and this amount of songs for this character. One would be really good here and we need a big number here.' You think, 'Right, it's got to go on a musical journey, i.e. it's got to be fast-paced and then a slow song then a sad one and then it gets happier.' It's got to move with the book, the story. We've given each character stereotypical songs from their era. So the mum's got a Vera Lynn-y number. Bridget's got a different mix of stuff.

How have you found writing as a character, because you would normally write from a personal perspective?

I've found it a lot easier. Although I have to say I did find the character of Bridget really irritating and frustrating. I found it quite difficult to get into her character, but once I'd got there I found writing the songs quite easy. She was such a foreign character from myself.

Have you free licence to create in your sound and style?

Yes, that's why they enlisted me and Greg. They definitely wanted Bridget's songs to have that range of references that I have and that storytelling aspect.

No . . . actually I found it quite refreshing because, no offence to musical audiences, but they're not the same as people who come to gigs or festivals. You can be really camp and naff and it's fine. You don't have to try and be within a cool box.

'Knock 'Em Out' has startling inventiveness: did it start with your spoken introduction?

My husband loves that song. He says, 'You sound like such an idiot on that.' It is different. I was in Manchester when I wrote that . . . it's so different from the way that I write now. I can visualize the room where I was. I was making up songwriting at that point. I didn't know how to write a song and that was what came into my head. Are you talking about that opening *OK here's a song about anyone*? I think that bit was done at the end of the song, weirdly . . . yeah . . . I don't know . . .

So the verse that begins *cut to the bar* would have been the original introduction?

Wait, is that how the first verse starts, *cut to the bar* . . . (*reading the lyric sheet*) . . . All these songs I did with Darren and Tunde . . . I've just got no idea where I was. I think just looking at it . . . at the time I was very influenced by Mike Skinner from The Streets. He used to do a lot of this talky stuff, didn't he? Maybe I did start off with this. It feels to me like . . . what I used to do with Future Cut was standing in front of the microphone and doing whatever came out. So it was total ad-libbing. Then these bits *cut to the bar* would have been more structured. I would definitely have sat down and written this out, and this.

How long would that have taken you?

Two hours. 'Smile' took me literally half an hour, forty-five minutes. This is a blast from the past, all of this.

The great line at the end is *I've got to go my house is on fire*.

(*Laughs*) On the original, original version which I posted on MySpace there's a bit where it goes, *I've got AIDS*, but it got cut.

Do you remember writing 'Him'?

Yes, that's my favourite song. It's sort of questioning, isn't it? The record company really weren't into it and didn't want to put it onto the record. I really put my foot down: 'No, it has to stay.' At the time I wrote that second album I was really questioning life: 'What are we doing here? How do we justify all this crap we're getting on with?' I think you see that in 'The Fear' and 'Him'. I was genuinely really confused and baffled by . . . probably something to do with the amount of drugs I was taking.

'Kabul Shit' is in the same mould of contemplating the world. There's a great line in 'Him': *do you think He's ever been suicidal? His favourite band . . .*

. . . *is Creedence Clearwater Revival*: that came first. I remember thinking about questions that you'd ask God. I wouldn't even ask God what his favourite band was because it would obviously be Creedence Clearwater Revival, and then it was coming up with a rhyme.

Doesn't matter 'cause I'm packing plastic and that's what makes my life so fuckin' fantastic: **was that a reference in 'The Fear' to the record shop Plastic Fantastic where you worked in Ibiza?**

No, *packing plastic* means credit.

I am a weapon of mass consumption.

That's a real Lily-ism; it's what we are, isn't it?

It's really surprising how all these one-liners were originated in the studio without any notes or recorded ideas.

Wordplay is my thing. It always has been. I play these stupid games with people at home or when I'm out drinking. It's always wordplay, puns, rhyme. That's just the way my brain works and it happens with just me and a pen, just thinking.

Was 'LDN' inspired by the William Wordsworth poem 'Composed Upon Westminster Bridge'?

Yeah, that was one of the poems I started to study for GCSE English at school. I remember thinking, 'I want to write about London,' and re-looking at that poem online and thinking, 'That's what he thought, what do I think?' I was looking at his viewpoint or how he began to tell the tale of what he felt at that particular moment.

'Fuck You' started with the working titles 'GWB' and 'Guess Who Batman'?

They were anagrams of George W. Bush and that's who the song was first directed at. It became broader than that.

'Nan You're A Window Shopper'.

That was loosely a cover of 50 Cent, 'Window Shopper'. I can't tell where half of these ideas come from . . . they just come. It started with the title 'Window Shopper' and I thought, 'Who do I know who's a window shopper? My nan, she's always going out shopping and never buying anything.

Will you continue to write songs and record?

Yeah. That's my plan. I haven't signed a new deal. I'll keep writing until I feel like I've got something that's worth playing to people.

Has the ambition changed, do you still perceive yourself having a musical career?

Not in the same way, because of Ethel, and I'd like to have more kids. (*In January 2013 Lily had a second child—Marnie Rose.*) It's definitely a harder decision for a woman to make than it is for a man to make, especially a woman with children, because you're not just making records any more. In order to see them through you've got to go on these long tours. It's incredibly time-consuming and not really something very well suited to small children.

The last decade has seen a significant emergence of British female songwriters.

I really feel a woman having a point of view has only recently become an acceptable notion. Even though in the late Sixties, Seventies and Eighties things started to get a lot easier for women, it took a long time for people to accept that women might want to express themselves creatively as well as in the workplace, or that they might have something that's worth listening to or something that people might be interested to hear. I just happened to come along at a time when people were ready to accept it. I don't think it was me breaking down any barriers. It was just luck. I don't think of myself as a female songwriter. I just do what I do.

LAURA MARLING

1 October 2007. A 17-year-old singer readies herself for a show at London's Soho Revue Bar. After the soundcheck, the venue manager asks to see her identification and then refuses her permission to play, as she is under age to perform in licensed premises. Undeterred, the singer takes to the street and entertains the audience outside the venue. It is an act of good faith and integrity. Conversations with her conscience are a recurring theme in Laura Marling's work.

In the current musical climate, songwriting rests more firmly in female hands than at any other time in British pop. The nation's women writers are now topping the charts and selling records in their millions. But despite Marling's considerable talent her commercial profile remains relatively low. Her music seems more fitting to the era of the late Sixties and early Seventies when the work of Janis Ian, Carole King, Laura Nyro, Buffy Sainte-Marie, Melanie, Joni Mitchell and Carly Simon in America was complemented by Sandy Denny and Joan Armatrading in the UK. Indeed, Laura herself expresses the wish that she was 'in a time where people could make money out of making music', before asserting, 'I could never change my songwriting in order to sell more records.'

The sole female singer-songwriter is still a rarity. There is a focus today on the kind of collaboration that has propelled Adele, Amy Winehouse, Duffy, Florence Welch, Leona Lewis, Emeli Sandé and, as we have seen, Lily Allen, into the mainstream. The producer and songwriting teams that dominated Tin Pan Alley before the explosion of Lennon and McCartney have been reinvented or replaced by the staggering popularity of television talent competitions and schools of songwriting apprenticeship. The modern emphasis is on the technical ability of the voice and the presence of the star. Marling's music doesn't fit that pattern. She is a writer troubled by the pursuit of 'art for art's sake', genuinely questioning why she writes and endures the subsequent and inevitable demands of touring and promotion. It is an irony that her four albums challenge the proliferation of manufactured music because of the economics of her natural artistry.

Marling regards songwriting as a self-indulgent and obsessive pursuit. She rarely writes during contented periods of her life, and like Cat Stevens in the Seventies, she is on a road of self-discovery. Laura was a regular churchgoer until the age of twelve, before exploring the possibilities of Buddhism. She is not religious, but is definitely on a quest to consolidate faith. Biblical and mythological imagery can be found liberally scattered across her song sheet: in communion, the fall of man, fate, angels, sin, Paracelsus' Undine, Judgement Day, God and the 'Devil's Resting Place'. In 2009 she toured her music in churches, in 2011 in cathedrals. These are not glamorous venues for a performer, but that is in part Marling's intention. She continues, as she began, to see performance as a shared experience with the audience.

A humble basement, The Bosun's Locker in west London, was the catalyst for Marling's emergence into the musical mainstream. Once again the King's Road ley line that had brought together Led Zeppelin, the Sex Pistols and Pet Shop Boys seemed to play its part. The venue had launched the careers of Mumford And Sons, Johnny Flynn and Marling's first band, Noah And The Whale. Laura describes a monthly event there as an all-inclusive gathering of like-minded musicians and audience. Instrumentalists and players would freely lend their ideas to one another. Where music had previously been a form of escapism, the opportunity to be with kindred spirits offered the young songwriter a valuable support network. In 2009, she hosted *Laura Marling & Friends* at the Royal Festival Hall. For a 19-year-old songwriter, it was an incredible achievement. As guests performed, and in between her own contributions, she reclined with musicians on a ragged sofa up-stage. It was a democratic gesture of openness, gratitude and bewilderment at her meteoric rise to success. Marling's desire to build connections between performer and audience led to her 2011 live art installation, Experiments in Awkwardness. This was built around a simple idea of taking two complete strangers into a room together to hear her perform a song live. It deliberately challenged the perceived boundaries of performance by direct interaction.

The historian of the English imagination, Peter Ackroyd, observed: 'The theme of exile and travel, whether mental or physical, is a constant feature of Englishwomen's writing.' This theme lies at the heart of Marling's work. Her music seems to yearn for a spiritual centre and a safe home of her own making. *Thank you naivety for failing me again*, she whimpers in 'Saved These Words'. In conversation, Laura is honest and revealing, her analysis of her writing state of mind quite profound. She questions, 'Is songwriting my saviour or is it my downfall?' Her writing is a knowing entry into a psychological darkness. As a result, philosophical control is integral to her make-up in a battle between logic and art. She asks in 'Master Hunter', *you want a woman who will call your name?* Her reply is blunt; with a subtle nod of appreciation to Bob Dylan: *it ain't me, Babe / No, no, no.*

'Don't Ask Me Why' is made up of strands of self-confession to *those of us who are lost and low.* Marling writes with inbuilt defences, and although not impenetrable, they are reluctantly acknowledged: *looking for answers in unsavoury places.* Her writing is mostly shrouded in metaphor or addressed to third persons, as songs capture the transition from innocence to knowing, from childhood to the uncertainties of adulthood. In 'Where Can I Go?' she ruminates, *Truth about desire they say is a need to breathe for another day*; in 'I Was An Eagle' she defiantly asserts, *I will not be a victim of romance.* 'The Beast' conjures an unknown presence. It is one of her most adventurous and uncomfortable compositions. Marling delivers the vocal in half-speech, a Hampshire echo of Lou Reed's Long Island deadpan. The narration is surrounded by a sense of darkness delivered by overdriven guitars. The author wrestles with inner demons and allows her character, the Beast, shifting roles within her third album, *A Creature I Don't Know.* At times, the Beast is the creator, but it also becomes others, and moves with unknown and undefined force. Strength and love crusade against weakness and hate. Marling's first album, *Alas I Cannot Swim*, explored similar themes. Marling characterized her writing as 'optimistic realism', with a cleansing running melody of water. A second release demonstrated a new, confident inner strength and honesty: *I speak because I can to anyone I trust enough to listen.*

Marling's creativity takes much from the role of women in literature. *Calling Sophia goddess of power*: the line draws on an ancient belief that Sophia was the female counterpart of God. Marling is drawn by the concepts of gender worship. She was enthralled by the books of Canadian and Anglican priest Robertson Davies and particularly his philosophical novel *The Rebel Angels.* Reading inspires Marling's thoughts. *The beast was a creature I don't know* was assimilated from a Jehanne Wake novel, *Sisters of Fortune*, into an unused lyric and later a piece of prose. 'Salinas' developed from reading an introduction to John Steinbeck's Glastonbury tale, *The Acts Of King Arthur And His Noble Knights*, in which the American author's widow revealed her sycophantic reverence for him. Marling was appalled. Her exploration of women is not a political stance, but a fascination with gender differences. 'What He Wrote' was provoked by reading Second World War letters published in a newspaper. A woman's correspondence exposed a soldier's wife deserted and left 'rigid with anger' as the call to arms took her husband away. Stolen, unspoken desire resonated with the shy songwriter.

Poetry also offers a source of stimulation: 'This Be The Verse' by Philip Larkin informed Marling's 'Tap At My Window' ... *Mother, I blame you with every inch of the being you gave ... Father ... how can you watch as I push her away?* In the spring of 2013 she composed 'Under The Greenwood Tree', an adaptation of Shakespeare's poem, for an RSC production of *As You Like It.*

Laura Beatrice Marling was born 1 February 1990 in Eversley, Hampshire.

DANIEL RACHEL

She was educated at Leighton Park Quaker School on a music scholarship, but failed in English, both at GCSE and A Level. Her attention had been diverted by a recording deal offered by Virgin Records. As a child she had aspirations to be a children's writer, but found the discipline of continuous prose beyond her capability. At sixteen, the family's 'Little One' moved to Kew. Six years later, in December 2012, she left London to rent an apartment in the Silverlake quarter of Los Angeles. The young Marling was taught guitar by her father, and he passed on to her his passion for Joni Mitchell. She grew up listening to her parents' eclectic record collection, where James Taylor, Leonard Cohen, Neil Young and Steely Dan stood alongside modern writers like Nina Nastasia, Diane Cluck and Bonnie Prince Billy. Her appreciation of live performance came from Ryan Adams, and the first CDs she bought were *Lenny Kravitz—Greatest Hits* and Joni Mitchell's *Court And Spark*. Marling may have assimilated a good deal from the past, but she invents the present with immense originality. As Ralph Vaughan Williams observed, 'The folk song is as old as time itself; in another aspect it is no older than the singer who sang it.'

The music industry has responded with accolades to each of Marling's successive releases. She was nominated for both the 2008 and the 2010 Mercury Prize. In 2011 she won the award for Best Female Solo Artist at the Brits. She was nominated again twelve months later, while 'Rambling Man' received a nomination in the best original song category at the BBC Radio 2 Folk Awards. Her last three albums have been top-five hits. Marling favours live performance in the studio, with her band recording from one room directly to tape. Her fourth album, *Once I Was An Eagle*, was recorded in LA in a mere ten days. Marling recorded her voice and guitar parts in the first day. Her music has travelled successfully to America, Australia and Europe, and was further enriched by a British Council cultural exchange in 2009. Traditional Rajasthani musicians The Dharohar Project collaborated on 'Devil's Spoke', invigorating Marling's song with dramatic rhythm and chant whilst incorporating their own work 'Sneh Ko Marg'. The Anglo-Indian alliance of Western musicianship and Eastern scales refers back to the music of George Harrison and Jimmy Page, and, like the Led Zeppelin guitarist, Marling increasingly favours tunings to reawaken the mystery of her instrument. Her guitar on *A Creature I Don't Know* is all set to the open strings D G D G B D. The second string was then often flattened by a half or full tone to create minor and seventh variation. The opening four-song suite on *Once I Was An Eagle* drones from a detuned bottom E string. Across the record ascending and descending scales are explored both on the guitar and in voice, often straying from traditional Western melody. The dynamics of the guitar playing summon the adventurous and dark paths of both Jimmy Page and Richard Thompson. Everything about Laura Marling suggests development and change: a force of restless creativity. Her aspirations are undeclared, but in conversation she gives out the distinct feeling of an uneasy and unsettled vocation. Before the recording of her fourth album, Marling toured America in a rented car. She drove herself to each gig, often alone, and played new songs in small venues. In June 2013 she played a seventeen-night residency in a former Victorian school house in east London, converted to reflect the themes of her songs. Marling performed unannounced in small rooms before playing a headline set in the Eagle Ballroom.

We settled down to chat outside a coffee shop in north London's Exmouth Market. She was wrapped in a long camel-skin coat with matching nicotine-light cigarettes. She has frequently spoken of her discomfort with people knowing so much about her without ever having met her—an inevitable consequence of musical popularity. I had recently seen Laura perform at Winchester Cathedral, a setting whose scholarly past complemented the songwriter's cultured present. Both the concert and our later conversation proved that in her hands English is a traditional yet still modern and vital language. As she wrote in 'Don't Ask Me Why': *I took the wind from the sea / I took the blood from an arrow / I took the wisdom of spring.*

It seems appropriate to end this book with a question I asked at the beginning to Ray Davies: why are you a songwriter?

I think out of necessity is the reason why I keep doing it: it's a necessary exercise. I don't know the reason why I started doing it.

What would the exercise be?

I've had to struggle to accept that some people have a creative need and some people just don't and are quite happy going about life without the need to express something. I would never have considered myself one of the other people who need to be creative because I find it can become an excuse. If I don't have an outlet in which to express myself, be it through songwriting or other mediums of writing, I do become, get a bit jittery and get a bit odd. I think it's a necessary thing and a blessing for that.

Can you explain your state of mind when you are writing a song?

I guess it varies but it's becoming more apparent to me the situation in which I tend to write songs—which is late at night. My biggest thing, and this will probably come up with all the questions that you ask, is that I hate the idea of once somebody proclaiming themselves an artist is perusing art for the sake of art. I was intrigued by what you were going to do because I find talking about songwriting so embarrassing, because it's such a self-indulgent pursuit of art and living in an artistic way. Well, it's quite brave to do that. I've got this constant tussle of whether by putting myself in those situations where the songs are written, am I indulging in a kind of lifestyle that perpetuates that kind of behaviour? Is it my saviour or is it my downfall?

Suggs was reluctant to label himself as a songwriter because he saw it as a lofty term that applied to people like Bob Dylan. His songs came because they seemed to just tumble out.

From seeing other people and other songwriters that I admire, the ones that really stand out are the ones that are brave enough to give themselves over to their art.

Have you done that?

No, and I don't intend to. They are now solitary, untouchable, barely real existences.

So you're fighting being a creative spirit or being a writer? You reluctantly put songs out?

Well, this is the thing; it's a complete contradiction, I suppose, because I do it and I am very grateful for having that outlet. I'm very grateful for doing a job that I love, but I would never completely give myself over to pursuing life for the sake of my creativity, or I hope I wouldn't. You can so easily become alienated or completely disconnected from what is reality. Music is not the be-all and end-all of anybody, I don't think. In the grand scheme of things, what my music or my songwriting means to other people is not grand enough for me to tip myself over the edge.

Are you aware of when a song is coming to you?

Yes, I think so. I think I know when the situation arises. There's too much clutter in my brain and it does literally feel like big chunks of mess that have come out. I'm pretty unawares as I write. I'm pretty bad company for a couple of days before a song is written.

Why would that be?

Preoccupied, I think. Not by thinking about how I'm going to write a song, but whatever I'm thinking about. I suppose melody is an afterthought. When I do sit down to write a song—I've always got a guitar around and I'm always playing guitar when I'm at home—I guess I'll be coming up with little melody lines and chord sequences all the time without really thinking about it. Then suddenly a song will just come out with one of those chord structures I've been playing with. It just seemed, I don't know, the right time.

Do you record little ideas and later build on them?

No, it's all from memory. I'm a complete technophobe. Sometimes if I finish a song very quickly then I write it down because I'll definitely forget it the next day. But I can't read or write music so I do write down chords and stuff.

Can you just sit and write a song at will because you want to?

I've tried, and it's awful, awful, awful, awful.

Because you've put undue pressure upon yourself?

Yes. I do it as an exercise sometimes: just writing for the sake of writing. Actually that's a lot easier; you can be a lot more absent-minded, but because you've got a guitar in front of you and you're trying to write a song then you end up trying to write a song about what you think a song should be written about, and it's always a disaster.

Because it's not coming from a true place?

Yeah.

Writing a song is a marriage between the guitar and the pen. You wouldn't isolate the two forms?

No, I never have. It would be incredibly convenient if you could.

I read recently Bob Dylan said that your intellectual mind can hinder the creative impulse.

Ah, nice. Well, that's interesting. I mean, it depends what he means by that. I take that as what I just said about not allowing oneself to be completely taken over by creativity, which I think is a sensible thing, personally. I don't know if Mr Dylan would agree. Also . . . I have to give a little credit to not knowing anything. That's probably why I write, because I've got so many questions unanswered. And also I don't know my instrument very well, which has helped me a lot. I was never taught the guitar properly and I was never taught music properly. So maybe in that way my lack of intellect has somehow helped my creativity.

Naivety in not knowing an instrument allows a freedom to explore—is that how it is?

Yes, definitely, in some ways the not knowing . . . you don't know what potential mistakes you could make. The not knowing is quite important.

Do you detune the guitar a lot or play with tunings?

Yes. My dad taught me the guitar. He's a mad Joni Mitchell fan so every tuning I learnt was a drop D, D A D G A D variation so I never really learnt on normal tuning.

Does open tuning mean you are unaware of the chords you are playing: is it sounds and shapes that you are finding?

Yes, shape and sounds, which is infuriating for my band, absolutely infuriating. I couldn't tell you what key any of my songs are in. I assume most of them are similar because of the tone of my voice.

Is the creative process therapeutic? There is a lot of darkness in your work, referred to either directly, obliquely, or through character. Do you recognize that?

Yeah, definitely, and that's why I say I'm equally grateful for it and fearful of it. That's obviously one side of my personality that seems to write songs—not that I have a split personality, as a liner note—that place that I'm in whenever I write songs, which does tend to be a similar kind of therapeutic and quite a dark place. My fear of it is that I would ever try and pursue that darkness; the exorcism is such a relief and then you kind of get to a place where you're sort of unhappy. That's a bit worrying! That's why I can't sit down and write a song whenever I want to and that's why I try and live life simply and normally as possible. I don't indulge in the thrills around songwriting and being creative, or I try not to. It is so tempting. The older I get the more aware I am of that.

Are you ever surprised by what you've written when you look back or reread?

Yeah, yes, I am. I don't sometimes really realize how much of a subconscious thing songwriting can be. Particularly on the last album (*A Creature I Don't Know*), there were some lines in it that I didn't even hear until we were mastering it, which was nice and then also again quite scary. I felt as I heard those lines, 'Oh gosh, it's a bit much, isn't it?' I suddenly thought how much of this I am actually in control of. I can preach my logic and my wariness of everything, but then ultimately the long-term illogical in my life has been songwriting and music and its effect on me and on other people and how much we're in control of that. Which is why the conclusion I've come to is that art and creativity in all its forms is incredibly brave, and thank God there are people who've done it before us to make us feel like it's OK to be that brave—not to pat myself on the back.

What is the editing process in your writing; does everything come in a single outpouring?

Everything comes as it comes, and I don't think I've ever gone back and taken out lyrics. It is very much an extension of my personality. I have good self-editing before it gets out, to some extent. I'm not that brave, I couldn't give away everything. I guess that bit happens before it even hits the page, as it were.

Do you practise?

I'm terrible with my voice. I never really considered my voice an instrument. I smoke and drink coffee and do terrible things. I've been lucky, but that's because I'm young. I play guitar whenever I can because I enjoy it.

How conscious are you of repeating yourself?

Mmm, well, I don't think I've had the opportunity to yet, but I can definitely see it coming. Every time I've written an album it's felt very obvious to me that that's an album done and some sort of wider issue dealt with. Not psychological issue, but topic. Each of them have their own goals they're achieving. I don't really realize this until after. So I think every time I start to write again . . . there are breaks in writing, it's not constant . . . I've been writing for a new album and its different questions, but it's still me and there's still things from the last album that I didn't conclude. So there will be things that crop up again. I'm a different person from what I was when I wrote that album, and my life was different then. I was going to release two albums, *I Speak Because I Can*, and another one close after, and that would have been repetition. I thought, 'It's already been said,' and the songs weren't as good either, and then my circumstances changed and I wrote *A Creature I Don't Know*.

You literally had a batch of songs that you were happy to cast aside and start again? Did you recognize that in the writing stage?

We recorded most of them with the band. We had it pretty much ready to go. It wasn't as good. Maybe I'd overindulged that thought, that idea, and taken it too far and it had got a bit boring.

Do you write with a pen?

A left-handed fountain pen.

Is that important?

Yeah. Those are the kind of things that are really embarrassing because they're so . . . it's like people who only write on typewriters and stuff. I got given a left-handed fountain pen two years ago. I'd never written with a fountain pen before. I thought it was so brilliant, so elegant, I'm never going to go back.

Do you have to write on the same pad or paper?

No. I've got hundreds of half-filled notebooks and things like that. The best advice I've had, from a friend of mine who's a writer, was always buy a cheap notebook so you don't feel pressure to fill it with glorious things. So that's what I do.

Can you expand on how you use your notebook?

It's my . . . I pick one to put in my handbag. I'm terrible; I buy so many of them and they get half loved and half thrown away. I don't write a diary. Most of them are filled with quotes from books and from newspapers and torn-out articles and things like that. It's usually the way that sentences are structured or words are used or something's described so beautifully. That's just a hobby and obviously quite helpful for mild plagiarism in songwriting . . . occasionally bits of poetry and bits of songwriting; mostly it's citations.

A coming-together of your mind's influences. When I listen to your music, lines and stanzas seem quite free of form, but read on a lyric sheet I was surprised how they fall into more familiar patterns.

In writing lyrics in a formation that is standard? I don't know, I can't quite tear it apart. I don't know why the couplets or whatever come out the way they do. I'm a big fan of everything rhyming.

Which I don't feel comes out in the way you put over melodies. The rhymes are not so obvious to me from your delivery.

Really? I don't know. Dylan's the king of it: the flow of the rhythm of words making it sound like it rhymes. I've always been aware of that.

Leonard Cohen said, 'The interesting moments in writing are when you inform yourself of something.'

Mmm . . . again, it depends what he meant by that. There are so many times in retrospect I've been aware of writing about something. And sometimes you go, 'Oh right, OK, I should probably have thought about that.' Things are so deeply ingrained in your behaviour that you recognize something in your songwriting. It's like cognitive behavioural therapy . . . the same patterns. He is the king of just nailing something on the head lyrically; making something so complicated so simple in one lyric. That's the kind of thing you can only do subconsciously. You can't force a really perfect metaphor because it just sounds too laboured. He's the king of not sounding laboured. It all sounds like he's a genius but I bet he's not a genius. I bet he's just somebody very engaged with that side of his brain. He might be a genius!

Do you write conversations with people you can't have conversations with?

Yes! Did you read that somewhere? It's a great exercise. A godfather of mine . . . he's just a brilliant mind. There's a few people like this in my life who point me in the direction of inspiration. At the beginning of my lyrical relationship with him he introduced me to an old Iranian poem called 'There's a Boy Across the River But Alas I Cannot Swim'; *with an arse like a peach* is the next line, which I obviously kept quite quiet. We were talking a lot about the relationship between early Christian writing and Greek mythology and the beginning of Western literature and how they contradict each other. A lot of the second album is about that. The third album, he introduced me to a Canadian writer called Robertson Davies. I read six of his books, all of which I plagiarized horribly in this album. They were so brilliant, the ideas of femininity; he worshipped women but was also deeply religious, and I'm not religious at all. I found it really difficult to believe that somebody I thought was so brilliant could have such a different opinion to me. I desperately, desperately wanted to go and meet him. I knew I was going to Toronto where he was a professor at the university. I phoned up and found that he had died ten years before, quite prematurely actually. I was so devastated. So this family friend of ours said, 'Have you ever tried writing letters to people you know you can't get a response from?' Having started a conversation in that way, it's really interesting what you come up with. That is just an exercise not particularly to do with songwriting, but it's an incredible way of realizing what questions you want to ask and what answers you want to have, actually, and how much of them you can answer yourself.

The theatre director Max Stafford-Clark similarly wrote letters to the late George Farquhar during the rehearsal process of *The Recruiting Officer*. Do you ever take those ideas and use them lyrically?

No: I suppose some of it might have crept in. I learnt a lot . . . when I'm writing I have focuses, like people, that aren't real but they're sort of . . . Robertson Davies and some of his characters were a huge focus in my mind when I was writing that album, because of the way he viewed women and put them on such a pedestal and was consistently disappointed by them. So a lot of it, in some way, may be conversationally directed at him, but it's hard to say which parts directly.

What is the importance of femininity in your writing?

In my writing as well as my life, the idea of femininity . . . My most prevalent thing in my being is my femininity and that realization, that understanding that I was feminine and not masculine—which is an obvious thing. You understand that at one and a half—it became very important for me to question the given ideas of femininity; also it ties in to what I do. When I first started doing interviews they'd have make-up artists there. I'd be like, 'I look fine, thank you.' That became an important part of my day-to-day life, establishing I don't need to look this way or behave like this. Femininity is intrinsic to your being. It's not how you dress. It's not how you walk. It's not how you talk. It's how you think. It's an incredibly powerful thing, as is masculinity, but I will never understand that so I don't waste my time trying to.

Is there femininity in songwriting?

Definitely, there's a Freudian femininity in songwriting for me in that everything I feel is as a woman, and I feel as womankind. I find that really interesting. The tone of most of the songs is shared woes of being feminine. Also the incredible power it comes with. I think essentially a big part of songwriting and life in general is wanting to be understood and wanting to understand people and be understood by another person. Ultimately people don't want to be lonely. Understanding myself is a huge reason why I write songs, and being understood is the reason why I play them live and put them out.

A lot of your words are more figurative than literal. There's a balance, it seems, between this is me but maybe I don't want you to see me, so I'll disguise . . .

Ha, yes, but just as I could sit here and tell you all my deepest, darkest desires so you would understand me . . . there's a certain level of acceptability. You can be understood to a certain level. I hate the idea that somebody might listen to my songs, or be told to listen to my songs, in order to understand me. It shouldn't be as penetrating as that. It should just be a communal understanding; a deep and meaningful conversation—that is not the intention.

We're back at the *Guardian* cryptic crossword that you were doing when I arrived: you might get some way but you won't complete and understand the whole. I'm interested in your musical household.

My mum's a gardener and my dad was a studio manager. He played guitar and was a songwriter but never pursued it really. He taught me guitar.

Does he continue to have a role in your writing as you've developed and left home?

In some ways; if anyone was ever to see my dad play guitar they'd know exactly where I'd got it from. He's got a unique way of playing the guitar. His influences are obviously very different to mine. Whenever I go home there's always a special time designated for just me and him to play guitar with each other, which is nice and good because I massively dislike writing with people and even jamming. Mainly because I can't read music and I never know what key we're in. Also, playing music is such a personal exercise for me that I struggle with other people around. He's opened my eyes to a few different sounds and tunings and ways of playing. He's invaluable in that way.

Who do you trust to play new songs to?

I guess my close friends. There's two of them and that's only because they ask, and they only ask because they're polite. They know it's my pursuit. They're not involved in music, but it is nice to play it to them and to some extent they might know where things have come from, but they won't know everything. Then the next person would be Ethan, my producer, and we'll come up with arrangements, and then the band.

Can you recall your first attempts at writing songs?

I've tried to forget desperately but I remember them all! And appallingly, some of them found their way, I don't know how, onto the Internet.

I've not heard them.

Please don't, if you want to retain any amount of enjoyment of my music. I recorded them for my GCSE music tech. Damn! I remember being fourteen or fifteen and writing songs about what you think songs should be written about. The very first song I wrote and completed was 'Failure', which was on the first album.

You're kidding: that's such a brilliant song. I'm really shocked to hear that—I'll start with that one just to make life easy! *If he made me in his image, then he's a failure too.*

Damning words. There were some pretty terrible ones following that . . . they're full of teenage rage and they're quite funny, I suppose. I remember writing 'Failure' at the piano on the guitar at my parents' house and my dad hearing me do it and going, 'That's good.' I remember thinking, 'I'm doing good.' I can't remember the process of writing it.

Do you use the piano to write?

I used to a lot, but I now live in a tiny flat up four flights of stairs so I don't have a piano. I'm not at all capable on the piano, but it's quite fun sometimes.

Two or three songwriters have told me they use the piano to visualize their melodies. When you get a melodic idea, how do you develop it and make it grow?

I've never approached it that way of considering a song as lyrics, melody and chords. They all come as one. Occasionally I might have a melody in mind and find the chords to go behind it, but that's quite rare.

I'd like to read one of your own lyrics from 'Rambling Man': *It's funny how the first chords you come to are the minor notes that come to serenade you.* **Is there an element of truth in the attraction of minor keys?**

Yes, it's self-perpetuating. Once you do indulge in melancholy it's addictive. It's much easier to be unhappy than happy. But that lyric, I wasn't consciously talking about myself. I project a lot of the confusion of songwriting and who I am into other people and characters.

Many of your vocal melodies are within your guitar playing. 'I Was Just A Card' is an obvious example. Does one lead the other?

I remember writing that distinctly because it was the first, and the rest of the album was written in the tuning that 'I Was Just A Card' was written in. I remember just fiddling with my guitar and thinking, 'That sounds nice up here.' I had a nylon string guitar around. The first sort of guitar I learnt to play was classical, so finger-picking melody has always been there. I've only just re-discovered it since I started Spanish guitar again.

I'd heard people making comparisons with your music and Leonard Cohen, which made me listen again to some of his records. The main similarity was in the style of playing on the nylon guitar. Is that coincidence?

I'd like to say it was coincidence. I was brought up on Leonard Cohen. What's the album with 'Avalanche' on? (*Songs Of Love And Hate*.) All those songs that you can very much tell it's a nylon string guitar, and a very distinctive way of playing it. There's one song in particular that when I played it to Ethan in the studio he was like, 'It's quite similar to a Leonard Cohen song, isn't it?' It is, and there's nothing to be done about it. I'm surprised it's only happened that obviously once in my songwriting, considering . . . the stuff I listen to is not actually that varied. I go back to the same thing over and over again.

What are those perennial records for you?

Leonard Cohen. Joni Mitchell. I can hear bits of Bob Dylan a lot creeping through, Neil Young and to some extent Judee Sill and that Sixties sound. That's the stuff that directly influences my songwriting. My first musical love was punk: Patti Smith, Television and rock 'n' roll. Just before I wrote the last album I got obsessed with records recorded in 1969. I picked up two that I'd never heard of: Jim Sullivan, *UFO*, and Jim Ford, *Harlan County*. I thought, 'These are the best things I've ever heard.' I was also quite bored at this point. I wasn't touring and I'd just finished recording the album so I had nothing else to do. I spent my time in record shops looking for records made in 1969.

I'm surprised to hear about your love of punk. Neil Tennant shares the same passion. It's always surprising how catholic people's tastes can be when the influence has no obvious bearing upon their records. You were a part of a 'community' in west London?

Of all the people one might consider part of the community, I'm probably the most accepting of the fact that it *was* a community secretly. When we were starting out, everyone suddenly got a bit wary that we were all going to be lumped in together, and our music was also different. So everyone was, 'No, it's not a scene. There's no "community", we just know each other.' I think that was a shame because the whole point why people started calling it a community or a scene is because our music and our playing gigs was just bringing people together. Who gives a fuck about the music? It was getting people together and playing or witnessing or being part of a crowd, or whatever.

Was that important to you developing as a songwriter?

Massively. I was part of Noah And The Whale and then subsequently Mumford And Sons; before they were known as that they were my backing band. I wouldn't have met any of those people and my music would have been different, and particularly if I hadn't met Charlie (*Fink*). All those people gave me an idea that you could play any music you wanted. Nobody was going to make any money anyway, so just do what you want. It sounds bizarre, but at the tender age of sixteen I'd never considered that I'd write. It was around the time of Lily Allen and Kate Nash, which is fine, but I so easily could have got signed and just been turned into another. I was grateful that in a way I had that protection. By meeting all these people I was crowded. Sometimes in a crowd it gives you the opportunity to be individual and do what you want. Be a bit more brave.

Do you feel out of time? There are so many performers with writing teams around them and a drive for commerciality led by television. You're very much not a part of that, but you have records seeping into the mainstream.

There's a big part of me that wishes I was making music in a time where people could make money out of making music. I do work hard and put out records and tour a lot, but it feels like a job sometimes when it's not the songwriting bit, when it's not the bit that feels natural. I could never change my songwriting in order to sell more records, and equally I couldn't bear to sell my soul to sell more records either. If the music's good then people will listen to it. If it's not to their taste then they won't. You can't force music on anybody. I think that's another part of not wanting to give myself over to it completely, because it's not really real life. I made a very conscious choice not to do anything that made me uncomfortable, made me really disassociate my name from myself. When we have to do promo for albums I hate seeing my face, I just can't bear it. I hate the idea that people might read an article about me, that they're misled or whatever. I find that side of it really difficult, but it's necessary.

Does the tattoo on your left wrist inform your thinking towards songwriting?

It's Latin, *Nulli Praeda Sumus*, which means, 'We are prey to none.' It's heinous, ridiculous, but I love how antiquated it is and that it's been our family motto for hundreds of years. I'm a big sucker for things like that.

In 'Goodbye England (Covered in Snow)' the emotion with which you sing a line reduces me to tears, which previously only 'Anchorage' by Michelle Shocked has done: *We will keep you little one, safe from harm, like an extra arm you are part of us.* Can you talk about the writing of that song?

The best way of putting the song into context is what I was doing at the time of writing it: I was travelling more than I'd travelled before. It was the first time I'd been far enough away from childhood to really miss my parents. I'd been living a legitimately adult life in London for three years and suddenly I was away in very foreign places and I really missed home and my boring village I grew up in. Also it was a time I was having to do a lot of stuff on my own. I was becoming very aware I was a solo artist: I'd left Noah And The Whale; the guys from Mumford And Sons were about to go off and do their thing full time; I was about to lose a lot of protection and safety.

Within that song is also the line *there's a mind under this hat*, which is obviously important to you . . . that people know that you are intelligent, well read . . . ?

. . . ha, what is the need? In that context, the line before that is *and I tried to be a girl who likes to be used, I'm too good for that*: that's very simple, pop-psychology femininity, feminism. I found that . . . I don't know . . . it's sort of self-explanatory, really.

Do you remember writing 'The Muse'?

Yep, that was not that long ago. 'The Muse' was the last song written for the album. I was really excited I was going to do it all on my own: single for the first time in six years and I was on a bit of a slight power trip. I found myself pursuing inspiration. I wanted very, very pure beauty. That pursuit of beauty and inspiration: you touch one inch of it and it falls apart, which is what aesthetic beauty is: skin, paper. The song was meant to be funny, light-hearted. I don't know if we quite pulled it off as that.

The piano defines much of the direction of the song.

I tried to arrange that song at home, and when I took it to the band, my keyboard player—I'd never seen his face light up so much: 'This is boogie-woogie stuff!' 'Oh God, just try to be restrained.' He's brilliant. You know my band—because I'm titled a solo musician, they really do not get enough credit. Pete (*Roe*) is one of the most phenomenal musicians I've ever met and a great songwriter. Their stamp is all over the album.

How do you approach arranging at home?

A friend of mine is an engineer who sometimes helps me out. All my instruments are in storage. I have to make quite a thing of it, dragging them all into the flat. And just for four days or whatever I record all the songs and put very basic arrangement around them. It usually starts with bass and drums and keyboards, then cello synth or backing vocals: very simply.

Do those ideas stay true and inform the song, beyond natural musical exaggeration and expansion?

It certainly did on this album.

Religious words dominate your writing.

I've been there and back with religion and faith, several times. It's a very prominent thing in my life. I do think that everybody has a space for some kind of faith in their·head. They want it, but it can be so damning. Love and faith are two things that have brought me so much joy and have let me see the best part of humanity and the very worst, and on a personal scale, not a world scale. I'm not talking about warfare or crimes of passion. I'm talking about in my day-to-day life. I've seen the best and the worst of people in love and faith. Faith is more logical than love; a very common subject matter for me.

Do you naturally relate your observations and collated thoughts and readings to faith?

I'm constantly looking for a way to be understood and constantly looking for a way to relay things to people: my thoughts or my musings. That's why I collect pieces from books that really nail things: that sum up things so brilliantly or explain things so wonderfully. I suppose the rest that I can't find quotes for, that I can't find explanations for, is what I try and sum up or explain or tear apart.

And the house you were born in is crumbling at the corner / Sagging skin and feet of crows. **Do you recall writing 'Cross Your Fingers'?**

I was in the midst of an incredible bout of fear of death. I still to this day don't really know why. I was obsessed by age. The thought of getting older terrified me. It was such a dark image; now I couldn't think any more differently. Once you've got that background to it I'm sure the lyrics sound a bit simpler.

'All My Rage' has an engaging almost yodel-style melody . . .

. . . that kind of skipping. I'd only written it because somebody had given me an Appalachian dulcimer. It's got four strings: two high drones and one string that you can play melody on. Again, it was meant to be light-hearted. We recorded that album in sequence and I was still umming and ahhing about recording it for the end of the album because it didn't really fit with the rest of it. It ended up being a bit of fun. We all went to the pub and got a bit trolleyed and then came back and recorded it.

It has a sense of the round from folk tradition. Can you place yourself in the moment when you wrote 'Devil's Spoke'?

Soon after writing that song I stopped romanticizing situations. It was an embellished situation in my life: the classic unchangeable, awful man.

It quite obviously draws on Dylan's 'It's Alright Ma, I'm Only Bleeding'.

I don't even know that song.

Oh right, yes, it does have that . . . When I listen to some of my songs I do hear that Dylan rhythm, lyrically. It's a good rhythm to use.

With 'Sophia', did you have a sense of what the end point was going to be at the outset?

No, I never know . . . it just blows along because it wants to. It felt like that song was going to be at the end of an album and that there should be some conclusive or defiant ending.

And you felt that as you were writing the song?

I must have done. I don't remember particularly thinking, 'Now how can I achieve that?' but it probably did enter my mind.

When you write, do you have the song's structure in mind?

I don't, but my dad would always drum into me that a song is verse, chorus, verse, chorus, middle eight. I've always had that basic ingrained structure in my head. Sometimes songs are one long, meandering, bizarre collection of sections.

This is a quote from you about 'The Beast': 'The electric guitar sound is like a character in the song, almost as important as the lyrics.'

I wrote it on a nylon string but I arranged it with electric guitars on it. That song was really interesting because even as I was taking it into the studio I was like, 'This is a boring song: it's going to be really boring for people to listen to but for some reason it has to be on the album.' Then suddenly Ethan got this sound going and Pete and Marcus got their guitars out and it made sense. It felt more like a story. Usually I'd say that the songs are finished and then they're arranged. That song was finished in the studio.

The menacing spoken delivery is in keeping with the controlled guitar, almost like a tamed beast, as it were. I expected live the feedback might be more ferocious in a Velvet Underground style, but it remained restrained.

When we started playing it I'd never played with somebody playing a full drum kit with sticks, and I couldn't physically sing loud enough to get heard over the drums, even though the drums were in a booth and I was in a room with everybody else. That is now important in how we perform it, in that it sounds like a struggle. It's not a comfortable song to play or to listen to. It's not satisfying. There is some importance in the general uncomfortableness of all the instrumentation.

Was the talk-singing part of the original idea?

That was just in the studio, in the moment.

Have you defined what the Beast is?

I know what the Beast is. It's just a figurative darkness, a character, a capability of darkness and the temptation of it.

What initiated Experiments In Awkwardness?

I was having to do a lot of festivals and I dislike them immensely. I do like playing them when I get there, but the idea of festivals is very contradictive and silly: everybody getting together to form a little community and ruin a perfectly beautiful patch of land for three days or whatever. That's my cynical side. I thought it might be interesting to try and take people out of the idea of this enormous amount of people in one space and take them into somewhere very calm and very quiet and make them feel incredibly uncomfortable. We would invite two people who didn't know each other into a tent or caravan. I would have to gauge the situation very quickly and find a position to sit in that is very full on. Then I would try and sing them a song looking them in the eye and not say anything and leave. Sometimes I did it and sometimes I couldn't do it. Everybody has an amazing innate sense of who's in control of the situation. Sometimes I would go in and feel completely in control of the situation, and I'd take it on board and I'd look them in the eye and I'd sing them a song and it would be incredibly awkward for both of us. Then sometimes it was so obvious to me that they were in control and I was going to have to look at the floor. Not only were they in the room with somebody they'd never met before and left alone for quite a bit of time to chat awkwardly, but then suddenly this very unexplained, very strange and I imagine very uncomfortable situation was put upon them. We got people to write down what they thought and some people really liked it and just enjoyed it as an experience, either to be closer to me as a songwriter, or to listen to music. Some people disliked it immensely and were angry that I'd put them through this incredibly awkward six minutes. It was an interesting thing for me to see what I could do and what I was comfortable with, and also to see people's reaction to it. And also whether people would like to or not. More people liked it than I thought they would. I found I wanted people to be a bit more angry. I wanted people to feel the vulnerability that I feel when I'm on stage. The vulnerability I feel when things are expected of me that I can't deliver. I'm just normal and sometimes I can walk into a room and look people in the eye and sometimes I can't. I hoped people might pick up on that and maybe consider how they felt being put on the spot just as much as I was.

Do you have any final thoughts on your body of work with regard to a path for the future?

So far with what I've put out I'm very proud of it, and as I said earlier on I think I've been very brave and it's been very important to me in my life. I intend to continue to do it as long as I need to do it, whether making money out

Medly
Master Arnber
~~PB~~ New Song (Help me)

Once
Where can I

Little love

Sophia

Hera

& Rosie
Saved these words

Guidex Document Wallet - A4
Buff 21142, Blue 21143, Green 21144, Orange 21146, Red 21148,
Assorted 21140.

Laura Marling handwritten set list, Grand Ballroom Hotel, London, 16 June 2013 of it or it becomes less of a priority as in touring and stuff like that. I can't see myself touring it, labouring it forever. The better my guitar playing's got the more questions I have.

Do you have an ideal of a song that you're trying to write?

No, not really. I'd like to try different styles and genres of music. I don't have any music goals. I have life goals, which are linked in some way.

ACKNOWLEDGEMENTS

Inviting songwriters to partake in a book without a publishing deal and by an author without any track record opens few doors. I needed help and I would like to heap praise on a good many people who have given it.

It starts with Richard Thomas, who I talked about in the introduction. He recognized the book would fill a gap in the market and played a significant role in introducing me to managers, literary agents and publishing houses. Simon Fowler is my oldest friend, and also the first person who agreed to meet and talk over his songwriting processes. It was a brilliant conversation and gave me confidence that this far-fetched idea was a possibility. I am desperately embarrassed he is not in the first edition of the book.

Without the twenty-seven songwriters I have spoken with *The Art of Noise* could not have happened. I offer my humblest gratitude to each and every one of them. The conversations were enabled by a host of people who have made the respective chapters possible by way of access to back catalogues, archives, or simple good-will. They are:

Chaz Jankel: Lee Harris, Jemima Dury, Sav Ramzi, and Steve at East Central One.

Paul Weller: Steve Cradock and Claire Moon. Ruth at Century books.

Ray Davies: Chris Metzler (exceptional persistence, willing and friendship), Kerry Michael, Sarah Lockwood, Linda McBride and Klaus Schmalenbach.

Billy Bragg: Peter Jenner, Matt Brown and Sarah Wills.

478

Mike Barson, Suggs and Chris Foreman:	Jamie Spenser, Clive Langer, Hugh Gadsdon, Mel Stephenson, Gareth White, Garry Blackburn, and at the eleventh hour Tony Murphy.
Sting:	Laura Wilson, Kate at Lake House, and Clare Fisher. Tracy Bufferd and Nicole VanGiesen, in New York, for being so direct and making communication so easy.
Neil Tennant and Chris Lowe:	Christina Skinner, Melisa Green, Angela Becker, Javier de Frutos and Julie Leveque.
Chris Difford and Glenn Tilbrook:	(for meeting twice due to my technical stupidity: a gentleman) Matt Thomas, Suzanne Hunt, David Bocking and David Bailey.
Noel Gallagher:	Natalie Hicks and the lovely Kat Killingley.
Johnny Marr:	Joe Moss and Ben Wileman.
Andy Partridge:	John Leckie, Sister Rachel, Sandy Beech, Steve Young and Declan Colgan.
Joan Armatrading:	Stewart Grant, Ruth Bowditch and Julie Baker.
Mick Jones:	Janine at Notorious, Sophie Brugere, Johnny Green (a pleasure to know), Robin Banks (thank you father; it would never have happened without you), Lucinda Mellor and Robert Gordon McHarg III.
Jimmy Page:	Joan Hudson, Brother Ben, and the always friendly Michael Loney.
Robin Gibb:	Patrick Rackow (without you it would never have happened), Mick Garbutt, Hik Sasaki, Eleanor Sherman and Dwina Murphy Gibb.
Bryan Ferry:	Isaac Ferry (sterling support), Gillian Fleet and Gemma Corry Reid.
John Lydon:	Michala Stuart, Rambo Stevens ('persistence will pay, Daniel') and Scott Murphy.

ACKNOWLEDGEMENTS

| **Damon Albarn:** | Brídín Murphy Mitchell, Tanyel Vahdettin, Anna Woodhall, Chris Morrison and Charly Hutchings. |

| **Lee Mavers:** | Jona Cox and Simon Ryan. |

| **Laura Marling:** | Laura Taylor. |

| **Annie Lennox:** | Jude Kelly and Tara Goldsmid Paterson (for your patience with my relentless onslaught of requests). |

| **Lily Allen:** | Todd Interland and Polly Hadden-Paton. |

| **Jarvis Cocker:** | Lucy Hurst and the thoroughly brilliant pair: Jeannette Lee and Kelly Kiley. |

A special thank you to Jon Webster for agreeing to meet me, help me and actively provide introductions and leads.

Many other thanks are necessary to: Angus Deayton, Owen O'Neil, Gill Taylor, Rebecca Sichel-Coates, Nicola Joss, Brian Message, Sally-Anne McKeown, Moira Bellas, Darrell Gilmour, Jake Kirner, Shaun Bowen, Paul Gambaccini, Tony King, Tamsin Lion, Katharina von Hellberg (for a wonderful stay in Munich), Ben Parsons, Régine Moylett, Matt Clifford (for belief and persistence), Bill Curbishley, Geoff Barradale, Paul Pattinson (for reassuring legal advice), Stuart Bell, Jane Rose (for always and immediately returning calls and emails), Sarah Yeoman and Lucie Panton.

In the book publishing world, thank you Jake Arnott, Kevin Conroy Scott, Simon Petherick (you were the first to say 'yes'—it would have been Beautiful!). In the music publishing world: Hannah Wilson, Edith Lobo, Nico Evans, Henrietta Haines, Leah Webb and Mel Johnson.

Special thanks to my literary agent, Carrie Kania: Simon said you were the best in London, you proved it so x. All at Picador and at St. Martin's Griffin (I am so thrilled to be on the imprints) and especially Paul Baggaley (a joy to work with, for shaping and editing the book, and for campaigning on my behalf) and Kris Doyle (for rolling up your sleeves and making it happen). Rachel Wright (for a wonderful copyedit that made my gibberish sound intelligent).

Thank you: Lawrence Impey (always a pleasure to share coffee and cake with), Yan Calmeyer Friis, Chris Metzler, and all the photographers who lent their work to the UK original, *Isle of Noises*.

Finally to friends and family: Martin Betts (your belief, knowledge and endless interest has spurred me on), Helen Tulley (for legal advice and putting

480   my mind at ease), Brother Saul (also for legal advice) and Marc Olivier (for explaining chords I hope one day to be able to play).

    Lastly, I have always been obsessed about music and four people have listened to virtually every record, by every artist, on repeat for most waking hours, for all our lives together. Without Susie, Lily, Eleanor and Lottie I would never have become an author. xxxx

LIST OF ILLUSTRATIONS

G M Sumner / EMI Music Publishing Ltd, London W1F 9LD. Image © Sting Archive

197 'Fragile' Words and Music by Gordon Matthew Sumner © 1987. Reproduced by Permission of G M Sumner / EMI Music Publishing Ltd, London W1F 9LD. Image © Sting Archive

199 The Police, Wembley Arena, 20 October 2007 © Lawrence Impey

206 'Rook' Words and Music by Andy Partridge © 1990. Reproduced by Permission of EMI Virgin Music Ltd, London W1F 9LD. Image © Andy Partridge

213 'The Disappointed' Words and Music by Andy Partridge © 1992. Reproduced by Permission of EMI Virgin Music Ltd, London W1F 9LD. Image © Andy Partridge

227 Harri Kakoulli diary entry, 1975. © www.packetofthree.com

232 Glenn Tilbrook and Chris Difford, Greenwich Baths Rehearsal Rooms, 1975. © Lawrence Impey

250 Madness ticket, Birmingham Odeon, 30 October 1985. © Daniel Rachel Archive
Madness set list, Birmingham Odeon, 30 October 1985. © Daniel Rachel Archive

288 Red Wedge at the Birmingham Odeon, 27 January 1986: (top left—bottom right) Billy Bragg; Mick Talbot; Paul Weller; Lloyd Cole; Andy Rourke and Johnny Marr; Paul Weller, Billy Bragg and Jimmy Somerville; Mark Bedford and Suggs; Cathal Smyth. © Daniel Rachel
Red Wedge ticket, Birmingham Odeon, 27 January 1986. © Daniel Rachel Archive

302 'A New England' Words and Music by Billy Bragg © 1983. Reproduced by Permission of Sony/ATV Music Publishing Ltd, London W1F 9LD. Image © Billy Bragg

304 Billy Bragg at Berry Street Studio, London, July 1984. © Nicki Rodgerson

331 'Being Boring' Words and Music by Christopher Lowe and Neil Tennant ©1990. Reproduced by permission of Cage Music Limited / Sony/ATV Music Publishing (UK) Ltd, London W1F 9LD. With kind thanks to Neil Tennant

358 *The La's* by The La's. Artwork © Ryan Art

406 'The Death of You and Me' Words and Music by Noel Gallagher © 2011. Reproduced by permission of Oasis Music / Sony/ATV Music Publishing (UK) Limited, London W1F 9LD. Image © Noel Gallagher

409 'Don't Look Back In Anger' Words and Music by Noel Gallagher ©1995. Reproduced by permission of Oasis Music / SM Publishing UK Limited, London W1F 9LD. Image © Noel Gallagher

475 Laura Marling handwritten set list, Grand Hotel Ballroom, London, 16 June 2013. © Daniel Rachel Archive

BIBLIOGRAPHY

Books, magazine articles, film, television and radio programmes consulted during the writing of this book.

RAY DAVIES

Davies, Dave, *Kink*, Hyperion 1996

Davies, Ray, *Waterloo Sunset*, Penguin 1997

Davies, Ray, *X-Ray: The Unauthorized Autobiography*, Viking 1994

Hinman, Doug, *The Kinks: All Day and All of the Night*, Backbeat 2004

Hudd, Roy, *Roy Hudd's Book of Music-Hall, Variety and Showbiz Anecdotes*, Robson 1998

Kitts, Thomas M., *Ray Davies*, Routledge 2008

Marten, Neville, and Hudson, Jeff, *The Kinks*, Sanctuary 2001

Rogan, Johnny, *The Complete Guide to the Music of The Kinks*, Omnibus 1998

Rogan, Johnny, *The Kinks: The Sound and the Fury*, Elm Tree 1984

Savage, Jon, *The Kinks: The Official Biography*, Faber and Faber 1984

Autumn Almanac—*The Ray Davies Story*, Smooth Operations / Radio 2 1991

The Davies Diaries, prod. Stewart Cruikshank, BBC radio 2000

I'm Not Like Everybody Else: The World of Ray Davies and The Kinks, dir. Vanessa Engle, BBC 1995

Ray Davies: The World From My Window, dir. Matthew Longfellow, ITV 2004

ROBIN GIBB

Black, Johnny, *The Rogue Gene*, MOJO June 2001

Buskin, Richard, *Stayin' Alive*, Sound On Sound 2005

Bee Gees: In Our Own Time, dir. Skot Bright, Pen / Bright Entertainment 2010

Cook, H., Hughes, A., and Bilyeu, M., *The Ultimate Biography of the Bee Gees: Tales of the Brothers Gibb*, Omnibus Press 2001

Keppel Road: The Life & Music of the Bee Gees, South Bank Show, dir. Tony Cash, LWT 1997

Radio interview with Roger Scott, Radio Academy 1989

Too Much Heaven: The Story of the Bee Gees, prod. Joe Bishop, BBC Radio 2 1997

JIMMY PAGE

Hoskyns, Barney, *Trampled Under Foot: The Power and Excess of Led Zeppelin*, Faber and Faber 2012

Wall, Mick, *When Giants Walked The Earth: A Biography of Led Zeppelin*, Orion 2008

Yorke, Ritchie, *Led Zeppelin: From Early Days to Page and Plant*, Virgin 1999

Jimmy Page and Robert Plant: No Quarter (Unledded), dir. Aubrey Powell, Warner Music Vision 1995

Led Zeppelin DVD, prod. Jimmy Page and Dick Carruthers, Warner Music Vision 2003

Robert Plant: By Myself, prod. Chris Rodley, BBC2 2010

Wired, interview with Plant, Channel 4 1998

BRYAN FERRY

Balfour, Rex, *The Bryan Ferry Story*, M. Dempsey 1976

Bracewell, Michael, *Re-Make / Re-Model*, Faber and Faber 2007

Buckley, David, *The Thrill of It All: The Story of Bryan Ferry and Roxy Music*, André Deutsch 2004

Rigby, Jonathan, *Both Ends Burning*, Reynolds & Hearn Ltd 2005

Rogan, Johnny, *Roxy Music—Style with Substance: Roxy's first ten years*, Star 1982

Stump, Paul, *Unknown Pleasures: a Cultural Biography of Roxy Music*, Quartet 1998

The Bryan Ferry Story, BBC Radio 1 1994

Interview with Richard Skinner, BBC Radio 1 1985

More Than This: The Roxy Music Story, dir. Bob Smeaton, Eagle Rock Entertainment 2008

Roxy Music: Total Recall—A History 1972–1982, dir. Phil MacDonald, Virgin Vision 1989

The Thrill Of It All: Roxy Music, Sugar Productions / BBC Radio 2 2011

Whistle Test Extra, interview with Richard Skinner, BBC2 1986

Without Walls: This is Tomorrow, Channel 4 1992

JOAN ARMATRADING

Mayes, Sean, *Joan Armatrading: A Biography*, Weidenfeld & Nicholson 1990

Desert Island Discs, BBC Radio 4 1988

Joan Armatrading: Track Record, A&M Video 1983

Joan Armatrading Music Special, Metro Radio 1988

Kaleidoscope, talking to Paul Gambaccini, BBC Radio 4 29/7/88

Who's That Girl with Janice Long, BBC Radio 1 12/05/84

CHAZ JANKEL

Balls, Richard, *Sex and Drugs and Rock 'n' Roll: The Life of Ian Dury*, Omnibus 2000

Birch, Will, *Ian Dury: The Definitive Biography*, Pan Macmillan 2010

Drury, Jim, *Ian Dury and the Blockheads: Song by Song*, Sanctuary 2003

Dury, Jemima, ed., *'Hallo Sausages': The Lyrics of Ian Dury*, Bloomsbury 2012

Ian Dury: Spasticus Autisticus, dir. Franco Rosso, Channel 4 1983

Jukebox Heroes: Ian Dury, dir. Paul Pierrot, BBC1 2002

JOHN LYDON

Lydon, John, with Zimmerman, Keith, and Zimmerman, Kent, *Rotten: No Irish, No blacks, No dogs: the authorized autobiography*, Coronet 1994

Myers, Ben, *John Lydon: The Sex Pistols, PiL & Anti-Celebrity*, Independent Music Press 2004

Savage, Jon, *England's Dreaming*, Faber and Faber 1991

Classic Albums: Never Mind the Bollocks, Here's The Sex Pistols, dir. Matthew Longfellow, Eagle Rock Entertainment 2002

The Culture Show: John Lydon Special, prod. John Mullen, BBC2 2010

The Filth and The Fury: A Sex Pistols Film, dir. Julien Temple, Film4 2003

That Was Then . . . This Is Now, dir. David G. Croft, BBC2 1998

MICK JONES

The Clash: The Complete Chord Songbook, Wise Publications 2004

Gilbert, Pat, *Passion Is A Fashion: The Real Story of The Clash*, Aurum 2009

Gray, Marcus, *Return of the Last Gang in Town*, Helter Skelter Publishing 2001

Gray, Marcus, *Route 19 Revisited: The Clash and London Calling*, Vintage 2011

Green, Johnny, and Barker, Garry, *A Riot of Our Own: Night and Day With The Clash*, Indigo 1997

Salewicz, Chris, *Redemption Song: The Definitive Biography of Joe Strummer*, Harper Collins 2006

Strummer, J., Jones, M., Simonon, P., Headon, T., *The Clash*, Atlantic 2008

Joe Strummer talking to Alan Whiting, Radio 1 4/9/1984

Rude Boy, dir. David Mingay , Buzzy Enterprises 1980

That Was Then . . . This Is Now, dir. Anya Camilleri, BBC2 1989

Viva Joe Strummer: The Clash and Beyond, dir. Mike Parkinson, WHE 2005

Westway to the World, dir. Don Letts, 3DD 2000

Wired, Channel 4 6/5/1988

PAUL WELLER

Hewitt, Paolo, *The Jam: A Beat Concerto*, Omnibus 1983

Reed, John, *Paul Weller: My Ever Changing Moods*, Omnibus 1996

Watson, Lawrence, and Hewitt, Paolo, *Days Lose Their Names and Time Slips Away*, Boxtree 1995

Weller, Paul, *Suburban 100*, Century 2007

Willmott, Graham, *The Jam: Sounds From The Street*, Reynolds & Hearn 2003

The Complete Jam, prod. Joe Cavanagh, Universal 2002

Highlights and Hang-Ups, dir. Pedro Romhanyi, Universal 1995

Into Tomorrow, dir. Stuart Watts, Universal 2007

Paul Weller: Modern Classics on Film 90–01, prod. Joe Cavanagh, Universal 2004

STING

Clarkson, Wensley, Sting, Blake 1996

Sting, *Broken Music*, Simon & Schuster 2003

Sting, *Lyrics*, The Dial Press 2007

Article by Steve Adams, *Record Collector*, June 1993

The Far East, The Near East And The Extremely Near East, Old Grey Whistle Test Special, BBC2 1980

The Police in Montserrat, BBC 1981

Sting! Bring On the Night, dir. Michael Apted, A&M Sound Pictures 1985

Sting's Winter Songbook, dir. Jim Gable, BBC1 2009

ANDY PARTRIDGE

Twomey, Chris, *Chalkhills and Children*, Omnibus 2002

XTC & Farmer, Neville, *XTC Song Stories*, Helter Skelter Publishing 1998

Interview with Todd Bernhardt, *myspace .com/toddbernhardt*

CHRIS DIFFORD AND GLENN TILBROOK

Difford, Chris, and Tilbrook, Glenn, with Drury, Jim, *Squeeze Song By Song*, Sanctuary 2004

Squeeze: Take Me I'm Yours, dir. Bob Smeaton, BBC4 2012

MADNESS

Edwards, Terry, *Madness: One Step Beyond*, Continuum 2009

Madness; The Madness Story So Far, Limited Edition Magazine, Gamester Publications 1982

Miles, Barry, *The 2-Tone Book for Rude Boys*, Omnibus 1981

Reed, John, *House Of Fun: The Story of Madness*, Omnibus Press 2010

Suggs, *Suggs and the City*, Headline 2009

The Nutty Boys Cracked (Return of The Mad 7), Adrian Thrills, NME 2/04/1983

Divine Madness video commentary, Virgin Records 2005

486

Five Years of Madness, Mike Smith, BBC Radio 1 1984

Madness: One Step Beyond, BBC Radio 1 1992

Madness: Take It or Leave It, Dave Robinson, Stiff Records 1981

Young Guns Go For It: Madness, dir. Kate Meynell, BBC 2000

ANNIE LENNOX

O'Brien, Lucy, *Annie Lennox: Sweet Dreams Are Made of This*, Sidgwick & Jackson 1991

Sutherland, Bryony, and Ellis, Lucy, *Annie Lennox: The Biography*, Omnibus 2002

Waller, J., and Rapport, S., *Sweet Dreams: The Definitive Biography of the Eurythmics*, Virgin 1985

BILLY BRAGG

Back To Basics with Billy Bragg, IMP 1985

Bragg, Billy, *The Progressive Patriot: A Search For Belonging*, Bantam Press 2006

Collins, Andrew, *Still Suitable For Miners: Billy Bragg*, Virgin 1998

Billy Bragg, South Bank Show, dir. David Thomas, LWT1985

Man in the Sand: Billy Bragg & Wilco, dir. Kim Hopkins, BBC 1999

JOHNNY MARR

Carman, Richard, *Johnny Marr: The Smiths and the Art of Gun-Slinging*, IMP 2006

Fletcher, Tony, *A Light That Never Goes Out: The Enduring Saga of The Smiths*, William Heinemann 2012

Goddard, Simon, *The Smiths: Songs That Saved Your Life*, Reynolds & Hearn 2002

Middles, Mick, *The Smiths: The Complete Story*, Omnibus 1985

Rogan, Johnny, *Morrissey and Marr: The Severed Alliance*, Calidore 2006

Woods, Paul, A., ed., *Morrissey In Conversation: the Essential Interviews*, Plexus 2007

The Smiths, South Bank Show, dir. Tony Knox, LWT 1987

Young Guns Go For It: The Rise And Fall Of The Smiths, dir. Mike Connolly BBC 1999

NEIL TENNANT AND CHRIS LOWE

Heath, Chris, *Pet Shop Boys, Literally*, Viking 1990

Heath, Chris, *Pet Shop Boys Versus America*, Viking 1993

Hoare, Philip, and Heath, Chris, *Pet Shop Boys Catalogue*, Thames & Hudson 2006

Pet Shop Boys: A Life in Pop, dir. George Scott, Parlophone 2006

LEE MAVERS

Macefield, M. W., *A Secret Liverpool: In search of The La's*, Helter Skelter Publishing 2011

DAMON ALBARN

Maconie, Stuart, *3862 Days: The Official History of Blur*, Virgin 1999

Roach, Martin, *Blur: The Whole Story*, Omnibus 1996

Roach, Martin, and Nolan, David, *Damon Albarn: Blur, Gorillaz & other fables*, IMP 2007

Blur End of a Century, South Bank Show, dir. Gerald Fox, LWT 1999

Blur—Starshaped, dir. Matthew Longfellow, PMI 1995

Gorillaz: Bananaz, dir. Ceri Levy, Gorillaz Productions Limited 2008

No Distance Left To Run, dir. Dylan Southern, Parlophone 2010

Parklife: The Blur Story, BBC Radio 1 1999

NOEL GALLAGHER

Abbot, Tim, *Oasis: Definitely*, Pavilion 1996

Furmanovsky, Jill, *Was There Then*, Ebury 1997

Hewitt, Paolo, *Getting High: The Adventures of Oasis*, Boxtree 1997

Mathur, Paul, *Take Me There: Oasis—the Story*, Bloomsbury 1996

Middles, Mick, *Oasis: Round Their Way*, IMP 1996

Shaw, Harry, *Oasis Talking*, Omnibus 2002

Lock the Box DVD, dir. Dick Carruthers, Big Brother 2006

Oasis: Lord Don't Slow Me Down, dir. Baillie Walsh, Big Brother 2007

Oasis—What's the Story?, BBC Radio 2 2002

JARVIS COCKER

Sturdy, Mark, *Truth and Beauty: The Story Of Pulp*, Omnibus 2003

No Sleep Till Sheffield—Pulp Go Public, dir. Mike Connolly, BBC2 1995

120 Minutes, interview with Jarvis Cocker, MTV 1993

Pulp: Do You Remember The First Time?, Radio 1 1998

Songbook: Jarvis Cocker, Sky Arts 1 2009

The Story of 'Common People', dir. Paul Grant, Colin Stone, BBC3 2006

LILY ALLEN

Howden, Martin, *Living Dangerously*, John Blake Publishing 2008

Wolfson, Bella, *'Smile': The Story of Lily Allen*, Omnibus 2010

Lily Allen: Still Alright?, dir. Jon Clements, Remedy Productions 2007

LAURA MARLING

Laura Marling & Friends, Live from the Royal Festival Hall, dir. Fred & Nick, Virgin 2010

GENERAL

Ackroyd, Peter, *Albion: The Origins of the English Imagination*, Chatto 2002

Bradford, Chris, *Heart and Soul: Revealing the Craft of Songwriting*, Sanctuary 2005

Byrne, David, *How Music Works*, Canongate 2012

Denselow, Robin, *When The Music's Over: The Story of Political Pop*, Faber and Faber 1989

Emerick, Geoff, and Massey, Howard, *Here, There and Everywhere*, Gotham Books 2006

Harris, John, *The Last Party: Britpop, Blair and the Demise of English Rock*, Fourth Estate 2003

Hodgkinson, Will, *Song Man*, Bloomsbury 2007

Larkin, Colin, *The Encyclopaedia of Popular Music*, Omnibus 2011

Martin, George, ed., *Making Music*, Barrie & Jenkins 1988

Massey, Howard, *Behind the Glass*, Backbeat 2000

Read, Mike, *Major to Minor: The Rise and Fall of the Songwriter*, Sanctuary 2000

Reynolds, Simon, *Rip It Up and Start Again*, Faber and Faber 2005

Roach, Martin, *The Right To Imagination and Madness*, IMP 1994

Roberts, David, ed., *British Hit Singles and Albums*, Hit Entertainment 2004

Ross, Alex, *Listen To This*, Fourth Estate 2010

Ross, Alex, *The Rest Is Noise: Listening to the Twentieth Century*, Fourth Estate 2008

Simons, David, *Studio Stories*, Backbeat 2004

Strong, Martin C., *The Essential Rock Discography*, Canongate 2006

Thatcher, Margaret, *The Downing Street Years*, Harper Collins 1993

Waterman, J. Douglas, ed., *Song*, Writers Digest Books 2007

Webb, Jimmy, *Tunesmith: Inside the Art of Songwriting*, Hyperion 1998

Zollo, Paul, *Songwriters on Songwriting*, Da Capo Press 1997

PUBLISHING CREDITS

RAY DAVIES

All of My Friends Were There Raymond Douglas Davies: Davray Music Ltd/ Carlin Music Corp.

Dead End Street Raymond Douglas Davies: Davray Music Ltd/Carlin Music Corp.

Oklahoma USA Raymond Douglas Davies: Davray Music Ltd / Sony/ATV Music Publishing Llc / Sony/ATV Music Publishing (UK) Limited.

Come Dancing Raymond Douglas Davies: Davray Music Ltd / Sony/ATV Music Publishing Llc / Sony/ATV Music Publishing (UK) Limited.

Where Have All The Good Times Gone Raymond Douglas Davies: Davray Music Ltd / Carlin Music Corp.

Well Respected Man Ray Davies: Edward Kassner Music Co Ltd.

Set Me Free Ray Davies: Edward Kassner Music Co Ltd.

Autumn Almanac Raymond Douglas Davies: Davray Music Ltd /Carlin Music Corp.

Americana Raymond Douglas Davies: Davray Music Ltd / Sony/ATV Music Publishing Llc / Sony/ATV Music Publishing (UK) Limited.

Sitting In My Hotel Raymond Douglas Davies: Davray Music Ltd / Sony/ATV Music Publishing Llc / Sony/ATV Music Publishing (UK) Limited.

Motorway Raymond Douglas Davies: Davray Music Ltd /Sony/ATV Music Publishing Llc / Sony/ATV Music Publishing (UK) Limited.

Celluloid Heroes Raymond Douglas Davies: Davray Music Ltd / Sony/ATV Music Publishing Llc / Sony/ATV Music Publishing (UK) Limited.

Australia Raymond Douglas Davies: Davray Music Ltd / Carlin Music Corp.

Wonderboy Raymond Douglas Davies: Davray Music Ltd / Carlin Music Corp.

Sweet Lady Genevieve Raymond Douglas Davies: Davray Music Ltd / Sony/ATV Music Publishing Llc / Sony/ATV Music Publishing (UK) Limited.

Fancy Raymond Douglas Davies: Davray Music Ltd / Carlin Music Corp.

Session Man Raymond Douglas Davies: Carlin Music Corp.

Look A Little On The Sunny Side Davies, Raymond Douglas / Davray Music Ltd / Sony/ATV Music Publishing Llc / Sony/ATV Music Publishing (UK) Limited.

ROBIN GIBB

You Win Again Gibb, Barry Alan / Gibb, Maurice Ernest / Gibb, Robin: Hugh Crompton Songs / Warner Chappell Music Ltd / Universal Music Publ International MGB Ltd.

Holiday Gibb, Barry Alan / Gibb, Robin: Hugh Crompton Songs / Gibb Brothers /

Universal Music Publishing MGB Limited.

The Echo Of Your Love Gibb, Barry Alan.

Marley Purt Drive Gibb, Barry Alan / Gibb, Maurice Ernest / Gibb, Robin: Hugh Crompton Songs / Gibb Brothers / Universal Music Publishing MGB Limited.

Stayin' Alive Gibb, Barry Alan / Gibb, Maurice Ernest / Gibb, Robin: Hugh Crompton Songs / Gibb Brothers / Universal Music Publ International MGB Ltd.

With The Sun In My Eyes Gibb, Barry Alan / Gibb, Maurice Ernest / Gibb, Robin: Hugh / Gibb Brothers Music / Universal Music Publ International MGB Ltd.

You Don't Have To Say You Love Me Donaggio, Pino / Pallavicini, Vito / Napier-Bell, Simon / Wickham, Vicki Heather: Accordo Edizioni Musicali S R L /Kassner Associated Publishers Limited.

JIMMY PAGE

Bron Y Aur Stomp Plant, Robert / Jones, John Paul / Page, Jimmy: Flames Of Albion Music Inc / Warner Chappell Music Inc / Warner Bros Inc / Warner/Chappell North America Limited.

Thank You Plant, Robert / Page, Jimmy: Flames Of Albion Music Inc / Warner Chappell Music Inc / Warner Bros Inc / Warner/Chappell North America Limited.

Immigrant Song Plant, Robert / Page, Jimmy: Flames Of Albion Music Inc / Warner Chappell Music Inc / Warner Bros Inc / Warner/Chappell North America Limited.

BRYAN FERRY

Mother Of Pearl Ferry, Bryan: BMG Rights Management (UK) Limited.

If It Takes All Night Ferry, Bryan: BMG Rights Management (UK) Limited.

Thrill Of It All Ferry, Bryan: BMG Rights Management (UK) Limited.

If There Is Something Ferry, Bryan: BMG Rights Management (UK) Limited.

Prairie Rose Manzanera, Phil / Ferry, Bryan: E G Music Ltd (GB 1) / Universal Music MGB Limited / BMG Rights Management (UK) Limited.

Street Life Ferry, Bryan: BMG Rights Management (UK) Limited.

In Every Dream Home A Heartache Ferry, Bryan: BMG Rights Management (UK) Limited.

Dance Away Ferry, Bryan / E G Music Ltd (GB 1) / Universal Music MGB Limited.

Slave To Love Ferry, Bryan: BMG Rights Management (UK) Limited.

Casanova Ferry, Bryan: BMG Rights Management (UK) Limited.

JOAN ARMATRADING

Mama Papa Armatrading, Joan Anita Barbara: Giftwend Ltd / Hornall Brothers Music Ltd.

Down To Zero Armatrading, Joan Anita Barbara: Westminster Music Ltd.

How Cruel Armatrading, Joan Anita Barbara: Magem Songs Limited.

Ma-Me-O-Beach Armatrading, Joan Anita Barbara: Imagem Songs Limited / Imagem Songs Limited.

A Woman In Love Armatrading, Joan Anita Barbara: Giftwend Ltd / Hornall Brothers Music Ltd.

Love And Affection Armatrading, Joan Anita Barbara: Magem Songs Limited.

Willow Armatrading, Joan Anita Barbara: Magem Songs Limited.

All A Woman Needs Armatrading, Joan Anita Barbara: Giftwend Ltd / Hornall Brothers Music Ltd.

If Women Ruled The World Armatrading, Joan Anita Barbara: Giftwend Ltd / Hornall Brothers Music Ltd.

Play The Blues Armatrading, Joan Anita Barbara: Giftwend Ltd / Hornall Brothers Music Ltd.

Me Myself I Armatrading, Joan Anita
Barbara / Magem Songs Limited.

All The Way From America Armatrading,
Joan Anita Barbara: Onward Music
Ltd.

IAN DURY

Plaistow Patricia Nugent, Stephen Lewis /
Dury, Ian Robins: Warner Chappell
Music Ltd.

Billericay Dickie Nugent, Stephen Lewis /
Dury, Ian Robins / Jankel, Chaz:
Templemill Music Ltd / Warner
Chappell Music Ltd.

Dance Of The Crackpots Turnbull, John
George / Dury, Ian Robins: Warner
Chappell Music Ltd.

This Is What We Find Gallagher, Michael
William / Dury, Ian Robins: Warner
Chappell Music Ltd.

England's Glory Dury, Ian Robins /
Melvin, Roderick Martin: Templemill
Music Ltd / Warner Chappell Music
Ltd.

What A Waste Dury, Ian Robins / Melvin,
Roderick Martin: Templemill Music
Ltd / Warner Chappell Music Ltd.

My Old Man Nugent, Stephen Lewis /
Dury, Ian Robins: Templemill
Music Ltd / Warner Chappell Music
Ltd.

Blockheads Dury, Ian Robins / Jankel,
Charles Jeremy: Templemill Music Ltd
/ Warner Chappell Music Ltd.

Delusions Of Grandeur Gallagher, Michael
William / Dury, Ian Robins: Warner
Chappell Music Ltd.

Manic Depression (Jimi) Gallagher,
Michael William / Dury, Ian Robins:
Templemill Music Ltd / Warner
Chappell Music Ltd.

Common As Muck Payne, David Stanley /
Dury, Ian Robins / Jankel, Chaz:
Templemill Music Ltd / Warner
Chappell Music Ltd.

Reasons To Be Cheerful (Part Three) Payne,
David Stanley / Dury, Ian Robins /
Jankel, Chaz: Andrew Heath Music

Ltd / London Publishing House Ltd /
Warner Chappell Music Ltd.

Sweet Gene Vincent Dury, Ian Robins /
Jankel, Charles Jeremy: Templemill
Music Ltd / Warner Chappell Music
Ltd.

Don't Ask Me Dury, Ian Robins / Jankel,
Charles Jeremy: Andrew Heath
Music Ltd / London Publishing
House Ltd / Warner Chappell Music
Ltd.

Bed Of Roses Dury, Ian Robins / Jankel,
Charles Jeremy: Templemill Music Ltd
/ Mute Song Limited / Bucks Music
Group Ltd.

Honeysuckle Highway Dury, Ian Robins /
Jankel, Charles Jeremy: Templemill
Music Ltd / Mute Song Limited /
Bucks Music Group Ltd.

Spasticus Autisticus Dury, Ian Robins /
Jankel, Charles Jeremy / Warner
Chappell Music Ltd / Heathwave
Music Ltd.

Passing Show Dury, Ian Robins / Jankel,
Charles Jeremy: Templemill Music
Ltd / Warner Chappell Music Ltd.

Clevor Trevor Dury, Ian Robins / Jankel,
Charles Jeremy: Templemill Music Ltd /
Mute Song Limited / Bucks Music
Group Ltd.

JOHN LYDON

Anarchy In The UK Matlock, Glen / Jones,
Stephen Philip / Lydon, John / Cook,
Paul Thomas: Rotten Music Ltd /
Warner Chappell Music Ltd / A
Thousand Miles Long Inc.

Albatross Lydon, John / Wardle, John
Joseph / Levene, Keith: Rotten Music
Ltd / Warner Chappell Music Ltd /
EMI Virgin Music Ltd.

Death Disco Lydon, John / Walker, James
Donat / Wardle, John Joseph / Levene,
Keith: Warner Chappell Music Ltd /
EMI Virgin Music Ltd / Rotten Music
Ltd.

Public Image Lydon, John / Walker, James
Donat / Wardle, John Joseph / Levene,

Keith: Warner Chappell Music Ltd / EMI Virgin Music Ltd / Rotten Music Ltd.

Chant Lydon, John / Dudanski, Richard / Wardle, John Joseph / Levene, Keith: Virgin Music Ltd / Rotten Music Ltd. / Warner Chappell Music Ltd.

Rise Lydon, John / Laswell, Bill O: More Cut Music / BMGPlatinum Songs US / BMG Rights Management (UK) Limited / Rotten Music Ltd.

Dog Lydon, John / Warner Chappell Music Ltd.

Grave Ride Lydon, John: Warner Chappell Music Ltd.

Sun Lydon, John: Warner Chappell Music Ltd.

Tie Me To The Length Of That Lydon, John / Atkins, Martin Clive: Complete Music Ltd / Rotten Music Ltd / Warner Chappell Music Ltd.

Warrior Lydon, John / McGeoch, John Alexander / Smith, Bruce Neal / Dias, Allan Richard: EMI 10 Music Ltd / Domino Publishing Company Limited / Rotten Music Ltd / Bug Music Ltd.

This Is Not A Love Song Lydon, John / Atkins, Martin Clive / Levene, Keith: Complete Music Ltd / EMI Virgin Music Ltd / Rotten Music Ltd / Warner Chappell Music Ltd.

Whatcha Gonna Do About It Potter, Brian August /Samwell, Ian Ralph: Fanfare Music Co Ltd.

Bodies Jones, Stephen Philip / Rotten, Johnny / Cook, Paul Thomas / Vicious, Sid: Rotten Music Ltd / Warner Chappell Music Ltd / A Thousand Miles Long Inc / Universal Music Publishing Limited.

Worry Lydon, John / McGeoch, John Alexander / Smith, Bruce Neal / Dias, Alan: Rotten Music Ltd / Warner Chapell Music Ltd.

God Save The Queen Matlock, Glen / Jones, Stephen Philip / Rotten, Johnny / Cook, Paul Thomas: Rotten Music Ltd / Warner Chappell Music

Ltd / Warner Chappell Music Ltd / A Thousand Miles Long Inc.

MICK JONES

White Riot Jones, Mick / Strummer, Joe / Simonon, Paul Gustave / Headon, Topper: Nineden Ltd / Universal Music Publishing Limited.

1977 Jones, Mick / Strummer, Joe / Simonon, Paul Gustave / Headon, Topper: Nineden Ltd / Universal Music Publishing Limited.

Garageland Jones, Mick / Strummer, Joe / Simonon, Paul Gustave / Headon, Topper: Nineden Ltd / Universal Music Publishing Limited.

English Civil War Trad / Jones, Mick / Strummer, Joe / Simonon, Paul Gustave: Nineden Ltd / Universal Music Publishing Limited.

Midnight Log Jones, Mick / Strummer, Joe / Headon, Topper: Nineden Ltd / Universal Music Publishing Limited.

The Magnificent Seven Jones, Mick / Strummer, Joe / Headon, Topper: Nineden Ltd / Universal Music Publishing Limited.

If Music Could Talk Jones, Mick / Strummer, Joe / Simonon, Paul Gustave / Headon, Topper: Nineden Ltd / Universal Music Publishing Limited.

The Sound Of The Sinners Jones, Mick / Strummer, Joe / Headon, Topper: Nineden Ltd / Universal Music Publishing Limited.

Beyond The Pale Jones, Michael Geoffrey / Strummer, Joe / Bad Songs Ltd / B-A-D Songs Ltd / Casbah Productions Ltd / Bucks Music Group Ltd.

The Beautiful People Are Ugly Too Jones, Mick / Strummer, Joe / Headon, Topper: Nineden Ltd / Universal Music Publishing Limited.

Idle In Kangaroo Court Jones, Mick / Strummer, Joe / Headon, Topper: Nineden Ltd / Universal Music Publishing Limited.

PAUL WELLER

Beat Surrender Weller, Paul John: Stylist Music Ltd / Universal Music Publishing MGB Limited.

Wasteland Weller, Paul John: Stylist Music Ltd / Universal Music Publishing MGB Limited.

That's Entertainment! Weller, Paul John: Stylist Music Ltd / Universal Music Publishing MGB Limited.

My Ever Changing Moods Weller, Paul John: Stylist Music Ltd / Universal Music Publishing MGB Limited.

Walls Come Tumbling Down Weller, Paul John: Stylist Music Ltd / Universal Music Publishing MGB Limited.

In The City Weller, Paul John: Stylist Music Ltd / Universal Music Publishing MGB Limited.

Down In The Tube Station At Midnight Weller, Paul John: Stylist Music Ltd / Universal Music Publishing MGB Limited.

The Changingman Weller, Paul John / Lynch, Brendan: Solid Bond Productions Ltd / Universal Music Publishing MGB Limited.

Wake Up The Nation Dine, Simon Paul / Weller, Paul John: Stylist Music Ltd / Universal Music Publishing MGB Limited / Sony/ATV Music Publishing (UK) Limited.

The Eton Rifles Weller, Paul John: Stylist Music Ltd / Universal Music Publishing MGB Limited.

Porcelain Gods Weller, Paul John: Solid Bond Productions Ltd / Universal Music Publishing MGB Limited.

Woodcutter's Son Weller, Paul John: Solid Bond Productions Ltd / Universal Music Publishing MGB Limited.

Science Weller, Paul John: Stylist Music Ltd / Universal Music Publishing MGB Limited.

Start Weller, Paul John: Stylist Music Ltd / Universal Music Publishing MGB Limited.

Savages Weller, Paul John: Stylist Music Ltd / Universal Music Publishing MGB Limited.

Town Called Malice Weller, Paul John: Stylist Music Ltd / Universal Music Publishing MGB Limited.

Man In The Corner Shop Weller, Paul John: Stylist Music Ltd / Universal Music Publishing MGB Limited.

Ghosts Of Dachau Weller, Paul John: Stylist Music Ltd / Universal Music Publishing MGB Limited.

Peacock Suit Weller, Paul John: Stylist Music Ltd / Universal Music Publishing MGB Limited.

Larson Larson Weller, Paul John / Dine, Simon Paul: Stylist Music Ltd / Universal Music Publishing MGB Limited.

STING

Every Breath You Take Sumner, Gordon Matthew / GM Sumner.

Love Is The Seventh Wave Sumner, Gordon Matthew / GM Sumner.

Every Little Thing She Does Is Magic Sumner, Gordon Matthew / GM Sumner.

Fragile Sumner, Gordon Matthew / GM Sumner.

Fields Of Gold Sumner, Gordon Matthew / Steerpike Ltd.

Can't Stand Losing You Sumner, Gordon Matthew / GM Sumner.

Don't Stand So Close To Me Sumner, Gordon Matthew / GM Sumner.

ANDY PARTRIDGE

This Is Pop Partridge, Andy: Allydor Ltd / EMI Virgin Music Ltd.

1000 Umbrellas Partridge, Andy: EMI Music Publishing Ltd.

Statue of Liberty Partridge, Andy: EMI Music Publishing Ltd.

No Language In Our Lungs Partridge, Andy: EMI Music Publishing Ltd.

River Orchids Partridge, Andy: EMI Music Publishing Ltd / Notting Hill Music (UK) Ltd.

Wrapped In Grey Partridge, Andy: EMI Music Publishing Ltd.

Chalkhills And Children Partridge, Andy: EMI Music Publishing Ltd.

Dear God Partridge, Andy: EMI Music Publishing Ltd.

A Dictionary of Modern Marriage Partridge, Andrew John: Allydor Ltd / EMI Virgin Music Ltd.

I'd Like That Partridge, Andy: Idea Records Ltd (PRS) / Notting Hill Music (UK) Ltd.

Senses Working Overtime Partridge, Andy: EMI Music Publishing Ltd.

Snowman Partridge, Andy: Allydor Ltd / EMI Virgin Music Ltd.

Sgt. Rock Is Going To Help Me Partridge, Andy: Allydor Ltd / EMI Virgin Music Ltd.

When You're Near Me I Have Difficulty Partridge, Andy: Allydor Ltd / EMI Virgin Music Ltd.

CHRIS DIFFORD AND GLENN TILBROOK

Love's Crashing Waves Difford, Christopher Henry / Tilbrook, Glenn Martin: EMI Virgin Music Ltd / UV Administration.

Vicky Verky Difford, Christopher Henry / Tilbrook, Glenn Martin: Javeberry Ltd / Universal Music Publishing Limited.

Melody Motel Difford, Christopher Henry / Tilbrook, Glenn Martin: EMI Virgin Music Ltd / UV Administration.

Cool For Cats Difford, Christopher Henry / Tilbrook, Glenn Martin: Javeberry Ltd / Universal Music Publishing Limited.

Letting Go Difford, Christopher Henry / Tilbrook, Glenn Martin: EMI Virgin Music Ltd / UV Administration.

Up The Junction Difford, Christopher Henry / Tilbrook, Glenn Martin: Javeberry Ltd / Universal Music Publishing Limited.

Labelled With Love Difford, Christopher Henry / Tilbrook, Glenn Martin: EMI Virgin Music Ltd.

If I Didn't Love You Difford, Christopher Henry / Tilbrook, Glenn Martin: EMI Virgin Music Ltd / UV Administration.

Black Coffee In Bed Difford, Christopher Henry / Tilbrook, Glenn Martin: EMI Virgin Music Ltd.

Is That Love Difford, Christopher Henry / Tilbrook, Glenn Martin: EMI Virgin Music Ltd / EMI Virgin Music Ltd.

Piccadilly Difford, Christopher Henry / Tilbrook, Glenn Martin: EMI Virgin Music Ltd.

It's Not Cricket Difford, Christopher Henry / Tilbrook, Glenn Martin: Javeberry Ltd / Universal Music Publishing Limited.

I've Returned Difford, Chris / Tilbrook, Glenn Martin: EMI Music Publishing Ltd.

Cold Shoulder Difford, Christopher Henry / Tilbrook, Glenn Martin: EMI Virgin Music Ltd / UV Administration.

MADNESS

The Good People of Lud Smyth, Cathal Joseph.

House Of Fun Barson, Michael / Thompson, Lee Jay: EMI Music Publishing Ltd.

One Step Beyond Campbell, Cecil Eustace: Melodisc Music Ltd.

Our House Foreman, Christopher John / Smyth, Cathal Joseph: EMI Music Publishing Ltd.

Bed And Breakfast Man Barson, Michael: EMI Music Publishing Ltd.

Johnny The Horse Smyth, Cathal Joseph: EMI Music Publishing Ltd.

The Liberty Of Norton Folgate Barson, Michael / McPherson, Graham / Smyth, Cathal Joseph: Peermusic (UK) Ltd / Peermusic (UK) Ltd / Peermusic (UK) Ltd.

All I Knew McPherson, Graham: EMI Music Publishing Ltd.

Shut Up Foreman, Christopher John / McPherson, Graham.

Waiting For The Ghost Train Barson,

Michael / Bedford, Mark William / Foreman, Christopher John / McPherson, Graham: EMI Music Publishing Ltd.

Mrs Hutchinson Barson, Michael: EMI Music Publishing Ltd.

Driving In My Car Barson, Michael / Bedford, Mark William / Foreman, Christopher John / McPherson, Graham: EMI Music Publishing Ltd.

Aeroplane Barson, Michael / McPherson, Graham: EMI Music Publishing Ltd.

ANNIE LENNOX

Legend In My Living Room Lennox, Annie / Vettese, Peter John: EMI Music Publishing Ltd / La Lennoxa Music Co Ltd / Universal Music Publishing MGB Limited.

There Must Be An Angel (Playing With My Heart) Lennox, Annie / Stewart, Dave: D-N-A Ltd / Universal Music Publishing MGB Limited.

Here Comes The Rain Again Lennox, Annie / Stewart, Dave: Universal Music Publ International MGB Ltd.

Love Is A Stranger Lennox, Annie / Stewart, Dave: Logo Songs Ltd / Metcom Music Limited / Universal Music Publ International MGB Ltd.

Savage Lennox, Annie / Stewart, David Allan: D-N-A Ltd / Universal Music Publishing MGB Limited.

Thorn In My Side Lennox, Ann / Stewart, David Allan: D-N-A Ltd / Universal Music Publishing MGB Limited.

Would I Lie To You Lennox, Ann / Stewart, David Allan: D-N-A Ltd / Universal Music Publishing MGB Limited.

A Star Greaney, Micky: Little Symphonies for the Kids / Copyright Control.

BILLY BRAGG

To Have And To Have Not Bragg, Billy: Sony/ATV Music Publishing (UK) Limited.

A New England Bragg, Billy: Sony/ATV Music Publishing (UK) Limited.

Between The Wars Bragg, Billy: Sony/ATV Music Publishing (UK) Limited.

Greetings To The New Brunette Bragg, Billy: Sony/ATV Music Publishing (UK) Limited.

The Myth Of Trust Bragg, Billy: Sony/ATV Music Publishing (UK) Limited.

Handy Man Blues Bragg, Billy: Sony/ATV Music Publishing (UK) Limited.

Brickbat Bragg, Billy: Sony/ATV Music Publishing (UK) Limited.

I Keep Faith Bragg, Billy: Sony/ATV Music Publishing (UK) Limited.

The Boy Done Good Bragg, Billy / Marr, Johnny: Chrysalis-Music-Ltd / Sony/ATV Music Publishing (UK).

Mr Tambourine Man Dylan, Bob: Special Rider Music / Sony/ATV Music Publishing Llc / Sony/ATV Music Publishing (UK) Limited.

Goalhanger Bragg, Billy: Sony/ATV Music Publishing (UK) Limited.

The Space Race Is Over Bragg, Billy: Sony/ATV Music Publishing (UK) Limited.

Valentine's Day Is Over Bragg, Billy: Sony/ATV Music Publishing (UK) Limited.

The Few Bragg, Billy Bonkers: Sony/ATV Music Publishing (UK) Limited.

Ideology Bragg, Billy Bonkers: Sony/ATV Music Publishing (UK) Limited.

The Short Answer Bragg, Billy: Sony/ATV Music Publishing (UK) Limited.

Tank Park Salute Bragg, Billy: Sony/ATV Music Publishing (UK) Limited.

England Half English Bragg, Billy / Barker, Martyn / Edmonds, Louis S / Edwards, Simon John: Union Productions Ltd / Universal Music Publishing MGB Limited / Sony/ATV Music Publishing (UK) Limited.

M for Me Bragg, Billy: Sony/ATV Music Publishing (UK) Limited.

Something Happened Bragg, Billy: Sony/ATV Music Publishing (UK) Limited.

Take Down The Union Jack Bragg, Billy: Sony/ATV Music Publishing (UK) Limited.

The Saturday Boy Bragg, Billy Bonkers: Sony/ATV Music Publishing (UK) Limited.

Richard Bragg, Billy: Sony/ATV Music Publishing (UK) Limited.

Must I Paint You A Picture Bragg, Billy Bonkers: Sony/ATV Music Publishing (UK) Limited.

Sexuality Bragg, Billy / Marr, Johnny: Chrysalis-Music-Ltd / Sony/ATV Music Publishing (UK) Limited.

Walk Away Renee monologue Bragg, Billy.

JOHNNY MARR

This Charming Man Morrissey, Steven Patrick / Marr, Johnny: Artemis Muziekuitgeverij B V / Warner/ Chappell Artemis Music Limited / Marr Songs Ltd / Universal Music Publishing Limited.

Reel Around The Fountain Morrissey, Steven Patrick / Marr, Johnny: Artemis Muziekuitgeverij B V / Warner/Chappell Artemis Music Limited / Marr Songs Ltd / Universal Music Publishing Limited.

Suffer Little Children Morrissey, Steven Patrick /Marr, Johnny: Artemis Muziekuitgeverij B V / Warner/ Chappell Artemis Music Limited / Marr Songs Ltd / Universal Music Publishing Limited.

Cemetry Gates Morrissey, Steven Patrick / Marr, Johnny: Artemis Muziekuitgeverij B V / Warner/ Chappell Artemis Music Limited / Marr Songs Ltd / Universal Music Publishing Limited.

How Soon Is Now Morrissey, Steven Patrick / Marr, Johnny: Artemis Muziekuitgeverij B V / Warner/ Chappell Artemis Music Limited / Marr Songs Ltd / Universal Music Publishing Limited.

PET SHOP BOYS

Can You Forgive Her Tennant, Neil Francis / Lowe, Chris: Cage-Music-Ltd / Sony/ATV Music Publishing (UK) Limited.

Paninaro Tennant, Neil Francis / Lowe, Christopher Sean: Cage-Music-Ltd / Sony/ATV Music Publishing (UK) Limited.

Why Don't We Live Together Tennant, Neil Francis / Lowe, Christopher Sean: Cage-Music-Ltd / Sony/ATV Music Publishing (UK) Limited.

So Hard Tennant, Neil Francis / Lowe, Chris: Cage-Music-Ltd / Sony/ATV Music Publishing (UK) Limited.

Suburbia Tennant, Neil Francis / Lowe, Christopher Sean: Cage-Music-Ltd / Sony/ATV Music Publishing (UK) Limited.

How Can You Expect To Be Taken Seriously Tennant, Neil Francis / Lowe, Christopher Sean: Cage-Music-Ltd / Sony/ATV Music Publishing (UK) Limited.

Being Boring Tennant, Neil Francis / Lowe, Chris / Cage-Music-Ltd / Sony/ATV Music Publishing (UK) Limited.

What Have I Done To Deserve This? Willis, Allee / Tennant, Neil Francis / Lowe, Chris: Cage-Music-Ltd / Sony/ATV Music Publishing (UK) Limited / Texascity Music Inc / MCA Texascity Music Inc.

Opportunities Tennant, Neil Francis / Lowe, Chris: Cage-Music-Ltd / Sony/ATV Music Publishing (UK) Limited.

West End Girls Tennant, Neil Francis / Lowe, Chris / Cage-Music-Ltd / Sony/ATV Music Publishing (UK) Limited.

Rent Tennant, Neil Francis / Lowe, Christopher Sean: Cage-Music-Ltd / Sony/ATV Music Publishing (UK) Limited.

Casanova In Hell Tennant, Neil Francis / Lowe, Christopher Sean / Cage-Music-Ltd / Sony/ATV Music Publishing (UK) Limited.

Nothing Has Been Proved Tennant, Neil Francis / Lowe, Christopher Sean:

Cage-Music-Ltd / Sony/ATV Music Publishing (UK) Limited.

LEE MAVERS

Freedom Song—Mavers, Lee Antony.
Timeless Melody Mavers, Lee Antony.
Son Of A Gun Mavers, Lee Antony.
Feelin' Mavers, Lee Antony.
Looking Glass Mavers, Lee Antony.
I.O.U. Mavers, Lee Antony.
Way Out Mavers, Lee Antony.
Who Knows Mavers, Lee Antony.
I Can't Sleep Mavers, Lee Antony.
The Lonesome Death Of Hattie Carroll Dylan, Bob: Special Rider Music / Sony/ATV Music Publishing Llc / Sony/ATV Music Publishing (UK) Limited.
Failure Mavers, Lee Antony.
Callin' All Mavers, Lee Antony.

DAMON ALBARN

Demon Days Albarn, Damon / Hewlett, Jamie Christopher: Gorillaz / EMI Music Publishing Ltd.
Girls and Boys Albarn, Damon / Coxon, Graham Leslie / James, Steven Alexander / Rowntree, David: EMI Music Publishing Ltd.
Editions Of You Ferry, Bryan: BMG Rights Management (UK) Limited.
Why Don't Women Like Me? Formby, George / Cottrell, Jack / Bennett, Bud: Harrison Music Co Ltd.
Parklife Albarn, Damon / Coxon, Graham Leslie / James, Steven Alexander / Rowntree, David: EMI Music Publishing Ltd.
Country House Albarn, Damon / Coxon, Graham Leslie / James, Steven Alexander / Rowntree, David: EMI Music Publishing Ltd.
Out Of Time Albarn, Damon / James, Steven Alexander / Rowntree, David: EMI Music Publishing Ltd.
Hong Kong Albarn, Damon / Hewlett, Jamie Christopher: Gorillaz / EMI Music Publishing Ltd.

Clint Eastwood Albarn, Damon / Hewlett, Jamie Christopher / Jones, Teren Delvon: Gorillaz / EMI Music Publishing Ltd / Happy Hemp Music / Universal Music Publishing Limited.
Essex Dogs Albarn, Damon / Coxon, Graham Leslie / James, Steven Alexander / Rowntree, David Alexander De Horne: EMI Music Publishing Ltd.
On Melancholy Hill Albarn, Damon / Hewlett, Jamie Christopher: Gorillaz / EMI Music Publishing Ltd.
The Marvelous Dream Albarn, Damon: Chrysalis-Music-Ltd.

NOEL GALLAGHER

D'You Know What I Mean? Gallagher, Noel Thomas: Oasis Music / Creation Songs Ltd / SM Publishing (UK) Limited.
Wonderwall Gallagher, Noel Thomas: Oasis Music / Creation Songs Ltd / SM Publishing (UK) Limited.
Badge Gallagher, Noel Thomas.
Cast No Shadow Gallagher, Noel Thomas: Oasis Music / Creation Songs Ltd / SM Publishing (UK) Limited.
Supersonic Gallagher, Noel Thomas: Oasis Music / Creation Songs Ltd / SM Publishing (UK) Limited.
Live Forever Gallagher, Noel Thomas: Oasis Music / Creation Songs Ltd / SM Publishing (UK) Limited.
Half The World Away Gallagher, Noel Thomas: Oasis Music / Creation Songs Ltd / SM Publishing (UK) Limited.
Stand By Me Gallagher, Noel Thomas: Oasis Music / Creation Songs Ltd / SM Publishing (UK) Limited.
Let There Be Love Gallagher, Noel Thomas: Oasis Music / Sony/ATV Music Publishing (UK) Limited.
Force Of Nature Gallagher, Noel Thomas: Oasis Music / Creation Songs Ltd / SM Publishing (UK) Limited.
The Masterplan Gallagher, Noel Thomas: Oasis Music / Creation Songs Ltd / SM Publishing (UK) Limited.

Mucky Fingers Gallagher, Noel Thomas: Oasis Music / Sony/ATV Music Publishing (UK) Limited.

Don't Look Back In Anger Gallagher, Noel Thomas: Oasis Music / Sony/ATV Music Publishing (UK) Limited.

Some Might Say Gallagher, Noel Thomas: Oasis Music / Creation Songs Ltd / SM Publishing (UK) Limited.

Champagne Supernova Gallagher, Noel Thomas: Oasis Music / Creation Songs Ltd / SM Publishing (UK) Limited.

Little By Little Gallagher, Noel Thomas: Oasis Music / Creation Songs Ltd / SM Publishing (UK) Limited.

JARVIS COCKER

I Never Said I Was Deep Cocker, Jarvis Branson / Mackey, Stephen Patrick / Stafford, Simon Edward / Orton, Ross: Warner/Chappell Music Publishing Limited / Universal Music Publishing Limited / Imagem London Limited.

Love Is Blind Cocker, Jarvis Branson / Senior, Russell / Mackey, Stephen Patrick / Banks, Nick: Twist And Shout Music / Conexion Music Limited.

97 Lovers Cocker, Jarvis Branson / Senior, Russell / Doyle, Candida / Mansell, Peter Duncan: Twist And Shout Music / Conexion Music Limited.

Dishes Cocker, Jarvis Branson / Mackey, Stephen Patrick / Banks, Nicholas David / Doyle, Candida Mary: Island Music Ltd / Universal.

Sheffield: Sex City Cocker, Jarvis Branson / Enior, Russell / Mackey, Stephen Patrick / Banks, Nick: Island Music Ltd / Universal.

Acrylic Afternoons Cocker, Jarvis Branson / Enior, Russell / Mackey, Stephen Patrick / Banks, Nick: Island Music Ltd / Universal.

I Spy Cocker, Jarvis Branson / Enior, Russell / Mackey, Stephen Patrick / Banks, Nick / Island Music Ltd / Universal.

Babies Cocker, Jarvis Branson / Enior, Russell / Mackey, Stephen Patrick /

Banks, Nick: Island Music Ltd / Universal.

Mis-Shapes Cocker, Jarvis Branson / Senior, Russell / Mackey, Stephen Patrick / Banks, Nicholas David: Island Music Ltd / Universal.

Bad Cover Version Cocker, Jarvis Branson / Mackey, Stephen Patrick / Banks, Nick / Doyle, Candida Mary: Island Music Ltd / Universal.

Catcliffe Shakedown Banks, Nick / Cocker, Jarvis Branson / Doyle, Candida / Mackey, Stephen Patrick: Island Music Ltd / Universal.

The Last Day Of The Miners' Strike Bacharach, Burt F. / Cocker, Jarvis Branson / Mackey, Stephen Patrick / Banks, Nick: Island Music Ltd / Universal / New-Hidden-Valley-Music Company / Warner/Chappell Music Publishing Limited.

Sliding Through Life On Charm Faithfull, Marianne / Cocker, Jarvis Branson / Mackey, Stephen Patrick / Banks, Nicholas David: Island Music Ltd / Universal / EMI Music Publishing Ltd.

You're A Nightmare Cocker, Jarvis Branson / Senior, Russell / Mackey, Stephen Patrick / Banks, Nick: Island Music Ltd / Universal.

LILY ALLEN

Nan, You're A Window Shopper Marley, Bob / Babalola, Iyiola Babatunde / Lewis, Darren / Jackson, Curtis James: Universal Music Corporation / Universal Music Publishing International Ltd / Universal/MCA Music Limited / Fifty Six Hope Road Music Limited.

Shame For You Cobbs, Willie C / Mackichan, Blair Nicholas Somerled / Allen, Lily Rose Beatrice: Universal Music Publishing MGB Limited / Embassy Music Corp / Carlin Music Corp / Katrina-Music.

LDN McCook, Thomas / Allen, Lily Rose Beatrice / Babalola, Iyiola Babatunde /

Lewis, Darren Emilio: Universal
Music Publishing Limited /
Sparta-Florida Music Group Ltd.
Not Big Kurstin, Greg / Allen, Lily Rose
Beatrice: EMI April Music Inc / EMI
Music Publishing Ltd / Kurstin Music.
It's Not Fair Kurstin, Greg / Allen, Lily Rose
Beatrice: EMI April Music Inc / EMI
Music Publishing Ltd / Kurstin Music.
Knock Em Out King, Earl / Babalola, Iyiola
Babatunde / Lewis, Darren Emilio /
Allen, Lily Rose Beatrice: Shirley S
Music Company / Don Williams
Music Inc / Fairwood Music Ltd /
Universal Music Publishing Limited.
Him Kurstin, Gregory Allen: Allen, Lily
Rose Beatrice Publishing Ltd /
Universal Music Publishing Limited.
The Fear Kurstin, Gregory Allen: Allen,
Lily Rose Beatrice Publishing Ltd /
Universal Music Publishing Limited

LAURA MARLING

Saved These Words Marling, Laura
Beatrice: Chrysalis-Music-Ltd.

I Am A Master Hunter Marling, Laura
Beatrice: Chrysalis-Music-Ltd.
Don't Ask Me Why Marling, Laura
Beatrice: Chrysalis-Music-Ltd.
Where Can I Go? Marling, Laura
Beatrice: Chrysalis-Music-Ltd.
I Was An Eagle Marling, Laura Beatrice:
Chrysalis-Music-Ltd.
I Speak Because I Can Marling, Laura
Beatrice: Chrysalis-Music-Ltd.
Sophia Marling, Laura Beatrice:
Chrysalis-Music-Ltd.
The Beast Marling, Laura Beatrice:
Chrysalis-Music-Ltd.
Tap At My Window Marling, Laura
Beatrice / Smith, Iotha.
Failure Marling, Laura Beatrice / Smith,
Iotha: Chrysalis-Music-Ltd.
Rambling Man Marling, Laura Beatrice:
Chrysalis-Music-Ltd.
Goodbye England (Covered in Snow)
Marling, Laura Beatrice:
Chrysalis-Music-Ltd.
Cross Your Fingers Marling, Laura
Beatrice: Chrysalis-Music-Ltd.

INDEX